Global Political Economy

Global Political Economy

FIFTH EDITION

Edited by
John Ravenhill

OXFORD
UNIVERSITY PRESS

OXFORD
UNIVERSITY PRESS

Great Clarendon Street, Oxford, ox2 6DP,
United Kingdom

Oxford University Press is a department of the University of Oxford.
It furthers the University's objective of excellence in research, scholarship,
and education by publishing worldwide. Oxford is a registered trade mark of
Oxford University Press in the UK and in certain other countries

Second edition 2008
Third edition 2011
Fourth edition 2014

Impression: 2

Published in the United States of America by Oxford University Press
198 Madison Avenue, New York, NY 10016, United States of America

British Library Cataloguing in Publication Data

Data available

Library of Congress Control Number: 2016953998

ISBN 978–0–19–873746–9

Printed in Great Britain by Bell and Bain Ltd, Glasgow

Preface and Acknowledgements

The contributors to this book are delighted that it has proved sufficiently popular with instructors and students that the publishers have commissioned a fifth edition. As always, contributors have substantially revised their chapters for the new edition to reflect contemporary developments in the global economy.

My thanks to the contributors for the work they have put into their chapters, and for complying with the tight schedule required in publishing a book of this type.

For this edition, we welcome two new authors—Ann Capling and Silke Trommer—who have taken over responsibility for the chapter on the global trade regime. Health problems prevented Gil Winham, who had authored this chapter in all previous editions, from contributing this time. We all wish Gil well and are particularly grateful for his being willing to permit us to include materials from earlier editions in the revised trade chapter.

Preparation of a volume of this size is a major task, which would not have been possible without the able assistance of Caleb Lauer, a PhD student in the Balsillie School of International Affairs, who had the major responsibility for preparing the manuscript to OUP's requirements. Caroline Cottet was responsible for updating the tables and figures in Chapters 6 and 11. Terry d'Andrea updated the PowerPoint® slides that are part of the online resources for the book.

My principal debt, as always, is to my wife, Stefa Wirga, who has provided encouragement and support throughout the project from its original conceptualization.

JOHN RAVENHILL

Economics for non-economists

Students in Global Political Economy courses are often concerned about their lack of background in economics. While we provide concise explanations in this book for all of the key concepts that we use (and the book contains a comprehensive Glossary), students often want to go beyond this basic information to improve their knowledge of economics. The following books are useful introductions, written with the non-specialist in mind:

James Gerber, *International Economics*, 6th edn (Prentice Hall, 2013)

John Black, Nigar Hashimzade, and Gareth Myles, *Oxford Dictionary of Economics*, 4th edn (Oxford University Press, 2012)

Donald Rutherford, *Routledge Dictionary of Economics*, 3rd edn (Routledge, 2012)

Donald Rutherford, *Economics: The Key Concepts* (Routledge, 2007)

For those who are comfortable with basic economic concepts, the following are the best introductory overviews of major theoretical approaches to international economics:

Paul Krugman and Maurice Obstfeld, *International Economics: Theory and Practice*, 10th edn (Pearson, 2014)

Peter B. Kenen, *The International Economy*, 4th edn (Cambridge University Press, 2000)

New to this Edition

- A new chapter on the Global Trade Regime, written by Professor Ann Capling and Dr Silke Trommer.
- Increased coverage of the rise of new actors, especially the BRICs, and the role of developing economies in global governance.
- The chapter on production has been moved earlier in the book to form a newly organized Part II looking at global trade and production.

Brief Contents

Detailed Contents

List of Figures

List of Boxes

List of Tables

Abbreviations

ACP	Africa, the Caribbean, and the Pacific	DSB	dispute settlement body
ACU	Asian Currency Unit	DSF	Debt Sustainability Framework
AFL–CIO	American Federation of Labor–Congress of Industrial Organizations	DSM	Dispute Settlement Mechanism
		DSU	Dispute Settlement Understanding
AFTA	ASEAN Free Trade Area	EBRD	European Bank for Reconstruction and Development
AIG	American International Group		
ANZCERTA	Australia–New Zealand Closer Economic Relations Trade Agreement	EC	European Community
		ECLA	Economic Commission for Latin America
APEC	Asia-Pacific Economic Cooperation	ECLAC	Economic Commission for Latin America and the Caribbean
ASEAN	Association of Southeast Asian Nations		
BCBS	Basel Committee on Banking Supervision	ECOSOC	[United Nations] Economic and Social Council
BIS	Bank for International Settlements	ECOWAS	Economic Community of West African States
BRICs	Brazil, Russia, India, and China	ECSC	European Coal and Steel Community
CACM	Central American Common Market	ECU	European Currency Unit
CAP	Common Agricultural Policy	EEC	European Economic Community
CARICOM	Caribbean Community and Common Market	EFTA	European Free Trade Association
CEO	chief executive officer	EKS	Èltetö-Köves-Szulc method
CER	Closer Economic Relations	EMEs	emerging market economies
CERDS	Charter of Economic Rights and Duties of States	EMS	[1] electronic manufacturing service; [2] European Monetary System; [3] Environmental Management System
CFA	Communauté Financière Africaine [African Financial Community]		
		EPA	Environmental Protection Agency
CFCs	chlorofluorocarbons	EPZs	export processing zones
CITES	Convention on International Trade in Endangered Species of Wild Flora and Fauna	EU	European Union
		FAO	Food and Agriculture Organization
CMIM	Chiang Mai Initiative Multilateralization	FASB	Financial Accounting Standards Board
COCOM	Coordinating Committee for Multilateral Export Controls	FDI	foreign direct investment
		FSA	firm-specific advantages
COMECON	Council of Mutual Economic Assistance	FSB	Financial Stability Board
COMESA	Common Market for Eastern and Southern Africa	FSC	Forest Stewardship Council
		FSF	Financial Stability Forum
COP	Conference of the Parties	FSOC	Financial Stability Oversight Council
COREPER	Committee of Permanent Representatives	FVA	fair value accounting
CPIA	Country Policy and Institutional Assessment	FX	foreign exchange
CPMI	Committee on Payments and Market Infrastructures	G7	Group of Seven
		G8	Group of Eight
CPR	common pool resources	G10	Group of Ten
CSAs	country-specific advantages	G20	Group of Twenty
CUSFTA/CUSTA	Canada–US Free Trade Agreement	G77	Group of Seventy-Seven
DA	district attorney	GATS	General Agreement on Trade in Services
DAC	Development Assistance Committee	GATT	General Agreement on Tariffs and Trade
DDA	Doha Development Agenda		

GCC	Gulf Cooperation Council
GDP	gross domestic product
GEF	Global Environment Facility
GEIs	global economic institutions
GEMs	global economic multilateral organizations
GEMI	Global Environmental Management Initiative
GFC	Global Financial Crisis
GM	General Motors
GNI	gross national income
GNP	gross national product
GPE	global political economy
GVCs	global value chains
HIPC	heavily indebted poor countries
IADI	International Association of Deposit Insurers
IAIS	International Association of Insurance Supervisors
IASB	International Accounting Standards Board
IBM	International Business Machines
IBRD	International Bank for Reconstruction and Development
ICCO	International Cocoa Organization
ICO	International Coffee Organization
ICP	International Comparison Program
ICSG	International Copper Study Group
ICSID	International Centre for Settlement of Investment Disputes
ICT	information and communications technology
IDA	International Development Association
IDB	Inter-American Development Bank
IEPL	international extreme poverty line
IFC	[World Bank] International Finance Corporation
IFI	international financial institution
IFRS	international financial reporting standards
ILO	International Labour Organization
IMF	International Monetary Fund
IO	International Organization
IOM	International Organization for Migration
IOSCO	International Organization of Securities Commissions
IPCC	Intergovernmental Panel on Climate Change
IPE	international political economy
IR	international relations
ISI	import-substitution industrialization
ISO	[1]International Organization for Standardization; [2] International Sugar Organization
ITA	[1] Information Technology Agreement [WTO)]; [2] International Trade Administration
ITO	International Trade Organization

ITTO	International Tropical Timber Organization
JFC	[World Bank–Civil Society] Joint Facilitation Committee
JV	joint venture
LAC	Latin America and the Caribbean
LDCs	less developed countries
LIC	low income country
LLDC	landlocked developing countries
LMU	Latin Monetary Union
LOS	Law of the Sea
LTCM	Long-Term Capital Management (American hedge fund)
M&As	Mergers and Acquisitions
MAFF	Ministry for Agriculture, Forestry, and Fisheries (Japan)
MAI	[OECD] Multilateral Agreement on Investment
MDGs	Millennium Development Goals
MDRI	Multilateral Debt Relief Initiative
MEOs	multilateral economic organizations
MERCOSUR	Common Market of the South
MFA	Multifiber Arrangement
MFN	most-favoured nation
MIC	middle income country
MIGA	[World Bank] Multilateral Investment Guarantee Agency
MITI	Ministry for International Trade and Industry (Japan)
MNC	multinational corporation
MNE	multinational enterprise
NAFTA	North American Free Trade Agreement
NAM	non-aligned movement
NAMA	non-agriculture market access
NASA	US National Aeronautics and Space Administration
NEC	Nippon Electric Company
NGO	non-governmental organization
NIDL	new international division of labour
NIEs	newly industrializing economies
NIEO	New International Economic Order
NTBs	non-tariff barriers
NTMs	non-tariff measures
ODA	Official Development Assistance
OECD	Organisation for Economic Co-operation and Development
OEMs	original equipment manufacturers
OPEC	Organization of the Petroleum Exporting Countries
PC	personal computer
PD	Prisoner's Dilemma
PGA	Peoples' Global Action
PIER	politics of international economic relations

POPs	persistent organic pollutants		TPRM	Trade Policy Review Mechanism
PPP	purchasing power parity		TRIMs	Trade-Related Investment Measures
PRSPs	Poverty Reduction Strategy Papers		TRIPs	Trade-Related Aspects of Intellectual Property Rights
PSIA	Poverty and Social Impact Analysis			
PTA	preferential trade agreement		UN	United Nations Organization
PWC	Post-Washington Consensus		UNCED	United Nations Conference on the Environment and Development
PWT	Penn World Tables			
R&D	research and development		UNCTAD	United Nations Conference on Trade and Development
RMB	renminbi			
RNGMA	Regional Nature of Global Multinational Activity Survey		UNDP	United Nations Development Programme
			UNEP	United Nations Environment Programme
RTA	regional trading agreement		UNFCCC	United Nations Framework Convention on Climate Change
RTAA	Reciprocal Trade Agreements Act			
SADC	Southern African Development Community		UNGA	United Nations General Assembly
SADCC	Southern African Development Coordination Conference		UNICEF	United Nations Children's Emergency Fund
			UNIDO	United Nations Industrial Development Organization
SAPs	structural adjustment programmes			
SDGs	Sustainable Development Goals		USAID	United States Agency for International Development
SDR	special drawing rights			
SDT	special and differential treatment		USTR	United States Trade Representative
SFM	sustainable forest management		VW	Volkswagen
SIDS	Small Island Developing States		WC	Washington Consensus
SMEs	small and medium-sized enterprise		WCED	World Commission on Environment and Development
SMU	Scandinavian Monetary Union			
SSA	sub-Saharan Africa		WEU	Western European Union
SSM	Special Safeguard Mechanism		WHO	World Health Organization
SWFs	sovereign wealth funds		WIDER	[UN] World Institute for Development Economics Research
SWIFT	Society for the Worldwide Interbank Financial Telecommunication			
			WTO	World Trade Organization
TFA	Trade Facilitation Agreement		DSU	Dispute Settlement Understanding
TNC	transnational corporation		WWF	World Wide Fund for Nature

About the Contributors

Vinod K. Aggarwal is Travers Family Senior Faculty Fellow and Professor in the Travers Department of Political Science, Affiliated Professor at the Haas School of Business, and Director of the Berkeley APEC Study Center at the University of California, Berkeley. He is Editor-in-Chief of the journal *Business and Politics*. His most recent book (with Sara Newland) is *Responding to the Rise of China* (Springer).

Ann Capling is Professorial Fellow in Political Science at the University of Melbourne. Her publications include *Beyond the Protective State: The Political Economy of Australia's Manufacturing Industry Policy* (with Brian Galligan); *Australia and the Global Trade System: From Havana to Seattle*; *Governments, Non-state Actors and Trade Policy Making: Negotiating Preferentially or Multilaterally?* (with Patrick Low)—all published by Cambridge University Press.

Peter Dauvergne is Professor of International Relations at the University of British Columbia, Canada. His recent books include *Environmentalism of the Rich* (MIT Press, 2016); *Protest Inc.: The Corporatization of Activism* (Polity, 2014, co-authored with Genevieve LeBaron); and *Eco-Business: A Big-Brand Takeover of Sustainability* (MIT Press, 2013, co-authored with Jane Lister). He is the founding and past editor of the journal *Global Environmental Politics*.

Cédric Dupont is Professor of Political Science and Director of Executive Education at the Graduate Institute of International and Development Studies, Geneva. He has published widely on governance and negotiation processes at the global and regional levels. His current work focuses on investment arbitration.

Colin Hay is Professor of Political Science at Sciences Po, Paris and an affiliate Professor of Political Analysis at the University of Sheffield, UK, where he is founding Co-Director of the Sheffield Political Economy Research Institute (SPERI). His recent publications include *Civic Capitalism* (Polity, with Anthony Payne); *The Political Economy of European Welfare Capitalism* (Palgrave, with Daniel Wincott); *The Failure of Anglo-Liberal Capitalism* (Palgrave); and *The Legacy of Thatcherism* (Oxford University Press/British Academy, with Stephen Farrall).

Eric Helleiner is Faculty of Arts Chair in International Political Economy at the University of Waterloo. His recent books include *Forgotten Foundations of Bretton Woods: International Development and the Making of the Postwar Order* (Cornell University Press, 2014); *The Status Quo Crisis: Global Financial Governance After the 2008 Meltdown* (Oxford University Press, 2014).

Michael J. Hiscox is Professor of Government, Harvard University. His publications include *International Trade and Political Conflict* (Princeton University Press).

Anthony McGrew is Pro-Vice Chancellor, Professor of Global Public Policy and Director of the Confucius Institute at La Trobe University, Melbourne. His publications include (with D. Held) *Global Transformations*; *The Global Transformations Reader*; and *Global Governance*—all Polity Press. He is currently researching China's role in global governance institutions.

Louis W. Pauly is Professor and Chair of Political Science at the University of Toronto. His publications include *Opening Financial Markets* and *Who Elected the Bankers?* (both Cornell University Press); *The Myth of the Global Corporation* (Princeton University Press); and *Complex Sovereignty* (University of Toronto Press).

Nicola Phillips is Professor of Political Economy and Head of the Department of Politics at the University of Sheffield, UK. She is an editor of *Review of International Political Economy* and Chair of the British International

Studies Association. Her publications include *Development* (with Anthony Payne, Polity); and, as editor, *The Handbook of the International Political Economy of Governance* (with Anthony Payne, Edward Elgar); *Migration in the Global Political Economy* (Lynne Rienner).

John Ravenhill is Director of the Balsillie School of International Affairs, and Professor of Political Science at the University of Waterloo, Canada. His publications include *The Oxford Handbook of the International Relations of East Asia* (co-edited with Saadia Pekkanen and Rosemary Foot); *Crisis as Catalyst: Asia's Dynamic Political Economy* (Cornell); *APEC and the Construction of Pacific Rim Regionalism* (Cambridge University Press).

Eric Thun is Peter Moores Associate Professor in Chinese Business Studies at Oxford University's Saïd Business School. His publications include *Changing Lanes in China: Foreign Direct Investment*; *Local Governments and Auto Sector Development*—Cambridge University Press.

Silke Trommer is Lecturer in Politics, School of Social Sciences, University of Manchester, UK. Her publications include *Transformations in Trade Politics: Participatory Trade Politics in West Africa* (Routledge, 2014); and *Expert Knowledge in Global Trade* (with Erin Hannah and James Scott; Routledge, 2015).

Robert Hunter Wade is Professor of Political Economy, Department of International Development, London School of Economics, UK. His publications include *Governing the Market* (Princeton University Press); *Village Republics* (Cambridge University Press); and *Irrigation and Agricultural Politics in South Korea* (Westview Press). He won the Leontief Prize for Advancing the Frontiers of Economic Thought in 2008.

Matthew Watson is Professor of Political Economy, Department of Politics and International Studies, University of Warwick, and a UK Economic and Social Research Council Professorial Fellow. His publications include *Uneconomic Economics and the Crisis of the Model World*; and *The Political Economy of International Capital Mobility*; *Foundations of International Political Economy*, the last of which takes the same approach as his contribution here.

Guided Tour of Learning Features

We have developed a number of learning tools to help you develop the essential knowledge and skills you need to study global political economy. This guided tour shows you how to get the most out of your textbook.

Reader's Guides

Each chapter opens with a reader's guide outlining what you can expect to cover in the chapter.

Reader's guide

The twentieth century witnessed a remarkable emergence of international institutions, and nowhere was their impact greater than in international trade. Following decades of depression and war, a global trading regime was initiated with the creation of the General Agreement on Tariffs and Trade (GATT) in 1947, which expanded steadily in both scope and membership through the twentieth century and culminated in the establishment of the World Trade Organization (WTO) in 1995. Underpinned by the philosophy that open markets and non-discriminatory trade policies promote the prosperity of all countries, and issued with a powerful dispute settlement mechanism, the WTO has been hailed as the most prominent example of cooperation between countries. At the same time, the WTO has been subject to internal and external criticism and now faces a number of difficulties, particularly in its negotiation function. This chapter reviews the history, politics, and recent trends and challenges of the multilateral trade system.

Boxes

Boxes give you extra information on particular topics, define and explain key ideas, and challenge you to think about what you've learned.

BOX 14.2 ECOLOGICAL FOOTPRINTS AND SHADOWS

Ecological footprints

Bill Rees and Mathis Wackernagel created the concept of ecological footprint to measure the sustainability of human lifestyles. It translates human consumption of renewable natural resources into hectares of average biologically productive land. A person's footprint is the total area in global hectares (1 hectare of average biological productivity) required to sustain his or her lifestyle: food and water, clothing, shelter, transportation, and consumer goods and services. The concept allows an analyst to compare the average ecological impact of people from Africa to Australia to China to the United Kingdom to the United States. The average global ecological

continuing to worsen—and the wo now equal to about 1.5 planet eart Wide Fund for Nature (WWF) lan ecological deficit with the Earth'.

Sources: Wackernagel and Rees (1996); WWF (2006: 28–34); Global Footprint footprintnetwork.org).

Ecological shadows

This concept is designed to capture environmental impact of a nation sta

Key Points

Each main chapter section ends with key points that reinforce your understanding and act as a useful revision tool.

KEY POINTS

- Although considerable complexity is involved in attempting to isolate the economic effects of RTAs, evidence suggests that they have led to more trade among members than would otherwise be the case.
- RTAs do appear, at least in their early years, to have encouraged increased investment in member states.
- Economic simulations suggest that RTAs have had little aggregate effect on members' economic welfare.
- Little evidence exists that RTAs have produced significant trade diversion.

their own rules of origin,
for a rationalization of ag
adverse consequences tha
their supply chains.
5. Global negotiations that t
groupings reduce the num

The intuitively attractive
groupings simplify global neg
number of parties is counte
that regional groupings ofte
mon position in negotiation
the EU on agricultural issue
Once a regional grouping ha

Questions

End-of-chapter questions probe your understanding of each chapter and encourage you to think critically about the material you've just covered.

Further Reading

Take your learning further by using the annotated reading lists at the end of each chapter to find the key literature in the field, or more detailed information on a specific topic.

Weblinks

At the end of each chapter you will find an annotated summary of useful websites to help you with further research.

Glossary of Terms

Key terms appear in bold in the text and are defined in a glossary at the end of the book, identifying and defining key terms and ideas as you learn, and acting as a useful prompt when it comes to revision.

Guided Tour of the Online Resource Centre

www.oxfordtextbooks.co.uk/orc/ravenhill5e

The Online Resource Centre that accompanies *Global Political Economy* provides ready-to-use learning and teaching materials. These resources are free of charge and designed to maximize the learning experience.

FOR STUDENTS:

Timeline

Created to provide essential context, this timeline sets out the key events in global political economy.

Flashcard Glossary

A series of interactive flashcards containing key terms allows you to test your knowledge of important concepts and ideas.

Web Links

Carefully selected lists of websites direct you to the sites of institutions and organizations that will help develop your knowledge and understanding.

FOR LECTURERS:

These customizable resources are password protected, but access is available to anyone using *Global Political Economy* in their teaching.

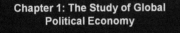

Chapter 1: The Study of Global Political Economy

Chapter by John Ravenhill

PowerPoint® Slides

PowerPoint slides complement each chapter and are a useful resource for preparing lectures and handouts.

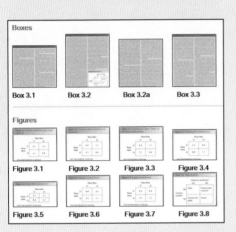

Boxes and Figures from the Text

Boxes and figures from the text have been provided in high resolution format for downloading into presentation software or for use in assignments and exam material.

PART I
Theoretical Approaches
to Global Political Economy

1

The Study of Global Political Economy

John Ravenhill

Chapter contents

Reader's guide

The contemporary international economic system is more closely integrated than in any previous era. The Global Financial Crisis, a decade on, continues to exert a profound influence on the global economy. The crisis and its aftermath provide a clear illustration of the relationship between trade, finance, international institutions, and the difficulties that governments face in coping with the problems generated by complex interdependence.

Before 1945, the spectacular increase in economic integration that had occurred over the previous century was not accompanied by institutionalized governmental collaboration on economic matters. International trade patterns also changed very little over several centuries before 1945. The end of the Second World War marked a significant disjunction: global economic institutions were created, the transnational corporation emerged as a major actor in international economic relations, and patterns of international trade began to change markedly from the traditional North–South exchange of manufactures for raw materials.

Since the emergence of global political economy (GPE) as a major subfield of the study of international relations in the early 1970s, GPE scholars have generated an enormous literature that has employed a wide variety of theories and methods. Most introductions to the study of GPE have divided the theoretical approaches to the subject into three categories: liberalism, nationalism, and Marxism. This threefold typology is of limited utility today, given the overlap between many of the approaches classified in different categories, and the wealth of theories and methodologies applied in the contemporary study of global political economy.

Prologue: the Global Financial Crisis

A decade after its onset, the Global Financial Crisis or, in the terminology favoured by the International Monetary Fund, the 'Great Recession', continued to exert a profound impact on the global economy. In the eurozone, unemployment rates remained in the double digits while those in Greece and Spain were double that. Youth unemployment rates in most euro-area countries were double the national average (http://www.oecd.org/std/labour-stats/HUR-Mar16.pdf). By mid 2015, banks in the euro area still had €900 billion in non-performing loans (IMF 2016: 33). The Great Recession, as we will discuss in more detail, appeared to have set the global economy on a course of lower investment, lower growth, and lower trade.

The Global Financial Crisis was triggered in September 2008 when the American financial services firm, Lehman Brothers, filed for bankruptcy, the largest single bankruptcy in United States history. The news triggered a massive sell-off of shares on Wall Street, the Dow Jones Index shedding more than 500 points (4.4 per cent), the biggest fall since the terrorist attacks of September 11, 2001. The effects of the bankruptcy soon reverberated around the world, marking the start of what became known as the Global Financial Crisis. In 2009, world output fell by over 2 per cent, the first such fall since the 1930s; and world trade declined by close to 40 per cent. A similar decline occurred in inflows of **foreign direct investment (FDI)**.

The fall in global output masked substantial differences in national and regional performance: the industrialized economies were among the worst hit, with output in the European Union (EU) falling by 4 per cent and that in the United States by 3.2 per cent. Among the less developed economies, some of the worst affected were those such as Singapore and Taiwan which were most dependent on international trade. Although China and India continued to grow strongly (at 8.7 and 5.6 per cent, respectively), the 36 per cent decline in the price of oil, and the 19 per cent decline in the prices of non-fuel commodities in 2008, a repercussion of the drop in world manufacturing output, had a severe impact on many less developed economies. Output in Mexico slumped by nearly 7 per cent, in Brazil by 0.4 per cent, while growth rates in Africa declined from the 2008 figure of 5 per cent to under 2 per cent (all data from IMF 2010b: Table 1.1). The dollar value of Africa's exports shrank by one-third in 2009 (Miller 2010).

The problems of Lehman Brothers stemmed in large part from its involvement in the sub-prime mortgage market. Lehman Brothers, like many other financial services firms, had become a substantial player in securitizing these mortgages (see Box 1.1).

BOX 1.1

Sub-Prime Lending and Securitization

Loans characterized as 'sub-prime' are those that are regarded by the market as carrying a higher-than-usual element of risk. Typically, they have been contracted with borrowers who, for a variety of reasons that might include limited experience in borrowing, poor credit history, or low or unreliable income, are regarded as more likely than average to default on their loans.

To offset the increased risks of lending in the sub-prime market, financial institutions took advantage of the practice of securitization, which had initially developed in the 1970s. Before that period, providers of mortgage finance typically held the loans they had made until borrowers repaid them: in other words, they bore all the risk of the lending and usually financed the loans from their own resources. As the demand for mortgage finance rose, however, and lenders became increasingly concerned about risk, they developed the practice (often with the assistance of other financial institutions) of pooling the loans; the pool was then split into shares that were on-sold to investors as tradeable securities (bonds) that carried either a fixed or floating interest rate. The investors in these securities thereby assumed much of the risk attached to the loans. The practice of 'securitization' spread from the United States to Europe in the late 1980s.

In the 1990s and the first decade of the current century, financial institutions developed ever more sophisticated means for pooling and on-selling loans. Individual securities were increasingly split into tranches, each of which carried a different level of risk: the higher tranches had the first claim on any income that the lender received; the lower tranches would be the first to absorb any losses. At the beginning of 2009, securitization accounted for approximately 28 per cent of outstanding credit in the United States: the figures for the UK and the eurozone were 14 and 6 per cent, respectively (IMF 2009b: box 1.2).

That problems that began in the home lending market in the United States could plunge the world into its worst recession since the 1930s is powerful testimony to the integration of the contemporary global economy. Difficulties originating in the US financial sector were quickly transmitted to financial institutions in other advanced economies and then to the 'real' economy when banks curtailed their lending (and, in many instances, had to be bailed out by their governments). Firms (and households) lacked the finance not only to invest for the future but even to conduct their daily operations. Finance for international trade dried up. The world economy quickly went into reverse. With the slowdown in production, the demand for and prices of raw materials fell substantially. Hit by falling prices for their exports and by a curtailment of inflows of public and private lending, output in many developing economies either went into reverse or declined below the rate of population growth. The World Bank estimated that the recession would increase the number of people living in poverty by 65 million (see Chapter 12 in this volume by Robert Hunter Wade), and further delay realization of the Millennium Development Goals (see Chapter 13 in this volume by Nicola Phillips).

The International Monetary Fund (IMF 2010: xii) suggested that the crisis-induced write-downs of bad loans by financial institutions cost around $2.3 trillion (including $230 billion in mortgage lending in the US alone)—imposing a potentially massive burden on the public purse for the recapitalization of these institutions. Because governments had to issue bonds to cover the costs of their bail-outs of financial institutions, risk was in effect transferred from private to public balance sheets. The bail-outs, coupled with the costs of the stimulus packages that most countries introduced to fight the recession, and with a steep reduction in tax revenues owing to the economic downturn, left public finances in most industrialized economies in a parlous state. The IMF anticipated that the average budget deficit in industrialized economies was 10 per cent of **gross domestic product (GDP)** in 2009, and 8.5 per cent in 2010. As a consequence, the ratio of public debt to GDP exceeded 100 per cent in many of the eurozone economies, the United States, and Japan (where it was in excess of 200 per cent in 2012) (IMF 2012a: Table 2.1). The steep increase in sovereign debt threatened the credit ratings of some countries, particularly those in southern and eastern Europe, and left all governments with a challenge as to how to reconcile income and expenditure in the future.

On several key dimensions, the downturn precipitated by the recession was sharper than that of the 1930s. In the first year of the recession, global output and global trade fell more rapidly than in the 1930s. Similarly, global stockmarkets fell more precipitously—by 50 per cent in the first 12 months (compared with only slightly over 10 per cent in the 1930s) (Eichengreen and O'Rourke 2010). How the recession most differed from the 1930s, however, was that the initial downturn was not so protracted—with recovery in global trade, output, and in stockmarkets beginning in the second half of 2009, this recovery in itself being a reflection of the effectiveness of concerted responses at the national and global levels (see later).

One reason for the severity of the recession that began in 2008 was that, unlike previous post-war downturns, all regions of the world were in economic decline simultaneously. The extent of the crisis provided evidence that not just a quantitative increase in interdependence had occurred in recent years but also a qualitative change. As the World Trade Organization (WTO) noted, the rapid spread of the recession worldwide was caused in part by the increasing presence of global supply chains in countries' trade (see Chapter 7 in this volume by Eric Thun). With components crossing national frontiers many times before a manufactured product reaches its final destination, a decline in the major global markets for finished products quickly affects trade—and then employment—in other parts of the world. Moreover, the extent of the recession, and the rapidity with which all regions of the world were affected, posed both practical and conceptual challenges for national and international governance. For the global financial institutions (the International Monetary Fund, the World Bank), the cessation of private and public lending posed a severe challenge to their efforts to minimize the impact of the recession on developing economies (and exposed the inadequacies of the resources they had available to fight recession).

Few observers anticipated the recession (or, at least, the severity with which it would strike). The world economy had enjoyed a sustained long boom, continuing on an upward trajectory despite the bursting of the 'dot.com' bubble and the shock of the 2001 terrorist attacks. For students of global political economy, however, the possibility that the processes of globalization might be interrupted or even thrown into reverse should come as no surprise (see Chapter 10 by Anthony McGrew in this volume). The causes of the crisis were similar to those that have afflicted the world previously (albeit with some new twists, reflecting aspects of contemporary financial globalization).

The recession was triggered by the bursting of an asset price bubble—in this instance, the inflated US housing market. The term 'bubble' was coined in the United Kingdom in 1720, following the crash of the South Sea Company, and the passing in that year of the so-called 'Bubble Act'—more formally, 'An Act to Restrain the Extravagant and Unwarrantable Practice of Raising Money by Voluntary Subscription for Carrying on Projects Dangerous to the Trade and Subjects of the United Kingdom'. As in previous crises, the collapse of the asset price bubble caused panic among investors, whose uncertainty over whether they could recoup the money they had paid, inter alia, for houses, caused them to flee the market (see Chapter 9 by Louis W. Pauly in this volume). Investor panic had significantly exacerbated the other major financial crisis to affect the global economy in the previous quarter of a century—that which afflicted East Asia in 1997/98 (Noble and Ravenhill 2000; Radelet and Sachs 2000). And, as with previous crashes, the bubble was associated with behaviour that was either outside the law or certainly contrary to its spirit—the 2,200-page report issued in March 2010 by Anton R. Valukas, an examiner appointed by the US Trustee to investigate the causes of the Lehman bankruptcy, for instance, found that Lehman had used accounting sleight of hand to conceal the extent of its bad loans (de la Merced and Sorkin 2010). The excesses of the 'irrational exuberance' of the financial sector in the run-up to the financial crisis have been memorably captured in numerous movies including *Inside Job*, *The Big Short*, and *The Wolf of Wall Street*.

The globalization of finance did introduce some elements to the financial crisis that had not been seen before. The growth of financial intermediation, of which an important aspect was the securitization of mortgage debt, had two important consequences. The first was that what began as a national problem (defaults on US mortgages) was quickly transformed into a global crisis. The new mortgage-backed financial instruments had been marketed globally by American and European investment banks—with the consequence that, once the bubble burst, various institutional investors, ranging from local councils in Australia and Norway to the London Metropolitan Police's pension fund, suffered significant losses. In a low-inflation environment, these investors had been attracted to financial instruments that offered potentially higher rates of return than those available on more familiar investments and, in doing so, had either discounted or not understood the risks involved.

The second consequence was that the complexity of the new financial instruments exacerbated the problem of panic because of the uncertainty created in transactions among financial institutions (for a detailed discussion of the new 'structured financial products' see IMF 2008: ch. 2). Financial institutions found it very difficult to determine exactly what their liabilities were. Once panic set in, they were reluctant to lend to one another—and, here, another dimension of financial globalization entered the equation: the increasing dependence of bank-lending on funds borrowed in the international wholesale market, rather than on their own deposits or capital. The extreme case was that of Iceland, where the country's banks had been the main source of its international debts, which were estimated in 2008 to amount to $276,622 for every resident. In 2008/09 alone, the three largest Icelandic banks had €11 billion of debt obligations maturing, a figure approaching the country's total annual GDP (Brogger 2008). When no new financing was forthcoming, the banks collapsed. The debts were so great that the private banks could not be bailed out by the country's central bank and the losses of the financial sector were expected to total $90 billion (Wade 2009b). Financial sector deregulation in Iceland had, in Robert Wade's words, created an 'accident waiting to happen' (Wade 2009b: 14). The value of Iceland's currency measured against the euro more than halved during 2008. Iceland may have been the extreme case but similar instances of reckless behaviour by financial institutions were commonplace in Europe (especially the UK) and the United States (financial institutions in most other regions of the world had been more conservative in their approach, in part because of better regulatory frameworks introduced in response to crises in the 1980s and 1990s).

The recession undermined triumphalist notions that governments had learned to master the factors driving business or economic cycles more generally, or that unregulated markets would generate optimal outcomes. A striking feature of the early governmental response to the recession was the acknowledgement of the inadequacies of previous policy approaches, particularly in the area of financial sector regulation ('Major failures in the financial sector and in financial regulation and supervision were fundamental causes of the crisis', admitted the Group of Twenty (G20) leaders in the communiqué from their London summit (G20 2009*a*: para. 13). One of the challenges faced by governments in the wake of the financial crisis was how to improve regulation of the financial system, and to decide whether this might best be pursued at the national, regional, or global level.

The recession prompted unprecedented policy interventions at the national and global levels, and produced significant changes in global economic governance—with the emergence of the G20 as the principal intergovernmental body for global economic management (Box 1.2). The crisis also saw the revitalization of the International Monetary Fund when the G20 agreed to make an additional $850 billion available to the **international financial institutions (IFIs)** and to endorse a more flexible response from the Fund to countries experiencing financial problems (see Chapter 8 by Eric Helleiner in this volume).

At the national level, most G20 economies implemented stimulus packages that the IMF estimated were equivalent to 1.5 per cent of their GDP in 2009 and 1.25 per cent in 2010. Half of the G20 countries cut personal income taxes; a third cut indirect taxes such as value-added taxes and excise duties. Three-quarters of the G20 members increased government expenditures on infrastructure, primarily on transportation networks (IMF 2009*a*: 18). Many also increased expenditures on programmes for the most vulnerable. The concerted international response was testimony to how the governance of the global economy had changed since the great depression of the 1930s. And although governments implemented measures designed to stimulate local industries, the widespread resort to beggar-thy-neighbour protectionist policies that characterized the 1930s was avoided. G20 leaders pledged repeatedly not to introduce protectionist measures or restrictions on investment. According to

---

BOX 1.2

The G20

The Group of Twenty (G20) Finance Ministers and Central Bank Governors was established in 1999, following the financial crises that had primarily afflicted East Asia but which also spread to other developing economies, to bring together 'systemically important' industrialized and developing economies to discuss key issues in the global economy. The inaugural meeting of the G20 took place in Berlin, on 15–16 December 1999.

The membership of the G20 comprises Argentina, Australia, Brazil, Canada, China, France, Germany, India, Indonesia, Italy, Japan, Mexico, Russia, Saudi Arabia, South Africa, Republic of Korea, Turkey, the United Kingdom, and the United States. The European Union, represented by the rotating Council Presidency and by the European Central Bank, is the twentieth member of the G20. To facilitate policy coordination with the global financial institutions, the Managing Director of the International Monetary Fund and the President of the World Bank, plus the chairs of the International Monetary and Financial Committee and Development Committee of the IMF and World Bank, also participate in G20 meetings on an *ex officio* basis.

The G20 remained a relatively low-profile and low-key grouping of finance ministers and central bankers until the 2008 recession, when an inaugural meeting of the political leaders of the G20 was held in Washington, DC, in November. The elevation of the G20 to summit status was recognition on the part of the leaders of the principal industrialized economies that their own grouping (the Group of Eight (G8)—see below) was

not sufficiently representative to effectively manage the problems of an increasingly globalized economy. In particular, it was acknowledgement of the growing importance of the major developing economies—especially China, India, and Brazil. At their meeting in Pittsburgh in September 2009, the G20 leaders formalized the status of the grouping by designating 'the G20 to be the premier forum for our international economic cooperation' (G20 2009*b*: para. 19).

The Group of Seven (G7) industrialized countries had been established in 1975, the first of a series of annual meetings where politicians and officials from the world's leading economies discussed issues relating to macroeconomic policy coordination, trade, and financial policies, and relations with developing countries.

Six countries were present at the initial meeting in Rambouillet in France: Britain, France, (West) Germany, Italy, Japan, and the United States. Canada joined the group in 1976, at its second meeting. In 1977, the group allowed participation by a representative of the European Community. From 1994 onwards, the G7 met with representatives of Russia at each of its meetings; at the Birmingham meeting in 1998, Russia was accorded full membership, transforming the G7 into the G8. On 24 March 2014, the original G7 nations voted to suspend Russia from the organization in response to the country's annexation of Crimea. The G7 continues to exist alongside the G20.

For more details on the G20, see www.g20.org for the G7/G8, see www.g7.utoronto.ca

the WTO, trade restrictions imposed after the crisis affected only 4.1 per cent of global merchandise imports (cited in World Bank 2015c: 173). By 2011, the value of global trade and production (but not foreign direct investment) had recovered to its pre-crisis levels. This surprisingly rapid recovery, according to one commentator, demonstrated that 'the system worked' (Drezner 2014).

For some observers, however, particularly those in Europe and the United States, the global recession did reflect one dimension of beggar-thy-neighbour policies that were at least as important in contributing to the recession as were regulatory failures: the mounting imbalances in international trade and payments, which they attributed primarily to China's determination to avoid a rapid appreciation of its currency against the US dollar. One of the missions with which the G20 has tasked the IMF is to analyse 'whether policies pursued by individual G20 countries are collectively consistent with more sustainable and balanced trajectories for the global economy' (G20 2009b: para. 7), a coordinating role that the IMF has singularly failed to perform since its foundation. With slow rates of growth lingering in many industrialized economies a decade after the onset of the crisis, governments in several major economies attempted to push down their exchange rates in an effort to stimulate demand for their exports—a worrying trend towards beggar-thy-neighbour policies that contributed to the severity of the Great Depression of the 1930s.

A decade after the onset of the Global Financial Crisis, there were increasing fears that it had produced a medium-term downward shift in global economic growth (Figure 1.1). Global GDP was more than 4.5 per cent below what it would have been had post-crisis growth rates been equivalent to the long-run pre-crisis average. After a sharp recovery in the immediate aftermath of the crisis, the growth in global GDP has been on a downward trend (Figure 1.2). The international financial institutions have repeatedly referred to the performance of the global economy in the years since the financial crisis as disappointing and 'mediocre'. Figure 1.2 suggests a downward trend has also occurred in the growth of global trade.

The Global Financial Crisis may have produced a downward shift in growth rates for several reasons. Investment rates in many economies have been lower since 2008–9. Various factors underlie this decline. Businesses, especially small and medium-sized enterprises, in a number of economies have found it more difficult to raise capital because lenders have become more risk-averse. Conservatism in lending has also been encouraged by new international principles governing the capital adequacy of banks (the Basel III Accord—see Pauly, Chapter 9 in this volume), which require banks to hold a higher ratio of

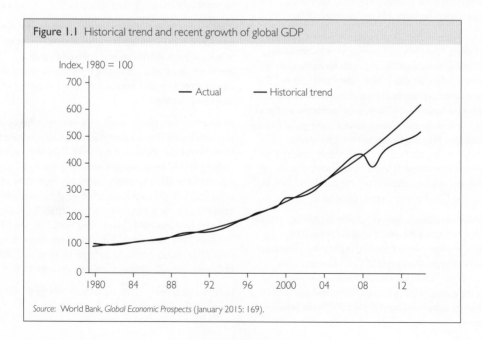

Figure 1.1 Historical trend and recent growth of global GDP

Index, 1980 = 100

— Actual   — Historical trend

Source: World Bank, *Global Economic Prospects* (January 2015: 169).

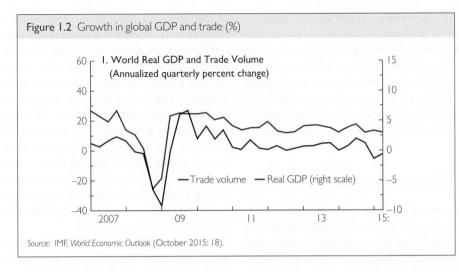

Figure 1.2 Growth in global GDP and trade (%)

1. World Real GDP and Trade Volume
(Annualized quarterly percent change)

— Trade volume — Real GDP (right scale)

Source: IMF, *World Economic Outlook* (October 2015: 18).

high-quality liquid assets to cash outflows than in the past. Businesses have become reluctant to invest in an environment of reduced consumer demand, itself exacerbated in some countries by fears of deflation (the expectation that prices will decline in the future). Foreign Direct Investment in aggregate remains substantially below its pre-financial crisis peaks (UNCTAD 2015*b*). Current lower levels of expenditure on research and development may lead to lower levels of innovation and productivity in the future. Unemployment may encourage some workers to leave the workforce permanently.

Much of the slowing of global trade has involved developing economies. Their recent economic performance, however, points to the role of factors other than the financial crisis itself in constraining their performance. Early optimism regarding developing countries' speed of recovery from the crisis has turned to pessimism because of the slow growth in some of their principal markets (notably Europe and China), the withdrawal of funds from developing country capital markets, and the decline in commodity prices since mid 2011. Here, China has played a particularly important role, a reflection of notable changes in the distribution of economic influence discussed in the second part of this chapter. From 2003 to 2008, China's metal consumption grew at an annual average rate of 16 per cent, accounting for fully 80 per cent of the increase in world demand. China now accounts for half of the world's consumption of base metals and alone is fully responsible for one half of the world's steel production (IMF 2015*c*: 41). The slowdown in China's growth in the middle of the second decade of this century has affected the economies of developing economies both directly (through reduced demand for their exports) and indirectly (through suppressing the prices of commodities). The World Bank estimates, for instance, that a 1 per cent decline in China's growth produces a 0.6 per cent decline in growth in Latin America and the Caribbean (World Bank 2015*c*: 78).

The Global Financial Crisis and the responses of the international community to it provide an excellent illustration of many of the themes of this book:

• the growing interdependence of countries in a globalizing economy;

• the vulnerability of the contemporary global financial system to periodic crises;

• the speed with which developments in one part of the world economy are transmitted to others;

• the increased significance of private actors in the contemporary global economy, especially in the financial sector;

• the way in which crises prompt governments to seek collaboration to regulate international markets—but concurrently the difficulties that states have in coordinating their behaviours to take effective action;

• the significant and evolving role of international institutions in responding to crises; and

• the manner in which the increased severity of financial crises has had an impact on poverty and inequality.

Although, as will become evident in later chapters, contributors to this book hold a variety of perspectives on the question of whether there is such a thing as a 'global' economy, all would accept that we live in a *globalizing* economy that differs in some fundamental ways from anything that the world has previously experienced. The following section briefly sketches how the world economy evolved to reach its present state.

The world economy pre-1914

The 'modern world economy', most historians agree, came into existence in the late fifteenth and sixteenth centuries. It was in large part a response to a deepening economic crisis within feudal systems as agricultural productivity declined (Wallerstein 1974). This was a period in which despotic monarchs in Western Europe, seeking to consolidate their power against both internal and external foes, pushed to extend the boundaries of markets. In this era of **mercantilism**, political power was equated with wealth, and wealth with power (Viner 1948). Wealth, in the form of bullion generated by trade surpluses or seized from enemies, enabled monarchs to build the administrative apparatus of their states and to finance the construction of military forces. The new concentration of military power could be projected, both internally and externally, to extract further resources. The consolidation of the state went hand in hand with the extension of markets. Gradually, most parts of the world were enmeshed in a Eurocentric economy, as suppliers of raw materials and 'luxury' goods. Britain adopted domestic reforms largely pioneered by the Netherlands (which had the world's highest per capita income in the seventeenth and eighteenth centuries) to supplant the Dutch in many world markets: armed conflict and the use of the Navigation Acts (1651–1849), which restricted the use of foreign vessels in British trade, enabled it to monopolize trade with its ever-expanding empire.

The era of mercantilism did not, however, bring a notable increase in overall global wealth. Before 1820, per capita incomes in most parts of the world were not significantly different from those of the previous eight *centuries* (they increased by less than an average of one-tenth of 1 per cent each year between 1700 and 1820). And despite the striking extension of the global market during the seventeenth and eighteenth centuries, the vast majority of commerce continued to be conducted within individual localities until the advent of the Industrial Revolution. The introduction of steam power in the first half of the nineteenth century revolutionized transportation, both internally and internationally. And in the second half of the nineteenth century, further technological advances—the introduction of refrigerated ships, the laying of submarine telegraph cables—contributed to a 'shrinking' of the world and to a deepening of the international division of labour. The value of world exports grew tenfold (from a relatively small base) between 1820 and 1870: from 1870 to 1913, world exports grew at an annual average rate of 3.4 per cent, substantially above the 2.1 annual increase in world GDP (Maddison 2001: 262, table B–19, and 362, table F–4).

Trade was becoming increasingly important to world welfare, yet the pattern of international commerce in 1913—indeed, even in 1945—was not dramatically different from that of the eighteenth century. The industrialized countries of the world—essentially a Western European core to which had been added the United States and Japan by the turn of the twentieth century—exported principally manufactured goods, while the rest of the world supplied agricultural products and raw materials to feed the industrialized countries' workforces and to fuel their manufacturing plants (as a relative latecomer to industrialization, and an economy with significant **comparative advantage** in agricultural production, the United States was an exception to this generalization: cotton remained the single most important export for the United States in 1913, contributing nearly twice the value of exports of machinery and iron and steel combined; it was not until 1930 that machinery exports exceeded those of cotton, although by 1910 the US had become a net exporter of manufactured goods (data from Mitchell 1993: 504, table E3; and Irwin 2003)).

With the exception of the United States, trade among the industrialized countries in manufactured goods remained relatively unimportant. In 1913, for example, agricultural products and other primary products constituted two-thirds of the total imports of the United Kingdom. To be sure, some changes had occurred in the composition of imports. Although the 'luxury' imports of the previous centuries—sugar, tea, coffee, and tobacco—had become staples in the diet of the new urban working and middle classes, their aggregate importance in European imports had shrunk relative to other commodities, notably wheat and flour, butter and vegetable oils, and meat (Offer 1989: 82, Table 6.1).

For the early European industrializers, trade with their colonies, dominions, or with the other lands of recent European settlement, such as Argentina, was more important than trade with other industrialized countries. For the United Kingdom, a larger share of imports was contributed by Argentina, Australia, Canada, and India together than by the United States, despite the latter's importance in British imports of cotton for its burgeoning textiles industry. These four countries also took five times the American share of British exports in 1913 (Mitchell 1992: 644, table E2). Similarly, Algeria was a larger market for French exports in 1913 than was the United States.

Tariffs continued to constitute a significant barrier to international trade, even in what is often termed the 'golden age' of liberalism before 1914. Most industrialized countries (the significant exceptions being the United Kingdom and the Netherlands) had actually raised the level of their tariffs in the last three decades of the nineteenth century to protect their domestic producers against the increasing import competition that had been facilitated by lower transport costs. In 1913, the average tariff level in Germany and Japan was 12 per cent, in France 16 per cent, and in the United States 32.5 per cent (Maddison 1989: 47, Table 4.4). The post-1870 increase in tariffs offset some of the gains from lower transportation costs. Lindert and Williamson (2001) estimate that nearly three-quarters of the closer integration of markets that occurred in the century before the outbreak of the First World War is attributable to these lower transport costs (see McGrew, Chapter 10 in this volume).

Governments continued to erect barriers to the movement of goods in the second part of the nineteenth century, but capital and people moved relatively freely across the globe, their mobility facilitated by developments in transportation and communication. From 1820 to 1913, 26 million people migrated from Europe to the United States, Canada, Australia, New Zealand, Argentina, and Brazil. Five million Indians followed the British flag in migrating to Burma, Malaya, Sri Lanka, and Africa, while an even larger number of Chinese are estimated to have migrated to other countries on the Western Pacific rim (Maddison 2001: 98). The opening up of the lands of 'new settlement' required massive capital investments—in railways in particular. By 1913, the United Kingdom, France, and Germany had investments abroad totalling over $33 billion: after the 1870s, Britain invested more than half its savings abroad, and the income from its foreign investments in 1913 was equivalent to almost 10 per cent of all the goods and services produced domestically (Maddison 2001: 100).

The spectacular growth in international economic integration was not accompanied by any significant institutionalization of intergovernmental collaboration. Even though the Anglo-French Cobden–Chevalier Treaty of 1860 had introduced the principle of **most-favoured nation status** (MFN) into international trade agreements (see Box 1.3), governments conducted trade negotiations on a bilateral basis rather than under the auspices of an international institution.

The international financial system was similarly characterized by a lack of institutionalization. The rapid growth of economic integration was facilitated by the international adoption of the **gold standard** (see Box 1.4). The origins of the nineteenth-century gold standard lay in action by the Bank of England in 1821 to make all its notes convertible into gold (although Britain had operated a de facto gold standard from as early as 1717). The United States, though formally on a bimetallic (gold and silver) standard, switched to a *de facto* gold standard in 1834 and turned this into a de jure arrangement in 1900. Germany and

---

BOX 1.3

Most-Favoured Nation Status (MFN)

Under the most-favoured nation (MFN) principle, a government is obliged to grant to any trading partner with which it has signed an agreement treatment equivalent to the best ('most preferred') it offers to any of its partners. For example, if France signed a trade treaty with Germany in which it reduced its tariffs on imports of German steel to 8 per cent, it would be obliged, under the most-favoured nation principle, if it signed a trade treaty with the United States, also to reduce its tariffs on imports of US steel to 8 per cent. The MFN principle is the foundation for non-discrimination in international trade, and is often asserted to be the 'cornerstone' of the post-1945 trade regime (see Capling and Trommer, Chapter 5 in this volume). The MFN principle makes a significant contribution to depoliticizing trade relations because: (a) countries are obliged to give equivalent treatment to all trading partners, regardless of their economic power; and (b) countries cannot discriminate in their treatment of the trade of certain partners simply because they do not like the political complexion or policies of the governments of these countries.

BOX 1.4

The Gold Standard

A gold standard requires a country to fix the price of its domestic currency in terms of a specific amount of gold. National money (which may or may not consist of gold coins, because other metallic coins and banknotes were also used in some countries) and bank deposits would be freely convertible into gold at the specified price.

Under the gold standard, because the level of each country's economic activity is determined by its money supply, which in turn rests on its gold holdings, a disequilibrium in its balance of trade in principle would be self-correcting. Let us assume, for example, that Britain is running a trade deficit with the United States because inflation in Britain has made its exports relatively unattractive to US consumers. Because British exports do not cover the full costs of imports from the United States, British authorities would have to transfer gold to the US Treasury. This transfer would reduce the domestic money supply, and hence the level of economic activity in Britain, having a deflationary effect on the domestic economy, and depressing its demand for imports. In the United States, the opposite would occur: an inflow of gold would boost the money supply, thereby generating additional economic activity in the United States and increasing inflationary pressures there. Higher levels of economic activity would also increase the country's demand for imports. Changes in the money supplies in the two countries brought about by the transfer of gold, therefore, would bring their demand for goods back into balance and lead to a restoration of the ratio of the two countries' prices to that reflected in the exchange rate between their currencies.

In principle, the gold standard should act to restore equilibrium automatically in international payments. Central banks, however, were also expected to facilitate adjustment by raising their interest rates when countries were suffering a payments deficit (thereby further dampening domestic economic activities and making domestic investments more attractive to foreigners) and, conversely, to lower interest rates when their economies were experiencing a payments surplus. For most of the period from 1870 to 1914, the Bank of England played by the rules of the game fairly consistently. Other central banks—including those of France and Belgium—did not. They frequently intervened to attempt to shield the domestic economy from the effects of gold flows (to 'sterilize' their effects) by buying or selling securities (thereby reducing or increasing the volume of gold circulating in the domestic economy).

The gold standard was vulnerable to shocks, which were often transmitted quickly from one country to another. The discovery of gold in California in 1848, for example, led to an increase in the US money supply, domestic inflation, and an outflow of gold to its trade partners, which in turn raised their domestic price levels. Countries on the periphery were particularly vulnerable to shocks: interest-rate increases in the industrialized countries, for example, often drew capital from the periphery, leaving the peripheral countries with the major burden of adjustment.

For further discussion, see Eichengreen (1985) and Officer (2001).

other industrializing economies followed suit in the 1870s. Because every country fixed the value of its national currency in terms of gold, each currency had a fixed exchange rate against every other in the system (assume, for example, that the United States sets the value of its currency as $100 per ounce of gold, while the United Kingdom sets its value at £50 per ounce of gold: the exchange rate between the two currencies would be £1 = $2).

The great contribution of the gold standard to facilitating international commerce was that economic agents generally did not have to worry about foreign exchange risks: the possibility that the value of the currency of a foreign country would change vis-à-vis their domestic currency and thus, for example, reduce the value of their foreign investments. British investors in American railways could be confident that the dollars

they had bought with their sterling investments would buy the same amount of sterling at the date their investment matured, and that the US Treasury would convert the dollars back into gold at this time. Meanwhile, they received interest on the sums invested. Confidence in the gold standard did not rest on any international institution but rather on the commitment of individual governments to maintain the opportunity for individuals to convert their domestic currencies into gold at a fixed exchange rate. Ultimately, the implementation of the gold standard rested on the assumption that governments had both the capacity and the will to impose economic pain on their domestic populations when deflation was needed in order to bring their economy back into equilibrium when experiencing trade deficits. These domestic costs became less acceptable with the rise of working-class political representation, and with the growth of expectations that a fundamental responsibility of governments was to ensure domestic full employment.

KEY POINTS

- The modern world economy came into existence in the fifteenth and sixteenth centuries.

- Despite the significant changes that occurred in the three centuries before the outbreak of the First World War, the fundamental composition and direction of international trade remained unchanged.

- Neither in the field of trade nor of finance was any significant international institution constructed in the years before 1914.

- Advances in technology were the main driving force behind the integration of markets, and they facilitated the enormous growth in investment and migration in the nineteenth century.

- The great merit of the gold standard was that it provided certainty for international transactions because it largely removed the risk of foreign exchange losses.

The world economy in the interwar period

The outbreak of the First World War was a devastating blow to cosmopolitan liberalism: it destroyed the credibility of the liberal argument that economic interdependence in itself would be sufficient to foster an era of peaceful coexistence among states. The war brought to an end an era of unprecedented economic interdependence among the leading industrial countries. As discussed in the chapters by McGrew and Hay in this book (see Chapters 10 and 11), for many industrialized economies, indicators of economic openness and interdependence did not regain their pre-First World War levels until the 1970s.

The war devastated the economies of Europe: subsequent political instability compounded economic disruptions. Economic reconstruction was further complicated by demands that Germany make reparations for its aggression, and that Britain and other European countries repay their wartime borrowings from the United States. The economic chaos of the interwar years was a sorry reflection of the inability of governments to agree on measures to restore economic stability, and of their resort to beggar-thy-neighbour policies in their efforts to alleviate domestic economic distress. Although the collapse of international trade in the 1930s is the feature of the interwar economy that figures most prominently in stories of this era, the most fundamental problem of the period was the inability of states to construct a viable international financial system.

The international gold standard broke down with the outbreak of war in August 1914, when a speculative attack on sterling caused the Bank of England to impose exchange controls—a refusal to convert sterling into gold and a de facto ban on gold exports. Other countries followed suit. Leading countries agreed to reinstate a modified version of the international gold standard in 1925. They failed to act consistently, however, in re-establishing the link between national currencies and gold. The United Kingdom restored the convertibility of sterling at the pre-war gold price, despite the domestic inflation that had occurred in the intervening decade. The consequence was that sterling was generally reckoned to be overvalued by at least 10 per cent, making British exports uncompetitive. It proved very difficult for the British government to establish an equilibrium in its **balance of payments** without imposing severe deflation domestically. Other countries—notably France, Belgium, and Italy—restored convertibility of their currencies at a much lower price of gold than had prevailed before 1914.

The resulting misalignment of currencies was compounded by higher trade barriers than had existed before 1914, the absence of a country/central bank with the resources and the will to provide leadership to the system, and by a failure of central banks to play by the 'rules of the game' of the gold standard. Their inclination to intervene to 'sterilize' the domestic impact of international gold flows was symptomatic of a more fundamental underlying problem: in an era when the working class had been fully enfranchised, when trade unions had become important players in political systems, especially in Western Europe, and when governments were expected to take responsibility for maintaining full employment and promoting domestic economic welfare, the subordination of the domestic economy to the dictates of global markets in the form of the international gold standard was no longer politically acceptable. Polanyi (1944) is the classic statement of this argument; on the misguided attempts by Britain to restore the convertibility of sterling at pre-1914 levels, see Keynes (1925).

The abandonment of the international gold standard followed another speculative attack on sterling in the middle of 1931. The Bank of England lost much of its reserves in July and August of that year, and Britain left the gold standard in September, a move that precipitated a sharp depreciation of the pound (testimony to its overvaluation in the brief period in which the gold standard was restored). Other countries again quickly followed in breaking the link between their currencies and gold. By then, the world economy was in depression, following the shocks to the world economy transmitted from the United States after the Wall Street collapse of October 1929. The gold standard almost certainly exacerbated the effects of the depression, because government efforts to maintain the link between their currencies and gold constrained the use of expansionary (inflationary) policies to combat unemployment and low levels of domestic demand (Eichengreen 1992).

The world economy was already in depression before the US Congress, in response to concerns about the intensification of import competition for domestic farmers, passed the infamous Smoot–Hawley Tariff of 1930. This raised US tariffs to historically high levels (an average *ad valorem* tariff of 41 per cent, although tariff rates were already very high as a result of the Tariff Act of 1922, the Fordney–McCumber Tariff). Retaliation from US trading partners quickly followed, with European countries giving preferential tariff treatment to their colonies. The value of world trade declined by two-thirds between 1929 and 1934, and became increasingly concentrated in closed imperial blocks.

As in the pre-1914 period, international institutions played no significant role in the governance of international economic matters. The League of Nations had established an Economic and Financial Organization with subcommittees on the various areas of international economic relations. It enjoyed success in the early 1920s in coordinating a financial reconstruction package of £26 million for Austria. It also held various conferences aimed at facilitating trade by promoting common standards on customs procedures, compilation of economic statistics, and so on. But the economic and political disarray of the interwar period simply overwhelmed the League's limited resources and legitimacy: the move to restore international economic collaboration awaited effective action by the world's leading economy, the United States. This began with the passage by Congress in 1934 of the Reciprocal Trade Agreements Act (RTAA), which gave the president the authority to negotiate foreign trade agreements (without Congressional approval). The RTAA and the subsequent signature before 1939 of trade agreements with 20 of America's trading partners laid the foundations for the multilateral system that emerged after the Second World War (the reasons why US trade policy changed so dramatically between 1930 and 1934 have been a focus of significant work in international political economy; see Hiscox 1999; Irwin and Kroszner 1997).

> **KEY POINTS**
>
> - Misalignment of exchange rates contributed to the problems of economic adjustment in the 1920s.
> - The world economy was already in recession before tariffs were raised in the early 1930s—but higher tariffs exacerbated the decline in international trade.
> - States did not negotiate any significant institutionalization of international economic relations in the interwar period.

The world economy post-1945

The world economy that emerged after the Second World War was qualitatively different from anything experienced before. John Ruggie, a leading theorist of political economy, has identified two fundamental principles that distinguish the post-war economy from its predecessors: the adoption of what Ruggie (1982), following Polanyi (1944), terms **embedded liberalism**, and a commitment to **multilateralism** (Ruggie 1992).

Embedded liberalism refers to the compromise that governments made after 1945 between safeguarding their domestic economic objectives, especially a commitment to maintaining full employment, on the one hand, and an opening up of the domestic economy to allow for the restoration of international trade and investment on the other. The 'embedding' of the commitment to economic openness—the liberal element—within domestic economic and political objectives was attained through the inclusion of provisions in the rules of international trade and finance that allowed governments to opt out, on a temporary basis, from their international commitments should these threaten fundamental domestic economic objectives. Moreover, an acknowledgement of the legitimacy of the principle that governments should give priority to the pursuit of domestic economic objectives was also written into the rules of the game. The adoption of the principle of embedded liberalism was a recognition by governments that international economic collaboration rested on their capacity to maintain domestic political consensus—and that international economic collaboration was, fundamentally, a political bargain. This recognition explains, for example, why the agricultural sector was for many years excluded from trade liberalization: the domestic political costs for governments of negotiating freer trade in agricultural products were judged to be so high as to jeopardize otherwise politically feasible trade liberalization in other sectors.

The institutionalization of international economic cooperation is another fundamental change in international economic relations in the post-war period. Neither in the period of relative stability of the pre-First World War gold standard era nor in the chaos of the 1930s did leading economies create significant international economic institutions. A commitment to multilateralism is one of the defining characteristics of the post-1945 order. For Ruggie (1992: 571), multilateralism is not merely a matter of numbers—it involves collaboration among three or more states, not necessarily all members of the system—but it also has a *qualitative* element in that the coordination of relations is on 'the basis of "generalized" principles of conduct—that is, principles which specify appropriate conduct for a class of actions, without regard to the particularistic interests of the parties or the strategic exigencies that may exist in any specific occurrence'. A

classic example is the most-favoured-nation principle, with its requirement that products from all trading partners must be treated in the same manner regardless of the characteristics of the countries involved. This principle for the conduct of trade contrasts, for example, with the largely bilateral trade agreements of the interwar years, where governments, rather than applying a generalized principle to their trade relations, discriminated in their treatment of individual trading partners.

The commitment to multilateralism that developed in the late 1930s and during the Second World War bore immediate fruit in the founding of the **Bretton Woods** multilateral financial institutions: the International Monetary Fund and the World Bank (see Box 1.5). Note, however, that these global or universal institutions, membership of which is open to all states in the international system, are just one form of multilateralism. For the whole of the period since 1945, but especially since the mid 1990s, regional institutions have also played an important role in international economic (as well as security) affairs (see Ravenhill, Chapter 6 in this volume). States have increasingly enmeshed themselves in a dense web of multilateral institutions.

The unprecedented rates of economic growth achieved in the years after 1945 attest to the success of the pursuit of multilateral economic collaboration in this period. Global GDP grew at close to 5 per cent in the period 1950–73. Although the recessions that followed the oil price rises of 1973–4 and 1979–80, and the debt crises that afflicted Latin America and Africa, contributed to a slowing of growth in the

---

BOX 1.5

Bretton Woods

In 1944, the Western allies brought together their principal economic advisers for a conference at the Mount Washington Hotel in the village of Bretton Woods, New Hampshire, to chart the future of the international economy in the post-war period. The 44 governments represented at what was officially known as the United Nations Monetary and Financial Conference agreed on the principles that would govern international finance in the post-war years, and to create two major international institutions to assist in the management of these arrangements: the International Monetary Fund; and the World Bank (formally known as the International Bank for

Reconstruction and Development). For details of the discussions at the conference, see van Dormael (1978) and Helleiner (2014a).

These institutions and the rules for managing international finance that were agreed became known collectively as the Bretton Woods regimes. In 1947, a United Nations Conference on Trade and Employment in Havana, Cuba, drew up a charter (www.wto.org/english/docs_e/legal_e/havana_e.pdf) for an International Trade Organization (ITO), to complement the Bretton Woods financial institutions. The ITO never came into existence, however—see Capling and Trommer, Chapter 5 in this volume.

quarter-century after 1973, world GDP nonetheless grew at an average of 3 per cent per annum, a faster rate than during any period before 1945 (Maddison 2001: 262, Table 8–19). Moreover, world trade grew more rapidly than world production: world exports expanded by close to 8 per cent per annum in the years 1950–73, and by 5 per cent annually in the subsequent 25-year period (Maddison 2001: 362, table F–4). The internationalized sector consequently grew in importance in most economies, with important implications for the balance of domestic political interests on trade policy issues (see Hiscox, Chapter 4 in this volume).

Aggregate rates of growth, however, disguised substantial variations across different regions of the world economy. The gap between rich and poor widened substantially (see Figure 1.3). In 1500, little difference had existed in per capita incomes across various regions of the world. Incomes per head in the United States did not exceed those of China until the second quarter of the eighteenth century. By the third quarter of the nineteenth century, however, a marked gap had developed between incomes per capita in the United States and Western Europe on the one hand, and those of the rest of the world. Per capita incomes in Africa and in most parts of Asia stagnated (and in

China actually regressed for a century). Despite the economic turmoil and slower rates of growth of the interwar years, the absolute gap between the industrialized economies and the rest of the world continued to widen: the divergence increased rapidly in the post-1945 era. Only a handful of previously **less developed countries** (**LDCs**), mostly in East Asia, made significant progress in closing the gap. Africa, meanwhile, became increasingly detached from the globalizing economy: its exports, measured in constant prices, barely expanded in the years between 1973 and 1990. The poor export performance contributed to falls in per capita income that occurred in the majority of years between 1973 and 1998. By the latter date, the average per capita income in Africa was no more than Western Europe had experienced in 1820 (all data drawn from Maddison 2001). Growing international inequality has been a fundamental part of the modern globalizing economy (see Wade, Chapter 12 in this volume).

Another defining characteristic of the post-1945 international economy was the growth in the number of **transnational corporations** (**TNCs**) (also referred to in some chapters of this volume as multinational enterprises). A growth of significant private economic

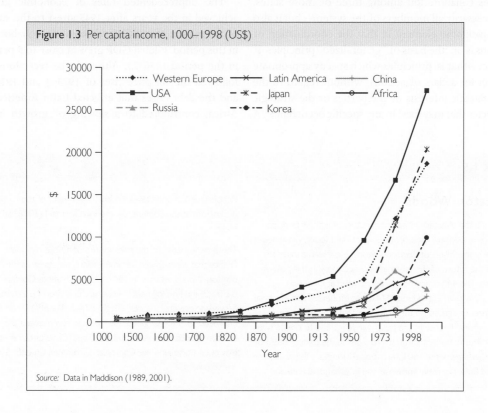

Figure 1.3 Per capita income, 1000–1998 (US$)

Source: Data in Maddison (1989, 2001).

enterprises with international operations had accompanied the emergence of the modern world economy in the fifteenth century. These, however, were primarily trading companies, such as the East India Company, specializing in moving goods between national markets. And when foreign investment took off in earnest, in the half-century before the First World War, the vast majority of it was **portfolio investment**—that is, investment in bonds and other financial instruments that did not give investors management control over the borrowing company. Companies that engaged in foreign direct investment—that is, the ownership and management of assets in more than one country for the purposes of production of goods or services (the definition of a TNC)—were relative rarities before 1945 (with some notable exceptions, such as the major oil companies and IBM). In the post-Second World War years, FDI took off, and has grown more rapidly than either production or international trade (see Thun, Chapter 7 in this volume).

The TNC has become the key actor in the globalizing economy. By 2009, it was estimated that there were 82,000 TNCs in operation, controlling more than 810,000 subsidiaries worldwide (UNCTAD 2009*b*: 18). By 2014, the global stock of FDI amounted to about $26 trillion, and the value added by TNC subsidiaries was equal to about 10 per cent of the world's GDP. Moreover, sales by the subsidiaries of TNCs were nearly 50% more than the total value of world trade: an estimated $36 trillion (UNCTAD 2015*b*: 18). Whereas in the period before 1960, the vast majority of FDI and TNCs came from the United States, in subsequent years the American presence has been supplemented by corporations with their headquarters in Europe, Japan, Korea, and, increasingly, in less developed countries such as Brazil, China, and India (for further discussion, see Dicken 2015). **Sovereign wealth funds** have also become major sources of foreign investment.

The activities of TNCs, in turn, have fundamentally transformed the nature of international trade. Both the composition and direction of trade have changed dramatically since 1945. Whereas in the interwar years the composition of trade differed little from that of the previous centuries—that is, it was based on the exchange of raw materials and agricultural products for manufactured goods, since the post-war reconstruction of Europe and Japan, the principal component of trade has been the international exchange of manufactured goods. At first, this trade was

primarily among the industrialized countries. In many instances, it involved **intra-industry trade**, that is, the international exchange of products from the same industry. For example, intra-industry trade occurs when Sweden exports Volvo cars to Germany and imports BMW vehicles from Germany. As this example suggests, product differentiation by brand name often provides the basis for intra-industry trade, and bears little resemblance to the comparative advantage-based explanation for trade that underlies conventional economic theory. In the last quarter of a century, the growth in intra-industry trade has occurred not so much in the exchange of finished products but of components that are often moved across several national boundaries before assembly and then exported to their final markets—a process that economists have termed the 'fragmentation' of production.

Since the 1980s, in particular, less developed countries have also been integrated into the international production networks led by TNCs (see Thun, Chapter 7 in this volume). Many developing countries have changed the structure of their tariffs to give preference to the processing and assembling of components that are subsequently exported. The World Trade Organization estimates that at the turn of the century such processing activities accounted for more than 80 per cent of the exports of the Dominican Republic, close to 60 per cent of the exports of China, and nearly 50 per cent of the exports of Mexico (WTO 2000*a*). This participation in global production networks is the most significant factor in a dramatic change in the commodity composition of the exports of less developing countries. Contrary to some popular impressions, by the end of the 1990s manufactured exports constituted 70 per cent of the total exports from the developing world. The share of manufactures in their exports had increased threefold since the end of the 1970s (UNCTAD 2001: xviii).

Reference to these less developed economies provides a timely reminder of another dramatic change in international economic relations since 1945—a huge augmentation in the number of independent states in the system. As noted in Box 1.5, only 44 countries were represented at the Bretton Woods conference, which was dominated by the industrialized countries of Europe and North America, but also included a few of the long-independent countries of Central and South America. Within two decades, almost all of the colonies of the European countries had gained their independence. This development had profound implications for the international system. One was simply the consequence of an increase in both the number of states and in the diversity of the international community: the number of states in the system more than doubled. Collaboration in international economic relations and the management of various dimensions of this collaboration became increasingly complex, illustrated very clearly in the trade sphere by the difficulties in negotiating the Uruguay and Doha Rounds of WTO talks (see Capling and Trommer, Chapter 5 in this volume, for details of these discussions; and Aggarwal and Dupont, Chapter 3, for a discussion of the problems that larger numbers pose for collaboration). The growth in the number of less developed countries also brought institutional changes, most notably in the foundation of the United Nations Conference on Trade and Development (UNCTAD) in 1964. And the new arithmetic in the international system generally, and particularly within the United Nations system, contributed to a change in international norms with the adoption, first, of decolonization (Jackson 1993), and then of development as core norms of the modern system.

Another defining characteristic of the contemporary system contributed to the enshrining of the development norm—the vast expansion in the number of non-governmental organizations (NGOs), many of which were focused on the alleviation of poverty (for further discussion of this topic, see the chapters in this volume by Wade and Phillips). NGOs have also been prominent in global environmental affairs (see Dauvergne, Chapter 14 in this volume) and, increasingly, in international trade. Relations between industrialized and less developed countries, and issues relating to global poverty and inequality, emerged as an important dimension of the study of international political economy, the evolution of which is discussed in the next section of this chapter.

KEY POINTS

The post-war international economy was qualitatively different from anything that preceded it, on several dimensions:

- states made a commitment to multilateralism, reflected in the construction of institutions at the global and regional levels;

- the world economy grew at unprecedented rates after 1945—the internationalized component of economies became more significant as trade and foreign investment grew more rapidly than production;
- TNCs and FDI emerged as key agents in the process of internationalization;
- the composition and direction of international trade changed dramatically, with intra-industry trade among industrialized economies constituting the majority of aggregate world trade; and
- the number of countries in the international system rose substantially.

The study of global political economy

The emergence of global political economy as a distinct subfield

Global political economy (GPE) developed as a significant subfield in the study of international relations in the 1970s. As has so often been the case in political science, the emergence of a new subject area was a response both to real-world changes and to trends in theorizing within and outside the discipline (see Box 1.6).

In the early 1970s, the global economy entered a period of turbulence following an unprecedented period of stable economic growth. The 'long boom' from the early post-war years through to 1970 benefited developed and less developed economies alike. Because of the comparative stability of this period, it was commonplace to regard international economic relations as a relatively uncontentious issue area that could be left to technocrats to manage. All this changed in the late 1960s, however, when the US economy encountered increasing problems because its commitment to a **fixed exchange rate** constrained its policy options at a time when domestic inflation was being fuelled by high levels of government expenditure—domestically, on social programmes, and internationally on the pursuit of the Vietnam War. In August 1971, a new era of instability in the global economy was ushered in when the Nixon administration unilaterally devalued the dollar (for further discussion, see Helleiner, Chapter 8 in this volume). In doing so, it set in train events that

BOX 1.6

What's in a Name? International Versus Global Political Economy

When international relations scholars began to examine economic issues in depth, the new subfield inherited the rather misleading adjective 'international' as the leading word in its title. Commentators have often pointed out that 'international' relations is a misnomer for its subject matter in that it confuses 'nation' with 'state', and fails to acknowledge the significance of private actors in global politics. But labels, like institutions, are often 'sticky'—once adopted, it is difficult to displace them, even if a better alternative is available. The abbreviation, IPE, has become synonymous with the field of study. Even though we prefer 'global political economy' for the title of the book because it reflects more accurately the contemporary subject matter of this field, many of the contributors follow conventional usage in employing the abbreviation IPE and in referring to 'international' political economy.

While the study of global political economy achieved a new prominence in the 1970s, a variety of work in what would now be recognized as the field of GPE was published much earlier than this. A prominent example is Albert Hirschman's (1945) study of asymmetries in Germany's economic relations with its East European neighbours. Much of the work in the field of development economics that blossomed in the post-war period included a significant focus on political and international components. And the Marxist tradition of political economy remained vibrant, particularly in Europe.

To confuse matters, the study of economics was known in the eighteenth and nineteenth centuries as political economy (see, for example, John Stuart Mill's (1970), *Principles of Political Economy* [first published in 1848]). The titles of some leading journals in the field of economics—for example, the *Journal of Political Economy*, first published in 1892—reflect this older usage.

were to end the system of fixed exchange rates, one of the pillars of the Bretton Woods financial regime.

The new instability in international finance reinforced perceptions that the global economy was about to enter an era of significant upheaval. Commodity prices had risen substantially in the early 1970s; Western concerns about the future availability and pricing of raw materials were compounded by the success of the Organization of the Petroleum Exporting Countries (OPEC) during the Arab–Israeli war of 1973 in substantially increasing the price of crude oil. Less developed countries believed that they could use their new-found 'commodity power' to engineer a dramatic restructuring of international economic regimes, a demand they made through calls at the United Nations for a **New International Economic Order (NIEO)** (see Phillips, Chapter 13 in this volume). Industrialized economies were already having difficulty in coping with a surge in imports of manufactured goods from Japan and the East Asian **newly industrializing economies (NIEs)**, causing them to revert to various discriminatory measures to protect their domestic industries, in disregard of their obligations under the international trade regime. In trade and finance regimes alike, new pressures were causing governments to seek to rewrite the rules governing international economic interactions.

At this time of the greatest instability in international economic relations since the depression of the 1930s, interstate relations in the security realm, which had been the principal focus of the study of post-war international relations, appeared to be on the verge of entering a new era of collaboration. The United States was winding down its involvement in Indo-China; Henry Kissinger was negotiating détente with the Soviet Union; and President Nixon's visit to China in 1972 appeared to presage a new epoch in which China would be integrated peacefully into the international system. For many scholars of international relations, the traditional agenda of the discipline was incomplete and the preoccupation of the dominant, realist approach with security issues and military power seemed increasingly irrelevant to the new international environment (Keohane and Nye 1972; Morse 1976).

The new turbulence in international economic relations prompted political scientists to take an interest in a subject matter that had previously been left largely to economists. It was not, as some commentators suggested, that international economic relations had suddenly become 'politicized'. Politics and asymmetries in power had always underlain the structure of global economic relations, seen, for example, in the content of the various financial regimes negotiated at Bretton Woods. Rather, what was novel was that the turbulence of the early 1970s suggested that the fundamental rules of the game were suddenly open for renegotiation.

Political scientists' new interest in international economic relations also coincided with the abandonment by the economics profession of what had previously been taught and researched as institutional economics. As the discipline of economics aspired to more 'scientific' approaches through the application of statistical and mathematical models, so it increasingly abandoned the study of international economic institutions. Political scientists discovered a vacuum that they quickly filled: the field of global political economy was born.

What is GPE?

Global political economy is a field of enquiry, a subject matter whose central focus is the interrelationship between public and private power in the allocation of scarce resources. It is not a specific approach or set of approaches to studying this subject matter (as we shall see, the full range of theoretical and methodological approaches from international and comparative politics has been applied to the study of international political economy).

Like other branches of the discipline, GPE seeks to answer the classic questions posed in Harold D. Lasswell's (1936) definition of politics: *who gets what, when, and how?* This definition explicitly identifies questions of *distribution* as being central to the study of politics. It also points implicitly to the importance of power—the concept that is at the heart of the study of political science—in determining outcomes. Power, of course, takes various forms: it is classically defined in terms of relationships—the capacity of one actor to change the behaviour of another (Dahl 1963). But power is also exercised in the capacity of actors to set agendas (Bachrach and Baratz 1970; Lukes 1974), and to structure the rules in various areas of international economic relations so as to privilege some actors and to disadvantage others (Strange 1988).

Consider, for example, the international financial regime. As the world's largest economy (and single most important market for many other countries in the global system), the United States has been able, over the years, to exercise relational power: to force changes in the behaviour of other countries—notably, to accept changes in their exchange rates (as, for example, in the Nixon administration's breaking of the fixed exchange rate between the dollar and gold, and the forced appreciation of the North-East Asian currencies against the dollar following the **Plaza Accord**).

The rules of the international financial regime have also been structured so that they privilege the more economically developed states in the system: not only do the wealthy industrialized economies enjoy more votes within the IMF and the World Bank under the weighted voting system employed in the two major **international financial institutions** (**IFIs**) (Box 1.7), but the industrialized economies (in part because of arrangements they have negotiated among themselves) have also largely escaped the discipline imposed by the IMF on countries that run persistent balance of payments deficits. Until the recession of 2008–9, no industrialized country had sought assistance from the IMF since Britain and Italy did so in 1976. Despite running huge deficits in its balance of payments, the United States has not been subject to IMF discipline because it can take advantage of the international acceptability of the dollar to print more money to finance its trade deficits.

Besides a focus on questions of distribution and of power, two of the fundamental concerns of political science, students of global political economy have also been preoccupied with one of the central issues in the study of international relations: which conditions are more favourable for the evolution of cooperation among states in an environment where no central enforcement agency is present? For many observers, this problem of 'cooperation under anarchy' is even more pertinent in the economic than in the security realm. This is because greater potential exists in the economic sphere, particularly under conditions of interdependence, for cooperation on a win-win basis, but states have a considerable temptation to 'cheat' by attempting to exploit concessions made by others while not fully responding in kind (see Aggarwal and Dupont, Chapter 3 in this volume).

Much of the early GPE work in the 1970s and early 1980s, particularly in North America, married two of these central concerns—the distribution of power within the global economy, and the potential for states to engage in collaboration. Conducted at a time when many perceived US economic power to be waning, this work focused on the link between hegemony and an open global economy (see Box 1.8).

Approaches to the study of global political economy

Following the publication of Robert Gilpin's (1987) magisterial overview of the then emerging field of

BOX 1.7

Voting in the International Financial Institutions

When the allied powers decided at Bretton Woods to create two international financial institutions, they agreed on a formula for voting rights that represented a compromise between the principle of sovereign equality and the realities of markedly unequal economic power. Members' voting power has two components: 'basic votes', assigned equally to all members; and (a much larger number) of weighted votes that are linked directly to the money members subscribed to the two institutions. Quotas have been adjusted over the years as the membership of the institutions has expanded, but the G7 industrialized countries still control 43 per cent of the votes in the IMF, while more than 40 African countries together have less than 5 per cent of the total votes.

Eight countries—China, France, Germany, Japan, Russia, Saudi Arabia, the United Kingdom, and the United States—have their own representative on the 24-member IMF Executive Board, which is responsible for the day-to-day running of the institution. Others are arranged in various groups, with a single executive director casting their collective votes. The same countries have their own executive directors on the 26-member World Bank Board of Directors: the remaining seventeen directors represent the Bank's other 180 member states; the Bank's President is also a member of the Board of Directors.

In the IMF, 'Ordinary' Decisions require a simple majority, whereas 'Special' Decisions require an 85 per cent 'supermajority'. The United States, with 16.67 per cent of the total votes at the IMF, can unilaterally block 'Special Decisions', such as changes in the IMF's Charter or use of its holdings of gold. Voting, however, is relatively rare, with most decisions being carried by consensus.

Criticisms of the failure of IMF quotas and voting rights to reflect the growing significance of developing economies were increasingly voiced after the East Asian financial crises of 1997–8. This criticism led to proposals to reform quotas and to increase the number of basic votes assigned to each country. The first stage was an 'ad hoc' increase in the quotas of China, Korea, Mexico, and Turkey (ranging from about a 20 per cent increase for Turkey to about 80 per cent for Korea), which took effect in 2007. In the wake of the financial crisis and the G20's decision to double the resources available to the IMF, the Fund's

Executive Board approved far-reaching reforms. The increase in quotas would be distributed in a manner such that the share of emerging market and developing economies would double. Voting power in the Fund would more closely reflect the relative size of countries in the global economy. The ten largest members of the Fund would be the United States, Japan, the four largest European economies (France, Germany, Italy, and the United Kingdom) and Brazil, China, India, and the Russian Federation. China would be the single largest beneficiary of the redistribution, with its voting rights increased by 50 per cent. The United States, whose weight in the global economy is actually under-represented in its IMF voting rights, would retain its veto power (for details of the new quotas and voting rights see http://www.imf.org/external/np/sec/memdir/members.aspx). The Executive Board would also be restructured with all Executive Directors being elected; two European seats would disappear to be replaced by two Directors from emerging economies. The changes, which require approval of countries with 85 per cent of the Fund's voting rights were introduced in January 2016.

By convention, since the foundation of the two IFIs, the United States has nominated the president of the World Bank, and (West) European countries the managing director of the IMF. In an unusual move in 2000, however, the Clinton administration in the US vetoed the German government's first-choice nominee for the post of managing director of the IMF. Although the appointment of the nominees is subject to a formal vote within the Fund and the Bank, other members have only the option of either voting for or against the nominated candidate rather than proposing alternative names. The dominance of the US and Europe in choosing the CEOs of the IFIs has increasingly been contested; in the process that led to the appointment of Christine Lagarde as Managing Director of the Fund in June 2011, however, developing economies were unable to reach agreement on an alternative candidate.

The Washington, DC location of the two IFIs facilitates US influence over their operations. For more detailed discussion of the representativeness and accountability of the IFIs, see Woods (2003) and Xu and Weller (2015).

Unlike the IFIs, the Geneva-based World Trade Organization operates on the principle of one member, one vote, but its members have never voted: decision-making is by consensus, see Capling and Trommer, Chapter 5 in this volume.

---

global political economy, most introductions to the subject have identified three principal categories of theoretical approaches to GPE. In Gilpin's original terminology (he changed some of his labels in the updated version of his book: Gilpin 2001), these were liberalism, nationalism, and Marxism. Of these three labels, only liberalism has been used universally in other categorizations. Other writers have substituted **statism**, 'mercantilism', 'realism', or 'economic nationalism' for nationalism. The approaches that

BOX 1.8

Power and Collaboration

The theory of hegemonic stability suggests that international economic collaboration in pursuit of an open (or liberal) economic order is most likely to occur when the global economy is dominated by a single power (because this country, the hegemon, will have both the desire and the capacity to support an open economic system—the dominant economy is likely to benefit most from free trade; moreover, its relatively large size will give it leverage over other states in the system). Theorists pointed to the experience of the mid-nineteenth century when Britain was the hegemonic power, and to the period of US dominance from 1945 to 1971, as demonstrating the relationship between hegemony and an open world economy. In contrast, the interwar period, when no single country enjoyed equivalent pre-eminence, was characterized by a breakdown in international economic collaboration. The decline in the relative position of the US

economy in the 1960s, following the rebuilding of the Western European and Japanese economies, appeared to coincide with renewed closure (a rise in protectionism in response to imports from Japan and the East Asian NIEs) and the general turbulence in global economic regimes noted above.

Subsequently, however, the hegemonic stability argument was undermined both by trends in the real world and by new theoretical work. In the 1990s, countries extended their collaboration on international economic matters, especially in trade, despite a relatively more even dispersion of economic power in the global system.

For statements of the hegemonic stability argument, see Kindleberger (1973) and Krasner (1976); for alternative theoretical perspectives see Keohane (1984, 1997), Snidal (1985b), and Pahre (1999). For further discussion, see Aggarwal and Dupont, Chapter 3 in this volume.

Gilpin subsumed under the label Marxism have variously been identified as 'radical', 'critical', 'structuralist', 'dependency', 'underdevelopment', and 'world systems'.

In itself, the use of a variety of labels points to one of the problems with the 'trichotomous' categorization of approaches to the study of GPE: the (sometimes misleading) lumping together of substantially different perspectives within a single category. Moreover, the trichotomous categorization does not capture the wealth of methodological and theoretical approaches used in the contemporary study of GPE, or provide an accurate signpost to the breadth of fascinating questions that currently preoccupies researchers in the field. For these reasons, we do not use such conventional categorization in this book. So common is the trichotomy in introductions to GPE, however, that it is worth investing a little time in understanding the underlying foundations of the categorization. Matthew Watson's chapter in this volume examines the historical origins and subsequent intellectual lineage of the principal theoretical perspectives on GPE (see Chapter 2).

Much of the best work in global political economy in recent years has been less concerned with prescription than with explanation—for example, how differences in political institutions shape policy decisions, and why some sectors of the economy are more successful than others in seeking protection (see Hiscox,

Chapter 4 in this volume); why it is easier for states to collaborate on some issues rather than others (see Aggarwal and Dupont, Chapter 3 in this volume); why states have increasingly pursued trade agreements at the regional instead of the global level (Ravenhill, Chapter 6 in this volume); why states have been unable to agree on an effective regime for dealing with international debt (Pauly, Chapter 9 in this volume); and why some global environmental regimes are effective while others are not (Dauvergne, Chapter 14 in this volume). Of course, policy prescriptions often follow from such theoretically informed analysis, and they are far more specific than those of the 'get the state out of the market' variety.

Since the early 1980s, the study of global political economy has been enriched by the application of a diverse array of theoretical and methodological approaches, but neither their subject matter nor the methodologies employed allow easy categorization. Take, for example, the role of ideas in shaping policy agendas, in helping states to reach agreement in various international negotiations, and in legitimizing current economic, political, and social structures. Ideas have been the central focus of work firmly within the Marxist tradition, which builds on the arguments of the former Italian communist party leader, Antonio Gramsci, on how ideas help ruling classes to legitimate their domination (Cox 1987; Gill 1990). But ideas have also been pivotal to quite different approaches, drawing on the work of the German so-ciologist, Max Weber. Work from this perspective ex-amines the role that ideas play in defining the range of policy options that governments consider, and in providing a focal point for agreement in international negotiations (Hall 1989; Goldstein and Keohane 1993; Garrett and Lange 1996). Also derived from Weberian analysis are constructivist approaches, which empha-size the significance of ideas in constituting actors' perceptions of their interests and identities, rather than taking these for granted—examples of the appli-cation of constructivist analysis to IPE include Colin Hay (Chapter 11 in this volume), Haas (1992), Burch and Denemark (1997), Hay and Rosamond (2002), Ab-delal, Blyth, and Parsons (2010). And cross-fertilization has occurred across different approaches—for exam-ple, the Gramscian idea of hegemony has been used by writers from a non-Marxist perspective, such as Ikenberry and Kupchan (1990), and finds resonance in Joseph Nye's (1990) concept of 'soft' power.

Likewise, turning to **methodology**, we find similar methods employed by scholars from dramatically dif-ferent theoretical traditions. Consider rational choice approaches, for example. Since the mid 1990s, rational choice has dominated many areas of the study of po-litical science, particularly in universities in the United States. Its origins lie in economic theory; the focus is primarily on individuals, the factors that lead them to choose preferred courses of action, and how strategic interaction generates uncertainty. In GPE, rational choice analysis has been prominent in the recent study of the determinants of trade policy preferences, and why international institutions, including the European Union, take particular forms, what the effects of insti-tutions are, and why some institutions survive longer than others (Frey 1984; Martin 1992; Garrett and We-ingast 1993). Vaubel (1986, 1991) has applied rational choice analysis in an examination of the behaviour of the officials of the IMF. Such work is very much in the mainstream of contemporary political science. But rational choice methods have also been applied by theorists working within the Marxist tradition—for ex-ample, Roemer (1988), and Carver and Thomas (1995).

Although rational choice methods have become dominant in some circles within North American political science, a large number of scholars of GPE would find it difficult to accept the argument made at the turn of the century by one proponent of rational choice methods that GPE 'is today characterized by growing consensus on theories, methods, analytical

BOX 1.9

Epistemology, Ontology, and Methodology

Epistemology is the study of knowledge and justified belief. It is concerned with questions about the necessary and sufficient conditions of knowledge, the sources of knowledge, and how knowledge is created. Ontology is the study of being and of what 'exists'. It is concerned with the identification of the core objects of study, their characteristics, and their relationships to other objects. Methodology refers to a procedure or set of procedures used to study a subject matter.

frameworks, and important questions' (Martin 2002: 244). Diversity in **ontology, epistemology**, and **meth-odology** continues to characterize the international study of global political economy (see Box 1.9). Many scholars find this rich mix of theories and methodolo-gies a cause for celebration rather than concern. This is certainly the view of the contributors to this vol-ume, which reflects much of the current lively debate in the study of GPE.

KEY POINTS

- The field of global political economy emerged in the early 1970s in response to developments in the world economy, in international security, and in the study of economics and international relations.

- GPE is best defined by its subject matter rather than as a particular theory or methodology.

- Approaches to the study of GPE have conventionally been divided into the three categories of liberalism, nationalism, and Marxism.

- This trichotomous division is of questionable contemporary utility because of the variation in approaches included within each of the three categories.

- The contemporary study of GPE is characterized by the application of a wealth of theories and methodologies.

- Most of the contemporary work in GPE focuses on positive theory: that is, attempting to explain why things happen, rather than on policy prescription.

The first part of this volume looks at some of the approaches that have addressed the key concerns of theorists of GPE: what conditions are most conducive to the emergence of collaborative behaviour among states on economic issues, and what are the determinants of the foreign economic policies of states? It then examines the evolution of trade relations, first at the global and then at the regional level. Chapter 8 reviews the development of the global financial regime since 1944; the following chapter addresses the causes of financial crises and the reasons why international collaboration to date has been ineffective in devising strategies to combat them.

The chapters in the second part of the book examine various aspects of the debate about globalization: whether in fact the contemporary economy is global and whether it differs, qualitatively or quantitatively, from previous eras of economic interdependence; and the extent to which enhanced globalization constrains the policy options available to states. In the last part of the book, we examine the impact of globalization on world poverty and inequality; how globalization has changed the relations between industrialized and less developed economies; and the impact of globalization on the environment.

? QUESTIONS

1. What were the principal factors that determined the severity of the recession of 2008–9?

2. In what ways did the recession of 2008–9 change global economic governance?

3. What were the principal features of the classical period of mercantilism?

4. What were the reasons for rapid economic growth in the nineteenth century?

5. How did the gold standard operate automatically to bring the payments position of countries into equilibrium?

6. What were the principal reasons for the breakdown of international economic relations in the interwar period?

7. What are the defining characteristics of the post-1945 world economy?

8. What factors led to the emergence of GPE as a significant field of study?

9. What is GPE?

10. What are the main weaknesses with the traditional threefold categorization of approaches to GPE?

FURTHER READING

Cohen, B. J. (1977), *Organizing the World's Money: The Political Economy of International Monetary Relations* (New York: Basic Books). The first major study from a GPE perspective of global financial relations.

Cohen, B. J. (2008), *International Political Economy: An Intellectual History* (Princeton, NJ: Princeton University Press). The most detailed examination of the development of contemporary international political economy.

Cooper, R. N. (1968), *The Economics of Interdependence* (New York: Columbia University Press). A pioneering work that laid the foundations for the emergence of GPE as a significant field of enquiry in the 1970s.

Crane, G. T. and Amawi, A. (eds) (1997), *The Theoretical Evolution of International Political Economy: A Reader*, 2nd edn (New York: Oxford University Press). An excellent compilation of selections from classical and contemporary writing on global political economy.

Gilpin, R. (1987), *The Political Economy of International Relations* (Princeton, NJ: Princeton University Press). The most theoretically sophisticated of the early introductory books on GPE.

Hirschman, A. O. (1945), *National Power and the Structure of Foreign Trade* (Berkeley and Los Angeles, CA: University of California Press). A pioneering study of the relationship between power and foreign economic relations, focusing on the interwar experiences of Nazi Germany.

Keohane, R. O. (1984), *After Hegemony: Cooperation and Discord in the World Political Economy* (Princeton, NJ: Princeton University Press). The most thorough assessment of the relationship between the distribution of power and collaboration among states on international economic matters.

Maddison, A. (2001), *The World Economy: A Millennial Perspective* (Paris: Development Centre of the Organisation for Economic Co-operation and Development). Excellent source of historical statistics on the development of the world economy.

Palan, R. (ed.) (2013), *Global Political Economy: Contemporary Theories*, 2nd edn (London: Routledge). The most comprehensive survey of contemporary theoretical approaches to global political economy.

Paul, D. E. and Amawi, A. (eds) (2013), *The Theoretical Evolution of International Political Economy: A Reader,* 3rd edn (New York: Oxford University Press). An excellent compilation of selections from classical and contemporary writing on global political economy.

Schwartz, H. M. (2010), *States versus Markets: The Emergence of a Global Economy*, 3rd edn (London: Macmillan). Provides an unusual historical perspective on the contemporary global economy by tracing its development since the 1500s, with emphasis placed on the links between the emergence of the modern state and the modern global economy.

Strange, S. (1971), *Sterling and British Policy: A Political Study of an International Currency in Decline* (London: Oxford University Press). A pioneering work on the relationship between politics and international financial policies.

Strange, S. (1988), *States and Markets* (London: Pinter). An idiosyncratic introduction to global political economy that is organized around the theme of structural power.

Wallerstein, I. (1974), *The Modern World-System* (New York: Academic Press). The first volume of a multi-part work examining the emergence of the modern world economy.

WEBLINKS

www.g7.utoronto.ca University of Toronto G8 Information Centre.

www.imf.org International Monetary Fund.

www.worldbank.org World Bank.

www.unctad.org United Nations Conference on Trade and Development (UNCTAD).

www.opec.org Organization of the Petroleum Exporting Countries.

www.eh.net/encyclopedia/article/officer.gold.standard Gold Standard—EH.Net Encyclopedia.

www.amosweb.com/gls Glossary of economic terms.

ONLINE RESOURCE CENTRE

For additional material and resources, please visit the Online Resource Centre at:
www.oxfordtextbooks.co.uk/ravenhill5e

2

The Nineteenth-Century Roots of Theoretical Traditions in Global Political Economy

Matthew Watson

Chapter contents

Reader's guide

This chapter focuses on the historical origins and the subsequent intellectual lineage of what many textbooks inform the beginning student are the three core theoretical positions within contemporary global political economy (GPE): realism, liberalism, and Marxism. In doing so it also seeks to explain why feminist scholarship, which has been so important to the more recent evolution of GPE theory, is generally included in the textbooks only as some sort of afterthought. The search for historical pre-emptions is always important, because it reminds the student of any subject that contemporary perspectives are part of a longer tradition of thought. It is even more significant in GPE because its introductory texts tend not to rework its roots from scratch. Instead, they often rely on populist intellectual histories that are simplistic in the extreme. The problem is that the modern-day variants of realism, liberalism, and Marxism are treated as the authoritative ones, with the original statements of something approaching those positions then being fitted to their closest modern-day equivalent. This, though, is to read the history of ideas the wrong way round. Meanwhile, the search for the foundations of feminist GPE is typically sidestepped altogether, which in this instance means that the history of ideas remains conspicuously *unread*. By taking the alternative option of trying to present students with a clear idea of exactly what united and what divided the main theoretical positions in contemporary GPE at their point of origination, this chapter provides important contextual evidence about the way in which those positions have subsequently evolved into their modern form. The result is that it is possible to collapse a number of the rigid lines of demarcation that are drawn in introductory textbooks between competing theoretical positions in GPE. At the same time, it also becomes possible to identify the intellectual propositions that did most to divide the eighteenth- and nineteenth-century theorists so as to compare them with today's accounts of the most similar GPE positions.

Introduction

The purpose of this chapter is to provide a broad overview of the subject field of GPE as a whole, but without simply repeating the introductions to the field that dominate other textbooks. Indeed, those introductions will often appear in the pages that follow as objects of criticism. I take issue with them primarily for their lack of attention to GPE's historical roots, and for allowing this to contribute to the reproduction of a number of important misreadings of the paths from foundational political economy debates to where GPE is located today. Straight lines are all-too-often invoked to link the old to the new, but almost always this involves the selective reading of historical positions to make them match modern-day ones. My aim is to question the account of the three main theoretical positions through which introductions to GPE are typically taught—realism, liberalism, and Marxism—and to urge students to go beyond these accounts and explore for themselves the specialist history of economic thought literature that offers alternative perspectives on those positions. This will also enable me to take the first steps in making good the gap that exists in almost all GPE textbooks where a discussion of gender issues and an appreciation of the historical role of women writers in political economy really ought to be.

There is what might be called a 'textbook GPE', then, which usually provides a student's first exposure to the subject field. Yet there are also other ways of learning about theoretical traditions in Global Political Economy, whereby GPE is brought together much more clearly with the study of the history of economic thought. These are generally treated as being two completely separate practices, but there is no good reason why this should necessarily be the case.

This chapter should therefore not be read as if it is a direct substitute for usual introductory textbook chapters on GPE theory, because I am attempting to do something quite distinct. It is, of course, very important that students become aware of the standard textbook account of how modern-day GPE realism, liberalism, and Marxism differ from one another, as well as why feminist GPE still largely gets presented as a marginal pursuit, as these will be the themes that they encounter more and more as their studies progress. Yet this should not be at the expense of trying to understand how these modern-day positions may be somewhat less than faithful to the arguments from the history of economic thought that they claim as their precursors. For instance, the analytical ends to which modern-day liberals put the eighteenth-century political economy concept of 'the market' often look completely different to how eighteenth-century scholars originally used it. It is also possible to identify a shared commitment across the centuries for liberals to talk about an abstract 'economic man', but the meaning of that abstraction differs markedly in its implied behavioural characteristics between the eighteenth century (when they often bordered on the effeminate) and today (when a hyper-masculinity pervades the contemporary *Homo economicus*). *Homo economicus*, the Latin term designed to capture the reduction of the human essence to something straightforwardly economic, is used in economic theories today to describe rational and self-interested beings capable of deciding the optimal strategy for pursuing their goals. These in turn are usually assumed to be linked directly to the unthinking and unreflexive accumulation of wealth. As a characterization of normal economic behaviour this particular *Homo economicus* would have been unrecognizable to the eighteenth-century theorists who saw 'economic man' as a social signaller intent on the display of status and unconcerned about frittering away his resources if this made that display more eye-catching.

Critically minded students therefore have much to gain from learning about the tendency for the main theories of GPE to have become detached from their historical moorings as well, as for others to be overlooked because they seem to lack such moorings. All is not necessarily as clean and as clear-cut in the intervening history as is so often suggested in the introductory textbooks to the field. My focus, in the first instance, is on the original interventions themselves that have provided GPE with a distinctive pre-history, including studying the arguments that their authors made in their own words. It is only by doing this that it is possible to reveal some of the peculiarities of the way in which the standard introductory GPE texts present their subject field's pre-history. I then hope to show that GPE and the history of economic thought can be combined in fruitful ways.

Teaching global political economy through the textbooks

Most GPE scholars were taught their trade having first studied international relations (IR) courses. Perhaps predictably, given this background, the question-asking framework associated with IR continues to loom large as a template for GPE (Phillips 2009). The same three-way distinction between realism, liberalism, and Marxism has been transposed in pretty much identical form from one to the other. Indeed, Robert Gilpin— author of the best-selling GPE textbook, *The Political Economy of International Relations* (1987), in addition to being one of the first generation of IPE scholars who, according to Benjamin Cohen (2008b), set the parameters within which the field continues to be located today—describes these positions as 'the three ideologies' of GPE (Gilpin 1987: 25; see also Gilpin 1975: 21).

The specific choice of descriptor is instructive. He could have called them three separate starting points for GPE. However, this would have implied that, at some stage, students would be required to branch out from those starting points in order to comprehend what is at stake by beginning there. He could also have called them three separate theoretical bases for understanding the world around us. However, the art of working within a theoretical perspective is always to question the limits that perspective imposes on original thought as a means of ultimately transcending it. Gilpin is clear about why he instead uses the word 'ideology' to describe realist, liberal, and Marxist GPE. He wants to capture a sense of self-contained,

coherent world-views, capable of imposing meaning on any experience of the world, and equally capable of encapsulating whole systems of thought and belief (Gilpin 1987: 25–6).

Students can turn to pretty much any introductory IPE textbook to find out how the subject field might be divided using this three-way split in Gilpin's specific sense. My intention in this chapter is rather different. The textbook introductions generally display very little focus on the historical roots of these three competing traditions of GPE's orthodox pedagogy. In specifying those roots rather more precisely, it becomes possible to show the limitations of conceiving of Gilpin's three ideologies of GPE as self-contained, coherent world-views. Doing so also undermines the rationale for calling them 'ideologies' in the first place.

The reason why this way of thinking continues to hold such a spell over GPE textbooks has much to do with how the chronology of the field continues to be understood. Almost every appraisal of the subject field begins by commenting on GPE's youth relative to other fields (Gill and Law 1988; Onuf 1997; Pearson and Rochester 1998; Dash et al. 2003). The year 1970 tends to be positioned as the beginning of history as far as GPE is concerned. The subject field was forged amid attempts to explain events that were a particular feature of distinctively modern times. Specifically, GPE results from concerns to reflect on the future of world economic affairs following the collapse of the **Bretton Woods** system of international economic management amidst the disturbances of the early 1970s (Krasner 1976; Gilpin 1987; Frieden and Lake 1995; Grieco and Ikenberry 2003). That system had brought seemingly unparalleled stability to the economies of the Western alliance. **Marshall Aid** had allowed the US to recycle its massive post-war trading surpluses while also simultaneously allowing countries in Western Europe and East Asia to fast-forward the process of economic reconstruction through securing extremely high growth rates and employment rates. From the perspective of the stagnant growth, the enhanced joblessness, the collapsing profits, and the escalating inflation of the 1970s, the immediate post-Second World War era looked like a 'golden age' of almost limitless economic possibilities (Kitschelt et al. 1999). Given such a context, the task that the early GPE scholars set themselves was how to envision the conditions of renewed systemic stability (Murphy and Tooze 1991: 17).

This intimate connection between the birth of GPE and the onset of what seemed to be qualitatively new economic conditions made it possible for the early GPE scholars to pay something less than full attention to the implications of the history of political economy for their new subject field. After all, developments within the most recent phase of the modern world economy could be said only to require the most up-to-date methods and approaches from the existing academic literature. 1970 represents an important birth date for GPE, then, in two distinct ways. It not only provided the early GPE scholars with a set of concrete historical facts to try to explain. It also provided them with some dominant theoretical constructions to organize the attempt to make sense of the surrounding world.

Looking back from today, GPE's birth date provided the subject field with two very important originating biases. The contextual assumption of foregone stability continues to cast a large shadow over contemporary GPE, providing a means of distinguishing normatively between the work of those who are willing to suppress the possibility of a new social order in the interests of international economic stability and the work of those who are not. Equally, the approaches that were just coming to prominence in GPE's parent field of IR in the early 1970s—primarily **rational choice theory**—continue to provide the basis for methodological disputes in GPE today. The frameworks in which rational choice theory was most readily applied at the time—realism, liberalism, and Marxism—were thus easily elevated to be GPE's standard fare. Feminist economics was developed later in the 1970s, often in direct opposition to the rational choice approach, and therefore it did not have the same sort of claim to easy incorporation into textbook GPE.

Rational choice approaches are based on the abstract assumptions of **utility-maximizing behaviour** through which *Homo economicus* makes his presence felt in the world. The exponents of these approaches believe that, by reducing all human behaviour to this single instinct, action is provided with the degree of replicability and predictability that they treasure so highly in their analyses. By remaining loyal to what Jonathan Kirshner (2011: 205) has called a 'hyper-rationalist' mode of explanation, a seemingly rigorous basis is provided on which to claim that a given type of policy will always be selected because it reflects the generic enactment of self-interest that it is assumed will always be in play. Those who are less sympathetic to the encroachment of rational choice theory within GPE are concerned that the theory itself attempts to naturalize a specific conception of economic **agency**. It is institutionally suited only to life lived within generally **free market economies**, so it is an analytical error, the unsympathetic commentators say, to elide this one institutional arrangement with all possible forms of economic life that might be lived (or, indeed, *are* being lived right now). To adopt that approach is akin to turning GPE into an element of the free market **hegemony** that the subject field's scholars might otherwise wish to critique. It is simply not possible from this perspective to gain sufficient autonomous theoretical space to comment on the political structures of world order if the theory being used itself both reflects and reinforces those structures (Cox 1981).

The general ideological shift towards the embrace of pro-market positions in the early 1970s therefore occurred at the same time as rational choice theory rose to prominence. As a consequence, writing GPE's history as if there is nothing of relevance before 1970 has the potential to inadvertently bind it to the very modern predilection for viewing the world through the interlocking prisms of pro-market ideology and rational choice theory. This was neither an ideology nor a theory that was in any way prominent when GPE's longer-term roots were being laid down in alternative forms of political economy scholarship in the eighteenth and nineteenth centuries, but the subsequent emphasis on the modern does provide a means of reinterpreting the older scholarship as if it spoke directly to today's intellectual concerns. The realism, liberalism, and Marxism of the GPE textbooks are cut off from their longer-term historical roots precisely to the extent to which they are incorporated into an academic agenda already wholly permeated by the influence of the market agency displayed by *Homo economicus*.

The biggest problem with this, to my mind, is not the fact that these changes have occurred per se, because theoretical perspectives are always likely to evolve due to the changing concrete circumstances that they are trying to explain. Rather, it is the fact that these changes have occurred without significant reflection on their origins from either the advocates or the detractors of the distinctively modern approaches. The theory of utility-maximizing behaviour has not materialized out of thin air, fully formed and merely awaiting incorporation into GPE. Rather, it has its own specific intellectual history. Its prominence in the other social sciences mirrors the effects of the so-called **Formalist Revolution** in economics in the 1940s and 1950s, through which the logical form that was used to express explanatory arguments was first allowed to take precedence over their economic content (Blaug 1999). This was the time when the leading edge of economics initially began explicitly to be modelled as a mathematical science, with the **mathematical tractability** of the implied economic relationships considered to be more important than whether or not those relationships had genuine economic meaning in a sense that corresponds to lives that can actually be led. Deirdre McCloskey (1990: 223) has called this the rise of a purely 'blackboard economics'. The hyper-rationalist individual who instinctively maximizes **utility** is perfect for such an exercise, because this individual is mathematically tractable rather than genuinely economic, but it should go without saying that this is not the sort of person that you could ever expect to meet on a day-to-day basis.

Terence Hutchison (1998) has argued that what McCloskey calls blackboard economics deserves the methodological label of 'ultra-deductivism'. This is to stipulate a number of first-principle behavioural characteristics and then to read off all actual economic behaviour from those characteristics by treating them as unchallengeable **axioms** of conduct. None of the founders of the positions that have evolved into modern-day GPE realism, liberalism, and Marxism, however, adopted anything approaching ultra-deductivism as their leitmotif. This was a development most closely associated with the work of the English economist, Nassau Senior, in the 1820s. He first began to write about an abstract persona that evolved into the 'economic man' that is today so familiar from rational choice theory but would have seriously stood out from previous accounts of normal economic behaviour. Senior was also the first to treat this abstract persona as the basis of economic enquiry, thus creating a competitor to the prior concern for understanding the individual relative to the concrete historical circumstances of his or her constitution. The emergence of neoclassical economics through the **Marginalist Revolution** of the 1870s (see Box 2.1) began to popularize such a shift, but it was not truly cemented until the culmination of the Formalist Revolution some eight decades later.

This brief historical sketch is important because of the particular way in which textbook GPE deals with matters of intellectual history. That treatment is sparing at best, attempting to consolidate the modern-day positions of realism, liberalism, and Marxism through appeal to a limited number of key precursors. The realist position is typically described as having its roots in the work of Friedrich List (1789–1846) and possibly Alexander Hamilton (1755–1804), the liberal position in Adam Smith (1723–90) and possibly David Ricardo (1772–1823), and the Marxist position, perhaps most obviously, in Karl Marx (1818–83) and possibly Vladimir Lenin (1870–1924). It is very rare to get more than a couple of sentences to say what these authors were famous for and how this is reflected in GPE today. But even this is not the end of the difficulties. For there seems to be—for want of a better expression—something of a nineteenth-century overlay placed on their work. That is, wherever possible, what is presented as the authoritative reading of GPE's intellectual forebears is how their work had come to be read by the time of the Marginalist Revolution of the 1870s.

A series of mutually reinforcing restrictions is therefore apparent. Textbook GPE limits its own start date to around 1970 and thus locks the subject field into the hyper-rationalist modes of reasoning that were becoming increasingly popular at that time. The broader social scientific heritage to which it belongs thus places on a pedestal the rationalist foundations laid down in neoclassical economics. Whereas 1970 is usually set as Year Zero for the history of GPE, then, 1870 serves a very similar role for its pre-history. Anything that was written in political economy before that time tends to be presented as it came to be viewed through a marginalist perspective in the 1870s. The textbook GPE reading of intellectual history, sparse as it is, therefore lines up directly to support the same rationalist themes as if they are the entirety of both the subject field's history and pre-history.

This nineteenth-century overlay is more apparent the further back in time we have to go to when the original text was written. It is necessary to reiterate just how little is included about intellectual history within textbook GPE. Still, though, a rather strange historiographical trend is visible. Hamilton is often made to look how List spoke about him, for instance, rather than the analysis concentrating on what he said for himself. The Smith that appears is often in the guise of where List in particular but also Marx thought that he had gone wrong, rather than through an analysis of how events of his own time had influenced his thinking. Ricardo tends to be presented

BOX 2.1

Neoclassical Economics and the Marginalist Revolution

Neoclassical economics focuses almost all of its attention on instances in which behaviour can have a rational calculus of costs and benefits imposed upon it. The aim is to use this calculus to offer an ostensibly detached, objective description of economic events that matches the standards of scientific rigour by being cleansed of the disruptive influence of philosophical debate (Schumpeter 1954/2006). The analyst is thus supposedly able to comment on economic affairs from beyond the boundaries of his/her own particular world-view. Such concerns relegate the significance of clear normative position-taking, thus providing economic enquiry with a technical veneer. The methodologist of economics, John Neville Keynes, once distinguished between the 'science' and the 'art' of economics, in order to emphasize that economists' attempts to engage in methodologically rigorous enquiry (the science) must also be set within the context of explicit acknowledgement that all economic enquiry is always undertaken with specific purposes in mind (the art) (Keynes 1891/1970). David Colander has recently picked up on this distinction to suggest that the twentieth-century dominance of neoclassical theory has led to the disappearance of the 'art' of economics (Colander 2001). Economic theory always proceeds according to preconceived social ends but, in trying to emphasize the purely technical prerequisites of modern theory, this is something that neoclassical economists typically attempt to disguise.

Historically speaking, neoclassical economics is itself a complex amalgam of different positions that possess a familial resemblance but otherwise have their own theoretical emphases (see Watson 2005: ch. 2). There are even three distinct starting points for neoclassical theory in the Marginalist Revolution of the 1870s, to be found in the contrasting work of William Stanley Jevons (1835–82), Carl Menger (1840–1921), and Léon Walras (1834–1910). As these three worked out of Manchester, Vienna, and Lausanne, respectively, there were rival English-speaking, German-speaking, and French-speaking traditions of neoclassical economics right from the start. However, despite these differences, all three traditions have a similar core in a recognized way of thinking, all emphasizing what they took to be the distinctively economic behavioural characteristic of maximizing at the margin. This was economizing behaviour in the literal sense of the word, seeking to make the most of whatever means were at hand.

The earliest neoclassical economists disagreed, however, on what the individual would attempt to maximize. Jevons (1871/1970) contrasted pleasure and pain to say that the maximization of net utility mattered most; Walras (1874/1984) emphasized the experience of scarcity constraints to suggest that the individual would focus on maximizing '**rareté**'; Menger (1871/1950) allowed his economic agents to maximize anything they put their minds to as long as they did not shirk from the maximizing path. The important point for current purposes, though, is not what each thought people maximized but the fact that they each used the technique of trying to isolate economic decisions taken at the margin. This allowed for the identification of optimal strategies within the context of equilibrium models, as well as for the later insertion of the rationality assumption to explain how the individual might come to know instinctively exactly what the optimal strategy is in any set of circumstances. These features of the early neoclassical economists' work remain visible today in most of textbook GPE, albeit they are almost never explicitly acknowledged as such.

through the thoughts of his late nineteenth-century political champions and not in his own words. And so the list goes on. In general, the views of those who came after Senior had activated the ultra-deductivist moment in the history of economic thought are imprinted on the views of those who came before. The idea of a nineteenth-century overlay is not perfect, however, because even Marx is in danger of having his nineteenth-century work interpreted in textbook GPE through what Lenin added to it in the twentieth century, as this is where the 'G' is usually thought to have originated in Marxist GPE. But still the same pattern is evident. This is all about newer work being used as the lens through which to speak about older work,

however much this is to read the history of economic thought in reverse chronological order.

The existence of something approaching a nineteenth-century overlay also helps to explain GPE's puzzling treatment of feminist scholarship within the textbooks. For some years now, feminism has been the source of many of the most vibrant, important, and challenging studies of global economic management. Yet it remains largely marginalized from textbook GPE, presented as something of a postscript to avoid accusations of having omitted it altogether rather than being placed centre stage in the discussion. It is often parcelled up with other avowedly anti-mainstream approaches under the broader label 'critical GPE', to be learnt not as an indelible part of the subject field's core but only once familiarity with the established core of realism, liberalism, and Marxism has first been established. Feminist scholarship can thus quickly be reduced to something that looks with fresh eyes at the world described by realism, liberalism, and Marxism, when it would be preferable to engage with it explicitly in its own terms.

Feminist scholarship is adversely affected in this regard by being a relative newcomer to the GPE scene. Its origins can be traced to the development of a distinctly feminist economics in the 1970s and an equally distinctly feminist international relations theory in the 1980s. As a result, both of these foundational approaches post-date the initial attempts to lay down the textbook assumptions about what GPE is designed to deliver knowledge of. The fact that this is where the nineteenth-century overlay comes into operation leads to the double marginalization of feminist scholarship. There was nothing approaching a nineteenth-century tradition of feminist political economy that can now be harked back to that can act as the modern subject field's pre-history.

Yet this does not mean that there were no women active in the field of political economy in the nineteenth century. As the final section in this chapter will show, there were certainly women writing very authoritatively *about* economic matters in that period, although they generally lacked recognition as being the authors *of* new departures in economic theory even when such acknowledgement was due. This influence of women writers in political economy has been all too readily expunged from more recent accounts of its history. Anne Sisson Runyan made the following telling point in this regard almost 20 years ago now, but it has not received anything like the attention it deserves. 'The most often told story of [G]PE is about men, states, and markets. Even in contemporary retellings of this story in standard [G]PE textbooks, the "making" of [G]PE as a field is routinely traced to … men' (1997: 79).

The following sections represent an attempt to capture how the nineteenth-century overlay operates in textbook GPE. To do so, it makes sense to concentrate in the first instance on the issue that did most to divide nineteenth-century economists: namely, the **free trade** policies resulting from the general ascendancy of **laissez-faire** ideology. The most celebrated of the critics, Friedrich List, is treated much more as a dependable authority figure in GPE than he is in the

history of economic thought. Indeed, in textbook GPE, the disputes between realist and liberal positions are very often presented initially through an account of List's work, despite the pre-history of liberalism being much the longer of the two. It is therefore with List that I start.

KEY POINTS

- The presentation of realism, liberalism, and Marxism specifically as ideologies is itself evidence of the transformation of the original positions from how they were first formulated in the eighteenth and nineteenth centuries.

- The move towards rational choice theory-inspired variants of GPE realism, liberalism, and Marxism mirrors prior changes in economics orthodoxy.

- 'Textbook GPE' privileges nineteenth-century understandings of political economy when discussing the pre-history of its own field.

- Feminist scholarship continues to be marginalized within textbook treatments of GPE, despite its many notable successes in recent years.

GPE realism and the nineteenth-century nationalist political economy tradition

The fact that scholars even consider it worthwhile to teach realism as one possible basis for GPE reveals something potentially interesting about the subject field's origins. Realism, of course, is a standard theoretical approach in IR, but a fair degree of creative licence is then required to transpose it into a readily recognizable political economy approach. In and of itself, realism has no political economy content. The aim of realist GPE is simply to explain how one state seeks to impose its national interest at the expense of other states' national interests in bargaining situations that occur either bilaterally or multilaterally. This might then be applied, for instance, to bargaining situations governing international trade, **foreign direct investment**, or **cross-border production**. Yet there is no reason why the question of interstate bargains needs to be tackled with any regard whatsoever for theories of political economy. Rational choice approaches to the structure of such bargains might mirror rational choice approaches to economic

The International Relations Roots of GPE Realism

The intellectual lineage of GPE realism can be traced to the founding texts of modern IR realism, drawing immediate notice to its distance from a genuine political economy tradition. It represents an attempt to synthesize two separate strands of thought: structural and historical realism. Modern structural realists tend to follow Hans Morgenthau's lead (1948/60) in anthropomorphizing the state and therefore treating state behaviour as epiphenomenal of essential human characteristics. By making the further assumption that it is human nature to be self-serving and to chase gains solely for oneself, combatively self-interested actions are consequently inscribed into the very logic of state behaviour. In contrast, modern historical realists work within a tradition that originates with E. H. Carr (1939/46). Here, the emphasis is on developing historically contextualized explanations for how the instinct for combatively self-interested actions might be balanced in any given instance by the perceived need for a state to demonstrate to rival states that it is acting within the bounds of international political norms. The structural logic of state behaviour might therefore always be offset by historically conditioned concerns for turning away from exercising full-on aggression towards other states. But this in itself is further assumed to reflect the rational decision to try to store up more resources of political credibility now for use in self-interested ways in the future. Although the link is nowhere fully fleshed out by GPE scholars, all forms of GPE realism therefore rely on the methodological changes first enacted in economics as its orthodoxy evolved in iterative stages from Nassau Senior through the Marginalist and Formalist Revolutions.

The questions on which this style of GPE focuses are by no means insignificant ones. The state is evidently an important actor in shaping its citizens' experiences and expectations of the world economy, and to suggest otherwise solely in the search for intellectual space that transcends realist GPE would be unhelpful. It is clearly an issue of note for GPE scholars to understand how states position themselves against one another in international economic negotiations: for instance, those that are conducted under the auspices of the **World Trade Organization** (WTO), **the International Monetary Fund**, and the **World Bank**. It also helps to focus attention on how states position themselves with respect to the balance of political forces within their respective societies so that they can decide on the character of their negotiating positions in the first place: for instance, whether they seek to forward a business-friendly image or emphasize the need to clamp down on corporate tax avoidance in the interests of pursuing more extensive social policy goals.

decision-making found elsewhere within the subject field, but this on its own does not necessarily mean that a political economy tradition can be easily invoked in realist GPE (see Box 2.2). The invocations that do take place infer a wholly invented tradition, whereby contemporary GPE realism is re-described as the logical heir of classical nineteenth-century political economy nationalism. This is a standard refrain of pretty much all introductory textbooks in the subject field. Yet, in its own terms, it is unconvincing. To treat the two as synonymous styles of study separated only by distance in time systematically distorts the objectives of classical nineteenth-century political economy nationalism.

The political economy foundations of nineteenth-century economic nationalism

The most famous account of classical nineteenth-century political economy nationalism is Friedrich List's *National System of Political Economy*. For this reason, it is perhaps understandable that so many introductory GPE textbooks have sought pre-emptive forms of analysis in List's work to act as a link to modern-day GPE realism (e.g. Gilpin 1987; Gill and Law 1988; Frieden and Lake 1995; O'Brien and Williams 2004). However, such a link requires that a disservice be done to List by forcing him to talk to a distinctly modern-day intellectual agenda on the question of how states derive their economic interests. For GPE realists, this is simply a matter of devising strategies to enhance short-term economic bargaining power, but for List it always involved complex trade-offs between emphasizing short- and long-term economic goals. It also involved successfully managing the expectations of society if the long-term objective of overall national **economic development** was to be prioritized over the short-term objective of the immediate enrichment of society. Fleshing out the distinctiveness of List's position in this regard, it is more than possible to go directly against the introductory GPE texts by depicting classical nineteenth-century political economy nationalism as an anti-realist perspective.

List was adamant (1841/2005a: 18–22; 1841/2005b: 34–5) that what counted as the national economic interest changed with respect to the stage of development exhibited by a country. Stated straightforwardly like this, there is unlikely to be much here to which most realists would today object, but first impressions might well be misleading. Modern-day realists assume that the national economic interest will change over time as the country's level of development changes, but that in each individual time period it will cohere internally as a singular and unproblematic entity. In List's work, by contrast, 'the' national economic interest was nothing of the sort. It was in fact a series of competing national economic interests played out at a single moment in historical time but over markedly different timeframes as, one after another, political obstacles to the next stage of development had to be overcome.

List's specific concern (1841/2005b: 191–2, 216–18; 2005c: 44–52) was to show why a newly politically unified but still only partially industrialized Germany should revoke its commitment to Britain's nineteenth-century laissez-faire policy. He insisted that this should be the policy of choice, even if it temporarily restricted ordinary Germans' consumption possibilities by stopping them from accessing cheap British imports. List is often treated as if he were a critic of free trade per se, but this was not so. His argument was only that free trade was wrong for Germany in the particular historical setting in which he was situated (List 1841/2005a: 107, 121; List 1841/2005b: 37–8, 65–6, 87–9). Germany, he wrote, should seek a better position to engage in free trade *alongside* Britain once it had developed into Britain's industrial equal. Free trade was still the ultimate goal of List's nationalist political economy, then, only just not yet. He first wanted a nationalist economic identity to be forged by winning the German people over to the idea that their consumption of British goods was detrimental to long-term German national economic self-determination.

The second big difference between List's work and that of modern-day GPE realists is that he point-blank rejected their statist **ontology**. Instead, in clearly elaborated terms to introduce what is almost certainly the most important chapter of his most important book, List announced his commitment—both political and theoretical—to a nationalist ontology. He wrote that (1841/2005b: 70): 'Between each individual and entire humanity … stands THE NATION, with its special language and literature, with its peculiar origin and history, with its special manners and customs, laws

and institutions'. He even placed the claim in capital letters in an attempt to make it impossible to miss (albeit the contents of the GPE textbooks suggest without lasting success).

A new generation of List scholars in GPE has begun to highlight this neglect of the nation in its attempts to ask what a nationalist economic ontology would look like today from a Listian perspective (e.g. Levi-Faur 1997; Crane 1998; Helleiner 2005). This work suggests that there is no simple one-to-one correspondence between List's nationalist economic ontology and the sorts of **protectionist policies** that he advocated for Germany in the specific circumstances it faced in the mid-nineteenth century. While List definitely did favour the introduction of certain carefully specified barriers to trade because he believed such protection to be consistent with German national economic interests at that specific time, the realm of national economic interests is much broader than the single case that he described and can therefore lead to many different types of policies today. Indeed, one of the major lessons to emerge recently from this type of work is that economically liberal policies can be the preference derived from adopting an economically nationalist ontology (Abdelal 2001). In other words, in an attempt to satisfy perceptions of the national interest today 'the nation' can be incorporated into liberal economic structures just as easily as into any other type of policy. The contextual factor of globalization leads many GPE scholars to assume that it is actually *easier* to construct liberal policies from a nationalist ontology today than it is the protectionist policies that List advocated for Germany in his day.

The continuing appeal of List's *National System*

The enduring appeal of List's work for scholars reacting to the political realities of the neo-liberal era is that it is so avowedly anti-market. Hence it becomes a ready means of asserting the right to autonomy for developing countries seeking political shelter from the disruptive influence of international economic norms (Veseth 2005: 47). Just as List had argued that the imposition of the British policy choice of laissez-faire served to frustrate German development aspirations in the nineteenth century, so, too, do many people today suggest that development space is systematically squeezed by the neo-liberal agenda of global governance institutions (see Phillips, Chapter 13 in this volume). List's *National System* appears to be a valuable resource to appropriate in this respect, because introductory GPE textbooks draw a smooth line of descent from Adam Smith's *Wealth of Nations* to contemporary **neo-liberalism**, while List was a wholly uncompromising critic of Smithian liberalism. Once again, though, all is not what it first seems.

List's attack on Smith was deliberately provocative, but it did not necessarily represent Smith's work fairly. List opened up space for his crusade against Smithian liberalism by deliberately caricaturing Smith's economics and turning his often ambivalent comments on the exposure of everyday life to market dynamics into undiluted and largely unthinking support for laissez-faire. Historians of economic thought are generally unimpressed when later theorists put words into earlier theorists' mouths, and this is why they tend not to rate List's work anywhere near as highly as GPE scholars do. The phrase 'laissez-faire', for instance, was not one that Smith used in his own work; moreover, at repeated points throughout *The Wealth of Nations* he presented his preferred policy solutions in terms that depart routinely from such assumptions (Viner 1928/89: 141). Indeed, Smithian liberalism often contained clear antiliberal arguments, perhaps most famously including praise of the palpably protectionist **Navigation Acts** for their far-sighted positive impacts on the wealth of the British nation (Smith 1776/1981: IV.ii.30). List ignored all such arguments, though, in his attempts to create clear-blue water for his own version of nationalist political economy. He therefore turned his back on textual accuracy in the search for more convenient depictions of his number one adversary, consistently attributing laissez-faire inclinations to Smith's work.

One issue on which List appears to fit his Smith caricature rather better than Smith does is the colonial question. Much of the interest in List today results from attempts to find feasible policy space beyond the unapologetic pro-market activism he attributed to Smith (e.g. Palan, Abbott, and Deans 1999: 80; Balaam and Veseth 2008: 34). List's *National System* is appealed to as an example of how things might be different today, and how developing countries might gain freedom from the policy script presented by global governance institutions through the strategic 'disinvention' of laissez-faire. He was particularly critical of German politicians who had tied the country's economy to the free trade rules established by Britain, urging them to renege on their international commitments and to follow their own course instead (Payne and Phillips

2010). The existing policy allowed German consumers to benefit from cheap British goods, but List believed that the British were the main beneficiaries by using market relationships to dump their country's production surplus in Germany. He argued that this made his own country nothing more than a trade captive of the leading industrial power (List 1841/2005c: 44–52). In effect, he said, Germany had become an economic colony of Britain (List 1841/2005b: 188–92; 216–17).

The parallels today are usually drawn with the WTO. The WTO has replaced Victorian Britain as the author of international commitments governing the flow of traded products, but the contents of the commitments remain the same. Both focus on rolling back the impediments to free trade. Equally, from a Listian perspective, both are inattentive to the process through which the advanced industrialized countries came to prominence in the sphere of international trade by deliberately restricting their initial exposure to world markets. List argued that, in his day, free trade was the policy of the strong, but that such strength had initially been built behind a structure of productive protection. He accused Britain of having 'kick[ed] away the ladder by which [it] has climbed up, in order to deprive others of the means of climbing up after [it]'. Other countries were thus disqualified from copying its first-mover advantage when engaged upon their own development (List 1841/2005c: 46). Advanced industrialized countries are accused today of using the WTO to enforce similar double standards by not allowing developing countries to protect their domestic industries until the time that they are able to join the free trade regime on equal terms. List's evocative phrase of 'kicking away the ladder' continues to be used to describe such effects (Chang 2003).

It would be somewhat one-sided, however, to try to depict List unequivocally as a friend of the developing world through his ostensibly anti-market rhetoric. It is certainly true that he objected vehemently to what he saw as deliberate British attempts to keep Germany underdeveloped and hence to treat it as some sort of imperial subordinate. Yet this merely reflected his fervent wish that, sometime in the not-too-distant future, Germany might be able to act on the world stage as Britain's equal (Shafaeddin 2005: 43). List still believed that there was a natural hierarchy of states, and his desire was purely to see Germany take its rightful place in that hierarchy. Given the time at which he was writing, this meant participating aggressively alongside other European powers in the struggle for overseas territorial acquisitions (List 1841/2005c: 71, 110). Part of the process of becoming Britain's equal was therefore to rival the scale and the significance of its empire. There is nothing in the *National System* that stands as a critique of imperial pretensions and the associated making of global markets. The colonial instinct is fine, List seems to have been saying, as long as Germany is the colonizer and not the colonized, the promoter and not the recipient of a self-interested laissez-faire (Harlen 1999: 739). Smith's *Wealth of Nations*, by contrast, is crammed full of criticisms of European colonial policy.

Textbook GPE, however, is also dominated by accounts of Smith's work that very much mirror List's in focus. On many points, it is true, Smith was a highly sympathetic critic of market processes in general, if not in terms of their extension in the colonial question. Yet he remained a critic, nonetheless, because of the way in which market processes turned a person's intrinsic worth into a monetary price (Force 2003). He understood this outcome to be a regrettably dehumanizing effect of the market economy and a clear impediment to the sustenance of functioning social organisms. The introductory texts through which GPE is taught have typically missed the fact that Smith was not the gung-ho advocate of the marketization of everything that he was made to appear in List's characterization of the *Wealth of Nations* (1841/2005b: 70). Smith explicitly denounced the utility theories of human nature through which the market frame was imposed on everyday life (Griswold 1999). Instead, the whole of his economic theory begins from the premise of how first to construct and then reproduce a functioning society.

KEY POINTS

- A very straightforward conception of state power lies at the heart of the explanatory frameworks of all realist approaches to the study of international economic affairs.

- Despite the tendency to regard them as synonymous, the statist ontology of realist GPE bears no resemblance to List's nationalist ontology as outlined in his classic work, *National System of Political Economy*.

- List's arguments add a level of complexity to the concept of national economic interest not apparent in realist GPE, but the distinctiveness he claimed for his own conception results in large part from deliberately caricaturing the work of his liberal predecessors on the same question.

- The historical relationship between realist GPE, List's *National System*, and Smith's *Wealth of Nations* is far more complicated than the standard textbook GPE account allows.

GPE liberalism and the nineteenth-century appropriation of the Smithian political economy tradition

The integrity of Smith's original writing might well have suffered at the hands of List's exaggerated style of criticism, but neither was Smith entirely innocent of having done much the same to a previous generation of political economy writers. He created the space for his alternative to the dominant economic ideas of the day—an alternative he described as exemplifying a system of natural liberty rather than being liberal per se (Fitzgibbons 1995)—by reducing the complexities of other people's texts to a straightforward anti-liberal dogma (Rashid 1998). In an attempt to differentiate his *National System* from *The Wealth of Nations*, List heaped praise on seventeenth- and eighteenth-century writers of the British Mercantilist School for their advocacy of the system of tariffs and trade restrictions that supported their country's developmental aspirations (e.g. List 1841/2005a: 69–70; 1841/2005b: 87–9). It is more than a little ironic, then, that no such self-conscious and self-organizing school existed in economic thought until Smith defined it in that way to suit his own ends as a critic. Nobody at the time could have purposely belonged to a school that had to wait until some decades later to be defined into existence in a post-hoc and wholly self-serving fashion using fairly crude pigeonholing devices. The historical roots of GPE liberalism therefore do not necessarily have the most illustrious or pristine of origins.

Moreover, there is an important element of the specialist Smith studies literature that questions whether it is reasonable to view him as a liberal at all (Henderson 2006). Certainly his work contains many of the philosophical features of that which came to delineate the embryonic liberal tradition in the following century. His concern was with specifying the conditions of existence under which people can recognize themselves as autonomous individuals within a broader social structure. Yet the work that came to set the tone for what became known as liberalism took the European Enlightenment starting point of 'reason' to be the source of such autonomy. Smith, by contrast, followed in the Scottish Enlightenment footsteps of his teacher, Francis Hutcheson, by emphasizing 'sentimentality' instead (McLean 2006: 46–8). People learned appropriate expressions of sociability from this perspective not by being able to rationalize the best possible response to prevailing circumstances but through imaginative acts enabling them to experience vicariously the types of feeling currently affecting fellow members of society. This is a process that Smith (1759/1982: I.i.2) called 'sympathy', and it is only through successful sympathetic enactments that people become aware not only of their autonomous status within society but also of the need to act in socially acceptable ways so as to preserve that status.

These elements of Smith's work are almost entirely disregarded in GPE's introductory textbooks. It might be possible to find single sentences that say in addition to *The Wealth of Nations* he was also the author of *The Theory of Moral Sentiments*, but that tends to be about as far as it goes. The Smith that overwhelmingly is presented to GPE students is that of *The Wealth of Nations* and, moreover, it is usual for this Smith to be reduced to a single observation from that most heterogeneous of texts. The renowned Smith scholar, Jacob Viner (1928/89: 126), has argued that a person must hold some pretty unusual economic ideas if they cannot read some pre-emption of their own theories back into *The Wealth of Nations*, such is its breadth of historical, theoretical, and philosophical coverage. However, the GPE textbooks tend to pick out just one comment to represent the supposedly authentic Smith, when in the middle of a much longer passage about the significance of choosing the right language if socially acceptable economic relations were to be reproduced he wrote the following: 'It is not from the benevolence of the butcher, the brewer, or the baker, that we expect our dinner, but from their regard to their own interest' (Smith 1776/1981: I.ii.2). This has typically been accepted in GPE—albeit incorrectly according to specialist Smith studies scholars—as evidence of his pre-emptive endorsement of the modern liberal justification of economic self-interest. His dismissal of mercantilist credos is also read in this light, as a reaction against the infringements upon individual economic self-determination, but in truth it was much more complicated than that.

Smith's political and moral critiques of mercantilism

To start at the beginning, though, Smith did devote a significant proportion of the 950 pages of *The Wealth of Nations* to refuting the core propositions of **mercantilism**. In particular, he sought credible counter-arguments founded on philosophical principles of natural liberty to two books: Thomas Mun's (1571–1641) *England's Treasure by Forraign Trade* and

Bernard Mandeville's (1670–1733) *Fable of the Bees*. Mun's (1664/1928) treatise, published posthumously by his son, was a celebration of England's eminent position in seventeenth-century international trade relations, which he attributed to a strong state capable of structuring the country's commercial activities so as to produce continual trade surpluses. Imports were discouraged by the use of tariffs, quotas, and subsidies. However, the English used their state strategically—through military means if necessary—to ensure that similarly restrictive practices were not imposed against their goods. The result was a net inflow of precious metals as other countries serviced their trade deficits with England. For many of the people who Smith lumped together as a single Mercantilist School, the hoarding of precious metals made possible by trade surpluses was the measure of the nation's wealth, rather than this being represented by the overall productive capacity of the economy as a whole.

Mandeville (1714/1997) extended Mun's analysis to argue that the state should ensure that its citizens did not follow its lead by attempting to hoard their wealth. He suggested that individual saving might well be seen as a private virtue, but that it was in fact a public vice. The impetus for export activity could only be maintained under the full utilization of domestic productive potential, and this, in turn, required the state to be on its guard against domestic under-consumption. Every effort should thus be made to encourage spending rather than saving, with the state acting coercively if necessary. Mandeville's best-remembered text is most famous for its celebration of a host of individualistic and often antisocial character traits (Hundert 1994). He positively eulogized selfish behaviour aimed at rather tawdry acts of personal display, because he treated these as the lifeblood of the consumption mentalities that kept the growth rate of the economy high (Goldsmith 1990).

Even though Smith presented his attack on mercantilism in terms of economics, it is not in fact an economic critique that is most prominent in this part of his work. Instead, it is a combination of political and moral critiques that most notably stands out. Starting with Smith's critique of Mun, the important historical fact to keep in mind here is that Mun was simultaneously a member of the Standing Commission on Trade established in Britain in 1622 and a member of the committee of the **British East India Company**. Smith's political critique of mercantilism focused on the obvious conflict of interests contained in situations such as this. He is often wrongly judged to have been against the whole process of modern government as an unnecessary distraction to the otherwise natural workings of the market economy: textbook GPE, for instance, often talks of little else. Yet Smith repeatedly used his own work to highlight the indispensability of government to how markets form, as well as to how they are reproduced in everyday economic life through outlawing certain market-bound behaviours because of their antisocial consequences (Fleischacker 2005). It was not government per se that drew Smith's ire, so much as clear corruption of the process of government when it was captured by particular vested interests. Mun's treatise, he thought, reduced to a straightfor-wardly self-interested account of what would be good for his own company (see Box 2.3).

Smith's moral critique of mercantilism was also a critique of self-interested behaviour, but this time centred on what he saw as the unfortunate, even disreputable, activities being advocated by Mandeville.

In order to make his displeasure absolutely clear he described Mandeville as the purveyor of a 'licentious system' of philosophy, one that was 'wholly pernicious' (Smith 1759/1982: VII.ii.4.6). At the time of writing his *Theory of Moral Sentiments*, Smith found himself caught between two very different accounts of the moral basis of the newly emergent commercial society and its attendant market economy. On the one side, there was Mandeville, armed with a completely instrumental defence of commercial and market-based ethics. In Smith's reading, Mandeville paid no attention at all to respectable manners, validating all sorts of antisocial behaviour as long as it helped to advance economic interests and caused the economy to grow. Gratuitous displays of personal wealth invited no moral condemnation, even if they were paraded in the context of other people's poverty, because it meant that more money was circulating within the economy. Obsequiousness to the rich, praising and

BOX 2.3

Smith on the British East India Company

The British East India Company was granted an English Royal Charter in 1600 to act on behalf of the sovereign in meeting the country's commercial objectives as laid down by the government (Robins 2006). However, it operated at a significant distance from the oversight that the government could apply to it. The British East India Company's sphere of activities was nearly two years' round-trip away from home. This provided it with a large degree of autonomy, which it used to seize for itself monopoly rights in the territories in which it was active. It generally treated those territories as colonial possessions ripe for asset- and resource-stripping. It imposed a form of martial law for this purpose, denying local people their social and economic rights in the interests of repatriating **balance-of-trade** surpluses to England. Smith made his feelings on this issue plain (1776/1981: IV.vii.b.44) by writing that to prohibit a people 'from making all that they can of every part of their own produce, or from employing their stock and industry in the way that they judge most advantageous to themselves, is a manifest violation of the most sacred rights of mankind'. Always an opponent of colonization, Smith found the British East India Company's activities wholly objectionable (Muthu 2008).

Perhaps feeling himself unable to take on directly the Company's supporters and paid employees in government, Smith set his sights instead on the economic *means* that the

British East India Company used to generate balance-of-trade surpluses. He endeavoured to cast 'odious imputation' upon the specific system of government in operation in England during the British East India Company's ascendance. Attacking the commercial restraints that were used to profit the Company at the expense of building the economic capabilities of the acquired territories became his chosen means of attacking the power that the Company had appropriated at everyone else's expense (Smith 1776/1981: IV.vii.c.107). In one conceptual move, Smith was able to show that the political conflicts of interest sustaining the monopoly positions of exclusive stockholding corporations was bad both for the countries that were being colonized *and* for the ordinary citizens of the colonizing countries. He wrote that:

Since the establishment of the English East India company ... the other inhabitants of England, over and above being excluded from the trade, must have paid in the price of the East India goods which they have consumed, not only for all the extraordinary profits which the company may have made upon those goods in consequence of their monopoly, but for all the extraordinary waste which the fraud and abuse, inseparable from the management of the affairs of so great a company, must necessarily have occasioned.

(Smith 1776/1981: IV.vii.c.91)

He railed against the 'absurdity' of continuing to tolerate such a situation (Smith 1776/1981: IV.vii.c.91).

then aspiring to emulate their consumption for nothing other than its own sake, was also considered fine, because this, too, triggered new economic activity. To Mandeville, the creation of a civilized market order was not the priority; the creation of a dynamic market economy was, and he was able to rationalize whatever behavioural traits underpinned it. Smith disagreed. In his view, a dynamic market economy was not a reasonable objective if it could only be bought at the cost of fundamentally antisocial behaviour.

However, Smith did not disagree with Mandeville to such an extent that he allied himself with the chief proponent of the other side of the debate, Jean-Jacques Rousseau. In his *Discourse on Inequality*, Rousseau implied that human life was increasingly not worth living if economic expediency was to be raised above respectable public ethics (Rousseau 1755/2003). He was a strong supporter of the republican proposition that the virtue of the individual overshadows all other considerations, going as far as to regret the entire move into the commercial stage of society, because for him this was associated with the unavoidable corruption of the individual as a moral entity (Hörnqvist 2000). The very possibility of luxury consumption within such a society, he said, was sufficient to turn everyone away from the path of virtue and to glorify instead in the possession of commodities for its own sake. He depicted a future of socially obstructive individuals permanently on the lookout for the commendation of their fellows purely for the riches they could display. His conclusion was that life surrounded by commerce and markets necessarily forced people to lose their virtue.

Smith on self-command

The longer-term historical roots of liberal GPE date to Smith's attempts to construct a middle way between the ethics-free zone of Mandeville's economics and the economic restrictions of Rousseau's ethics. However, the ethical basis of Smith's thought has been almost completely written out of the GPE account of liberalism. As Stephen Rosow (1997) has argued very persuasively, this is as narrow an understanding of liberalism as there has been in that approach's whole history. When GPE scholars talk about liberalism, it is almost always as a set of economic principles, rather than Smith's wider-ranging system of natural liberty. It is true that he sided with Mandeville against Rousseau on the latter's insistence that progress into the

commercial stage of society was necessarily at odds with human happiness. Yet he shared many of Rousseau's concerns about the corrupting influence of luxury consumption and the need, contra Mandeville, to restate the value of virtue in the face of that corruption. He thus set out to construct a philosophical account of moral activity that would be specifically suited to the commercial stage of society. It is an account oriented to the articulation of what McCloskey (2006) calls the 'bourgeois virtues'.

The enactment of bourgeois virtues entails learning how to exhibit a politeness of manners, deliberately reining in the urge for self-display in anything other than the most restrained way. Smith called this learning the virtue of self-command (Smith 1759/1982: VI.iii.11). Tutoring oneself to self-command means being able to understand the effects of other people's hardship and to respond accordingly to one's success with only muted celebrations. Moderation of emotions all round is the order of the day in such a world (Smith 1759/1982: I.ii.intro.2). This eliminates at a stroke the gratuitous parade of possessions so beloved of Mandeville's consumers, as well as the obsequiousness to the rich that encourages the parade of possessions in the first place. Throughout *The Theory of Moral Sentiments*, Smith suggested that, whether or not society functions successfully under the influence of market-based institutions depends on whether or not self-command is enacted successfully among the population as a whole.

Smith therefore praised deliberate acts of impartiality and insisted that all individuals should experience dutiful sensations to act conscionably with respect to other members of society. The purpose of government when understood from this perspective is to design social institutions to ensure that people live within the bounds of acceptable behaviour (Raphael and Macfie 1982). Conspicuous self-interest that List, among others, later attributed to Smith must therefore be contrasted with Smith's concerns that market-based institutions were only legitimate if they encouraged people to act im*partially*. Yet this is precisely the sort of juxtaposition between what Smith was deemed to have said and what he did say that most GPE scholars and, to my knowledge, all introductory GPE textbooks tend to overlook in preference for populist readings of his work (e.g. Underhill 1994; Grieco and Ikenberry 2003; Brawley 2005; Oatley 2006). In particular, they emphasize much more recent political arguments about the '**invisible hand**'. In doing so,

Smith is turned into a simple apologist for all things market-based.

Maybe the reason why this elision is made so often nowadays is that the invisible hand reading fits neatly with the main claims of rational choice theory and with the distinctively nineteenth-century history of economic thought that has been handed down from the Marginalist Revolution. If people are to act as instinctive utility maximizers they must have a context in which such instincts might be realized and also a mechanism to trigger them. Somewhat fortuitously, perhaps, abstract accounts of 'the market' associated with modern-day GPE liberalism provide both the context and the mechanism. If the behavioural environment is shaped solely by a disembodied market logic, then there can be no non-economic impediments to the activation of even the most extreme variants of *Homo economicus*. Moreover, that same logic also guides the individual to the equilibrium position associated with utility maximization. The unfortunate point, though, when trying to superimpose this purely modern-day reading back onto Smith is that he was as opposed to using the economic concept of equilibrium as he was to the philosophical proposition that people are governed by innate utility considerations.

> ### KEY POINTS
>
> - Smith was guilty of artificially homogenizing existing writings in the mercantilist tradition to open up the space for his alternative system of natural liberty.
> - The textbook GPE account of *The Wealth of Nations* often ignores completely all of his philosophical reflections.
> - Associating Smith's insights solely with the populist rendition of the invisible hand concept is a complete red herring as far as specialist Smith scholarship is concerned.
> - Smith believed that individuals are duty-bound to act impartially via self-command.

GPE Marxism and the nineteenth-century Marxian political economy tradition

The historical roots of Marxist GPE are much more frequently discussed within the subject field as a whole than are the historical roots of either nationalist or liberal GPE. Global political economists in general appear to be more comfortable constructing positions that are recognizably part of a lineage that appeals in some way to Marx than they are doing likewise for either List or Smith. Nonetheless, an important division is still visible on the question of 'which' Marx to hark back to.

Some contributions in Marxist GPE are rooted in a normative Marx, who makes the avowedly political case for a new type of society. The lineage here is usually to *The Communist Manifesto* (Marx and Engels 1848/1948). Others, however, are rooted in an analytical Marx, who makes the intellectual case for breaking with the liberal traditions of post-Smithian classical economics. The lineage here is usually to the *Grundrisse* (Marx 1973) or to *Kapital* (Marx 1930). Despite this difference, all are united in their refusal to take the social basis of capitalism for granted. They ask searching questions about the likely effects of the capitalist system on those who have to live within it and, in particular, why they should be expected to consent to its reproduction. This is to be contrasted with what Marx called the 'bourgeois economics' of Smith and the other classical economists, who he said were only interested in how the capitalist system might be organized to grow more effectively.

As has already been shown, though, this is not really to take Smith's texts at face value, and once again we encounter a selective nineteenth-century rereading of eighteenth-century scholarship as a means of activating a new political economy tradition. Had he genuinely been interested solely in the capitalist accumulation imperative, Smith would have had no need to articulate his views quite so clearly in opposition to those of Mandeville. Marx was consequently partly right in his overall objection to Smith's work—Smith certainly exhibited no desire to leave behind the commercial stage of society in its entirety, only to civilize it—but not wholly so. The language Marx used to describe Smith's alleged shortcomings is also noteworthy. His brusqueness was of the sort that is driven by exasperation that potentially important insights on the human condition of capitalism were not pushed to their logical political conclusion. Marx did, after all, borrow many of his starting propositions directly from Smith. Understanding the historical roots of Marxist GPE accordingly requires at least some appreciation of the relationship between the two men's work.

The foundations of Marx's political economy

The whole of Marx's political economy is grounded in the opening premise that the capitalist system can only be a dynamic entity when the needs of that system are forcibly prioritized over the rights of individuals to live as autonomous human beings (Marx 1973). The reproduction of the capitalist system overrides that autonomy by turning individuals into a functional part of the system. People might believe that they work to satisfy basic existential needs, that they work to be able to finance leisure time, or that they work to provide themselves with the material possessions they associate with a life of comfort. Yet, for Marx, this in itself is an element of false consciousness: an inability to see things for what they really are and to form interests accordingly. Within a capitalist system, he said, people in fact work solely in order to preserve the smooth running of the system itself through preserving the momentum towards **capital accumulation**. In effect, no individual is more than a tiny cog in a huge economic machine, and it is the well-being of the machine that takes precedence over the defence of truly human existence. In Marx's view, the incorporation of the individual as a commodified input into the capitalist system necessarily has dehumanizing effects (Marx 1930) (see Box 2.4).

Given this, it is easy to see why Marx thought that the act of labour was so important to life in a capitalist society. The subjugation of the needs of the individual to the reproduction of the capitalist system in effect reduces the essence of human life to mere labouring activities (Wolff 2002: 27). Even then, Marx was eager to show that labourers do not receive full recompense for the value of their labouring activities. He drew a politically charged distinction between labour and labour power, arguing that the average capitalist will always seek to reduce wages as far as possible and preferably to the point at which they become the equivalent of labour power, even though it is labour that is physically expended in the production process. Labour power represents the costs of sustaining the workers who have been incorporated into the capitalist system. Yet it is labour that adds value to the commodities being produced, and thereby it is labour that creates the potential for the capitalist to take profits out of the system. The more that capitalists are able to enforce a structural difference between labour and labour power, the more they will be able to reward themselves with handsome profits. Marx described

---

BOX 2.4

Smith and Marx on Alienation

Smith used *The Wealth of Nations* to outline his model of the commercial economy. He placed the concept of **division of labour** centre stage, showing that the growth of the economy and the consequent enrichment of the nation both depend on the degree to which work takes place within specialized units. The depth of the institutionalization of the market follows closely the incorporation of workers into ever-more finely detailed patterns of specialization (Smith 1776/1981: I.iii.1). This was socially beneficial, according to Smith, because it was here that the potential was concentrated for lifting people out of poverty. However, it was by no means an unequivocal social good, because there were palpable psychological costs involved when forcing the division of labour onto people through the move towards routinized factory work. Smith (1776/1981: V.i.f.51) was even prepared to describe the ensuing state of mind as a 'drowsy stupidity'.

On this most fundamental of assumptions about everyday experiences under capitalism there is thus very little to choose between Marx and Smith. Marx developed from first principles

a thoroughly thought-through and conceptually robust notion of **alienation** to replace Smith's (1776/1981: V.i.f.60) simple observation about 'mental mutilation, deformity and wretchedness', but it would be difficult to demonstrate that they were doing anything other than talking about the same essential process. The only real difference—major though it is—relates to what they then inferred. Smith offered state-financed education as a palliative to the psychological drudgery of repeating the same basic work tasks day in, day out: the dehumanizing effects of workers' incorporation into a division of labour were to be balanced by publicly funded mental stimulation outside of work hours. For Marx, this was Smith at his most bourgeois. The education palliative was merely a means of imposing false consciousness, he said, and it was therefore part of the problem through which workers failed to see that the interests of the capitalist system did not coincide with their own interests. Individuals are socialized into the necessity of production before being coerced into a social structure that facilitates specifically capitalist production. Obedience is paramount, and the creativity occasioned by mental stimulation is discouraged for fear that it will corrupt the standardization of commodities.

this as the logic of **surplus value extraction**, and he believed it to be a fundamental logic inscribed into the very essence of the capitalist system. To ensure the dynamism that guarantees its survival as a system, employers under capitalism must require employees to add more economic value in production than they are compensated for in terms of wages. This can be explained using the labour theory of value, which links the effort expended in the production process to the monetary rewards taken from it. It therefore provides important insights into who gets their fair share and who does not.

Perhaps unusually, the labour theory of value did not attain its purest form in its original articulation. It began life with a number of qualifications introduced by Smith, had further qualifications added by Ricardo (1821/2002), and was only latterly stripped back to its bare essentials by Marx. Smith began by saying that it was not only the physical labour provided by workers that gave products their underlying value. He believed that entrepreneurial labour could also legitimately be reflected in the price of a commodity (this is a feature of his concept of 'natural prices'). Following from this, Ricardo argued that the organizational labour provided by the firm was also part of the value inscribed upon a product (this is a feature of his defence of profits). The most famous articulation of the labour theory of value, though, came from Marx. He built on the work of the so-called **Ricardian Socialists** of the 1820s–40s. They had forwarded a radical interpretation of the dynamics of price formation by arguing that the integrity of the labour theory of value rested on it meaning exactly what it said in its title. In other words, the intrinsic value of a commodity should be seen as having been determined by the inputs workers provide for the production process via their physical labour and by nothing else.

The political implications of such a view were clear: the social structure of ownership should be fundamentally reorganized to prevent anyone else benefiting from the efforts of workers in the production process. Ronald Meek (1974) suggests that this argument led directly to the development of neoclassical economics. The break that marginalist scholarship enacted from the labour theory of value meant that the ruling elite felt less politically threatened (De Vroey 1975). Marx, though, took the opposite path, fully embracing the radical implications of the work of the Ricardian Socialists. He treated social deference to organizational and entrepreneurial labour as further

examples of the phenomenon of false consciousness. The returns that capitalists took from the economy were rewards for their privileged social position, he said, and not rewards for effort per se.

The fact that surplus value extraction continued to be tolerated proved to Marx that capitalism could only operate via a logic of exploitation. The contractual basis of the wage labour nexus defends a situation in which workers remain unpaid for part of the work they are obliged to do. A procedural injustice is clearly perpetrated in this instance and, given that this experience is fundamental to the reproduction of capitalism as a functioning system, for Marx, capitalism could never be just. Indeed, from his perspective, the whole essence of capitalism is that it forcibly submits the vast majority of any given society—via the process of false consciousness—to implicit consent to the injustices that are committed against them. This is the point of departure for the normative Marx to build upon the insights of the analytical Marx in order to advocate the move to a brand new society capable of transcending the logic of exploitation on which capitalism depends. The organizational basis for prosecuting such a move arises from the fact that exploitation and injustice are not solitary experiences under capitalism. Rather, they are shared to a greater or lesser degree by everyone who has to work to finance their own subsistence. Marx thus depicted society as riven into two classes relating to their respective positions in the production process. On the one hand, there are the capitalists—the bourgeoisie—who benefit from the surplus value extraction that permeates right to the heart of the capitalist system. On the other hand, there are the workers—the proletariat—who bear the indignity of having surplus value forcibly extracted from them.

Interestingly, there is very little by way of outright condemnation of the activities of individual business leaders in either the *Grundrisse* or *Kapital*. Certainly there is no evidence of the sustained hostility against the monopolizing spirit to be found in *The Wealth of Nations*, where Smith took every opportunity he could to decry business activities which led to 'a conspiracy against the publick' (Smith 1776/1981: I.x.c.ii.27). Whereas Smith took the concentration of capital through monopoly as a sign of diminished social propriety in the actions of business leaders, Marx treated it as the manifestation of a simple system requirement. One capitalist was necessarily in competition with all others, and if this meant forcing the destruction of rival capitals in a bid for survival then so be it: "Accumulate, accumulate! That is Moses and the prophets!" (Marx 1867/1996: 309). This was a system imperative, according to Marx, not the slapdash enactment of antisocial behaviour (Catephores 1989: 32). He focused his analysis at the level of the system imperative to such an extent that there was no need for him to comment on the rationality—flawed or otherwise—of any individual within the system. It was therefore always going to be something of a stretch to make his original insights compatible with the notion of a Marxist ideology of GPE suited to the age of rational choice theory.

Modern 'structuralist' extensions of Marx's political economy

Proponents of Marxist GPE have typically stayed loyal to the outlines of Marx's original analytical formulations in the 150 + years since they were initially devised. They generally seek to uncover exploitative dynamics in modern processes of international production, and they present such dynamics as infringements of global justice enacted through new geographical patterns of surplus value extraction. Thus, one particularly prominent line of research involves attempts to investigate the way in which large companies with multinational operating facilities today make profits for themselves and their shareholders through globalizing their production in the search for maximum monetary gain. Such research focuses in particular on the potential for labour power to command different prices in different countries, as well as on how this creates opportunities for **multinational corporations** to enforce ever-greater discrepancies between the labour they command and the labour power they are obliged to recompense. The policy-making apparatus of the state might always be called upon to defend workers' rights and to meliorate the tendency towards proletarian exploitation. Yet Marxist GPE scholars have pointed increasingly to the development of a **transnational capitalist class** as a by-product of the contemporary trend towards globalization (see e.g. van der Pijl 1998; Sklair 2001). Members of a transnational capitalist class have allegiance to no state and are therefore able increasingly to escape the impact of regulatory policies introduced by state managers in the interests of workers' rights. If this is true, then the fundamental antagonism between bourgeoisie and proletariat identified by Marx is likely to be experienced in its purest form today within specifically international

production processes. The labour theory of value continues to provide interesting insights in this regard.

A 'structuralist' approach to Marxist GPE has developed in an attempt to capture this point, conceptualizing the world economy as a single, integrated capitalist system existing within a single, integrated political space of exploitation. Structuralists, however, will often pay only limited attention to reconstructing Marx's explanatory framework in its own terms (Rosenberg 2002), because their real starting point is instead in Lenin's efforts to internationalize fundamental Marxian themes (Lenin 1917/96). In a pamphlet of the same name, Lenin argued that imperialism had become the 'highest stage of capitalism' by the start of the twentieth century, as well as that, as such, the new dynamism within the capitalist system centred on the relationship between states. Marx's original class-based analysis was retained, but Lenin asked how class-based relationships had been transformed across national borders now that capitalism had become a world system.

He argued that domestic bourgeoisies in advanced European countries had increasingly become international bourgeoisies through their willingness to strike class compromises at home. Their acquiescence to the granting of workers' rights domestically was met by a need to increase the level of surplus value extraction overseas in the interests of maintaining underlying levels of profitability for the national economy as a whole. Colonial links provided the ideal political context in which this could be achieved. As a consequence, imperialism was seen to have important economic effects both at home and abroad. Given the willingness of many scholars to treat contemporary conditions of globalization as just the latest phase of economic imperialism (see e.g. Hoogvelt 1997; Hardt and Negri 2000; Petras and Veltmeyer 2001), the structuralist approach to GPE has retained many adherents. They are usually to be found today practising either World Systems Theory or Dependency Theory. In its most up-to-date guise, World Systems Theory is based on the assumption that the world divides into economic regions of core, periphery, and semi-periphery (see e.g. Wallerstein 1979). Dependency Theory, meanwhile, is based on the assumption that the continued distorted development of poorer countries results from the need to defend the conditions that have led to the development trajectory of more economically advanced countries (see e.g. dos Santos 1970). In both cases the efforts made by advanced industrialized countries to maintain their position of economic advantage is treated as a rational reflection of the existing global balance of power.

Modern-day structuralist extensions of Marxism therefore involve at least a partial break with Marx's own intellectual trajectory. This is not a complete break, because the aspiration for a better world free of the logic of economic exploitation remains visible in modern-day GPE literatures that trace their origins to Lenin. In this respect, the normative Marx remains alive and well, thereby justifying the retention of the label 'Marxist' in order to describe it. However, the analytical Marx is not necessarily as prominent. As befits the continued presence of the normative Marx, modern-day Marxist GPE seeks its essence in a fundamental challenge to prevailing neo-liberal conditions of world order. Yet it does not always reveal its historical roots in the analytical Marx's efforts to undermine the way in which Smith's system of natural liberty came to dominate the concepts of orthodox economic discourse. It certainly does little to show the struggle in which Marx had to engage in order to break free of Smithian thinking, given that he so often took Smith's conceptual starting points as his own. Smith's theory of the capitalist economy as an engine for the creation of economic value reappears—albeit in admittedly revised form—in Marx's work, as does his embryonic account of alienation.

KEY POINTS

- Marx insisted that all economic experiences should be placed in their correct historical context and understood in relation to the evolution of the capitalist system from one time period to the next.

- Marx's theory problematizes the concepts of bourgeois economics to show how they work to legitimize exploitation within the capitalist system.

- Marxist GPE is an all-encompassing critique of capitalist society, from the exploitation it enforces upon its members to the false consciousness that masks the real dynamics of this exploitation within the normal workings of everyday life.

- In order to keep pace with changes to the economy, twentieth-century extensions of Marxism increasingly came to place more emphasis on the international dimension of economic affairs, but they have done so through partial divorce from their political economy origins in Marx's own work.

GPE feminism and the nineteenth-century popularization of classical economics for women

The nineteenth century witnessed significant social struggle over who should be taught political economy and what should be the content of their learning. In Britain—still at that time the world's leading economic nation and, according to Marx, the cradle of economic theory—women were at the forefront of that struggle, both as those seeking education and as the educators. Spurred on by Mary Wollstonecraft's campaign for co-educational schooling (Darling and Glendinning 1996: 23), a number of women writers took on the task of showing how the concerns of classical economics need not remain a purely male preserve (Chapman 2015: 55). The names of Maria Edgeworth (1768–1849), Jane Marcet (1769–1858), and Harriet Martineau (1802–76) do not appear as central figures in most histories of nineteenth-century economic thought, because by their own account they were not adding to the cumulative stock of economic knowledge. Yet it remains a shame that their activities in bringing economic theory to the people whose lives were increasingly regulated by it remain generally overlooked. After Wollstonecraft had successfully undermined the notion of a uniquely feminine 'modesty' (Richardson 2002: 36), Edgeworth, Marcet, and Martineau occupied the resulting pedagogical space to show that there might be no limits to who should be comfortable speaking the leading economic principles of the day. Edgeworth began the trend of opening up economic education by writing specifically for children; Marcet wrote for young women about to embark on adult life; Martineau wanted to reach as many people among the adult population as she could.

The writings of these women were also representative of a more general trend. They endorsed Jeremy Bentham's application of his utilitarian philosophy to the sphere of education, using their work to emphasize the advantage to the nation as a whole in having ever wider sections of the population well drilled in practical affairs (Henderson 1995: 50). Up until that time, in Britain at least, education tended to be used as a marker of status within a class-bound society. It therefore focused on disseminating a knowledge base biased towards classical antiquity, usually conducted in either Greek or Latin. Marcet wrote in the Preface to her *Conversations on Political Economy* that her aim was 'to bring within the reach of young persons a science which no English writer has yet presented in any easy and familiar form' (Marcet 1839/2009: xxxvii). This was, after all, the heyday of the Society for the Diffusion of Useful Knowledge, a Whiggish organization established under the promptings of the free-trader statesman Lord Brougham to enable a greater degree of mass self-education (Berg 1980: 292).

Some of the leading philosophers and economists of the day got in on the act, James Mill writing *Elements of Political Economy* and John Ramsay McCulloch *Principles of Political Economy* for very similar audiences to those that Edgeworth, Marcet, and Martineau were targeting. Yet the men's work achieved none of the popularity and contemporary critical acclaim that was bestowed upon the women's. It is perhaps for this reason that the women's work was met by a decidedly sniffy attitude from those who latterly wished to stick up for what Runyan (1997: 79) has so compellingly called the mainstream economic story of 'men, states, and markets'. Joseph Schumpeter (1954/2006: 477) waved an airily dismissive hand in his account of an economics 'so delightfully simple as to be capable

of being taught to every school girl'. Alfred Marshall, even more poisonously, drew attention to the divide he perceived between the real theoretical work being undertaken by the men and whatever it was the women could be considered to be doing. At century's end he made the following portentous prediction: 'Never again will ... a Mrs. Marcet, or a Miss Martineau earn a goodly reputation by throwing [economic principles] into the form of a catechism or of simple tales, by aid of which any intelligent governess might make it clear to the children nestling around her where lies economic truth, and might send them forth ready to instruct statesmen and merchants how to choose the right path in economic policy' (Marshall 1897: 117).

As will become only too evident, there is no linear path that ties the content of the best-known economic work written by women in the nineteenth century to the content of feminist GPE today. But this is one issue where similarities are difficult to miss. Both have had to endure significant hardship when struggling for recognition and attempting to safeguard their own legacy (see Box 2.5).

BOX 2.5

Edgeworth, Marcet, and Martineau: Adam Smith's 'Daughters'?

There is a well-worked tendency for the history of economic thought to be presented through the prism of intergenerational evolution. This is a relatively easy way to capture the sense of the centre of gravity of economic theory as it moves over time. For instance, it becomes possible using this presentational device to provide much more nuanced accounts of neoclassical economics than when thinking of it as a single, undifferentiated entity: the insights of the first-generation marginalists (Jevons, Menger, Walras—see Box 2.1) might be usefully contrasted with what later-generation marginalists subsequently brought to the debate (Pareto, Marshall, Hicks, Samuelson, etc.). However, the same way of thinking can also collapse into unhelpful 'parental' metaphors. Nowhere is this more unfortunately manifested than in the reduction of Edgeworth, Marcet, and Martineau to nothing more than the 'daughters' of Adam Smith, the 'father' of economics (Polkinghorn and Thomson 1998).

There is certainly a link back to Smith here, but to say that this is *all* there is runs the risk of seriously trivializing the contributions to popular understandings of economics made by women in Britain in the early nineteenth century. Edgeworth perhaps provides the most obvious connection, having received a copy of *The Wealth of Nations* as a commemorative gift from her father to mark the end of her education and her progress into adulthood.

The most important stories that she wrote for parents to read to their children—'The Cherry Orchard', 'Lazy Lawrence', 'The Bracelet of Memory'—all appropriate major themes from Smith's most famous work. The noted Smith scholar, Vivienne Brown (1994), suggests that *The Wealth of Nations* was in any case written in monological form for Smith to urge his readers to adopt his chosen perspective on the economic issues of the day. It was therefore perhaps not a huge jump for Edgeworth to adapt a similar structure and tone for promoting basic Smithian principles.

However, the same nineteenth-century overlay that dominates textbook GPE could be said to be in operation here. As the intellectual historian Bob Black (1976) has argued, by the early nineteenth century Smith was already being read less for his abstract theory and more for his free trade instincts. The Smith whose image re-emerges in Edgeworth's stories is a Smith for her age rather than for his. As the free trade lobby became better organized as the nineteenth century advanced— particularly through opposition to the Corn Laws—Marcet's and Martineau's work revealed even more of the nineteenth-century readings of *The Wealth of Nations*. Marcet and Martineau thus echoed List and Marx in placing their own template over Smith's work. In their case, the writings of David Ricardo (1772– 1823) and Robert Malthus (1766–1834) acted as important intermediaries: it was *The Wealth of Nations* read through their labour theory of value and population theory respectively rather than in its own terms.

Marcet's and Martineau's use of fictional representations of economic principles

Marcet and Martineau could both count among their friends and acquaintances the leading British economists of their day. They were able to call upon these personal contacts to open up the black box of theoretical abstractions and to bring a series of basic economic principles to life as something of explicit relevance to everyday experiences. They did so using fictional prose through which readers were able to overcome their uncertainties on abstract economic matters by being shown how a 'guide' was able to direct the uninitiated into an increasingly sophisticated understanding of economics. Marcet published the first of seven editions of her *Conversations on Political Economy* in 1816 as part of a wider series of *Conversations* that introduced her readers to all sorts of different scientific material. Martineau, meanwhile, published her *Illustrations of Political Economy* in 25 monthly instalments, each one as a novella, between 1832 and 1834. Both Marcet and Martineau alighted on a set format for their work, focusing on didactic, self-contained stories that 'corrected' the initial misgivings of an ingénue so that the 'true' principles of political economy might enjoy an ever expanding support base.

The content of Marcet's and Martineau's characterizations means that their relationship to feminist GPE today is rather complex. The first thing to note, of course, is that even the fact that women were supporting themselves financially through writing something other than romance fiction was a rarity in itself. Moreover, both set themselves against nineteenth-century gender norms through which the education of girls was to focus on matters of social practice and imagined social standing to enhance their prospects of being identified as a suitably dutiful and deferential wife. The guide in Marcet's stories, for instance, reacts stridently to the suggestion that it might be of little consequence if young women were to display a 'happy ignorance' of political economy debates: 'When you plead in favour of ignorance, there is a strong presumption that you are in the wrong' (Marcet 1839/2009: 9). Martineau went even further in flipping contemporary gender norms on their head. In confronting social anxiety at the time about the onset of industrialization in 'The Hill and the Valley', she used a female character (Mrs Wallace) to get a male character (Mr Armstrong) to challenge his deeply held doubts as to whether this equated unequivocally to

progress. He expects her to second his objections, as a duty both to nature and to his opinion. However, she guides both what his eyes will see in recognizing the intrinsic beauty of an ironworks and the economic judgement that he will allow himself to come to when seeing their raw masculine form on the landscape (Martineau 1832–4, number 2: 51–79). At the same time, she exposes the implicit effeminacy of his previous regret that nature was being swallowed up by the rush towards industrial capitalism (Freedgood 1999: 219). Yet even though Martineau occasionally began to describe a radical utopia in which women enjoy full equality with men, Marcet's guide spoke of a future in which women would remain dependent upon and resolutely subordinate to men. Furthermore, both saw their task as popularizing the writings of male economists that emerged from a society exhibiting often exorbitant male privilege.

The structure of Marcet's writing is particularly interesting in this regard: her *Conversations* were precisely that. She wrote in a dialogical form (see Wallbank 2012: 127) because this is what provided the best opportunity of 'introducing objections, and placing in various points of view, questions and answers as they had actually occurred' to Marcet herself. 'It will be observed, accordingly', she continued in her Preface, 'that the questions are generally the vehicle of some collateral remarks contributing to illustrate the subject' (Marcet 1839/2009: 39, 29–40). It is instructive that the question-asker is Caroline, an adolescent of never-quite-specified age whose naivety serves as the perfect foil for the wisely Mrs B. to play her designated role of patient tutor. The characters of Caroline and Mrs B. stand in for the intellectual journey that Marcet recognizes she must have undertaken, having herself started out as an economic ingénue before becoming familiar with the essence of political economy (Henderson 1995: 53). Caroline speaks the opinions of what, at the opening of the nineteenth century, counted as conventional hierarchical morality. She does so in a well-intentioned manner, challenging the ever more obvious encroachment of Ricardian and Malthusian political economy as an alternative source of morals, but her characteristic flippancy never spills over into the explicitly threatening way of the contemporary radical presses. This style of polite questioning enables Mrs. B. to calmly work through her argument that the latest insights of the classical economists are perfectly compatible with the prevailing moral structure. Caroline is repeatedly persuaded into acquiescence with the existing social order as it is reflected in the work of Ricardo and Malthus.

Martineau took a different view of the relationship between political economy and morality. Marcet had Mrs. B. facing down the suggestion that the amoral pursuits of capital accumulation advocated by the classical economists were a direct menace to the system of manners established during the Enlightenment. Martineau, by contrast, believed that the classical economists had set down a new template for morality based on individual choice and that conventional morality of the type espoused by Caroline should give way to it (Klaver 2003: 54). The characters who control the flow of the narrative in Martineau's stories are all more than willing to embrace this modern view of the world as their own. Her guides lead the reader through situations in which the solution to social problems comes when people learn how to better match their own actions to what basic economic principles suggest they should do (Goodlad 2004: 48). Whereas Marcet's *Conversations* are all about making economics safe to engage, Martineau's *Illustrations* are all about elevating it to a pedestal from which it will help individuals to reconstitute their fundamental sense of self.

Martineau was not writing long after Marcet, but quite a lot had changed in the interim to disturb the political status quo reflected in their respective works. Free trade campaigners had become much more prominent in their opposition to the protectionist Corn Laws, with the context already set for the abolitionists' ultimately successful People's Bread campaign (see Pickering and Tyrell 2000: 119). McCulloch had also begun his own personal crusade to impose the view that Ricardo's work—the intellectual inspiration, remember, for Britain's nineteenth-century free traders—represented the teleological endpoint of all conceivable economic theories designed to better the lot of ordinary people (Poovey 2008: 226). Martineau's *Illustrations*, moreover, began to be published in 1832, the year of the Great Reform Act, after which time much more care had to be given to expressing a system of morals that resonated beyond the aristocracy (Hawkins 2015: 151).

Marcet, Martineau, and the politics of their time

Feminist GPE arose from the women's liberation campaign and still speaks very clearly to political strategies for social empowerment. Feminists today typically embrace intersectionality studies, through which the barriers to social advancement are theorized across multiple, often interlocking dimensions. Breaking down institutionalized gender stereotypes remains a central task of all feminist scholarship, allowing insights to be gained into the difference between the lives that women currently lead and the lives that they could lead in a more equal society. The demand for equality, of course, spreads far and wide, because social privileges continue to be organized across categories including class, race, and sexuality as well as gender. It is for this reason that it is common to see feminist GPE scholars today aligning their studies of gender with the politics of other liberation campaigns. From this perspective, Marcet's and Martineau's work, radical though it was on so many different counts, appears to betray an inherent political conservatism. This can be seen in both who they were writing for and the content of their message.

Taking these issues in turn, Marcet was clear that she was addressing young women of particular breeding and with certain prospects. The aristocratic and landed elites had very little to fear from the *Conversations*, because the 'propagation of useful truths' that formed the centre point of Marcet's mission were 'truths' as understood from an elite perspective (Marcet, cited in Polkinghorn 1993: 48). Despite the increasing prominence of mass educational tracts in the early nineteenth century, she was unwilling at first to concede that the labouring classes were a natural audience for her work. She later relented to a degree when writing *John Hopkins's Notions of Political Economy* in 1833, where the title character was a labourer thinking through how his life is influenced by practical manifestations of abstract economic principles (Marcet 1833/2009). But the basic message of that book is that there are inalienable market-bound laws of price and wage determination and, as a consequence, Hopkins should be grateful for his lot.

Martineau, by contrast, was adamant from the start of her writing career that it was necessary to engage the working classes. However, opinion is divided as to how successful she was in this regard, and not just because the subscription price of the *Illustrations* was clearly beyond the means of most working people. She certainly believed that greater economic equality would only be possible—thus transcending the situation in which a wealthy elite was 'pampered above-stairs while others are starving below' (Martineau 1832–4: v)—when the masses understood the forces that were lined up against them. In particular, she wanted them to see that the 'truths' passed down by the classical economists revealed the extent to which political decisions that protected landowners' privileges kept them poor. At the same time, though, suspicions abound that the language Martineau used means that she wrote *about* the working classes and not *for* them (Huzel 2006: 56). Feminists today tend to be very attentive to the need to tone down their academic prose so as not to deliberately exclude others who are fighting for their own liberation (see Tooze and Murphy 1996: 697 for the need for GPE theorists as a whole to avoid exclusionary language). Martineau, however, made her working-class characters speak a lofty language that would have been unfamiliar, even anathema, to them (Logan 2004: 38).

This is merely one example of the overwhelming political optimism that runs throughout her work. Putting middle-class words into working-class mouths reinforced Martineau's wider claim that the working classes could improve their own conditions of existence by beginning to act as though they had the same opportunities as the middle classes: aping their aspirations, taking on their affectations, etc. (Freedgood 1999: 224). Her writings identify very few structural impediments within society that the poor and the oppressed cannot overcome through the right display of character (Feller 2000: xii). Her consistent self-help advocacy explains the stories Martineau wrote around the time of the Great Reform Act backing Whig Poor Law reform. 'Cousin Marshall' in particular aims to overturn the contemporary view of parish assistance to the poor as charitable, kindly, and noble (Martineau 1833). Rather, she said, it was evidence of unjustified interference into the natural workings of the laissez-faire economy, which could only lead to heightened dependence from those seeking assistance. Her approach to matters of empire was exactly the same. She opposed a commercially oriented colonialism for the distorting impact it had on patterns of trade, but she was anything other than anti-imperialist (Çelikkol 2011: 67). In classic Malthusian style, colonial territories offered the possibility of spatial overflows into which the surplus population of Britain could be poured. The willingness to emigrate in the spirit of self-help might also serve the patriotic duty of releasing the pressure on subsistence food supplies back at home.

These same basic political themes are also always present in Marcet's work. Whereas Martineau's early unconditional support for laissez-faire began to be qualified as she took an increasing interest in the rights of women, slaves, and free thinkers, Marcet hardly wavered from her opening position (McDonald 2001: 155). At the very least, over the many editions of the *Conversations* Mrs. B. took no backward step from her assertion that laissez-faire is best for everyone (Frey 2009: 39). Caroline responds to her guide's promptings by declaring: 'All that you have said reconciles me, in a great measure, to the inequality of the distribution of wealth' (Marcet 1839/2009: 401). In the political world that Marcet had Mrs. B. create, the responsibility for escaping the worst deprivations of early nineteenth-century poverty lay with the poor alone. Marcet's later *Rich and Poor* (1851) was by no means the commercial success of the *Conversations*, but it revealed more of her view that the differential social opportunities available across class boundaries could be explained by the classes' differential moral standing. This is why her work, taken as a whole, reads akin to nineteenth-century conduct books (Cooper 1997: 31). The exportation of surplus British workers to labour colonies is thus justified in relation to spreading not just the English race but also the prevailing English system of manners to other parts of the world.

> ## KEY POINTS
>
> - Most histories of economic thought treat the subject—erroneously—as an exclusively male preserve in the nineteenth century.
> - The women writers who popularized classical economics in Britain in the nineteenth century must be seen as products of their own society, and the political content of their work differs greatly from feminist GPE today.
> - Marcet and Martineau used a storytelling form populated by fictional characters to try to reach sections of society who might otherwise have remained ignorant of basic political economy principles.
> - There is a clear Malthusian theme contained in Marcet's and Martineau's thinking on matters of economic policy, which today can seem like really rather callous treatment of the poor.

Conclusion

So, what can be distilled from this whistle-stop tour around the historical roots of contemporary GPE? The objective has been to caution against many of the introductory textbook accounts of those roots in an effort to signal to students what might easily be overlooked if the textbooks' rather simplistic characterizations are accepted at face value. Great care should be taken whenever one is confronted with a straight line drawn between the political economy tradition of an earlier time and the political economy tradition of a later time. Even if the traditions seem to share the same name, whether partly or wholly, things tend not to stay the same for long. This is because theories are dynamic entities constantly under pressure to change from two distinct sources. One is internal to the theory itself, as scholars attempt to further its development by rendering it more sophisticated and hence resetting its outer limits of applicability. The other is external to the theory, as scholars realize that changes in the real-world relationships that the theory purports to explain require different emphases within the theory.

While it would be unrealistic to expect anything other than the outline of a theory to remain in place over a protracted period of time, much of genuine value can be learned if the time is taken to compare the modern-day version of a theory with its original articulation. This is what I have attempted to do in this chapter for GPE realism, liberalism, and Marxism, as well as showing that GPE's typical nineteenth-century overlay tends to rob feminist scholarship of a similar understanding of its roots. There was no obvious feminist tradition at the time at which the Marginalist Revolution laid down the rationalist assumptions that had become more-or-less pervasive when GPE was first imagined into existence around 1970. One hundred years prior to that women economists were busy popularizing other people's ideas rather than being given the intellectual space to develop their own. By engaging in these strategies of comparison across different centuries, the embedded assumptions of the modern-day versions can be brought clearly to the surface, shining the spotlight on assumptions that

were not originally present but now are. It also invites students to try to forward plausible reconstructions about what it was in the intervening environment that caused the new assumptions to be added, especially if they were originally consciously rejected.

It is a potentially infinite process to specify such factors in fully comprehensive fashion. I need to be clear that I have only been able to scratch the surface of the original contributions of List, Smith, Marx, Edgeworth, Marcet, and Martineau in my attempt to demonstrate just how far GPE realism, liberalism, Marxism, and feminism typically depart from their work while still claiming that it is in their intellectual DNA. Much more can be done to set each author's work within the context of its time to isolate the ways in which the prevailing historical conditions influenced the content of the original theory. And this is before giving any thought to how economic theory developed from the eighteenth century onwards beyond its traditional European heartlands. Historical contextualization of this nature allows further errors of analogy between newer and older theories to be brought to light. In addition, it makes it possible to identify a number of claims made in the introductory textbooks about older forms of political economy scholarship that simply do not stand up to scrutiny.

This brings the chapter full circle by way of conclusion. I hope I have demonstrated that theoretical traditions within GPE are not self-contained, coherent ideologies at all. In fact, there is—or at the very least there is the possibility of there being—serious competition over ownership of any of GPE's main theoretical labels. Yet this possibility might only be unlocked through increasing awareness of the historical roots of contemporary GPE. History matters, then, and a turn to situate GPE more assuredly within the history of economic thought is very much to be advocated.

 QUESTIONS

1. What can be gained in our understanding of contemporary GPE by attempting to uncover the historical roots of the political economy traditions in which modern positions are located? In other words, why should we read classic texts?

2. To what extent does the typical textbook structure of liberalism versus realism versus Marxism obscure the significance of societal cleavages such as gender, race, sexuality, and religion?

3. Would it be fair to criticize GPE theories for taking the development profile of Western market capitalism and treating it as a generic feature of economic life, thus implying that all other countries will also have the same experience?

4. What are the main features of nationalist political economy in both its original and reworked Listian forms? Is it possible to point to examples in the modern world of nationalist insights continuing to inform the management of international economic affairs?

5. What emphasis should be placed on Smith's sympathy principle? How different might liberal GPE look if this aspect of his work were to be prioritized more?

6. Is Marxism still relevant in contemporary GPE? What features of the world that Marx described are still recognizably with us today?

7. How different does the pre-history of feminist GPE look compared to the pre-histories of realist, liberal, and Marxist GPE? Is the fact that there is no simple nineteenth-century overlay to place on top of contemporary scholarship a good or a bad thing for feminist GPE?

8. To what extent do many GPE theorists incorporate the key insights of neoclassical economics without acknowledging explicitly that this is what they are doing?

 FURTHER READING

General

Watson, M. (2005), *Foundations of International Political Economy* (Basingstoke: Palgrave Macmillan). This is for students who find my account of the practice of GPE convincing, as the themes of the current chapter are surveyed in much greater depth here.

History of economic ideas

Backhouse, R. (2002), *The Penguin History of Economics* (London: Penguin). This book is written with the beginning student in mind, and, as such, it is a more accessible introduction to the history of economic thought than those that address the student who already has some training in economics.

Barber, W. (2001), *A History of Economic Thought*, repr. edn (London: Penguin). This book attempts similar things to Backhouse, also assuming no prior economics training from its readership in presenting an accessible history of economic thought.

Blaug, M. (1996), *Economic Theory in Retrospect*, 5th edn (Cambridge: Cambridge University Press). This is almost certainly the most comprehensive account of the different ways in which the economy has been studied in the history of economic thought. However, it is written from a perspective that assumes the student has some prior background in economics debates, but this will not necessarily be the case for beginning GPE students.

Heilbroner, R. (2000), *The Worldly Philosophers: The Lives, Times, and Ideas of the Great Economic Thinkers*, 7th edn (London: Penguin). This is an accessible text where the author's aim is not to dazzle his readers with the technicalities of the argument, but to bring the basic ideas he is discussing to life. It performs the same sort of function as Backhouse and Barber, as it is aimed at the same sort of readership.

Landreth, H., and Colander, D. (1994), *History of Economic Thought*, 3rd edn (Boston, MA: Houghton Mifflin). This book covers much of the same territory as Blaug, and would serve as a more than acceptable substitute for it. Again, though, it is written assuming that the reader has some background training in the theories, methods, and language of economics.

Robinson, J. (1964), *Economic Philosophy*, rev. edn (Harmondsworth: Penguin). This is written less as an introduction to the history of economic thought and more as an attempt by the author to carve out her own view of how economic analysis should proceed. Nonetheless, it is a very good read and students will learn much from it.

Samuels, W., Biddle, J., and Davis, J. (eds) (2007), *A Companion to the History of Economic Thought*, 2nd edn (Oxford: Blackwell). This book offers extensive commentary and criticism on existing attempts to provide a plausible historiography of economic ideas. Thirty-nine chapters cover nearly 700 pages of scholars writing on their research specialisms.

However, as with Blaug and with Landreth and Colander, this is probably not for students who possess no prior knowledge of rudimentary economic debates.

Introductions to the classical political economists

Heilbroner, R. (1986), *The Essential Adam Smith* (New York: W. W. Norton). This is a very good introduction to the work of Adam Smith. Heilbroner provides excerpts from all of Smith's published work, each of which is preceded by a useful introduction.

Hollander, S. (1987), *Classical Economics* (Oxford: Basil Blackwell). This is a very good introduction to the field of classical political economy as a whole. However, there is a chance that beginning GPE students might find it a little bit daunting, as it is written by a respected economist for an audience of fellow economists.

Wheen, F. (1999), *Karl Marx* (London: Fourth Estate). This is perhaps the most readable of all biographies of Marx, and it tries to draw out the intellectual inspiration underpinning his work from a broader assessment of his life.

Wolff, J. (2002), *Why Read Marx Today?* (New York: Oxford University Press). This is an introductory book about Marx's ideas, and it will not present the non-economist with similar problems to those they might experience when reading Hollander. The content of the book follows directly from the self-explanatory title.

Classic texts

Despite all the above advice on further reading, nothing beats the rewards that come from going back to a classic text and discovering what is in it for oneself. I would very much advocate, then, that students attempt to familiarize themselves with at least some of the classic texts mentioned by name in this chapter.

WEBLINKS

www.blupete.com/Literature/Biographies/Philosophy/BiosEcon.htm Students can work their way around the alphabetical listings on this site to find the bibliographies of most of the great economists in history.

http://oll.libertyfund.org This is the link to the online library of the Liberty Fund, which holds fully searchable electronic versions of many of the most important texts in the history of liberal political economy. www.marxists.org/subject/economy/index.htm This is a comprehensive site that allows students to explore both Marx's work and his reflections on the context in which it was written. Importantly, it also contains links to a detailed glossary of terms to be found in the writings of Marxist political economists.

http://pandora.simons-rock.edu/~eatonak/LTV-FAQ.html This is a site that allows students to get to the heart of what made the labour theory of value so attractive to the classical political economists. It is organized very helpfully around a series of 'frequently asked questions'. Students seeking to contextualize what can be found here with what superseded the labour theory of value should then begin searching for content surrounding the 'subjective theory of value'.

ONLINE RESOURCE CENTRE

For additional material and resources, please visit the Online Resource Centre at:
www.oxfordtextbooks.co.uk/ravenhill5e

3

Cooperation and Conflict in the Global Political Economy

Vinod K. Aggarwal and Cédric Dupont

Chapter contents

Reader's guide

How can one understand the problems of collaboration and coordination in the global political economy? In situations of global **interdependence**, individual action by states often does not yield the desired result. Many argue that the solution to the problem of interdependence is to create international institutions, but this approach itself raises the issue of how states might go about creating such institutions in the first place. This chapter examines the conditions under which states might wish to take joint action and provides an introduction to game theory as an approach to understanding interdependent decision-making. It then discusses the conditions under which international institutions are likely to be developed and how they may facilitate international cooperation. We then examine dimensions of institutional variation, with a discussion of factors that shape the design of international institutions.

Introduction

It is now commonplace to hear about the phenomenon of globalization. Much of the current analytical debate on globalization has its roots in the international political economy literature on interdependence of the early 1970s (Cooper 1972; Keohane and Nye 1977). At that time, political scientists began to identify the characteristics of the changing global economy, including the increased flows of goods and money across national boundaries as well as the rise of non-state actors as a challenge to traditional conceptions of international politics.

Although increasing interdependence among states was a relatively new phenomenon when considered against the baseline of the 1950s, high levels of interdependence had existed in earlier historical periods, including the period prior to the First World War (Bordo, Eichengreen, and Irwin 1999; McGrew, Chapter 10 in this volume). This interdependence, however, was not matched by high levels of institutionalization, in stark contrast to the post-Second World War Bretton Woods organizations of the International Monetary Fund (IMF), the World Bank, and the General Agreement on Tariffs and Trade (GATT, and now its successor, the World Trade Organization (WTO)). The problems that institutions such as the IMF faced with the breakdown of the Bretton Woods dollar-based standard in 1971(Reinhart and Trebesch 2016), the movement towards trade protectionism that appeared to undermine the GATT, and instability in the oil market with the 1973–4 oil crisis also drove the debate on interdependence in the early 1970s.

A key issue in considering the implications of interdependence revolves around the question of how to achieve collaboration and coordination among states. In particular, scholars have focused on how states respond to perceived problems in the global economy that they cannot deal with solely on their own. An important starting point is to distinguish interdependence from interconnectedness based on the costs of interaction. 'Where interactions do not have significant costly effects, there is simply interconnectedness' (Keohane and Nye 1977: 9). With costly effects (or high benefits), however, we can consider countries as mutually dependent on each other, or interdependent. In attempting to cope with interdependence, then, countries will be faced with making decisions that will affect their direct well-being, and thus the sharing of costs and benefits can be potentially controversial.

This chapter considers the problem of collaboration by first characterizing situations that might require states to work with each other to achieve a desired outcome. It then turns to a focus on basic game theory as an analytical tool to tackle the nature of collaboration and coordination efforts. Finally, we consider how institutions might play a role in enhancing the prospects for cooperative behaviour.

Globalization and the need for international cooperation

According to international economics textbooks, worldwide economic openness has clear benefits. Integrated world markets help to ensure an optimal allocation of factors of production and therefore help to maximize both aggregate world welfare and individual national welfare. By contrast, sealing off national borders fosters economic inefficiency and has negative consequences for poverty alleviation and development prospects. Yet, in practice, the benefits of globalization cannot always be realized by states pursuing independent policies; cooperative action is required.

The process of global integration forces significant adjustments in production patterns across states. In particular, the changing distribution of costs and benefits from trade liberalization can result in strong political opposition, both for and against further liberalization. Adjustment has been all the more difficult in that it leads to unpredictable outcomes and instability in the prices of traded goods. This has proven particularly problematical for many developing countries because they strongly rely on a few primary commodities for the bulk of their exports (UNDP 2011; UNCTAD 2014). Not only have the prices of most non-fuel commodities tended to decline over the long term, but also they have been increasingly volatile (UNDP 2011; UNCTAD 2012b; UNGA 2013). From this perspective, the price surges from 2003 to mid 2008, in 2009–10, and in spring 2012 may not be indicative of a long-term reversal and the abrupt drop of prices in the second half of 2008 is an acute reminder of the long-term boom-and-bust pattern in commodity terms of trade (Spatafora and Tytell 2009; IMF 2012b). Ultra-specialization by some countries in specific commodities has therefore, on the one hand, brought severe adjustment costs and, on the other hand, failed to provide stable and increasing revenues and significantly hurt their growth prospects (Cavalcanti, Mohaddes, and Raissi 2012). Developing countries that rely on the export of manufactures have also faced significant adjustment challenges. For example, many Latin American countries have increasingly faced a loss of market share in the United States and Europe with the rapid rise of the Chinese export juggernaut.

Liberal analysts often argue that countries will be able to manage the process of adjusting to a rapidly shifting division of labour. From their perspective, the prospect of growth in a large number of newly competitive sectors, combined with state capacity to provide social and fiscal transfers, should serve as means to address the challenges of world competition. Yet developing countries, in particular the poorest among them, often have a pre-industrial economic structure. As a consequence, economic openness has brought about a radical transformation of their socio-economic structures, particularly in rural areas, leading to massive migration flows to urban areas. The state structures of developing states are often simply unable to cope with such a rapid and radical transformation. This has led to chaos and, in many instances, to famine and violence as well as to further political instability and insecurity. For their part, rich countries often face strong domestic lobbies in agriculture, textiles, steel, and other older sectors of the economy, creating pressure for trade distorting restrictions of various kinds including subsidies, tariffs, quotas, **voluntary export restraints**, and the like (see Hiscox, Chapter 4 in this volume).

Given these political constraints, countries may either be unwilling or unable by themselves to sustain processes of economic liberalization. We need to distinguish between two situations. Facing political difficulties, some countries may no longer view international economic cooperation as beneficial and will adopt a national mercantilist approach, relying on selective domestic economic closure while pushing for market access abroad. For most countries, however, such a choice would be politically too costly given previous international commitments but also because they still consider cooperation to be valuable in the medium to long run. Reneging on economic liberalization mostly comes from the difficulty of resisting domestic demands for some protectionism or from the hope of levelling or tilting the international playing field in their favour. In the latter case, the temptation by some countries to slow or halt liberalization may induce others to reconsider their commitments, leading to an action–reaction cycle that slows global integration and decreases economic welfare.

International cooperative action may therefore be required to avoid the unfortunate effects of this **temptation to free ride**. This temptation varies according to the sociopolitical organization of countries and to their degree of economic flexibility. On the sociopolitical dimension, the political insulation of governments from lobbying by those who are affected by

adjustment costs can ease the process of economic liberalization, as was the case in the first wave of globalization in the second half of the nineteenth century when few countries had democratic systems of government. But with the spread of democracy, such political insulation has drastically diminished, forcing governments to at best 'talk' protectionist or worse, adopting protectionist policies during economic recessions. Another way to make liberalization politically palatable has been the development in some countries of corporatist deals between the government, unions, and business to share the costs of adjustment. The temptation to free ride also depends on the economy of countries and on its flexibility, particularly regarding labour markets, as well as labour skill levels. More generally, countries with deregulated markets, and few and lean state-owned companies should be less tempted to free ride on the globalization process because adjustment would be less costly.

International cooperation may also be required to remedy what we call the 'inhibiting fear' that countries may feel when facing a decision to either engage in economic liberalization or to continue it. Although countries may be convinced that liberalization will yield benefits, they may be hesitant to risk the instability that might come from the ebb and flows of the international market. This fear is particularly problematical in the domain of financial liberalization. In contrast to trade integration, financial integration has produced sudden and violent shocks to national economies (see Pauly, Chapter 9 in this volume). The massive increase in capital flows in the last 15 years has been accompanied by extreme volatility, particularly for developing countries that have been experiencing sharp fluctuations in the flow of short-term capital (Calvo and Talvi 2005; Edwards 2005; Reinhardt and Rogoff 2009). As John Ravenhill discusses in Chapter 1, the series of crises that hit East Asia in the period 1997–8 led to drastic economic contractions. South Korea's growth rate dropped seven percentage points below its pre-crisis, five-year-average growth rate, Indonesia's performance was similar, and Thailand's was even worse (Eichengreen and Bordo 2002). Recent work on the Asian financial crises and the Argentinean crisis in 2001, both at the aggregate and case-specific levels, has shown that governments are highly vulnerable to such profound economic contractions. On average, the chances of losing office in the six months immediately following a currency crash seem to be twice as likely as at other times (Frankel 2005). Long believed to be limited to the developing world, this financial and political reality has nowhere been more vivid than in Greece since 2010, threatening to destroy the whole European monetary union. Economic globalization has created profound and far-reaching policy challenges to states that, in turn, have an impact on key pillars of their economic and political organization.

International cooperative action in the financial realm may reassure countries by promises of assistance either by individual states or international institutions before or during difficult times. This may facilitate states' adjustment efforts in responding to shocks and prevent them from taking the wrong action at the wrong time, which could lead to massive negative contagion effects. As with trade, the need for international support varies across countries depending on the sociopolitical and economic characteristics that we have discussed. The inadequate response of rich states and financial institutions to the problems faced by countries affected by the financial crises of the late 1990s led many countries to rapidly build up their holdings of foreign reserves to counter speculative attacks on their currency. Reserves now amount to more than 30 per cent of developing countries' GDP, enough to finance almost one year of imports. But this individual response has come at a significant price. Most central banks hold foreign exchange

reserves in the form of low-yielding, short-term US Treasury (and other) securities; the accumulation of reserves by developing countries created an important opportunity cost (the difference between what governments might have earned by investing these assets elsewhere versus keeping them in low-yielding securities). In most cases, for instance, investing the same amount in the domestic economy would have yielded a significantly higher return. According to a recent study, the income loss due to this difference in yields amounts to close to 1 per cent of GDP (Rodrik 2006*b*). Leaving aside the question of whether this insurance against the vagaries of financial integration comes at an acceptable price, such a solution is only available to a small number of countries, and therefore is not a viable alternative to international action to provide liquidity to countries facing financial crises.

Finally, when countries address the issues of 'temptation to free ride' and 'inhibiting fear', they may encounter a third problem—how to negotiate the distribution of gains and losses from a possible agreement. This 'where to meet' problem can be seen in cases of international cooperation such as a decision on how much to contribute to common support funds, how and to what extent to intervene in currency markets, and in the trade-off between quotas, tariffs, and subsidies in trade negotiations (see Box 3.1). For example, as part of the bargaining over the creation of

BOX 3.1

Goods and the Problems of Cooperation

In examining the problem of collaboration, we can use the concept of 'type of goods' to examine more rigorously the problem of incentives to free ride, fear that one's counterparts will fail to follow good policies, and the distributive conflicts that might ensue over where to meet. In a capitalist economy, private firms produce goods such as wheat, clothing, computers, and services such as financial products, insurance, and the like. Such goods are generally referred to as private goods, based on two characteristics: the goods are generally excludable and are not joint in consumption. The concept of *excludable* means that goods can be withheld from those who do not pay for them; *not joint in consumption* means that when a consumer utilizes the good, it is exhausted and cannot be used by others without additional production. In addition to private goods, other goods may be desired, such as national defence or parks. These goods are characterized by the lack of ability to create exclusion and

the jointness of their consumption, and they are known as public goods. Because anyone can have access to these goods once they are produced, consumers will misrepresent their demand for such goods as they can obtain them once they are produced and 'free ride'. In such cases, the private sector will not produce public goods, and governments will coerce citizens to pay for such goods through mechanisms such as taxation. If a good is characterized by lack of exclusion and lack of jointness, then such a good is referred to as a common pool resource. Examples of such goods include fish in the oceans, or even, as a limiting case, a public park. Thus, if the ocean is overfished, fish will cease to reproduce and die out. Similarly, while parks are often seen as public goods, too many users of a park create crowding, which impairs the enjoyment of the good for others. Private actors will be particularly reluctant to produce such goods, and even governments will be concerned about the problem of too many users. Finally, inclusive club goods refer to goods that may be excludable and yet be joint in consumption. These include goods such as software, music, and literature,

BOX 3.1 (continued)

which the private sector has a great incentive to produce. Once a unit of the good is produced, it can be distributed at either little or no cost. Indeed, firms may quickly develop a monopoly in the production of such goods if they are the first movers who make the good, and thus face regulation. For example, if a firm launches a satellite to beam television programmes to consumers, while the initial cost of securing a rocket to put the satellite in orbit will be great, once the satellite is in operation, the programmes can be disseminated to large numbers of consumers. Private firms will generally attempt to regulate consumption by encoding the transmission to prevent free riding. Alternatively, governments may simply regulate the industry and consumer behaviour to prevent consumption without paying (for example, penalties for copyright infringement).

Figure 3.1 summarizes the four types of goods.

How do the problems of creating various types of goods play out in the international arena, and what obstacles do states face in achieving cooperation? Consider the case of cooperation with respect to global warming. It is now well documented that emissions of greenhouse gases, in particular CO_2, due to human activity (in particular the burning of fossil fuels) have reached levels that lead to an important warming of average temperatures on earth with potentially dramatic impact on populations in the medium to long term. Yet, because reducing the emissions of greenhouse gases is a costly process that may require deep restructuring of energy production and use, the negotiations over how much or how quickly to limit those gases has been an internationally contentious issue. The public good nature of the problem can be seen in the incentives to free ride by various countries who wish to benefit from the reduction in emissions of greenhouse gases but do not want to bear the costs of reducing their emissions. There is a severe distributive conflict ('where to meet') as actors debate the levels of

reduction for developed and developing countries. The latter fear to derail economic development to fight a phenomenon largely associated with the economic development since the mid 1800s of current developed economies. With respect to crowding, at the extreme, limiting global warming has common pool resource properties, because jointness may be impaired if one country (or a small number of countries) produces a huge amount of emissions that then spread evenly in the atmosphere.

In 1992, States recognized the need to take action to limit global warming with the adoption of United Nations Framework Convention on Climate Change (UNFCCC) that established the Conference of the Parties (COP) as its highest authority to develop an international climate change regime. So far the most important pillar of this regime has been the Kyoto protocol adopted in 1997 by the COP and entered into force in 2006. The protocol set binding targets for the reduction of greenhouse gases by 37 industrialized countries (the so-called Annex I countries) as well as a general commitment for all groups of countries. The originality of the protocol is that it defines 'flexible mechanisms' to help industrialized economies meet their targets, including the trading of emission 'rights', the transfer of 'clean energy' technology to developing nations (the so-called Clean Development Mechanism) as well as the possibility of joint implementation. But whereas the flexibility of implementation for industrialized economies and the lack of binding commitments for developing countries were essential for the adoption of the Kyoto protocol, they have severely limited its impact on the limitation of global warming. There is a clear need to do more, including by developing countries, and within a stronger monitoring framework. Yet discussions have been impeded by severe distributive conflicts (on financial commitments in particular) both within industrialized countries and between industrialized and developing countries. The agreement reached in December 2015 at the 21st meeting of the Parties in Paris brought hope of change and progress towards the objective of curbing warming. According to the agreement, all parties have to 'undertake ambitious efforts' (art. 3) in the view of reaching the objective to hold 'the increase in the global average temperature to well below 2 °C above pre-industrial levels' (art. 2). Although the pace and intensity of efforts will take into account differences in levels of economic development, the Paris agreement extends the obligation of taking concrete action to all countries. This came about at the price of significant financial assistance given by developed countries to developing ones, which could open new discussions on the distribution of costs and benefits.

With respect to inclusive club goods, the debate over standards also illustrates the problem of 'where to meet'. If a firm convinces its government to advocate the choice of its standard

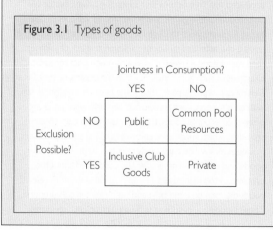

Figure 3.1 Types of goods

		Jointness in Consumption?	
		YES	NO
Exclusion Possible?	NO	Public	Common Pool Resources
	YES	Inclusive Club Goods	Private

BOX 3.1 (continued)

in international negotiations, the firm may be able to gain a significant advantage over its competitors. Even less firm-driven choices may influence costs and benefits, and lead to possible conflict. For example, the implementation of international financial reporting standards (IFRS) developed under the auspices of the International Accounting Standards Board (IASB) led to fierce debates and discussions within the European Union before its final implementation in January 2005. The IFRS

cornerstone is the notion of fair value accounting (FVA) that aims at assigning market values to assets. Whereas this had been the standard adopted in the Anglo-Saxon world, continental European firms had relied on a more 'prudent' way with a valuation based on the balance sheet and a low valuation of assets. The move towards a new standard significantly increased the risk of hostile takeover of companies that would become suddenly more attractive due to 'hidden' reserves.

a **common pool of resources** to support financial stability, there is likely to be considerable debate about the criteria for which country should contribute how much. This burden-sharing decision has often been a problem historically. Intervention in currency markets is also controversial. Although some national intervention to maintain stable currencies may be warranted in that it helps governments to obtain various national economic objectives such as controlling the rate of inflation, the US has often accused Japan and China (and other East Asian states) of manipulating their exchange rate to gain a competitive advantage in trade.

Burden-sharing problems may also be part of the problem of trade liberalization. A good example has been the ongoing conflict with respect to the reduction of agricultural support schemes used by developed countries (and often by developing countries as well) to protect their farmers. Addressing the free riding temptation has been hampered by the difficulty to find an agreement at a lower level of support.

KEY POINTS

- International cooperation can help to address three typical problems associated with the process of global integration: a temptation to free ride, an inhibiting fear, and a need to find meeting points in situations where collaboration will produce differing costs and benefits to governments.

- A country's need for international cooperation depends on its sociopolitical structure as well as on the structure and flexibility of its economy.

- Different types of problems associated with the process of global integration call for different solutions to address the three typical problems, ranging from the provision of binding rules to facilitating mechanisms.

International cooperation: a strategic interdependence approach

Our discussion so far has highlighted the potentially important role of international cooperation in enhancing the prospects for global economic integration. Yet, as the 'where to meet problem' shows, such cooperation may itself entail varying costs and benefits for participating states and its successful negotiation is therefore not a foregone conclusion. To further explore the challenges of international cooperation, we can utilize a game-theoretic approach to examine interdependent decision-making. A country's choice depends both on its cost–benefit evaluation of the various outcomes and on its expectations regarding the choices of other actors. Game theory provides useful tools to analyse actors' behaviour in such a context. Key features of actors' interactions are captured through 'games' that describe the choices available to actors (players in the game), their evaluations of potential outcomes, as well as the information they have when they make their choices.

To keep this chapter's discussion of game theory as parsimonious as possible, we focus on simple games with two persons and two strategies per person (see Box 3.2). We further assume that actors have extensive knowledge of the other actor's preferences but that they cannot observe his or her actual choices. Obviously, in real-life situations, actors may have less information about preferences and/or may be able to observe the other's behaviour. Our modelling choices may appear to oversimplify real-life examples but, as several authors have already shown, simple models can clearly reveal the decisions that governments face in attempting to deal with fundamental aspects of interdependence (Cooper 1975; Snidal 1985; Martin 1992; Zürn 1992; Aggarwal and Dupont 1999; Drezner 2007).

BOX 3.2

Game Theory and Its Critics

Game theory has become a standard tool for analysis of situations of interdependence in social sciences. Aside from its predictive aim, game theory has a strong appeal for anyone engaged in explanation, investigation, or prescription. It often makes ostensibly puzzling processes intelligible, without attributing causality to factors such as the incompetence, irresponsibility, or lack of concern of decision-makers.

Whatever its value, however, the use of game theory poses severe methodological problems that have prompted intense debates in the literature. Critics have traditionally emphasized (1) the overstretching of the concept of rationality and (2) the gap between abstract theoretical concepts and real phenomena. Regarding the notion of rationality, most applications of game theory assume that players, interacting under conditions of imperfect information, possess a very high computational ability. To make their decisions, players must evaluate a host of possible worlds on the basis of the knowledge commonly shared with others or privately known. This kind of situation often implies that players engage in comparative reasoning about a large set of possible worlds. Leeway in their interpretation often leads to a myriad of possible equilibria, which significantly decreases the predictive power of game theory. To avoid this indeterminacy, most game theorists have refined the concept of 'rationality' to allow the selection of one or very few equilibria among the vast initial array. For example, one might assume that people always choose to buy the cheapest product available (even though we know that many people buy based on brand name, reputation, or other factors) because it makes the choices of actors easier to map. Most of these refinements to the concept of rationality thus lack empirical grounding.

A more recent controversy has focused on the empirical contribution of rational choice approaches to politics, including game-theoretic work. A variety of pathologies have prevented rational choice theory from improving our understanding of politics. In particular, rational choice theorists are, according to these critics, method-driven rather than problem-driven. In other words, instead of focusing on building models that accurately reflect decision-making in the real world, game theorists (according to critics) are more concerned with constructing elegant models. As a consequence, game theorists tend to neglect issues of empirical testing and therefore to undermine the scientific value of rational choice theory.

Although there clearly remain weaknesses in most game-theoretic analyses of international relations, the link between theory and empirics has clearly improved over the last decade. Users of game theory have used different techniques to check the validity of their models based on a comparison with reality. The dominant approach has been indirect testing through statistical analysis using either large-N data sets or a series of case studies. Another approach has been to use case studies to trace the behavioural attitude of actors and check them with specific predictions of models.

Each of the three typical problems discussed in the previous discussion can be depicted with a specific game. We address them in turn and then focus on situations that represent mixed situations.

'Free riding temptation': the Prisoner's Dilemma

As we have seen, global economic integration remains fragile due to countries' political difficulties in implementing potentially costly economic changes—albeit ones that are economically positive. They may be tempted to free ride on others' policy changes to take advantage of their gains from their trading partners opening their markets, which may in turn affect others' policy choices, and possibly bring an end to global economic liberalization. This situation is aptly captured with the game called the Prisoner's Dilemma (PD).

The PD models a situation in which two individuals are involved in a robbery and are caught near the scene of the crime. The district attorney (the DA or prosecutor) does not have sufficient evidence to convict either of the suspects of robbery unless at least one of them reveals additional information to him, but he has some evidence to convict both of them of a lesser crime (for instance, reckless driving or carrying a firearm). The DA wants more information to convict both suspects for a long period. The two prisoners are placed in separate interrogation rooms. The DA tells each prisoner that if they confess and reveal the truth, they will get a much lighter sentence. If both prisoners confess (Strategy S2 in the game depicted in Figure 3.2) however, they get a heavier sentence than they would have received if they had both remained silent (Strategy S1 in Figure 3.2) where they would have been charged with the lesser crime (when both confess, the DA has the evidence to convict both on the more serious

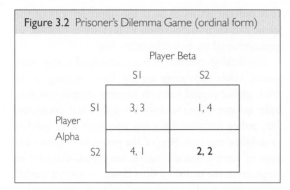

Figure 3.2 Prisoner's Dilemma Game (ordinal form)

another actor), is unstable because each actor can improve his or her own welfare by individually switching strategy to the cells in the upper-right or lower-left corners of the matrix.

Within international political economy, the PD has been widely used to illustrate the problem of reciprocal trade liberalization (Grossman and Helpman 1995; Hoekman and Kosteki 1995; Maggi 1999). The difficulties in monitoring partners' trade policies, and the potential political benefits to governments from open export markets and closed domestic markets often push states to back out of their commitments to reciprocate trade liberalization measures. As Conybeare shows (1984), this argument particularly applies to countries with large domestic markets, as these countries are less dependent on the success of trade liberalization (this makes the utilities of the lower-right cell in Figure 3.2 relatively acceptable) and such countries can also positively affect world prices through their tariff policy (imposing a tariff on imports lowers the price that other countries will receive for their exports). For smaller countries, though, the PD is not an adequate depiction of their trade situations. Rather, smaller countries tend to have preferences that reflect the game of chicken, a situation that we discuss later.

Another typical application of the PD in international political economy has been in examining the collective management of resources. Whereas countries producing particular commodities traded on world markets would prefer a situation where they all manage production so as to keep prices sufficiently high—by forming a cartel such as OPEC (Organization of Petroleum Exporting Countries)—individual countries face the temptation to 'cheat' by increasing extraction or production of those commodities so as to maximize their individual income. As a result, acting collectively to keep commodity prices stable—in commodities such as coffee, tin, and even oil—has been a daunting task, particularly for developing countries.

offences). Confessing to the DA could bring the minimal sentence if the other one does not confess but could also lead to a lengthier sentence if the other also confesses. Remaining silent, on the other hand, may lead to either a moderate sanction if the other prisoner remains silent, or the maximum penalty if the other one speaks to the attorney. Facing this situation, and unable to communicate, the logical strategy for both prisoners is to choose to confess. They do so because confessing to the DA is individually always a safer strategy than remaining silent. The key point of the PD game is that actors may face a structure of interaction that prevents them from reaching a cooperative solution even though such a solution would be optimal for both of them.

This story can be generalized using the game depicted in Figure 3.2. The numbers in the various cells indicate the preferences of players on an ordinal ranking scale, with four being the most preferred situation and one the least preferred. In the following figures, the first number in each box refers to Player Alpha's preference, while the second number refers to Player Beta's preference (thus '4,1' is Alpha's most preferred outcome and Beta's least preferred outcome).

As Figure 3.2 shows, both players have a dominant strategy (confess, Strategy 2) that leads to what is called the **Nash Equilibrium** outcome, which is in the lower-right cell of the matrix. A Nash Equilibrium is an outcome in which none of the players can improve his (her) situation by changing his (her) individual strategy. But if both players switch to Strategy 1 (remain silent) in the matrix in Figure 3.2, each of them gets a better outcome (upper left cell). Yet ironically, this collectively optimal situation, also known as a **Pareto-optimal outcome** (Pareto-efficient outcomes are defined as outcomes from which no actor could become better off without worsening the pay-offs to

'Inhibiting fear': assurance games

The second typical problem that a country seeking to enter international cooperation faces comes from the uncertainty of benefits and costs linked to integration in the world economy. Global economic integration brings its full benefits when most countries are part of it and adopt appropriate policies. When some countries make mistakes, or if liberalization policies lose momentum, international markets may react abruptly. If states become paralysed by this likelihood, the whole world may revert to a much lower level of integration. This situation is best modelled through another category of game—assurance games.

One specific example of an assurance game is 'Stag Hunt', depicted in Figure 3.3. The name of the game comes from the story of two hunters chasing a stag. They go out before dawn and take positions on different sides of an area where they think a stag is hiding. They have a mutual understanding to shoot only at the stag (Strategy S1 in the game depicted in Figure 3.3). Shooting at any other wild animal, say a hare (Strategy S2), would lead them to miss shooting the stag because the stag would be frightened by the noise and stay put in its hiding place. As time goes by and as dawn arrives, however, both hunters start thinking that going back home with a hare might be better than continuing to wait for the stag to come out of hiding. If each of them thinks that the other one will eventually yield to the temptation to shoot at a hare, they will both end up killing a hare—a better outcome than not catching anything but clearly much less attractive than sharing a stag.

In Stag Hunt, players share a single most preferred outcome—i.e. a Pareto-optimal Nash Equilibrium—but they do not have dominant strategies. As a result, there is a second, Pareto-deficient, equilibrium outcome. In such a game, reaching the Pareto-optimal equilibrium is not a foregone conclusion. Doubts about the willingness of one's counterpart to choose strategy S1 (shoot the stag) might push a player to choose strategy S2 (shoot a hare), which guarantees for that individual the highest minimal gain. Yet, such an outcome is rather unlikely because of the attraction of the upper-left cell. In contrast to the PD game, it is not the temptation to reap additional gains that

may prevent actors to be in the upper-left cell of the game but their anticipation of a possible mistake or unintentional move by the other one.

Financial globalization has features of a stag hunt game. With increasing capital flows among countries, global capital markets become deeper and provide greater opportunities for individual countries. Yet, policy mistakes by some countries may quickly destabilize markets. Fear of the potential negative impact of such a destabilization may lead countries to implement measures to slow down or restrict capital movements. Such a move may lead to changes in other actors' expectations and quickly drive the world, or at least a region of the world, to a much lower level of integration. This new situation could have the advantage of being less risky for countries but is unlikely to bring as many opportunities for investment and therefore reduce growth prospects.

'Where to meet': coordination games

Whereas market liberalization is essential for global economic integration and increased prosperity, sustainable global integration requires some market supervision. This supervision in turn requires co-operative action by countries. The difficulty, however, is that there are often many ways to supervise markets and countries may differ on their preferred coordination point because potential solutions vary in their costs and benefits. This strategic context corresponds to a game of coordination. In the specific game depicted in Figure 3.4, actors have to choose *among* Pareto-optimal outcomes. Its name, 'Battle of the Sexes', comes from the story of a husband and wife who have to decide where to spend their evening after work. They either can go to the opera or watch

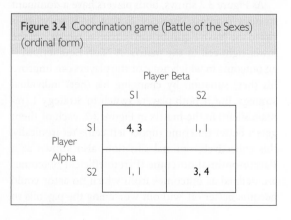

Figure 3.3 Assurance game (Stag Hunt) (ordinal form)

| | | Player Beta | |
		S1	S2
Player Alpha	S1	4, 4	1, 3
	S2	3, 1	2, 2

Figure 3.4 Coordination game (Battle of the Sexes) (ordinal form)

| | | Player Beta | |
		S1	S2
Player Alpha	S1	4, 3	1, 1
	S2	1, 1	3, 4

a football match. Neither spouse derives much pleasure by being without the other one but they differ on the best choice. The husband would prefer to watch football (strategy S1 in Figure 3.4) whereas the wife would prefer the opera (strategy S2 in Figure 3.4). In the story, both are getting off of work and have to rush to either the stadium or opera. They cannot communicate with each other (say the batteries of their cell phones are dead!), and have to meet at one of the locations. If each of them follows their preferred solution, they end up at different locations, which both regard as a bad outcome. Perversely, if both of them want to please the other one by choosing the location that they know that their partner prefers, they also end up being separated. Thus, they have to somehow implicitly coordinate, with one making a concession and the other getting his/her first choice. Figure 3.4 provides a generalization of that story.

In the Battle of the Sexes, none of the players has a dominant strategy. Player Alpha prefers to play Strategy 1 when Player Beta chooses Strategy 1 and prefers Strategy 2 when Player Alpha chooses Strategy 2. With Player Beta having the same preferences as Alpha, the game has two equilibrium outcomes—the upper-left and lower-right cells in Figure 3.4. These two outcomes are clearly Pareto-superior to the two other possible outcomes, but actors will disagree on which one to choose. Player Alpha prefers the upper-left cell whereas Player Beta prefers to end up in the lower-right cell. Both players want to avoid being separated but each player prefers a different outcome.

In international political economy, efforts by developed countries to choose mutually compatible macroeconomic policies typically reflect games of coordination (Putnam and Bayne 1987). For instance, when there is high volatility in financial and exchange rate markets, coordinated responses by leading countries would often be best but each country would like to choose the policy mix that best fits its own domestic constraints. Coordination was a key challenge in efforts to address the 2008–9 Global Financial Crisis and the ensuing 2009–12 global recession. Whereas major central banks were able to coordinate their actions to contain the stress in financial markets to a reasonable extent, governments have had more difficulty in implementing concerted fiscal responses. Some countries, such as the United States, engaged in large fiscal stimulus, while others were more reluctant to use fiscal policy out of concern for the health of public finances. This asymmetry fuelled a concern for free riding where a country would benefit from the efforts of its neighbours, as their stimulus plans boost its exports without affecting its fiscal stance. As a result, countries resorting to large stimulus tended to adopt 'nationalist' or protectionist policies to channel government funding to national firms. To offset this suboptimal dynamic, major economies have promoted the use of a new informal grouping—the G20—as a forum in which heads of states have repeatedly committed to concerted plans of action and pledged to refrain from protectionist measures. Yet, despite high hopes following the meetings held in London and Pittsburgh in 2009 (Cooper 2010), the new forum has gradually lost momentum and the governance of international financial matters looks very similar to the pre-crisis situation (Helleiner 2014b).

Another prominent example is the choice of international monetary system (Cooper 1975). Discussions between the USA and Great Britain during the Second World War regarding the architecture of the future international economic order revealed that, although both countries agreed on the absolute need for coordination, they fought over the details of the new order, with each trying to impose its own plan. A more recent example was the debate within the European Union over the design of monetary union, which saw Britain, France, and Germany proposing different solutions for some economic and monetary convergence between member states as well as for rules of fiscal behaviour within the monetary union (Wolf and Zangl 1996). At the global level, in the aftermath of the recent Global Financial Crisis, Russia and China have aired the idea of finding an alternative to the current dollar-dominated system. They have not however been able to push this onto the financial agenda of the G20 whose performance on matters of monetary and financial governance has fallen short of expectations (Vestergaard and Wade 2012; Helleiner 2014b).

Mixed situations: Chicken, Called Bluff, and Suasion

We now turn to games that capture situations in which more than one typical problem of cooperation may be present or in which the actors may view the structure of the problem differently. We begin with the game of Chicken that combines the features of the temptation to free ride as well as distributive tensions between the actors. This game, depicted in Figure 3.5, builds on the story of two cars, travelling in opposite directions,

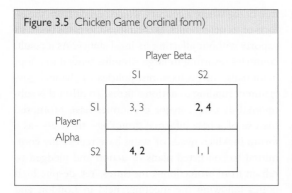

Figure 3.5 Chicken Game (ordinal form)

speeding down the middle of the road towards one another. Inside each car sits a driver who wants to impress his respective passenger that he is a tough person (i.e. demonstrate resolve). The best way to do so is to continue driving straight down the middle of the road (strategy S2 in the game depicted in Figure 3.5)—even when the car coming in the opposite direction comes dangerously close. Yet, if at least one driver does not swerve, the outcome will be disastrous and both cars will crash, killing everyone. To avoid this unfortunate outcome, at least one driver will have to yield and swerve (strategy S1 in Figure 3.5), but both would like the other one to be the 'Chicken' who swerves.

The distributive tension between two equilibrium outcomes is a typical feature of the coordination games discussed earlier. But in contrast to those games, the game of Chicken has a third outcome that is collectively optimal—the compromise solution in the upper-left cell. As in the PD, however, this outcome is not stable and actors have a strong temptation to revert to one of the two equilibriums represented in boldface in Figure 3.5. As such, the Chicken game helps to capture more complex situations faced by countries attempting to engage in international cooperation (Stein 1982).

In the context of the global political economy, Chicken games are useful depictions of the complex structure of burden sharing that occurs within a group of powerful players. For instance, when there is monetary and financial stability in the global economy, the US and the EU may tend to resist making public commitments to international cooperation unless there is a clear sign that the other party will act similarly. Getting out of a trade negotiation stalemate or dispute can also be a Chicken-like situation in which each actor is unwilling to agree on any asymmetric solutions.

To this point, we have only considered cases where actors have symmetrical preferences. We now

examine two interesting *asymmetric* games, the first of which has one player whose preferences are those of the PD game, and a second player with a structure of preferences of the Chicken game. The resulting asymmetric game, known as the game of 'Called Bluff', is depicted in Figure 3.6.

Player Alpha has PD preferences with a dominant strategy to play S2, whereas Player Beta has Chicken preferences with a preferred choice of S2 if Alpha chooses S1 and a choice of S1 if Alpha chooses S2. Yet in this game, owing to the asymmetry in pay-offs, Beta knows that Alpha has a dominant strategy of S2, Beta therefore should choose S1, leading to the equilibrium outcome in the lower-left cell in Figure 3.6. Here, Player Alpha gets his most preferred outcome, whereas Player Beta gets her second worse outcome. This scenario can be used to analyse situations where stronger countries or actors can take advantage of the other's weakness and shift the burden of cost of cooperative action onto the weaker party. This outcome is caused by the difference in actors' sensitivity (vulnerability) to the need for cooperation itself. The player with the less dependence on the need for cooperation (Beta in Figure 3.6) is able to free ride on the other player (Alpha in Figure 3.6). Given the lack of capacity of the weaker actor to sustain cooperation alone, this often leads to a breakdown of international action.

A good illustration of this situation is the monetary policy of Germany and Japan in the 1960s, in the context of the Bretton Woods fixed exchange rate system. The stronger player, the United States, asked these countries to revalue their currencies to help boost the competitiveness of US exports and relieve the pressure on the dollar. These countries refused to undertake significant revaluations, which thus had increasingly costly implications for the US economy and, ultimately under the Nixon administration, the US simply forced the burden of adjustment on the weaker

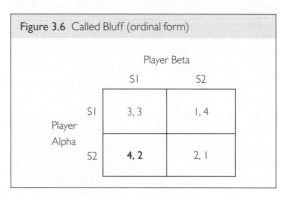

Figure 3.6 Called Bluff (ordinal form)

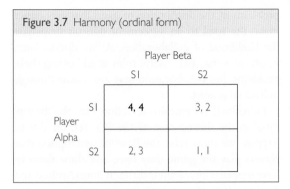

Figure 3.7 Harmony (ordinal form)

		Player Beta	
		S1	S2
Player Alpha	S1	4, 4	3, 2
	S2	2, 3	1, 1

countries by breaking the link between the dollar and gold and imposing a 10 per cent across-the-board tariff. This action led to the end of the Bretton Woods system (see Helleiner, Chapter 8 in this volume).

A second case of asymmetry is a game with one player having preferences oriented towards cooperation and the other one having Chicken preferences. In the game of 'Suasion', Player Beta has preferences similar to a player in the Chicken game but Player Alpha has preferences that are typical of another game, the game of Harmony. The basic feature of Harmony games (see Figure 3.7) is that both players not only dislike acting separately (as in the case of coordination games) but they also do not differ on the best outcome. They both therefore have a dominant strategy to do the same thing. Cooperation is, so to speak, naturally guaranteed (as, for instance, in nineteenth-century liberal assumptions about international economic relations, which argued that everyone would generally be made better off with free trade and open markets more generally).

Combining a player with Chicken preferences and a player with Harmony preferences yields the game depicted in Figure 3.8, known as the game of 'Suasion' (Martin 1992).

Figure 3.8 Suasion (ordinal form)

		Player Beta	
		S1	S2
Player Alpha	S1	4, 3	3, 4
	S2	2, 2	1, 1

The predicted outcome of the Suasion game shares some similarity with that of the game of Called Bluff illustrated in Figure 3.6. Both games feature a situation in which one player gets its most preferred outcome. However, the difference between these two games is that in Suasion, the 'stronger' player (Alpha in Figure 3.8) gets his second best outcome, which results from the choice of his dominant strategy (S1 in Figure 3.8). Put into the context of international cooperation, this clearly reflects a situation in which an actor perceives the benefits of international action to be much more than its associated costs. Because this actor (Alpha) absolutely wants to carry through action at the international level and is assumed to have the capability to do so, other actors (Beta) are in a situation whereby they will let him (Alpha) undertake the bulk of the effort, and will enjoy the benefits at low or no costs to themselves.

One can view this as a situation as one of the tyranny of the weak, which is in sharp contrast to the game of Called Bluff. Note, however, that the stronger player is not forced into an asymmetric outcome by the behaviour of the weak, but by his own preferences. From this perspective, the Suasion game features an opportunistic attitude by the weak rather than a deliberately tyrannical outlook. Martin (1992) argues that this game illustrates the Western world's restriction of technology exports to the Soviet Union during the Cold War. Control of technology sales to the Soviet bloc was done through the Coordinating Committee on Export Controls (COCOM). Within it, however, the United States had a dominant strategy to control technology whereas European states were more opportunistic. They could benefit from sales to the Soviet bloc without jeopardizing the overall balance of power between the two blocs. The US was dissatisfied with this situation and had to persuade Europeans to participate fully with COCOM.

More generally, this type of game relates to situations where one actor (or group of actors) can undertake actions that are immune (up to some degree) to the free riding behaviour of other countries. For example, tax havens in small countries were 'tolerated' by bigger countries as long as the latter could use capital movement restrictions to secure financial stability. When capital restrictions were dismantled, there were significant increases in the efforts to circumvent the free riding behaviour of tax havens. Such free riding became politically intolerable with the advent of the Global Financial Crisis, which required global coordination efforts. The G20 countries put signifi-cant pressure on 'renegade' countries with the prepa-ration of a blacklist by the Organisation for Economic Co-operation and Development (OECD).

KEY POINTS

- Each of the typical problems of international cooperation can be viewed through the lens of strategic decision-making.

- Game theory can help us analyse interdependent decision-making.

- Cooperation can be expected to fail either due to actors' incentives to cheat, to actors' sensitivities to distribution issues, or to lack of confidence in the other actor's behaviour.

- Problems of distribution and free riding may be combined in real-world situations; some games are able to model these combinations.

- Differences in resources or in the perceived need for cooperation result in situations of asymmetric burden sharing.

International cooperation: a variety of solutions

The discussion of cooperation problems in the global political economy highlights the varied nature of the challenges facing actors. We now turn to the question of how to address these challenges. In particular, we focus on the role that international institutions can play in addressing cooperation problems. Our analysis begins with situations where the problems can be ad-dressed without institutions and then turns to cases where institutions help the process of cooperation.

International action without international institutions

In most of the games that we have examined, indi-vidual actions by both players lead, or may lead, to an outcome that we can characterize as collectively opti-mal because there is no welfare loss. Yet, this notion of optimality tends to be short sighted because the asymmetric outcomes of the Called Bluff, Suasion, Chicken, and even coordination games are optimal only in terms of a narrow view of *collective welfare*. Such a conception of welfare does not obviate the

problems of the distribution of gains that may either make the road to an agreement difficult or plague the likelihood of collaboration. As we discuss later, institutions may play useful roles in addressing these problems, but collaboration may also occur through individual actions.

Individual, decentralized, action can also be op-timal in the thorny case of the PD. Yet, for this to happen, we must relax the Baseline assumption that players play the game only once and allow them to have repeated interactions through time (Axelrod and Keohane 1986; Taylor 1987; Sandler 1992; Cornes and Sandler 1996). When players expect to meet again in the future, they may be more willing to cooperate. Yet even under such conditions of iteration, however, co-operation is not a foregone conclusion. For example, if the expected net value of cooperation is too low (for example, actors may overly discount the impor-tance of future iterations owing to a dire economic or political situation at home for governments), the temptation to free ride cannot be overcome. The PD demonstrates that, if defection by one actor would generate high costs for the other actor (resulting in a lengthy prison sentence in PD), or if actors cannot gather information easily, actors may not reach a Pa-reto-optimal outcome.

Applied to the case of trade liberalization, repeated interaction is not sufficient to ensure cooperative behaviour for governments that are under heavy do-mestic pressure, as the temptation to reap immediate political gains through defection may simply be too great. Domestic pressure may be particularly high in democratic countries where economic groups or citizens have easy access to the political sphere, in countries with a political system that tends to fa-vour coalition governments, or in countries without strongly embedded social consultation mechanisms. Conversely, the cost of defection may be too high when actors invest heavily in cooperative efforts and value the outcome produced by cooperation. In such cases, they are significantly more reluctant to jeopard-ize cooperation, even if others have undertaken free riding behaviour.

A world without international institutions is also not universally effective in securing the exchange of goods. As long as trading partners have access to other markets for their products, an institution-free world can work in the context of global trade, because coun-tries can simply turn to another market if a breach in the trading relationship occurs. Yet if there is only one partner that is interested in the goods produced, or if it would be more costly to trade with other partners, such an option does not exist. If a country cannot threaten to sell its goods elsewhere, another country may take advantage of it. Another important qualification for successful institution-free contexts is if one (or both) of the parties has made relation-specific investments. In such a case, these investments will discourage defection and may encourage cooperative behaviour.

What other factors might impede cooperation when actors cannot rely on international institutions? Monitoring will be much more difficult if states only have limited information gathering capability. If an actor has so little information that, for example, it is unsure whether the other actor 'defected' on the last round, then the prospect of repeated interactions does not increase the chances of cooperation. Similarly, an expanding number of states, with an expanding range of trade products that use increasingly sophisticated policies to intervene in markets, makes monitoring trade policies increasingly difficult. It is therefore more difficult to detect non-compliance without the help of a third party.

The role of institutions

As our discussion earlier suggests, actors may need help to sustain collectively optimal outcomes. One way that individuals might be able to coordinate their choices to achieve desired goals might be through the creation or use of international institutions or regimes. International regimes have been defined broadly as 'sets of principle, norms, rules and decision-making procedures upon which actors' expectations converge' (Krasner 1983). To refine this definition, we can distinguish between the principles and norms, or 'meta-regime', and the regime itself, defined as the rules and procedures to allow us to distinguish between two very different types of constraints on the behaviour of states (Aggarwal 1985). In this case, we can use the term institution to refer to the combination of a meta-regime and a regime—rather than Krasner's definition. Note that an institution is not the same thing as an international organization: one can find areas of international collaboration where there are well-defined principles, norms, rules, and procedures for actors' behaviour in the absence of an organization such as the IMF. We structure our discussion in the following sections around three major functions of institutions (see Table 3.1).

Table 3.1 Problems, games, and institutional roles

	From problems to institutional solutions		
	'Free riding temptation'	**'Inhibiting Fear'**	**'Where to meet'**
Strategic game	Prisoner's Dilemma	Stag Hunt (Assurance games)	Battle of the Sexes
Illustrations	Trade liberalization	Financial integration	Managing adjustments
	Debt rescheduling	Trade specialization	Multilateral negotiations
Role(s) of institutions	Channel to enforce contracts – monitoring/surveillance – sanctioning mechanisms – policy transfer	Enhancers of cooperation – pools of resources – suppliers of knowledge and capacity	Providers of solutions to distributive conflicts – negotiation fora – agenda setting – linkages
Examples of institutional solutions	*Monitoring/Surveillance*: Articles IV and VIII of IMF; Trade Policy Review mechanism WTO; *'Sanction'*: Conditionality IMF; DSB's authorization of sanctions WTO *Policy transfer*: Common Trade policy and Economic and Monetary Union in the European union	*Pools of resources*: quota system in IMF *Suppliers of knowledge and capacity*: WTO (technical cooperation), World Bank, IMF, UNCTAD	*Negotiation fora*: WTO General Council; Executive Boards IMF and World Bank; UNCTAD *Agenda setting*: IMF and World Bank staff

First, institutions can act as channels for the third-party enforcement of agreements. To successfully overcome players' temptation to free ride, international institutions should be strong, meaning that member countries should have specific and binding obligations. In particular, agreements that credibly restrain actors' temptation to free ride in trade and monetary policy, for instance, need to rely on some sort of enforcement mechanism delegated to an international institution. At its strongest expression, in the European Union or in the WTO, such a mechanism relies on an organization—the EU has two such entities, the Commission and the Court of Justice—with supranational power to monitor, evaluate, and sanction (if needed) the behaviour of its members.

The chances of a cooperative agreement can also be enhanced through a different kind of centralization—one that ensures a prompt and undistorted dissemination of information. This type of facility helps identify the requirements of multilateral action and protects against possible defections. Enforcement can also be achieved through either positive incentives, as when the IMF provides funds to countries that are following its policy recommendations, or through punitive action as when the WTO rules against a particular state policy.

Second, international institutions can help craft responses to situations characterized by distributive tensions among states. They can help states choose one among several collective outcomes and eliminate some sharply asymmetric outcomes. Institutions may also be useful for gathering information about the preferences of actors, and through appropriate use of agenda setting, may help find focal point solutions for both cost sharing and benefit splitting. Institutions with a firmly and widely established meta-regime tend to perform these tasks extremely well. In contrast, institutions lacking a strong meta-regime may have difficulty generating possible solutions that are attractive to all members. This has often been considered as the source of difficulties for the GATT, and its successor the WTO. Deep disagreements among GATT members led to the creation of another forum, the United Nations Conference on Trade and Development (UNCTAD), in the 1960s, and to serious hurdles in the negotiations of the extension of the scope of GATT/WTO, as recently revealed during the Doha Round of negotiations. The members of UNCTAD had shared principles and norms that they felt were not importantly addressed in GATT/WTO.

Third, international institutions can do a lot to allay actors' fear or reluctance to engage in cooperative behaviour. Rather than enforcing a particular outcome, institutions should enable actors to reach it (by pooling resources, for example). To help the integration of developing countries into the global financial system, the IMF provides cheap credit opportunities through the contributions subscribed by all members. The World Bank finances the development of basic infrastructure in developing countries to help them reduce poverty. At the European regional level, the European Monetary System (EMS) has relied on a decentralized system of very short lending facilities among members to help them defend the parity grid that served as an anchor to the set of national currencies.

To address enforcement and distribution problems, institutions can establish rights for members that either define mechanisms of exclusion or determine compensation schemes. In relation to our previous discussion of games and cooperation, careful institutional design can sometimes 'privatize' the benefits of cooperation, reducing the temptation to free ride. The reduction of trade barriers almost always applies to countries that belong to particular clubs, be they regional (see Ravenhill, Chapter 6 in this volume) or global. Assigning rights and obligations can also produce decentralized cooperation when institutions also provide information about the preferences of actors and reduce the costs of their discussions to their minimum. When actors are more certain about who owns and is responsible for what (a result of the assignment of rights and obligations), cooperation may result.

Under these conditions, as Coase (1960) suggests, actors do not need any centralized power to remedy the problem of negative **externalities** (situations where an individual's action negatively affects the well-being of another individual in ways that need not be paid for according to the existing definition of **property rights**) (Conybeare 1980; Keohane 1984) but should find a mutually satisfactory solution through financial compensation. The crucial aspect, in the Coasian framework, is establishing liabilities for externalities. The history of international monetary agreements provides several examples of the difficulties associated with determining satisfactory schemes assigning responsibilities to the involved parties. For instance, the collapse of the fixed exchange rate systems was largely due to the inability of IMF members to redistribute the burden of adjustment from the USA to Germany and Japan. Difficulties in the so-called European Snake in the early 1970s induced member states to design the EMS in such a way as to put the responsibility on strong currency members (in particular Germany) to intervene as much as weak currency members in defending existing parities.

Our brief discussion of the roles of institutions reveals the value associated with information gathering and dissemination. Long-term enforcement requires identifying prospects for defection, finding a focal point based on the constellation of positions, and informing actors of the overall global context. Therefore, a major activity of international institutions is to collect information about actors' behaviour, preferences, and the state of the international environment.

KEY POINTS

- Institutions are key instruments for resolving enforcement, distribution, and assurance problems.

- Institutions help assign rights and obligations to benefactors of cooperation as well as in defining those benefactors.

- Institutions help make the international scene an information-rich environment.

The formation and evolution of institutions

We have seen that institutions can help cooperation in several ways. But how might institutions be formed in the first place? And what factors may impact the design of institutions? We begin with a broad discussion from the literature on international relations and then turn to more specific issues. In examining institutions, five different approaches in international relations have been brought to bear on this problem: Neorealism, Neorealist institutionalism, Neo-liberal Institutionalism, Cognitivism, and Radical Constructivism (Aggarwal 1998).[1]

Neorealists assume that in an anarchic international system, states must rely primarily on their own resources to ensure their security. For neorealist scholars, thus, regimes and international institutions have no significant role in international relations because

---

[1]The term Radical Constructivism was first used by Haas (1992); for a more recent synthesis, see Duffield (2007).

power considerations are predominant in an anarchic world (Waltz 1979; Mearsheimer 1990). In this view, as we have discussed earlier, collaboration will only be sustainable if states highly value future interactions, have symmetric resources, and are highly interdependent.

Still within a power-based tradition, though, some scholars have examined changes in and the effects of international institutions. In this literature, labelled Neorealist Institutionalism, the central concern is on how regimes affect the distribution of costs and benefits of state interaction. For analysts in this school (Krasner 1983; Aggarwal 1985; Krasner 1991; Knight 1992), institutions have distributional consequences (in other words, the benefits of cooperation may be unequal) and can be used as devices to seek and maintain asymmetric gains. They can more broadly help control other actors' behaviour, both at home and abroad (Aggarwal 1985). For example, within the domestic context, state elites can argue that their hands are tied and thus attempt to circumvent pressure for particular actions from domestic actors. Examples of this include the Mexican government signing onto the North American Free Trade Agreement (NAFTA) (tying the hands of the Mexican government to a more open market posture in the face of domestic protectionist groups) or the American use of the Multi-Fiber Arrangement (MFA) to prevent textile and apparel interests from pressing for excessive protection.

A central theme in this literature has been the role of hegemonic powers in fostering the development of institutions through both positive and negative incentives (Kindleberger 1973; Gilpin 1975; Krasner 1976). Benevolent hegemons, for example, may provide **public goods** (a special type of good, e.g. national defence, that cannot practically be withheld from an individual without withholding them from all—the 'nonexcludability criterion'—and for which the marginal cost of an additional person consuming them, once they have been produced, is zero; the 'nonrival consumption' criterion) because their large size makes it worthwhile for them to take action on their own to overcome collective action problems. But while suggesting that regimes may form when powerful states desire them, this approach does not tell us much about the nature of regimes. Moreover, scholars in this school overemphasize tensions arising from the differences in the distribution of benefits between actors and downplay the possibility that actors may not necessarily and as acutely think in comparative terms but focus on the positive impact of institutions on their situations. Finally, this approach has little to say about actors' desire to pursue multilateral versus bilateral solutions to accomplish their ends.

Building on these criticisms of the Neorealist approach, Neo-liberal institutionalists have examined the specific incentives for states to create institutions—as opposed to simply engaging in ad hoc bargaining. This body of work, taking off from seminal research by Oliver Williamson, examines the role of institutions in lowering the costs involved in choosing, organizing, negotiating, and entering into an agreement (what he calls transaction costs), and has garnered a considerable following in the field of international relations (Keohane 1984). As we have seen, institutions provide many useful functions in helping actors to coordinate their actions or achieve collaboration. This theoretical approach assumes that collaborative action is primarily demand driven—that is, actors will create institutions because they are useful—but does not really specify a mechanism for how they would go about actually creating them.

An important theme of this work has been how existing institutions may constrain future institutional developments (Keohane and Nye 1977; Keohane 1984). One aspect of this constraint is the possibility that existing institutions with a broad mandate will affect the negotiation of more specific institutions, leading to the 'nesting' of regimes within one another (Aggarwal 1985). Thus, while the notion of transaction costs and sunk costs (the investments that actors have made in specific institutions) are central elements in this thinking, the role of regimes in providing states with information and reducing organizational costs can be distinguished from the role of existing institutions in constraining future actions.

A fourth approach to examining institutional innovation and change places emphasis on the role of expert consensus and the interplay of experts and politicians (Haas 1980; Haas 1992). New knowledge and cognitive understandings may lead decision-makers to calculate their interests differently. For example, work by Ernst Haas focused on the efforts of politicians to use linkages across various issues (sometimes from quite distinct areas) to create new issue packages in international negotiations. The objective is to provide benefits to all, in an effort to facilitate the formation of international regimes (Haas 1980).

Lastly, 'Radical Constructivists', while focusing on the role of ideas, argue that reality is in fact constructed in the minds of decision-makers. These scholars, drawing from Ernst Haas's work, go much further than Haas in suggesting, 'power and interest do not have effects apart from the shared knowledge that constitutes them as such' (Wendt 1995). Analysts in this school see norms and values as being dominant causal forces and ascribe considerable power to institutions in not only constraining actors, but in fundamentally altering how they conceive of their basic interests. In summarizing their view, Peter Haas notes that this school argues that 'there is no 'objective' basis for identifying material reality and all claims for objectivity are therefore suspect' (Haas 1992). The subjective element in states' decision-making makes it more difficult to objectively evaluate the role that institutions might play or how they might be constructed.

The characteristics of international institutions

The five general approaches just discussed are a useful starting point for the understanding of how institutions are created and of the key drivers of their subsequent evolution, but they clearly are of limited help to understand specific variations in the forms of institutions. Based on the existing literature and on our own work, we characterize institutions in terms of their membership, the stringency of their rules (the degree to which they constrain state behaviour), their scope, their membership, the extent of delegation of power from member states to institutional bodies, and the centralization of tasks within the institution (see Box 3.3).

The Bretton Woods institutions, the WTO, and UNCTAD have quasi-universal *membership*. By contrast, the Group of Seven most industrialized countries only welcomed one new member in the last 30 years (Russia formally joined the Group in 1997, transforming it into the G8). Moreover, it is interesting to underline that the G7/8 remains autonomous from the larger G20, with the latter becoming the most visible global economic steering forum. Similarly, most regional integration arrangements have remained selected clubs with limited membership (see Ravenhill, Chapter 6 in this volume). Membership also varies in terms of the type of actors who can participate. While most institutions remain state-centric, some have started to include private actors. For instance, the Financial Stability Forum (FSF) was created in 1999 and upgraded to the Financial Stability Board by

BOX 3.3

IMF and WTO: Selected Organizational Characteristics

Set up in order to promote international monetary cooperation, the International Monetary Fund exerts a surveillance function over member states' financial and economic policies and provides financial and technical assistance to member states. Day-to-day business is conducted by the Executive Board, a restrictive body with 24 Executive Directors representing directly or indirectly all members. The IMF's five largest shareholders—the USA, Japan, Germany, France, and the United Kingdom—along with China, Russia, and Saudi Arabia have their own seats whereas the other 16 Executive Directors are elected by groups of countries. The Executive Board gets its powers from the Board of Governors, the highest authority of the IMF in which each member has a seat. To assist it in the conduct of IMF affairs, the Executive Board in turn selects a Managing Director who is the chief of the operating staff of the Fund of 2,800 employees, with half of them being economists.

Within the Executive Board, the normal *de jure* decision-making mode is simple majority, but important issues are decided by qualified majority, either 70 per cent (suspension of one member's rights in case of non-respect of obligations) or by 85 per cent (e.g. modification of quotas, change in the seats of the Executive Board, provisions for general exchange arrangements). Qualified majority voting increases the power of the biggest contributors, in particular the USA, which has a veto power over issues requiring 85 per cent majority decisions. De facto, however, voting rarely occurs in the Executive Board. Instead, Executive Directors use consensus to adopt decisions.

The institutional structure of the WTO differs significantly from the IMF model. It reflects very clearly what the organization considers to be its primary role, that is, a forum for the negotiation of liberalization agreements. In the WTO, the principal institutional structures are a ministerial Conference meeting every two years; the General Council, and three councils in the area of goods, services, and intellectual property.

All members have a seat in these councils. The default decision-making mode is consensus but decisions may also be made at unanimity (suspension of MFN treatment), at 75 per cent majority (interpretation of an existing multilateral agreement, or a waiver of an obligation for a particular country), or with two-thirds majority (for admission of new members for instance).

The WTO General Council also serves as the Trade Policy Review Body that adopts reviews of member states' trade policies. Reviews are conducted on the basis of a policy statement by the Member under review and a report prepared by economists in the WTO Secretariat. That Secretariat, headed by a director-general, has around 630 staff and its main function is one of administrative and technical support to WTO councils, committees, and working groups.

Delegation of authority in the WTO is therefore restricted to the mechanism for solving trade disputes between members. Delegation is conferred first to small groups of experts (three or five) who are established when members fail to settle disputes in a conciliatory way. Panel members are independent individuals under instruction from no government. Their role is to make an objective assessment of the dispute and issue a report with findings and recommendations (establishing the legality of member states' policies in the case under dispute). This report has then to be adopted by the General Council serving as the Dispute Settlement Body. The latter, however, can only reject the panel report by consensus.

The second body with delegated authority from the member state is the Appellate Body, which reviews appeals made by member states on panel reports. The seven members of the Appellate Body serve for four-year terms and are legal experts with international standing. The appeal can uphold, modify, or reverse the panel's legal findings and conclusions. As for the case of panel reports, the Dispute Settlement Body must endorse the appeal report. Rejection is only possible by consensus.

For more information, see http://www.wto.org and http://www.imf.org

the G20 in 2009 (Helleiner 2014*b*) to promote international financial stability groups representatives from national ministries, international financial institutions, and sector-specific groups (insurance, accounting standards, securities commissions). Controversy continues at the WTO over whether non-state actors should be permitted to participate in deliberations. (For other efforts paying particular attention to membership issues see Sandler (1992), Koremenos, Lipson, and Snidal (2001) and Aggarwal and Dupont (2002)).

The second dimension, *stringency of rules*, covers both the precision and the obligation of rules in the literature on legalization of world politics (see Aggarwal 1985 on regime strength, and Abbott and Snidal 2000 on legalization). From this perspective, authors have often contrasted the so-called European and Asian models of regional economic integration. The first one is built upon a wide set of specific and binding rules (called the *acquis communautaire* in the jargon of European integration) whereas the second is built upon declarations, intentions, and voluntary commitments (Ravenhill 1995, 2001). The lack of any precise and concise definition of a balance of payments problem in the IMF severely affected the constraining power of this institution in preventing its members from running imbalances.

Third, we consider the *scope* of agreements defined as issue coverage (Aggarwal 1985; Koremenos Lipson and Snidal 2001). The evolution of the GATT from its origins in 1947 to the creation of WTO in 1995 reveals an important increase in the scope of the agreements. Whereas GATT initially focused on the liberalization of trade in goods, the WTO covers services, agriculture, as well as trade-related aspects of intellectual property rights and investment. Similarly, the G7/8 agenda has drastically expanded from a focus on macroeconomic management at its creation in the mid 1970s to a broad range of international security and economic issues, including terrorism, energy, environment, and arms control in the 1990s and early 2000s. At the other end of the range, one finds sector-specific institutions such as the International Organization of Securities Commissions (IOSCO), the International Associations of Insurance Supervisors (IAIS), and International Accounting Standards Board (IASB), as well as product-specific organizations such as the International Coffee Organization (ICO), the International Cocoa Organization (ICCO), the International Copper Study Group (ICSG), and the International Sugar Organization (ISO).

The fourth dimension is the extent of *institutional delegation*, the authority ceded by members to an institution, a dimension central to several existing studies (Abbott and Snidal 2000; McCall Smith 2000; Dupont and Hefeker 2001; Hawkins, Lake, Nielson, and Tierney 2006). International agreements may or may not include the creation of institutional organs, and these organs may or may not be given some autonomy from members for making new rules or monitoring and enforcing existing ones.

The extent of delegation may vary significantly across organs of the same institution. For instance, while the dispute settlement process in the WTO features an independent Appellate Body, the governing body of the organization—the General Council—relies upon consensus decision-making and the members have kept the size and the prerogatives of the secretariat down to a minimum. At the regional level, the extent of delegation strongly distinguishes the European Union from the small secretariats found

in other regional institutions. Whereas the EU includes organs with supranational power, governments remain in full control of negotiation and implementation processes in most other regional agreements, including the NAFTA, the Association of Southeast Asian Nations (ASEAN), and the Asia-Pacific Economic Cooperation (APEC) grouping.

A fifth dimension is *institutional centralization* (Koremenos, Lipson, and Snidal 2001). Is there a concentration of tasks performed by a single institutional entity? Centralization may refer to such tasks as the diffusion of information, monitoring of members' behaviour, or the imposition of sanctions, as well as the adoption of new rules or modification of existing ones. Strong administrative bodies are natural candidates for the centralization of many tasks, as exemplified by the case of the European Commission in the European Union, or the administration of the IMF or the World Bank. Yet, in the latter two, key decisions and tasks go through the Executive Board with a limited membership of 24 countries or groups of countries represented by Executive Directors elected by member states (see Helleiner, Chapter 8 in this volume).

It is often difficult to understand these five dimensions as being separate but they are conceptually distinct. As an example, although it is hard to imagine an agreement with lax rules and high delegation, strict rules do not necessarily imply high delegation (good instances are the numerous bilateral treaties on investment and to a lesser extent bilateral free trade treaties). Similarly, centralization and delegation may reinforce each other but none of them requires the other one. Conferences or councils of head of governments and states centralize most of the activities of several regional economic organizations (including monitoring, and dispute settlement). Yet, decision-making remains either consensual (where no state publicly dissents from the agreement) or based on unanimity.

Explaining institutional design

How can one account for institutional variation on these five dimensions? Consistent with a functionalist approach to the study of international institutions, we should expect the five dimensions to be affected by the type of problems that institutions should address (Stein 1982; Snidal 1985; Aggarwal and Dupont 1999; Koremenos, Lipson, and Snidal 2001; Ostrom 2003). In Table 3.1, we linked our three typical problems with specific roles for international institutions.

Keeping these in mind, the 'temptation to free ride' problem is the one that clearly calls for strong rules, with delegation and centralization to international bodies. Cooperation is difficult and thus requires relatively strong institutions. In such cases, membership tends to be restricted to well 'socialized' governments. An inclusive membership makes monitoring more difficult and costly, and thus creates many opportunities for members to free ride.

As for scope, on the one hand, enforcement of the agreements is more likely to occur when institutions have a broad scope and are able to connect different issues ('issue linkage'). Linkages across issues help in deterring defection on a single issue when actors have broad interests (McGinnis 1986; Lohmann 1997). For example, members of the WTO cannot subscribe to the agreement on goods (GATT) without also accepting the agreement on services (GATS) as well as the agreements on intellectual property rights (TRIPs) and investment (TRIMs), and the dispute settlement mechanism. On the other hand, adding issues to an institution's agenda requires strong capacity to monitor behaviour, which may often not be present. In the context of the Doha Round of talks within the WTO, now collapsed, there was increasing concern about the negative impact of the willingness to support an all or nothing approach—to make the WTO a single undertaking as a means to achieve a negotiation breakthrough (Elsig and Dupont 2012).

The 'inhibiting fear' and 'where to meet' problems call for quite different institutional features. For these cases, there is a positive link with centralization for the pooling of resources, knowledge, and information provision, or the reduction of costs of negotiations. Addressing the 'inhibiting fear' may require some clear and binding rules on access to resources and knowledge. Yet in these cases, restricting the size of membership may not be a strong prerequisite for success. Solving distribution problems may require a softening of rules to allow some room for different interpretations of the agreements. Delegation of power is not essential in both situations, except for a potential benefit of agenda setting power to find mutually acceptable solutions.

As for scope, there is no clear link between 'inhibiting fear' and issue coverage. But a diverse set of issues can provide greater ground for compromise when players have different preferences and when they do not assign equal value to all of the issues. For instance, trade liberalization and monetary cooperation in the

European Community has often been facilitated by the development of social or regional policies or packages to 'compensate' countries that might not immediately be major beneficiaries of the other policies. But, as the case of agriculture in the GATT/WTO shows, having different issues on the agenda is not helpful when countries categorically exclude certain issues from consideration in making trade-offs. Finally, with respect to membership, selected, restrictive groupings tend to reinforce the fear of being left out and thus should be avoided to address the 'inhibiting fear' problem. As for problems of distribution, more members may on the one hand help in the quest for new solutions. Yet, new members may also add as many new conflicts as complementarities among players.

As we have seen, then, different types of problems call for appropriate institutional design. Although focusing on general tendencies in institutional design in view of the problems they need to address provides a useful first step, we are still faced with some anomalies. For instance, given that trade liberalization is widely portrayed as embodying a 'temptation to free ride', how can one explain that some institutions (for instance European Free Trade Association) that focus on trade liberalization have remained informal and thus lack organs with delegated power? Why is it that some institutions do not have clear rules and preconditions for membership (for instance GATT/WTO or the EU until the early 1990s)? And lastly, why do some countries prefer very loose rules in designing institutions (such as ASEAN and APEC)?

To increase our ability to understand such choices, we can consider three other key influences. First, an important issue is what we call *potential participants* in the institution. In particular, the number of these actors and their relative power—two factors considered by Koremenos, Lipson, and Snidal (2001)—as well as their overall financial and 'social' capital (Ostrom 2000) influence the design of institutions. Relatively little concern about membership rules in GATT 1947 can be accounted for by the fact that the international system was much smaller and more homogeneous than the one that emerged in the 1960s as a result of decolonization. Similarly, the need to define strict criteria for entering the EU only became salient when the iron curtain fell and former communist countries with still very different political systems expressed an interest in joining the EU. Turning to the financial and social capital among potential actors, the disparities in size of financial reserves held by East Asian economies surely explains the very decentralized form of the regional financing arrangement known as the Chiang Mai Initiative (an East Asian mechanism that is intended to provide emergency finance to member economies facing a run on their currencies). In turn, the fact that there has been little formalization of relationships between central banks in the developed, democratic world builds upon a joint understanding and on a high level of expertise on how to address problems.

Second, the *information and knowledge available to actors* affects institutional design. Institutions comprised of actors with rich and reliable information usually require less centralization or less delegation (Coase 1960; Williamson 1975; Koremenos, Lipson, and Snidal 2001), as illustrated with the loose structure of the European Free Trade Association from its creation in 1960 to its upgrading in 1993. The founding members of that association—the United Kingdom, Denmark, Norway, Sweden, Austria, Switzerland, and Portugal—did not have the mutual distrust that characterized French–German relationships in the EC and information from partner countries was thus considered by all members to be rich and reliable. Existing knowledge about the issue area(s) covered by the agreement may affect the stringency of rules, the delegation of power, issue scope, and membership. Poor knowledge about the issues at stake tends to make actors wary of making hard commitments (rules and delegation)—a tendency particularly present in the discussions in the domain of the environment (see Dauvergne, Chapter 14 in this volume). Better knowledge may affect issue scope and the contours of membership as clearly illustrated by the key influence of the work of the Intergovernmental Panel on Climate Change (IPCC)—the intergovernmental body that reviews and assesses the scientific information on climate change—on the evolution of commitments in the domain of climate change. In trade, whereas the politics of trade liberalization may call for careful selection of members for inclusion in the WTO, the widespread belief in the veracity of international trade theory (which argues that global membership yields the greatest efficiency in the allocation of resources) helps to account for the pressure to universalize increasingly membership in this institution.

Third, and finally, we can focus on the *outside institutional setting*. When actors create new institutions, they generally do not do so in a vacuum. Thus, when new institutions are developed, they often must be reconciled with existing ones. One approach to achieving such reconciliation is by nesting broader and narrower institutions in hierarchical fashion. Another means of achieving harmony among institutions is through an institutional division of labour, or 'horizontal' linkages (Aggarwal 1998). The challenge of institutional reconciliation is not, however, unique to the creation of new ones. In lieu of creating new institutions, policy-makers might also modify existing institutions for new purposes. For instance, faced by seemingly intractable balance of payments problems in Africa in the 1990s, the IMF developed new **structural adjustment** facilities that overlapped substantially with those of the World Bank. When modifying institutions, members therefore must also focus on issues of institutional compatibility. Moreover, bargaining over institutional modification is likely to be strongly influenced by existing institutions.

A few examples will illustrate these ideas. One can think about the problem of reconciling institutions from both an issue area and a regional perspective (Oye 1992; Gamble and Payne 1996; Lawrence 1996a). Nested institutions in an issue area are nicely illustrated by the relationship between the international regime for textile and apparel trade (the Long Term Arrangement on Cotton Textiles and its successor arrangement, the Multifiber Arrangement that was phased out completely in 2005) with respect to the broader regime in which it was nested, the GATT. When the Executive Branch in the US faced pressure from domestic protectionist interests simultaneously with international pressures to keep its market open, the American administration promoted the formation of a sector-specific international regime under GATT auspices. This nesting effort ensured a high degree of conformity with both the GATT's principles and norms as well as with its rules and procedures (Aggarwal 1985, 1994). Although the textile regime deviated from some of the GATT's norms in permitting discriminatory treatment of developing countries' exports, it did follow the **most-favoured nation** (MFN) norm, which called for developed countries to treat all developing countries alike.

The Asia-Pacific Economic Cooperation grouping (APEC), created in 1989, illustrates the concept of regional nesting. APEC's founding members were extremely worried about undermining the GATT, and sought to reconcile these two institutions by focusing on the notion of 'open regionalism'—that is, the creation of APEC would not bar others from benefiting from any ensuing liberalization in the region. APEC members saw this non-discriminatory liberalization as a better alternative to using Article 24 of the GATT, which permits the formation of discriminatory **free trade areas** and **customs unions**, to justify this accord (see Ravenhill Chapter 6 in this volume). Rather than forming an institution that could conflict with the promotion of GATT initiatives, therefore, APEC founding members attempted to construct an institution that would complement the GATT. Furthermore, APEC members wanted to avoid undermining existing sub-regional organizations, in particular ASEAN. This clearly restricted the level of obligation and delegation that could have been transferred to the newly created pan-regional organization (Dupont 1998).

An alternative mode of reconciling institutions would be to simply create 'horizontal' institutions to deal with separate but related activities, as exemplified by the division of labour between the GATT and the Bretton Woods monetary system (IMF and World Bank). In creating institutions for the post-Second World War era, policy-makers were concerned about a return to the 1930s era of competitive devaluations, marked by an inward turn among states and the use of protectionist measures. These 'beggar-thy-neighbour' policies were found across economic issue areas, and individual action by each state worked to the detriment of all. As a consequence, the founders of the Bretton Woods monetary system also turned their focus to creating institutions that would help to encourage trade liberalization. By promoting fixed exchange rates through the IMF and liberalization of trade through the GATT, policy-makers hoped that this horizontal institutional division of labour between complementary institutions would lead to freer trade.

Finally, on a regional basis, one can see the development of the European Economic Coal and Steel Community and the Western European Union (WEU) as horizontal organizations. The first was oriented towards strengthening European cooperation in economic matters (with, of course, important security implications), while the WEU sought to develop a coordinated European defence effort.

Conclusion

This chapter has sought to provide a systematic analysis of the problem of collaboration in global political economy through the lenses of types of problems,

games, and institutions. We have seen that states may need to collaborate or to coordinate their actions to keep economic globalization on track because they may face problems of free riding, an inhibiting fear that their efforts will lead to instability for their economy, and the need to find coordination points that have varying costs and benefits to the participants.

The problem of free riding or the difficulty of finding a coordination equilibrium is a common one on a number of issues, including trade, monetary cooperation, the environment, human rights, and the like. Despite some limitations, game theory provides useful insight into the diverse set of problems that states may face in collaborating or in coordinating their actions. One of the most commonly used games, the PD, has been utilized to show that in many issue areas, actors have a strong incentive to defect despite the potential joint gains that they may receive. Yet as we have shown, many problems in international political economy are not PD games, but instead may be better characterized as Chicken, Assurance, Suasion, or even Harmony games. By carefully examining the types of problems that actors face in a particular issue area and the structure of pay-offs, game theory provides insight into the constraints on joint action.

It is worth keeping in mind that the preferences that go into creating games are often assumed by many analysts—particularly those in the neorealist institutionalist and neo-liberal institutionalist camps. Where do preferences come from and are such preferences amenable to change? It is on this dimension that constructivist arguments focusing on the role of experts, changing knowledge, and possible shifts in preferences through learning may provide significant insight that can help us to create more logically compelling games.

Once we can establish the basic game structure that actors face, we can better examine what role institutions might play in ensuring more favourable outcomes. In some cases, contrary to the perspective often taken by neo-institutionalists, institutions may not really be necessary for ensuring cooperative state action. Hence, we examined the types of situations in which self-help might lead to a positive outcome versus those in which institutions might play a genuinely useful role in overcoming collective action problems.

The role of institutions in fostering collaboration itself raises two puzzles. First, how might states collaborate in the first place to create institutions? This in itself raises an analytical problem that various theories have attempted to address. As we have seen, hegemons may have strong incentives to create institutions to constrain the behaviour of other actors and possibly their own domestic lobbies. Other approaches such as neo-liberal institutionalism focus on the strong incentives that major states may have in creating institutions and suggest that small numbers of actors may be able to overcome the usual collective action problems that may lead to free riding behaviour. To better understand the process of institutional design, we focused on five dimensions to characterize institutions: membership, the stringency of their rules, their scope, the extent of delegation of power from member states to institutional bodies, and the centralization of tasks within the institution. The types of problems which actors face can partially account for specific institutional characteristics. Yet other factors also influence the design of institutions. These include the potential participants in the specific issue area, the knowledge and information available to actors, and the pre-existing institutional context. In particular, with respect to

the last factor, the Asian financial crisis of 1997–8 and the ongoing proliferation of trade agreements raises an important issue about reconciling new and old institutions. The Asian financial crisis generated considerable conflict when some Asian countries sought to create an Asian Monetary Fund. In the end, this effort faltered in the face of IMF and US opposition, but East Asian countries have since aggressively sought to create regional monetary mechanisms and the biggest emerging countries have created their own multilateral development bank—the New Development Bank BRICs. In trade, the problems of the Doha Round have been accompanied by the proliferation of new bilateral and regional agreements with the development of new rules for international production networks. The extent to which such arrangements will continue to coexist with the WTO in a sort of two-pillar system (Baldwin 2016) or further undermine the WTO remains a crucial question that will have important implications for prospects of continued economic liberalization in the global economy.

 QUESTIONS

1. Why does globalization increase the pressure for international collaboration?
2. What is the most frequent problem of collaboration in global political economy?
3. What is the thorniest situation of collaboration in global political economy?
4. How can game theory help us understand problems of collaboration?
5. Can enforcement really be carried out in international political economy?
6. How can institutions help overcome obstacles to collaboration?
7. What is the link between the types of problems that countries face in the global economy and their choice of an institution?
8. What are some key characteristics that can be used to describe international institutions?
9. What theories or variables help to account for the choice of specific international institutional characteristics?

FURTHER READING

Aggarwal, V. K. (ed.) (1998), *Institutional Designs for a Complex World: Bargaining, Linkages and Nesting* (Ithaca, NY: Cornell University Press). A collective volume that focuses on the relationships between institutions and the stability of dense institutional settings.

Aggarwal, V. K. and Dupont, C. (1999), 'Goods, Games and Institutions', *International Political Science Review*, 20/4: 393–409. The original and technical presentation of our theory that links goods, games, and institutions.

Cooper, R. N. (ed.) (1989), *Can Nations Agree?* (Washington, DC: Brookings Institution). An insightful collection of work on coordination attempts of economic policies among nations outside of institutional settings.

Hasenclever, A., Mayer, P., and Rittberger, V. (eds) (1997), *Theories of International Regimes* (Cambridge: Cambridge University Press). A collective volume on developments on theories of international regimes with application to all domains of international politics.

Kaul, I., Grunberg, I., and Stern, M. A. (eds) (1999), *Global Public Goods* (New York: Oxford University Press). A collective volume with a range of examples of global public goods in economics, politics, and environment with interesting lessons for the future provision of such goods.

Keohane, R. O. (1984), *After Hegemony: Cooperation and Discord in the World Political Economy* (Princeton: Princeton University Press). The classic work on the links between regime change and change in power distribution.

Kormenos, B., Lipson, C., and Snidal, D. (2001), 'The Rational Design of International Institutions', *International Organization*, 55/4: 761–99. Introductory article to the latest collective work on institutional design, using insights from game theory and considering various facets of institutions.

Krasner, S. D. (ed.) (1983), *International Regimes* (Ithaca, NY: Cornell University Press). The seminal collective volume on international regimes that includes the classic definition of regimes as well as a range of examples in various domains of international politics.

Olson, M. (1965), *The Logic of Collective Action: Public Goods and the Theory of Groups* (Cambridge, MA: Harvard University Press). Classic work on collective action and the conditions under which groups of actors may produce public goods.

Sandler, T. (1992), *Collective Action: Theory and Applications* (Ann Arbor: University of Michigan Press). A comprehensive treatment of the problem of collective action using both basic and advanced formal analytical tools.

Snidal, D. (1985), 'Coordination versus Prisoner's Dilemma: Implications for International Cooperation', *American Political Science Review*, 79: 923–42. The seminal article on the contrast between PD and coordination games applied to international relations.

Taylor, M. (1987), *The Possibility of Cooperation* (Cambridge: Cambridge University Press). An advanced treatment of the problem of cooperation using repeated games.

Yarbrough, B. V. and Yarbrough R.M. (1992), *Cooperation and Governance in International Trade* (Princeton: Princeton University Press). An elegant analysis of the problem of governance in trade approached through the lens of transaction costs.

WEBLINKS

www.gametheory.net Game theory.

http://www.globalpublicgoods.org Global public goods.

ONLINE RESOURCE CENTRE

For additional material and resources, please visit the Online Resource Centre at:
www.oxfordtextbooks.co.uk/ravenhill5e

4

The Domestic Sources of Foreign Economic Policies

Michael J. Hiscox

Reader's guide

How should a nation manage its economic ties with the rest of the world? How should the government regulate flows of goods, people, and investment to and from foreign nations? Intense, often rancorous, debates over foreign economic policies break out regularly in politics in all countries. Indeed, how governments should now be dealing with the multiple facets of 'globalization' is perhaps the single most pressing political challenge of our time. It is an issue that has been debated in national legislatures and lecture halls across the world; it has mobilized nationalist populist movements at one end of the political spectrum, and transnational environmental and human rights organizations at the other; and it has led to violent protests and demonstrations in the streets of London, Paris, Berlin, and New York. What are the battle lines in these political debates? How are policies decided in different countries? How do differences in political institutions shape these policy decisions? And how do new ideas and information about policy options filter into politics? This chapter examines each of these questions, focusing on the domestic politics of trade, immigration, investment, and exchange rates.

Introduction

Each government must make choices about how best to manage the way its own economy is linked to the global economy. It must choose whether to open the national market to international trade, whether to liberalize trade with some nations more than with others, and whether to allow more trade in some sectors of the economy than in others. Each government must also decide whether to restrict international flows of investment in different sectors, and whether to regulate immigration and emigration by different types of workers. And it must either fix the exchange rate for the national currency or allow the rate to fluctuate to some degree, in response to supply and demand in international financial markets.

Of course, if every government always made the same choices in all these areas of policy, things would be very simple for us as scholars (and much more predictable for the citizens of the world). But governments in different countries, and at different moments in history, have often chosen radically different foreign economic policies. Some have closed off their national economies almost completely from the rest of the world, imposing strict limits on trade, immigration, and investment—an example is China in the 1960s, which kept itself isolated almost completely from the rest of the world's economies. In other situations, governments have adopted the opposite approach, allowing virtually unfettered economic exchange between their citizens and foreigners—ironically, Hong Kong in the 1960s may be the best example of this type of extreme openness. Most governments today adopt a mixture of policies that fall somewhere in the middle ground between these two extremes, imposing selective controls on activities that affect some sectors of their economy, and restricting exchanges with some foreign countries more than with others. Understanding why governments make the particular choices they do requires careful attention to the political pressures they face from different domestic groups and the political institutions that regulate the way collective decisions are made and implemented.

Politics, we know, is all about who gets what, when, and how. Different individuals and groups in every society typically have very different views about what their government should do when it comes to setting the policies that regulate international trade, immigration, investment, and exchange rates. These competing demands must be reconciled in some way by the political institutions that govern policymaking. To really understand the domestic origins of foreign economic policies we thus need to perform two critical tasks:

1. Identify or map the policy preferences of different groups in the domestic economy.

2. Specify how political institutions determine the way these preferences are aggregated or converted into actual government decisions.

The first step will require some *economic* analysis. How people are affected by their nation's ties with the global economy, and thus what types of policies they prefer to manage those ties, depends primarily on how they make their living. Steelworkers, for example, typically have very different views from wheat farmers about most foreign economic policies, because these policies rarely affect the steel and wheat industries in a similar fashion. Of critical importance here are the types of assets that individuals own, and how the income earned from these assets is affected by different policy choices.

The second step calls for *political* analysis. How political representatives are elected, how groups organize to lobby or otherwise influence politicians, and how policies are proposed, debated, amended, and passed in legislatures, and then implemented by government agencies, all depend on the structure of political institutions. Democratically elected leaders face very different institutional constraints from military dictators, of course, and even among democracies there is quite a wide range of institutional variation that can have a large impact on the behaviour of policymakers.

These two analytical steps put together like this, combining both economic and political analysis in tandem, are generally referred to as the *political economy* approach to the study of policy outcomes. In the next two sections, we shall consider each of the two analytical steps in some detail, examining the domestic sources of policies in the areas of trade, immigration, investment, and exchange rates. We shall then shift gears a little, and consider the ways in which ideas and information might affect policymaking. We shall also discuss linkages between the different policy dimensions and non-economic issues, focusing on environmental and human rights concerns, and how they feature in debates over foreign economic policies. Finally, in the conclusion, to link all this to the discussion of international collaboration and coordination in Chapter 3, we shall briefly consider the impact of domestic politics on bargaining over economic issues between governments at the international level.

Policy preferences

The guiding assumption here is that, when it comes to taking positions on how to regulate ties with the global economy, individuals and groups are fundamentally concerned with how different policy choices affect their incomes. Of course, people may also have important non-material concerns that affect their attitudes towards foreign economic policies. Many people are concerned about the ways in which globalization affects national security, for example, and they worry about its impact on traditional cultures, on the world's environment, and on human rights; and these concerns may have a direct impact on their views about the regulation of international trade, immigration, and investment. We shall discuss some of these important considerations in more detail later in the chapter. But we begin here with the simplest possible framework in which economic policies are evaluated only in terms of their economic effects. Given that organized producer groups have almost always been the most vocal participants in domestic debates about foreign economic policies, and the debates themselves have been couched mainly in economic terms, this seems an appropriate way to begin.

Trade

The dramatic growth in international trade during the last five decades has intensified political debate over the costs and benefits of trade openness. In the United States, the controversy surrounding the creation of the North American Free Trade Agreement (NAFTA) in 1993 was especially intense, and similar arguments have arisen in Europe over the issue of enlargement of the European Union, and over attempts to reform the Common Agricultural Policy (CAP). Rapid trade policy reforms have also generated a significant political backlash in many developing nations, and recent years have witnessed violent protests and demonstrations by groups from a variety of countries that hope to disrupt meetings of the World Trade Organization (WTO). Political leaders around the world frequently voice concerns about the negative effects of trade, and the need to protect their firms and workers from foreign competition.

What is behind all this political turmoil and protest? At first glance, it may seem puzzling that there is so much conflict over trade. After all, the most famous insight from international economics is the proof that trade provides mutual gains; that is, when countries exchange goods and services they are all generally better off. Trade allows each country to specialize in producing those goods and services in which it has a **comparative advantage**, and in doing so world welfare is improved (see Box 4.8 at the end of this chapter).

While there are gains from trade for all countries *in the aggregate*, what makes trade so controversial is that, among individuals within each country, trade creates winners and losers. How trade affects different individuals depends on how they earn their living. To flesh out this story, economists have traditionally relied on a very simple theory of trade devised by two Swedish economists, Eli Heckscher and Bertil Ohlin. In the **Heckscher–Ohlin model** of trade, each nation's comparative advantage is traced to its particular endowments of different factors of production: that is, basic inputs such as land, labour, and capital that are used in different proportions in the production of different goods and services. Since the costs of these inputs in each country will depend on their availability, differences in factor endowments across countries will create differences in comparative advantage. Each country will tend to export items whose production requires intensive use of the factors with which it is abundantly endowed relative to other nations; conversely, each country will import goods whose production requires intensive use of factors that are relatively scarce. Countries well endowed with land, such as Australia and Canada, are expected to export agricultural products (for example, wheat and wool), while importing products that require the intensive use of labour (for example, textiles and footwear) from more labour-abundant economies like China and India. The advanced economies of Europe, Japan, and the United States, well endowed with capital relative to the rest of the world, should export capital-intensive products (for example, automobiles and pharmaceuticals), while importing other types of goods from less developed trading partners where supplies of capital are scarce compared to supplies of labour and land.

Building on this simple model of trade, Wolfgang Stolper and Paul Samuelson (1941) derived a famous theorem in 1941 that outlined the likely effects of trade on the real incomes of different sets of individuals within any economy. According to the Stolper–Samuelson theorem, trade benefits those who own the factors of production with which the economy is relatively well endowed, but hurts owners of scarce factors. The reasoning is straightforward: by encouraging specialization in each economy in export-oriented types of production, trade increases the demand for locally abundant factors (and bids up the earnings of those who own those factors), while reducing demand for locally scarce factors (and lowering the earnings of owners of such factors). In Australia and Canada, the theorem tells us, landowners should clearly benefit from trade, while workers can expect lower real wages as a consequence of increased imports of labour-intensive goods. In the United States, the theorem predicts that trade should benefit owners of capital and landowners at the expense of workers. The converse should hold in relatively labour-abundant (and capital-scarce) developing economies such as China and India, where trade will raise the wages of workers relative to the profits earned by local owners of capital.

By revealing how trade benefits some people while making others worse off, the Stolper–Samuelson theorem thus accounts for why trade is such a divisive political issue. The theorem also provides a neat way to map the policy preferences of individuals in each economy. In each nation, owners of locally *abundant* factors should support greater trade openness, while owners of locally *scarce* factors should be protectionist (see Box 4.1).

There is a good deal of evidence in the histories of political conflict over trade in a variety of nations that fits with this simple prediction (see Rogowski 1989). In Australia, for example, the first national elections in 1901 were fought between a Free Trade party representing predominantly rural voters, and a Protectionist party supported overwhelmingly by urban owners of capital and labour. A very similar kind of political division characterized most debates over trade policy in Canada in the late nineteenth century, with support for trade openness emanating mainly from farmers in the western provinces. In Europe and Japan, in contrast, much of the opposition to trade over the last century or so has come from agricultural interests, anxious to block cheap imports of farm products from abroad. In the United States and Europe, at least since the 1960s, labour unions have voiced some of the loudest opposition to trade openness and called for import restrictions aimed at protecting jobs in labour-intensive industries threatened by foreign competition.

On the other hand, political divisions and coalitions in trade politics often appear to contradict this simple model of preferences. It is quite common to see workers and owners in the same industry banding together to lobby for protective import barriers, for example, in contemporary debates about policy in the United States, even though the Stolper–Samuelson theorem tells us that capital and labour are

---

BOX 4.1

The Repeal of the Corn Laws

The story of the repeal of Britain's protectionist Corn Laws in 1846 is perhaps still the best-known example of a political clash over trade policy that fits nicely with the Stolper–Samuelson theorem. With the revival of foreign trade after the Napoleonic Wars, policy debates in Britain began to focus on the protectionist Corn Laws that restricted importation of various grains (wheat, rye, barley, and oats, as well as peas and beans), defended resolutely by the landowning elite. Pressure for reform came most strongly from manufacturers, especially textile producers in Leicester and Manchester, anxious to reduce labour costs (see McCord 1958). It was these manufacturers who formed the leadership of the Anti-Corn Law League in 1838, and a cotton manufacturer, Richard Cobden, became the League's most famous advocate. The push for reform soon drew a larger following among both the urban middle and working classes, and attracted support from the working-class Chartist reform movement, which organized the 'bigger loaf' campaign in the 1840s. The effects were soon felt in Parliament, transformed by the Great Reform Act of 1832 and the enfranchisement of voters in the large industrial centres of the West Riding. Cobden himself entered Parliament

in 1841, campaigning with the cry, 'You must untax the people's bread!' and the League stepped up its campaign with a storm of pamphlets, petition drives, public meetings, and addresses to labour unions. The widespread economic distress of the early 1840s had a great impact on the Tory Prime Minister, Robert Peel. He introduced a sliding scale for grain duties in 1841 and then reduced those rates in 1842 and 1844, in an attempt to ease the food crisis, but this aroused fierce opposition from landed interests and from within Conservative ranks. The failure of the potato crop in 1845, and the ensuing food crisis, gave Peel the pretext to go further. Amid reports of widespread starvation, the prime minister pushed through a bill to repeal the Corn Laws altogether, with support from both Liberals and Radicals. The conflict over repeal split the Conservatives irrevocably. Once 'purified' of their Peelite faction, the Tories (known for years as the Protectionists) were increasingly isolated on the trade issue in Parliament. Peel's supporters, including William Gladstone, gravitated to the Liberals, and their free trade platform drew on an immense base of support among urban industrialists, the middle classes, and workers. Gladstone's first budget as prime minister in 1860 effectively eliminated all remaining protectionist duties in Britain.

supposed to have directly opposing views about trade in these economies. So what is going on here? The critical problem is that the theorem is derived by assuming that factors of production are highly mobile between different industries in each economy. An alternative approach to mapping the effects of trade on incomes, often referred to as the **specific factors model**, allows instead that it can be quite costly to move factors of production between different sectors in the economy. That is, different types of land, labour skills, and capital equipment often have a very limited or specific use (or range of uses) to which they can be put when it comes to making products. The plant and machinery used in modern manufacturing industries is very specialized: the presses used to stamp out automobile bodies are designed only for that purpose, for example, and cannot be adapted easily or quickly to perform other tasks. Steel factories cannot easily be converted into pharmaceutical factories or software design houses. Nor can steelworkers quickly adapt their skills and become chemical engineers or computer programmers.

In the specific factors model, the real incomes of different individuals are tied very closely to the fortunes of the particular industries in which they make their living. Individuals employed or invested in export industries benefit from trade according to this model, while those who are attached to import-competing industries are harmed (see Jones 1971; Mussa 1974). In the advanced economies of Europe and the United States, the implication is that owners and employees in export-oriented industries, such as aerospace, pharmaceuticals, computer software, construction equipment, and financial services, should be much more supportive of trade than their counterparts in, say, the steel, textiles, and footwear industries, which face intense pressure from import competition. There is much evidence supporting these predictions in the real world of trade politics, especially in the debates over trade in the most advanced economies, where technologies (and the skills that complement them) have become increasingly specialized in many different manufacturing and service industries, and even in various areas of agriculture and mining production (see Magee 1980; Hiscox 2002). In the recent debates over regional and multilateral trade agreements in the United States, for example, some of the most vociferous opposition to removing barriers to trade has come from owners and workers aligned together in the steel and textile industries.

The leading research on the political economy of trade now assumes routinely that the specific factors approach is the most appropriate way to think about trade policy preferences, at least in the contemporary context in the advanced economies (see Grossman and Helpman 1994; Rodrik 1995), so we shall rely on it for the most part in the discussions later. This model, it is worth noting, is still nested within the broader Heckscher–Ohlin theory that explains trade according to differences in factor endowments. Newer theories of trade, motivated by some clear evidence that not all trade seems to fit well with this simple endowments-based theory (for example, Europe, Japan, and the United States all importing automobiles from each other), have made some significant departures from the standard Heckscher–Ohlin framework. One innovation is to allow that technologies of production and tastes among consumers may vary substantially across countries. Such differences might affect the types of products an economy will be likely to export and import, but the predictions about trade policy preferences derived from the specific factors approach are not otherwise affected: individuals engaged in export industries favour trade, while those in import-competing industries oppose trade. A more complicated innovation in trade theory allows for the possibility of **economies of scale** and other sources of firm-specific cost differences (Melitz 2003). In some industries requiring large investments of capital, the largest firms may enjoy such a dramatic cost advantage over smaller firms that those markets tend to be dominated by only a few, very large, corporations. In such cases, in which firms compete with one another and with foreign rivals for different market niches, trade may have different effects for firms in the same industry (Osgood 2016). These types of complexities are difficult to incorporate into a broadly applicable model of trade, however, so we shall not pursue them here. Although it might be noted that large firms enjoying economies of scale in production also tend to engage in foreign investment and locate parts of their enterprise in different countries. Later, we shall discuss the political implications of this type of multinational investment in more detail.

Immigration

Of course, globalization is not simply a matter of trade in goods and services; it also involves international flows of the factors of production themselves—the migration of workers between nations, and international investment and lending that transfers capital across borders. There is not a radical difference between how we analyse these phenomena and how we examine trade, but neither is the analysis identical in terms of the economic effects and the policy preferences we anticipate for different sets of individuals within each nation.

Political debates about immigration policy have been rising in volume and intensity in recent years in almost all Western economies. On the one hand, immigration is seen by many as an economic and cultural lifeline that can supply firms in key industries with skilled workers while also injecting new artistic and intellectual life into the nation. On the other hand, many people are concerned that immigrants take jobs away from local workers and create ethnic enclaves that can Balkanize a nation and lead to more crime and other social ills. These latter concerns have encouraged the recent imposition of much tighter immigration controls in many countries, while also nurturing the growth of extremist anti-immigrant political movements in several European countries and increasing the incidence of hate crimes directed toward immigrants. The debate seems certain to continue in the years ahead, and to grow fiercer.

Historically, immigration has almost always been more politically controversial than has trade. The issue is still so sensitive that tight restrictions on immigration are nearly universal. Again, as with limits on trade, such restrictions make little sense if we look only at the *aggregate* welfare effects of international labour flows. It is easy to demonstrate that when labour is free to migrate to countries where it can be more productive (and earn correspondingly higher wages), there will be an increase in total world output of goods and services (see Krugman and Obstfeld 2000: ch. 7). And total output must also increase in any economy that allows more immigrants to enter. This expansion in production makes it possible, in principle, for everyone to enjoy higher standards of living. Migration flows can actually serve the same economic purpose as trade flows, responding to price signals to improve economic efficiency. Indeed, in the standard Heckscher–Ohlin model of trade described earlier, trade is simply a function of country differences in endowments of labour and other factors, and so international movements of goods and factors are, in fact, substitutes for one another. Countries abundantly endowed with labour, such as China and India,

and in which wages are thus quite low compared to wages paid elsewhere, are not only natural suppliers of labour-intensive exports for the world market, but are also natural suppliers of labour itself (that is, emigrants).

As we already know, however, what matters most for politics is not that aggregate welfare gains are possible from exchanges (of goods or factors) between economies; what matters most is that some people gain and others lose. Which individuals are most likely to oppose immigration? Again, the standard economic analysis emphasizes the importance of the different types of productive factors—including land and capital, as above, with an additional distinction made between high-skilled labour (or 'human capital') and low-skilled or blue-collar labour. What is critical, as you will have already guessed, is the impact that immigration can have on relative supplies of factors of production in the local economy. If immigrants have low skill levels, as is typically assumed when discussing the effects of immigration in the advanced economies of Europe and North America, allowing more immigration will increase the local supply of low-skilled labour relative to other factors. The effect is to lower the real wages of all low-skilled workers, as the new arrivals price themselves into employment by accepting lower pay, while raising the real earnings for local owners of land, capital, and skills, as demand for these other factors increases. Of course, if a nation only allows *high-skilled* workers to immigrate, the effect will be lower real wages for high-skilled workers, but higher real earnings for low-skilled workers and owners of land and capital.

The basic results from this simple model of the impact of immigration—often referred to as 'factor-proportions' analysis (see Borjas *et al.* 1996; Borjas 1999)—are widely applicable. Immigration always harms local workers with similar skill levels to those of the arriving workers, while benefiting local owners of other factors. Even if we allow for high levels of trade, which can partially offset the impact of immigration as economies adjust to the change in factor supplies by importing less of some goods that can now be produced locally at a lower cost, the effects are always in the same direction—although they may become very small in size, and even disappear altogether, if the local economy is small relative to other economies (Leamer and Levinsohn 1995). The effects are even generally the same if we allow that the skills of workers can be highly 'specific' to particular industries, though the impact of immigration on earnings will be larger for high-skilled (specific) workers in some industries than in others. Any inflow of unskilled labour will be especially valuable for high-skilled workers in sectors that use unskilled labour more intensively, for example, but it will still benefit all high-skilled workers since output (and demand for their skills) will rise in each industry. Conversely, an inflow of any type of high-skilled labour will generate the largest decline in earnings for high-skilled workers in the same industry (those who own the same specific skills as the immigrants). But it will also hurt high-skilled workers in other industries in the local economy whose earnings will suffer, albeit in a relatively minor way, as demand for their types of specific skills falls in response to the expansion taking place in the industry into which the skilled immigrants have moved.

So, again, we have a very simple and generally applicable way of identifying the policy preferences of individuals. Individuals can be expected to oppose any policy that would permit immigration of foreign workers with similar skill levels, but they will support other types of immigration. Individuals who make their living from ownership of land and capital are likely to be the strongest supporters of more open immigration laws. If we look at the political debates over immigration laws in particular countries, the alignment of organized interests often seems to fit with these expectations. The most vocal opposition to changes in immigration laws that would permit more

low-skilled immigration often comes from labour unions representing blue-collar workers. In the United States, for example, the AFL–CIO has traditionally taken a very tough stance in favour of restrictive immigration laws and border control measures aimed at stemming illegal immigration into the country from Mexico (Tichenor 2002: 209). American business and farm associations have taken a very different position, often lobbying for more lenient treatment of illegal immigrants and for larger quotas in various non-immigrant working visa categories. In similar fashion, trade union federations in Britain, France, and Germany have raised protests about enlargement of the European Union and the possible influx of low-skilled workers into their economies from new member countries in Southern and Eastern Europe. Organizations representing high-skilled workers have not shied away from immigration politics either, often lobbying to restrict inflows of immigrants with skills that match their own and would thus pose a competitive threat in the local labour market—the American Medical Association, for example, the organization that represents doctors in the United States, has pushed hard to limit the number of foreign doctors granted visa status while also making it more difficult for them to obtain licences to practise (see Box 4.2).

This simple approach to the political economy of immigration restrictions is very useful, at least as a first step towards understanding the political forces that are likely to shape policy outcomes. It is extremely

---

BOX 4.2

The 'New World' Closes Its Doors to Immigrants

Beginning in the 1840s and 1850s, there was a huge surge in emigration from England, Ireland, and other parts of Europe and Asia to the 'New World' economies in North and South America and Australasia, where labour was relatively scarce and wage rates comparatively high. The rudimentary border controls and open policy towards immigrants in these frontier economies meant that labour flows responded quite quickly to economic events—and, in particular, to gold rushes and other 'booms' associated with the construction of railways and the birth of new industries. Over time, however, as labour unions became more organized and politically influential in the New World economies, greater restrictions were imposed on immigration. The political pressure for limits on immigration became

especially strong during economic recessions, when local rates of unemployment often rose swiftly, and labour groups blamed new immigrants for taking jobs away from 'native' workers (see Goldin 1994). Between the 1880s and the 1920s, all the New World economies gradually closed themselves off to immigration (see O'Rourke and Williamson 1999). In the United States, the first bans were imposed on Chinese immigrants in 1882, and then on all Asian immigrants in 1917, when a tough literacy test was also introduced as a way of limiting inflows of low-skilled workers. In 1921, the Emergency Quota Act placed severe restrictions on all new arrivals. The strongest political support for these measures came from north-eastern states with highly urbanized populations working in manufacturing industries, where labour unions were particularly well organized and vocal.

difficult, however, to analyse the politics of immigration without examining non-economic concerns among individuals related to questions of culture and identity. Immigration policy, after all, has a profound impact on who makes up the nation itself. In this way, it is quite different from trade policy. A great deal of research suggests that divisions among individuals over immigration policy are most strongly related to fundamental differences in cultural values associated with ethnic and racial tolerance and cosmopolitanism (e.g. Espenshade and Calhoun 1993; Citrin *et al.* 1997; McLaren 2001; Hainmueller and Hiscox 2007; Hainmueller, Hiscox, and Margalit 2015). This question of whether preferences related to non-economic issues have a profound effect on attitudes towards foreign economic policies is one that we shall return to later.

Foreign investment

Capital can also move from one country to another. These movements usually do not take the form of a physical relocation of some existing buildings and machinery from a site in one nation to another site abroad (the equivalent to worker migration). Instead, they take the form of financial transactions between citizens of different nations that transfer ownership rights over assets: a firm in one country buys facilities abroad that it can operate as a subsidiary, for example, or individuals in one country buy shares in foreign companies, or a bank in one country lends money to foreign firms. All such transactions increase the stock of capital available for productive use in one country, and decrease the stock of capital in another country.

The dramatic increase in the volume of international capital flows since the 1960s, outstripping the increase in trade, has had a profound impact on the international economy. Short-term flows of capital in the form of **portfolio investment** (purchases of company shares and other forms of securities, including government bonds), which can change direction quite rapidly in response to news and speculation about changing macroeconomic conditions and possible adjustments in exchange rates, have had a major impact on the choices governments can make when it comes to monetary and exchange rate policies (see Pauly, Chapter 9 in this volume). Longer-term capital flows in the form of 'direct foreign investment' (where the purchase of foreign assets by a firm based in one country gives it ownership control of a firm located on foreign soil), have perhaps been even more

politically controversial since the activities of these multinational firms have had major and highly visible effects in the host nations in which they manage affiliates (see Thun, Chapter 7 in this volume). Many critics of multinational corporations fear that the economic leverage enjoyed by these firms, especially in small, developing nations, can undermine national policies aimed at improving environmental standards and human rights. The political debate over direct foreign investment is thus highly charged.

Tight restrictions on both short- and long-term investment by foreigners have been quite common historically, although the controls have been much less strict than those typically imposed on immigration. Clearly, these controls cannot be motivated by a desire for economic efficiency. If such controls are removed and capital is allowed to move freely to those locations in which it is used most productively (and where it will be rewarded, as a result, with higher earnings), it is easy to show that the total output of goods and services will be increased in both the country to which the capital is flowing and in the world economy as a whole. Again, this expansion in aggregate production makes it possible, in principle, to raise the standard of living for people everywhere. International investment, just like the migration of workers examined earlier, can serve the same economic purpose that is otherwise served by trade. International flows of capital substitute for the exports of capital-intensive goods and services in the benchmark Heckscher–Ohlin model. In general, then, we can expect that the advanced industrial economies of Europe and the United States, which have abundant local supplies of capital for investment, and in which rates of return on capital are thus quite low compared with earnings elsewhere, are the natural suppliers of capital (as well as capital-intensive goods) to poorer nations, in which capital is in relatively scarce supply (see Box 4.3).

One point worth making here about the likely direction of capital flows concerns the distinction between lending and portfolio flows of capital and direct foreign investment (see Ravenhill, Chapter 1 in this volume). It is reasonable to imagine that the former types of international investment are driven purely by the quest to maximize (risk-adjusted) rates of return on capital, in line with the Heckscher–Ohlin model. With the caveat that capital-poor developing countries are often politically unstable, and high levels of risk can deter investors, we should, nevertheless, expect large flows of capital from the industrial nations to the developing world. It is much less clear

BOX 4.3

Investment, Imperialism, and the 'Race for Africa'

Beginning in the 1870s, vast quantities of investment capital flowed from the centres of finance in Western Europe to the rest of the world, providing the capital necessary to develop railways and telegraph networks, ports, and new mining industries in eastern and central Europe, the Americas, and much of Asia. In the following decade, the political context in which these foreign investments were made began to change drastically as an intense race developed among the major powers for political control of territories in Africa and Eastern Asia. Governments in Britain, France, Germany, and Belgium made imperial expansion in these regions their most urgent foreign policy priority. Seizing political control of territories in which there was often no clear or stable governing authority, or

at least not one capable of defending the area from conquest by outside force, was a way to safeguard the investments that were being made in these territories (mostly in the production of raw materials, such as cotton, silk, rubber, vegetable oils, and other products of tropical climates, as well as railways and ports, that were all very vulnerable to seizure). These imperial policies were supported most strongly by financial interests and conservative parties, typically backed by commercial and shipping industries as well, and by military leaders anxious about the security implications of falling behind rivals in the control of strategic territories and ports. British economist, J. A. Hobson (1902/1948), and following him, Lenin (1917/1996), famously interpreted the imperial expansion of this time as the natural consequence of owners of capital needing access to new investment opportunities overseas; imperialism was, in Hobson's terms, 'excessive capital in search of investment'.

that economy-wide differences in rates of return are critical for explaining patterns in direct foreign investment. There is certainly a considerable amount of direct investment by European, American, and Japanese firms in developing nations, with many firms setting up a 'vertical' multinational structure of enterprises that locates land or labour-intensive parts of the production process in developing nations. But the vast bulk of direct foreign investment in the modern world economy, in fact, takes the form of capital flows between the industrial economies themselves, with firms creating 'horizontal' structures in which similar functions are performed in facilities in different locations (see Graham and Krugman 1995: 36). This type of investment does not fit well with the standard Heckscher–Ohlin predictions based on factor endowments, and is best explained instead by the special advantages that firms in some industries gain by jumping borders (and trade barriers), and by internalizing transactions within the firm itself. Firms that rely heavily on specialized technologies, and management and marketing expertise, may have a hard time selling these kinds of intangible assets to foreign companies it would like to work with as suppliers or distributors; instead, it may make far more sense to keep all these relationships within the firm (see Hymer 1976; Caves 1982). Many of these types of horizontal multinational firms also appear to have been established to secure access to foreign markets into which they might not otherwise be able to sell because they faced trade barriers. This

'tariff-jumping' motive was a big factor in motivating Japanese auto firms to set up manufacturing facilities in both Europe and North America beginning in the 1980s. The implication is that there is often a strong connection between the effects of trade policies and investment (and investment restrictions), a topic we shall return to in the final section of the chapter (see also Thun, Chapter 7 in this volume).

Now, putting aside the aggregate welfare gains that the international movement of capital makes possible, which individuals are likely to benefit from such capital flows, and which individuals will lose out? Here, we can simply apply the logic of the same 'factor-proportions' approach we used earlier to outline the effects of immigration. We might distinguish between different types of capital, in the same way that we distinguished between low- and high-skilled labour above, and set apart lending and short-term or portfolio investment flows from direct foreign investment. But to keep things simple here, we shall just consider them all as a single form of capital. What is critical here, of course, is the impact that inflows of any foreign capital have on relative supplies of factors of production in the local economy. Allowing more inflows of capital from abroad will increase the local supply of capital relative to other factors, and thus lower real returns for local owners of capital. At the same time, inflows of investment will raise the real earnings of local owners of land and labour by increasing demand for these other factors of production.

Again, even allowing for the fact that trade flows can partially offset the impact of international movements of factors of production—economies may adjust by importing lower quantities of some goods that are now less costly to produce at home—the direction of the effects on the incomes of different groups is always the same. Local owners of capital are disadvantaged by inflows of foreign capital; while local landowners and workers (in all categories) are better off. These effects may diminish in size in cases in which the local economy is small relative to others, as we noted earlier when discussing the income effects of immigration, but they are always working in the same direction. And, again, in parallel with the analysis of immigration flows, these income effects are not affected drastically by allowing that capital can take forms that are highly 'specific' to particular industries—though the effects may be larger for owners of some types of capital than others. This is especially relevant when we think about direct foreign investment, which typically involves the relocation of a particular set of manufacturing or marketing activities that require very specific types of technologies in a particular industry. An inflow of any type of specific capital will, of course, result in a decline in earnings for local owners of capital in the same industry; it will also hurt all others who own specific types of capital used in different industries—in a more marginal way, of course—as demand for their assets will fall in response to the expansion taking place in the industry favoured by foreign investment.

We can thus expect that policies allowing greater inflows of foreign capital will be strongly opposed by individuals who own capital in the local economy, but such policies will be supported by local landowners and workers. There is some evidence that does fit well with these basic predictions. Perhaps the best example involves the way European and American auto companies have supported restrictions on the operations of local affiliates of their Japanese rivals since the 1980s. In Europe, auto firms pushed hard for an agreement with Japan that included cars produced in Japanese affiliates within the limits set on the total Japanese market share of the European auto market. In the United States, after some initial hesitation (perhaps reflecting the fact that they had themselves set up numerous foreign transplant firms around the world), the US auto firms supported a variety of proposals for 'domestic content' laws that would have placed local affiliates of Japanese auto makers at a considerable disadvantage by disrupting their relationships with parts suppliers at home (Crystal 2003). The 'big three' American firms (Ford, General Motors, and Chrysler) also seized the opportunity to demand high local content requirements in the **rules of origin** for autos in the negotiations over the 1993 North American Free Trade Agreement, ensuring that they would have a major advantage over Japanese transplants producing cars in Mexico for the North American market. Interestingly, the workers we would expect to be strongly supportive of incoming Japanese investment in the auto industry, represented by the United Auto Workers union, were in fact quite lukewarm—perhaps because they had long advocated that tough domestic content rules be applied to American firms, to prevent them from transplanting their parts manufacturing facilities to Canada and Mexico, and perhaps also in response to concerns that the foreign transplants setting up in southern American states such as Tennessee (Nissan) and Kentucky (Toyota) were not employing union members.

Foreign investment tends to be even more politically controversial in developing nations, where the behaviour of large foreign corporations can have profound effects on the local economy and on local politics. One particular concern among critics of multinational firms has been the role that several large corporations have apparently played in supporting authoritarian governments that have restricted political organization among labour groups, limited growth in wage rates, and permitted firms to mistreat workers and pollute the environment (see Evans 1979; Klein 2002). While the evidence is not very clear, in some cases, local owners of capital may well have muted their opposition to investments by foreign firms in order to support authoritarian policies adopted by military regimes: in Nigeria, for example, where Shell (the European oil company) has long been the major foreign investor, or more recently in Myanmar, where Unocal (an American oil and gas firm) is the key foreign player. But the basic competitive tension between local capitalists and foreign firms (whose entry into the economy bids down local profits) is typically very obvious even in these unstable and non-democratic environments, as local firms have often encouraged their governments to impose severe restrictions on foreign investments, including onerous regulations stipulating that foreign firms use local rather than imported inputs, exclusion from key sectors of the economy, and even nationalization (seizure) of firms' assets (Jenkins

1987: 172). Newer evidence suggests that, as we might expect given the preferences of labour in capital-poor developing nations, left-wing governments backed by organized labour have made the strongest efforts to lure foreign firms to make investments (Pinto 2003).

So far, we have considered only the issue of whether governments relax restrictions on *inflows* of foreign capital. Of course, governments can and often do act to influence how much investment flows out of their economies. And the same holds for labour flows, as governments often try to affect *emigration* as well as immigration—many governments, in countries as diverse as Australia, Canada, and India, are worried about a 'brain drain' of skilled workers and professionals, for example, and have adopted a range of policies to discourage or tax such labour flows. But the issue of outward direct investment, often involving the 'outsourcing' of jobs by multinational firms to their affiliates in labour-abundant (low-wage) nations, has become an especially salient political issue recently in Europe and the United States. The political divisions over the issue are largely what we expect from the factor-proportions theory: those who own capital are strongly opposed to any restrictions on their ability to invest it abroad in order to earn higher profits, but restrictions on outward investment are strongly supported by local workers, who understand that capital outflows will reduce their real earnings. In the United States, for example, the most ardent advocates of legislation that would raise the tax burden on profits earned abroad by American corporations has been the AFL–CIO and those workers among its membership that have been hit hardest by outsourcing (for example, labour unions in the textile and auto industries). Interestingly, these labour unions have often had support from environmental and human rights groups concerned that competition among developing countries to attract new investments from multinational firms may produce a **race to the bottom** in environmental and labour standards. Coalitions of labour unions and human rights groups have waged campaigns to try to force US corporations to adhere to strict codes of conduct abroad. We shall discuss these types of multi-issue political coalitions below.

Exchange rates

Of course, a critical difference between transactions that take place between individuals living in the same country and transactions between people in different countries is that the latter require that people can convert one national currency into another. If a firm in Australia wants to import DVDs from a film studio in the United States, for example, it will need to exchange its Australian dollars for US dollars to pay the American company. The rate at which this conversion takes place will obviously affect the transaction: the more Australian dollars it takes to buy the number of US dollars required (the price of the DVDs), the more costly are the imports for movie-loving Australian buyers. All the trade and investment transactions taking place every day in the world economy are affected by the rates at which currencies are exchanged.

Before the First World War, almost all governments fixed the value of their currency in terms of gold, thereby creating an international monetary system in which all rates of conversion between individual currencies were held constant (for further discussion of this international **gold standard**, see Ravenhill, Box 1.4 in this volume). Between the Second World War and 1973, most currencies were fixed in value to the US dollar, the most important currency in the postwar world economy. In this system, often referred to as the **Bretton Woods** system (see Ravenhill, Box 1.5 in this volume), the United States agreed to guarantee the value of the dollar by committing to exchange dollars for gold at a set price of $35 per ounce. Since 1973, when the Nixon administration officially abandoned the fixed rate between the dollar and gold, all the major currencies have essentially been allowed to fluctuate freely in value in world financial markets (see Helleiner, Chapter 8 in this volume). Among developing nations, however, many governments continue to fix the value of their currency in terms of dollars or another of the major currencies (see Frieden *et al.* 2001). And groups of nations in different regions of the world, including the members of the European Union, have made separate efforts to stabilize exchange rates at the regional level, even progressing to the adoption of a common regional currency.

The fundamental choice each government must make involves deciding whether to allow the value of the national currency to fluctuate freely in response to market demand and supply, or instead fix the value of the currency in terms of some other currency or external standard—typically, the currency of a major trading partner or, as was common in the past, gold (a precious metal valued highly in most societies throughout history). When a government chooses to fix the value of the national currency, it sets the official rate of exchange and commits itself to buy the currency at that fixed rate when requested to by private actors or foreign governments. Between a 'pure float' and a fixed exchange rate there are intermediate options: a government can choose a target value for the exchange rate and only allow the currency to fluctuate in value within some range around the target rate. The wider this range, of course, the more policy approximates floating the currency (see Box 4.4).

When it comes to trade, immigration, and investment, economists agree almost universally on the policy choice that is best for maximizing national (and world) output, and hence general standards of living: removing barriers to all types of international exchange is optimal, because it allows resources to be allocated in the most productive way. There is no similar consensus, however, on the best approach to currency policy. Fixing the exchange rate has both pros and cons, and it is not always clear which are larger. By eliminating fluctuations in the exchange rate, fixing makes international trade and investment less costly for firms and individuals, since they will not need to worry that the benefits from these international transactions will be affected adversely by some sudden, unexpected shift in exchange rates. By doing away with exchange rate risk, fixing allows the economy to benefit more fully from international trade and investment. But what is the downside? What does the government give up by pledging to buy or sell its own currency on request at the official rate of exchange? The answer, in short, is control over **monetary policy**.

A nation's monetary policy regulates the supply of money (and the associated cost of credit) in order to manage aggregate levels of economic activity, and hence levels of inflation and unemployment. Governments typically use monetary policy to counter economic cycles: they expand the supply of money and lower the cost of credit during recessions to increase economic activity and promote job creation, and restrict the supply of money and raise the cost of borrowing during 'booms' to slow economic activity and control inflation. When a government commits to fixing the exchange rate, it effectively gives up the ability to tailor monetary policy to manage domestic economic conditions. To see why, just imagine what happens to money supply if, at the given exchange rate, the nation's residents spend more on foreign goods, services and assets in any given period than foreigners buy from firms and individuals in that nation: the country's **balance of payments**, which registers the

BOX 4.4

The Politics of the Rising Dollar

Between 1980 and 1985, the US dollar rose by approximately 50 per cent in value against the Japanese yen and by roughly similar amounts against the German Deutschmark and the British pound. The rapid dollar appreciation placed immense strain on US producers of traded goods and services, and by 1985 the Reagan government was being lobbied strenuously by a large variety of groups asking for some kind of action to halt the rise (see Destler and Henning 1989). The strongest pressure came from groups in a broad collection of export-oriented sectors, including grain farmers, firms such as IBM and Motorola in the computer industry, and Caterpillar, a large exporter of construction equipment and machinery. The voices of these exporters were swelled by protests coming from firms in import-competing industries, including the major auto companies and the steel-makers. The initial reaction from the Reagan administration was to sit tight and characterize the rise of the dollar as a sign that the rest of the world held the United States and its economy in high esteem. The government had set a course to restrain inflation when entering office in 1981, and had raised US interest rates considerably. Taking action to devalue the dollar would have thrown into substantial doubt this commitment to defeat inflation. After their initial pleas were rebuffed by the White House, however, many groups from the steel, auto, and textiles industries began demanding new forms of trade protection instead, bombarding Congress with calls for trade barriers that would make up for the competitive effects of the dollar appreciation. It was this threat of runaway protectionism in Congress that finally prompted the government to take action on the dollar. In 1985, the White House reached an agreement with the governments of Japan, Germany, Britain, and France, which became known as the Plaza Accord (a reference to the lavish New York hotel in which it was negotiated). This deal provided for a cooperative effort to manage a gradual depreciation of the dollar against the other currencies, with each government agreeing to alter its macroeconomic policies in such a way as to ease demand for the dollar compared with other currencies (for example, the Reagan government agreed to lower interest rates and to make a new effort to reduce the size of the US budget deficit). By giving up some control over macroeconomic policy, in coordination with other governments, the White House was able to reverse the rise of the dollar and ease the strain imposed on US producers of traded goods and services.

value of all transactions with the rest of the world, will be in deficit. This means that that there is less overall demand for the country's currency than for the currencies of other countries (needed for residents to buy foreign products and assets). To satisfy this excess demand for foreign currencies and to maintain the exchange rate at the fixed level, the government will be a net buyer of its own currency, selling off its reserves of foreign currencies (or gold). The automatic effect of maintaining the fixed exchange rate in these conditions, then, is to reduce the total supply of the nation's money in circulation and slow domestic economic activity. Just the opposite should occur when the nation runs a balance of payments surplus: excess demand for its currency compared to other currencies will require that the government increases the supply of its money in circulation, thus stimulating economic activity.

In effect, then, fixing the value of the currency makes monetary policy a hostage to exchange rate policy. Even if a government sets the exchange rate at a level that it hopes will generate no balance of payments deficits or surpluses, since the balance of international transactions in any period will depend heavily on external economic conditions and events in foreign countries, it has very little control. A recession abroad, for example, will reduce purchases of a nation's products by foreigners and lead to a deficit in the balance of payments, and so, if currency values are fixed firmly, this recession will be 'transmitted' to the home nation by the subsequent reduction in its money supply.

The crux of the choice between fixed and floating exchange rates is the choice between stability and policy control: a stable exchange rate will increase the economic benefits attainable from international trade and investment, but this requires giving up the ability to adjust monetary policy to suit domestic economic conditions. Governments in the most advanced economies have generally decided that policy control is more important to them than exchange rate stability, at least since the early 1970s. Governments in smaller, developing nations have mainly chosen exchange rate stability over policy control. In part, this is because these countries tend to rely more heavily on trade and foreign investment as sources of economic growth. This choice is also more attractive for governments in smaller countries trying to defeat chronic inflation. Government promises to deal with runaway inflation in these countries may not be regarded as credible by private actors if governments in the past have shown a tendency to act irresponsibly (for example, by printing and spending large amounts of money) when facing electoral challenges. Since the expectations that private actors have about government policy feed directly into the prices (and wages) set, inflationary expectations can have devastating effects. In such circumstances, fixing the nation's currency in terms of the currency of a major trading partner with a comparatively low rate of inflation can serve an important function, providing a way for the government to commit itself more credibly to a low-inflation monetary policy. In essence, by committing to keep the exchange rate fixed, the government is ceding control of monetary policy in a very clear and visible way, and anchoring inflation at home to the inflation rate in the partner country (see Giavazzi and Pagano 1988; Broz and Frieden 2001).

In terms of the effects on aggregate welfare, the wisdom of fixing exchange rates is thus not always crystal clear. The best or most preferred policy for different sets of individuals within each country can similarly be difficult to identify. Consider first the case in which we assume that factors of production are mobile between sectors in the domestic economy (they are not 'specific' to particular sectors), and so we can apply the logic of the Stolper–Samuelson theorem and factor-proportions analysis. Since exchange rate volatility serves, in effect, as an added barrier or cost to international trade and investment flows, we have a place to begin when trying to map the policy preferences of individuals: in each economy, owners of locally abundant factors are more likely to support a fixed exchange rate, while owners of locally scarce factors are more likely to prefer a floating rate. In the capital-abundant, labour-scarce advanced economies of Europe and the United States, we might thus expect a simple class division over exchange rate policy: fixed rates benefit owners of capital at the expense of workers. We could expect the reverse alignment of class interests in the labour-abundant, capital-scarce economies of, say, China and India. In such countries, greater exchange rate certainty should encourage more trade and greater inflows of foreign investment, and both types of international flows will benefit workers at the expense of local owners of capital.

But, here, we cannot think about exchange rate stability without also thinking about monetary policy control. In general, workers might be expected to oppose fixed exchange rates in most circumstances, since they are likely to bear greater costs than others when monetary policy can no longer be used to avert economic downturns resulting in higher levels of unemployment. Owners of capital, on the other hand, care less about unemployment rates than they do about keeping inflation in check, which is typically much easier for the government to achieve (as noted earlier) when monetary policy is committed to keeping the exchange rate fixed. Just as in the case for the nation as whole, then, owners of labour and owners of capital may have to make a difficult choice about where they stand in terms of the trade-off between the effects of greater currency stability and less monetary policy control. In contemporary, labour-scarce Europe, for example, workers would seem to be better off along both dimensions if exchange rates were more flexible, while owners of capital should prefer fixed rates. There is some evidence that fits in with this interpretation. Labour unions in Western European countries generally provided the most vocal opposition to government policies aimed at fixing or stabilizing exchange rates in the 1970s and 1980s, particularly in France and Italy. But the record is mixed. While the labour-backed Socialist government that came to power in France in 1981 initially abandoned exchange rate stability as a goal, by 1983 it was committed to a fixed currency peg (see Oatley 1997). In fact, during the interwar period in Europe, left-wing governments tended to keep their currencies fixed to the gold standard longer than other governments (Simmons 1994). And looking across a broader range of countries, in which labour is the locally abundant factor and capital is scarce, the preferences of these broad classes of individuals when it comes to exchange rates becomes even more difficult to predict.

Perhaps one major reason why it is difficult to find compelling evidence to support simple class-based interpretations of exchange rate politics is that individuals tend to see things very differently depending on the industries in which they are employed and invested. If we allow, as in previous discussions above, that factors of production are typically very specific to particular industries, we get a very different picture of the alignment of individual preferences on the exchange rate issue. And the picture is also much clearer. Individuals employed or invested in sectors that invest or sell in foreign markets are likely to favour exchange rate stability, since fluctuations in rates impose costs on their international transactions and because they have a relatively small economic stake in domestic (versus foreign) macroeconomic conditions. Those individuals associated with firms and banks that invest heavily in foreign markets, for example, and export-oriented sectors that sell a large proportion of their output abroad, should thus tend to support fixed exchange rates. On the other hand, owners and employees in import-competing industries and those producing non-traded services (for example, building, transportation, sales) whose incomes depend overwhelmingly on domestic economic conditions, are likely to favour flexible exchange rates that allow the government more control over monetary policy. There is some compelling evidence supporting these predictions, especially in the debates over exchange rate policy in the most advanced economies. In Europe in recent decades, for example, the strongest support for fixing exchange rates (and ultimately, for creating a common European currency) has come from the international banks, multinational firms in a diverse range of industries (including auto firms such as BMW and Mercedes), and from export-oriented sectors. The strongest opposition to fixed rates has tended to come from owners and labour unions associated with import-competing industries such as coal, steel, and textiles, especially in nations such as France and Italy that have battled relatively high rates of inflation (see Frieden 1994). In developing nations, recent studies have indicated that governments are more likely to float their currency when the import-competing manufacturing sector accounts for a large proportion of the local economy (Frieden et al. 2001).

Finally, when a government does decide to fix or stabilize its currency, it must also decide the level at which to set the exchange rate. Whether the currency should be 'stronger' (that is, take a higher value versus other currencies) or 'weaker' (a lower value) is a second, important dimension of exchange rate policy. Even when the currency is floating, in fact, if it happens to move strongly in one direction or another, the issue can become a salient one, since the government may be called upon to intervene in an effort to raise or lower the exchange rate towards some new target. What is interesting in this regard is that the alignment of the various groups in terms of preferences for fixing versus floating the currency are not quite the same as the way they are positioned on the issue of the actual rate that should be set or targeted. A stronger currency will harm those in both export-oriented and import-competing industries, since it will make their products less attractive to consumers relative to the foreign alternatives. Individuals in these sectors should prefer a weaker currency. But a weaker currency will harm all others in the local economy by eroding their purchasing power when it comes to buying foreign goods and services. Owners and employees in non-traded sectors should prefer a stronger currency, as should any multinational firms or international banks that are investing abroad and purchasing foreign assets (Frieden 1994). In the real world of politics, in cases in which the level of a nation's exchange rate has, in fact, become a salient political issue, these types of coalitions do appear to emerge. Devaluation of the US dollar became a major election issue in the 1890s, for example, with the rise of the Populist movement, supported predominantly by export-oriented farmers who demanded a break from the gold standard in order tó reset the dollar exchange rate at a lower level. The Populists were opposed most strongly by banking and commercial interests in the north-eastern states, who favoured a strong dollar (see Frieden 1997).

KEY POINTS

- According to the Stolper–Samuelson theorem, trade benefits those who own the factors of production with which the economy is relatively well endowed, and hurts owners of scarce factors.

- In the alternative 'specific factors' model, individuals employed or invested in export industries are the ones who benefit from trade, while those who are attached to import-competing industries are disadvantaged.

- The leading research assumes that the specific factors approach is the most appropriate way to think about the effects of trade in the contemporary advanced economies.

- Immigration harms the real earnings of local workers with similar skill levels to those of the arriving workers, while benefiting everyone else in the host country.

- Inflows of foreign capital will hurt individuals who own capital in the local economy, while benefiting all local landowners and workers.

- Individuals attached to firms and banks that invest abroad or export a large proportion of their output are likely to favour a fixed exchange rate. On the other hand, owners and employees in import-competing industries and those producing non-traded services are likely to favour a flexible exchange rate.

- A stronger currency will harm those in both export-oriented *and* import-competing industries, while benefiting all others in the local economy.

Institutions

Once we have specified the preferences of different individuals and groups on any particular issue, we need to think about how much influence they will have over policy outcomes. This is where political institutions come in to play. Political institutions establish the rules by which policy is made, and thus how the policy preferences of different groups are weighed in the process that determines the policy outcome. It is appropriate here to start with the broadest types of rules first, and consider the formal mechanisms by which governments and representatives in legislative bodies are elected (or otherwise come to power). These broad features of the institutional environment have large effects on all types of policies. But, then, we can move on to discuss more specific aspects of the legislative process and administrative agencies that have implications for the formulation and implementation of trade, immigration, investment, and exchange rate policies.

Elections and representation

Perhaps it is best to start with the observation that the general relationship between democratization and foreign economic policymaking is a matter that is still open to considerable theoretical and empirical doubt. Part of the puzzle is that there is a great deal of variation in the levels of economic openness we have observed among autocratic nations. In autocratic regimes, the orientation of policy will depend on the particular desires and motivations of the (non-elected) leadership, and there are different theoretical approaches to this issue. Non-elected governments could pursue trade and investment liberalization, on the one hand, if they calculate that this will increase their own power or wealth (for example, through taxation) by increasing national economic output. Such policies may be easier to adopt because autocratic leaders are more insulated than their democratic counterparts from the political demands made by any organized domestic groups that favour trade protection and limits on foreign investment (Haggard 1990). Perhaps this is an apt description of the state of affairs in China, as it has been opening its economy gradually to trade and investment since the 1980s, and non-democratic governments in Taiwan and South Korea pursued trade liberalization even more rapidly in the 1960s. On the other hand, autocratic governments may draw political support from small, powerful groups that favour trade protection. Many such governments appear to have used trade and investment barriers in ways that were aimed at consolidating their rule (Wintrobe 1998). The experience in Sub-Saharan African nations since the 1960s, and in Pakistan and Myanmar, seems to fit this mould. Without a detailed assessment of the particular groups upon which a particular authoritarian regime depends for political backing, it is quite difficult to make predictions about likely policy outcomes under non-democratic rule.

In formal democracies that hold real elections, the most fundamental set of political rules is the set that defines which individuals get to vote. If the franchise law gives more weight to one side in a policy contest compared to others, it can obviously have a great impact on policy outcomes. Where only those who own land can vote, for example, agricultural interests will be privileged in the policymaking process. If this landowning elite favours trade protection, as it did in Britain in the years before the Great Reform Act of 1832, then such a policy is almost certain to be held firmly in place. By shifting political power away from landowners and towards urban owners of capital and labour, extensions of the franchise had a major impact on all forms of economic policy during the late nineteenth and early twentieth centuries in Europe, America, and elsewhere. In England, the extension of voting power to the middle and working classes, achieved in the reforms of 1832 and 1867, had the effect of making free trade politically invincible—with a huge block of workers along with the urban business class supporting trade openness, and only a tiny fraction of the electorate (the traditional rural elites) against it, a government that endorsed tariffs or restrictions on investment would have been committing electoral suicide. In the United States and Australia, on the other hand, where labour and capital were in relatively scarce supply, the elimination of property qualifications for voting and the extension of suffrage had exactly the opposite effect, empowering a larger block of urban voters who favoured high tariffs. In general, extensions of the franchise to urban classes tend to produce more open policies toward trade, immigration, and investment in labour and capital-abundant countries, but more closed or protectionist policies in labour- and capital-scarce economies.

The precise rules by which representatives are elected to national legislatures are the next critical feature of the institutional environment. Scholars have suggested that, in parliamentary systems in which legislative seats are apportioned among parties according to the proportion of votes they receive ('proportional representation'), narrowly organized groups have far less impact on policymaking in general than they do in electoral systems in which individual seats are decided by the plurality rule (see Rogowski 1987). Parliamentary systems with proportional representation tend to encourage the formation of strong, cohesive political parties which appeal to a national constituency and have less to gain in electoral terms by responding to localized and particularistic demands in marginal or contested districts (McGillivray 1997). Other types of systems, in contrast, tend to encourage intra-party competition among individual politicians and the development of a 'personal vote' in each particular electoral district, and are thus more conducive to interest-group lobbying. The implications for foreign economic policies are usually spelt out in very clear terms: we expect that proportional representation systems with strong political parties (for example, Sweden) will typically produce lower levels of trade protection and other restrictions than alternative types of electoral systems (for example, Britain, the United States) in which particular local and regional interests have a greater influence.

These conclusions about the impact of particularistic groups in different types of electoral systems rest upon a critical insight derived from theoretical work on collective action in trade politics: that there is a fundamental asymmetry between the lobbying pressure generated from groups seeking protectionist policies, and the lobbying pressure that comes from groups who oppose such restrictions. The main reason for this is that restrictions on imports and other types of exchange, when imposed one at a time, tend to have very uneven effects. As we know from the analysis of the specific factors model earlier, the benefits of a tariff on a particular good are concentrated on the owners of capital and labour engaged in that particular industry. If the tariff is substantial, these benefits are likely to be quite large as a share of the incomes of those individuals, and thus they will typically be willing to spend a good deal of their time and energy (and savings) lobbying to ensure they get the tariff they want. The stakes are very high for them. In contrast, the costs of the tariff are shared among all the owners of other types of specific factors in the economy; they are dispersed so broadly, in fact, that they tend to be quite small as a fraction of the incomes of these individuals. Thus, it is unlikely that those hurt by the new tariff will be prepared to devote resources to lobbying against the policy proposal. Collective political action will always be much easier to organize in the relatively small groups that benefit from a particular trade restriction than in the much larger groups (the rest of the economy) that are hurt by the restriction (see Olson 1965). Perhaps the best example of this logic is the extraordinary political power that has been demonstrated by the small, highly organized agricultural groups in Europe, the United States, and Japan since the 1950s. These groups, which together represent a tiny fraction of the population in each political system, have been able to win extremely high (if not prohibitive) rates of protection from imports and lavish subsidies (see Tyers and Anderson 1992).

Other aspects of electoral institutions may also play a role in shaping policy outcomes (see Box 4.5). In general, smaller electoral districts in plurality systems may be expected to increase the influence of sectoral or particularistic groups over elected representatives, and thus lead to higher levels of protection (Rogoswki 1987; Alt and Gilligan 1994). In larger districts, political representatives will be forced to balance the interests of a greater variety of industry groups when making decisions about policies, and will be less affected by the demands of any particular industry lobby, and a larger share of the costs of any tariff or restriction will be 'internalized' among voters within the district. From this perspective, upper chambers of parliaments, which typically allocate seats among representatives of much larger electoral districts than those in lower chambers, tend to be less inclined toward trade protection and other types of restrictive foreign economic policies. Meanwhile, in legislative chambers in which seats are defined along political/geographical lines without regard for population (for example, in the United States Senate, where each state receives two seats), agricultural, forestry, and mining interests in underpopulated areas typically gain a great deal more influence over policymaking than they can wield in chambers (for example, the United States House of Representatives) where legislative seats are defined based on the number of voters in each district.

We have generally been focusing on trade policies, since most of the past research on the effects of

---

BOX 4.5

The Institutional Foundations of the Gold Standard

Why was the gold standard, the system of fixed exchange rates that appeared to work so well in bringing order and stability to the global economy between the 1880s and 1914, so difficult to re-establish in the 1920s? One very important reason has to do with the major changes in political institutions that took place in Western nations around the time of the First World War. The gold standard required that governments give up control of monetary policy in order to keep the value of their currencies fixed in terms of gold (and one another). In essence, macroeconomic policy was held hostage to exchange rate policy, so that currency values were stable. This was especially difficult for small economies that happened to run large balance of payments deficits at the set rates of exchange. To maintain their exchange rates, they were forced to reduce the supply of their money in circulation and raise interest rates, thereby reducing economic activity at home and increasing unemployment. If they were already in the middle of an economic recession, this meant making the downturn even worse. Governments could only follow through with this type of commitment to a fixed exchange rate if the economic costs of recession—which fell predominantly upon workers who lost jobs and income, and small businesses and farmers driven into debt—did not have direct political consequences in terms of their ability to remain in office. This changed in many nations around the start of the twentieth century, when electoral laws were reformed, extending the franchise to larger proportions of the population (including workers who had previously been denied the right to vote in many places). Around the same time, labour organizations, including trade unions and labour parties, grew in political strength in almost all the Western economies, using strikes to push for political reforms while gaining significant electoral representation for the first time. Given these profound changes in the lie of the political land, the attempts to recreate the gold standard in the interwar period appear to have been doomed from the outset. Governments elected by much broader segments of the population were increasingly unwilling to give up their ability to manage domestic economic conditions, especially during recessions, in order merely to maintain the gold parity. Eventually, after weathering several smaller crises, the system collapsed when governments began to abandon the gold standard completely after 1929 in response to the onset of the Great Depression.

institutions has tended to concentrate on tariff levels. But recent studies also suggest that differences in electoral institutions can have a significant impact on exchange rate policies. In particular, in plurality systems in which elections are all-or-nothing contests between the major parties, governments appear to be far less likely to fix exchange rates and give up control over monetary policy than governments in proportional representation systems (see Clark and Hallerberg 2000). It appears that the costs of having ceded control over monetary policy in plurality systems, should the government face an election contest during an economic slump, are much higher than elsewhere. This difference also appears to be more pronounced for governments in plurality systems, in which the timing of elections is predetermined by law (Bernhard and Leblang 1999).

Legislatures and policymaking rules

The rules that govern the way national legislatures go about making laws can have profound effects on the way the preferences of individuals and groups are aggregated into different types of foreign economic policies. These rules determine the way new policies are proposed, considered, amended, and voted upon. They structure the interactions among different legislative and executive bodies, and establish which branches have what types of agenda setting and veto power over policy.

Most of the recent research on the impact of legislative institutions on foreign economic policies has been focused on American trade policy. The point of departure for many studies is the infamous Smoot–Hawley Tariff Act of 1930, which was such a disaster that it helped to inspire a fairly radical change in the rules by which Congress has dealt with trade policy ever since. The core of the legislative problem, as many see it, is the possibility for **logrolling** or vote-trading between protectionist interests. The benefits of a tariff or trade restriction can often go to an import-competing industry located almost entirely in one electoral district, with the costs borne generally by individuals across the rest of the economy. In such cases, lobbying pressure by these industries can generate a protectionist logroll when tariffs are being set by voting among members of a legislature: each member of the legislature will propose generous protective measures for industries in his or her own district without accounting for the costs they impose on individuals elsewhere.

To gain support for these measures, each member will vote in favour of similar measures proposed by other legislators. If members can vote indefinitely on a sequence of such proposals, a policy that includes every new tariff can be the equilibrium outcome (supported by each legislator's belief that a vote against another's proposal would induce others to retaliate by offering an amendment to withdraw protection from the defector's district). The result of such unchecked logrolling is a vast array of protective measures, such that all individuals are far worse off than they were before the bill was passed (see Weingast *et al.* 1981).

According to conventional wisdom, the Smoot–Hawley tariff was just such a logrolling disaster, and Congress reacted to it in a remarkably sensible way by redesigning the rules governing the way trade policy was made. Specifically, Congress delegated to the executive branch the authority to alter US trade policy by negotiating reciprocal trade agreements with other countries. This practice of delegating negotiating authority to the president has been continued since 1934. By delegating authority over policy to the president, who would presumably set trade policy to benefit all individuals within the one, *national* electoral district, this innovation eliminated the spectre of protectionist logrolling completely, and ensured that all the costs of trade protection were fully 'internalized' by a decision-maker accountable to all voters. In addition, by empowering the president to negotiate trade agreements that elicited reciprocal tariff reductions from other countries, the change helped to mobilize support for trade liberalization among export interests who could now expect improved sales abroad as a result of tariff reductions at home.

The lessons drawn from this case are almost certainly overstated, and the conventional account has some gaping inconsistencies. In particular, there appears to have been no learning at all on the part of members of Congress between 1930 and 1934: the congressional voting records indicate that, among the members voting on both bills, almost all those who voted for Smoot–Hawley in 1930 voted against the Reciprocal Trade Agreements Act (RTAA) (see Schnietz 1994). Moreover, it is not at all clear that protectionist logrolls have been an otherwise unsolvable problem for tariff legislation in the US Congress (or elsewhere)—what of all the cases in which *liberalizing* bills were passed by legislatures in the absence of delegation? In the US Congress itself, the major acts passed by the Democrats when in control of government before the 1930s (the Wilson Tariff of 1894 and the Underwood Tariff of 1913) stand out in this regard. Examples also abound in the legislative histories of other Western democracies. It should not be a mystery as to why. In parliamentary systems, political parties play critical roles in controlling the legislative agenda. In proportional representation systems these parties compete for a share of the national vote, and so legislation designed to appease district-specific interests holds little appeal. Even in plurality rule systems, however, the majority party that forms a government typically imposes strict control over the policy agenda in a way that prevents such self-defeating logrolls. Finally, the notion that presidents, simply by dint of having a large (national) constituency, must be champions of freer trade is hopelessly ahistorical. Here, again, we cannot ignore the critical role played by political parties. In the US case, the Republican base of support between the 1840s and 1940s was concentrated among manufacturing interests in the north-east and Midwest states and was staunchly protectionist, and a long list of Republican presidents championed high tariffs in

election campaigns and backed the most protectionist of Republican tariff bills in Congress (see Hiscox 1999). More generally, in all the Western democracies, political parties typically have very distinct core constituencies among the electorate, defined in regional or class terms, to whom they are principally accountable when designing policies. Whether a government allows protectionist amendments during legislative deliberations of policy, and whether a president supports trade liberalization, will depend on their partisan affiliation and the preferences of their party's core electoral base.

Despite the distortions, the story of the RTAA still holds some valuable lessons for thinking about ways in which legislative rules can affect foreign economic policies (see Box 4.6). The explicit institutional connection that the RTAA forged between tariff reductions at home and reciprocal reductions in tariffs abroad certainly played a role in generating increased support for trade policy reform among export-oriented industries, and thus made it easier for all policymakers to support trade liberalization. This link is now more-or-less

---

BOX 4.6

The Reciprocal Trade Agreements Act of 1934 (RTAA)

In 1930, the US Congress passed the infamous Smoot–Hawley Tariff Act, which raised import duties on a vast array of manufactured and agricultural goods (some to over 200 per cent), and was dubbed the 'worst tariff bill in the nation's history' even before it was passed. Retaliation from other countries, in the form of higher tariffs, was swift and substantial, and the subsequent sharp decline in world trade and the collapse of the fragile international monetary system increased the depth and scope of the Great Depression. The 1930 tariff bill was widely regarded as a case of protectionist logrolling run wild. The Senate alone made 1,253 amendments to the original House bill, and duties on over 20,000 items were altered (see Pastor 1980: 77–8). When the Democrats won control of the White House, and majorities in Congress, in 1932, they looked for a way to make a change. Rural interests still made up a large part of the Democrats' electoral base, especially in the south, and still strongly favoured trade and the party's traditional anti-tariff platform. Unilateral tariff reductions were politically sensitive in the middle of a recession, however, and were not popular at all among workers, who had thrown their support behind the Democrats in the 1932 campaign. Franklin D. Roosevelt's

secretary of state, Cordell Hull, a long-time advocate of free trade, instead designed new legislation that would permit the president to negotiate bilateral treaties with trading partners, to restart trade by making reciprocal reductions in import duties. Passed as the Reciprocal Trade Agreements Act in 1934 (RTAA), the legislation granted the president authority (for three years) to negotiate alterations of up to 50 per cent in the existing import duties. When that initial authority expired in 1937, Congress renewed it and continued to do so in the decades that followed. Beginning in 1974, the president's authority was expanded to cover negotiations over a range of non-tariff barriers to trade (NTBs), although various procedural and monitoring provisions were also introduced to constrain executive behaviour, and the Congress maintained the power to approve or reject any trade agreement by vote (under the so-called 'fast-track' provision that prohibited amendments and set a firm time limit for a ratifying vote). The delegation of policymaking power to the executive branch, which can aggregate the costs and benefits of protection across the entire nation and bargain for reciprocal changes in the policies of other governments to open foreign markets to American exports, is credited with reorienting US trade policy away from protectionism in the decades since 1934 (see Destler 1995; Gilligan 1997).

routine for policymaking in most Western governments as a consequence of their membership commitments in the WTO. For nations outside the WTO, however, most of them being developing countries, where attempts to liberalize trade policy have a poor political track record, this does suggest that governments are more likely to succeed with trade reform if they can do so as part of a bilateral or regional free trade agreement with major trading partners.

The RTAA also offers a lesson about group access to lawmakers that is often overlooked. Up to 1934, congressional committee hearings were pivotal in shaping the trade legislation voted on in the US House and Senate. The hearings format, which assigned particular days for receiving testimony on the duties to be levied on different commodities, was especially convenient for industry group lobbying. This system was changed completely in 1934. After the RTAA, hearings were typically limited to general discussions about whether to extend the president's negotiating authority and, after 1974, whether to implement previously negotiated agreements (under 'fast-track' provisions that prohibited amendment). Closing off this very direct channel by which groups had been able for years to lobby for changes in duties on particular items may have had the most profound effect on trade policymaking in the United States. In general, *any* type of policymaking rule that provides routine access for organized groups to exert lobbying pressure to change particular features of legislation will make trade protection and other forms of restriction more likely—including open legislative hearings and 'commissions' or industry advisory panels set up within government agencies to gather opinions from producer and labour groups (see Alt and Gilligan 1994; Verdier 1994).

Legislative institutions can also influence other types of foreign economic policies. One line of work by scholars has been focusing on the general differences between multi-party coalition governments and single-party majority governments. Coalition governments appear to have less incentive than majority governments to alter their monetary policy prior to elections, to try to boost economic activity in an 'opportunistic' fashion, since voters find it difficult to assign blame or credit to any single party within the coalition. An implication seems to be that coalition governments are also much more likely than other types of government to adopt fixed exchange rates and give up control over monetary policy (see Bernhard and Leblang 1999).

Bureaucratic agencies

Lastly, there is the issue of how foreign economic policies are implemented or administered by the bureaucratic agencies of each government. The rules that are established to regulate these agencies, and the way they make decisions, can play a powerful part in shaping policy outcomes. Legislatures delegate the responsibility for implementing their laws to these agencies, establishing the rules by which they are to operate, the ways in which their performance is monitored and evaluated, and so on. Built into these relationships between the legislature and the bureaucracy, however, there is always some measure of 'slack'—that is, some room for bureaucrats to manoeuvre, free from legislative interference. This bureaucratic independence can have important effects in terms of foreign economic policies.

When it comes to the implementation of trade policies, for example, there is often a real fear that the bureaucratic agencies that administer various aspects of trade laws may develop far too cosy a relationship with the sectors of the home economy that they are supposed to be regulating. This danger of bureaucratic 'capture' appears to be very real. In the US case, the Departments of Commerce and Agriculture are both regarded as unapologetic advocates of protection for their 'clients'—American business firms and farmers. Indeed, the International Trade Administration (ITA), located within the Department of Commerce, is renowned for having 'gone native'. Charged with making rulings on petitions from US companies claiming that foreign firms are **dumping** products below cost in the American market, the ITA finds in favour of local firms in around 99 per cent of cases (see Bovard 1991).

This problem is by no means unique to the American system. In Japan, the Ministry of International Trade and Industry (MITI), and the Ministry Agriculture, Forestry, and Fisheries (MAFF), have long been known for their extremely close ties with Japanese industry, and the farming and fishing communities (see Okimoto 1988: 310). While MITI was for many years applauded by Western observers as the model for a new kind of autonomous state bureaucracy, capable of targeting subsidies expertly to particular manufacturing industries that would excel in competition with foreign producers (Johnson 1982), comprehensive evidence from recent studies indicates that MITI, in fact, allocated support to favoured industries in a highly political and ineffective way, a situation much like bureaucracies elsewhere (see Beason and Weinstein 1993).

In general, extreme cases aside, the interplay between bureaucratic independence and accountability is complex. In some issue areas, greater independence is generally regarded as desirable. Central banking is perhaps the most important case. The general problem, which we have discussed briefly above, is often referred to as the time inconsistency of monetary policy. Governments have an incentive to allow an unexpected rise in inflation that boosts economic activity, especially when facing an election. But since private actors know this, any promises a government may make to keep inflation in check may not be considered credible. Even if the government has all the best intentions, private actors might, nevertheless, keep inflation expectations high. By delegating control over monetary policy to an independent central bank that is insulated from any political temptations to alter monetary policy, the government can beat the problem. Moreover, independent central banks also appear to play an important part in shaping currency policies. Recent studies have indicated that governments in countries with independent central banks are less likely to engage in electorally motivated manipulations of exchange rates (Clark and Reichert 1998). And a related claim is that governments that can commit credibly to low inflation by establishing an independent central bank are less likely to need to fix their exchange rate in order to gain anti-inflationary credibility. Central bank independence and fixed exchange rates, in other words, can function as policy substitutes (see Clark and Hallerberg 2000).

- Proportional representation systems with strong political parties typically generate lower levels of trade protection and other restrictions than plurality rule systems, in which particular local and regional interests have a greater influence.
- Small electoral districts in plurality rule systems tend to increase the influence of sectoral or particularistic groups over elected representatives when compared to larger districts, and thus lead to higher levels of protection.
- In plurality rule systems, in which elections are all-or-nothing contests between the major parties, governments are less likely to fix exchange rates than governments in proportional representation systems.
- Whether a government allows protectionist logrolling in a legislature, and whether a president supports trade liberalization, will depend on their partisan affiliation and the policy preferences of their party's core electoral constituency.
- An explicit institutional connection that links tariff reductions at home with reciprocal reductions in tariffs abroad (for example, a free trade agreement), can generate much stronger support for trade policy reform among export-oriented industries.
- Rules that provide access for organized groups to exert lobbying pressure to change particular features of legislation make trade protection and other forms of restriction more likely.
- The delegation of policymaking authority to bureaucratic agencies or bodies independent from national legislatures may not produce policies less affected by lobbying from protectionist interests, since groups may gain privileged access to decision-makers in such agencies.
- The existence of an independent central bank makes it less likely that a government will choose to fix the exchange rate.

KEY POINTS

- Restrictions on the franchise can give more weight to one side relative to others in contests over foreign economic policies. Extensions of the franchise to urban classes tend to produce more open policies toward trade and investment in labour and capital-abundant countries, and more closed or protectionist policies in labour and capital-scarce economies.
- Collective action is easier to organize in the relatively small groups that benefit from a particular trade restriction than in the much larger groups that are hurt by the restriction, so the strongest lobbying pressure tends to come from protectionist groups.

Conclusions, extensions, and complications

There is really no such thing as the 'national interest' when it comes to foreign economic policy—or rather, there is no single national interest; there are many. Different individuals have very different conceptions of what is best for the nation and, not coincidentally, what is best for themselves, when it comes to setting foreign economic policies. This chapter has attempted to outline the principal divisions that usually characterize domestic political battles over trade, immigration, investment, and exchange rates. These divisions, as we have seen, tend to fall along either class or industry lines. Owners of capital and workers are typically pitted against one another when it comes to restrictions on inflows of labour or capital, for example, but they tend to take the same position in each industry on trade and exchange rate issues since the effects of policy can be very different for different sectors of the economy.

Once we know who wants what, the next task involves figuring out who gets what they want from the political process. This second step involves understanding how policies are decided in different countries, and thus how differences in political institutions affect economic policy choices. Our ultimate goal is to work out why governments in different countries often choose very different types of trade, immigration, investment, and exchange rate policies. We might also hope to form some reasonably accurate predictions about what our governments are likely to do in the future. Understanding why governments make the choices they do, and predicting what they will do next, requires careful attention to the political pressures they face from domestic groups, and to the ways in which the preferences of these groups are aggregated into collective decisions by political institutions. But there are at least three additional complications to this simple analytical picture that we should discuss briefly here. The first is related to the knowledge or information that individuals have about the effects of different policies, and about the preferences of others; the second extension involves allowing for linkages between the various policy issues, and between these issues and other non-economic policy concerns; and the third complication involves international bargaining, and the ways in which we might think about the connection between domestic politics and international politics.

Information and the role of ideas

Who gains and who loses? And who wins the political contest between those who gain and those who lose? Answering these questions in each issue area is at the heart of the standard political economy approach we have outlined earlier. In keeping with traditional assumptions, we have been taking it for granted that individuals know what they want, know what others want, and know what types of policies will have what kinds of effects. These are heroic assumptions.

A great deal of the most recent research in both economics and political science has, in fact, tried to depart from this notion that people have full or complete information about their world, examining the effects of uncertainty, asymmetry in information among actors, and changes in knowledge that might be attributable to learning and the impact of new ideas. It is useful in this respect to distinguish between two basic types of information that individuals may be missing: people may be lacking knowledge about the effects of different policies on economic outcomes, or they may not have full knowledge about other people (including government leaders) and their preferences. We can discuss each of these informational problems separately.

What if we allow that individuals are not sure about the effects of different types of policies? It took us some time to disentangle the various effects of trade, immigration, investment, and exchange rate policies above, with the help of several simplifying assumptions, so this does seem an important question to pose. This clearly provides a large window through which new ideas, in the form of new beliefs about cause-and-effect relationships between policies and outcomes, might have a significant impact on policymaking. This is the view espoused by John Maynard Keynes (1936: 383) in his famous contention that 'the ideas of economists and political philosophers, both when they are right and when they are wrong, are more powerful than is commonly understood. Indeed the world is ruled by little else.'

Several prominent scholars have, indeed, argued that foreign economic policies have changed markedly in response to new ideas about these policies and their effects. The abandonment of mercantilist restrictions on trade and investment by most European governments in the nineteenth century has been attributed, in large measure, to the ideas of Adam Smith and David Ricardo and the development of classical trade theory (Kindleberger 1975; Bhagwati 1988) (see Box 4.7). The multilateral liberalization of trade and investment among Western economies in the era after the Second World War, allowing governments considerable scope for managing their domestic economies to avoid recessions, has similarly been traced to the refinement of classical and neoclassical economic theories and the ideas of Keynes himself (Ruggie 1982; Goldstein 1993). More recently, the rush to liberalize trade by governments in developing nations has been attributed to a learning process and the discrediting

BOX 4.7

The Rise of Free Trade in Europe

The publication of *The Wealth of Nations* by Adam Smith in 1776 stands out as an intellectual landmark in the history of thinking about international trade, pointing out the critical role that trade plays in encouraging specialization and the resulting gains in efficiency and wealth. Smith adroitly punctured the old doctrine of mercantilism, which favoured expanding exports while restricting imports and hoarding gold, making it clear that national wealth is defined not by stocks of gold but by how much citizens can consume with the resources they have at their disposal. But the modern theory of international trade really began with the arrival of David Ricardo's *Principles of Political Economy and Taxation* in 1817. Ricardo demonstrated that trade is mutually beneficial for all countries, even a country that cannot produce anything more efficiently than other nations in terms of the costs of its inputs. As long as the costs of production are different in different nations, Ricardo's analysis showed that it must be true that, in terms of the opportunity costs of

production (the value of other things that might have been produced with the inputs used to make a given item), each nation will be better at producing some things than others, and thus there is a basis for specialization and exchange that will leave both countries better off. This 'law of comparative advantage', which Paul Samuelson has called the most beautiful law in economics, has had a profound impact on all scholarly and political debates about trade ever since. That the cause of free trade was taken up enthusiastically by the leading English political economists, including John Stuart Mill, all inspired by Ricardian theory, and that these ideas also spread rapidly throughout Europe during the nineteenth century, has led many scholars to suggest that the broad shift away from trade protectionism in Europe (which began in 1846 with the repeal of the Corn Laws that Ricardo himself had attacked) was a result in large measure of a profound change in the way leaders understood the economic effects of trade (see Kindleberger 1975; Bhagwati 1988).

of the idea that rapid development could be achieved by **import-substitution** policies (see Krueger 1995). Competing ideas about cause-and-effect relationships often appear in policy debates, and dominant ideas are frequently embedded within policymaking institutions as the foundations for rules followed by bureaucratic agencies (Goldstein 1993). Yet, there remains much debate about the degree to which these types of ideas are independent of the interests that might be served by them. Max Weber's famous analogy compared ideas to 'switchmen' who determine the tracks along which human behaviour, pushed by interests, travel (Weber 1913/1958). From a more sceptical perspective, one might suggest that the individuals who gain and lose the most from any economic policy, such as tariffs on trade, have all the knowledge they need about its effects, and need no new ideas from economists to help them out; the policies just reflect the wishes of those interested actors who have the most political clout, and the ideas that attract our attention are just the ones sprinkled like holy water over the new legislation (to borrow an equally memorable metaphor from Kindleberger (1975: 36)). The relationship between ideas and interests is still very murky, and will remain so until we have a better understanding of where new ideas about policy come from, and what explains which ideas catch on and spread.

But by focusing only on the role of new ideas and how they might change knowledge about policies, we may be missing the bulk of the iceberg here when it comes to the impact of incomplete information. We noted in the discussions earlier that while foreign economic policies such as tariffs on imported goods generate real costs for a large set of owners and workers in all the other (non-protected) sectors of the economy, these costs are dispersed across such a large number of individuals that the 'per person' losses can be extremely small. Not only will it not pay for those affected to take political action to oppose the tariff in these cases, it may not even pay for them to spend any time or resources acquiring accurate information about the policy and its effects. Public opinion experts typically regard foreign economic policies as a particularly complex set of issues, about which survey respondents have very low levels of information (see Bauer *et al.* 1972: 81–4). Survey responses to questions about these issues tend to vary drastically with simple changes in question wording, making it very difficult to pinpoint where the public stands on any given policy question at any particular point in time (see Destler 1995: 180). One implication is that voters may be very susceptible to issue framing or manipulation by political leaders and organized lobby groups whenever these issues become more prominent. Recent research on political communication and public opinion has highlighted this possibility (e.g. Manheim 1991; Zaller 1992: 95). To the extent that this type of influence can be exercised, the politics of globalization may be regarded, at least to some degree, as a competition in issue framing among organized interests on different sides of the debate trying to sway public opinion to their side. This did appear to be an important dimension of the intense debate over NAFTA in the United States in 1993 (Holsti 1996: 52).

Another interesting implication of incomplete information among voters is that it may provide an explanation for why governments so often seem to do very inefficient things when setting foreign economic policies. Economists are fond of pointing out that, if a government really wanted to redistribute income to particular groups of owners and employees, using restrictions on trade is a very inefficient way to go about it. It would be far better just to make a direct, lump-sum payment to these individuals and avoid the inefficiencies generated by trade barriers that prop up uncompetitive industries. But if the costs to taxpayers of such direct payments are more visible (because they must appear, say, in the government's annual budget), they are more likely to generate a backlash among the voters on whom the burden falls. If this is true, it may make sense for a government to use trade policies to redistribute income to favoured groups, because these policies provide an effective disguise in a low-information environment (see Tullock 1983). From this perspective, the use of trade protection can be characterized as 'optimal obfuscation' (Magee et al. 1989).

Finally, what happens if we allow that individuals, even if they are fully informed about the effects of foreign economic policies, may nevertheless be uncertain about the motivations or intentions of the government managing those policies. One circumstance in which this type of incomplete information can become important is when setting exchange rate policy, as we have discussed above. Since governments have an incentive to print money and allow a burst of inflation when facing an election, any promises they make to keep inflation in check may not be considered credible by private actors, who understand that the government has an incentive to bluff and portray itself as 'tougher' on inflation than it really is. The problem is that no one can be sure that the government values its low-inflation reputation enough (relative to how much it wants to gain re-election) to keep its pledge; even if the government had followed through with its promises, private actors might, nevertheless, keep inflation expectations high. If there is no independent central bank to which control of monetary policy can be ceded, governments in these circumstances are likely to be drawn more to fixing the exchange rate, especially in countries that have a history of chronic inflation. Fixing the value of the currency is a way for the government to signal to private actors that it is committed to keeping inflation under control by raising the potential costs to itself should it fail.

Another important context in which incomplete information about the government may play a key role in shaping policies is the case in which a government is attempting to reform trade policy in the face of stiff opposition from groups in import-competing industries. In such cases, since the government may, indeed, have an incentive to back down if it encounters a major political revolt, any promises it makes in advance to hold fast to the reforms may not be considered credible by the groups (who know very well that the government could just be trying to bluff its way through the painful reforms). Thus, even if the government does fully intend to stick with the reforms, it might have to weather a long and costly (and perhaps even violent) political protest. Again, tying its own hands in some clear and visible way can be an especially attractive policy option for a government in this situation, and by signing an international trade treaty with a major regional partner it might be able to do the trick. This desire to make a credible commitment to trade reform is widely held to have been one reason why the Mexican government initiated the negotiations that produced the NAFTA agreement in 1993, after two decades of failed efforts to lower trade barriers unilaterally (see Whalley 1999).

Combinations of policies and issue linkages

Up to this point, we have been examining one type of foreign economic policy at a time. It is clear, however, that the effects of different policy instruments often depend on how *other* policies are set. In the basic Heckscher–Ohlin model, trade and factor movements are *substitutes* for one another—more of one type of international flow will generally mean less of another, and vice versa. If exports of labour-intensive products can move easily across a border between a labour-abundant economy (where wages are low) and a labour-scarce economy (where wages are high), this will tend to equalize labour costs over time, reducing the incentives for workers themselves to try to migrate between countries. If exports between the countries are blocked or impeded, more workers are likely to try to cross the border into the country that pays higher wages. When a dam is placed in front of flows in one channel it tends to divert flows into other channels.

This interaction among policies can become very interesting, because we know that while trade and factor flows are substitutable in general terms, they, in fact, have different types of effects on individuals. Individuals may thus have preferences for different combinations of policies. Perhaps the best example concerns the relationship between trade flows (and trade barriers) and direct investment. There is a great deal of evidence that firms engage in direct investment in markets as a way of 'jumping' trade barriers that would inhibit exports, and they even seem to reduce exports and invest more to stave off anticipated pressure for tariffs among local firms—a phenomenon known as 'quid pro quo foreign investment' (Bhagwati *et al.* 1987; Blonigen and Feenstra 1996). Local firms may be able to raise trade barriers, since they should have the lobbying support of their workers, whose jobs are endangered by high levels of imports, but they are less likely to win restrictions on inward direct investment by foreign firms, since workers in the industry will benefit from any new inflows of capital. Indeed, the best *policy combination* for local workers in an industry facing competition from a (relocatable) foreign producer is a high tariff *and* no restrictions on inward foreign investment. Local firms would prefer restrictions of *both* types of exchange, but would accept any restrictions rather than none at all if these are the politically feasible options. This political logic helps to explain the common pattern in policies towards the automobile industry in Europe and North America, where restrictions on imports were negotiated with Japanese auto firms but no restrictions were imposed to block the same firms from investing heavily in production facilities within both markets.

Exchange rate policy can also be 'in play' at the same time as trade policy. Trade policy and exchange rate policy are partially substitutable: a 1 per cent depreciation of the currency is equivalent to a 1 per cent across-the-board tariff on imports and a 1 per cent subsidy for all exports. But, clearly, the coalition that supports depreciation—those invested and employed in both import-competing and exporting industries—is different from the coalition that would support higher tariffs (import-competing interests). Exchange rate policies tend to be more rigid than trade policies, in general, mainly because the credibility of monetary policy commitments is undermined by frequent shifts in policy. But when there is an opportunity for the government to alter the exchange rate, intense lobbying for protection by import-competing groups (or even just the threat of it), may induce export interests to help persuade the government to weaken the currency—an outcome that would ease the competitive pressure on producers threatened by imports, while not harming (benefiting, in fact) those engaged in export industries. This seems to have been the case in the United States in the early 1980s, as the value of the US dollar rose dramatically. While the White House appeared to prefer to leave both its currency and trade policies unchanged, fearing a spate of protectionist legislation from Congress in response to lobbying by firms and unions in import-sensitive sectors, and hearing support for depreciation from export interests as well, it moved in 1985 to weaken the value of the dollar. Similarly, in many Latin American countries in the 1980s and 1990s, governments attempting reforms aimed at lowering barriers to trade were able to render these changes more politically palatable to threatened sectors by devaluing exchange rates at the same time (see De Gregorio 2001).

Perhaps even more important, in some ways, than these connections between different foreign economic policies are the linkages that have been made with increasing frequency in recent policy debates between these policies and a variety of *non-economic* issues. Some of these linkages are not new. Trade and investment policies have always been connected in various ways to the issue of national security. Most governments place tight controls on trade in weapons and dangerous chemicals, for example, and restrictions on foreign investment in strategically important industries (such as, energy, airlines, and broadcasting) are also common. And governments have strong incentives to lower barriers to trade and investment more rapidly among alliance partners than with other nations in the international system, as the experience in Europe after the Second World War (and among the industrialized democracies more generally) makes clear (see Gowa 1994). All individuals within an economy tend to share similar concerns about national security, so this form of issue linkage tends to affect policymaking in a fairly straightforward way, generating more support among all citizens for policy options that appear to contribute to national security. But foreign economic policies are now linked more regularly with a range of other non-economic issues, about which individuals tend to have more varied opinions. Most importantly, trade and investment are now frequently linked to discussions of environmental policy and to human rights issues in the political debates about globalization in Western democracies.

How do these issue linkages affect the analysis of the politics of trade and investment? The clearest impact is the involvement of a variety of organized environmental and human rights groups in recent debates over regional trade agreements and the WTO (see Destler and Balint 1999). The members of these groups care deeply about addressing environmental and human rights problems in their own countries and in other countries around the world; and they either believe that globalization is making these problems worse and thus should be restrained in some way, or they argue that trade and investment provide economic leverage which can and should be used to persuade governments in developing nations to improve environmental and labour standards and democratic institutions. The position taken by many of these groups is that all trade agreements, including the WTO itself, should include provisions for minimum environmental and labour standards that would be enforced (if necessary) by the imposition of trade sanctions. Many environmental groups have also lobbied for changes to the existing rules of the WTO, so that laws that discriminated against foreign products on environmental grounds (for example, import bans on tuna caught using nets that also endanger dolphins) would be permissible. But environmentalists and human rights activists have also expressed grave concerns about the behaviour of multinational firms in developing nations, with much of the focus being on whether these large corporations are moving production to areas in which they can pollute and otherwise damage the environment, or run 'sweatshop' factories in which they mistreat and underpay workers, avoiding the regulatory supervision that would prevent such behaviour in their home countries. The policies recommended by these groups, and in particular by human rights organizations worried by the lack of democratic institutions in countries such as China,

typically involve a more proactive use of economic sanctions—that is, Western governments cutting off trade with, and investment to, such 'problem' nations until their leaders make significant political reforms. Consumer boycotts aimed at particular corporations that are investing in such nations are usually warmly recommended too (although these types of consumer actions represent private market behaviour and are thus not a question of public policy).

One important general development has been the formation of what might be called 'Baptist and bootlegger' coalitions between some of these issue groups, and the business and labour organizations that have an economic stake in restricting international trade and/or investment. This type of coalition gets its name from American politics in the era of Prohibition, when strong support for the ban on alcohol sales came from Baptists, on moral grounds, and from bootleggers, who made large fortunes selling alcohol on the black market (see Yandle 1984). In recent debates over the NAFTA in the United States, for example, environmental groups such as the Sierra Club joined with labour unions in lobbying against the agreement, on the grounds that it did not contain provisions that would ensure a substantial improvement in environmental and labour standards in Mexico (see Destler and Balint 1999: 42–5). And recent 'anti-sweatshop' campaigns, organized by human rights groups and student activists, and targeting foreign investment and outsourcing by US apparel manufacturers to nations such as Vietnam, Bangladesh, and China, have been backed financially and supported enthusiastically by American textile worker unions and firms producing locally.

The concern among many analysts, especially among those who generally support international economic integration for its ability to raise living standards in all countries, is that these types of political coalitions may be hijacked by their protectionist members who support restrictions on international trade and investment, *regardless* of whether they have any positive (or negative) long-term effects on environmental conditions or human rights standards. It would be far better, many argue, to pursue improvements in environmental and human rights standards by working towards separate international treaties dealing with those precise issues in a more direct way, perhaps by compensating developing nations for making costly improvements to their environmental and labour laws. Sanctions could severely limit economic growth in the very poorest developing countries, where governments are likely to resist making political concessions (especially democratic reforms that increase the risk that they will be toppled from power). The issues are complex, however, and the political problems difficult. The 'Baptists' are drawn to supporting economic sanctions rather than other policy instruments (for example, new international treaties, or foreign aid grants to nations that improve their environmental standards), because they have calculated that these alternatives are politically infeasible. With the support of the 'bootleggers' for restrictions on trade and investment, however, they might stand a greater chance of getting something done that will have beneficial effects.

The general point here is that our simple, one-issue-at-a-time approach to the analysis of foreign economic policies becomes much more complicated when we allow that different policy instruments are often up for grabs at the same time and have partially substitutable effects, and if we take into account the fact that a variety of groups are often interested in using the tools of foreign economic policy to advance non-economic types of goals. Often, it is the institutional context in which government decisions are made (many of the features of which we have discussed earlier) that determines which types of policy instruments are more adjustable than others, and which types of political coalitions are more viable than others. The most comprehensive and persuasive accounts of economic policymaking will take all these complexities into account.

International bargaining and domestic politics

Finally, recalling the discussion by Aggarwal and Dupont in the previous chapter, it is worth pausing here briefly to consider the ways in which the domestic politics of foreign economic policies may be translated into international-level bargaining over these same issues. What we really require here is a theoretical model of the policymaking process that takes into account all the incentives and constraints operating among actors at both domestic and international levels. This is the type of model that Putnam (1988) famously envisioned, using the metaphor of the **two-level game**. A government engaged in international economic negotiations, in fact, plays two different

political 'games' at the same time, he suggested, with its actions constituting 'moves' that must be seen, not only in the context of the demands made by individuals and groups in *domestic* politics, but also in view of the bargaining power it has when negotiating *international* agreements with other governments. Government leaders negotiate with other leaders at the international level over the terms of economic agreements, and in those negotiations the relative size and strength of the economy can make a tremendous difference to the terms that can be demanded. But the leaders must be attuned to the preferences of the domestic groups whose support they need to remain in office, and the set of international deals that would be ratified or supported by these groups at home.

To date, theoretical work along these lines has focused mainly on differences between the preferences of legislative and executive branches of government, and their different agenda-setting and vetoing powers, and how these features of domestic politics affect the outcomes of international negotiations and agreements (see Evans *et al.* 1993; Milner 1997a). Much of the attention has been directed to the so-called 'Schelling conjecture', which holds that a hawkish domestic constituency—represented in the simplest models as a legislature that prefers very little international cooperation—can, in fact, improve the bargaining power of the executive branch in its dealings with foreign counterparts (Schelling 1960: 28–9). Recent work has also focused on how executive–legislative divisions affect the credibility of governments during international negotiations (for example, Martin 2000), and whether international agreements are negotiated to allow for greater flexibility in cases when future changes in domestic political coalitions might lead to substantial shifts in the types of policies a government can implement (Downs and Rocke 1995).

While being full of insights about the effects of domestic political institutions on the prospects for international cooperation, this line of work has so far paid very little attention to the roles played by organized interests and voters in shaping legislative and executive preferences on particular policy issues. In fact, to date, standard political economy models of trade politics, emphasizing the role played by organized lobby groups in the formulation of policy, have not at all been linked to two-level game models of negotiations over trade and other economic agreements. Moreover, the existing work on two-level games tends to concentrate overwhelmingly on parameters that operate only on one level—domestic politics in the home nation. Features of the strategic relationship between nations, such as the economic and military asymmetries that might affect relative bargaining power, or common ties to alliances or international institutions that might affect incentives to cooperate, are largely ignored. We clearly need a better two-level mousetrap: a model that incorporates a fuller representation of organized interests and lobbying at the domestic level, while also allowing for the ways in which incentives and constraints are generated at the international level.

In practice, most international political economists work with partial theories that focus on one set of causal variables operating at one level. Some argue that the features of the international system, such as the distribution of economic power, and any specific nation's position within it, impose broad but important constraints on what governments can and cannot do when setting policies. Others, in keeping with the orientation of this chapter, argue that the prime focus of our attention should be placed on what is going on within nations—their particular sets of political institutions, and the preferences and lobbying activities of different group of individuals—since it is these things that primarily determine the policies chosen by governments. But, in principal, almost all scholars recognize that politics at both the domestic and international levels should be a feature of any complete analysis of foreign economic policy. Integrating theoretical insights about politics at these two levels is an extremely complex and challenging task that still remains, to a very large extent, undone.

KEY POINTS

- To understand the domestic origins of foreign economic policies, we need to perform two main tasks: first, to map the policy preferences of different groups in the domestic economy; and then to specify how political institutions affect the way that these preferences are aggregated into government decisions.

- Policy preferences depend mainly on the types of assets people own, and how the income earned from those assets is affected by different policies.

- Political institutions affect policy outcomes by defining who has a vote, how political representatives are elected, and how policymaking takes place in legislatures, and is delegated to presidents and government agencies.

- New ideas about cause-and-effect relationships appear to have had a large impact on foreign economic policies in different eras. The relationship between ideas and interests is far from clear, however, and we need a better understanding of where new ideas about policy come from, and what explains which ideas catch on and spread.

- Foreign economic policies involve a complex set of issues about which most voters have very low levels of information. As a result, the politics of globalization may be regarded to some degree as a competition in issue framing among organized interests.

- If private actors have incomplete information about the degree to which the government is committed to policy reforms, the government may have an incentive to tie its own hands in some visible way (for example, by fixing the exchange rate, or signing a trade treaty) to signal its intentions in a credible way.

- Since the effects of a change in one type of foreign economic policy may depend on choices made about other types of policy, individuals may have preferences over different combinations of policies that are closely related (for example, tariffs and restrictions on inward investment induced by tariffs).

- Trade and investment policies are also linked to discussions of *non-economic* issues. One important development has been the formation of 'Baptist and bootlegger' coalitions between environmental and human rights groups concerned about globalization, and business and labour organizations that have an economic stake in restricting international trade and investment.

- Governments may be thought of as playing political games at two levels, their actions constituting moves that are both responses to demands made by groups in *domestic* politics, and responses to offers made by other governments in *international* negotiations.

- We need a better theory of two-level games that incorporates fuller representations of both domestic and international politics. In practice, most international political economists employ partial theories that focus only on variables operating at a single level.

QUESTIONS

1.   If the economic case for trade liberalization is so strong, why is it that governments continue to impose barriers to trade and are engaged so frequently in trade disputes?

2.   Trade theory does not imply that every individual within each nation will benefit from the lowering of trade barriers, just that aggregate benefits will exceed aggregate losses. Who stands to benefit most from trade liberalization in the advanced economies of Europe, Japan, and the United States, and who is most likely to be disadvantaged? What about the situation in developing nations with different types of factor endowments?

3.   Can these different groups of individuals reach some kind of agreement so that trade liberalization can benefit everyone? What are the political obstacles to this type of agreement?

4.   Is it inappropriate to think only, or primarily, in terms of economic gains and losses when evaluating the effects of increased international trade? How important are other types of concerns (for example, national security, income inequality, environmental hazards, human rights abuses) in the political debates that determine policy outcomes?

5.   What types of electoral and policymaking institutions tend to mitigate the effects of lobbying by protectionist groups when it comes to the determination of trade policy? Are electoral systems based on proportional representation likely to generate less protection than plurality systems?

6.   Do the economic effects of immigration shape the political struggles over changes in immigration law? Or do the politics of immigration reflect other types of cultural and social divisions within host countries?

7.   What are the economic effects of foreign investment for the source country and for the host country? Does foreign investment generate a 'race to the bottom' in labour and environmental standards in developing countries? Does it inhibit democratic reform?

8.   What economic and political changes during the twentieth century led to the abandonment of fixed exchange rates among the advanced economies? Why do many developing countries continue to fix their exchange rates?

FURTHER READING

Trade

Ciuriak, D., Lapham, B., Wolfe, R., Collins-Williams, W. T., and Curtis, J. (2015), 'Firms in International Trade: Trade Policy Implications of the New New Trade Theory', *Global Policy* 6/2: 130–40. Examines the implications for trade policy of the literature on firm heterogeneity.

Destler, I. M. (1995), *American Trade Politics*, 3rd edn (Washington, DC: Institute for International Economics). This is required reading for anyone interested in how US trade policy is made. It provides a comprehensive analysis of American political institutions and policymaking.

Hayes, J. P. (1993), *Making Trade Policy in the European Community* (London: Macmillan). This book provides a thorough discussion of the processes of trade policymaking in the European Community.

Helpman, E. (2014), 'Foreign Trade and Investment: Firm-Level Perspectives', *Economica*, 81/321: 1–14. Examines how recent research has changed the analytical frameworks used to understand trade by incorporating product differentiation, monopolistic competition, and firm heterogeneity.

Hiscox, M. J. (2002), *International Trade and Political Conflict* (Princeton: Princeton University Press). An analysis of historical changes in levels of factor specificity in several Western nations, relating these changes to shifts in political alignments in trade politics.

Krueger, A. O. (1995), *Trade Policies and Developing Nations* (Washington, DC: Brookings Institution). An engaging discussion of trade liberalization in developing nations.

Rogowski, R. (1989), *Commerce and Coalitions* (Princeton: Princeton University Press). A sweeping analysis of coalitions in trade politics in a variety of historical contexts, based on an application of the Stolper–Samuelson theorem.

Immigration

Borjas, G. J. (1999), *Heaven's Door: Immigration Policy and the American Economy* (Princeton: Princeton University Press). A provocative analysis of the effects of immigration in the United States in recent decades.

Fetzer, J. S. (2000), *Public Attitudes toward Immigration in the United States, France, and Germany* (Cambridge: Cambridge University Press). This book uses available survey data to compare public attitudes towards immigration and the determinants of anti-immigrant sentiments.

Tichenor, D. J. (2002), *Dividing Lines: The Politics of Immigration Control in America* (Princeton: Princeton University Press). A very impressive history of immigration politics in the United States.

Investment

Crystal, J. (2003), *Unwanted Company: Foreign Investment in American Industries* (Ithaca, NY: Cornell University Press). An excellent study of political debates about inward direct foreign investment in the United States.

Graham, E., and Krugman, P. R. (1995), *Foreign Direct Investment in the United States* (Washington, DC: Institute for International Economics). This book provides a comprehensive analysis of the economic and political effects of inward foreign investment.

Moran, T. (1998), *Foreign Direct Investment and Development* (Washington, DC: Institute for International Economics). An excellent study of the effects of direct foreign investment in developing nations.

Exchange rates

Frieden, J., Ghezzi, P., and Stein, E. (eds) (2001), *The Currency Game: Exchange Rate Politics in Latin America* (New York: Inter-American Development Bank). A very interesting collection of research on the politics of exchange rate policies in Latin America.

Henning, R. C. (1994), *Currencies and Politics in the United States, Germany, and Japan* (Washington, DC: Institute for International Economics). This book provides a clear and detailed discussion of exchange rate policymaking in the United States, Germany, and Japan.

Simmons, B. A. (1994), *Who Adjusts? Domestic Sources of Foreign Economic Policy during the Interwar Years* (Princeton: Princeton University Press). An impressive analysis of the political determinants of exchange rate policies adopted by Western nations in the interwar period.

Institutions

Gilligan, M. (1997), *Empowering Exporters: Reciprocity and Collective Action in Twentieth-Century American Trade Policy* (Ann Arbor, MI: University of Michigan Press). A fine study of the importance of institutionalizing reciprocity in trade policymaking.

Hiscox, M. J. (1999), 'The Magic Bullet? The RTAA, Institutional Reform, and Trade Liberalization', *International Organization*, 53/4: 669–98. A critical review of research on the RTAA that emphasizes the role of political parties and their core constituencies in the of politics institutional change.

Rogowski, R. (1987), 'Trade and the Variety of Democratic Institutions', *International Organization*, 41/2: 203–23. A classic analysis of the ways in which different types of electoral institutions affect trade policy outcomes in democracies.

Wintrobe, R. (1998), *The Political Economy of Dictatorship* (Cambridge: Cambridge University Press). An excellent analysis of policymaking in non-democratic regimes.

Extensions and complications

Elliott, K. A., and Freeman, R. (2003), *Can Labor Standards Improve under Globalization?* (Washington, DC: Institute for International Economics). This book provides a comprehensive review of the debates about whether trade and investment policies should be linked to agreements about improving labour standards in developing nations.

Goldstein, J., and Keohane, R. O. (eds) (1993), *Ideas and Foreign Policy: Beliefs, Institutions, and Political Change* (Ithaca, NY: Cornell University Press). An important collection of essays discussing the impact of new ideas on foreign policy outcomes.

Graham, E. (2000), *Fighting the Wrong Enemy: Anti-Global Activists and Multinational Enterprises* (Washington, DC: Institute for International Economics). A compelling analysis of the effects of direct foreign investment in developing nations that argues that criticisms made by environmental and human rights groups are misguided.

Irwin, D. (1996), *Against the Tide: An Intellectual History of Free Trade* (Princeton: Princeton University Press). A sweeping account of theoretical developments in economics that support the case for trade liberalization.

WEBLINKS

For regular research reports and briefs on policy issues:

www.piie.com Peterson Institute for International Economics.

For theoretical background on international economics and helpful beginner guides:

www.internationalecon.com International Economics Study Center.

www.amosweb.com/gls Amos World Economics Glossary.

For data and analysis of public opinion on international economic issues:

www.pewglobal.org PEW Global Attitudes Project.

www.pipa.org Program on International Policy Attitudes (PIPA).

For data on world trade, migration, and investment:

www.wto.org/english/res_e/statis_e/statis_e.htm WTO's International Trade Statistics.

http://laborsta.ilo.org ILO's International Labour Migration Database.

http://unctad.org/en/Pages/Publications/World-Investment-Directory.aspx UNCTAD's World Investment Directory.

For information and statistics on trade, immigration, investment, and exchange rate policies:

http://wits.worldbank.org/wits World Integrated Trade Solutions Database of Trade and Trade Control Measures.

www.wto.org/english/tratop_e/dda_e/tnc_e.htm WTO's Negotiations Committee.

www.ustr.gov United States Trade Representative (USTR).

http://ec.europa.eu/trade European Union Trade Policy.

www.meti.go.jp/english Japanese Trade Policy.

www.migrationpolicy.org Migration Policy Institute.

www.imf.org/external/np/tre/tad/exfin1.cfm IMF's Country Finances and Exchange Rates.

www.federalreserve.gov Federal Reserve Board.

www.bankofengland.co.uk Bank of England.

www.ecb.int European Union Central Bank.

www.boj.or.jp/en Bank of Japan.

ONLINE RESOURCE CENTRE

For additional material and resources, please visit the Online Resource Centre at:
www.oxfordtextbooks.co.uk/ravenhill5e

Appendix 4.1 The Theory of Comparative Advantage

BOX 4.8

The Theory of Comparative Advantage

The case for free trade was stated succinctly by Adam Smith. In *The Wealth of Nations*, he wrote: 'If a foreign country can supply us with a commodity cheaper than we ourselves can make it, better buy it of them with some part of the produce of our own industry, employed in a way in which we have some advantage' (iv.ii.12). The idea here is simple and intuitive. If a country can produce some set of goods at lower cost than can a foreign country, and if the foreign country can produce some other set of goods at a lower cost, then clearly it would be best for the country to trade its relatively cheaper goods for the foreign economy's relatively cheaper goods. In this way, both countries can gain from trade. This is the theory of trade according to absolute advantage.

David Ricardo, working in the early part of the nineteenth century, realized that absolute advantage was a limited case of a more general basis for international trade (the idea was originally stated by another economist, Robert Torrens, in *Essay on the External Corn Trade*, published in 1815, but most historians of

economic thought believe that Ricardo reached his conclusions independently). Consider Table 4.1. Portugal can produce both cloth and wine more efficiently, i.e. with less labour input than England (it has an absolute advantage in the production of both commodities). Ricardo argued that, nonetheless, it could still be mutually beneficial for both countries to specialize and trade.

The logic of comparative advantage rests on the *opportunity costs* of producing goods across countries; that is, the amount of one good that has to be given up to produce another good. In Table 4.1, producing a unit of wine in England requires the same amount of labour as required to produce two units of cloth. Production of an extra unit of wine means forgoing production of two units of cloth (that is, the opportunity cost of a unit of wine is two units of cloth). In Portugal, the labour required to produce a unit of wine would only produce 1.5 units of cloth (that is, the opportunity cost of a unit of wine is 1.5 units of cloth in Portugal). To concentrate on wine production in Portugal requires giving up relatively less cloth output than would be the case in England. Similarly, if England produced only cloth, the amount of wine production forgone would be relatively smaller than if Portugal did so.

Portugal is thus relatively better at producing wine than is England: if Portugal concentrated on producing wine, it would give up a smaller volume of cloth production than would England. Portugal is said to have a *comparative advantage* in the production of wine. England is relatively better at producing cloth than wine, so, England is said to have a comparative advantage in the production of cloth.

Because relative or comparative costs differ, it can still be mutually advantageous for both countries to trade *even though Portugal has an absolute advantage in producing both commodities*. For international welfare to be maximized, Portugal should specialize in the product in which it is relatively most efficient; and England, in the commodity in which it is relatively least inefficient.

Table 4.2 shows how trade might be advantageous. Costs of production are as set out in Table 4.1. In this example, England is assumed to have 270 person hours available for production. Before trade takes place, it produces and consumes eight units of cloth (requiring 120 person hours of labour input) and five units of wine (150 person hours). Portugal has fewer labour resources, with a total of 180 person hours of labour available for production. Before trade takes place, it produces and consumes nine units of cloth (requiring 90 person hours of labour input) and six units of wine (90 person hours). Total production for the two economies combined is 17 units of cloth and 11 units of wine.

If both countries now specialize, with Portugal producing only wine and England producing only cloth, and all their labour resources are devoted to

Table 4.1 Comparative Costs of Production (Cost Per Unit in Person Hours)

Country	Cloth	Wine
England	15	30
Portugal	10	15

Table 4.2 Production before and after trade

Country	Production before trade		Production after trade	
	Cloth	Wine	Cloth	Wine
England	8	5	18	0
Portugal	9	6	0	12
Total	17	11	18	12

the single product, England can produce (270 divided by 15) units of cloth and Portugal (180 divided by 15) units of wine. Total production by the two economies is 18 units of cloth and 12 units of wine. Specialization, according to comparative advantage and international trade, therefore, has enabled overall welfare to increase because total production has gone up by one unit of cloth and one unit of wine.

For trade to take place, the ratio of the price of the two goods must be lower than the domestic opportunity costs of production; that is, a bottle of wine will have to sell for somewhere between 1.5 and 2 bales of cloth. Note that the theory says nothing about distributional questions; that is, where in this range the price will settle, and thus who will gain most from trade.

The simple theory of comparative advantage makes a number of important assumptions:

• There are no transport costs.

• Costs are constant and there are no economies of scale.

• There are only two economies producing two goods.

• Traded goods are homogeneous (i.e. identical as far as the consumer is concerned).

• Factors of production (labour and capital) are perfectly mobile internally but not internationally.

• There is full employment in both economies.

• There are no tariffs or other trade barriers.

• There is perfect knowledge, so that all buyers and sellers know where the cheapest goods can be found internationally.

Despite the lack of correspondence between the contemporary globalized economy and these assumptions, most economists believe that the fundamental principle that Ricardo identified still holds.

PART II

Global Trade and Production

5

The Evolution of the Global Trade Regime

Ann Capling and Silke Trommer

Chapter contents

Reader's guide

The twentieth century witnessed a remarkable emergence of international institutions, and nowhere was their impact greater than in international trade. Following decades of depression and war, a global trading regime was initiated with the creation of the General Agreement on Tariffs and Trade (GATT) in 1947, which expanded steadily in both scope and membership through the twentieth century and culminated in the establishment of the World Trade Organization (WTO) in 1995. Underpinned by the philosophy that open markets and non-discriminatory trade policies promote the prosperity of all countries, and issued with a powerful dispute settlement mechanism, the WTO has been hailed as the most prominent example of cooperation between countries. At the same time, the WTO has been subject to internal and external criticism and now faces a number of difficulties, particularly in its negotiation function. This chapter reviews the history, politics, and recent trends and challenges of the multilateral trade system.

Introduction

Today, the global trade regime is a rules-based political system where the rules flowing from international agreements that seek to promote and stabilize economic exchanges between countries are ranged against the regulations of national governments that often restrict those exchanges. The purpose of the international rules is to reduce the protectionism of national regulations, but even more, to reduce the uncertainty and unpredictability of international trade relations, and to promote stability. The task of this chapter will be to show how this global trade regime has been established through the actions of trading countries over the past 150 years, how it became institutionalized in the WTO, and why it is facing difficulties now.

The global trade regime is based on three components: trade, national regulations, and international agreements. Trade and national regulations have been a theme and counterpoint throughout much of history, in the sense that when national regulations receded, trade flourished; and when those regulations intensified, trade languished. To this combination can be added the third factor of international agreements, by which countries attempt to establish international rules that would restrict their own (and other countries') capacity to distort or interrupt international trade through national regulation. Rules and regulations are inherent in our highly ordered lives, and the irony is that in order to reduce regulation of one kind, it requires the intercession of rules of another kind. The important issue is where the rules or regulations come from, and whether their purpose is to reduce or expand the scope of our economic activity.

Trade, which is a staple of our modern global political economy, is also a historic phenomenon. It was important to many ancient and medieval powers. More than 2,000 years ago, the 'Silk Road', a vast overland and maritime network of trade routes, connected China with Europe, North Africa, Arabia, Central Asia, and India. Trade lay at the centre of state revenue and state power in ancient Athens; Ptolemaic Egypt; the Italian city states of Venice, Florence, and Genoa; and the German Hanseatic League. The importance of trade to state wealth and power was exemplified by ancient Athens, which developed through commercial activities and at its height was totally dependent on trade. Athens exported silver and olive oil, and the shards of pottery urns that have been discovered throughout the Mediterranean region have charted the boundaries of its trade over time. In return, the Athenians were dependent on the import of grain, which was essential to maintain the population of Athens in an arid region.

In examining the global trade regime, trade is by necessity the starting point, but government is equally part of the story. This point has been observed by many writers, but perhaps was expressed most effectively by John Condliffe, as follows:

> ❝ The beginnings of trade are to be found in the enterprise of groups and individuals, but regulation and taxation of trade are almost as old as trade itself. In tracking history, if enterprise is the theme, regulation is the counterpoint. As soon as the track begins to be beaten out, established authority intervenes to control and levy tolls upon the traders. ❞

(1950: 27)

The earliest means of regulating trade were tolls, exacted by local leaders for permission to pass through territory, or to trade, or simply for protection. Tolls were an expression of military control and political sovereignty, and if one controlled territory, one could exact tribute through tolls at will. This resulted in a great hindrance to trade, especially in Europe, which was divided into many small jurisdictions during the Middle Ages.

A more modern method of regulation than tolls was the tariff, or customs duty, which is a percentage tax added to the price of traded goods. Tariffs are still with us today, but they are among the oldest functions of government. The purpose of early tariffs, whether on imports or exports, was to raise revenue. Tariffs were effective for this purpose, and by the beginning of the eighteenth century, duties on imported goods had come to be the chief source of revenue in European countries. A further function of the tariff was to protect domestic producers from foreign competition.

Today, protectionism is the main purpose of the tariff. The revenue function is less important in developed countries, as governments have found other means to raise revenues, although the tariff is still an important source of revenue in **less developed countries** (**LDCs**). Other forms of protection have also arisen, collectively known as **non-tariff measures** (**NTMs**) (also, **non-tariff barriers** (**NTBs**)). These measures have now become more important than tariffs, the latter having been greatly reduced by successive trade negotiations under the GATT.

The regulations that have restricted trade in recent decades have been the work of national governments. But those same governments have also reached international agreements with other governments attempting to constrain the extent to which domestic policies would restrict the free flow of international trade. These agreements started as simple undertakings between peoples as to how their commercial relations would be conducted, and trade agreements are almost as old as trade itself. For example, commercial treaties have been discovered between the kings of ancient Egypt and Babylonia, giving the parties the right to exact duties on the merchandise of traders or travellers. In more modern times, such treaties have been instrumental in establishing the rules whereby trade could be carried on between different political jurisdictions.

The next sections scrutinize these international agreements and their historical evolution to the present day.

KEY POINTS

- The international trade regime is based on three components: trade, national regulations, and international agreements.

Historical antecedents: 1860 to 1945

The golden age of liberalism

During the nineteenth century, there was a vibrant international debate on the merits of free trade (Irwin 1996). In Britain, Adam Smith (*The Wealth of Nations* 1776) argued for the benefits of free trade based on his **absolute advantage** theory whereby global welfare would rise if every country focused on producing the product that they are best at making. David Ricardo (*On the Principles of Political Economy and Taxation* 1817/2002) subsequently introduced the notion of **comparative advantage** to argue that even for countries that are not best at producing anything, the free trade argument still holds. According to Ricardo, this is because we need to ask how much of the production of one product we give up to in order to be able to produce another. If we compare opportunity costs of

production, a country that does not hold an absolute advantage in any product can still be comparatively better at producing the product than the country holding the absolute advantage. Specialization and exchange still increases global welfare in this scenario. Their ideas provided the intellectual underpinnings for the free trade movement in Britain and western Europe. The most prominent opponents of free trade were Alexander Hamilton (*Report on the Subject of Manufactures* 1791) and Friedrich List (*National System of Political Economy* 1841) who advocated interventionist trade policies and tariffs for **infant industry promotion** (Gilpin 1987). Their ideas influenced tariff and trade policy in the United States (US) and Germany. Even as free trade swept through Europe in the mid-nineteenth century, the US retained a policy of high tariffs to protect its emerging manufacturing industries.

A campaign for free trade began among British merchants in the second quarter of the nineteenth century. The campaign was part of a broader effort of political reform in British society, and its eventual success resulted in part from the political realignment introduced by the Reform Act of 1832 (as discussed by Hiscox in Chapter 4 in this volume). The campaign was led by Richard Cobden, who demonstrated the importance of pragmatic leadership in promoting the idea of free trade. In 1848 Britain repealed the Corn Laws, which had restricted imports of wheat and other grains, and implemented a series of administrative and diplomatic measures over the next two decades that put free trade into practice.

Other European powers also liberalized their trade during the third quarter of the nineteenth century but unlike Britain, they did this through the negotiation of trade treaties rather than through unilateral liberalization. The Cobden–Chevalier treaty of 1860 between Britain and France prompted the governments of other European countries to seek similar commercial treaties with France, beginning with Prussia in 1865, and then followed by a flurry of liberalizing trade agreements across Europe (Rosecrance 1986).

A key element of the Cobden–Chevalier treaty was a **most-favoured nation** (MFN) clause, whereby the tariff concessions granted by France and England to each other were automatically extended to other countries with whom they concluded bilateral trade agreements. This led to the emergence of a network of interlocking bilateral trade agreements across Europe, with MFN as the linchpin that joined them together. Although short-lived, this system of liberalized and non-discriminatory trade was a precursor to the multilateral trade system that was established a century later (Brown 2003).

The brief period of liberal commercial exchange that started in the 1830s lasted until the 1870s. This period was dominated economically by Great Britain. The Napoleonic Wars of the early 1800s had left British manufacturing capabilities unscathed, and following the wars, Britain's economic strength allowed it to become the leading creditor country in the world. Britain provided aid and loans to European nations and had large exports of foreign investment, mainly to the US and British colonies in Asia. Britain also led the world in industrial and technological innovation and was the biggest exporter and importer. For the British, free trade was the principal commercial policy of the nation until well after the First World War.

The European commitment to free trade was considerably less enduring than the British, and it turned around quickly in the face of depression after 1870. As a result of a series of rapid technological improvements in the mid 1850s, the **comparative advantage** in grain growing shifted to the New World, with the result that grain prices fell sharply in European markets. At the same time, a slump occurred in industrial production, which continued for over two decades in the form of low prices and low return on capital for manufactured products. International competition became severe, and in all countries there were strong pressures for protection against imports. One by one, national governments succumbed to the pressures, and reversed the period of relatively free trade that had been established prior to the 1850s. Austria-Hungary raised tariffs in 1876, and Italy followed in 1878. In 1879 Germany shifted to a protectionist policy and, because of its size in the European economy and its philosophy of nationalism and **mercantilism**, it set a protectionist tone for the overall system. France responded to German protectionism with restrictions of its own and, for its part, the US continued the protectionism it had pursued throughout the nineteenth century. The UK, the Low Countries, and Switzerland, however, resisted the move towards higher tariffs, but by the end of the century, the UK was the only major nation practising free trade (Kindleberger 1951).

The depression that began in the 1870s also ushered in a lengthy period of protectionism that lasted until after the Second World War. Growing nationalism and war in 1914 exacerbated the protectionist trend that

was already well established in response to the economic conditions of the late 1800s. The First World War broke up an imperfect but workable equilibrium between internal economic policies, trade, and payments that had existed under the **gold standard** of the nineteenth century. The war produced enormous dislocation that was even more serious in economic terms than the destruction that had occurred. The results were maladjustments to the free flow of labour, capital, and goods, which created impediments to economic activity that lasted well into the 1930s.

Continued war planning also played an important role in the European mentality after 1919. In the realm of economic policy, war planning took the form of **mercantilism** and 'beggar-thy-neighbour' policies, inspired by Nazi Germany but copied by some European countries and Japan. The practice of mercantilism, like war itself, was an expression of nationalism in economic policy, designed to place the interests of the nation ahead of the wider community. Great Britain, the US, and many other countries abandoned the **gold standard** in the early 1930s and governments introduced a range of blunt measures to restrict trade, including prohibitions, quantitative restrictions, and exchange controls. Openly discriminatory trade relations developed quickly. Germany established preferential trade agreements with East European countries. In 1932, Great Britain abandoned its century-old commitment to non-discriminatory liberal trade when it established the Imperial Preference system through a combination of tariff increases and tariff preferences for the British Empire. During the interwar period, governments made efforts at the international level to negotiate international agreements to restrict the use of tariffs and non-tariff measures and to stabilize exchange rates. These agreements failed due to lack of support from key governments (Shonfield 1976).

Reciprocal Trade Agreements Act of 1934

The US had emerged from the First World War as the largest trading nation in the world; hence, it was likely that domestic events affecting US trade capabilities would have a wide impact on commercial relations in the international system. This was the case with two events of the early 1930s that were major watersheds in modern trade policy: the Smoot–Hawley tariff of 1930, and the Reciprocal Trade Agreements Act of

1934 (RTAA). The former was the culmination of a trend towards protectionism that had begun in the late nineteenth century, while the latter was the beginning of a trend towards liberalism that was interrupted by the Second World War but then continued into the present. These two events were major watersheds in modern trade policy.

The Smoot–Hawley Act of 1930 raised US duties to historic levels and increased the scope of tariff coverage. It represented a new level in the long movement by nations towards closing off their economies to foreign imports. In the wake of the combined effects of the Great Depression, and the Smoot–Hawley tariff and the retaliation by foreign countries that it precipitated, world trade fell by about two-thirds by the mid 1930s. The breakdown of trade after 1930 was alarming to Western governments, but even more alarming was the process that had led to that breakdown. The Smoot–Hawley Act was written in congressional committees that were essentially unable to master the detail that had become inherent in any major tariff legislation. Because of this economic illiteracy, and because of the general sympathy towards protectionism that had been created by the Great Depression, Congress essentially extended protection to all those groups that demanded it. The spectacle was that of a gross excess of the democratic process and a loss of control over the economy by both the US president and the congressional leadership. During the legislative debate, 1,000 American economists and the governments of numerous countries protested against the Act, but to no effect. The Smoot–Hawley tariff provoked widespread retaliation by other countries, contributing to tariff increases around the world and openly discriminatory trade relations (Irwin 2011).

The breakdown of international trade took its toll on public sympathy towards protectionism. The tariff became an issue in the presidential election of 1932, and was attacked by Democratic candidate Franklin D. Roosevelt as contributing to the Depression. Following his election, Roosevelt appointed Cordell Hull as secretary of state, a man committed to the view that free trade was an essential ingredient in world prosperity, and an even more important ingredient in international peace and stability. Hull and his officials began working with Congress to prepare new tariff legislation, and two years later the legislation was enacted under the title Reciprocal Trade Agreements Act (RTAA) of 1934.

The RTAA produced a revolution in US and even international trade policy (Haggard 1988). The central element of the RTAA was that it empowered the president to lower (or raise) tariffs up to 50 per cent from Smoot–Hawley levels in the course of trade negotiations with other countries. From the standpoint of American politics, the RTAA transferred tariff-setting policy to the presidency, which could organize itself bureaucratically for the task, and away from the Congress, which had ultimately proven to be incapable of discriminating between the many appeals brought by constituents for protection. This transfer substantially increased the control the government exercised over trade policy, and it has been an essential part of the US trade policy structure ever since 1934. From the standpoint of international politics, the RTAA advanced the notion that setting tariff rates should no longer be exclusively a unilateral policy by a nation state, but, rather, was a bilateral matter to be settled through negotiation. This action was reminiscent of the efforts by Michel Chevalier in the previous century to use commercial and political negotiation to reduce trade restrictions between France and Britain, and it began the changeover from a protectionist trade policy that had existed since the 1870s.

The US government pursued reciprocal trade agreements with other countries as far as economic circumstances after 1934 would allow. By 1939, the US had concluded 21 agreements, which made reductions in about a thousand duties. All agreements were made on an MFN basis, which slowed the negotiation because it engaged more parties, but also for the same reason extended the impact of the agreements. The RTAA agreements were successful in increasing the flow of international trade. More importantly, they provided a corpus of experience in trade liberalization that became integrated after the Second World War, which was demonstrated by the fact that most of the GATT articles drawn up in 1947 were taken from various agreements reached during the previous decade under the RTAA system. It also underlines the leadership of the US in the international trading system in the twentieth century.

The reciprocal trade program was concurrent with a sea change in US and world public opinion regarding protectionism and free trade. What appeared to have changed in the US and elsewhere was the principle of free trade versus protectionism, or more precisely, the expectations that people held as to which principle was just and would ordinarily prevail as a general rule.

This change created a more favourable economic context for the major changes in the global trade regime that occurred after the Second World War.

KEY POINTS

- Organized efforts to establish freer and non-discriminatory trade in Europe began in the middle of the nineteenth century.

- A lengthy period of protectionism was initiated by the world depression that began in the 1870s, and then continued as a result of the world wars and depression of the first half of the twentieth century.

- Efforts to establish a liberal international trading system were begun with the US RTAA of 1934.

The birth of the GATT

Post-war economic situation

The ascendancy of the US in the early post-war period was immediately evident in the play of international policymaking. In terms of security policy, the US took over the leadership of the Western alliance. The US enjoyed a preponderant position in the formation of the United Nations and other post-war international organizations. Reconstruction aid to Europe through the **Marshall Plan** further demonstrated the primacy of the US in the Western system. In addition, US economic hegemony could be demonstrated by figures representing three important areas of the international economic system, namely international monetary payments, trade, and foreign investment. In 1947, the US held about 70 per cent of the monetary gold stock of the world. Even a decade later, this figure had not dropped below 59 per cent of the world's stock (Cooper 1968). There was an acute shortage of US dollars over this period, and the dollar itself began to serve as a reserve currency for international payments. Regarding trade, by 1950 the US accounted for nearly 17 per cent of world trade, and its share was about 1.5 times the share of the UK, the next leading nation (Krasner 1976). Throughout the decade of the 1950s, the US increased its preponderance in world trade. By 1960, US trade was 20 per cent of overall world trade, over twice as large as that of the next leading nation (the

UK), and roughly equal to the combined total of the three leading European economies, namely the UK, France, and West Germany. Finally, with regard to foreign investment, the US went from an initial accumulated stock of foreign investment of $7 billion in 1946 to over $100 billion in 1973. The latter figure represented 51 per cent of total world foreign investment in that year (UN Commission on Transnational Corporations 1978). The second-ranking nation in foreign investment in 1973 was the UK with 13.5 per cent, or about one-quarter of the US total. In sum, all the major indicators of international economic performance demonstrate that the US was in a unique position of leadership in the first two decades of the post-war period.

US leadership rested relatively easily on other Western nations because the security concerns of the Cold War with the Soviet Union encouraged those nations to be more willing to follow than they might otherwise have been. However, any system where one nation is dominant is likely to reflect the values of that nation, which was the case of the trade regime set up under the GATT after 1947. One American value that was carried forward to the international system was an emphatic belief that trade liberalization was the driver for full employment and economic growth. For the Americans, trade liberalization was an attractive goal in ideological terms and it was also consistent with the US national interest, since the US was favourably positioned to benefit from freer trade. This was problematic for the Europeans; because of the uncertain circumstances facing their economies after the war and their emphasis on maintaining low levels of unemployment, they believed that full employment and economic growth were a precondition of trade liberalization.

A second and equally important American value was that of multilateralism, intended to guarantee non-discrimination between all countries participating in the trade regime. The Americans blamed the collapse of international trade on the discriminatory trading blocs created by the Europeans in the interwar years, most notably the Imperial Preferential trade system created between Great Britain, India, and the British Dominions in 1932. The Europeans did not share the American enthusiasm for non-discrimination and multilateralism, promoting instead the virtues of economic regionalism, which later came to fruition in the formation of the institutions that led to the present-day European Union

(EU). Similarly, some members of the Imperial Preferential system were keen to preserve their preferential trade relations with Great Britain and the other Dominions.

A third American value was a legal approach to international trade relations, complete with the conception of a code of international trade law backed up by a mechanism for settling disputes between parties. For their part, the Europeans were wary of a codified approach to international trade relations, and sought instead to preserve their right to administrative discretion. They preferred to build up a post-war trading system on practice rather than formal legal commitments (Gardner 1969).

As a result of the different approaches taken by the US and its allies the trade regime was based on compromise in the face of policy disagreements. This compromise, which effectively established a middle ground between various forms of unfettered economic liberalism and Keynesian domestic interventionism has been characterized by Ruggie (1982) as **embedded liberalism**. It is important when assessing the global trade regime to recall that it has always been based on a negotiated consensus, and that in the real world consensus is often only achieved through compromises that are unpalatable to the purists.

The rules of the GATT

Led by the US, the Second World War allies attempted to create a new structure for the international system following the war. An essential part of this attempt was the **Bretton Woods** Conference of 1944, which established the **International Bank for Reconstruction and Development** (**World Bank**) and the **International Monetary Fund** (**IMF**). Along with these efforts in the development and monetary fields, the allies met in several conferences to establish an international trade regime. To that end, countries concluded and signed an agreement to establish an **International Trade Organization** (**ITO**) in 1948, which was to complete the triad of functional organizations in the area of international economic relations. However, the US Congress failed to ratify the agreement, and without US involvement the ITO would have been irrelevant. In place of the ITO, countries relied on the GATT, established in 1947, to provide structure for the rapidly expanding trade system. The GATT itself was simply a contract embodying trade rules for industrial and manufactured products that were negotiated during a multilateral tariff negotiation in 1947.

The GATT was signed by 23 countries and came into force in 1948. Its rules and principles are codified in the 35 articles of the General Agreement (Jackson 1969).

BOX 5.1

Most-Favoured Nation Principle (MFN)

The most-favoured nation principle (MFN) was introduced into the US reciprocal trade agreements of the 1930s and incorporated as Article I of the GATT in 1947. It required GATT Contracting Parties to extend to all signatories the benefits of any agreement that it might reach with any other country (that is, the 'most-favoured nation'). The GATT provided a forum and a legal regime within which countries were encouraged to negotiate and to reach agreements to lower tariffs on a reciprocal basis. These negotiations were normally undertaken on a bilateral basis between the principal supplier and the principal buyer of a good. For example, in the 1950s, the US, as the major buyer of wool (to clothe its troops fighting the Korean war) negotiated tariff reductions with Australia, the principal supplier of wool. These negotiations were conducted on a bilateral basis but the resulting lowered tariff would be accorded to all countries exporting wool to the US. In this example, it would be assumed that Australia would reciprocate by offering concessions to the US.

The effect of the MFN principle was to eliminate discrimination between trade partners, as countries were in principle obliged to have one MFN tariff that applied to all countries, and therefore were prohibited from applying different tariffs on the same product coming from different countries. Non-discrimination introduced the problem of free-riding, where a country might take unreciprocated benefits from a lowering of tariffs by other countries, but this was regarded as a lesser problem than that caused by overtly discriminatory tariff policies. The overall purpose of MFN and non-discrimination was to create a unified multilateral trading system, and to prevent the international trade system from degenerating into a fragmented and discriminatory system of regional preferences. The recent proliferation of preferential free trade agreements (also known as regional trade agreements), which are inherently discriminatory, has heavily compromised the norm of non-discrimination in the global trade regime.

Its overall objective was to reduce tariffs and limit the use of non-tariff barriers to trade, such as quotas, in the economic sectors where it applied. In addition to liberalization, the most important principles of the GATT are non-discrimination, reciprocity, development, and safeguards (Zacher and Finlayson 1981).

The cornerstone of the GATT is non-discrimination, which is embodied in Articles I and III of the GATT. Article I is known as the most-favoured nation principle (see Box 5.1). It requires that any advantage—such as a lowered tariff—granted by one contracting party to any other country would immediately be accorded to all other contracting parties. This obligation—strongly promoted by the US—attacked the practice of discriminatory tariff preferences, which were commonly employed for political reasons before the Second World War, and which compartmentalized and therefore reduced the flow of trade between nations. The US prevailed on this matter, but not before it compromised with the British and French, allowing them to maintain preferential trade arrangements for their colonies. Another major exception to the MFN principle is Article XXIV, which allows the formation of regional trade agreements and **customs unions**, subject to specific conditions. The Article XXIV exception anticipated the creation of the European Economic Community—the precursor to the EU. It was also supported by the Americans who were at the time preparing a then-secret US–Canada free trade agreement that ultimately never entered into force (Chase 2006).

A second dimension of non-discrimination is the National Treatment rule (Article III), which obliges nations to treat imported products no less favourably than domestic products with respect to taxes and all laws and regulations affecting the product's placement on the domestic market. Article III removed a whole range of policy tools (such as internal taxes or distribution requirements) that governments traditionally used to extend preferential treatment to domestic producers. Under the 'General Exceptions' of Article XX, governments nonetheless reserved the right to take measures that serve a restricted list of public policy goals, such as the protection of public morals, the protection of human, animal or plant life or health, or the conservation of exhaustible natural resources. In general, Article I ensured that a country could not discriminate externally between countries and Article III ensured it could not discriminate internally within countries.

Another important principle of the GATT, **reciprocity**, is a normal aspect of negotiations in general. In international trade, reciprocity has been promoted as a political imperative where nations give trade concessions in the form of tariff reduction or market access in order to get similar benefits from their partners. Reciprocity allows governments to mobilize export interests to support liberalization (because they will benefit from concessions granted by other countries) in the face of domestic interest groups that will lose as a result of trade liberalization (see Hiscox, Chapter 4, in this volume). The norm of reciprocity is promoted through the GATT's methodology for tariff negotiations, which were to be conducted 'on a reciprocal and mutually advantageous basis' and 'directed to the substantial reduction of tariffs'.

In the GATT's early history of trade negotiations, reciprocity was a guiding beacon as countries began the process of dismantling tariff protectionism. Reciprocity ran into difficulties when developing countries began to accede to the GATT as a result of the decolonization process. The developing countries comparative advantages lay mainly in areas that were not covered under the GATT, namely agriculture and textiles. In various negotiations beginning in the mid 1950s, attempts were made to mitigate the obligations of GATT membership for developing countries through the concept of **special and differential treatment (SDT)**. This involved exemptions from the negotiating principle of reciprocity, preferential access for developing country exports to rich country markets (i.e. better than MFN treatment), and development assistance to help developing countries compete in export markets (Hoekman and Kostecki 2009). Efforts to accommodate the special needs of developing countries are a continuing aspect of the trade regime, as evidenced in the WTO Doha Round trade negotiations (discussed later in this chapter).

The GATT signatories agreed that significant tariff reductions could only be achieved if escape clauses and exceptions could be included in the new international trade regime and this flexibility is reflected in the above-mentioned exceptions and the GATT's various **safeguards** provisions. For example, Article XII allows governments to reimpose trade restrictions in the face of balance-of-payment difficulties while Article XIX permits governments to raise tariffs for a period of time when a particular industry is confronting significant problems as a result of tariff reductions. The intent of Article XIX was to ensure that problems in specific industries did not compromise the general process of liberalization.

The rules of the GATT provided a basis for governance in a narrow, but fundamentally important, sector of international relations. The GATT was never intended to function as an international organization; it was only ever intended to be a temporary agreement until the ITO Charter came into force. The fact that the GATT came to look and function like an international organization is the result of a largely unplanned and incremental accretion of political and legal powers. It was institution-building by accident.

KEY POINTS

- Following the Second World War, the US was a preponderant presence in the world economy, and took a leadership role in post-war planning.

- Trading nations established the GATT in 1947, and attempted in 1948 to create an ITO, which failed to receive ratification by the US Congress.

- The objectives of the GATT were to promote economic growth and prosperity through the expansion of international trade. This was to be achieved through the reduction of tariffs and the elimination of discrimination in industrial and manufactured products.

- The GATT rules provided a rudimentary basis for the regulation of international trade.

The GATT to 1994

GATT negotiations to 1979

The GATT was established to support the trade negotiations in 1947, and following that date the GATT sponsored multilateral negotiations in 1949 (Annecy), 1951 (Torquay), 1956 (Geneva), 1960–1 (the Dillon Round), and in 1963–7 (the Kennedy Round). Further negotiations were the Tokyo Round (1973–9), the Uruguay Round (1986–93), and the problem-riddled WTO Doha Round, discussed later in this chapter. Of these nine negotiations, the first four after 1947 took up important institutional matters, such as the accession of new members, but they did not make significant progress in liberalizing trade. One reason is that European recovery from the war did not occur as quickly as expected, as evidenced by the fact that

European currencies were not made fully convertible until 1958, which made it difficult for these countries to increase their exposure to international competition. In practice, the US was the preponderant actor in the early negotiations, and offered most of the tariff concessions.

The Kennedy Round of 1963–7 emerged as the first significant negotiation in GATT since 1947 (Preeg 1970). The Kennedy Round was the first GATT negotiation at which the nations of the European Community (EC) participated as a single unit, which was the first time Europe and America engaged in a major negotiation across the Atlantic on an apparent basis of equality and reciprocity. Several new topics were introduced to the negotiating agenda including agriculture, the special treatment of developing countries that had emerged as new players in the GATT as a result of the decolonization process from the 1950s onwards, and non-tariff measures. The inclusion of agriculture was significant, as agriculture trade was highly distorted by interventionist policies designed to detach domestic prices from international markets. However, disagreement between the US and the EC stymied progress on bringing agriculture into the discipline of the GATT rules.

The Kennedy Round led to significant tariff cuts on industrial goods in developed countries. The negotiation also produced an anti-dumping code that helped to standardize national policies geared to prevent unfair competition in international trade, and an international grain agreement that established price ranges for wheat and provided for multilateral sharing of food aid to developing countries. These efforts at rule-making were significant 'firsts' in trade cooperation through the GATT, as it represented the willingness of governments to expand the purview of the regime in order to tackle long-standing problems in the trade system. It was also the first negotiation to explicitly address developing country concerns, culminating in the formal endorsement of the principle of non-reciprocity for developing countries, codified as Part IV of the GATT.

At the close of the Kennedy Round in 1967, the GATT secretariat sought to convince the major trading nations to extend liberalization into the area of non-tariff barriers to trade (Evans 1971). This initial effort was unsuccessful, but by the early 1970s chaos in the international monetary system and increasing use of non-tariff barriers in response to the surge of exports from Japan and the **newly industrializing**

economies (**NIEs**) resurrected fears of trade protectionism and convinced national governments to begin a new negotiation in the GATT.

The agreements reached at the Tokyo Round were the most comprehensive and far-reaching results achieved in trade negotiations since 1947 (Winham 1986). The results fell into three categories: six legal codes that dealt with NTBs (plus a sectoral code for trade in aircraft); tariff reductions; and a series of revisions of GATT articles primarily of interest to developing countries. The six codes updated and expanded aspects of the trade law of the GATT, and were the most important part of the Tokyo Round accords. These covered, respectively, customs valuation procedures, import licensing, technical standards for products, subsidies, and countervailing duty measures, government procurement, and anti-dumping duty procedures. However, negotiations on a safeguards code failed. The general thrust of the code negotiations was to effect a 'constitutional reform' of GATT law, and to improve the openness, certainty, and non-arbitrariness of the rules governing international trade.

The second category of results from the Tokyo Round was tariff reductions. Tariff negotiations had been the main item of business in the six multilateral negotiations that were held under GATT auspices through the Kennedy Round of 1967. Tariffs were not the major focus of the Tokyo Round, yet the average reductions of about 35 per cent of industrial nations' tariffs achieved in this negotiation were comparable to the reductions of the Kennedy Round. The reductions covered more than $100 billion of imports, and were phased in over an eight-year period beginning in 1980 (Cline 1983). Once again, however, agriculture proved to be an intractable issue, with the US and the EC agreeing to remove the two major issues in agriculture trade—market access and the use of subsidies—from the negotiating table halfway through the round.

The third category of Tokyo Round results was a proposed series of revisions to GATT Articles known as the 'framework' agreements. Negotiations on this subject were initiated by Brazil, intending to clarify GATT obligations and ease those obligations for developing countries. The framework agreements covered subjects such as safeguard actions for development purposes, trade measures taken to correct payments deficits, export controls, and deviations from MFN for developing countries. A major outcome of these negotiations was the 'Enabling Clause', which allowed GATT signatories to accord differential and more favourable treatment to developing countries, without according the same treatment to other countries.

Notwithstanding the Enabling Clause, developing countries were disappointed with the results of the Tokyo Round, as it failed to tackle non-tariff measures used by developed countries to restrict imports in industry sectors where developing countries were competitive, including food products, textiles, clothing, and footwear, iron and steel, shipbuilding, and consumer electronics (United Nations Conference on Trade and Development 1982). However, the active involvement of a large number of developing countries in the Tokyo Round negotiation was unprecedented in the GATT and it set the scene for the Uruguay Round a decade later.

The Tokyo Round underscored the extent to which multilateral negotiations had become a point of departure for managing the international trade system. In contrast with past GATT negotiations, which were largely limited to the reduction of tariffs, the Tokyo Round was a rule-making exercise of major proportions. Furthermore, the agreements of the Tokyo Round constituted legal rules that reached further into the nation state and impacted on domestic regulatory systems more deeply than was the case with most international agreements.

KEY POINTS

- Multilateral trade negotiations were conducted in the GATT to reduce tariff protectionism on a reciprocal basis.

- The Kennedy Round (1963–7) was the first significant tariff-cutting round under the GATT.

- In the Tokyo Round (1973–9), countries focused on the more difficult task of reducing non-tariff measures that afforded protection in international trade. These measures were regulated through the negotiation of international codes of conduct.

- The Tokyo Round demonstrated the importance of multilateral negotiation to the management of the international trade system.

The Uruguay Round

The next major effort to establish further the global trade regime was the Uruguay Round negotiation, which was launched at a GATT ministerial meeting in

Punta del Este in September 1986 (Croome 1995). The path to the Uruguay Round was difficult as there was deep division among the major players about the desirability of new multilateral trade negotiations. The US was the most vigorous advocate of a new round, partly to counter growing protectionist pressures at home but also to expand the GATT regime to include new topics such as services, investment, and intellectual property, which were issues of particular concern to US business and industry. The US also wanted to deal with high levels of agricultural protectionism, especially in the EC and Japan. The US position was supported by a group of major agriculture exporters including Australia, Canada, New Zealand, and a group of developing countries in South America and South-East Asia. But many other countries opposed the commencement of a new round; opponents included the EC and Japan, who wanted to maintain their agricultural trade barriers, and a group of ten developing countries (G10), led by India and Brazil, who insisted that they were not sufficiently developed to negotiate the new issues, such as services, on an equal footing with the developed countries. These divisions proved to be insurmountable. The 1982 GATT ministerial meeting, which was convened to launch a new round, ended in acrimony and it brought the GATT close to breakdown (Croome 1995).

The failure of the 1982 ministerial meeting fuelled views in the US that while its economy was the most open in the world, other countries were imposing obstacles to trade that could not be addressed through GATT negotiations. In response, the US began to negotiate bilateral and regional trade agreements with key trade and security partners, including Israel and Canada (Ostry 1997). This was a 'shot across the bow' of other GATT parties to indicate that the US commitment to multilateralism could not be taken for granted, and if it could not achieve its objectives through the GATT, it would work outside the multilateral trade system.

In 1985 the GATT Contracting Parties agreed to work towards the launch of a new round of negotiations. Ongoing opposition from the G10 to the inclusion of the new areas such as services, investment, and intellectual property impeded progress towards the launch. The impasse was ultimately overcome through the efforts of an informal working group of developed countries (including Australia, Canada, NZ, and some non-European countries) and 20 developing countries that were supportive of a new round

of negotiations. These developing countries were moving away from protectionist policies and **import-substitution industrialization** in favour of export-oriented development and they were keen to ensure that developed countries addressed issues of particular interest to them, most notably high levels of protection in agriculture, and textiles and clothing. Led by Colombia and Switzerland, this informal working group—the so-called 'Café au Lait' group—developed the negotiating mandate that became the basis for the Uruguay Round. The success of this coalition of like-minded countries marked a watershed moment in GATT/WTO history; henceforth, coalitional diplomacy was a central feature of multilateral negotiations, particularly in the face of conflicts between the major powers in the global trade regime.

The Uruguay Round was successfully launched after a week-long special ministerial session at Punta del Este in September 1986 (Winham 1998). The G10's opposition to the inclusion of services, investment, and intellectual property was overcome by agreement to separate those negotiations from the traditional GATT issues, which was expected to lessen the prospects that developed countries could force trade-offs between new and traditional subjects in the negotiation. A coalition of agriculture-exporting developed and developing countries, the Cairns Group, led by Australia, ensured that agriculture would have a prominent part in the negotiations (Capling 2001).

New issues: services, investment, and intellectual property

The agenda of the Uruguay Round (Box 5.2) comprised 15 negotiating groups arranged initially in four principal categories: market access (including the critical areas of agriculture and textiles); reform of GATT rules; measures to strengthen the GATT as an institution; and the new issues, specifically services, investment, and intellectual property. The new issues were included in the negotiation in order to make the GATT more relevant to developments in the world economy, and to respond to strong pressures coming from industry in developed countries (Preeg 1995).

As a combined result of communication, transportation, and technology revolutions and changes in the global financial system, services had come to account for well over half of the **gross domestic product (GDP)** of developed countries by the late 1980s, and they were beginning to account for an increasing

BOX 5.2

Uruguay Round Agreements

The GATT Uruguay Round began in September 1986, effectively concluded in December 1993, and formally concluded with official signatures at the Marrakesh Ministerial Meeting in April 1994. The Uruguay Round produced a wide range of agreements integrated under a common legal system. What is usually thought of as the 'WTO system' is contained in the Marrakesh Agreement Establishing the World Trade Organization (WTO) and the Dispute Settlement Understanding (DSU). The WTO Agreement established the WTO as an international organization, and ensured that all the agreements negotiated at the Uruguay Round were accepted as a Single Undertaking, which required members to implement all the Uruguay Round agreements as a condition of joining the WTO. The dispute settlement system established by the DSU was also intended to apply to all areas of the Uruguay Round

Agreements; hence it is an integral part of the architecture of the WTO system.

The Uruguay Round Agreements comprise about 60 agreements of some 550 pages, covering subjects as widely diversified as agriculture, services, intellectual property, textiles and clothing, safeguards, rules of origin, sanitary and phytosanitary measures, and technical barriers to trade. These agreements can be accessed on the WTO website www.wto.org under the title 'Legal Texts of the WTO Agreements'. In addition, the Uruguay Round Agreements also included the GATT 1994, which effectively incorporated the GATT of 1947 into the WTO system. There were some additional agreements interpreting various provisions of the GATT, but there is historical and legal continuity from the basic rules and provisions of the GATT to the WTO trade regime.

---

proportion of international trade. Bringing services into the global trade regime required negotiators to incorporate GATT principles of transparency, national treatment and reciprocity, as well as newer principles such as market access, into an area of trade that was conceptually dissimilar from trade in goods, the normal milieu of GATT principles and practice (Arup 2000). Given the paucity of information on trade in services, negotiators first developed a common database on which substantive decisions could later be made. Second, a code of principles, which later became known as the General Agreement on Trade in Services (GATS), was negotiated to provide for a standard of treatment between countries of trade in services. Finally, the code of principles was to be applied to specific sectors of services trade.

For the GATT, the incorporation of services was not a straightforward matter. Services are not goods, which had always been the focus of GATT rules, but rather are processes in which skills and knowledge are exchanged in order to meet a particular consumer need. They can include processes as widely differentiated as engineering consulting, financial **intermediation**, tourism, transport, and shipping, and legal advice. Traditionally, most services were considered to be domestic activities but by the 1980s, services were becoming increasingly mobile across international borders. As services often require the provider and the consumer to be in close proximity, trade in services

often involves the international movement of people. This can occur through the physical movement of consumers to obtain services in a foreign jurisdiction (e.g. tourism, education, healthcare), or through the entry of service providers to the territory of the consumer (e.g. architects, engineers, management consultants). Some services require the provider to establish a commercial presence in another territory (e.g. foreign subsidiaries of hotels, universities, or insurance companies). A fourth type of international service trade is the cross-border supply of services, for instance online education or call centres, where services are provided from one territory to another over the telephone or internet.

One important obstacle to free exchange of services between countries is the reluctance of domestic authorities to grant foreign firms the right to establish and do business in their markets. Governments generally seek to provide consistent regulation over their own markets; this might require discrimination against trade partners that apply different standards from trade in services or it may require the protection of an entire service sector from international competitors. However, in the 1980s, many governments began to undertake regulatory reform of some of their services sectors through the breaking up of monopolies, privatization, and liberalization (e.g. public utilities, postal services, telecommunications, and national airlines). Combined with pressure from other sectors of the economy who wanted access to cheaper services, as well as changing consumer preferences, and facilitated by rapid advances in information communications technology, services increasingly became seen as contestable and tradeable—hence the willingness of governments to contemplate multilateral rules and disciplines in services trade.

Translating GATT principles such as non-discrimination and national treatment of foreign suppliers to the services sector proved to be a major conceptual challenge for the Uruguay Round negotiators, and private sector lobbying (particularly in the US financial services sector) played a significant role in advancing this work. The result of the negotiations was the creation of GATS, which established a code of conduct for all measures affecting trade in services. GATS Article I defines trade in services and specifies four modes of supply: cross-border supply, consumption abroad, commercial presence, and presence of natural persons. The GATS requires MFN treatment with some time-bound exceptions (Article II) and exemptions for regional trade agreements (Article V). National treatment (Article XVII) is required for any sectors that are listed in a member's schedule of commitments. The GATS explicitly recognizes the right of governments to regulate services in order to meet their national policy objectives, but requires that these regulations be applied in 'a reasonable, objective and impartial manner' (Article VI).

Annexed to the GATS is each member's schedule of commitments, which lists each service sector for which a member has granted market access and national treatment to foreign service suppliers. There is wide variation in these schedules. Developed countries included a greater number of services sectors in their schedules than developing countries, and the poorest developing countries scheduled very few commitments at all. Rarely did these scheduled commitments extend new market access; in most cases, they were simply a legal commitment to 'bind' existing regulatory regimes. While the GATS constituted an unprecedented extension of multilateral trade rules into a new area of trade, it achieved very little liberalization. That task was left to future negotiations in the WTO.

The two other new issues on the Uruguay Round agenda were investment and intellectual property. Investment was included because by the 1980s, it had become apparent that investment was interchangeable with trade, and, more important, that trade liberalization might be less valuable in stimulating international economic exchanges unless it is accompanied by the liberalization of investment regimes. However, investment has always attracted considerable regulation in importing countries because of the perceived risk to sovereignty associated with high levels of foreign investment in sensitive industries. In the Uruguay Round, the negotiation of a multilateral investment agreement eventually proved to be an unreachable goal, and the agreement that was reached on **Trade-Related Investment Measures (TRIMs)** dealt with only a small proportion of the issues raised in the negotiation.

Trade-Related Aspects of Intellectual Property Rights (TRIPs) was the third of the new issues. Intellectual property rights grant state protection to producers of new ideas. The Berne and Paris Conventions had provided for international cooperation on these rights since 1886 and 1896 respectively, but protection had not been mandatory in the international economy (Maskus 2000). Producers of high-tech products sought to internationalize the intellectual property protections they enjoyed in their home country, and producers' associations such as the Pharmaceuticals Manufacturers Association demanded constraints on generic industries that arguably did not recognize legitimate patents on drugs. Negotiations in the Uruguay Round began by addressing the problem of counterfeit goods in international trade, but developed countries—which asserted that inadequate protection of intellectual property rights was a serious non-tariff barrier to trade—quickly pressed for a broader negotiation over patents and copyrights. Developing countries, led by India and Brazil, viewed TRIPs protection as a potential barrier to trade in its own right, but they were more concerned over the monopolies effectively granted in developed countries for products such as pharmaceuticals, which they considered crucial to the public interest. The developing countries acquiesced on this issue because they felt their losses were compensated by gains elsewhere in the overall accord (e.g. agriculture, textiles, and clothing), and an agreement was concluded that set international standards for certain protections dealing with copyrights and patents (Winham 1998). However, the controversy over the TRIPs Agreement continued as a mainstay of WTO politics, as developing countries saw intellectual property rights as a mechanism by which developed countries could maintain a competitive edge relative to countries that lacked a sophisticated technological infrastructure.

Agriculture

At the outset of the negotiation, a coalition of 14 agricultural exporters from among the developed and developing countries formed under Australian leadership to promote the liberalization of global agricultural markets. Known as the Cairns Group, these countries played an important role in the early stages of the negotiation in bridging the differences between the US and the EU over agricultural trade and ensuring that agriculture was not put in the 'too hard basket', as had been the case in previous Rounds (Capling 2001). However, by January 1992, it became clear that the Uruguay Round was blocked, and the reason was the agricultural negotiation between the major players. Agricultural trade had long been a difficult problem for many countries in the GATT system, but in the Uruguay Round the inherent problems of agriculture were compounded because this issue pitted the interests of the US and the EU against one another. The US–EU differences stemmed mainly from the fact that, since the 1960s, Europe had established a protectionist policy under the Common Agricultural Policy, while the US was moving towards a comparative advantage in agricultural exports. The Uruguay Round thus turned into a politicized contest between the major players, and for 18 months the main activity of the multilateral negotiation was a series of bilateral encounters between US and EU officials, with the Cairns Group keeping pressure on the parties to reach agreement. This blockage halted progress in other areas and even between other countries. The US and the EU eventually reached a resolution of their differences in the 'Blair House' accords on agriculture, but agriculture continued to be the major stumbling block to a general agreement until very late in the negotiation. The Agreement on Agriculture was a significant achievement of the Uruguay Round. For the first time in history, agricultural tariffs were bound and the use of domestic and export subsidies was codified and restricted. Like the GATS, while it did not achieve much additional trade liberalization, it incorporated agriculture into multilateral trade rules and created a basis for future liberalization.

Developing countries

For most of the history of the GATT, the developing countries have been marginal players. The GATT itself was largely a creation of the US and its Western allies, and focused mainly on trade rather than economic development, which was the central concern of the poorer countries of Africa, Asia, and South America. Above all, the GATT took aim at the high level of tariffs in the trading system, and promoted the reduction of these tariff levels in developing countries (see Figure 5.1). By comparison, in terms of trade policy, most developing countries pursued a policy of **import-substitution industrialization**, which called for high protective tariffs to force consumers to purchase domestic-made products at the expense of imports. These policies encouraged developing-country governments to pursue trade policies of self-sufficiency, and to seek 'special and differential' benefits in GATT negotiations in lieu of accepting the multilateral rules of the GATT based on reciprocity. The upshot was that, as the GATT system matured, it became clear that one of the major threats to that system was its inability to be relevant to traders and governments in countries representing over two-thirds of the world's population. This threat was largely overcome in the Uruguay Round negotiation, for one of the results of the negotiation was that, for the first time, developing countries became fully integrated into the world trade regime.

Most developing countries did not support the initiation of the Uruguay Round. However, once developing countries agreed to negotiate, they quickly engaged in all the issues. As the round continued, it became clear that the capacity to determine the outcome of the Uruguay Round fell mainly to the two major trading powers: the US and the EU. At this point, a curious change took place: the major powers that had been so insistent on a new negotiation reached a deadlock, largely over agriculture, while the developing countries that had fought so hard against a new negotiation for most of the 1980s became the greatest advocates for its successful conclusion in the early 1990s. From 1991 until the conclusion of the Uruguay Round in December 1993, the developing countries kept the pressure on the majors to settle their differences, which was an important element in the multilateral agreement that was eventually reached.

The turnaround in the developing countries' position was one of the most interesting stories of the Uruguay Round (Winham 1998). It occurred, first, because developing countries were advantaged by two negotiating principles that underlay the Uruguay Round; namely, consensus and the single undertaking.

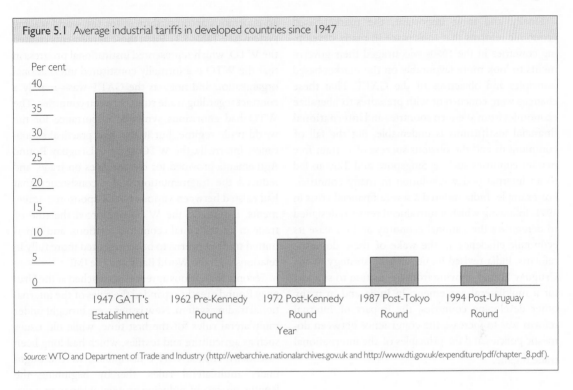

Figure 5.1 Average industrial tariffs in developed countries since 1947

Per cent

Source: WTO and Department of Trade and Industry (http://webarchive.nationalarchives.gov.uk and http://www.dti.gov.uk/expenditure/pdf/chapter_8.pdf).

Consensus—which was a traditional GATT principle for decision-making—meant that multilateral agreement required the passive support (that is, no formal opposition) of all participants. As a negotiating procedure, single undertaking meant that all issues were treated as a single package so that 'nothing was agreed until everything was agreed'. In effect, this required a balance of concessions from developed countries (e.g. in agriculture, textiles and clothing, and SDT (Special and Differential Treatment)) and developing countries (e.g. services, intellectual property) in order to make a deal acceptable to all members. The principles of consensus and the single undertaking combined to increase the power of small and middle-sized powers at the Uruguay Round, which was demonstrated dramatically at the 1988 ministerial meeting in Montreal when five Latin American countries prevented consensus on an interim package agreement because their concerns over agriculture were not being met by the US and the EC. This action empowered the developing countries, and led them to take a greater interest in the overall negotiation.

This procedural notion of the single undertaking should not be confused with the other meaning of the Single Undertaking as a set of legal obligations

that requires all parties to accept and implement all elements of a negotiated agreement. The Uruguay Round results were implemented as a Single Undertaking and any GATT members that wanted to join the WTO in 1995 had to accept all agreements negotiated in the round. This was a departure from the Tokyo Round non-tariff agreements which countries could adopt on an opt in/opt out basis. The Single Undertaking implied significant new obligations for many developing countries, which later proved to be contentious.

Despite the reality that developing countries continued to be economically disadvantaged in comparison to developed countries, the agreements reached at the Uruguay Round were relatively favourable to the interests of the former. Developing countries as a group benefited from agreements on agriculture, textiles, and clothing (and probably services), while they were generally disadvantaged on intellectual property and possibly anti-dumping practices. Most important, however, developing countries were advantaged by the institutional arrangements resulting from the Uruguay Round Agreements, namely the strong dispute settlement mechanism and the creation of the WTO itself.

Finally, and most important, the market-based economic reforms that took place in many developing countries in the 1980s encouraged their governments to look more favourably on the market-based principles and objectives of the GATT. That these changes were concurrent with pressures to liberalize economies from Western countries and **international financial institutions** is undeniable, but the fall of communism and the obvious success of certain free market countries such as Singapore and Taiwan led to an internal policy revolution in many countries. For example, India suffered a severe financial crisis in 1991, following which it introduced reforms designed to deregulate the national economy and increase its economic efficiency. In the wake of these domestic reforms, India revised its negotiating strategy at the Uruguay Round, moving from opposition to support for a multilateral agreement. In India and in many other developing countries, the impact of internal reform was to increase the congruence between domestic policies and the principles of the international trade regime.

Results

The Uruguay Round Agreements were concluded on 15 December 1993. In comparison to the results achieved in previous negotiations, they represented

an enormous accomplishment for the world trading system (see Table 5.1). First, these agreements created the WTO, which represented institutional progress in that the WTO is a formally constituted international organization and not—as the GATT was—mainly a contract regarding trade rules between countries. The WTO had enormous symbolic importance for the world trade regime, but it also had practical significance. Internally, the WTO and the Uruguay Round Agreements provided for clearer rules on trade, and reduced the fragmentation and inconsistency that had existed between various GATT-sponsored agreements. Externally, the WTO reinforced the role of trade in international economic relations, and it permitted trade concerns to be represented more fully in relations with the World Bank and the IMF.

Second, the various agreements reached at the Uruguay Round greatly expanded the rules of the international trading system. New issues were brought under multilateral rules for the first time, while old issues such as agriculture and textiles, which had long been essentially outside GATT disciplines, were brought under multilateral rules, thereby beginning the lengthy process of reducing protectionism in two sectors that had for a long time resisted the progression towards a more liberal world trade regime (Paarlberg 1997). Third, as a result of the Single Undertaking, which required that all negotiating parties accept all

Table 5.1 Results of GATT negotiations, 1960–94

Negotiation	No. of countries	Results
Dillon Round 1960–1	26	• Average tariff cut of 10% on $4.9 bn of trade
Kennedy Round 1963–7	62	• Average tariff cut of 35% on $40 bn of trade • Anti-dumping code • Part IV of the GATT for developing countries
Tokyo Round 1973–9	102	• Average tariff cut of 35% on more than $100 bn of trade • Six codes dealing with non-tariff measures, plus aircraft code • Revision of GATT articles for developing countries
Uruguay Round 1986–94	128	• Average tariff cut of 39% on $3.7 trillion of trade • 12 Agreements (including Agriculture, Textiles, Subsidies, Safeguards) • New issues: GATS and trade related • Aspects of intellectual property rights (TRIPs) • DSU • Creation of WTO, new legal footing for the multilateral trade regime

parts of the Uruguay Round Agreements as a condition of joining the WTO, developing countries took on far-reaching commitments. Effectively, the Uruguay Round brought the developing countries fully into the global trade regime. The Uruguay Round concluded at a time when many developing countries were undergoing substantial liberalization, when it was hoped that the confluence of change in the developing world and the deepening of the multilateral regime would engage trade more fully in the progress towards international development.

Finally, the Uruguay Round Agreements represented a further step towards a system based more on rules rather than power in international trade. The agreements advanced the rules-based nature of trade relations between countries, and thereby increased the economic security of smaller and middle-sized countries in their relations with larger powers. In particular, the agreements consolidated and considerably strengthened the dispute settlement system that had evolved under the GATT. The agreements created an obligation for countries to adjudicate an issue if a trading partner seeks this recourse. Conversely, countries are obligated not to use unilateral trade sanctions as an alternative to multilateral dispute settlement actions under the WTO. Both provisions were intended to increase the prospects that countries, regardless of their size and power, would be equal before the law in trade disputes.

KEY POINTS

- Developing countries resisted efforts by developed countries to establish a new GATT negotiation following the Tokyo Round.

- The Uruguay Round (1986–93) comprised a lengthy negotiating agenda, including new issues such as trade in services and TRIPs.

- The most difficult issue in the Uruguay Round was trade in agriculture, particularly between the major parties, the EU, and the US.

- The Uruguay Round was an enormous accomplishment for the international trade system. International rules were established in most important areas of international trade, the WTO was created, and a more effective dispute settlement system established. The developing countries became full participants in the WTO system.

The WTO

The establishment of the WTO marked a watershed in the evolution of the global trade regime. Its key functions are to reduce discrimination and promote market access opportunities in international commerce; to formulate rules of conduct for international trade in goods and services; to promote transparency of national laws and regulations; to promote dialogue and understanding on trade matters; and to settle trade disputes among nations. It has near universal membership (162 countries at the time of writing, with 26 more in the queue for accession). Major powers that had remained outside of the GATT have since joined the WTO, including China (2001) and the Russian Federation (2012).

Organization and functions

Institutionally, the WTO is headquartered in Geneva and headed by a Ministerial Conference which convenes every two years, although as shown in Table 5.2, exceptions have occurred.

The Ministerial Conference brings together trade ministers of all member countries and is the WTO's top decision-making organ. The General Council acts on behalf of the Ministerial Conference between these meetings. Members typically have permanent representations in Geneva and state officials at ambassadorial level come together regularly in order to carry out the functions of the WTO. The General Council may also convene as the Dispute Settlement Body (DSB), which adopts reports on international trade disputes, and as the Trade Policy Review Body, an organ tasked with the systematic, regular examination and publication of individual members' domestic trade policy measures. The Council for Trade in Goods, the Council for Trade in Services, and the TRIPS Council are subsidiary bodies operating under the guidance of the General Council and are supported by a large number of committees and working groups addressing topics as diverse as Agriculture, Trade and Environment, and Trade in Financial Services. The Trade Negotiations Committee was set up at the launch of the Doha Round of multilateral trade negotiations to supervise the overall conduct of negotiations under the authority of the General Council. It oversees the work of subcommittees that negotiate on individual subjects. The political organs are aided in their work by the

Table 5.2 WTO ministerial conferences	
Year	**City**
1996	Singapore
1998	Geneva
1999	Seattle
2001	Doha
2003	Cancún
2005	Hong Kong
2009	Geneva
2011	Geneva
2013	Bali
2015	Nairobi

Source: WTO (www.wto.org/english/thewto_e/minist_e/minist_e.htm).

Table 5.3 GATT/WTO directors-general		
Name	**Time in office**	**Country of origin**
Eric Wyndham-White	1948–68	UK
Olivier Long	1968–80	Switzerland
Arthur Dunkel	1980–93	Switzerland
Peter Sutherland	1993–5	EC
Renato Ruggiero	1995–9	EC
Mike Moore	1999–2002	New Zealand
Supachai Panitchpakdi	2002–5	Thailand
Pascal Lamy	2005–13	EC
Roberto Azevedô	2013–present	Brazil

Source: WTO (https://www.wto.org/english/thewto_e/dg_e/dg_e.htm).

WTO's Director-General, with the support of a small Secretariat of 639 staff in 2015 (WTO 2015c).

Unlike other international economic institutions, the WTO works on a one-country/one-vote basis. In keeping with the consensus practice inherited from the GATT, a decision is adopted when no member actively disagrees. In other words, there is no need for all 160-plus WTO members to agree that a decision shall be taken. It suffices if no member vetoes the decision. Although decision-making by consensus puts all members on equal footing in procedural terms, a country's influence in WTO politics is generally determined not only by the size of its market, but also by the quality of its representation in Geneva. Two simple statistics indicate that although the WTO is based on democratic procedural principles, not every member is automatically empowered to have their trade concerns heard. First, there are significant variations in the size of members' permanent representations in Geneva. While big trading nations such as the US, the EU and China have separate, well-staffed WTO missions in addition to their UN missions and diplomatic representations to Switzerland, the LDCs' missions had 4.1 staff members on average in 2008, with many of them simultaneously representing their country in all international organizations in Geneva as well as taking on consular functions (DiCaprio and Trommer, 2010). With scarce human resources, representing one country's interest in a large number of WTO councils, committees, working groups, and negotiations can be an impossible task.

Second, Table 5.3 shows Directors-General of the GATT/WTO since 1947 by country of origin. It indicates that the overwhelming majority of Directors-General have come from a small cohort of developed country members.

The WTO is a 'member-driven' organization, meaning that the members and not the Secretariat are mainly responsible for setting the agenda and carrying out the functions of the organization (Blackhurst 1998). The WTO's role is to provide for a transparent and predictable system of international trade. Three elements are essential to this, namely (1) making international trade rules, (2) providing a forum for dialogue on international trade issues, and (3) adjudicating trade disputes among members.

In regard to its rule-making function, in a dynamic world economy, members periodically find the set of existing rules in need of reform. This may be the case when new issues gain pertinence that were not previously considered at the WTO, such as the increasing attention paid to the intersection of trade rules and environmental problems today. Members may also consider existing rules and concessions to be unsatisfactory. Many low- and middle-income countries continue to fight for market access in agriculture, for example, while trade policy communities in advanced countries have become concerned with the lack of rules in e-commerce. The WTO agreements and domestic law pertaining to international trade flows constitute the hard core of rules. These rules can be renegotiated in WTO negotiations under the basic negotiating principles carried over from the GATT, that is to say: consensus, single undertaking, and reciprocity. The single undertaking in principle excludes the possibility that new rules will apply in certain areas before the entire set of rules being negotiated across all areas has been agreed. As explored later in this chapter, this principle has gradually eroded during the Doha Round, particularly over the last two WTO ministerial conferences, and its status is currently unclear.

The second function of the WTO is to provide a forum for dialogue on international trade issues. This does not only occur through regular exchanges among country officials in Geneva. The Trade Policy Review Mechanism is also an important tool through which the WTO fulfils this function. The frequency by which a member's domestic trade policy regime is reviewed depends on its share of world trade. The main purpose of a review is information dissemination and transparency, but the reviews also help to evaluate whether members are in full compliance with their obligations under the WTO Agreements.

Third, the efficacy with which the WTO exercises its adjudication function makes the organization unique in the realm of international cooperation. Public international law is generally notorious for its lack of instruments to enforce legal obligations. Unlike in a domestic setting, where the judiciary relies on the executive's authority backed by its monopoly over legitimate violence to give effect to its decisions, there is no world government to assure that international legal provisions be adhered to. Ultimately, states in the international system need to police each other when it comes to the application of international law, and traditionally have done so, where they chose to, through ruptures in diplomatic relations, economic sanctions, or war. The institutional shift from GATT to WTO changed the domain of public international law with respect to the enforceability of rules. The institutional change was as simple as it was dramatic in legal and political impact, and it is explored in greater detail in the section that follows.

Dispute settlement

During the GATT years, legal procedures evolved whereby one contracting party could enter into consultations with another contracting party in cases where it believed that GATT obligations had been violated. If the two parties could not put their differences aside in consultations, the dispute was adjudicated by a GATT Panel of international trade experts. Once the panel issued its findings in a panel report, this was sent to the membership for adoption, a formal procedure through which the report became legally binding. Because decision-making by consensus effectively gives individual countries a power of veto, non-compliance with GATT reports became a problem from 1980 onwards (Hudec et al. 1993). To flip the political logic, the WTO's DSU stipulates that a report is adopted unless the DSB decides by consensus not to adopt it. This negative or reverse consensus rule effectively requires that the member in whose favour the dispute has been decided agrees in the DSB not to adopt the report. Needless to say, reverse consensus decision-making in the DSB has made the adoption of dispute settlement reports quasi-automatic under the WTO's Dispute Settlement Mechanism (DSM) (Palmeter and Mavroidis 1999).

To provide legal security, including the right to appeal, the DSU establishes a three-step process. The initiation of a proceeding retains the dispute settlement practices of the GATT years. Thus, dispute settlement procedures begin when one member requests consultations with another member over an alleged violation of WTO law. Only members can bring disputes to the WTO. Although there is no direct possibility for private parties to make recourse to the DSM, non-state actors including, notably, businesses can and do lobby their governments to file a complaint in Geneva. To date, the majority of disputes have been settled in the consultation stage, indicating that dialogue and negotiation remain crucial tools also within the WTO's dispute settlement function. Only if consultations have failed to produce a result within 60 days may the complaining member request the establishment of a panel and thus enter into a legal process of adjudication. Panels are made up of three or five international trade experts and are established by the DSB on a case-by-case basis. Legal hearings are held in WTO headquarters in Geneva, where both sides present their interpretation of WTO law and facts of the case, and other members who have a substantial interest in the dispute may make third-party submissions. Once a panel has issued a report, usually within six months from the date of its composition, the members may submit an appeal on legal questions before the panel report is adopted in the DSB. Appeals are heard before three of the seven members of the Appellate Body, which is a standing body of international legal experts that is appointed by the DSB for a four-year term. In addition to giving parties a right to appeal panel reports, the Appellate Body has been created with the intention of bringing consistency, coherence, and stability into the interpretation and application of WTO law, which is considered an important element of legal security in any legal system.

The ability to appeal is all the more important as the DSU contains provisions that can give effect to potentially hurtful sanctions in case of a member's non-compliance. A member that has been found to violate WTO law by the DSB is expected to bring its domestic trade policy regime in line with its WTO obligations. If the member does not comply with the recommendations of a report, it must enter into negotiations with the complaining countries in order to agree on mutually acceptable compensations, usually in the form of trade concessions such as tariff reductions on a product of interest to the other side(s). According to Article 22 of the DSU, if these negotiations do not succeed within 20 days, the complaining member 'may request authorization from the DSB to suspend the application to the Member concerned of concessions or other obligations under the covered agreements'. In order to make retaliation effective, members are not confined to issuing measures in the economic sector in which the violation has occurred. A notable example of this occurred in the famous *EC Hormones* case taken by the US against the EU. The report required the EU to lift its import ban on hormone-treated beef products because, in the eyes of the Appellate Body, the EU had not conducted a scientific risk assessment of the health risks associated with the products before implementing the ban. When the EU failed to comply, the US was not obliged to withdraw preferences in the beef sector, but instead introduced a 100 per cent *ad valorem* duty on a variety of agricultural products (Sien 2007).

In its short history since 1995, the WTO's DSM has been highly popular, as the dispute settlement statistics in Table 5.4 indicate.

However, in times when the WTO fails to update the trade law rulebook, some observers worry that

Table 5.4 Dispute settlement statistics, 1995–2015 (without retaliation requests)

Standard DSU complaints	498
Panel requests	356
Standard panel reports adopted	164
Standard Appellate Body reports adopted	100

Source: worldtradelaw.net

the DSM will become overburdened. If the rules of international trade are out of sync with developments in the global economy, there is a perceived risk that members might increasingly use dispute settlement in order to fill normative gaps in the trade regime. The danger is that the DSB may exceed its remit and lose legitimacy in the eyes of the membership. This risk exists, according to Article 3.2 of the DSU 'the DSB cannot add to or diminish the rights and obligations provided in the covered agreements'. In plain terms, this means that the DSB is prohibited from engaging in judicial lawmaking, as concessions and trade rules can only be made by members.

Attempting to walk the fine line between WTO law and politics, dispute settlement organs sometimes issue longwinded statements that can raise questions about how effectively the DSB can bite. In the *Turkey–Textiles* case, for example, the Appellate Body had to pronounce itself on the question, *inter alia*, of whether the customs union between the EC and Turkey fulfilled the conditions under which Article XXIV GATT permits members to enter into regional agreements. One requirement is that the members of a customs union liberalize 'substantially all the trade' between them. The term does not establish a concrete threshold, and members' interpretation of the provision and corresponding practice vary considerably. Asked to pronounce itself on the condition in *Turkey–Textiles*, the Appellate Body stated that 'it is clear … that "substantially all the trade" is not the same as *all* the trade, and also that "substantially all the trade" is something considerably more than merely *some* of the trade' (italics in original, paragraph 48). For those who had hoped that dispute settlement would bring some discipline into the ever-growing web of preferential trade agreements (see Ravenhill, Chapter 6, in this volume), the statement was disappointing. Overall, it illustrates the difficult balance that the Appellate Body often has to strike in order to solve disputes among members, without being seen to restrict the rights or expand on the obligations that have been agreed in negotiations. At the end of the day, even the WTO's rules-based system depends on the members' acceptance of the legitimacy of the DSM. Few are more acutely aware of the complex interplay of international politics and international law than WTO Appellate Body members.

In this interplay, it is not always evident to members whether their issues are better addressed by way of dispute settlement or in the course of negotiations. The episode of the cotton case, presented in Box 5.3, is a case in point.

The cotton case exposes another salient feature of the WTO DSM. Put simply, in WTO dispute settlement, size matters. As explained above, a proceeding normally starts when commercial interests of a member are at stake. At the same time, WTO dispute settlement is a highly technical exercise requiring

extensive and specialized legal expertise and experience. In many low-income countries and LDCs, government, and business are not organized to the degree where this kind of expertise is always readily available, nor may they dispose of the human and financial resources required to run a case in Geneva. To address this imbalance, a range of international lawyers do *pro bono* work for developing countries and LDCs and the Advisory Centre on WTO Law was created as an independent organization in Geneva in 2001 in order to provide legal capacity to these members. The size of a member, however, also matters at the implementation stage of a ruling. International trade flows are highly asymmetrical among members, making some countries trade-dependent on others for whom their trade may not represent a big percentage of overall trade flows. For example, many African countries conduct most of their trade with the EU. For the EU, even the African heavyweight Nigeria only accounts for 1.2 per cent of EU merchandise trade (DG Trade 2015). In this context, the possibility for members to compensate across WTO agreements can be a decisive factor

BOX 5.3

The *Cotton* Case

The domestic support measures that a number of WTO members provide for their domestic producers, users, and exporters of cotton are a long-standing issue in the global trade regime. While protecting domestic economic actors from variations in world market prices for cotton, the measures are perceived to reinforce these fluctuations and negatively impact on cotton producers abroad. The issue is particularly pressing given that cotton production provides the livelihoods of hundreds of millions of small-scale and family farmers across the developing world. WTO members have chosen to address the situation through different channels in the WTO. In 2002, the government of Brazil requested consultations with the US concerning its domestic support measures that Brazil deemed to constitute export subsidies for US cotton. In 2003, four African countries, Benin, Burkina Faso, Chad, and Mali—dubbed the 'Cotton 4'—raised the issue with the WTO Director-General and in the Trade Negotiations Committee. Their Sectoral Initiative in Favour of Cotton led to the creation of a Cotton Sub-Committee in the Doha Round in November 2004. At the WTO Ministerial Conference in Hong Kong in 2005, ministers agreed that all forms of export subsidies for cotton would be eliminated by developed

countries in 2006, that developed countries would provide duty-free and quota-free access for cotton exports from LDCs, and that trade-distorting domestic support for cotton would be reduced. Ten years later, the 2015 Nairobi Ministerial Conference issued a decision that obliges members to 'consider the possibilities' of improving market access for cotton. Whether the decision will translate into commercial value is questionable, given the vague language and members' inability to find consensus on the future of the Doha Round (discussed later in this chapter). Meanwhile, the panel decided the *US–Upland Cotton* case in favour of Brazil's complaint in 2004, which was confirmed by the Appellate Body in 2005. In 2008, the DSB authorized Brazil to retaliate by withdrawing concessions across a wide range of economic sectors, given the failure by the US to comply with the cotton ruling. In order to resolve the case, Brazil and the US announced the conclusion of a Framework for a Mutually Agreed Solution to the Cotton Dispute to the DSB in 2010. In 2014, the US and Brazil settled the dispute by agreeing that the US pay Brazilian cotton producers US$300 million in compensation. In return, Brazil agreed to refrain from taking any further trade measures against the US. In the current scenario, this does little to address the plight of small-scale cotton farmers in other developing countries.

in enabling a small, trade-dependent nation to retaliate against a trade giant. This was markedly demonstrated in the *US–Gambling* case that pitched the US against the tiny island state of Antigua and Barbuda. In this case, the Appellate Body sided with Antigua and Barbuda in arguing that certain US laws restricting the cross-border provisioning of online gambling services violated the market access commitments that the US had made under the GATS. When the US failed to comply with the DSB report, it was clear that retaliation in the services sectors was prone to economically hurt Antigua and Barbuda more than the US. In January 2013, the DSB thus authorized Antigua and Barbuda to suspend a number of concessions and obligations to the US under TRIPs instead. Although compensations were not made effective until ten years after the establishment of a panel on *US–Gambling* in 2003, the case demonstrates that the DSM can work for small members also. At the same time, like the *EC–Hormones* case, *US–Gambling* shows that although the DSM has teeth, ultimately there is no way to force a country to change its trade regime. In both cases, retaliation continues to date. Some countries have the ability to afford non-compliance, particularly in politically sensitive cases.

Despite these considerations, the DSM is popular among members and most members comply with most rulings most of the time. The effectiveness of its DSM has made the WTO attractive across the board of trade and trade-related interests. It has also been one important factor in its at times troubled relationship with civil society and trade critics. To this we turn in the next section.

> **KEY POINTS**
>
> - The WTO is an international economic institution that combines elements of procedural equality and factual political asymmetry among members.
> - Its main functions are making international trade rules, providing a forum for dialogue on trade issues for countries, and adjudicating international trade disputes among its members.
> - The WTO Dispute Settlement Mechanism is unique in international law and highly effective in assuring compliance with WTO obligations. Because economic power and legal expertise matter, not all countries have equal access to dispute settlement.

The WTO and civil society

The introduction of new issues in the Uruguay Round and the new enforceability of trade rules have contributed to increasing civil society interest in the global trade regime. A number of early WTO dispute settlement cases, such as *US–Gasoline* and *US-Shrimp Turtle* signalled to environmental groups that decisions taken in Geneva could impact on the regulatory victories they had registered at home. In both cases, WTO members successfully challenged domestic measures taken in the interest of environmental protection, namely certain aspects of the US Clean Air Act (in *US–Gasoline*) and an import prohibition on shrimp fished with nets that did not feature turtle excluder devices (in *US–Shrimp Turtle*). The DSB confirmed that members have the right, under GATT Article XX, to assure air quality or protect certain species. However, it found that the member—in both cases the US—could have implemented the environmental measures in a less trade restrictive manner, a condition also foreseen in Article XX. Neither domestic regulation was thus in line with its WTO obligations and needed to be amended. One bone of contention in the trade and environment debate today is the question of where the right balance between enabling trade flows and enabling environmental protection and preservation lies, and which governmental or international body is best placed to make the decision.

The unprecedented extension of international trade rules into domestic legal and regulatory systems, as a result of the Uruguay Round and the establishment of the DSM, attracted criticism from a broad range of civil society groups. In addition to their concerns about the impact of WTO agreements on domestic policy regimes, these groups were critical of the lack of transparency in trade policymaking, of the privileged access that governments afforded to business interests in trade policy matters, and of their inability to participate directly in WTO negotiations (Capling and Low 2010). The lowest point to date in the relationship between the WTO and civil society was reached during the 1999 Ministerial Conference held in Seattle. Negotiations collapsed over agricultural subsidies, competition, investment, and the dismay of many developing countries about long-standing institutional practices that effectively excluded them from the negotiating room. Meanwhile, in the streets of Seattle at least 40,000 protesters assembled and periodically clashed with armed police in a brawl that became known as the Battle of Seattle. Similarly outspoken, if less violent, protests that critiqued the WTO as being anti-democratic and biased in favour of the interests of rich nations and corporations were registered across the world at every ministerial conference held in the first decade of the twenty-first century.

Since the events of Seattle, efforts have been made to increase the WTO's transparency and engagement with civil society. Although the stillborn ITO foresaw extensive mechanisms of engaging with societal stakeholders, the *WTO Guidelines for Arrangements on Relations with Non-Governmental Organizations* do not go as far. While welcoming increased transparency and dialogue, the General Council notes in this document that it is not possible to involve NGOs directly in the WTO's work and that the appropriate level for taking public interest into account in trade policymaking is the domestic level (WTO, 1996). Nonetheless, NGOs can become accredited to attend plenary sessions at WTO Ministerial Conferences and can cooperate with the Secretariat to arrange issue-specific symposia. The WTO Secretariat has also established a dedicated NGO unit in its External Relations Division which is responsible for maintaining contact with the NGO community and channelling information flows between the WTO and civil society. Since 2001, the WTO opens its doors annually during a three-day Public Forum event where representatives from civil society, academia, business, the media, governments, parliamentarians, and intergovernmental organizations present their views on the multilateral trade regime. In the WTO's adjudicating branch, the Appellate Body held in *US–Shrimp Turtle* that it is permissible for dispute settlement organs to use unsolicited NGO submissions as *amicus curiae* briefs.

While it is common in many countries for business representatives to lobby their governments on WTO matters, civil society has also provided impetus on a number of initiatives at the WTO. The first reports on the hardship that cotton farmers in Central and West Africa endure as a result of fluctuating world market prices, and that ultimately culminated in the Cotton Initiative, for example, came from the NGO community (Trommer 2014). The debate around trade and public health produced another pertinent example of a political process at the WTO where civil society organizations influenced the course of events at key junctures. As the HIV/AIDS epidemic ravaged sub-Saharan Africa, a controversy arose in the multilateral trade regime around flexibilities on patenting

rules in the TRIPs Agreement. Members such as the EU and the US were initially keen to actively defend the protection of intellectual property rights attained in the Uruguay Round. NGOs such as Médecins sans Frontières, Oxfam, and Treatment Action Campaign ran public relations campaigns across the world and lobbied heavily to support the developing countries' position that provisions in TRIPs enabling the use of generic drugs to combat national health epidemics should not be undermined. By building and maintaining a successful coalition around TRIPs flexibilities in the WTO, developing countries attained the adoption of the Doha Declaration on the TRIPs Agreement and Public Health at the Ministerial Conference in Doha (Abbott 2002). The declaration created a presumption that WTO members would be able to exercise their rights to procure generic medicines, and more important, that other members (particularly the US) would be unlikely to take dispute settlement actions against members that exercised those rights.

The episode is instructive because it shows that business and civil society organizations often use similar strategies and tools to get trade policymakers on their side (Sell and Prakash 2004). In the lead-up to the TRIPs Agreement, the business community successfully managed to sell policymakers the idea that patent protection, free trade and investment would be cornerstones of development across the global economy. In the lead-up to the Doha Declaration on TRIPs and Public Health, transnational NGOs managed to frame the HIV/AIDS crisis as a problem of excessive intellectual property protection that made HIV/AIDS medication unaffordable. In each case, agenda-setting, coalition-building, and normative framing were key components of a successful trade campaign.

Nonetheless, these cases remain the exception rather than the rule. Commentators of the evolving relationship between the WTO and civil society are divided along two broad lines. Some hold that the natural constituency of a trade organization is economic interests, including business, workers, and consumer representatives and they see more far-reaching societal engagement with a critical eye. Others argue that as the trade agenda expands to cover behind-the-border measures that aim at protecting the environment and society more broadly, excluding these interests from trade governance makes the WTO illegitimate. The question of the appropriate level and form of civil society input also remains unresolved. Under the current ad hoc modes of engagement, some worry that the type of civil society representation that effectively reaches trade policy circles reproduces existing biases in favour of well-resourced political actors from wealthy countries (Chimni 2006), and crowds out alternative voices from the debate (Hannah 2014). More recently, trade critics have turned their attention to regional trade agreements, which often include controversial subjects that are not negotiated at the WTO.

> ### KEY POINTS
>
> - The expansion of the trade agenda and the introduction of binding dispute settlement procedures drew the attention of broader societal interests to the global trade regime.
> - WTO initiatives to promote transparency and accessibility have improved the relationship between civil society and the WTO.
> - As trade negotiations have moved to new forums with the rise of preferential trade agreements, civil society mobilization on trade issues is less centred on the WTO today.

The Doha Round

With the adoption of the Doha Ministerial Declaration on 14 November 2001, members launched the WTO's first round of multilateral trade negotiations. The road to Doha was rocky and contained the seeds of many political problems that have plagued the round. From the outset, there were significant divisions between the major players in the WTO in terms of their negotiating interests and priorities. The EU wanted a new Round to include four new issues in the negotiating agenda, namely competition policy, investment, trade facilitation and government procurement—the so-called Singapore Issues. The US, which was lukewarm on the Singapore Issues, proposed reductions in trade barriers in industrial goods and raised the controversial issue of trade sanctions to protect domestic policies related to labour and the environment. For their part, developing countries rejected the inclusion of the Singapore Issues outright and argued that before any new negotiation could begin, further efforts should be made to redress the inequities resulting from the Uruguay Round results, notably in the areas of agriculture, textiles, and TRIPs.

Following the collapse of the Seattle meeting, which had been intended to launch a new Millennium Round in 1999, officials worked at the technical level to bridge gaps between WTO members. The EU and the US stepped back from their most contentious demands on investment and competition policy, and labour rights and the environment, respectively. By September 2001, the parties had achieved a single negotiating text, which is an essential precursor for the launch of a new round. By this time, it was clear that the major issues were those of particular importance to the developing countries, mainly relating to agriculture. When the 9/11 attacks struck in New York and Washington in the same month, a sense that the international community needed to stand as one gave political momentum to the Doha Ministerial Conference in November 2001. Having resolved the TRIPs/public health issue, ministers set out an ambitious work programme in the Doha Declaration covering, *inter alia*, agriculture, implementation issues, intellectual property, services, Singapore Issue, and trade and environment. As the focus of the negotiation was development, the agenda became known as the Doha Development Agenda (DDA). The DDA was scheduled to conclude on 1 January 2005.

The first ministerial meeting of the Doha Round took place in Cancún, Mexico, in September 2003. At the Ministerial Conference, it became clear that the old negotiating paradigm of the GATT, whereby a deal was struck once the US, the EU, Canada, and Japan were in agreement, could not be brought forward into the WTO. Spearheaded by Brazil, China, India, and South Africa, a group of developing countries formed a new coalition, known as the G20. The G20 demanded increased access to developed country markets for their agricultural products, an end to agricultural export subsidies, and the elimination of domestic support measures that act as export subsidies. The Cancún negotiations broke down over the Singapore Issues and agriculture, and the WTO members were unable to reach consensus on a Ministerial Declaration.

Following that setback, in 2004 WTO members adopted a new approach (the so-called July Package) which singled out the subjects of agriculture subsidies and tariffs, non-agricultural market access (mainly, industrial tariffs), and, to a lesser degree trade in services, for priority attention in the negotiations. Additionally, members agreed to drop all Singapore Issues except trade facilitation from the negotiating agenda, reaffirmed the importance of a sectoral negotiation on cotton, and agreed to pursue the matter in the negotiations on agriculture. Negotiations slowed in 2005, as the key stand-offs crystalized around agriculture, industrial tariffs, and services. With the EU unwilling to make substantial reductions on agricultural tariffs and the US unprepared to offer significant concessions on agricultural subsidies, developing countries were not willing to offer concessions in services or manufactured goods. By 2007, a profound malaise enveloped the Doha Round.

In July 2008, ministers from around 30 key members met in Geneva in a 'mini-Ministerial' to attempt to resolve the key blockages in the round. While progress was made on agricultural subsidies and industrial tariffs, the negotiations imploded over the Special Safeguard Mechanism (SSM) in agriculture, an issue that had attracted little attention until that point. The 2004 July Package had envisaged a mechanism that would enable developing countries to protect themselves from import surges or a collapse in import prices in foodstuffs. In 2005 the G33 coalition of developing country members had proposed a SSM methodology that would allow developing countries under certain conditions to increase duties on farm imports in excess of pre-Doha tariff ceilings. In a dramatic meeting of key WTO members (Australia, Brazil, China, the EU, Japan, India, and the US) on 29 July 2008, US demands for predictable market access for farm products clashed with the concerns of import-sensitive China and India and led to a collapse of negotiations.

After the failed mini-Ministerial meeting, the intensity of negotiations declined substantially and ministers did not negotiate DDA matters at the 2009 Ministerial Conference in Geneva. Not even the threat of resurgent protectionism in the wake of the Global Financial Crisis in 2008–9 was sufficient to prod leaders into bridging their differences for the sake of locking in much of the unilateral liberalization that had occurred in the preceding decade. In 2011 ministers formally declared that the Doha Round was at an impasse. Views diverged on whether the DDA was dead and should be buried, or whether the round had nonetheless brought about a number of notable decisions and needed to be concluded.

Disagreement also arose on whether the inability to conclude a round signalled that the WTO itself was in crisis. The 2011 Geneva Ministerial Conference directed members to explore new negotiating approaches. Over the course of the next two years,

various initiatives lead to a negotiating outcome that few had thought possible, namely the adoption of the Bali Package at the 2013 Ministerial Conference in Bali. The Bali Package included a new Trade Facilitation Agreement (TFA), a decision on LDCs, and a decision on agriculture. In order to reduce the cost of trading, the TFA obliges members to speed up their customs procedures and underlines the need for technical assistance for the poorest countries to implement the necessary reforms. The TFA will enter into force once two-thirds of the membership have ratified it (at the time of writing, one-third of WTO members had ratified it). The Bali Ministerial also witnessed the disintegration of the G33 developing country group, with India remaining in an isolated position demanding that the SSM issue needed to be permanently resolved before the Bali Package could be closed. The year 2014 saw a dramatic stand-off between the US and India over the Bali 'peace clause', which stated that no country would be barred from food security programmes even if it breached the support limits specified in the WTO Agreement on Agriculture. While India's issue was resolved in this instance, the episode demonstrated that members' trust of Doha process had long eroded.

The 2015 Ministerial Conference in Nairobi may well prove to be another watershed moment for the multilateral trade system. In terms of trade rules, members reached a historical agreement on the elimination of export subsidies in agriculture. They also reached decisions on SSM, Public Stockholding for Food Security Purposes, Cotton and LDCs. A group of members also reached a plurilateral deal on information technology. The devil for the DDA however lies in the detail of the Nairobi Ministerial Declaration. The text notes that 'many members reaffirm the Doha mandate', while others have 'different views on how to address negotiations'. This effectively means that there is no longer a consensus among WTO members on the Doha Mandate. The next months and years will show how the organization can proceed in a situation where its traditionally powerful members, the US, the EU, Japan, and to a lesser degree Australia, insist that it is time to move on from the round, while its newly powerful members, led by India and China, insist the main concerns underlying the Doha Mandate must be addressed.

Some of the problems that have plagued the DDA are intrinsic to the round itself including the high level of sensitivity of issues on the table (e.g. agricultural protectionism in rich and poor countries alike) and the vague and contested nature of its development agenda. WTO institutional features have also been blamed. The consensus principle—which effectively gives any member a veto—can be cumbersome and it can promote a lowest common denominator approach to decision-making. The obligation of Single Undertaking has made some countries resistant to the inclusion of new issues in the WTO agenda. A significant outcome of the Nairobi meeting is a return to plurilateral negotiations among subsets of WTO members. For developed countries, this will reintroduce a more flexible and supple approach to deal-making where smaller groups can advance their common interests within the WTO. However, many developing countries fear that this will reduce their power to shape deals within the WTO.

Since the launch of the Doha Round, the global economy has also changed dramatically. The contemporary global economic environment is increasingly characterized by economic crisis in 'the West' and the rise of 'the rest'. Emerging markets have reshaped trade patterns across the globe. In 2013 China replaced the US as the world's largest trading nation. Long gone are the days when the US and the EU could shape the contours of a deal and when developing countries were not expected to make 'concessions' in negotiations. Smaller developing countries and LDCs have continuously built negotiating capacity and have started to use coalition-building as an effective negotiating strategy.

Finally, the Doha Round has also exposed the difficult relationship between trade and development policy. In the Doha Declaration, the objectives specified by all signatories clearly identified the main concern to be the betterment of developing and least developed countries. This was expressed in statements of belief that trade could play a major role in economic development and the alleviation of poverty and in statements of action, such as the intent to place the needs of the developing countries at the heart of the Doha Work Programme. This shift has politicized negotiations, because it has brought controversies over the appropriate trade and development policy mix into the WTO's negotiating arena.

Over recent years, disagreement has arisen in trade policy circles on whether the inability to conclude a round signals that the WTO itself is in crisis. On the one hand, the WTO's rule-making function appears dysfunctional from the perspective of most members.

On the other hand, the WTO DSM remains popular and cannot easily be replaced by preferential trade deals, not least because these agreements lack the institutional support required for effective dispute settlement that the WTO Secretariat provides in the multilateral system. Over the second half of the course of the DDA it further became apparent that the US and the EU have abandoned multilateralism as their international policy preference and have shifted their rule-making activity to the bilateral realm. Many other members have since followed suit (see Ravenhill, Chapter 6, in this volume). It is safe to say that the future of the WTO is currently uncertain. In the final section, we discuss present challenges to the multilateral trade system.

KEY POINTS

- Disagreement over market access for agricultural goods, manufactures, and services has been at the heart of deadlock in the Doha Round negotiations.

- The rise of large and fast-growing economies has transformed the negotiating dynamics in the global trade regime. The US and the EU no longer exercise unrivalled dominance in multilateral trade negotiations.

- The emphasis on development issues exposed profound differences in members' understandings of the trade and development nexus.

- The greatest immediate challenge for the WTO is the potential demise of its negotiation function.

Challenges to the multilateral trade system

The Doha Round has focused on traditional trade issues, namely agriculture and industrial tariffs. While these are important issues, many contemporary issues that feature prominently in the global trading system in the twenty-first century, such as services and investment, are effectively missing from the WTO agenda. As a result, governments are resorting to alternative ways of pursuing their trade agendas, most notably through preferential trade agreements. This presents a significant challenge to the ongoing relevance of the WTO and, particularly, its rule-making function. In this final section, we briefly canvas the major challenges to the multilateral trade system and proposals for reform.

The nature of international trade is dramatically changing (see Thun, Chapter 7, in this volume). The phenomenon of Factory Asia is the exemplar of twenty-first century trade, based on the unbundling and spatial dispersion of production and made possible by abundant and accessible energy across the global economy, trade liberalization and the information communications technological revolution. Much of contemporary international commerce is conducted through regional supply chains, and it involves not just trade in goods but also investment and services (from communication and logistics, via trade finance, to outsourcing of essential business services). Richard Baldwin (2011) characterizes this as the 'trade-investment-services' nexus that requires twenty-first century trade rules including increased levels of intellectual property protection; investment assurances including rights of establishment and the right for investors to sue governments; assurances on capital flows (foreign direct investment and profit repatriation); the movement of people (technical and professional); and the provision of high-quality infrastructure. As Baldwin says, 'the bargain in a 21st century regional trade agreement is "foreign factories in exchange for domestic reforms" not "exchange of market access" as was the case for 20th century RTAs'. Critics reject these policy recommendations as the now infamous Washington Consensus under a new guise and insist that a balanced global economy will require trade rules that allow all countries to move beyond their comparative advantages, rather than locking in existing asymmetries (Ismail 2012).

So far, the demand for new rules to support the unbundling of production, the information and communications technology (ICT) revolution, and the intertwining of trade, investment, and services is being met by regional trade agreements, not by multilateral agreements negotiated in the WTO. The emergence of twenty-first century regionalism entails a number of potential risks, including the erosion of global trade rules and the return to a fragmented, pre-Second World War system of trade governance dominated by the great powers.

As governments and trade policy communities disengage with the WTO in favour of more exclusive forms of trade cooperation, there is a diminished understanding and appreciation of the role of the WTO in providing a rules-based system (Capling and Low 2010). This is problematic in that many twenty-first century trade challenges cannot be solved through unilateral action or regional trade agreements. For example, in relation to climate change the development of a WTO code on the use of border adjustments on imports from countries that are not using carbon mitigation schemes may be essential to avoiding protectionism and future trade conflicts. The protection of common pool resources such as ocean fisheries and solutions to emerging problems such as the use of export restraints on food, energy, and minerals can only be effectively dealt with through a global organization like the WTO.

One way to revive the WTO's rule-making function could be through the adoption of more flexible approaches to decision-making that would allow groups of members to move agendas forward inside the WTO through the use of plurilateral or 'critical mass' agreements. This approach is not new with the Tokyo Round codes and the WTO agreements on basic telecommunications, financial services, and information technology being examples of plurilateral agreements on rules and market access respectively. Provided that the obligations of plurilateral agreements fall only on the parties to the agreement, with the benefits being extended to all WTO members on an MFN basis, this approach to decision-making may be the best way forward for the WTO (Warwick Commission 2007). There is a concern, particularly among some developing countries, that a plurilateral approach would lessen the possibilities for trade-offs within the WTO, which could make it harder for them to secure wins in difficult areas such as agriculture. However, in the absence of new ways forward in the WTO, groups of countries will continue to pursue their agendas outside of the WTO, primarily through RTAs which have no benefits for non-members. And pressing global trade problems, which require global solutions, will remain unaddressed.

Conclusion

The start of the Doha negotiation was a reaffirmation of the evolution the world trade regime has taken since the middle of the twentieth century. The focus of the regime has been to create rules whereby countries can exchange goods and services with a minimum of interference from national governments, and the means to accomplish that task has been to reach agreements through international negotiation. Such agreements are an important form of regulation, or system management, in the international economy. Today, the regulation of trade is carried out as much through the negotiation of trade agreements, as through the actions of domestic agencies and the purpose has been to replace inward-looking national regulation with a broader conception of international rules. There is a need to keep an open transparent and non-discriminatory trade system because the alternatives—witnessed in the interwar period in the twentieth century—were so damaging to the interests of all countries.

The GATT, and now the WTO, are central features of the international trade system. Through negotiations in these institutions, analogous to lawmaking in domestic parliaments, countries have been able to establish a rules-based regime for regulating international trade. The negotiation process is critically important to the success of the WTO, but it is a fickle and sometimes fragile process. When it is successful, the rules of the regime are advanced, and all countries can be said to benefit from the greater stability and predictability that comes from a regime based on rules rather than on the play of power politics. But the negotiation process is not always successful, and just as an absence of consensus occasionally paralyses the legislative agenda in domestic parliaments, the absence of consensus also stops the WTO from dealing with problems that many members think need to be addressed. If there is a major difference between domestic parliaments and the WTO, it is that an impasse in the former rarely calls into question the survival of the institution, whereas when an impasse occurs in the WTO, there is always the fear that the organization will be eclipsed, and that countries will use other means, including unilateral actions, to resolve the problems they face in the international trade system.

As it looks to the future, the greatest challenge facing the WTO will be to incorporate countries at varying levels of development fully into one multilateral organization and particularly to do this as countries graduate from 'developing' to more fully 'developed' status. Included in the Preamble to the Marrakesh Agreement that established the WTO is a statement expressing the need that developing countries should 'secure a share in the growth in international trade commensurate with the needs of their economic development'. The Doha Round can be seen as a political wake-up call that the developing countries will use their negotiating power to realize their aspirations in the Doha negotiation and beyond. However, the outcome of the Nairobi meeting has altered that dynamic, with a return to a more piecemeal and focused approach to deal-making. This will reintroduce a level flexibility in multilateral negotiations not seen since the Tokyo Round, but the risk is that developing countries will lose some of their power to extract concessions and shape deals.

Since the 1950s, the GATT and WTO have endured despite many challenges, but the task of implementing a global and inclusive trade regime continues to be the most imposing test of all.

 QUESTIONS

1. What are the basic components of the international trade regime? Give examples.

2. What was the effect of the US RTAA of 1934?

3. What does non-discrimination mean in international trade and how is it put into effect by the rules of the GATT?

4. Does international trade liberalization depend on the leadership of a hegemonic power? Discuss with reference to Great Britain and the US.

5. What was the role of the developing countries in the Uruguay Round negotiation? Why was it historically significant?

6. What were the challenges encountered in negotiating rules for trade in services in the Uruguay Round negotiation?

7. How does the WTO differ from the GATT?

8. What is the WTO DSU? Why is it necessary? What are some of the difficulties with its operations?

9. What were the challenges for the WTO in conducting the Doha Round?

10. What are the major challenges facing the multilateral trade system and how could they be addressed?

FURTHER READING

Bhagwati, J. (1988), *Protectionism* (Cambridge, MA: MIT Press). A review of the history, ideology, and practice of the trade policy of protectionism.

Davis, C. L. (2012), *Why Adjudicate? Enforcing Trade Rules at the WTO* (Princeton: Princeton University Press). An investigation of the domestic politics of WTO adjudication and an analysis of the legalization of world politics.

Hoekman, B. M. and Kostecki, M. M. (2009), *The Political Economy of the World Trading System: The WTO and Beyond* (Oxford: Oxford University Press). An overview of the economics, politics, and institutional workings of the WTO.

Irwin, D. A. (2015), *Free Trade under Fire* (Princeton: Princeton University Press). An economic and political defence of the free trade idea.

Jones, K. A. (2010), *The Doha Blues: Institutional Crisis and Reform in the WTO* (Cambridge: Cambridge University Press). An analysis of the Doha Round and a plea for WTO institutional reform.

Matsushita, M., Schoenbaum, T., Mavroidis, P., and Hahn, M. (2015), *The World Trade Organization: Law, Practice and Policy* (Oxford: Oxford University Press). A WTO textbook by leading scholars of international trade law.

Narlikar, A. (2005), *International Trade and Developing Countries: Coalitions in the GATT and WTO* (London: Routledge). An analysis of coalition-building behaviour of developing countries in the multilateral trade system from the GATT to the Uruguay Round.

Ostry, S. (1997), *The Post-Cold War Trading System: Who's on First* (Chicago: University of Chicago Press). A history of international trade from 1945 onwards that blends economics, politics, and law into a rounded analysis of the subject.

Wilkinson, R. (2014), *What's Wrong with the WTO and How to Fix It* (Cambridge: Polity). A diagnosis of the ills of the WTO and a reform proposal that promises development for all.

Winham, G. R. (1992), *The Evolution of International Trade Agreements* (Toronto: University of Toronto Press). A review of trade agreements from antiquity to the mid Uruguay Round.

Case law cited

Appellate Body, *United States—Standards for Reformulated and Conventional Gasoline*, WT/DS2/AB/R, adopted 20 May 1996.

Appellate Body, *European Communities—Measures Concerning Meat and Meat Products (Hormones)*, WT/DS26/AB/R, adopted 13 February 1998.

Appellate Body, *United States—Import Prohibition of Certain Shrimp and Shrimp Products*, WT/DS58/AB/R, adopted 6 November 1998.

Appellate Body, *Turkey—Restrictions on Imports of Textile and Clothing Products*, WT/DS34/AB/R, adopted 19 November 1999.

Appellate Body, *United States—Subsidies on Upland Cotton*, WT/DS267/AB/R, adopted 21 March 2005.

Appellate Body, *United States—Measures Affecting the Cross-Border Supply of Gambling and Betting Services*, WT/DS285/AB/R, adopted 20 April 2005.

WEBLINKS

The main link for international trade is the WTO link: **www.wto.org**

Other useful information and statistical databases can be found on **www.unctad.org**

National ministries of international trade can be found with the help of search engines, such as **http://english.mofcom.gov.cn/** (China), ec.europa.eu/trade/(EU), or **www.ustr.gov** (US).

 ONLINE RESOURCE CENTRE

For additional material and resources, please visit the Online Resource Centre at:
www.oxfordtextbooks.co.uk/ravenhill5e

6

Regional Trade Agreements

John Ravenhill

Chapter contents

Reader's guide

The number of regional trade agreements has grown rapidly since the World Trade Organization (WTO) came into existence in 1995. Roughly one-half of world trade is now conducted within these preferential trade arrangements, the most significant exception to the WTO's principle of non-discrimination. Governments have entered regional economic agreements motivated by a variety of political and economic considerations. They may prefer trade liberalization on a regional rather than a global basis for several reasons. This chapter reviews the political economy of regionalism: why regional trade agreements are established, which actors are likely to support regional rather than global trade liberalization, the effects that regionalism has had on the trade and welfare of members and non-members, and the relationship between liberalization at the regional and global levels.

Introduction

When the Japanese Prime Minister, Junichiro Koizumi, and his Singaporean counterpart, Goh Chok Tong, signed a bilateral trade agreement in January 2002, Japan departed from the rapidly depleting ranks of WTO members that were not parties to a discriminatory trade arrangement. By the end of March 2016, of the WTO's 162 members only four, the Democratic Republic of the Congo, Djibouti, Mauritania, and Mongolia, were not parties to one or more regional trade agreements (RTAs) (for a complete listing of RTAs by country, see https://www.wto.org/english/tratop_e/region_e/rta_participation_map_e.htm). In the 20 years since the foundation of the WTO, members notified the organization of more than 400 new RTAs, more than twice the number notified to the **General Agreement on Tariffs and Trade** (GATT) in the period 1948–94. By 2016, the WTO and its predecessor had been notified of more than 400 regional agreements that were still in force (https://www.wto.org/english/tratop_e/region_e/region_e.htm accessed May 2016). Later in this chapter we examine the reasons behind this 'rush to regionalism'. First, we look at the different forms of regional trade cooperation.

Forms of regional trade cooperation

For most of the post-war period, the concept of regional economic integration was usually associated with an arrangement between three or more geographically contiguous states. The European Union (EU) is the best known of such agreements, but consider also East African Cooperation (Kenya, Tanzania, and Uganda), and the Andean Community of Nations (Bolivia, Colombia, Ecuador, and Peru). In recent years, however, a large number of preferential trade agreements (PTAs) have been signed that involve only two parties (for example, China–Hong Kong), and sometimes these bilateral agreements link parties that are not geographically contiguous (for example, Korea and Chile). Because non-global agreements are subject to the scrutiny of the WTO's Committee on Regional Trade Agreements, however, they are also frequently labelled 'regional'. Whether such terminology is appropriate is questionable (some commentators suggest that since many of the recent agreements are not 'regional' in the conventional geographical sense and do not free all trade between the parties, they are better termed 'preferential' rather than 'regional' or

'free' trade agreements). But it is not just the terminology that is problematic: the arguments of the large body of theoretical work on regional integration, which was developed with groupings involving multiple members from the same geographical region in mind, may not be applicable to arrangements that involve only two parties or those that involve states that are not geographical neighbours.

Table 6.1 demonstrates the complexity of the current configuration of 'regional' arrangements—essentially all strategies for trade liberalization that fall between unilateral action at the one extreme and negotiations at the global level in the WTO at the other. Bilateral agreements can occur either between neighbours or between countries that are far removed from one another. Regionalism, as conventionally understood, is a *minilateral* rather than a bilateral relationship, that is, one that involves more than two countries, on a geographically concentrated basis, for example, the North American Free Trade Area (NAFTA) or the Association of Southeast Asian Nations (ASEAN) Free Trade Area (AFTA) (Table 6.4 at the end of the chapter, lists the principal minilateral regional trade groupings). In recent years, however, two other forms of minilateral groupings have emerged among members that are geographically dispersed. *Trans-regional* groupings link individual countries located in different parts of the world. Good examples are the Trans-Pacific Partnership, signed in February 2016, whose membership comprises 12 countries from the Americas, Asia, and Oceania (Lim, Elms, and Low, 2012), and the Transatlantic Trade and Investment Partnership (which links the US and the EU), under negotiation at the time of writing in 2016. These are sometimes referred to as 'Mega-FTAs'. Many of the recently negotiated bilateral RTAs, for instance, US–Jordan, Singapore–New Zealand, link countries from different geographical areas. Meanwhile, *Interregional* arrangements join two established minilateral economic arrangements, as between the EU and MERCOSUR (Argentina, Brazil, Paraguay, and Uruguay), and ASEAN and the Australia–New Zealand Closer Economic Relations Trade Agreement (ANZCERTA). More than 25 trans-regional and interregional agreements are currently operational.

One of the few issues on which writers on regionalism agree is that there is no such thing as a 'natural' region. Regions are *social constructions* whose members choose how to define their boundaries. Consider, for instance, the EU: in its successive incarnations—European Economic Community, European Community,

Table 6.1 Example of the geographical scope of trade liberalization strategies

Unilateral	Bilateral		Minilateral			Global
	Geographically concentrated	Geographically dispersed	Geographically concentrated	Geographically dispersed		
	Bilateral within region	Bilateral trans-regional	Regionalism	Trans-regionalism	Inter–regionalism	
Trade liberalization in Latin America, SE Asia, Australia, and NZ in 1980s and 1990s	Australia–New Zealand CER[a] Trade Agreement (ANZCERTA)	Singapore–USA	NAFTA	Trans-Pacific Partnership Transatlantic Trade and Investment Partnership	EU–MERCOSUR ANZCERTA–AFTA	GATT/WTO

[a] CER = Closer Economic Relations.
Source: Adapted from Aggarwal (2001: 238).

and, now, the European Union—its membership has risen from its six founders to the current total of 28 (but this number will be reduced if 'Brexit' proceeds). And debates over EU membership for Turkey show that no consensus exists on either geographic or cultural criteria that could be used to distinguish the 'European' from the 'non-European'.

Regional trade agreements are one example of *regionalism*, which is a formal process of intergovernmental collaboration between two or more states. It should be distinguished from *regionalization*, which refers to the growth of economic **interdependence** within a given geographical area. RTAs are the most important exception that the WTO permits to the principle that countries should not discriminate in their treatment of other members. Parties to regional arrangements are obliged to notify the WTO of the details of their agreements; the Committee on Regional Trade Agreements has responsibility for ensuring that the agreements comply with the WTO's provisions (for agreements only involving developing economies, the responsibility lies with the Committee on Trade and Development).

The growth in the number of preferential arrangements has led to a marked increase in the share of global trade conducted within RTAs, now accounting for roughly one-half of world trade, but note that only a relatively small percentage of total trade conducted between partners in regional economic agreements actually benefits from treatment better than that offered to non-members—the **most-favoured nation** tariff may be zero; moreover, companies may decide not to do the paperwork required to gain the preferential access these agreements afford (see discussion later in this chapter).

Three sets of rules in the WTO permit the creation of RTAs:

- Article xxiv of the GATT lays down conditions for the establishment and operation of free trade agreements and customs unions covering trade in goods.
- The **Enabling Clause**, formally the 1979 Decision on Differential and More Favourable Treatment, Reciprocity and Fuller Participation of Developing Countries, permits regional agreements among developing countries on trade in goods.
- Article v of the General Agreement on Trade in Services (GATS) establishes conditions that permit liberalization of trade in services among regional partners.

At the start of 2016, 244 of the RTAs in force were under Article xxiv, 139 were under GATS Article v (the most rapidly growing category of agreement), and 41 were under the Enabling Clause (calculated from http://rtais.wto.org/UI/PublicMaintainRTAHome.aspx).

RTAs take various forms that range, in scope of cooperation, from **free trade areas** to **economic unions** (Box 6.1).

BOX 6.1

A Hierarchy of Regional Economic Arrangements

Regional integration arrangements are usually categorized as a hierarchy that runs from free trade areas through customs unions and common markets to economic unions. The terminology of 'hierarchy' is used because each level incorporates all the provisions of the lower level of integration. A hierarchy does not imply that particular regional arrangements will necessarily progress from a lower to a higher level of integration. Nor is it the case that regional partnerships inevitably begin at the lowest level and then move to 'deeper' integration: some arrangements, for instance, have been established as customs unions.

A *free trade area* exists when countries remove tariffs and non-tariff barriers (NTBs) to the free movement of goods and services between them. Governments, meanwhile, are free to choose how they treat goods and services imported from non-regional-partner states. Membership in one free trade area therefore does not prevent a country from establishing or joining other free trade areas: Mexico, for example, is a party to agreements with more than 30 countries. Because free trade areas impose relatively few constraints on national decision-making autonomy, they are the easiest of the regional arrangements to negotiate. More than 90 per cent of regional partnerships take the form of free trade areas. Examples include NAFTA, the Japan–Singapore Economic Partnership Agreement, and the Baltic Free Trade Area.

A *customs union* goes beyond the removal of barriers to trade within the region to adopt a common set of policies towards imports from countries outside the region. This includes agreement on a common level of tariffs (often referred to as a 'common external tariff') on all extra-regional imports. Such agreements inevitably cost governments autonomy in their foreign economic policies (joint institutions are usually required to negotiate and administer the common external trade policies). They will also have distributive effects, depending on the level at which the common external tariff is set for various items. Consequently, customs unions are usually more difficult to negotiate than are free trade areas. The relatively small number of customs unions includes the Andean Community, Caribbean Community and Common Market (CARICOM), Common Market of the South (MERCOSUR, comprising Argentina, Brazil, Paraguay, and Uruguay), and the Southern African Customs Union. Many have experienced difficulties in negotiating a common external tariff. Even in the EU, individual states maintained different tariffs on some products for more than 30 years after its formation. MERCOSUR's negotiation of a common external tariff took 15 years longer than anticipated, it applied to only three-quarters of total products, and even then was not accepted by two of its associate members, Bolivia and Peru.

A *common market* includes a customs union and also allows for free movement of labour and capital within the regional partnership. Such free flows of factors of production inevitably require governments to collaborate in additional policy areas to ensure comparable treatment in all countries within the common market. Historically, few governments have been willing to accept the loss of policymaking autonomy that occurs in a common market. The controversies that have arisen from the free flow of labour in the European Union illustrate the challenges posed by the deep integration produced by a common market. The Andean Community, CARICOM, the COMESA (Common Market for Eastern and Southern Africa) grouping, and MERCOSUR have committed themselves to work for the establishment of a common market but it is too early to judge whether their aspirations will be realized.

Why regionalism?

Economists assert that an economy's welfare can be maximized, other than in exceptional circumstances, if governments lower trade barriers on a non-discriminatory basis (either through unilateral action or through negotiations at the global level that adhere to the WTO's principle of non-discrimination). Regional trade agreements, on the other hand, can reduce global welfare by distorting the allocation of resources, and may even lead to welfare losses for their members (see Box 6.2). Moreover, from the political scientist's perspective, it is usually more efficient to negotiate a single agreement with a large number of states than to undertake a series of negotiations with individual states or with small groupings (because it both economizes on the resources needed for negotiations and increases the opportunities for trade-offs in reaching a package deal).

Why, then, has regionalism not only been attractive to governments throughout the post-war period but has apparently become increasingly so in the last two decades? Governments usually have multiple motives in entering an arrangement as complex as

BOX 6.2

The Costs and Benefits of Preferential Trade Agreements: Trade Diversion and Trade Creation

Jacob Viner (1950) was the first author to present a systematic assessment of the economic costs and benefits of regional economic integration, and to demonstrate, contrary to the then conventional wisdom, that a selective removal of tariffs might not be welfare enhancing. He argued that increased trade between parties to a regional arrangement can occur through two mechanisms. Trade *creation* occurs when imports from a regional partner displace goods that have been produced domestically at higher cost, goods that can no longer compete once the tariffs on imports from the regional partner are removed. Trade *diversion* occurs when imports from a regional partner displace those that originated outside the regional arrangement, the displacement occurring because the extra-regional imports are no longer price competitive when the tariffs on trade within the region are removed. Consider, for instance, a hypothetical example of what might happen with the implementation of the North American Free Trade Agreement (see Table 6.2). Let's assume that Indonesia was the lowest-cost source of imported cotton T-shirts for the United States. Before the implementation of NAFTA, when all countries faced the same level of tariffs on their exports to the US market, its T-shirts were preferred to the higher-cost production of Mexican firms. Assume that the tariff on T-shirts was 10 per cent, the cost of manufacturing and delivering an Indonesian T-shirt to the US was $5 while that for a Mexican T-shirt was $5.40. Adding the 10 per cent tariff to the costs of manufacturing and delivery, the price paid by the importer before NAFTA would be $5.50 for an Indonesian shirt and $5.94 for a Mexican shirt.

Following the implementation of NAFTA, however, the tariff on imported T-shirts from Mexico is removed. For the importer, the Mexican T-shirt is now the least expensive ($5.40) because it is no longer subject to tariffs, while the Indonesian product will still face a 10 per cent tariff and still costs the importer $5.50. Assuming that the importer chooses the lowest-cost product, imports will be switched after the regional scheme goes into effect from the lowest-cost producer (Indonesia) to Mexico, a relatively expensive producer, which now benefits from zero tariffs in the US market.

Several consequences follow from this trade *diversion*. The consumer in the USA *may* gain because the cost to the importer of purchasing a T-shirt falls from $5.50 to $5.40 (although the producer/wholesaler/retailer may be able to capture some or all of this gain). The US government, however, loses the tariff revenue (50 cents for each imported T-shirt) that it previously derived from taxing Indonesian T-shirt imports (the new imports from Mexico not being subject to a tariff). For the US economy as a whole, therefore, the potential gain to consumers is significantly exceeded by the loss of tariff revenue (which is, of course, a form of taxation income for the government). Considered again from the perspective of the US economy, real resources are wasted because more money is being spent than would be the case if free trade prevailed with both Indonesia and Mexico ($5.40 compared with $5.00 for each imported T-shirt). And, unless exceptional circumstances intervene, the Indonesian economy will also suffer a welfare loss because of the decline in export revenue it experiences (and with the loss of the US market, it may also have to lower the price of its T-shirt exports to compete in other markets).

If trade diversion outweighs trade creation, then the net effect of a regional scheme on its members' welfare can be negative.

Table 6.2 The potential for trade diversion after the removal of tariffs on intra-regional trade ($)

	Cost of production	Tariff cost pre-NAFTA	Cost to importer pre-NAFTA	Tariff post-NAFTA	Cost to importer post-NAFTA
Indonesia	5.00	0.50 (10%)	5.50	0.50 (10%)	5.50
Mexico	5.40	0.54 (10%)	5.94	Zero	5.40

a regional partnership: it would be naive to expect to find a single factor that explains governments' actions across all regional agreements. The combination of reasons why governments enter regional economic agreements includes political as well as economic factors.

Political motivations for entering regional trade agreements

Economic cooperation and confidence building

Regionalism frequently involves the use of economic means for political ends: the improvement of interstate relations and/or the enhancement of security within a region. In international relationships that have a history of conflict or where no tradition of partnership exists, cooperation on economic matters can be a core element in a process of confidence building.

The origins of post-war European economic integration provide an excellent example. The European Coal and Steel Community (ECSC), created by the 1951 Treaty of Paris, was the first of the institutions of what eventually was to evolve into the EU. The ECSC, founded by France, West Germany, Italy, Belgium, the Netherlands, and Luxembourg, pooled the coal and steel resources (perceived as critical to any military capacity) of its members by providing a unified market for these commodities; it also created a unified labour market in this sector. The underlying objective was to manage the rebuilding of Germany's economy after the Second World War and to integrate it with those of its neighbours, thereby helping to restore confidence amongst countries whose conflicts had embroiled the world in two major wars.

In a similar fashion, the Association of Southeast Asian Nations was founded in 1967 to promote economic cooperation in an attempt to build confidence and avoid conflict in a region that was the site of armed struggles in the Cold War era. Two of its founding members, Indonesia and Malaysia, had engaged in armed conflict in the period 1963–6 as the Indonesian government of President Sukarno attempted to destabilize the newly independent Malaysia. Over the years, ASEAN membership expanded and the organization successfully used cooperation on economic matters to overcome deep-seated interstate rivalries and suspicions. In 1999, one of the visions of ASEAN's founders was realized when its membership was expanded to include all ten of the countries of South East Asia (including Vietnam and Cambodia that had in the previous quarter of a century been at war with other ASEAN states and with one another).

In some instances, regional economic integration has been stimulated by a desire to enhance the security of regional partners against threats emanating from *outside* the membership of the regional arrangement. The Southern African Development Coordination Conference (SADCC), for instance, was founded in 1980 in an attempt to reduce members' dependence on South Africa during the apartheid era.

Regionalism as a reward for security partners

The negotiation of a regional trade agreement has been used by large powers, most notably the United States, to reward its security partners. Since the first RTA that the US negotiated, with Israel in 1985, Washington has used these arrangements to reinforce some of its key strategic partnerships. After the terrorist attacks of 11 September 2001, the Bush administration initiated a series of RTA negotiations with countries that were viewed as of key strategic importance to the United States (Higgott 2004; Kelton 2008). These agreements were used to reward or shore up allies (e.g. agreements with Jordan, Morocco, Bahrain, and Oman) or to promote existing security arrangements (e.g. Australia, Chile, and Singapore) (Aggarwal and Govella 2013).

Regional economic cooperation and the 'new security agenda'

Offers by industrialized countries in recent years to extend regional economic cooperation to their less developed neighbours have frequently been encouraged by concerns about 'non-traditional' security threats emanating from less developed partners. Such threats include environmental damage, illegal migration, organized crime, drug smuggling, and international terrorism. Regional cooperation may help address these issues directly, for example, through NAFTA's provisions on the environment, or, proponents hope, indirectly by promoting economic development and thereby ameliorating the conditions that were perceived as fostering the security threats. Concerns about new security threats played a part in European enthusiasm for new agreements with Mediterranean states, and in US interest in extending NAFTA to other Western Hemisphere countries.

Regionalism as a bargaining tool

Many of the regional economic agreements that developing countries established in the 1950s through the 1970s were motivated by a desire to enhance their bargaining power with **transnational corporations** (TNCs) and with trading partners. They were often inspired by the work of the UN's Economic Commission for Latin America, and its principal theorist, Raul Prebisch, whose ideas were subsequently taken up by writers from the dependency school. Prebisch (1963, 1970) had argued that regional integration was essential to provide a sufficiently large market to enable the efficient local production of goods that had previously been imported. Moreover, a regional partnership would enhance bargaining power with external actors if the partners negotiated with one voice. One approach, as in the Andean Pact (founded in 1969 by Bolivia, Chile (which withdrew in 1976), Colombia, Ecuador, and Peru) was to adopt a system of region-wide industrial licensing. The intention was to prevent TNCs from gaining concessions by playing off governments of the region against one another, and to use the carrot of access to a larger regional market to extract concessions from potential investors. None of these efforts was long-lived: they usually foundered on the unwillingness of the more developed economies in a region to give up, to the benefit of their less competitive neighbours, investments that they would probably otherwise have attracted.

Less developed countries (LDCs) have also used regional partnerships as a way of gaining more aid from donor countries and organizations. Over the years, various governments and international organizations have encouraged regional economic integration among developing countries and have set aside some of their aid budgets to promote regional projects. The EU has been a particularly enthusiastic supporter of regionalism in other parts of the world, providing both financial assistance and technical support for other regional schemes.

A World Bank study (2000: 20) notes that by pooling their diplomatic resources in a regional arrangement, LDCs are sometimes able to achieve greater prominence in international relations and to negotiate agreements that would not be available if they had acted individually, and to ensure election of their representatives to key positions in international organizations. The best example of successful pursuit of this strategy, the Bank suggests, is the Caribbean Community and Common Market (CARICOM).

But it is not just developing countries that have perceived regional economic partnerships as a means of enhancing their bargaining power. The Japanese Ministry of Economy, Trade and Industry, for instance, in advocating participation in discriminatory regional arrangements, pointed to the possibility that by facilitating partnerships with like-minded countries they could increase Japan's leverage within the WTO (METI 2000). The foundation of APEC (in 1989) was linked to perceptions that it could help to pressure the EU into trade concessions during GATT's Uruguay Round of trade negotiations (Ravenhill 2001). And some authors have suggested that the negotiation of the Treaty of Rome, which established the European Economic Community in 1957, was at least in part motivated by European countries' desires to increase their leverage against the United States in the upcoming GATT talks (Milward 1984, 1992).

Regionalism as a mechanism for locking-in reforms

Regional trade agreements can enhance the credibility of domestic economic reforms and thereby increase the attractiveness of economies to potential foreign investors (Rodrik 1989). Such considerations have become more important in an increasingly integrated global economy where countries are competing to stake their claims as preferred partners in global production networks (see Thun, Chapter 7 in this volume).

Commitments made within a regional forum can be more attractive to potential investors than those made in global institutions for several reasons. Countries' compliance with their commitments is likely to be more closely scrutinized within a regional grouping: the numbers of partners to be monitored is smaller than within the WTO with its 164 members, and any breaking of commitments is more likely to have a direct impact on regional partners and lead to swift retaliation. Some regional arrangements provide for regional institutions to monitor the implementation of agreements as well as for dispute settlement mechanisms. Moreover, repeated interactions with a small number of partners within regional arrangements may make governments more concerned about their reputations (their credibility as collaborators) than they would be within more diffuse multilateral forums (Fernandez and Portes 1998). Regional arrangements may be particularly effective in enhancing the credibility of commitments when LDCs enter partnerships with an industrialized country as, for instance, in Mexico's participation in NAFTA (Haggard 1997). And the possibility that the policy coverage of the RTA may be more comprehensive than agreements at the global level—embracing, for instance, rules on competition policy and on the treatment of foreign investment—further enhances the potential of regional arrangements as a device for signalling to potential foreign investors the seriousness of a government's commitment to reform.

Regionalism to satisfy domestic political constituencies

Often, the choice of trade policies faced by governments is not between liberalization at the global level and liberalization at the regional level, but between entering a regional agreement and undertaking unilateral liberalization. In contrast to a unilateral lowering of tariffs, which is often politically difficult for governments because domestic groups believe that the government is giving something away (tariff protection) and not receiving anything in return from other countries, a regional trade agreement provides a means for a government to ensure that it receives concessions (**reciprocity**) from its partners in return for those that it has offered. And, in so far as a regional agreement makes it easier politically for governments to undertake liberalization, and therefore enhances such activities, it may be beneficial not just to regional partners but to the wider international community.

'Protection for sale'

Even though mainstream economic theory suggests that welfare gains will be maximized when trade liberalization occurs on a non-discriminatory basis, governments may, nonetheless, prefer a regional (discriminatory) trade agreement. This alternative is attractive for domestic political economy reasons. The classic explanation was provided by Grossman and Helpman (1995). In their model, governments' policies towards trade are driven primarily by their desire to be re-elected. Their prospects will depend on their capacity to attract voters and campaign contributions. A country's policy stance consequently will reflect the relative power of its various special interests. The advantage of a regional trade agreements to governments is that they may be able to respond to protectionist pressures by excluding 'politically sensitive' non-competitive domestic sectors from the trade liberalization measures negotiated within a regional agreement, whereas such exclusion would be more difficult at the global level. Meanwhile, they will push for liberalization in those sectors where there are competitive domestic exporters.

Ease of negotiating and implementing agreements

The larger the number of states, the more likely it is that they will have a greater diversity of interests that will complicate negotiations. Moreover, the larger the number of members, the more difficult it is to monitor behaviour and to enforce sanctions in the event of non-compliance (Oye 1985; Keohane 1984). A regional agreement with a limited number of partners accordingly might be easier to negotiate and implement than one at the global level. This logic is particularly applicable to bilateral trade agreements.

On the other hand, numerous cases exist of large numbers of governments successfully concluding international agreements (within the United Nations, for instance, on issues that range from arms control to the environment to human rights: see e.g. Osherenko and Young 1993: 12). Kahler (1992) has argued persuasively that success in solving the numbers problem depends upon institutional design (a problem that the WTO has yet to address effectively). Mechanisms for discussing issues and voting procedures can be adapted to counter the problems of numbers and diversity. A larger numbers of participants may bring potential for greater gains and more opportunities for trade-offs among the parties.

In short, the international relations literature is inconclusive on the relationship between the number of participants and the successful negotiation and implementation of agreements. There are plenty of instances where regional negotiations have failed to produce agreements or have taken a very long time to complete (for instance, a bilateral free trade agreement between Japan and Korea was first proposed in 1998 but negotiations had not been successfully concluded by 2016). Of greater importance to shaping state action, however, are the perceptions that governments hold on this issue. And there is little doubt that many *believe* that regional agreements are easier to negotiate than those at the global level, given the numbers and diversity of WTO membership. The failure to conclude the Doha Round 15 years after negotiations began reinforced these beliefs.

Economic motivations for regionalism

Here, we can distinguish between two possibilities: (a) where governments, for economic reasons, prefer a regional economic agreement to unilateral liberalization or to a non-discriminatory multilateral agreement; and (b) where they prefer a regional agreement to the status quo.

Economic reasons for choosing regionalism over multilateralism

Regionalism enables continued protection of sectors that would not survive in global competition

Even though mainstream economic theory suggests that welfare gains will be maximized when trade liberalization occurs on a non-discriminatory basis, governments may, nonetheless, prefer a regional (discriminatory) trade agreement. This alternative is attractive, for instance, when they believe that domestic producers will be successful in competition with regional partners and will benefit from the larger (protected) market that a regional scheme creates, but that they would not survive a competition with producers located outside the region.

A more benign variant of this argument is that a reform-minded government may seek to enter a regional agreement as a way to gradually expose inefficient domestic producers to international competition, with the expectation that competition from regional partners will generate reforms that will eventually enable the sector to be exposed to full international competition. In this scenario, regionalism is a stepping-stone to broader liberalization.

Regionalism provides opportunities for 'deeper integration'

Regionalism may be more attractive than a multilateral treaty to pro-liberalization governments because it enables agreement on issues that would not be possible in the WTO where membership is more diverse. Since the early 1990s, a number of governments, such as those of the United States, Singapore, Chile, and Australia, which have been seeking to raise the tempo of trade liberalization, have turned to regional agreements in an attempt to promote 'WTO Plus' *deeper* integration. This concept refers to cooperation that goes beyond the traditional liberalization menu of removing tariff barriers. It may include, for instance, agreements on the environment, on the treatment of **foreign direct investment** (**FDI**), on domestic competition (anti-trust) policies, on intellectual property rights, on regulatory standards, and on labour standards—sometimes referred to as twenty-first-century trade issues (Baldwin 2011). The North American Free Trade Agreement was one of the first free trade agreements to incorporate provisions on many of these matters. As trade liberalization within the WTO reduced the significance of border barriers so matters of 'deeper integration' have grown in importance as governments seek to establish a level playing field with their partners. The Trans-Pacific Partnership, a negotiation that began in 2010 among twelve Asian and Pacific countries, has concentrated on these issues. So, too, have the negotiations for the Transatlantic Trade and Investment Partnership between the EU and the US (Ville and Siles-Brugge 2016).

A regional approach is more likely to facilitate reaching agreement on these politically sensitive issues if the partner states share certain characteristics, for example, similar levels of economic development. Regional agreements, especially bilateral free trade areas, may also enable more powerful states to bring their weight to bear more effectively on weaker parties, for whom the price of gaining security of access to a larger market may be to accept undertakings on issues of 'deeper integration', such as their treatment of foreign investment, etc. (on this issue of unequal bargaining power in regional agreements, see Perroni and Whalley 1994; Helleiner 1996).

Economic reasons for preferring regionalism to unilateralism or the status quo

Larger markets and increased foreign investment

Governments may not have the option of choosing between a regional agreement and an agreement at the global level: the latter may simply not be available at the time. The choice that governments then face is to stick with the status quo, to liberalize on a unilateral basis, or to seek a regional agreement. Besides the political advantages, noted earlier, that a regional agreement often has over unilateral action, economic advantages may also come into play. Coordinated liberalization on a regional basis broadens the geographical scope of liberalization and may also enable a widening of the product coverage of the agreement, thereby increasing the potential economic gains.

Compared with the status quo, a regional economic agreement can confer two principal economic benefits. First, it provides a larger 'home' market for domestic industries, possibly enabling them to produce more efficiently because of **economies of scale** (see Box 6.3). How significant an advantage is gained

---

BOX 6.3

Economies of Scale

In modern manufacturing, which frequently depends on the use of expensive machinery and on very large investments in research and development, large-scale production often enables firms to produce at a lower average cost per unit. These *economies of scale* can result not just from a more efficient use of machinery and of labour but also because specialist managers and workers can be employed, savings can be made in borrowing on financial markets (which generally charge higher rates of interest to smaller borrowers), raw materials can be purchased more cheaply when bought in bulk, and advertising costs are spread across a higher volume of output.

A related concept is *economies of scope*. These occur when firms can spread various costs (including, for instance, research and development, accounting, marketing) across various products, which may—although not necessarily—be related (for instance, production of calculators and of LCD screens for laptop computers).

from regionalism will depend on the number of partner economies and their relative size: a firm in a large economy is unlikely to make significant gains in economies of scale if the regional partnership is with only a couple of much smaller economies.

Second, regionalism can increase the attractiveness of an economy to potential investors. Companies that previously supplied the separate national markets through exports from outside the region may now find that the unified regional market is of sufficient size to make local production (and hence foreign investment into the region) attractive. Gains from FDI may be particularly significant when an LDC enters into a regional partnership with one or more industrialized economies. Companies may be able to take advantage of the relatively low-cost labour in the LDC to supply the whole of the regional market from factories established there. A frequently cited example is the dramatic increase that occurred in FDI into Mexico following the signature of NAFTA in 1994. Inflows of FDI to Mexico, which averaged $8 billion per year in the period 1990–5, rose to $14 billion in 1997 and to $24 billion in 2001 (UNCTAD 2002: 304, annex table B.1). Some evidence also exists of similar effects elsewhere, for example, FDI inflows to ASEAN increased after it negotiated its free trade area (UNCTAD 2003:

47, box ii.5). Here the focus is on the evolution of regional value chains (see Thun Chapter 7).

A related strategy is for governments to attempt to position their economies as regional hubs. For a number of activities, companies will wish to establish only one office in a geographical area (it might, for instance, be a central office responsible for procurement, or for providing management services to all of the company's regional subsidiaries). One of the reasons why some governments appear to have chosen to negotiate multiple RTAs is that this strategy enhances the prospects for attracting companies' 'regional' headquarters as the economy becomes a 'hub' for multiple regional 'spokes'. Singapore, an active proponent of RTAs, is a good example—it has a larger number of regional corporate headquarters than any other developing economy. Regional hubs may also be attractive to subsidiaries of TNCs seeking to take advantage of the preferential access the RTAs provide to third-country markets. For instance, US subsidiaries operating in Singapore enjoy duty-free access to the Japanese market for their production (subject to meeting the rules of origin in Singapore's economic partnership agreement with Japan—see Box 6.4), something not always available to them if they exported to Japan from their home base in the US.

BOX 6.4

Rules of Origin

Countries that enter into a free trade agreement inevitably are concerned that non-members should not exploit the benefits they provide to their partners. In particular, they fear that because free trade areas (unlike customs unions) do not have a common external tariff, non-members will send goods into the free trade area through the country with the lowest tariff, and then use the free trade provisions of the grouping to access other members' markets. This *trade deflection* will lead to a loss of tariff revenue for the economies with higher tariffs and possibly to greater competition for their domestic producers.

Consider, for instance, the following hypothetical example. Assume that Mexico has a 5 per cent tariff on cameras whereas Canada and the United States both have a 12 per cent tariff. If they were able to take advantage of the introduction of free trade under NAFTA, Japanese camera manufacturers would export their cameras to Mexico and supply Canada and the United States from the Mexican imports, enjoying duty-free access to these markets. Both the Canadian and US governments would lose tariff revenue that they would otherwise collect on

imports of Japanese cameras. And Japanese cameras (now subject to a lower NAFTA external tariff) would become more competitive than they otherwise would have been with cameras produced in Canada and the United States. To prevent free trade areas from causing trade deflection of this type, their members typically adopt what are called rules of origin. These are intended to ensure that goods will only benefit from the provisions of the free trade agreement if they can be considered to have 'originated', that is, to have been produced primarily in the partner country. Goods that are merely passing through the partner or, for instance, have been re-packaged as 'Made in Mexico', will not qualify for duty-free access to other members' markets. Determining where a product has originated has become increasingly difficult in an integrated global economy in which goods are often assembled from components manufactured in various countries.

Rules of origin typically take one or more of the following forms:

(a) *A value-added criterion*. This specifies that a particular percentage of the value of the export must have been generated within the partner country. For instance, to qualify as

BOX 6.4 (continued)

a local product for the purposes of NAFTA, 62.5 per cent of the value of an automobile must have been generated locally.

(b) *A change of tariff heading criterion*. The World Customs Organization has developed a 'Harmonized System Nomenclature' of tariff headings that classifies all products according to their degree of processing, ranging from raw materials through semi-processed products to finished manufactures. Under this criterion, a good is considered to have been produced domestically if a change in tariff heading results from the local processing/manufacture.

(c) *A specific processing criterion*. This stipulates that particular stages in the production of the export must be undertaken locally. For instance, cloth may only be considered a local product if weaving has been conducted locally.

(d) *A specific components criterion*. This establishes that particular parts of the finished good must have been manufactured locally for it to qualify for duty-free treatment. In NAFTA, colour television sets are considered to be local products only if their flat panel displays have been manufactured locally. Usually, rules of origin allow for 'cumulation' so that components sourced from partner countries are counted as if they have been produced domestically (so that, for instance, a colour TV manufactured in Mexico which contains a flat panel display manufactured in the US would be classed as a local product for NAFTA rules of origin purposes).

As is evident from these examples, rules of origin are usually product-specific and can be very complex. Specification of the rules of origin often constitutes the bulk of the agreements that establish free trade areas. Those for NAFTA, for instance, run to close to 200 pages of small print. They require detailed, complex negotiations. The complexity of rules of origin is often viewed as a barrier to developing economies' participation in international trade, especially when they have to cope with multiple sets of rules that govern trade with different partners.

The negotiation of rules of origin, moreover, whose product-specific provisions often appear to be arbitrary, offers an opportunity for domestic interests to attempt to seek protection against the effects of regional trade liberalization. Setting a high value-added criterion may make it impossible for rival producers in partner countries to qualify for duty-free access to the domestic market. And the requirement that a specific component be produced locally may increase the discrimination against non-members and exclude them from the enlarged regional market. For instance, Schiff and Winters (2003: 80) cite the example of tomato ketchup. Under the 1988 Canada–US Free Trade Agreement (CUSFTA/CUSTA), ketchup produced from imported tomato paste qualified as a local product and received duty-free treatment. When the CUSFTA was converted into NAFTA, however, the new rules of origin stated that ketchup would be considered a local product only if it contained tomato paste manufactured within NAFTA. The result was *trade diversion* from Chile to Mexico: whereas Chile accounted for more than 80 per cent of US imports of tomato paste before NAFTA, after the introduction of the NAFTA rules of origin Chile's share dropped to 5 per cent whereas that of Mexico rose to 75 per cent.

The political economy of regionalism

Private sector interests

It is straightforward, for instance, to suggest that when companies face high tariffs in markets where their competitors' products enter duty free because of the existence of free trade arrangements, they will lobby their governments to obtain similar arrangements. But other than for these 'defensive' reasons, when might companies support the establishment of a regional free trade area rather than prefer either continued protectionism or non-discriminatory liberalization?

To address this question requires a starting point that is far removed from the assumptions of trade theory as developed in neoclassical economics (which assumes constant returns to scale and immobile factors of production, that is, unit costs of production are the same regardless of the size of the production run, and factors of production—capital, for example—will not move across national boundaries). In particular, it rests on the possibility that companies will be able to produce more efficiently for a regional rather than a domestic market because they are able to capture economies of scale, on the increasing mobility of capital, and on observations regarding the geographical distribution of subsidiaries of TNCs.

The economies-of-scale argument assumes that regional integration is able to provide firms with the minimum market size required for them to capture scale economies, whereas the domestic market alone is too small for this to happen. But why would firms not prefer multilateral liberalization so as to gain access to even larger global markets? The reason is that a regional agreement will provide an opportunity to retain tariff and other barriers against competitors from outside the region. The logic is that of strategic trade theory, one component of which asserts that it is possible for governments to provide an advantage to their domestic companies if they offer a protected domestic market that enables them to realize economies of scale (Krugman 1990; for an application of the argument to the regional level, see Milner 1997b; Chase 2003, 2005).

The other departure from conventional trade theory rests on an acknowledgement that contemporary manufacturing often involves conducting various stages of production in different geographical locations to take advantage of local characteristics such as relatively low-cost labour or a concentration of product- or industry-specific skills. From the 1980s onwards, United States and European firms, facing intense competition in their domestic market from imports from East Asia, increasingly sourced components from relatively low labour-cost economies (see the discussion in Thun, Chapter 7 in this volume). The establishment of regional free trade areas facilitates this corporate strategy (and, here, it is appropriate to remember the North–South architecture of many of the new regional arrangements of the 1990s, for example, trade agreements between the EU and Eastern European and Mediterranean countries, NAFTA, and the Caribbean Basin Initiative). Moreover, the rules of origin, in NAFTA for instance, that allow components sourced from US companies to be counted towards requirements that goods must meet if they are to be deemed to have been manufactured in Mexico, serve as a protectionist device that provides further advantage to US-based corporations (for further discussion, see Cox 2000).

Even though TNCs disperse their activities to capitalize on local characteristics, their production and sales are frequently concentrated within one geographical region. This geographical concentration of activities is likely to cause many TNCs to put their efforts into lobbying for regional trading agreements rather than for liberalization at the global level, because their principal interest is in removing barriers to trade between those countries in which their own manufacturing plants and those of principal suppliers are located. This concentration on the regional level is encouraged by the better prospects there, compared with the global level, of pursuing the 'deeper integration' that TNCs need for efficient integration of their production networks—for example, agreements on the treatment that foreign investment will

receive, protection of intellectual property rights, and facilitation of the movement of skilled workers and management.

Economies of scale and regionalization of production may both incline companies towards lobbying for RTAs but their impact on the attitudes of labour is likely to be more ambiguous. On the one hand, the possibility of gaining larger market share, longer production runs, and higher profits through the realization of economies of scale offers the prospect to labour of additional employment, higher wages, etc. On the other, the opportunity that the negotiation of a free trade area provides companies to regionalize their production will be likely to worry labour unions in relatively high-wage countries that will fear that labour-intensive stages of production will be moved to those parts of the region with lower labour costs. It was not surprising, therefore, that companies with regionalized production networks lobbied in favour of NAFTA, whereas labour unions (together with American firms that produced solely within the US for the domestic market) expressed their concern that the agreement would generate, in the words of H. Ross Perot, a 'giant sucking sound' as US jobs were lost to Mexico (Chase 2003).

KEY POINTS

- Governments often enter RTAs for political reasons. These include: enhancing security; improving their international bargaining positions; signalling to potential investors the seriousness of their commitment to reforms; to satisfy domestic constituencies' demands for 'reciprocity'; and because they perceive regional agreements are easier to negotiate than those within the WTO.

- Economic motivations for regionalism include access to a larger 'domestic' market; possibilities for attracting additional FDI; the possibility of engaging in 'deeper integration'; and the opportunity afforded to continue to protect politically sensitive, globally uncompetitive industries.

The rush to regionalism

The rush to regionalism that began in the mid 1990s is the second major wave of RTAs since the Second World War: the first occurred in the early 1960s, largely in response to the 1957 establishment of the European Economic Community (regionalism, however, has a much longer history, dating back several centuries: the previous peak in regional activity occurred in the inter-war period, when industrialized countries responded to the Great Depression by attempting to form closed trading blocs with LDCs, in the case of European countries, with their colonies).

Many of the agreements negotiated in the 1960s linked LDCs together. In Africa, the growth of regionalism followed former European colonies gaining their independence in the late 1950s and early 1960s. As in South America, the other continent where regionalism took off in this period, the principal objectives of the regional agreements were to promote local **import-substitution industrialization (ISI)**, and to enhance the bargaining power of participants vis-à-vis external actors (in Asia, few regional economic partnerships, with the exception of ASEAN, emerged, not least because of the Cold War conflicts that divided countries in this part of the world). In marked contrast with the most recent wave of regionalism, the agreements among LDCs in the 1960s aimed to restrict imports from outside the region (in other words, they deliberately sought trade diversion—see Box 6.2—and to control foreign investors).

The landscape of interstate relations in South America and particularly in Africa soon became littered with the debris of failed regional arrangements. One reason was that few of the parties to regional arrangements were significant economic partners for one another. This was especially the case in Africa where the economies had been shaped in the colonial era to produce primary commodity exports for the European market. The share of intra-regional trade (that is, trade with regional partners) in countries' overall trade was often less than 5 per cent. A consequence was that liberalization of trade on a regional basis in itself brought the participants few immediate benefits.

Moreover, liberalization of trade within a region often exacerbated existing inequalities among the partner states. Where companies had a choice of a single country location to serve the unified, protected, regional market, they usually preferred the city where infrastructure was most developed. Industries therefore tended to cluster around 'growth poles' and shunned the poorer-resourced towns and cities in the least developed parts of the region. The less developed economies within a regional partnership frequently found that they faced significant costs from trade diversion as imports from outside the region were replaced by relatively high-cost production from their partner states. They also lost tariff revenue, on which many less developed economies depended heavily as a source of government funding (the loss occurring both because of the removal of intra-regional tariffs and from the diversion of imports from outside the region to goods sourced from regional partners).

Some regional arrangements (including ASEAN and the Andean Pact) in their early years attempted to address the problems caused by this unbalanced growth by pursuing a policy of industrial licensing: the location of new industrial plants would be agreed by governments and allocated across different parts of the region to ensure that the less developed gained a share of the benefits from integration. But such an approach was politically unpopular with the governments of the more developed partners. They perceived the losses in investment forgone and the generally negative responses from foreign partners as exceeding any gains they made from collaboration with their less developed regional partners.

Arguments about the distribution of benefits from regionalism led to the collapse of many of the schemes established in the 1960s, and to a heightening of tensions between regional partners. Contrary to the idea that regionalism might improve interstate security, disputes over the distribution of benefits from regional partnerships contributed in some instances to the onset of armed conflicts between former regional partners, for example, the 'soccer war' between former Central American Common Market members Honduras and El Salvador in 1969, and hostilities between former East African Community members Uganda and Tanzania in 1979.

New patterns in regional trade agreements

The failure of many RTAs among LDCs in the 1970s (Figure 6.1 shows how few schemes from the 1960s and 1970s are still in force today) occurred at a time when there was a considerable degree of pessimism about the prospects for the European Community. There, integration had proceeded more slowly than many had anticipated, and progress had been punctuated by increasingly acrimonious disputes among the member governments. By the middle of the 1970s, when worldwide economic conditions were more turbulent than at any time since 1945 because of the Organization of the Petroleum Exporting Countries (OPEC)-induced oil price rises and subsequent

Figure 6.1 Regional trade agreements notified to the GATT/WTO, 1948–2016

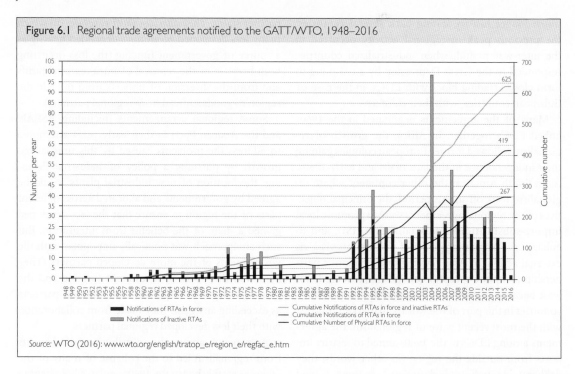

Source: WTO (2016): www.wto.org/english/tratop_e/region_e/regfac_e.htm

recession, regional integration no longer appeared to be a viable solution to the problems of interdependence that governments faced. To political leaders and academics alike, regional integration seemed increasingly obsolescent—the terminology the intellectual father of European integration studies, Ernst B. Haas (1975), applied at the time to theories of integration.

Two factors were to change the global context to make it far more favourable to regionalism in the 1990s. The first was the end of the Cold War. Regional economic agreements, like other aspects of international economic relations, are, in Aggarwal's (1985) terminology, 'nested' within the overall security context. A dramatic change in the security environment opened up new possibilities for partnerships among countries that had previously been on opposite sides of the Cold War divide. In Europe, the disintegration of the former Soviet Union and the 1991 break-up of the Council of Mutual Economic Assistance (COMECON; founded in 1949 by the Soviet Union as an alternative to the assistance that the US was providing Western Europe through the **Marshall Plan**), its membership expanded to include Czechoslovakia, East Germany, Poland, Hungary, Romania, Bulgaria, Mongolia, and Albania), opened the way for East European countries to enter into economic agreements

with the EU (and, for some, eventual membership in the EU). It also required new arrangements to be established amongst former Soviet bloc members if economic cooperation was to be sustained. Georgia, for instance, signed six free trade agreements with other former Soviet republics in the 1990s.

The concentration of new regional agreements in Europe in the 1990s underlines the importance of East European fragmentation for the growth in the number of RTAs (the enlargement of the EU in 2004 and 2007 subsequently made many of these treaties redundant). In Asia, also, the end of the Cold War broke down the barriers that had previously prevented regional economic integration. In 1991, China joined the APEC grouping, which included its former Cold War foes Japan, the US, and South Korea. In 2001, demonstrating the enormous improvement in relations that had occurred in East Asia over the previous decade, China began to negotiate a free trade agreement with ASEAN (see Figure 6.2).

The second contextual factor was the growth in global interdependence, and the ascendancy of neoliberal ideas in Western governments and in the **international financial institutions (IFIs)**. The growing integration of markets—for goods, services, and finance—placed increasing pressure on governments

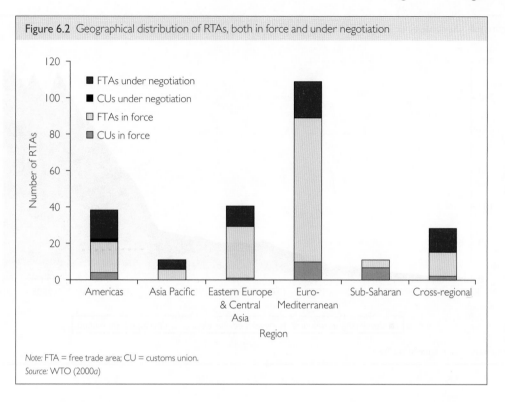

Figure 6.2 Geographical distribution of RTAs, both in force and under negotiation

Note: FTA = free trade area; CU = customs union.
Source: WTO (2000a)

to pursue market-friendly policies. Potential foreign investors quickly voted with their feet when faced by governments that attempted to impose conditions on them: indeed, from the early 1980s onwards, the balance of bargaining power between investors and governments shifted dramatically so that investors were increasingly able to demand concessions from host governments on issues such as taxation, rather than accepting restrictions on their activities. Similarly, financial markets were quick to punish governments that were perceived to be inward-looking or inclined towards interventionist measures.

In this new context, the regional arrangements that developed were often designed to enhance states' participation in the global economy, to signal their openness to foreign investment, and to seek access to the markets of industrialized countries. Unlike the arrangements from the 1960s and 1970s, the new regionalism frequently involved partnerships between industrialized and less developed economies, that is, they were often North–South rather than South–South in orientation. The North American Free Trade Agreement is the most prominent example; meanwhile, many less developed economies sought free trade agreements with the EU, and by the early years

of the new millennium, Japan had begun to negotiate free trade agreements with less developed economies in South East Asia and South America.

In the last decade, an increase in the number of agreements between industrialized and emerging economies has reflected a desire to facilitate the operation of production networks. Again, the focus has been less on traditional barriers to trade but on facilitating the movement of components around a region. Richard Baldwin has characterized these '21st Century Trade Agreements' as being driven by a new reciprocity: 'the basic bargain is "foreign factories for domestic reforms"—not "exchange of market access"' (2011: 1).

It was not just LDCs that responded to the increased market integration through seeking regional economic partnerships. The decision by European member states to deepen integration and to complete the implementation of a single internal market (brought into being by the Single European Act, signed in 1986), has been widely interpreted as an attempt to strengthen the capacity of European companies to compete in the new global market place (Sandholtz and Zysman 1989; Schirm 2002).

Figure 6.3 illustrates a number of the factors contributing to the explosive growth in regionalism in the

Figure 6.3 Cumulative numbers of RTAs in force 1950–2010 by country group

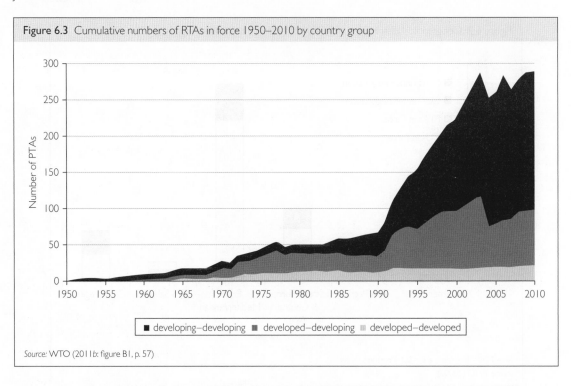

■ developing–developing ■ developed–developing ■ developed–developed

Source: WTO (2011b: figure B1, p. 57)

1990s. Transition economies (the former Soviet bloc countries) were involved in more than one-half of all RTAs signed in the 1990s (including 40 RTAs that only involved other transition economies). Reflecting the desire of Southern countries to seek alliances with Northern partners, there was also a dramatic jump in the number of RTAs linking developed with developing countries in the 1990s. In contrast, few of the agreements signed in the 1990s linked two or more developed economies. In the new century, however, with the proliferation of bilateral agreements (and the rise of China and India), developing countries began once more to negotiate a significant number of agreements among themselves. A variety of other factors also contributed to the growth of regionalism in the 1990s.

Frustration with the difficulties of negotiating global agreements

The GATT began as a relatively small international institution dominated by Western industrial countries (see Capling and Trommer, Chapter 5 in this volume). As more countries joined it, so the difficulties of reaching agreement among an increasingly diverse group on an agenda that was becoming more complex were

intensified. The consequence was that it took much longer to bring successive rounds of GATT talks to a conclusion.

When the Uruguay Round of GATT negotiations stalled, governments turned to regional agreements both as a substitute for a global agreement and as a means of increasing pressure on other countries to attempt to persuade them to make concessions in global talks. Similar considerations applied a decade later when the WTO prepared to launch a new round of global trade negotiations: membership of the WTO was approaching 150 economies and the agenda was yet more complex. The 'debacle in Seattle', the failure of the WTO's ministerial meeting in December 1999, convinced many governments (including some that had previously been hostile towards RTAs, for example, Japan, see METI 2000), that negotiation of a new global agreement would not bring early results and that they should therefore look to RTAs if they wished to advance their trade agendas. The deadlock in the Doha Round—and a more general frustration on the part of the US and the EU about the prospects for advancing their 'deeper' integration agenda in global institutions—were significant precipitants of the TPP and TTIP negotiations.

Bandwagoning and balancing: 'contagion' effects

The fact that post-war regional integration has come in two waves points both to the likelihood that common responses have occurred across various parts of the globe to the same stimuli (especially to increased economic interdependence), and to the possibility that regionalism in one part of the world triggers regionalism elsewhere through 'demonstration', 'emulation', or 'contagion' effects.

The establishment of the European Common Market in 1957, with its apparently positive impacts both on interstate relations and on the economies of its members, inspired a wave of imitations among LDCs. Similarly, the completion of the single internal market in the EU in 1992 and the establishment of NAFTA in 1994 led governments elsewhere to take a keener interest in becoming participants in regional agreements. The Japanese government report cited earlier, for instance, presented a detailed review of academic studies of existing regional arrangements, concluding that they generally had a positive effect on the welfare of member states. For many governments, therefore, the new interest in regionalism was primarily a defensive response to developments elsewhere. And some governments that were already party to regional arrangements sought new ones in an attempt to reduce their dependence on existing regional partners. Mexico, for instance, began negotiations for free trade arrangements with the EU and Japan as a means of reducing its heavy reliance on its NAFTA partners.

It was not just governments, however, that were prompted into action by regionalism elsewhere. The essence of preferential trade agreements is that they are discriminatory: non-members do not share the benefits they provide. Companies located in non-members therefore find that RTAs place them at a competitive disadvantage. They have an incentive to lobby their governments either to bandwagon by joining existing regional arrangements where such possibilities exist, or to negotiate a treaty that provides them with equivalent access to markets (Baldwin 1993). For instance, following the implementation of NAFTA and the signature of the Mexico–EU Free Trade Agreement, Japanese manufacturers found themselves at a disadvantage in competing in the Mexican market. Whereas their American and European counterparts enjoyed duty-free access to Mexico, Japanese companies faced tariffs that averaged 16 per cent. The main

business grouping, the Japan Federation of Economic Organizations, Keidanren, lobbied the government to sign a free trade agreement with Mexico that would give Japanese companies equivalent access to that enjoyed by their competitors (Solis 2003b; Manger 2005).

The proliferation of preferential trade agreements across the globe, with the potential competitive disadvantages they bring for non-participants, increases the incentives for governments either to join existing agreements or to seek similar arrangements for their own exporters (Oye 1992; Baldwin 1997).

The change in the US attitude towards preferential agreements

The United States government was the strongest supporter of a non-discriminatory multilateral approach to trade in the negotiations that led to the creation of GATT at the end of the Second World War. Not only had it been a victim of the discriminatory colonial trading blocs that the European powers had created in the inter-war period, but it believed that their closing off of international trade had made a significant contribution to the global recession of the 1930s. It was largely at US insistence that non-discrimination was enshrined as the cornerstone of the post-war global trade regime.

Washington, however, was willing to tolerate regional trading groupings that discriminated against its exports where it believed that these helped to achieve its political objectives through, for example, facilitating reconciliation between former enemies and strengthening the economies of the participants so that they would be less susceptible to the perceived communist threat. Security concerns trumped economic principles. The primary example was the European Economic Community (EEC). Washington had encouraged European recipients of **Marshall Plan** assistance (Box 6.5) to coordinate their plans (which led to the formation of the Organisation for European Economic Co-operation, the forerunner to the OECD, the Organisation for Economic Co-operation and Development). It put pressure on France to accommodate the rebuilding of Germany's industry and to devise a mechanism that would allay French concerns (which ultimately became the Schuman Plan for the European Coal and Steel Community). The US government supported the formation of the EEC in 1957, even though it was obvious that the new Community,

BOX 6.5

The Marshall Plan

Under the Marshall Plan, the US government provided $11.8 billion in grants and a further $1.5 billion in loans to assist in the rebuilding of European economies (and, in some instances, those of their colonies) in the years 1948–52. The United Kingdom received the largest volume of grants ($2.8 billion), followed by France ($2.5 billion), Italy ($1.4 billion), and West Germany ($1.2 billion). The Plan was an outgrowth of Washington's concerns about the perceived growth of Soviet influence in Europe. Funds were used for purposes such as

purchasing new machinery for factories, providing technical assistance to enable Europeans to become familiar with new technologies, and the rebuilding of roads, railways, and ports. The bilateral assistance provided to Europe under the Marshall Plan far exceeded the funds available from the International Bank for Reconstruction and Development (World Bank). The Organisation for European Economic Co-operation (which subsequently evolved into the Organisation for Economic Co-operation and Development (OECD)) was created to manage the Marshall Plan aid.

---

like the ECSC, would not be fully compatible with GATT requirements for RTAs and would discriminate against US exports. At the same time, it exerted pressure on the Europeans not to introduce any provisions that would increase discrimination against US economic interests. Its support for European integration was also accompanied by American initiatives in the GATT for new rounds of global negotiations with the objective of reducing overall tariff levels and thus the discrimination its exporters would face in the European market (the 'Kennedy Round', 1963–7, was the response to the EEC's creation, and the 'Tokyo Round', 1973–9, the response to the first enlargement of the Community when it admitted Denmark, Ireland, and the United Kingdom in 1973).

Washington's attitude towards regional economic agreements among LDCs was more ambivalent. Although it appreciated the possibility that regionalism might improve the security of the participants, its enthusiasm was tempered because of the anti-import and pro-interventionist frameworks that figured prominently in many of the regional schemes among less developing countries in the 1960s. Its support for regional economic integration among South American countries, therefore, was at best lukewarm. And, in other parts of the world, especially Asia, Washington opposed any movement towards a regional agreement from which it would be excluded.

The US attitude towards regional economic agreements changed in the early 1980s, as it despaired of the slow progress in global trade liberalization and bristled at the growing trade distortions generated by the European Community's Common Agricultural Policy (CAP). United States Trade Representative William Brock announced in 1982 that Washington was

willing to enter into RTAs. Negotiation of a free trade agreement with Israel quickly followed. The US also launched the Caribbean Basin Initiative, a programme of trade preferences for the island states of the region. Far more significant, however, was Washington's positive response to a Canadian proposal for negotiation of a free trade agreement. In one sense, this was not a dramatic departure in American trade policy. Washington had offered such an agreement to Canada on several occasions over the previous century only to be rebuffed by a Canadian government concerned about maintaining its economic independence. Nonetheless, the signature of the Canada–US Free Trade Agreement in 1988 sent a dramatic signal to other members of the international community. This was reinforced in the following years when the first Bush administration indicated its willingness to construct a 'hub and spokes' framework that would link the US in a series of free trade agreements with partners in Central and South America, Oceania, and East Asia.

The new approach to trade policy in the early 1990s was succinctly stated by Lawrence Summers, who became under-secretary of the Treasury for International Affairs in the first Clinton administration: that there should be a 'presumption in favor of all the lateral reductions in trade barriers, whether they be multi, uni, tri, plurilateral' (quoted in Frankel 1997: 5). In other words, the policy was one of 'anything goes' in trade policy so long as it contributed to trade liberalization, there no longer being a presumption that discriminatory regional agreements would be barriers to liberalization at the global level.

With the United States itself in the second half of the 1990s actively pursuing regionalism through NAFTA and advocating its extension into a Free Trade

Area of the Americas, it would have been difficult for Washington to maintain its opposition to regionalism in other parts of the world. The change in attitude was particularly important in facilitating the development of preferential trade arrangements in East Asia. Whereas Washington had vigorously opposed a proposal from Malaysian Prime Minister Mahathir Mohamad in the early 1990s for the creation of an East Asian Economic Group, which would have excluded the countries of North America and Oceania that were members of the rival APEC grouping, by the late 1990s it acquiesced in the creation of an equivalent grouping (ASEAN Plus Three, the ten ASEAN members plus China, Japan, and South Korea), and in numerous East Asian moves to negotiate bilateral free trade arrangements.

Making existing preferential trade arrangements compatible with WTO requirements: the EU's relations with developing economies

Some of the new free trade areas came into being because industrialized countries perceived that they needed to make their trade agreements with LDCs compatible with the WTO's regulations. Here, the EU has again been the most important actor.

The EU had previously constructed a network of preferential trade arrangements with the countries of the southern Mediterranean, and with the Africa, Caribbean, and Pacific grouping (ACP), which comprises over 70 countries, many of which had formerly been European colonies. These agreements had been negotiated in contexts entirely different from that prevailing in the second half of the 1990s. The arrangements with the ACP grouping were codified in the Lomé Conventions, the first of which had come into effect in 1975 at the height of the demands from less developed economies for the creation of a **New International Economic Order** (**NIEO**). Reflecting a context in which industrialized countries were responsive to the demands from less developed economies for special treatment, the Conventions offered duty-free access to the European market for most ACP exports without obliging the ACP countries to provide similar preferential treatment to European exports: in other words, they were non-reciprocal arrangements. (Treaties with southern Mediterranean countries, signed in 1975–7, offered similar duty-free access to the European market: the Mediterranean countries did

commit to lower their tariffs on imports from the European Community but the timetable for this process was not specified.)

Besides their general trade provisions, the Lomé Conventions also included special arrangements for specific products, including bananas, beef, rum, and sugar, on which some countries' export earnings were heavily dependent. These typically enabled their sale in European markets at prices much higher than those prevailing elsewhere. In some instances, they rested on a segmentation of the European market, with, for instance, exports of ACP bananas being subject to different treatment in the United Kingdom and in France than they received in Germany and the Netherlands. The EU, in fact, operated three different tariff regimes for bananas, even though, as a common market, it had supposedly adopted a common external tariff. The new commitment to realizing a single internal market in the EU in 1992 made it impossible to maintain this arrangement for ACP bananas.

In an attempt to preserve the special position of ACP bananas, the EU introduced an interventionist system of import licensing that discriminated against bananas coming from non-ACP countries (primarily Central and South America). Several of these producing countries challenged the new EU banana regime in the GATT; they were supported by the US government, which had been lobbied by the two giant US agribusiness firms, Dole and Chiquita, which handled most of the trade in Central and South American bananas. This lengthy and convoluted dispute took more than two decades before final resolution in 2012 (WTO 2012), and at one stage threatened to trigger a 'trade war' between the United States and the EU. Ultimately, a WTO Dispute Settlement Panel found that the European provisions on bananas contravened several of WTO articles. The Europeans eventually backed down, committing themselves to introducing arrangements that were compatible with their WTO obligations (Ravenhill 2004).

The dispute illustrated how the WTO makes it possible for LDCs to initiate a successful challenge against an aspect of the trade policies of an economic superpower, the EU. It also demonstrated the significance of the changed arrangements for dispute settlement with the transition from the GATT to the WTO. Unlike the situation under the GATT, when countries simply ignored dispute settlement judgements that they did not like, the EU had no viable alternative but to conform to the WTO's requirements. More important than the specifics of the banana dispute itself are the implications of the WTO's judgement for rules governing relations between industrialized and less developed economies.

In finding that the EU's banana regime contravened several of its provisions, the WTO rejected European arguments that the trade arrangements with the ACP were legitimized by WTO rules on RTAs and on special treatment for less developed economies. The WTO found that the Lomé Convention did not conform to its rules for regional trade arrangements because the ACP countries were not required to remove their tariffs on European imports (under the requirements of Article xxiv, all parties to a regional economic agreement must liberalize 'substantially all trade' between them). Moreover, the Convention did not conform to the rules on preferences for less developed economies because it gave special treatment to one group (the ACP) but not to other economies at similar levels of development. These rulings left the EU with only one other avenue for seeking WTO legitimacy for the Convention: to apply under Article ix of the WTO for a special waiver from the most-favoured-nation rule. But the requirements for such a waiver are more stringent under the WTO than they were in the GATT; the waiver is only for a fixed term and would not have prevented WTO members from subsequently challenging specific elements of the arrangements. In other words, a waiver would have provided little assurance to the ACP states that the provisions would not be disrupted in the future.

Faced with this dilemma, the EU decided that the only means through which it could provide long-term trade security for the ACP would be to abandon its previous approach and to negotiate arrangements that were compatible with WTO rules on RTAs (Article xxiv). It proposed, in the Cotonou Agreement of 2000, to do this through concluding a series of economic partnership agreements with groupings of ACP countries, which were to be negotiated by the end of 2007. By mid-2016, however, few of the agreements had been ratified and the country coverage in West and Central Africa was very limited. A similar decision had been made earlier regarding the trade agreements with the countries of the southern Mediterranean: in its Barcelona Declaration of 1995, the EU stated its intention to negotiate WTO-compatible free trade agreements with these countries. These were subsequently concluded with Tunisia (1995), Israel (1995), Morocco (1996), Jordan (1997), Egypt (1999), Algeria (2001), and Lebanon (2002).

KEY POINTS

- The RTAs of the 1960s and 1970s aimed to promote regional industrialization behind tariff walls.

- They often broke down because of disagreements over the distribution of benefits and costs from regional cooperation.

- The new regionalism differs from this previous wave in that participating countries are typically using agreements to increase their integration into the world economy. Many of the agreements link developed with developing economies.

- The origins of the new regionalism lie in the end of the Cold War; the perceived success of RTAs elsewhere; frustrations with the pace of trade liberalization at the global level; a desire to make existing preferential trade relations compatible with WTO rules; and a change in US attitudes towards regionalism.

The politics of regional deepening in the European Union: neo-functionalist and intergovernmental explanations

As indicated in Box 6.1, governments that enter regional agreements that involve more than the creation of a free trade area inevitably have to agree to establish institutions that 'pool their sovereignty' on policies that have to be determined at the regional level—for instance, the determination of common external tariffs and other common foreign economic policies in customs unions. The deeper the integration—that is, the broader the scope of policy issues on which members agree to cooperate—the greater will be the number of policy areas on which regional institutions will have to be given competence (except on issues where members agree to a policy of mutual recognition whereby they accept policies/standards in other members as if they were their own).

Political scientists have long been fascinated by the question of whether a regional arrangement, once established, generates its own momentum towards not only closer economic but also closer political integration. The vast majority of regional economic agreements take the form of free trade areas, which, because they do not require setting a common external tariff, provide little stimulus for the establishment of a regional institution to coordinate policies. Most free trade areas do provide a process for the resolution of disputes between the parties over the interpretation and/or implementation of the free trade area's rules, but this process is usually managed by secretariats within the governments of the member countries. For instance, although there is a NAFTA secretariat, which administers the dispute resolution procedures created by the agreement, this is a 'virtual' secretariat comprised of three sections located within the respective national governments. Very limited scope is available to such national agencies to act to promote deeper regional integration: indeed, the very lack of the creation of any alternative source of authority at the regional level is one of the attractions of free trade areas to many national governments. Even in those free trade areas where member governments have agreed to create a central secretariat, as in ASEAN, they often deliberately keep such institutions weak so that they do not develop as challengers to national governments.

With deeper integration, the scope for regional institutions to act autonomously may increase. The best example is the EU, the only regional agreement that has fully implemented a common market and moved beyond this to form an economic union. It has by far the most complex of governance arrangements of any regional grouping. As Helen Wallace (2000: 44) suggests, 'much of what makes the EU so interesting … is the density of institutions and the evidence of institutional creativity. EU institutions provide both opportunities and constraints, and they serve to channel and to structure the behaviour of political actors from the participating countries'.

The principal political organs at the regional level are a supranational secretariat, the European Commission ('supranational' because it is autonomous from the governments of the member states and its officials have the responsibility of promoting the interests of the EU as a whole rather than those of specific members), an institution comprised of ministers from the national governments (the Council of Ministers, which is supported by a committee of senior officials, known by its French acronym, COREPER, the Committee of Permanent Representatives), the European Parliament (directly elected since 1979 by voters in the member states), and the European Court of Justice (which is charged with interpreting the various EU treaties that member states have signed). The EU treaties now extend far beyond the liberalization of internal trade and the establishment of common foreign economic policies to include competition policies, environmental policies, common foreign and security policies, justice and home affairs (including human

rights), and regional development. The EU and its member states now constitute a complex web of multilevel governance, with authority for making and implementing policies on various issues being split between institutions at the regional level, at the national level and, in some instances, at the subnational level (for further discussion, see Kenealy, Peterson, and Corbett 2015; and Wallace *et al.* 2015).

Most of the theorizing in international relations on regionalism has concentrated on the European experience. The early years of European integration inspired the development of neo-functionalist analysis (Haas 1958; Lindberg 1963). This approach suggested how a regional grouping could generate a momentum of its own that would lead to a deepening of cooperation. The logic was that cooperation in one area of economic activity would produce pressures for cooperation in other areas as the costs of pursuing uncoordinated policies became increasingly evident to member states and their private sector actors, a process that the *neo-functionalist* theorists termed 'spillover'. Entrepreneurial leadership by key actors in regional institutions could intensify the pressures for further cooperation.

In the EU, the European Commission has the power to take initiatives in the various areas where the members have agreed that the EU has competence; it thus has the capacity to shape agendas and to push for further cooperation at the European level. The European Court of Justice's responsibility for interpreting the treaties and for adjudicating disputes between member states affords it an opportunity that extends into the realm of policymaking; over the last quarter of the twentieth century, some of its judgements significantly extended the scope of European competence.

One element of neo-functional theorizing emphasized the significance of the unintended consequences of previous actions and decisions. For instance, member states did not anticipate the important role that the Court of Justice would come to play in extending the scope of integration when they created a body that was intended to arbitrate disputes on the implementation of treaties. For theorists in the neo-functionalist tradition, the logic of spillover and the creative leadership provided by regional institutions can provide the integration process with a dynamic of its own (Sandholtz and Stone Sweet 1998 provide an example of theorizing from this perspective).

The neo-functionalist approach has consistently been challenged by scholars who assert that national states have primacy in the integration process. Stanley Hoffmann (1966) pioneered this challenge; the economic historian, Alan Milward (1992), subsequently developed the theme that integration in Europe is best interpreted as a strategy pursued by national states to strengthen their own positions. Andrew Moravcsik (1998) presents the most theoretically sophisticated articulation of this 'liberal intergovernmental' argument, suggesting that the major steps forward in European integration were driven not by the European Commission or the Court of Justice but by member governments that were responding in a rational way to domestic economic interests. Key decisions on integration reflect bargains struck among member states; the most significant European institution therefore is not the supranational Commission but the intergovernmental Council of Ministers. For writers in this tradition, to the extent that member states delegate authority to community institutions, such moves are 'calculated, rational, and circumscribed' (Bomberg and Stubb 2003: 11).

In this hotly contested debate, as is often the case in international relations theorizing, authors writing from one perspective have been reluctant to acknowledge that the arguments of the competing school have any legitimacy whatsoever. Because the EU embraces such a wide array of activities, and the competencies of its various actors and the balance of power between them have evolved over time, it is possible for both sides to this debate to find compelling examples that support their case. Rather than perceiving this issue as a dichotomy of government preferences versus the actions of **supranational institutions**, it would be more helpful to focus on the interaction between these two. Sandholtz (1993) has argued persuasively that state preferences themselves are not formed in a vacuum: membership in the EU itself has become an important influence on how governments define their interests—they are socialized into particular ways of thinking.

To date, the failure of those other regional schemes that aspire to become common markets to realize their aspirations inevitably limits to the European context debates about the role that supranational institutions can play in driving integration forwards. Meanwhile, it is too early to tell definitively whether the neo-functional logic of spillover will apply to some of the more significant free trade areas—most notably NAFTA—that were established in the 1990s, although little evidence has emerged to date to support such ideas (for discussion of the NAFTA case, see Capling and Nossal 2009).

> **KEY POINTS**
>
> - Corporations may prefer regionalism to global trade liberalization if it enables them to capture economies of scale while avoiding exposure to global competition.
>
> - Regionalism may be particularly attractive to companies that seek 'deeper integration' to facilitate the operation of regional production networks (through, for instance, provisions to safeguard investments).
>
> - Unskilled labour in industrialized economies is likely to oppose regional integration if this includes less developed economies with significantly lower labour costs.
>
> - Because most RTAs are free trade areas, they require little pooling of sovereignty and afford little scope for the emergence of sources of power at the regional level that rival national governments.
>
> - In the EU, evidence from different sectors at different periods of time supports arguments from both the intergovernmental and the neo-functionalist perspectives.

The economic consequences of regional integration

The discussion of trade diversion in Box 6.2 reminds us that no assumption can be made that RTAs will necessarily enhance the welfare of their participants. It is not straightforward to estimate the effect that RTAs have had on members' trade and their welfare more generally because the impact of many other variables has to be taken into consideration.

Regional agreements and members' trade

That the overall share of world trade conducted within RTAs has risen, as noted at the beginning of this chapter, reflects both an increase in the number of RTAs and an increase in the share of their total trade that members of some RTAs conduct with one another. Table 6.3 shows the share of intra-regional trade in members' total trade for the major minilateral RTAs.

The share of intra-regional trade in the total trade of members of some regional agreements rose dramatically: most notable here were the Andean Group, CARICOM, and MERCOSUR. In contrast, ASEAN states were little more important as trading partners for one another in 2014 than they had been 40 years before, despite implementing a free trade agreement

Table 6.3 Changes in the share of intra-regional trade in selected RTAs, 1970–2014

	1970	1980	1985	1990	1995	2000	2005	2008	2014
EU (1957)	59.5	60.8	59.2	65.9	62.4	66.2	66.5	65.4	63.4
NAFTA (1994)	36.0	33.6	43.9	41.4	41.5	46.4	43.0	40.0	41.4
CACM (1961)	26.0	24.4	14.4	15.4	21.7	13.7	15.0*	15.2*	n.a.
Andean Group (1988)	1.8	3.8	3.2	4.2	7.5	8.5	10.0	8.4	7.7
CARICOM (1973)	4.2	5.3	6.3	8.1	12.1	14.6	9.4*	10.2*	n.a.
MERCOSUR (1991)	9.4	11.6	5.5	8.9	19.2	20.6	15.7	16.0	13.5
ECOWAS (1975)	2.9	9.6	5.1	8.0	9.0	9.6	10.0*	7.9*	8.6
SADC (1992)	4.2	0.4	1.4	3.1	10.6	11.9	9.2*	10.4*	10.7
ASEAN/AFTA (1992)	22.4	17.4	18.6	19	22.0	22.8	25.1	25.0	24.0
GCC (1981)	4.6	3.0	4.9	8.0	6.8	5.0	5.8*	5.9*	n.a.

Note: Figures in parentheses refer to year in which the RTA came into force.

Sources: WTO (2003c: Table 1B.11); updated with author's calculations from data in https://www.wto.org/english/res_e/statis_e/its2015_e/its15_appendix_e.htm except for figures marked with an asterisk (*), which were calculated using data extracted from the IMF DOTS online database (accessed in February 2010) and may not therefore be directly comparable.

in the interim. The record of many African RTAs was mixed: the Southern African Development Community (SADC) was notable in increasing intra-regional trade, a reflection of the reintegration of the post-apartheid South Africa into the regional economy. In many of the groupings, we see a plateauing of the share of intra-regional trade in total trade in the 1990s. One factor for many groupings was the rise in importance of China as an extra-regional trading partner.

Simple statistics of this type, however, do not tell us whether the RTA itself has been a significant influence on trade among the member economies. Multiple factors other than the existence of a RTA can influence the volume of trade between any two countries. Among the most important of these are the size of the two economies, the levels of per capita income, the geographical distance between the two countries (and hence the transportation costs in trading), whether or not they share a common boundary, and whether or not their populations speak the same language. Such factors have to be built into any model that attempts to isolate the impact of the regional agreement itself on trade. Jeffrey Frankel (1997) constructed one of the early comprehensive models. He found that after

allowing for the various factors identified earlier, RTAs had a (statistically significant) positive impact on the trade between their members. This positive effect was particularly pronounced for agreements among less developed economies, including ASEAN and MERCOSUR, but trade among EU member states was also 65 per cent above the level that would otherwise have been expected in the absence of a RTA. These results echo those in several other studies. The evidence points strongly to preferential trade agreements having caused substantial changes in their members' international trade.

These results in themselves, however, do not distinguish between trade creation and trade diversion effects, and thus tell us little about the *welfare* effects of the RTAs. Again, isolating the causes of the increased trade is no easy task. The new preferences created for regional partners have to be viewed in the context of other changes in the participants' trade policies including, for instance, any reduction of their tariffs towards non-members of the regional agreement (as occurred in the 1980s and 1990s, both through unilateral liberalization and through implementation of GATT/WTO agreements).

The welfare effects of RTAs have been the subject of a very extensive literature in economics (a recent review can be found in WTO 2011*b*: 105–6). A major study by the World Bank (2000) finds that, although the ratio of intra-regional trade to **gross domestic product (GDP)** increased in all regional groupings reviewed, so too did the ratio of trade with extra-regional partners to GDP. In other words, not only did trade with regional partners grow in economic importance but so too did trade with countries outside the region. Consequently, the Bank concluded, while studies suggest that some trade diversion occurred in the EU, European Free Trade Association, and NAFTA, 'the picture is sufficiently mixed that it is not possible to conclude that trade diversion has been a major problem' (World Bank 2000: 48), a finding consistent with Frankel's (1997) comprehensive study (see also Krueger 1999).

That RTAs may distort members' trade patterns only to a limited extent is consistent with the lowering of MFN tariffs (and thus the preferential margins enjoyed by partner countries) that has occurred in the last two decades. In Canada, 55 per cent of all MFN tariff lines are duty free; in the United States, the figure is 43 per cent. As noted in the previous chapter, the average tariff level in industrialized countries on imports of manufactured goods is less than 5 per cent. A similar trend towards tariff reduction is also evident in most LDCs, with an inevitable consequence for the preferential margins that RTAs create.

In a study of the world's 20 largest importing economies, the WTO (2011*b*: 73–81) found that 50 per cent of imports came from partners in a preferential arrangement (excluding intra-EU trade) but that only a third of that total (16 per cent) was potentially subject to preferential access—either because MFN tariffs were zero or because the product was excluded from the RTA. In aggregate, only 3.8 per cent of global non-preferential imports had MFN tariff rates above 10 per cent. In ASEAN, for instance, in roughly two-thirds of the tariff lines, MFN and preferential tariffs are identical. For many of the others, the preferential margin is so small in the more developed economies (Singapore and Malaysia) that few companies have found it worthwhile to meet the rules of origin requirements and file the necessary paperwork: less than 5 per cent of all intra-ASEAN trade is estimated to take advantage of the preferential tariffs provided under the ASEAN Free Trade Agreement. Not only do many RTAs create few advantages for partners for many exports, but they also seldom help in the most heavily protected areas: when 'sensitive' sectors are protected by high MFN tariffs, governments frequently also exempt them altogether from the regional agreement or minimize the liberalization provided.

Scale economies, competition effects, and deeper integration

Regional trade agreements affect the welfare of their participants through impacts beyond those on trade itself. One argument made in support of RTAs is that they will lead to increased investment flows for participants—that may come from regional partners or from states outside the region whose investors are attracted by the enlarged regional market. As noted earlier, inflows of FDI into Mexico increased substantially after the signature of NAFTA. Similarly, the establishment of the European Community and the subsequent deepening of European integration through the completion of the single internal market led to substantial increases in FDI in the EU, both intra-regionally—that is, from one member state to another, and from external countries (Motta and Norman 1996).

The other means through which RTAs are often assumed to improve the welfare of participating countries is by increasing the size of the 'home' market. As noted earlier, this can be particularly important for firms dependent upon access to a market larger than that available within one country to achieve economies of scale. Moreover, regionalism may generate increased competition for domestic companies, thereby forcing them to become more efficient. Again, estimating these effects requires complex economic modelling with often 'heroic' assumptions.

Although the computer simulations that modellers have used reach dramatically different conclusions depending on the assumptions employed, the most frequent finding is that regional integration produces only a very limited positive aggregate effect on the *welfare* of the participating countries (on the Asia-Pacific region, for instance, see Scollay and Gilbert 2001). Supporters of regionalism suggest that these findings reflect the inability of the models to capture the 'dynamic' effects of regional integration, those that develop over time as companies benefit from scale economies and other efficiencies. Others argue that the majority of benefits from regionalism come from the beneficial effects of companies responding to increased competition rather than from realizing economies of scale, and that these competitive benefits can be achieved more effectively through non-discriminatory liberalization that exposes domestic companies to worldwide competition (Schiff and Winters 2003: 51–2).

In short, the verdict on the economic effects of regional trade arrangements is mixed and frequently inconclusive. Economic models suggest that there is little evidence that RTAs have generated significant trade diversion. They do appear, at least in the years immediately following their signature, to have been associated with increased inflows of FDI. Yet, their overall effects on the economic welfare of participants, if positive, have been of limited magnitude. And in the most sophisticated of regional schemes, the EU, welfare benefits arising from improved competitiveness in manufacturing have been at least partially offset by the welfare losses caused by the EU's Common Agricultural Policy.

KEY POINTS

- Although considerable complexity is involved in attempting to isolate the economic effects of RTAs, evidence suggests that they have led to more trade among members than would otherwise be the case.

- RTAs do appear, at least in their early years, to have encouraged increased investment in member states.

- Economic simulations suggest that RTAs have had little aggregate effect on members' economic welfare.

- Little evidence exists that RTAs have produced significant trade diversion.

Regionalism and the WTO: stepping stone or stumbling block?

The huge increase in the number of RTAs in the last 20 years has been accompanied by a lively debate about its relationship to trade liberalization at the global level. Will RTAs facilitate or obstruct global trade liberalization or, as in Bhagwati's (1991) terminology, are regional agreements 'stepping stones' or 'stumbling blocks'?

Several arguments suggest how regional agreements might facilitate global negotiations:

1. Reaching agreement on issues of deeper integration will be easier within regional groupings; these agreements can then serve as models for global treaties.

2. Regional agreements can enhance the competitiveness of domestic industries, paving the way for full liberalization.

3. Regional agreements improve the financial position of export-oriented interests, thereby providing them with the means and incentive to lobby governments for broader liberalization, which will translate into support for global trade talks.

4. When regional agreements provide companies from some countries with preferential access to a foreign market, their competitors in other countries will lobby their governments to sign agreements that will provide them with equivalent access. This attempt 'to level the playing field' will produce what Baldwin (1997, 2006) has called a 'domino' effect in regionalism, in effect, broadening the scope of liberalization. Baldwin (2006) has extended the argument by suggesting that, with the proliferation of RTAs, each with their own rules of origin, corporations will press for a rationalization of agreements because of the adverse consequences that they had on managing their supply chains.

5. Global negotiations that take place among regional groupings reduce the number of actors involved.

The intuitively attractive argument that regional groupings simplify global negotiations by reducing the number of parties is counteracted by the difficulties that regional groupings often have in reaching a common position in negotiations with outsiders (witness the EU on agricultural issues in global negotiations). Once a regional grouping has reached internal agreement on its own position, it may have little flexibility in bargaining with other actors. And there is no assurance that the common position adopted by a regional grouping will not be more restrictive than that held by a majority of its member states: in other words, the regional grouping can end up throwing its combined weight behind policies that might not have been supported by a majority of its members (or possibly the largest economies in the region), had they acted individually in the global negotiations. The recent proliferation of regional trade arrangements, many of which have overlapping memberships, suggests further complications should negotiations occur between 'regions' rather than between individual countries.

Until recently, little evidence existed to support arguments that agreement on contentious issues or on matters of 'deeper' integration could be reached more easily at the regional level. The EU, for instance, has found it very difficult to liberalize the most politically sensitive areas of trade, especially in agriculture. In the OECD's words, 'regionalism has often failed to crack the hardest nuts' (2002: 20). And few regional agreements have moved beyond the basics of removing tariffs to address the 'behind-the-border' barriers that many economists believe are more significant impediments to contemporary trade than tariffs themselves. Nonetheless, the recent wave of regionalism has provided greater encouragement for the argument that deeper integration on issues such as investment and the environment is more easily accomplished through negotiations among a limited subset of countries (for further discussion, see OECD 2002). Developments at the regional level on these issues, however, have yet to be translated into global agreements, so the idea that regional agreements will subsequently have a positive influence on global negotiations has yet to be substantiated.

The argument that regional agreements will enable industries to become internationally competitive, and therefore that an RTA will ease the path towards non-discriminatory liberalization, assumes that the level of competition at the regional level will be similar to that in the global marketplace to which firms will then be able to graduate. An alternative proposition is also intuitively plausible: that the regional market will be of sufficient size to enable firms to realize economies of scale, and that they will prefer to operate with the comfort provided by the external tariff of the regional grouping rather than be exposed to extra competition in the global market. Companies content with operating in the regional market may be financially strengthened through regional integration, and therefore may have an incentive to lobby against extending trade liberalization beyond the region.

Baldwin's arguments that RTAs create a virtuous circle in which companies will press governments for additional liberalization appears persuasive in the European context. It rests, however, on the proposition that these agreements create significant advantages for corporations in countries that have these agreements and, consequently, substantially disadvantage companies in countries that do not. In other parts of the world, however, where RTAs are shallower and less comprehensive, their effects are far more limited. Consequently, the political logic of Baldwin's argument has less force: because the agreements do not significantly disadvantage excluded parties, then these corporations may have little incentive to lobby for

equivalent agreements. Moreover, because of exceptions in the agreements, protectionist interests are not necessarily weakened (Ravenhill 2010).

Critics who see regional agreements as stumbling blocks in the path of global liberalization assert that:

- They magnify the influence of power disparities in international trade relations, enabling larger economies to impose their will on smaller partners, gaining them advantages through, for instance, the imposition of rules of origin that would not be achieved if liberalization occurred on a global basis Such agreements consequently generate popular resentment against trade liberalization in smaller, less developed economies.

- They lead to a diversion of scarce bureaucratic resources and political leadership away from global trade negotiations towards those at the bilateral and regional levels.

- They give rise to what Bhagwati (1995) has termed a 'spaghetti bowl' effect of numerous, crisscrossing preferential arrangements with a multiplicity of tariff rates and different rules of origin. The complexity of regulations provides opportunities for special pleading by interest groups and generally increases the costs of engaging in international trade. With countries being members of several RTAs, each with its own set of rules, companies face difficult decisions on where to establish subsidiaries and where to source their inputs (OECD 2002: 18).

- They provide exporters with the access to markets that they desire, thereby removing their incentive to lobby the government either for further liberalization at the global level, or for a further opening up of their domestic markets.

- They enable governments to exempt sensitive political sectors from liberalization, thereby energizing protectionist forces and *strengthening* political resistance against liberalization at the global level. Some commentators suggest that this has been the case, for instance, with the agricultural sector in Japan.

The exemption of sensitive sectors from liberalization rests on the possibility that regional arrangements will not be comprehensive in their product coverage because members are able to exploit the ambiguity of the WTO's rules on RTAs (Box 6.6

BOX 6.6

The World Trade Organization and Preferential Trade Agreements

Article xxiv of the GATT lays down the criteria that regional arrangements must meet to be regarded as legitimate by the WTO. Members' customs duties under the new agreement must not 'on the whole' be higher or more restrictive than those previously imposed by the individual countries. The preferential agreement, according to Article xxiv.8, must also eliminate duties and other restrictions on 'substantially all the trade' between participants.

These provisions have generated enormous controversy over the years. In particular, members have failed to reach agreement on defining and applying the phrase 'substantially all the trade'. The WTO notes 'there exists neither an agreed definition of the percentage of trade to be covered by a WTO-consistent agreement nor common criteria against which the exclusion of a particular sector from the agreement could be assessed'. The EU, a pioneer in negotiating preferential trade agreements, has argued that the Article xxiv.8 requirement has both a quantitative and a qualitative element, with at least 90 per cent of the trade between parties being covered and no major sector excluded. But other members have contested this interpretation, which raises its own problems of definition: how is the 90 per cent of trade to be measured (does it only refer to existing trade or to that which might take place should restrictions be removed)? And how does one define a 'major' sector? A reinterpretation of Article xxiv.8 was one of the items on the agenda in the Doha Round of multilateral negotiations, but one on which few observers believe there will be agreement.

The lack of consensus on the provisions of Article xxiv.8 has stymied the work of the WTO's Committee on Regional Trade Agreements, created in February 1996 to examine preferential trade agreements and their implications for the multilateral trading system. Members have been able to agree that only one of the large number of PTAs notified to the Committee since 1996 (the customs union between the Czech Republic and the Slovak Republic after the break-up of Czechoslovakia) was fully compatible with the relevant rules (and this treaty lapsed when

both countries joined the EU). Lack of consensus has prevented the Committee from finalizing its other reports. The WTO's record on this matter is similar to that of the GATT, which was able to agree on the compatibility with Article xxiv of only four of the more than 50 RTAs submitted to it for consideration. Political factors have dominated decision-making on this issue. Nowhere was this more evident than when a GATT Working Party was convened to consider whether the Treaty of Rome, which established the EEC in 1957, met the requirements for RTAs. Faced with a threat by the Europeans to quit GATT should their integration arrangements be found incompatible with the full requirements of Article xxiv (which they clearly were), the GATT Working Party failed to reach consensus in its deliberations. Ultimately, contracting parties' desire for integration in Europe to proceed (as much for security as for economic reasons) outweighed their concerns about the legality of the agreements. Subsequently, GATT and the WTO have simply failed to pass judgement on the vast majority of RTAs they have examined, including CUSFTA and NAFTA.

The rules relating to the establishment of preferential trading arrangements among less developed economies under the 'Enabling Clause' are even less restrictive than those under Article xxiv. They make no reference to coverage of trade, the complete elimination of duties, or to a timetable for implementation. They require only that the regional agreement not constitute a barrier to most-favoured-nation trade reductions or cause 'undue difficulties' for other members. RTAs notified to the GATT/WTO under the Enabling Clause include AFTA and MERCOSUR.

As part of the Doha Round negotiations, WTO members agreed on a new 'transparency mechanism' for RTAs. Members negotiating regional agreements are now obliged to provide early notification of an RTA to the WTO: the WTO Secretariat prepares a factual presentation on the agreement for consideration by the Committee on Regional Trade Agreements or the Committee on Trade and Development (see http://wto.org/english/tratop_e/region_e/trans_mecha_e.htm). How effective this new scrutiny of agreements will be remains to be seen.

---

summarizes these rules). For the WTO to regard RTAs as legitimate, duties at the regional level must not be higher on average than those imposed by individual members before the agreement, and the arrangements must cover 'substantially all the trade' between the parties. The first of these obligations is ambiguous because it takes no account of rules of origin and NTBs; moreover, a substantial gap often

exists between the tariff levels that countries have committed to in the WTO (so-called 'bound' rates) and the actual ('applied') tariffs they have put into force (these are usually lower). In entering a regional agreement, countries can therefore keep the regional tariffs below their bound levels while actually imposing higher rates than they previously applied to non-members.

The ambiguities of the second obligation—the requirement that RTAs should cover substantially all trade—are of even greater import because they have enabled countries to exclude politically sensitive sectors from regional agreements. The EU, for instance, did not include most of Mexico's and South Africa's agricultural exports in the free trade agreements it signed with these countries. Similarly, the Japanese government excluded the few agricultural products that Singapore exported to it from its free trade agreement with the island state.

Regional trade agreements that provide partial liberalization can provide exporters with what they want (access to foreign markets), while enabling governments to avoid tackling the problem of inefficient domestic industries. The result is a process of 'liberalization without political pain'. The continued protection that uncompetitive domestic industries enjoy by being exempted from regional liberalization may encourage them to lobby against any liberalization, whether at the regional or the global level. Meanwhile, the wider the network of preferential trade agreements, the less incentive will domestic exporters have for lobbying for liberalization at the global level (Ravenhill 2006*b*). Take Mexico as the current extreme example. It has more than 30 preferential trade agreements with partners on all continents that collectively account for more than 60 per cent of global GDP and more than 97 per cent of Mexican exports (the vast majority, of course, going to the United States). The signature of RTAs has substantially reduced the incentive for Mexican exporters to expend resources in lobbying for global liberalization.

Some observers have suggested that the difficulties in negotiating the Doha Round of WTO negotiations were exacerbated by its becoming an 'agriculture' round because manufacturing and service sectors showed little interest in lobbying for liberalization at the global level (in contrast to the Uruguay Round).

The evidence

The sometimes contradictory arguments on the relationship between RTAs and global trade liberalization rest on intuitively plausible hypotheses, but these are not easy to test. Moreover, the relatively brief period for which many of the new regional agreements have been operating makes it difficult to reach conclusions about their effects (and generalization is hazardous when the agreements themselves differ so markedly in their scope and content).

Two pieces of evidence support those who believe that RTAs have not been barriers to liberalization at the global level. The first is the successful conclusion of the Uruguay Round of GATT negotiations which, as documented in the previous chapter, produced major steps forward in liberalization at the global level (although most of the Uruguay Round's negotiations took place *before* many of the agreements that are part of the new wave of regionalism came into being). The second is that members of many of the RTAs, particularly those in South America, have lowered their barriers to non-member states more rapidly than did countries that were not members of regional agreements (Foroutan 1998). Although it is impossible to demonstrate a causal relationship here, the logic is straightforward: lowering barriers to non-members at the same time as entering a preferential trade arrangement reduces the risk of welfare loss through trade diversion. Critics of the new regionalism, however, point to evidence that after joining regional arrangements, Israel, Mexico, and MERCOSUR members, when encountering economic difficulties, all raised their tariffs against non-members but exempted their regional partners from this increased protectionism. Like so many other issues relating to the political economy of regionalism, the link between RTAs and global liberalization remains inconclusive. (See Table 6.4 for a list of websites maintained by most RTAs.)

KEY POINTS

- A lively debate among writers on RTAs has produced several plausible arguments suggesting that regionalism can facilitate or hinder trade liberalization at the global level.

- The proliferation of RTAs is of such recent origin that the evidence on its effects on global trade negotiations remains inconclusive.

- The success of the Uruguay Round refuted the popular arguments in the late 1980s that the world economy was about to fragment into three rival trading blocs. But the results of the Doha Round may be a more significant indicator of the effects of the new regionalism on liberalization at the global level.

Table 6.4 Membership of Minilateral Regional Trading Agreements

AFTA	ASEAN Free Trade Area www.asean.org/communities/ asean-economic-community/category/ asean-free-trade-area-afta-council	Brunei, Darussalam, Cambodia, Indonesia, Laos, Malaysia, Myanmar, Philippines, Singapore, Thailand, Vietnam
APEC	Asia-Pacific Economic Cooperation www.apec.org	Australia, Brunei, Darussalam, Canada, Chile, China, Hong Kong, Indonesia, Japan, Korea, Malaysia, Mexico, New Zealand, Papua New Guinea, Peru, Philippines, Russia, Singapore, Chinese Taipei (Taiwan), Thailand, USA, Vietnam
APTA	Asia-Pacific Trade Agreement www.unescap.org/tid/apta.asp	Bangladesh, China, India, Republic of Korea, Laos, Sri Lanka
CAFTA-DR	Dominican Republic–Central America–USA Free Trade Agreement	Costa Rica, Dominican Republic, El Salvador, Guatemala, Honduras, Nicaragua, USA
CAN	Andean Community www.comunidadandina.org	Bolivia, Colombia, Ecuador, Peru
CARICOM	Caribbean Community and Common Market www.caricom.org	Antigua & Barbuda, Bahamas, Barbados, Belize, Dominica, Grenada, Guyana, Haiti, Jamaica, Monserrat, Trinidad & Tobago, St Kitts & Nevis, St Lucia, St Vincent & the Grenadines, Suriname
CACM	Central American Common Market www.sice.oas.org/trade/camertoc.asp	Costa Rica, El Salvador, Guatemala, Honduras, Nicaragua
CEFTA	Central European Free Trade Agreement www.cefta.int	Albania, Bosnia and Herzegovina, Croatia, Kosovo, Macedonia, Moldova, Montenegro, Serbia
CEMAC	Economic and Monetary Community of Central Africa www.cemac.cf	Cameroon, Central African Republic, Chad, Congo, Equatorial Guinea, Gabon
CER	Closer Economic Relations Trade Agreement www.dfat.gov.au/fta/anzcerta	Australia, New Zealand
CIS	Commonwealth of Independent States www.cisstat.com/eng/site-map.htm	Azerbaijan, Armenia, Belarus, Georgia, Kazakhstan, Kyrgyz Republic, Moldova, Russian Federation, Tajikistan, Turkmenistan, Ukraine, Uzbekistan
COMESA	Common Market for Eastern and Southern Africa www.comesa.int	Burundi, Comoros, DRC, Djibouti, Egypt, Eritrea, Ethiopia, Kenya, Libya, Madagascar, Malawi, Mauritius, Rwanda, Seychelles, Sudan, Swaziland, Uganda, Zambia, Zimbabwe
EAC	East African Community www.eac.int	Burundi, Kenya, Rwanda, Tanzania, Uganda
EAEC	Eurasian Economic Community www.evrazes.com/en/about	Belarus, Kazakhstan, Kyrgyz Republic, Russian Federation, Tajikistan
ECO	Economic Cooperation Organization www.ecosecretariat.org	Afghanistan, Azerbaijan, Iran, Kazakhstan, Kyrgyz Republic, Pakistan, Tajikistan, Turkey, Turkmenistan, Uzbekistan

(Continued)

Table 6.4 Membership of Minilateral Regional Trading Agreements (continued)

ECOWAS	Economic Community of West African States www.ecowas.int	Benin, Burkina Faso, Cape Verde, Côte d'Ivoire, Gambia, Ghana, Guinea, Guinea Bissau, Liberia, Mali, Niger, Nigeria, Senegal, Sierra Leone, Togo
EEA	European Economic Area www.eeas.europa.eu/eea	EC, Iceland, Liechtenstein, Norway
EFTA	European Free Trade Association www.efta.int	Iceland, Liechtenstein, Norway, Switzerland
EU	European Union www.europa.eu	Austria, Belgium, Bulgaria, Cyprus, Czech Republic, Denmark, Estonia, Finland, France, Germany, Greece, Hungary, Ireland, Italy, Latvia, Lithuania, Luxembourg, Malta, Netherlands, Poland, Portugal, Romania, Slovakia, Slovenia, Spain, Sweden, UK
GCC	Gulf Cooperation Council www.gcc-sg.org/eng	Bahrain, Kuwait, Oman, Qatar, Saudi Arabia, United Arab Emirates
GSTP	Global System of Trade Preferences among Developing Countries www.wipo.int/wipolex/en/other_treaties/text.jsp?file_id=230619	Algeria, Argentina, Bangladesh, Benin, Bolivia, Brazil, Cameroon, Chile, Colombia, Cuba, Democratic People's Republic of Korea, Ecuador, Egypt, Ghana, Guinea, Guyana, India, Indonesia, Islamic Republic of Iran, Iraq, Libya, Macedonia, Malaysia, Mexico, Morocco, Mozambique, Myanmar, Nicaragua, Nigeria, Pakistan, Paraguay, Peru, Philippines, Republic of Korea, Singapore, Sri Lanka, Sudan, Thailand, Trinidad & Tobago, Tunisia, United Republic of Tanzania, Uruguay, Venezuela, Vietnam, Zimbabwe
LAIA	Latin American Integration Association www.aladi.org	Argentina, Bolivia, Brazil, Chile, Colombia, Cuba, Ecuador, Mexico, Panama, Paraguay, Peru, Uruguay, Venezuela
MERCOSUR	Southern Common Market www.mercosur.int	Argentina, Brazil, Paraguay[a], Uruguay
MSG	Melanesian Spearhead Group www.msgsec.info	Fiji, New Caledonia, Papua New Guinea, Solomon Islands, Vanuatu
NAFTA	North American Free Trade Agreement www.nafta-sec-alena.org	Canada, Mexico, USA
PAFTA	Pan-Arab Free Trade Area	Algeria, Bahrain, Egypt, Iraq, Jordan, Kuwait, Lebanon, Libyan Arab Jamahiriya, Morocco, Oman, Palestinian Authority, Qatar, Saudi Arabia, Sudan, Syrian Arab Republic, Tunisia, United Arab Emirates, Yemen
PICTA	Pacific Island Countries Trade Agreement	Cook Islands, Fiji, Kiribati, Marshall Islands, Micronesia, Nauru, Niue, Papua New Guinea, Samoa, Solomon Islands, Tonga, Tuvalu, Vanuatu
PTN	Protocol relating to Trade Negotiations among Developing Countries	Bangladesh, Brazil, Chile, Egypt, Israel, Mexico, Pakistan, Paraguay, Peru, Philippines, Republic of Korea, Serbia, Tunisia, Turkey, Uruguay
SADC	Southern African Development Community www.sadc.int	Angola, Botswana, DRC, Lesotho, Madagascar, Malawi, Mauritius, Mozambique, Namibia, Seychelles, South Africa, Swaziland, Tanzania, Zambia, Zimbabwe

SACU	Southern African Customs Union www.sacu.int	Botswana, Lesotho, Namibia, South Africa, Swaziland
SAFTA	South Asian Free Trade Agreement www.saarc-sec.org/areaofcooperation/ detail.php?activity_id=5	Bangladesh, Bhutan, India, Maldives, Nepal, Pakistan, Sri Lanka
SPARTECA	South Pacific Regional Trade and Economic Cooperation Agreement Trans-Pacific Strategic Economic Partnership	Australia, Chile, Cook Islands, Fiji, Kiribati, Marshall Islands, Micronesia, Nauru, New Zealand, Niue, Papua New Guinea, Samoa, Solomon Islands, Tonga, Tuvalu, Vanuatu, Brunei Darussalam, Singapore
TRIPARTITE	Tripartite Agreement	Egypt, India, Yugoslavia
UEMOA/WAE MU	West African Economic and Monetary Union www.uemoa.int	Benin, Burkina Faso, Ivory Coast, Guinea Bissau, Mali, Niger, Senegal, Togo

[a] Currently suspended, see www.mercosur.int/innovaportal/file/3862/1/dec_028-2012_es_reglam_suspension_paraguay.pdf

 QUESTIONS

1. How does the pattern of recent RTAs differ from that of the 1960s and 1970s?

2. For what economic reasons might governments prefer trade liberalization at the regional rather than global level?

3. What political benefits might membership of a regional agreement bring?

4. What are the likely sources of domestic political opposition to regionalism?

5. Why might companies lobby for liberalization at the regional rather than the global level?

6. What is 'deeper' integration?

7. What were the sources of the failure of many of the RTAs of the 1960s and 1970s?

8. Why did the United States government change its mind in the early 1980s on the desirability of RTAs?

9. How does trade creation differ from trade diversion?

10. Why are rules of origin regarded as a potential protectionist device?

11. What are the reasons behind the emergence of 'Mega-FTAs?'

12. What evidence is there that regional integration has had a positive impact on the economies of participating economies? And what has been its impact on non-members?

13. For what reasons might regionalism assist or impede trade liberalization at the global level?

FURTHER READING

General

Bhagwati, J. and Panagariya, A. (eds) (1996), *The Economics of Preferential Trade Agreements* (Washington, DC: AEI Press). An accessible overview of arguments by economists against regionalism.

Borzel, T. A. and Risse, T. (eds) (2016), *The Oxford Handbook of Comparative Regionalism* (Oxford: Oxford University Press). A major compendium of research on regionalism from a comparative perspective.

Crawford, J.-A. and Florentino, R. V. (2006), *The Changing Landscape of Regional Trade Agreements*, WTO Discussion Paper 12 (Geneva: World Trade Organization), http://wto.org/english/res_e/reser_e/discussion_papers_e.htm#n12 A comprehensive assessment of RTAs by two members of the WTO Secretariat.

Fawcett, L. and Hurrell, A. (eds) (1995), *Regionalism in World Politics: Regional Organization and International Order* (Oxford: Oxford University Press). An initial exploration of the new regionalism with overviews and case studies.

Fawn R. (ed.) (2009), *Globalising the Regional, Regionalising the Global* (Cambridge: Cambridge University Press). A contemporary overview of developments in regionalism in various parts of the world.

Frankel, J. A. (1997), *Regional Trading Blocs in the World Economic System* (Washington, DC: Institute for International Economics). The most comprehensive examination of the effects of RTAs.

Haas, E. B. (1975), *The Obsolescence of Regional Integration Theory* (Berkeley, CA: Institute of International Studies, University of California). A reconsideration of the relevance of early integration theory.

Mansfield, E. D. and Milner, H. V. (eds) (1997), *The Political Economy of Regionalism* (New York: Columbia University Press). A collection of articles from a political economy perspective on regionalism in general; it includes case studies of the principal geographical regions.

Moravcsik, A. (1998), *The Choice for Europe: Social Purpose and State Power from Messina to Maastricht* (Ithaca, NY: Cornell University Press). The most sophisticated statement of the liberal intergovernmental approach to regionalism.

World Bank (2000), *Trade Blocs* (New York: Oxford University Press). A review of the evidence on the economic and political effects of regionalism and their relevance to less developed economies.

World Trade Organization (2011), *World Trade Report 2011: The WTO and Preferential Trade Agreements: From Co-existence to Coherence* (Geneva: WTO). A comprehensive overview of the evidence of the effects of RTAs on the global trading system.

World Trade Organization (2012), Historic Signing Ends 20 Years of EU–Latin American Banana Disputes. 8 November. http://www.wto.org/english/news_e/news12_e/disp_08nov12_e.htm, accessed May 2016)

Africa

Bach, D. (ed.) (1999), *Regionalisation in Africa: Integration and Disintegration* (Bloomington, IN: Indiana University Press). A collection that examines the relationship between regionalism, regionalization, and state disintegration in Africa.

Bach, D. (2016), *Regionalism in Africa: Genealogies, Institutions and Trans-State Networks.* London: Routledge. A survey of the new African regionalism since the turn of the century.

Lee, M. C. (2003), *The Political Economy of Regionalism in Southern Africa* (Boulder, CO: Lynne Rienner). Examines the history of regionalism in the southern part of Africa, with special emphasis on SADC.

The Americas

Cameron, M. A. and Tomlin, B. W. (2000), *The Making of NAFTA: How the Deal Was Done* (Ithaca, NY: Cornell University Press). Analyses the negotiating process leading up to the signature of the NAFTA treaty.

Cason, J. W. (2013), *The Political Economy of Integration: The Experience of Mercosur* (London: Routledge). Examines Mercosur's integration record through an explicit comparison with the European experience.

Hufbauer, G. C. and Schott, J. J. (2005), *NAFTA Revisited: Achievements and Challenges* (Washington, DC: Institute for International Economics). The most comprehensive analysis of the effects in various sectors of NAFTA's implementation.

Nelson, M. (2015), *A History of the FTAA: From Hegemony to Fragmentation in the Americas* (London: Palgrave). A Gramscian account of the collapse of the FTAA proposals.

Roett, R. (ed.) (1999), *Mercosur: Regional Integration, World Markets* (Boulder, CO: Lynne Rienner). A collection of articles on integration among MERCOSUR members and their relations with the global economy.

Asia-Pacific

Aggarwal, V. K. and Morrison, C. E. (eds) (1998), *Asia-Pacific Crossroads: Regime Creation and the Future of APEC* (New York: St Martin's Press). A collection of articles on the foundation of APEC, the objectives of its founders, and its early impact.

Aggarwal, V. K. and Urata, S. (eds) (2006), *Bilateral Trade Agreements in the Asia-Pacific: Origins, Evolution, and Implications* (London: Routledge). Reviews the recent spate of bilateral agreements in the Asia-Pacific region.

He, B. (2016), *Contested Ideas of Regionalism in Asia* (London: Routledge). Examines contesting ideas underlying Asian regionalism.

Ravenhill, J. (2001), *APEC and the Construction of Asia-Pacific Regionalism* (Cambridge: Cambridge University Press). Applies the theoretical literature on regionalism to APEC's foundation and operating principles.

Europe

Hix, S. and Hayland, B. (2011), *The Political System of the European Union,* 3rd edn (London: Palgrave Macmillan). Applies contemporary political theory to the study of the EU.

Kenealy, D., Peterson, J., and Corbett, R. (2015), *The European Union: How does it Work?* 4th edn (Oxford: Oxford University Press). An introductory text on the EU.

Milward, A. S. (1992), *The European Rescue of the Nation-State* (London: Routledge). A historical review of European integration from an intergovernmental perspective.

Wallace, H., Pollack M. A., and Young, A. R. (eds) (2015), *Policy-Making in the European Union,* 7th edn (Oxford: Oxford University Press). The most comprehensive and theoretically sophisticated overview of the various dimensions of EU integration.

WEBLINKS

Table 6.4 lists addresses for the websites maintained by most RTAs.

www.wto.org/english/tratop_e/region_e/region_e.htm The WTO website's gateway to the organization's material on RTAs.

ONLINE RESOURCE CENTRE

For additional material and resources, please visit the Online Resource Centre at:
www.oxfordtextbooks.co.uk/ravenhill5e

7

The Globalization of Production

Eric Thun

Chapter contents

Reader's guide

Although companies have been investing abroad for centuries, the current era of globalization has created an unprecedented range of possibilities for global firms to reorganize and relocate their activities. This chapter analyses how advances in transportation and technology allow a firm to divide up a global value chain—the sequence of activities that lead to the production of a particular good or service—and how these decisions create new opportunities and challenges for both companies and the societies within which they operate. The first section of the chapter reviews the rise of global production and the forces that have led to dramatic increases in foreign direct investment (FDI) and outsourcing. The central questions for any firm involved in global production involves how to govern the value chain and where to locate different activities. The second section provides a framework for understanding these issues and the implications of the various choices. The third section applies these concepts to the case of East Asia.

Introduction

Multinational corporations (MNCs) are the most public face of globalization. Defined as firms that have operations in two or more countries, MNCs are a source of hope and promise to those who seek to harness the power of economic globalization for purposes of development, and a source of fear and opposition to those who view globalization as a threat to national sovereignty. MNCs are pervasive. At the time of the global economic crisis in 2008, there were some 82,000 parent MNCs, with over 810,000 affiliates. These affiliates employed approximately 77 million people—more than twice the labour force of Germany—and accounted for one-third of total world exports of goods and service (UNCTAD 2009*b*: 17). Sales from these foreign affiliates dipped after the crisis, but then rebounded strongly, reaching a record US$36 trillion in 2014 (UNCTAD 2015*b*: 18). MNCs are also very tangible. They are not anonymous buyers and sellers engaged in arm's-length trade. Through FDI, they own assets and employ people in foreign countries. They are the companies behind the most powerful global brands. To populations that are being buffeted by the invisible forces of globalization, MNCs serve as very visible symbols of forces they cannot control.

Foreign investment on the part of MNCs, however, is only the tip of the iceberg that is the globalization of production. Firms such as Nike and Apple do not own the foreign factories that make their products; they use contractors who work to their specifications. Nike has approximately 43,000 direct employees (Nike 2013: 75), but as of November 2015, its products were being manufactured by 948,732 workers in 5,698 factories in 41 countries (see end-of-chapter Weblinks; Nike Manufacturing Map). Apple has slightly fewer than 100,000 direct employees, the majority of which are in the United States, but has at least 459 factories and 1.1 million workers in the company's global supply chain (Apple 2015, note the higher level of ambiguity in the Apple numbers as compared to Nike). Apple iPhones, for instance, are all produced by contract manufacturing firms such as Taiwan's Foxconn, primarily in huge in facilities in China that employ hundreds of thousands of workers. Similarly, retailers such as the GAP and electronic giants such as Dell and Hewlett-Packard (HP) rely on specialized manufacturing firms to make their products, and focus primarily on design, marketing, distribution, and service.

Global value chains are important determinants of who gets what, when, and how in the global economy. There are two sides to the global production coin. From the perspective of 'home' countries—where the headquarters of multinational firms are located—the key question is what will be left behind when production moves abroad. Because outward investment from the home economy of a multinational will potentially be moving jobs, technology, and profits beyond national borders, it creates fears of a 'hollowing out' effect. Will outward investment and outsourcing

lead to an inexorable flow of jobs, technology, and profits to lower-cost countries? Will the competition for high value-added activities lead to a convergence of economic models? From the perspective of 'host' countries—the destinations of FDI and outsourcing—the question is whether they will be able to capture the high value-added activities, or whether they will be trapped into a dependent relationship with multinational firms in which they are limited to low value-added activities. Will the foreign firms contribute to the long-term development of the local economy, or will they inhibit the development of local firms? Will the foreign firms adhere to the social, political, and environmental standards of the local society, or will they behave in an imperialistic manner and/or engage in practices that would not be allowed in their home societies?

In both cases, the questions revolve around the distribution of resources, the bargaining leverage of the states that 'host' foreign investment, and the power of multinational firms to determine who gets which part of global production, and how this influences employment, the locus of knowledge and innovation, and the creation of profits in the world economy. This chapter will analyse how advances in transportation and technology have created new opportunities to divide up a value chain, how this creates new possibilities for global firms to reorganize and relocate the various activities that they engage in, and the opportunities and challenges these changes create for both home and host states and societies.

The rise of global production

There is nothing new about foreign investment or international production. In the sixteenth century, chartered trading companies established foreign production facilities for much the same reasons as firms did centuries later—internalization within the firm was a means of economizing on frequent transactions that inherently had to occur in a particular location, whether in order to access particular raw materials or markets. The Dutch East India Company, for example, established a saltpetre plant in Bengal in 1641, a print works for textiles ten years later, and employed 4,000 silk spinners by 1717. In an era when the full cycle of activity (export, transport, and sale of goods from home to foreign markets, import, transport, and sale of goods from foreign to home markets) could take anywhere from 18 to 30 months to complete, hierarchical coordination within the firm allowed a trading company to equate supply and demand more effectively (Carlos and Nicholas 1988: 403, 407).

In the nineteenth century, the Industrial Revolution spurred demand for raw materials, and companies sought to own and manage their sources of raw materials in order to reduce risk. For manufacturing companies, the result was vertical investments upstream and downstream, and a hub-and-spoke model of international production: raw materials were imported from the periphery, manufacturing took place at home, and finished goods were then distributed globally. In response to rising protectionism in the early twentieth century, firms began to make horizontal investments abroad: manufacturing capabilities were duplicated in foreign markets that were increasingly sheltered behind tariff barriers (Palmisano 2006: 128). In the 1920s and 1930s, for example, American companies such as General Motors, Ford, Firestone, Nabisco, General Foods, Hoover, ITT, and Honeywell rapidly increased the numbers of their manufacturing facilities in Europe. These were multinationals in the form that would dominate the global economy for much of the twentieth century. Certain activities, such as research and development, were concentrated in their headquarters, but other capabilities were duplicated in operations around the world. These companies pursued a multi-market strategy.

Numbers and trends

International production is not new, but its magnitude and the degree of fragmentation in global value chains is new. To an unprecedented degree, firms are able to break up their value chains and locate each discrete activity according to **competitive advantage** rather than geographical convenience. How can we measure the growth of global production?

One relatively straightforward indicator is the rapid increase in FDI prior to the global economic crisis that began in 2008. Between 1982 and 2008, according to the United Nations Conference on Trade and Development (UNCTAD) *World Investment Report*, the value of FDI inflows (in current prices) increased from $59 billion to $1,697 billion (UNCTAD 2009b: 3). The ratio of world FDI inflows to global gross domestic capital formation (a measure of domestic investment) increased from 2 per cent in 1980 to 12.3 per cent in 2008 (UNCTAD 2000: pp. xv–xvi; 2009b: 255).

After the crisis, flows of FDI dropped sharply initially, but have since returned to pre-crisis levels (UNCTAD 2015b: 18). Two trends are important to note about these massive flows. First, they are often quite concentrated. A relatively small number of countries dominate the flows of FDI and large 'mega-deals', often in the form of merger and acquisitions (M&As), can be a major driver. Just as the development of technology, regulatory changes, and new modes of finance led to a wave of corporate M&As in the United States at the end of the nineteenth century, as firms shifted from a regional to a national focus, the same factors have led firms to adapt a global focus over the last several decades (UNCTAD 1999: p. xx). Increasing regional integration and the introduction of a single currency in the EU, for example, created a wave of M&A activity in Europe, and horizontal acquisitions between firms in the same industry (which, in terms of value, accounted for 70 per cent of M&A activity at the end of the 1990s) represented the quickest route to global scale and scope for firms seeking to access new markets and complementary capabilities (UNCTAD 1999: pp. xix–xx).

A second important trend has been the rising importance of developing countries in these flows. As destinations for investment, FDI plays a crucial role in the development process in these countries. A developing country seeking external capital investment has four choices: official flows (from international development agencies and governments), commercial bank loans, portfolio flows (from institutional investors such as pension funds, insurance companies, and mutual funds), and FDI. Until the early 1990s, official flows were the dominant source of capital for developing countries, often in the form of loans that were made on concessional terms, but over the course of the 1990s there was a dramatic shift from public to private capital flows. This was partly the result of budgetary difficulties in developed countries, which led to a cutback in foreign aid, but it also reflected an ideological shift towards market-based approaches to public policy. By 2005, official flows to the developing world had largely dried up, and over half of the total resource flow to the developing world consisted of FDI ($334 billion). As is the case in the developed world, these flows tend to be concentrated, and a relatively small number of countries receive the lion's share of investment. The global recession that began in 2008 led to a surge in FDI to developing countries. This was partly because problems in the financial sector reduced the capacity of MNCs to invest in developed countries, and partly because many of the markets in the developing world fared better than developed markets during the crisis. Attracting FDI is important for developing countries, not just because it is the most stable form of foreign capital that is available, but as will be explained in greater detail later, because it is thought to have the potential to bring a package of benefits, including technology, managerial skills, and access to new markets. In recent years, developing countries have also become an important source of outward FDI. Cross-border investments on the part of developing country firms increased from 10 per cent in 2003 to 40 per cent in 2012 and has remained stable since then (UNCTAD 2015*b*: 11).

Although FDI represents a critical element of global production, it only measures global production that takes place under foreign ownership, and neglects the outsourcing of production. Simply defined, outsourcing is the reallocation of a particular task from within one firm to another, and the two are usually separated by having different ownership (Sako 2006: 503). There is overlap between the two categories—an American firm that uses a Korean manufacturer located in China is both outsourcing (from the perspective of the US firm) and reliant on FDI (from the perspective of the Korean firm)—but the distinction is important from an analytical perspective, because it points to the wide variety of governance forms in global value chains. And outsourcing need not necessarily be accompanied by any transborder flows of capital—firms may be linked simply by 'arm's-length' purchase arrangements, or the relationship may involve, for example, the transfer of expertise from purchaser to supplier.

Unfortunately, it is very difficult to determine the value of outsourcing transactions from general trade data. One possible measure is the growth of trade in intermediate goods (components that are neither raw materials nor finished products), with the expectation being that value chain fragmentation would lead to higher levels of trade in intermediate goods. In their analysis of United National COMTRADE data, Timothy Sturgeon and Olga Memedovic (2010: 12–14) find that trade in manufactured intermediate goods increased at the same rate as trade in final goods during the 1990s on a global basis, but increased substantially faster after 2001. Growth in developing countries was faster than in developed countries (3.4

times between 1992 and 2006 compared to 2.2. times), and within developing countries, growth in China and Mexico was particularly pronounced. There are also substantial differences between industries, with the highest percentage of trade in intermediate products in the electronics and automotive industries (Sturgeon and Memedovic 2010: 18). In these two industries, the rise of large-scale global suppliers was a very concrete manifestation of this trend. In electronics, electronic manufacturing services (EMS) firms grew from nothing in the early 1980s—when IBM began to look for key suppliers for its personal computers in 1981—to $170 billion in revenue in 2005. Foxconn became the largest of these firms in 2005, and by 2009 its revenue exceeded $60 billion, accounting for 26 per cent of the EMS market (Eccles, Serafeim, and Cheng 2012). These firms operate massive factories around the world, and manufacture much of the world's electronic goods. In 2011, for instance, Taiwanese contractors produced 94 per cent of the world's laptop computers. Similarly, in the auto industry, the largest supply firms are now almost as large as the assembly firms they serve. In order to save on development costs, take advantage of supplier knowledge, and maximize **economies of scale**, auto assembly firms outsource the design and manufacture of entire modules of a car to large supply firms. In 1992, there were only 28 US auto supply firms with annual sales between $1 billion and $5 billion, and five companies with sales higher than $5 billion. In 1998, these numbers were 47 and 13, respectively (Veloso 2000: 16). In 2009, there were 28 global auto component firms with sales greater than $5 billion. Although not quite as dramatic as in the electronics industry, the outsourcing of manufacturing was a dominant trend in the auto industry during the 1990s.

Why now?

Politics has played a key role in the expansion of global production. The liberalization of trade was a critical prerequisite for the globalization of production. When trade barriers are high, a multinational firm will invest in production facilities abroad in order to access foreign markets, but it will hesitate to relocate portions of the value chain that must be integrated with other global activities—the fragmentation of value chains requires low tariff barriers. The trade regime is the most prominent example of global cooperation in the post-Second World-War era. Chastened by the breakdown of the global economy during the interwar period, the United States began a return to liberalism with the passage of the Reciprocal Trade Agreements Act of 1934. After the Second World War, the trend of increased economic liberalism continued with each successive round of the **General Agreement on Tariffs and Trade (GATT)**, and the result was the rapid expansion of world trade. World exports increased by close to 8 per cent per annum between 1950 and 1973, and by 5 per cent for the subsequent 25-year period (Ravenhill, Chapter 1 in this volume).

The move towards a liberal trade regime at the international level had a corollary at the domestic level—a general trend towards market-based policies—and this expanded the range of options for global production. As Anthony McGrew explains in Chapter 10 of this book, the neo-liberal ideology associated with liberalization, deregulation, and privatization provided the normative infrastructure for economic globalization. In OECD states, governments across the political spectrum were instrumental in liberalizing national economies, and creating the policy and institutional frameworks that have enabled the growth of global trade and production.

Governments in the developing world used the expansion of global trade as an engine of growth. No region benefited more than East Asia. Scholars debate the extent to which economic growth in economies such as Korea and Taiwan was the result of government-led industrial policies (Amsden 1989; Wade 1990) as opposed to market-conforming policies (World Bank 1993), but reliance on export markets was clear in all these cases. Taiwan, for example, pioneered the use of export-processing zones—industrial parks where foreign firms could enjoy preferential trade and investment policies so long as their output was intended for export markets—at the same time as Japanese manufacturers were forcing American firms to reduce their costs by moving labour-intensive activities offshore. With the encouragement of the Taiwanese government and the United States Agency for International Development, General Instruments began manufacturing in Taiwan in 1964, and was followed over the next two years by 24 other American firms (Wade 1990: 94). This was in many important respects the beginning of the global manufacturing model that would dominate East Asia in the 1970s and 1980s—firms from high-wage economies began to

break apart their value chains and locate the manufacturing of each component according to competitive advantage. As the neo-liberal reforms took hold in China, Eastern Europe, India, and Latin America over the decades that followed, the scope of global manufacturing increased in turn.

At the same time as political changes were opening countries up to trade and investment, technology was extending the geographical reach of business, and making possible new forms of business organization. In many respects, this is an old story writ large. In the latter half of the nineteenth century, technology transformed the organization of business in the United States. As Alfred Chandler (1977: 75–80) has described, the spread of iron, coal, and machinery created the possibility of large-scale production in the United States, and the invention of the telegraph and expansion of railways created the means of communication and transportation that would allow these businesses to extend their geographical reach. These changes led to the emergence of the modern hierarchical corporation. Just as the telegraph and the railway allowed firms in the latter half of the nineteenth century to adopt a national rather than regional orientation, the improvement in transportation and technology in the latter half of the twentieth century allowed firms to adopt a global perspective. These changes led to the fragmentation of the value chain.

The first set of changes involved new forms of transportation. An obvious development was the introduction of commercial jet services in the 1950s. Less obvious, but probably even more important for world commerce, was the introduction of standardized shipping containers. Prior to the introduction of standardized steel and aluminium containers in the late 1950s, the process of loading and unloading cargo at the point of origin, at ports along the way, and at the destination was time-consuming and fraught with the possibility of loss and damage. Containers dramatically reduced the friction of transportation in global economy. Marc Levinson (2006: 7) provides a compelling illustration: a 35-ton container of coffee-makers in Malaysia can be loaded into a container at the factory door, taken to a port and loaded on to a ship, and then transported the 9,000 miles to Los Angeles in 16 days. A day later, the container will be on a unit train to Chicago. If the train were to carry the capacity load of one of the new mega container ships—which can carry over 8,000 6-metre-long containers—it would stretch over 37 kilometres. Once in Chicago, the container of coffee-makers is transferred immediately to a flatbed lorry headed to Cincinnati, the distribution centre for the retailer. The process is not only inexpensive—in this case, less than the price of a single first-class air ticket from Malaysia to the USA—it is completely automated and the transfers at each juncture in the journey are seamless; human hands will not touch the contents of the container between the factory and the destination. In the late 1950s and early 1960s, transport costs were often a higher barrier to trade than were import tariffs (as high as 25 per cent of the cost of some products, according to one study) and the result was that globalization of production was not a cost-effective strategy (Levinson 2006: 9). At the time of writing, when 90 per cent of world trade is transported in shipping containers, transport in many industries is a marginal part of a company's overall cost structure. From the perspective of transport cost, it almost does not matter if a firm is doing business with a factory on the other side of town or the other side of the world.

If container shipping reduced the hurdle of transport costs, the digital revolution and the shift to modularity made it possible to separate the activities of the value chain and scatter them across the globe. The electronics industry has been at the cutting edge of the modular revolution (Baldwin and Clark 2000). Until the 1960s, the designs of the different parts of a computer system were highly interdependent, and consequently, when any new product was introduced, the design process would have to begin again from the start to ensure that all the component parts were compatible. The result was time-consuming and expensive, because teams of engineers within a single company had to work together on each component; outsourcing was not possible, because the connections between different parts of the product design were complex and varied in arbitrary and non-obvious ways (Baldwin and Clark 2000: 171). Like craftsmen putting together a custom-built piece of furniture, the engineers had to work together, relying not on codified rules to piece together a machine but on tacit knowledge (information that cannot be written or coded in a set of instructions, but must be imparted by people working together).

The solution, introduced by IBM in the autumn of 1961, was to conceive of a family of computers—the System/360—that would include machines of different sizes and uses, but all of which would share the same instruction set and peripherals. A central office mandated the design rules that would determine how the different modules of the machine would interact with each other, and this allowed different teams of engineers to work independently on the aspects of each module that did not affect other modules (see Box 7.1). The shift to modularity increased the speed of the design process (because teams worked simultaneously), increased the rate of innovation (because teams could try any number of approaches so long as they adhered to the design rules for interacting with other modules), and created the flexibility needed to meet a variety of customer needs. Paradoxically, these advances also led to the end of IBM's dominance of the industry, because outside companies could perform the same role as internal company divisions, so long as they knew the design rules—easily specified as computer code—that would make their product compatible with an IBM machine (Baldwin and Clark 1997: 85). As a result, we now take it for granted that we can download photographs from a Canon camera to a Dell computer in order to print them on an HP printer. In other industries, the interfaces between modules are not always as easy to specify, but there is also a trend towards increasing modularity. As was pointed out in the previous section, auto assembly firms have been shifting responsibilities to their suppliers to as great an extent as possible. A Volkswagen truck factory in Brazil has taken this approach to the extreme. VW established the architecture of the production process and the interfaces that connect modules, but all the manufacturing is done by suppliers (Baldwin and Clark 1997: 87).

The ability to codify design information in digital form, particularly when combined with new forms of telecommunication to transmit this information, was a key enabler of globalization. As Suzanne Berger (2006: 76) explains, new software in the 1990s increased the ability of a wide variety of firms to digitize instructions and thus codify the interfaces within a product. This created new options with respect to location. Once engineers are able to specify the 'hand-off' between two different modules within a product utilizing software, there is no longer any inherent reason why designers and production staff have to be located within the same facility. The design firm transmits the design specifications electronically to the production facility, and as long as the production facility meets the appropriate standards, it can be located anywhere. The ability to codify design information does not inevitably lead to the fragmentation

BOX 7.1

Modular Production

In the classic work on modularity, Baldwin and Clark (1997, 2000) define a modular system as one that 'is composed of units (or modules) that are designed independently but still function as an integrated whole' (1997: 86). The structural elements of a module are connected powerfully to each other and relatively weakly to elements in other modules of the same system (2000: 63). Every product that consists of multiple modules will have an *architecture* that specifies what modules are part of the system and what the function of each will be; *interfaces* that describe in detail how the modules will interact, connect, and communicate; and *standards* for testing the extent to which a module conforms to the design rules (1997: 86). Sako (2003) specifies how modularity fulfils different roles across the life cycle of a product. In the design phase, the principle purpose of modularity is to reduce the lead time of the design process, and the cost of design and development. In the manufacturing phase, the objective is to increase operational efficiency by allowing the mixing and matching of standardized components, thus allowing for both the benefits of scale efficiencies and greater customization and variety. Finally, when the product is being used, consumers want a product that is easy to use, compatible with other products, easily upgraded, and easily and inexpensively maintained. The objectives of the different phases are not always compatible. The core concern of product designers, for example, will be to ensure that the design of each module is independent of other modules, and this may lead to tight **interdependencies** within the module. When the consumer has to make a repair, however, rather than being able to replace an individual component, he or she may find that an entire (and expensive) module must be replaced rather than an individual component.

Modularity does not lead inevitably to outsourcing, but it creates the possibility—it is difficult to outsource or separate the component parts of an integral product. Prior to the rise of mass production, for example, automobiles were made by craftsmen, and each vehicle had to be made in its entirety in a workshop because the component parts had to custom fit to each other. The workers were skilled in the principles of mechanical design and experienced with the materials with which they worked. As Womack, Jones, and Roos (1990) explain, production of the cars depended on the tacit knowledge of these craftsmen, and it was difficult to codify this knowledge reliably in a way that would make it readily accessible to outside firms; there was no standard gauging system, and machine tools at this point could not cut hardened steel. Because the craftsmen fitted each piece together individually, no two vehicles were exactly alike. The core innovation of Henry Ford was the development of a system that used a standard gauge and pre-hardened metal that would not warp during the manufacturing process, previously the major obstacle to standardizing the size of parts (Womack, Jones, and Roos 1990: 22–7). The introduction of interchangeable parts with standard interfaces made it possible for an auto firm to replace skilled craftsmen with unskilled assembly-line workers, and to outsource production of components. The benefits of outsourcing to a supply firm can be numerous: the supplier will be a specialist in the production of a particular component, it will be able to capture greater economies of scale (since it supplies many firms), and it will give the assembler greater flexibility to concentrate on other parts of the production process.

of the value chain—in some industries and some regions, firms may decide that it makes sense to co-locate distinct parts of the value chain—but it does create a wider variety of possibilities than existed previously.

The ideal type of this new breed of firm, according to Samuel Palmisano (2006: 129), the CEO of IBM, is the globally integrated enterprise. In contrast to the multinational company of old, 'the emerging globally integrated enterprise is a company that fashions its strategy, its management, and its operations in pursuit of a new goal: the integration of production and value delivery worldwide'. Whereas the technical changes of the late nineteenth century resulted in a tightening of corporate control—a strict hierarchy was needed to organize rapidly expanding operations—the technical changes of the late twentieth century have resulted in tremendous fluidity. This new breed of firm is being organized by functions rather than products or geography, and every firm must decide which functions it will continue to perform; which functions it will rely on outside partners to perform; and where in the world each function will be located. The results to these decisions, of course, have important implications not only for the competitiveness of individual firms and industries, but also for the well-being of the societies in which they operate.

KEY POINTS

- The globalization of production is not new, but the magnitude with which it takes place and the degree of fragmentation in global value chains *is* new.

- The increasing levels of global production can be measured in both the dramatic increases in FDI and the increasing importance of trade in components.

- Flows of FDI are concentrated heavily in developed economies, and dominated by mergers and acquisitions between large firms that are seeking the scale and scope that is increasingly necessary to compete in global markets.

- The increase in global production is a result of economic liberalization, improvements in transportation, and advances in technologies that facilitate modularization.

Global value chains: governance and location

In order to understand the implications of global value chains, it is necessary to distinguish between their different forms. For analytical purposes, it is useful to consider global value chains along two dimensions: governance (how to coordinate activities); and location (where to locate each activity). Although the two dimensions are closely linked, there are distinct scholarly literatures focused on each.

Governance

If a defining feature of economic globalization is that technology has increased the ability of firms to fragment the value chain, one of the key issues that must be understood is how coordination of the fragmented parts is achieved. Defined in its broadest sense, governance refers to any means of coordinating interdependent activities (Jessop 1998: 29). It is useful to think of the governance options for global value chains along a spectrum. At one end of the spectrum are pure market relations with foreign firms (for example, arm's-length trade relationships), and at the other end is hierarchical control of foreign operations (for example, FDI). Between these two endpoints are various forms of networks.

Traditional explanations of FDI focus on the end points of the governance spectrum, and transfer the classic 'make or buy' question from the domestic to a global context. As Sven Arndt and Henryk Kierzkowski

(2001: 2) write, 'fragmentation is not a new phenomenon; nor is outsourcing. Both go back to the beginning of the Industrial Revolution or even predate it.' What is new is the extent to which improvements in technology have tamed the 'tyranny of distance' and made it increasingly possible to consider the global organization of industry in the same terms as domestic. One clear option is to rely on arm's-length market relationships. As Robert Gilpin (2001: 279) notes, in the ideal world of a neoclassical economist, firms would not invest abroad. If markets are operating efficiently, information is costless, there are no barriers to trade or competition, and there are no advantages to be gained from economies of scale, there would be little reason for a firm to invest abroad because trade would be the logical means of reaching foreign markets and accessing inputs. Markets are efficient, prices summarize all relevant information, and actors are motivated by self-interest rather than coercion—coordination is seemingly effortless.

Why does a firm decide to make rather than buy a particular product or service in the domestic context? Economists explain vertical integration and hierarchical coordination as a response to **transaction costs**. As Ronald Coase (1937) argued, there are costs associated with using a market; even for the simplest transaction a buyer or seller must be found, a product or service evaluated, and a price negotiated. Oliver Williamson (1981: 1545) added to this explanation the problems inherent in human nature. **Bounded rationality** makes it impossible for actors to foresee every contingency that might affect an agreement between two actors, hence contracts can never be complete; the problem of **opportunism** means that each actor has to expect the other to act not only out of self-interest, but potentially with deceit and guile. In light of these assumptions, it is apparent that the costs of some market transactions are higher than others. It is necessary to identify and analyse the key dimensions along which transactions vary—the frequency with which transactions recur, the degree of complexity and uncertainty to which transactions are subject, and the degree of asset specificity—in order to determine whether hierarchical coordination (retaining all activities within the organization) is more appropriate than market coordination (Williamson 1975, 1981).

The same logic has been used to explain why firms engage in FDI rather than licensing, trade, or contractual relationships. The literature on FDI is large, but within it John Dunning's eclectic paradigm is one of the dominant strands (Dunning 1981). At its core is a transactional approach: a firm will create operations abroad when the net costs of an internal market (hierarchical coordination) are lower than the net cost of using arm's-length market relationships (Caves 1982). The *advantages of internalization* within the firm might stem from concerns about the costs and uncertainty of monitoring and negotiating the relationship with a licensee or contractor, or the firm might be eager to ensure that it captures all of the benefits of the advantages that it has over local firms. These *firm-specific advantages* (Dunning 1981) might involve a trademark, a particular technology or manufacturing process, economies of scale, or marketing power; or a firm might be reluctant to license such advantages to a foreign firm out of fear that it will be training a future competitor. There are costs to operating internationally—a foreign firm will rarely understand the local market as well as a domestic firm does, for example—so a multinational firm has to ensure that it protects what advantages it does hold. In addition, there may be *location-specific advantages* to setting up operations on foreign soil as opposed to establishing trade relations. The foreign firm may gain better access to information on the marketplace, an ability to respond more quickly to changes in the market, access to unique resources or capabilities, and/or ability to avoid protectionist trade barriers. In short, the potential costs of relying on markets and arm's-length relationships to govern a global value chain are weighed against the difficulty of controlling and operating subsidiaries that are within the firm but spread across great distances and unfamiliar territory through FDI.

Although the distinction between utilizing markets and hierarchy to govern global value chains is an important one, there is a range of possibilities in between these two endpoints. Just as firms within a domestic economy can form long-term relationships that cannot be characterized completely by markets or hierarchy, global value chains can take the form of a diverse variety of networks that are neither pure markets nor hierarchy. In the 1990s, Gary Gereffi and others (Gereffi and Korzeniewicz 1994) developed the framework of the global commodity chain to distinguish between different forms of global value chains (for a comparison of the theoretical concepts of commodity chains and value chains, and the evolution of this research agenda, see Bair (2005)). This approach identified different 'nodes' in a value chain—pivotal points in the production process (that is, supply of raw materials,

production, export, or marketing)—with the intent of analysing how control of various nodes translated into power and profit. Gereffi distinguished between two types of commodity chains: the buyer-driven chain; and the producer-driven chain. In a buyer-driven chain, large retailers, brand-named marketers, and trading companies use various combinations of branding, design, marketing, and sales expertise to exert control over a decentralized network of supply firms often located in the developing world. As any supplier to a large retailer such as Walmart or a brand such as Nike is painfully aware, these customers do not need ownership in order to exert control. In a producer-driven chain, large (and often capital-intensive) integrated enterprises play the key role in controlling forward and backward linkages—the auto industry is a classic example.

Over the following decade, a growing body of research on global value chains identified other forms of networks. Scholars distinguished between 'commodity suppliers' (firms that provided a standard product through arm's-length ties), 'captive suppliers' (firms that provide a specialized product using production equipment or processes that are dedicated to a particular customer), and 'turnkey' suppliers (firms that produce customized—and often sophisticated—products for customers using flexible production equipment that can be used for multiple customers) (Humphrey and Schmitz 2000; Sturgeon 2002).

There are clearly multiple means of coordinating a global value chain that involve neither markets nor hierarchy, and a key question is why one form is chosen rather than another. Gereffi, Humphrey, and Sturgeon (2005: 87) argue that three key variables determine the organization of a global value chain: (1) the complexity of inter-firm transactions; (2) the degree to which this complexity can be codified; and (3) the extent to which the suppliers have the necessary capabilities to meet the requirements of the buyers. As with traditional attempts to explain FDI, their approach places a heavy emphasis on the nature of the transaction, but with a particular focus on how modern technology allows some transactions to be translated easily into a set of digital instructions, while others cannot. In this respect, the approach reflects the new range of opportunities that are available to firms. *Market relations* will tend to prevail when transactions are not complex, product specifications are easily specified by the buyer, and supplier capabilities can easily meet these demands. A buyer of inexpensive plastic toys, for example, can easily switch from one supplier to another, and a simple contract will suffice. *Modular value chains* will occur when the interfaces between complex modules can easily be codified, and there are suppliers capable of providing the sophisticated modules on either side of the interface. Large auto supply firms or contract manufacturers in the electronic industry are prominent examples. *Relational value chains* involve complex transactions, product specifications that are not easily codified, and highly capable suppliers. The result is mutual dependence between firms, close relationships that involve the exchange of tacit knowledge and relationships that are regulated through reputation, geographical proximity, and social, ethnic, and/or family ties. In *captive value chains* both the complexity of transactions and the ability to codify this complexity is high, but the capabilities of suppliers are low. The lead firm in these cases must provide the core design elements of product and significant assistance to the supply firm, and because it does not want other customers to benefit from new supplier capabilities that may result, it seeks to lock the supplier into a 'captive' relationship. By not providing key design elements or complementary activities, for example, the supplier firm will remain dependent on the lead firm. Finally, when product specifications cannot be codified, products are complex, and highly competent suppliers cannot be found, a firm will rely on in-house capabilities and *hierarchical coordination* (Gereffi, Humphrey, and Sturgeon 2005: 86–7).

Why does the form of governance matter? As Raphael Kaplinsky (2000: 118) notes, if it was clear that the only losers from increased economic globalization were those who did not globalize, the solution would be clear—attract more FDI and promote exports. But clearly economic globalization has not benefited all participants: the trade/GDP of sub-Saharan Africa increased from 51 per cent to 56.1 per cent between 1985 and 1995, at the same time as its share of global output fell (Kaplinsky 2000: 119; 2005; see also Wade, Chapter 12 in this volume). How a country inserts itself into the global economy is as important as whether or not a country does so, and a primary contribution of value chain analysis is to identify the terms under which a firm is participating in the global economy.

First, the distribution of gains within a value chain is determined to a great extent by barriers to entry (Kaplinsky 2000: 127). When barriers to entry are low, increased globalization can lead to a decrease in income, because competition is greater; when barriers to entry

are high, a firm has the ability to dictate the terms (that is, the price it will receive and the role it will have) to others within the value chain. To an increasing extent, and in a dramatic shift from an era when manufacturing prowess was the key to successful development, power in the value chain now stems from intangibility (Kaplinsky 2000: 127). That is, a firm that depends on low wages to convert physical inputs into a physical product will consistently face downward pressure on its prices because it will face competition from ambitious firms throughout the developing world, while a firm that depends on intangible factors such as design, brands, or marketing is able to protect its position because its skills are not easily copied (Kaplinsky 2000: 127; Bair 2005: 165). A value chain framework highlights the barriers to entry by focusing attention on the switching cost at each link in the chain. Any factor that makes it more difficult for a customer to switch from one supplier to another, whether it be the complexity of the transaction, the ability to codify the transaction, or the unique capabilities of the supplier, will increase the power (and profits) of the supplier. A supply firm that is part of a relational value chain, for example, will have far more power than a firm that is part of a captive value chain, because the relationship with the customer is characterized by mutual dependence—the customer cannot shift easily to another supplier—and this allows it to demand a higher price for its products or services.

Second, the governance of value chains is an important determinant of the prospects for economic upgrading, commonly defined as increasing competitiveness by capturing a part of the value chain that involves higher value-added activities. This can be achieved by increasing the breadth of functions a firm undertakes, the complexity of product that is produced, or improving the process technology that is utilized in production (Bair 2005: 165). From a development perspective, of course, economic upgrading is a crucial objective—what form of insertion to the global economy will provide a local economy with the strongest prospects for upgrading the capabilities, and thus future prospects, of local firms? The value chain literature highlights the benefits that firms in developing countries receive from incorporation into global value chains. The lead firms of these networks demand low cost, high quality, and good service from their suppliers, and often take an active role in transmitting best practice through the network (Humphrey and Schmitz 2001). The extent to which a lead firm within a network is willing to assist a supplier will depend on the form of governance: it is less likely to assist a supplier that can easily begin working for a competitor than it is a supplier that is enmeshed in a relational value chain.

Third, the form of insertion within a global value chain has important implications for workers within firms, and strategies that lead to economic upgrading may not always lead to social upgrading. As a firm engages in economic upgrading, for example, there is often a tension between a firm's need to deliver the higher quality that buyers demand and the need to lower costs and respond quickly to (highly variable) customer demands. Often the balance is adjusted through the use of regular and irregular (i.e. temporary) workers, with the conditions and benefits measurably worse for the latter (Barrientos et al. 2011; Barrientos et al. 2016). The objective of the lead firm in the value chain is to exactly match the supply of products to exactly match demand, so as to reduce inventory costs and allow it to control product pricing (e.g. avoid discounting excess demand). In the widely quotes words of Apple CEO Tim Cook, 'Inventory ... is fundamentally evil. You want to manage it like you're in the dairy business: if it gets past its freshness date, you have a problem' (e.g. Chan et al. 2013: 107). While this approach keeps Apple stores in stock with the latest products, it also means that the competitive advantage that Apple looks for in suppliers (i.e. the supplier's source of economic upgrading) is flexibility, and this often stems from the use of temporary workers (e.g. 'student interns'), high amounts of overtime for workers, and highly pressurized work environments (Chan et al. 2013).

Finally, the governance of global value chains gives insight into the degree of leverage that outside actors have—whether this be a government, international organization, or a non-governmental organization (NGO)—to influence the behaviour of firms. An NGO in the United States that is interested in promoting fair labour standards in Nike factories, for example, might have very little leverage over the factories themselves. The factories are foreign-owned, and even if progress is made within one factory, it will inevitably be only a small part of a huge, decentralized network. The real power in this value chain lies with Nike, but this is also the point of vulnerability: the very intangibility of branding that makes it difficult for other firms to imitate the success of Nike also creates a potential danger if the brand becomes associated with sweatshop labour. But as Richard Locke (2003: 7–8) argues, even the power of Nike to effect change within its own supply chain will vary. Because shoe factories tend to be large and capital-intensive—partly a result of the elimination by industrialized countries of quotas on footwear imports in the mid 1980s—Nike has long-term relationships with a relatively small number of large Korean and Taiwanese suppliers, and the stability of these relationships facilitates the coordination of production processes and (sometimes) the implementation of Nike's labour code of conduct. Nike has much looser relationships with its apparel supplies because product cycles are short, factories tend to specialize in a particular segment, and these factories supply Nike's competitors as well as Nike. According to Locke, the different form of these relationships has the potential to alter Nike's influence with the suppliers and its ability to monitor their behaviour (2003: 9, see also Distlehorst, Hainmueller, and Locke 2016)).

Location

The second key dimension along which value chains vary is location. Decisions about the governance of a value chain—whether it makes more sense to make or buy a particular product or service, for example—do not necessarily relate to decisions about location. If a firm decides that it can rely on market relationships to source a particular input—that it can 'buy' rather than 'make'—it can either *outsource* production to a firm across the street or it can *offshore* production to a firm overseas (Sako 2006: 503).

Why do value chains become global? One standard explanation is that foreign investment and offshoring are part of an evolutionary process. Raymond Vernon (1971) argued that every product followed a life cycle beginning with development, proceeding to maturity, and culminating in standardization and obsolescence. Over the course of this life cycle, the **comparative advantage** of a country will shift as the emphasis moves from product innovation and development—a stage when it can be highly beneficial to have designers, suppliers, and customers in close proximity—to a standardized product that competes on the basis of cost. At the time that Vernon was writing, the United States economy was the clear leader in technological and entrepreneurial resources, and it had the most affluent and demanding domestic marketplace. Firms developed new products for the domestic marketplace, eventually began to export to foreign markets, and finally, as the product matured and became standardized, they moved production offshore so as to forestall the rise of foreign competitors and preserve monopoly rents. A similar evolutionary pattern was used by scholars in East Asia to describe the relationship between foreign investment and regional development, although the focus was on leading industries rather than on products. Like geese flying in formation, industrial structures were passed from advanced economies to developing economies: a less-developed economy would initially import products in leading industries from more advanced countries, imitation and import-substitution would lead to the development of indigenous industry, and eventually the indigenous industry would advance to the point where it too would begin to export. As Bruce Cumings (1984: 46) argues in the case of North-East Asia:

> the cycle in given industries—textiles, steel, automobiles, light electronics—of origin, rise, apogee, and decline has not simply been marked, but often mastered in Japan; in each industrial life cycle there is also an appropriate jumping off place, that is, a point at which it pays to let others make the product or at least provide the labor. Taiwan and Korea have historically been receptacles for declining Japanese industries. Regional integration, in other words, is a natural impulse of economic growth and development—the leaders move into higher value-added activities as their cost structures rise, and lower-cost followers replicate the industrial structures of those ahead.

These evolutionary approaches captured a key dynamic driving foreign investment in a world in which the forces of technology and product innovation were highly concentrated and the rate of change was slow and predicable, but as Mitchell Bernard and John Ravenhill (1995) ague, these approaches have difficulty in explaining the contemporary global economy. First, in a world of rapid technical change and product proliferation, the process of product and technological maturation that is predicted by the industry–life cycle model appears to be less and less common. Product life cycles—for example for mobile phones—are now matters of months rather than years. Second, it is not an entire production system that an advanced country manufacturer such as a Japanese company simply boxes up and ships to a low-cost labour site, it is only a *part* of the system that is transferred, and in most circumstances it is the labour-intensive part of final assembly. The forces of innovation and the backward

linkages remain behind in the advanced economy, and in the absence of an active state role to promote the development of indigenous industry in the developing economy, the result will be partial diffusion of technology, and what Bernard and Ravenhill call an intra-regional hierarchy of production. This is not to say that late developers cannot overcome their place in the hierarchy—the emergence of strong and powerful competitors from countries such as Korea and Taiwan since the mid 1990s is evidence of this—but their success cannot be assumed. Finally, the evolutionary approach has difficulty explaining why the majority of global foreign investment is between developed economies that have very similar industrial structures. Clearly, the overseas activities of firms are not simply about accessing low-cost labour to produce outdated products.

Another way of thinking about how location drives global production is to consider the advantages that a firm seeks in any given place. Some of these advantages will be obvious—natural resources, new markets, or low-cost labour—but they may also involve factors that relate to the culture, language, or politics of a particular region. These motivating drivers of investment are the location-specific advantages of Dunning's 'eclectic' paradigm: a firm will invest abroad (assuming that there are benefits to internalization) in order to access the immobile resources of a particular place. A similar emphasis on the advantages inherent in a particular location is at the core of Michael Porter's (1990) concept of a firm's 'home base'. The home base consists of factors of production (and particularly specialized factors such as educational systems, technology and innovation systems, and infrastructure); demand conditions (the quality and quantity of the home market); related and supporting industries that are internationally competitive; and the national circumstances and context that influence the strategy, structure, and competitive practices of local firms. The interaction of these four attributes (what Porter calls the 'diamond of national advantage') leads to the creation of geographically concentrated clusters of competitive strengths that are mutually reinforcing. One of the greatest advantages of a multinational firm, according to Porter (1990: 60), is that it has the advantage of being able to combine the strengths of its own home base with other locations in its global network; at every stage of the value chain, a global firm can decide where to locate activities, to maximize the benefits of its global reach. If global value chains are the means of connecting a network of far-flung capabilities, the key then becomes a case of understanding why certain locations will vary in their ability to develop particular capabilities.

The traditional approach of comparative political economy has been to focus on the nation state, and to explain economic outcomes as a result of the relationship between domestic state institutions, patterns of industrial policy, and social actors. Successive generations of this approach analysed how national institutional structures responded to the challenges of economic adjustment in the advanced capitalist world (Katzenstein 1978, 1985; Schmitter and Lehbruch 1979; Zysman 1984). The most recent approach in this tradition has focused on systematic differences in the way that national economies are organized (Hall and Soskice 2001). Firms must coordinate activities with a range of economic actors—investors, other firms (suppliers and clients), the organizations that represent workers, and their own employees (in particular)—and firms that operate in liberal market economies will have very different characteristics and strengths from firms that operate in coordinated market economies (see Hay, Chapter 11 in this volume). This 'varieties of capitalism' approach assumes that 'the most important institutional structures—notably systems of labour market regulation, of education and training, and of corporate governance—depend on the presence of regulatory regimes that are the preserve of the nation-state' (Hall and Soskice 2001: 4). The result is a stark departure from the traditional perspective of economics on comparative advantage because the advantages of a particular location are not endowed by nature, but are the result of a complex constellation of interrelated institutions. Firms in a liberal market economy, for example, may have an advantage in activities that emphasize radical innovation; firms in a coordinated market economy may have an advantage in activities that require incremental innovation and manufacturing excellence. The key point from the perspective of global production is that multinational firms have the potential to access the advantages of all systems, and in doing so they can compensate for weaknesses at home.

Although national institutions are clearly important in shaping general patterns of economic coordination within an economy, an exclusive focus on the nation state as the unit of analysis can obscure as much as it reveals. There is increasing evidence that, as Anwar Shah and Theresa Thompson (2002: 5) of the World

Bank put it, 'nation-states are too small to tackle large things in life and too large to address small things'. National governments do not have the same degree of autonomy to shape their national economies as they did in the past. As Colin Hay explains (Chapter 11 of this book), the extent to which globalization forces states to converge on a single economic model is the subject of fierce debate. While the resilience of distinct 'varieties' of capitalism is debated, few would question that nation states are increasingly aware of the international constraints on their economic policies. National governments that do not take into account international capital markets and foreign investors before making policy changes, for example, do so at their peril. At the same time as national governments are operating under greater constraints, decentralization—the process of devolving political, fiscal, and administrative powers to subnational units of government (Burki et al. 1999)—has been one of the dominant economic and political trends since the 1980s. This move towards decentralization started in advanced industrial nations, where free-market policy reforms were accompanied by a 'devolution revolution' that transferred authority and resources from central to local governments, and the approach was transferred to the developing world by the World Bank and development NGOs (Snyder 2001: 93).

The importance of regional economies is certainly not surprising to multinational firms that are seeking to access the best capabilities across the globe. If a firm wants to access high-tech capabilities in the United States, for example, the most capable firms are not scattered at random: they are clustered in places such as Silicon Valley in California; Route 128 outside Boston; or the Research Triangle in North Carolina. Why are national economic systems composed of disparate regional economies (Marshall 1920; Nadvi and Schmitz 1998)? One set of explanations focuses on the ability of firms in an industrial cluster to minimize transaction costs and maximize their share of specialized labour markets. For firms interested in design and technology, it is easier to identify new technologies and market trends; the flow of personnel between firms helps to disseminate knowledge; there is better access to highly specialized types of labour; and there may be better access to capital and other key inputs in a technology cluster (McKendrick, Doner, and Haggard 2000: 46). For firms involved with manufacturing and operations, there are also benefits to agglomeration, although they are slightly different. Firms will benefit from lower transport costs and reduced transport times; greater economies of scale; a greater ability to increase production rapidly; specialized pools of labour; better ability to monitor and coordinate with suppliers; and a greater ability to monitor and imitate the competition (McKendrick, Doner, and Haggard 2000: 46). A second (and not competing) set of explanations focuses on the political and economic characteristics of a particular region. In an era in which decentralization is a dominant political and economic trend, increasingly it is local institutions that help firms overcome the coordination problems of development (Thun 2006). The patterns of association in a region, types of intergroup relations, political representation, and forms of economic governance (both in the present and in the past) create different opportunities and constraints for economic actors, and these differences help to explain divergent economic outcomes within a single national economy (Locke 1995; Herrigel 1996).

KEY POINTS

- The activities within global value chains can be governed by a range of mechanisms, including market coordination, various forms of network coordination, and hierarchical coordination. The form of value chain governance is a key determinant of how power and profits are distributed among the key actors within the value chain.

- According to Dunning's eclectic paradigm, firms will engage in FDI when there are firm-specific advantages, location-specific advantages, and advantages of internalization.

- Gereffi et al. argue that the organization of a global value chain will vary according to the complexity of inter-firm transactions, the degree to which this complexity can be codified, and the extent to which the suppliers have the capabilities needed to meet the requirements of the buyers.

- When considering where to locate different parts of the value chain, firms must consider the cost of production and the competitive strengths and weaknesses of both nations and regions.

China as the world's factory

There is no better place to analyse the trends in global production than China; the rise of China as an economic power has corresponded with the globalization of manufacturing. In the three decades since China began to make the transition to a market economy, the country has come to dominate world manufacturing, and the impact of this manufacturing juggernaut is difficult to ignore. China has a significant impact on the global prices of the inputs it sucks in to fuel its economic growth (even to the extent that manhole covers and highway railings disappear from countries on the other side of the world when Chinese commodity prices create the incentive for thieves to sell scrap metal) and the global price of the outputs it manufactures. Increasingly, it is not only the most important source of manufactured goods, it is also the most important market.

The impact of China on global manufacturing is difficult to overstate. From the perspective of economies that compete with it, the situation is often portrayed as grim. In 2013, the United States recorded a trade deficit in goods of $318.4 billion with China, accounting for 46.3 per cent of the overall US goods trade deficit in that year, and when factories close in the United States and workers lose their jobs, China is an obvious target of political wrath (http://www.ustr.gov/countries-regions/china-mongolia-taiwan).

From the perspective of multinational firms, however, the situation is very different. Although it is not the common understanding of the term, China is the 'world's factory' in the sense that much of the world's factories are operating in China; China's trade performance is as much a testament to foreign companies that have invested in manufacturing operations in China as they are an indication of the strength of Chinese-owned companies. The country received US$129 billion in FDI in 2014, more than any other country in the world, and it has been a leading destination for foreign firms for decades (UNCTAD 2015b: 5); for reasons why Chinese FDI figures may be considerably overstated in official statistics, see Ravenhill 2006a: 661). These foreign-invested factories play a key role in Chinese manufacturing: over half of all Chinese exports are from foreign-invested factories, and over 80 per cent of technology-intensive exports are from foreign-invested factories (Rosen 2003: 22; Koopman 2008). Multinational firms benefit from Chinese production both when they invest in manufacturing facilities and when they outsource production to factories that produce in China (both foreign- and Chinese-owned). Consumers benefit from the low price of manufactured goods that are exported from China.

Location and global production

The patterns of foreign investment in China reflect the complex interaction of the multiple levels of location within which a multinational firm operates—the regional, the national, and the local—and the efforts of both firms and governments to balance concerns of efficiency, equity, and sovereignty in this highly dynamic process.

First, and most obviously, the investment flows have led to the integration of national economies in the region. In fact, it is more accurate to speak of China as a *regional production base* than a national production base. When China began to reform its economy at the end of the 1970s, a development approach that emphasized foreign investment had the benefit of allowing the leadership to avoid the ideologically sensitive issue of whether to allow private-sector investment within China, and it created the opportunity for China to acquire technical and managerial skills rapidly from foreign firms. Special economic zones were located initially in the mainland provinces that were across from Taiwan and Hong Kong—the primary sources of investment during the 1980s—and as preferential policies were gradually expanded to include the entire coastal region of China, Japan and Korea became important sources of investment as well. These countries did not transfer entire industries to China; they transferred the labour-intensive activities to China, and the subsidiaries established then imported higher value-added components from their home country.

The extent of regional integration is reflected in a dramatic increase in **intra-industry trade** between 1990 and 2005, the period when Asian countries were rapidly transferring their manufacturing operations to China. The percentage of the electronics trade between Japan and China that consisted of components increased from slightly over 10 per cent in 1990 to almost 60 per cent in 2005 (METI 2006: 25). It was estimated that two-thirds of the inputs for China's processing activities come from Hong Kong, Japan, Korea, and Taiwan (Ravenhill 2006a: 670). As a result of this intra-industry trade, the United States' trade deficit is with East Asia as a whole rather than with China: the high-wage economies export components to China for final assembly, and then the finished goods are exported to the United States. In 2003, China had a large trade surplus with the United States (about $125 billion), but an almost equally large deficit with its Asian trading partners (about $99 billion) (Hufbauer and

Wong 2004: 3). In trade statistics, a good that is shipped from China to the United States appears as an import from China even though the value added in China may be as little as 20–40 per cent (Ravenhill 2006a: 669).

The formation of these regional networks was driven by high costs in the countries that surrounded China, and facilitated by advances in technology. The production process in a garment factory, for example, is distinctly low-tech and labour-intensive—a factory consists of rows of women sitting at sewing machines—but the linkages between different parts of the garment value chain can be very high-tech, and these linkages create the opportunity to manage offshore production networks more effectively. Until the early 1980s, for example, textiles and garments were Taiwan's number one export (Gee and Kuo 1997: 52). During the 1980s, however, the rising cost of labour in Taiwan and a strengthening currency decreased Taiwan's competitiveness, and led Taiwanese firms either to upgrade into higher value-added activities or to move production overseas. Taiwan's apparel and accessory exports peaked in 1987 (at $5 billion), and then began a rapid decline as firms moved manufacturing to low-cost regions such as China (Gereffi and Pan 1994: 130–1). The result is what Gereffi and Pan call a triangular manufacturing system (see Box 7.2): a foreign buyer places orders with a Taiwanese firm with which it has had a long-term relationship; this firm then issues the manufacturing orders with offshore factories (that it either owns or contracts); and the final goods are then shipped to the foreign buyer (Gereffi and Pan 1994: 127).

At the same time that East Asia is a regional economy with manufacturing networks that cross national borders, *local economic clusters* are extraordinarily important in China. The factories of particular townships and villages will often specialize in a particular product, and then dominate world markets. For example, 80 per cent of the world's metallic-shell lighters come from the city of Wenzhou in Zhejiang province. Not far away, in the town of Qiaotou, 700 family-run factories produce 15 billion buttons and 200 million metres of zippers a year—again, they are the world leaders (Watts 2005; *China News Digest* 2006). Qingxi Township in the southern city of Dongguan specializes in PC production, and has become so important in the production of monitors, motherboards, keyboards, and PC boxes that the deputy director of IBM Asia remarked that 'If there is a traffic jam between

BOX 7.2

Triangular Manufacturing

Are companies always looking for low-cost labour? Not necessarily. The garment and apparel sector is a classic example of a labour-intensive industry, but actual decisions on where to locate production involves complex calculations of labour costs, quotas, and proximity to market. TW Industries, a Taiwanese garment manufacturer, is a typical example of a triangular manufacturing network (a pseudonym has been used to protect the confidentiality of an actual firm; the example is from Thun 2000). Its major customer is Gap, and because the two firms have a long history of working together, Gap continued to maintain its relationship with TW even after most Taiwanese garment manufacturing had relocated to less expensive regions. TW maintains its headquarters and one factory in Taiwan, and has a network of factories in China, Indonesia, and Cambodia.

The production process at TW begins when Gap uses a computer-assisted design system to send the master garment patterns via the internet to TW headquarters. The local factory, although high-cost, is maintained to make samples—the workers are highly dependable and turnaround is quicker—and these samples are sent back to Gap via express mail. When the sample is approved, the headquarters must decide where to locate the production run. First, the cost of production is obviously important. In addition to the Taiwanese factory, TW has factories in China, Indonesia, and Cambodia, and wages vary considerably. The monthly wages for a worker are $800 per month in Taiwan, $100 in a coastal province of China, $30–$40 in Indonesia, and $50–$60 in Cambodia. The cost of production is a combination of labour cost and productivity, of course, and the latter varies as well. Using the Taiwan productivity rate as an index of 100, China is a 95, Indonesia 40–45, and Cambodia 55–60. Second, politics plays a key role in location decision. Prior to the elimination of the **Multifiber Arrangement** in 2005, TW had to be sure to locate production in countries that had the quotas necessary for the final markets. Even after these quotas were eliminated, TW seeks to have a geographical distribution of production facilities in order to protect itself from the risk of new tariffs and quotas. Finally, the proximity to market is critical. Because clothing is influenced by fashion and trends, it can be extraordinarily time-sensitive. Much like a fruit or vegetable that will lose its value as it ages on a grocer's shelves, a piece of clothing that is yesterday's fashion must be

marked down dramatically in price. As a result, speed to market is absolutely critical: saving a few cents on labour costs is a pyrrhic victory if it causes a firm to miss a trend and the product ends up in a discount outlet rather than a department store display case. The calculation will vary by product: it continues to make sense to produce high-fashion items in high-cost areas such as New York or Los Angeles; relatively fashionable items will be produced in regions where they can get to market quickly (Mexico and low-cost regions of Europe are only hours away from major markets); and relatively stable items (such as men's tee shirts and underwear) will be produced wherever costs are lowest.

Managing the technology of the production network is of critical importance. Given the fashion-sensitive nature of much of the business, retailers want to keep inventories low. In fact, the ideal would be to have a factory behind the store, because this would allow the retailer to make each item of clothing as it is purchased. It would be possible to expand production when it became apparent that an item was becoming popular, and stop production of items that were not selling—discounting would never be needed. Obviously, this is not possible, but retailers try to use information technology to keep their inventories low and their supply chains as 'lean' as possible. The objective of lean retailing is to reduce the risk of selling a perishable good by continuously adjusting the supply of products offered to consumers at retail outlets so as to match the actual level of market demand (Abernathy et al. 1999: 55). Bar code and scanning technology will track sales at a retail store, for example, and this information will be sent to a distant factory at the close of business. The factory will not only manufacture the new clothing, but will place it on hangers, complete with price tags, and then air freight it back to the retail store. In some cases, the buyer is able to use specialized software systems and the internet to track the progress of an order through each stage of the production process.

The increasingly high-tech nature of the industry creates opportunities for Taiwanese firms because the emphasis of the global network shifts from achieving cost reductions through savings on labour costs (a primary weakness of the Taiwanese at home) to more effective management of the production network and the consequent ability to match supply to market demand more effectively (a potential strength of Taiwanese firms vis-à-vis companies with lower labour costs).

Dongguan and Hong Kong [where the port is located], 70 per cent of the world's computer market will be affected' (Enright, Scott, and Chang 2005: 62). Similar clusters can be found for bicycles, domestic

appliances, furniture, plastic flowers, air-conditioners, and shoes—virtually any product imaginable.

The formation of these clusters is partly the result of a natural tendency on the part of firms to seek agglomeration economies, but government policy also played a key role. Over the course of the reform period in China, the central government gave increasing autonomy to local governments to shape their own economic policies, and gave them fiscal incentives to do so successfully (Oi 1992). The slate with which local governments had to work, however, was not a clean one: the economic history, the structure of government institutions, and the types of firms in a region created different sets of possibilities for different places. Small and entrepreneurial firms in Zhejiang province benefited from a local government that supported (or at least did not obstruct) private-sector firms and the lack of competing state-owned enterprises (Whiting 2001). Firms in capital and technology-intensive industries in Shanghai benefited from a local government that invested heavily in firm development and guided the process of technology transfer from foreign-invested enterprises. Light industrial firms in Guangdong province took advantage of local policies that favoured exporting and foreign investment from ethnic Chinese networks. In a decentralized economy environment, the role of local policy is as important as national policy in shaping the framework of opportunities and constraints within which firms must operate.

The competitive pressures that lead to regional integration in East Asia, and the opportunity to access world-class and inexpensive manufacturing capabilities in the various industrial clusters of China creates strong pressure on the *national 'varieties of capitalism'* of multinational firms that invest in China. As Hay points out in Chapter 11, there is no topic in the field of global political economy that is more controversial than whether global capital, trade, and investment flows are leading towards a convergence of national institutions. This debate has a corollary in the literature on global production: when multinational firms and their suppliers move abroad, do they preserve certain characteristics of their home country? The characteristics of Japanese production networks, for example, are commonly perceived to be relatively closed when compared to American production networks—a result of the preferential trade relationships and cross-shareholding within Japanese corporate groups and long-term relationships between management and labour—and these characteristics have been seen as surprisingly durable when transferred abroad. The overseas subsidiaries of Japanese companies are less likely to employ local managers, less likely to rely on

local sourcing (except when Japanese affiliates were located in the local economy), and less likely to transfer research and development activities to overseas affiliates (Encarnation 1999; Ernst and Ravenhill 2000; Solis 2003a). According to this viewpoint, 'firms involved in global competition begin their lives under very different legal, social and political environments and histories ... [and] while firms from different nations may eventually converge on some best practice, convergence may not happen quickly or automatically' (McKendrick, Doner, and Haggard 2000: 9; see also Borrus and Zysman 1997). The durability of national foundations leads to unique corporate strategies, and alternate strategies lead to variation in the form of the production networks that bind regions together.

In China, both the durability of national approaches to investment and the intense pressures on these approaches are visible in the patterns of Japanese investment. When Japanese firms began to manufacture in China, for example, there was a strong tendency to continue to rely on Japanese suppliers. During the 1990s, the bulk of Japanese investment in China followed a predictable pattern: the objective of Japanese firms was to lower costs, and, in keeping with the concept of a regional hierarchy, production was moved to China but core components and design continued to come from Japanese firms. Because the focus of these firms was on export markets, the drive to lower costs could not be at the expense of quality, and it was easier to maintain quality standards while using tried-and-true suppliers. Over time, Japanese firms became more focused on the Chinese market and were forced to compete with low-cost Chinese firms and Western firms that were heavily taking advantage of low-cost suppliers. Gradually, the Japanese supply networks began to loosen. The extent to which Japanese production networks open to non-Japanese firms varies both by firm and industry, and they continue to be far more closed than other national networks, but the trend is an important one. As Dieter Ernst argues (2006: 183), it signals the end of an unequal division of labour in East Asia, one in which the higher value-added activities and technology remain in Japan, and only the labour-intensive activities move offshore, the beginning of a complex process of 'hybridization' of national production networks (Ernst and Ravenhill 2000: 242).

The industrial clusters of China represent a particularly pure version of globalization of production—they consist not of local firms that have developed slowly over time, but are composed primarily of highly competitive foreign firms that have co-located in China and feed off of each other's strengths—and this puts pressure on ties that were formed in the less competitive context of the home country.

The most recent phase of China's development process reflects the highly dynamic nature of global production: the same problems that led Taiwanese firms to relocate to mainland China in the 1980s—a strengthening currency and the increasing cost of labour—are now beginning to threaten the competitive advantage of firms in mainland China. Since 2001, wages in China's manufacturing sector have increased by an average of 12 per cent a year, and the strength of the currency is at an all-time high.

When a consideration of rising manufacturing cost in China is combined with other variables—e.g. transport costs, duties, the degree of labour content in a product, speed to market—firms begin to rethink the location of their manufacturing network. Firms that are labour intensive, mass producing, and mobile will search for the next source of low-cost labour (e.g. garments). Other firms will be concerned about labour costs, but the strength of the industrial clusters in China and the agglomeration effects will continue to outweigh rising costs. These firms will stay. There will also be those firms that move back to developed economies such as the US, given that differences in labour costs (particularly when adjusted for differences in productivity) are decreasing. The labour cost of equipment manufacturing is often as low as 5 per cent of total costs, and firms such as Caterpillar (construction equipment), NCR (ATM machines), and Ford (cars) have moved some production back to the US. Companies with products that have high shipping costs relative to value (e.g. plastic coolers, refrigerators, washing machines, large-screen televisions) or products for which speed to market is important (i.e. high-end garments) have also rebuilt capacity in the US. In a world of footloose global production, investment can flow out as fast as it flows in.

Governance and upgrading

The spectre of rising costs in China has created fears in Beijing of a 'middle-income trap'. When a developing country is able to compete on the basis of low-cost, growth is rapid and incomes begin to rise. As wages rise, firms are no longer able to compete with lower-cost producers and they must either make the transition into higher value-added products or risk being trapped at the middle-income level.

Will Chinese firms be able to upgrade their capabilities and move into higher value-added activities? Within China, the extent of the country's participation in global value chains has been a point of controversy. Although advocates of openness argued that foreign investment would ultimately increase self-reliance, as Chinese firms gained technology and managerial capabilities, sceptics claimed that Chinese firms were not capturing the gains from their participation in global production networks. In the wake of the rapid increase in inward FDI flows in the mid 1990s, the *Economic Daily* (*Jingji Ribao*), an authoritative economic paper in China, ran a series of articles that were highly critical of the impact that foreign investment was having on Chinese firms. Openness was not inherently bad, the commentary argued, 'but looking across the countries of the world, [we see] that opening up definitely cannot be without certain principles and certain limits'. It is important to 'pay attention to protecting national industries', the paper concluded (Fewsmith 2001: 173–4).

There is evidence to support this scepticism. In 2010, for instance, an iPhone 4 that retailed for $600 was manufactured in China by Foxconn, but only an estimated $6.53 (3.4 per cent) of the total factory price of $194.04 was added in China (OECD and WTO, 2012). The bulk of the cost ($187.51) came from imported materials and components, primarily from South Korea, Germany, Taiwan, and the United States. Apple, which provided design and marketing, profited the most. In short, the activities which required innovation and knowledge, and which are extremely difficult to imitate, take place outside of China; the activities which are labour-intensive and high volume take place inside China. Given the demands this places on labour and the rising cost of Chinese labour, not only did Chinese firms gain little from the production of the iPhone, increasing wages and the rising expectations of Chinese workers meant that even the location of the assembly activities in China might eventually move out of China.

In the automotive industry, the Chinese government utilized every weapon in its arsenal to utilize FDI as a means of promoting national firms, including forcing foreign firms to form joint ventures, transfer technology, and localize the sourcing of components, but success has still been limited: no Chinese firm has emerged as a major auto manufacturer in its own right (Thun, 2006). As in the case of the iPhone, the high cost of product development in the industry and the rapid advance of technology create high barriers to entry in the industry. Assembly firms such as Volkswagen (VW) and General Motors (GM) group products around common underbody platforms, outsource the design and production of large modules of the car to global suppliers, and then rely on these firms to supply the modules wherever in the world they decide to assemble the vehicles (Humphrey and Memedovic, 2003). Global platforms spread the costs of development more widely by creating greater economies of scale for each model, and outsourcing passes a good portion of the design burden for individual modules on to the supply firms. These same characteristics, however, make it very difficult for a local supply firm to become an upper-tier supplier in the network of a multinational firm (Humphrey and Memedovic 2003). Tier one global suppliers (e.g. such as Bosch, Denso, and Visteon) are often as large and powerful as their customers (e.g. firms such as VW and GM), and they must be able to cooperate on the design of new models with the assemblers. Unless they have foreign partners, local firms generally play a role only in the lower tiers—hardly an unusual outcome in developing countries (Humphrey and Memedovic, 2003)

Although there is evidence of familiar obstacles, China also gives evidence of a profound change in global production. The global value chain literature has traditionally assumed that the endpoint of the value chains—the final markets—are in the developed world and this shapes the nature of the upgrading challenge that local firms face. In a buyer-driven chain, for example, the core competencies of the lead firms are marketing, sales, and retail. Firms from developed markets could dominate these powerful positions in the value chain because they had the best understanding of their home markets. A firm from a developing country such as China is at a distinct disadvantage if it wants to create a brand that can compete with Nike in the United States. In a producer-driven chain, the core competencies of lead firms are technology and design. Again, developed markets demand the most advanced technology and design and this is the advantage of global firms. As Hubert Schmitz (2007: 420) has argued, the firms from developing countries faced both a marketing gap and a technology gap, and overcoming these shortcomings was the challenge of development.

Global value chains are increasingly being turned around, however, and their endpoints are in developing countries such as China. China, for instance, is now the largest market in the world for a wide variety of products, including beer (surpassing the US in 2002), automobiles (surpassing the US in 2009), food and groceries (surpassing the US in 2011), and smart phones (surpassing the US in 2011). This shift has the potential to drastically alter the upgrading challenges facing Chinese firms (Brandt and Thun 2010). For products that are technology intensive, the 'technology gap' confronting a local firm will be smaller than in export markets because a market with a lower average income level may prioritize features other than technical sophistication. A first-time car buyer in China, for instance, might be satisfied with 'good enough' quality and fewer features if the price is reasonable. Similarly, the 'marketing gap' that local firms face when exporting to developed economies will largely disappear when they focus on their domestic market. A foreign firm with powerful brands will continue to have strong advantages, but domestic firms might have a superior understanding of what the consumers want and how to reach them. In short, there will be cases when it is the foreign firm that faces a marketing and technology gap.

The extent to which the domestic market will create an advantage for domestic firms will vary by product, but it seems to be particularly important when there is a full range of market segments (Brandt and Thun 2016). The low-end market provides domestic firms with a segment that is naturally protected from higher-cost foreign firms, creating the space for these firms to develop capabilities and increase volumes. The size of the low-end segment also drives foreign firms to localize their activities (e.g. design and purchasing) in an effort to lower their cost structures and compete. Rather than use local suppliers only for commodity parts in the lower tier of the value chain, the foreign assembly firms begin to work much more closely with local suppliers because they are reliant on their low-cost capabilities (i.e. a shift from market to relational governance in the value chain). Each successively higher market segment provides domestic firms with the knowledge and the incentives that drive domestic upgrading. In both telecom equipment and construction equipment, for instance, domestic firms first dominated low-end segments which foreign firms were either ignoring or unable to compete in, and then gradually upgraded their capabilities until they were able to compete with global firms in all segments.

Conclusion

Firms have long been a product of their immediate geography. They have always been shaped strongly by the regulatory and legal institutions of the states within which they are formed, the inputs available to them (human capital, raw materials, and components), and the nature of the markets within which they compete. The intensity of these constraints has varied over time, however. As early as the seventeenth century, firms were looking to distant countries for raw materials not available at home. In the early twentieth century, they began to relocate (and replicate) manufacturing activities in major foreign markets in order to escape protectionist trade barriers. Foreign production has been commonplace for centuries. What is new in the current era of globalization is that geographical dispersion no longer precludes global integration. Firms are able to break up their value chain in ways that were not previously possible, make a decision about where each particular activity should be located, and then integrate these far-flung activities with advanced technologies.

The globalization of production creates opportunities and challenges for both developing and developed economies. From the perspective of developing economies, the massive flows of foreign investment and the increased willingness of multinational firms to outsource production has create a range of opportunities that were not previously present. Under the right circumstances, multinational firms are willing to take offshore not only the labour-intensive activities that have traditionally gone to the developing world, but also the higher value-added activities. There are two significant caveats, however. First, the flows of FDI are highly concentrated (and multinational firms often display a strongly herd-like mentality). Countries with

seemingly ideal investment climates can find themselves, through no fault of their own, without any investment. They might be too small; there might be a shortage of supporting industries and suppliers; they might not be easily accessible; or they might be located in what is otherwise a rough and dangerous neighbourhood. This problem is particularly harsh, of course, because private investment flows have largely replaced official sources of investment capital. In this environment, the poorest countries may easily find themselves worse off than in the past. Second, in those cases that are blessed with high rates of inward FDI, the gains for the domestic economy are far from guaranteed. Few countries are in as favourable a position as China to cope with the challenges of FDI, and yet even China continues to struggle with maximizing the benefits of foreign investment for indigenous firms. Indigenous Chinese firms often find themselves locked in a downward competitive spiral: because they usually compete in areas with low barriers to entry, competition is intense and profit margins thin, and they often have little to invest in research and development. State policy is critical, particularly the support that is given to local firms, but it must be more nuanced than in the past—investment that flows in can just as easily flow out when host governments impose conditions that are too onerous. Rather than strong-arming multinational firms into transferring technology and utilizing local suppliers, it is far more effective (and more difficult) to create a policy environment that will support the development of the capabilities that multinational firms are seeking in their supply base.

From the perspective of developed economies, the globalization of production allows firms to choose à la carte from a global menu of production sites. No longer constrained by the limitation of having to conduct all activities in one particular geographical setting, the parts of the value chain can be broken up and located separately, according to the competitive needs of any particular activity. This allows a firm to compensate for weaknesses in their home base without completely abandoning it. Although the hope is always that the higher value-added activities will remain at home, the danger is that the outflow will be too great and a hollowed-out economy will be left behind. In the case of the regional production networks of East Asia, the fears of hollowing-out in the advanced economies that surround China have not yet been realized. Quite the contrary, in fact—the combination of the growing Chinese market and the increase of imports of high value-added components into China has been an economic engine for the region. The gains, however, are not evenly distributed. It is the small and medium-sized enterprises in an economy that have the most difficulty in adjusting, and these are often the firms that provide the bulk of employment at home. Trading relationships that appear to be mutually beneficial in the aggregate can mask significant dislocation and, as in the developing countries, public policy must focus on increasing the capacity of smaller firms to take advantage of the potential gains of globalization. In the absence of balanced growth, the possibility of a backlash against globalization is all too real.

KEY POINTS

- The rise of global production creates new opportunities for developing countries, but also real risks: first, for those that are unable to attract FDI; and, second, for those able to attract FDI but unable to maximize the benefits for indigenous firms.

- Similarly, in developed economies, the gains from globalization are not evenly distributed, and in the absence of effective public policy this imbalance creates the possibility of a backlash against globalization.

? QUESTIONS

1. What have been the drivers of the globalization of production since the 1980s?

2. Why do multinational firms invest in equity stakes in foreign operations rather than form trading relationships with foreign firms?

3. What is modularity, and how does it increase the opportunities for global production?

4. How does the governance of a global value chain affect the prospects for upgrading in a developing country?

5. What factors does a firm need to consider when deciding where to locate production facilities?

6. What are the benefits of industrial clusters, and why do they form?

7. Why did China emerge as the world's factory, what were the implications of this trend, and what pressures threaten this trend?

8. From the perspective of a developing country, is a heavy reliance on FDI good or bad?

9. From the perspective of an advanced capitalist economy, is the offshoring of production good or bad?

≋ FURTHER READING

Abernathy, F. H., Dunlop, J. T., Hammond, J. H., and Weil, D. (1999), *A Stitch in Time: Lean Retailing and the Transformation of Manufacturing* (Oxford: Oxford University Press). A detailed and fascinating account of how information technology has transformed retailing in the clothing industry.

Baldwin, C. Y., and Clark, K. B. (1997), 'Managing in an Age of Modularity', *Harvard Business Review*, 75/5: 84–93. A classic account of how modularity creates new possibilities for structuring industrial sectors.

Bartley, T., Koos, S., Samel, H., Setrini, G., and Summers, N. (2015), *Looking Behind the Label: Global Industries and the Conscientious Consumer* (Bloomington and Indianapolis: Indiana University Press). An insightful look into how 'conscientious consumption' (such as student movements against sweatshop labour) have and have not impacted global production.

Berger, S. (2006), *How We Compete: What Companies around the World Are Doing to Make It in Today's Global Economy* (New York: Currency Doubleday). A highly readable and knowledgeable analysis of how different companies and countries are coping with the challenges created by the globalization of production.

Dunning, J. H. (1981), *International Production and the Multinational Enterprise* (London: Allen & Unwin). A classic work on FDI.

Gereffi, G., Humphrey, J., and Sturgeon, T. (2005), 'The Governance of Global Value Chains', *Review of International Political Economy*, 12/1: 78–104. This article provides a framework for analysing the structure of global value chains.

Kaplinsky, R. (2005), *Globalization, Poverty and Inequality: Between a Rock and a Hard Place* (Cambridge: Polity Press). This book provides a cogent analysis of why many countries have difficulty in capturing the benefits of globalization.

Levinson, M. (2006), *How the Shipping Container Made the World Smaller and the World Economy Bigger* (Princeton: Princeton University Press). A fascinating account of how something as simple as a shipping container transformed the global economy.

McKendrick, D. G., Doner, R. F., and Haggard, S. (2000), *From Silicon Valley to Singapore: Location and Competitive Advantage in the Hard Disk Drive Industry* (Stanford, CA: Stanford University Press). A detailed academic study of how decisions about location helped US firms to dominate the global hard disk drive industry.

Palmisano, S. J. (2006), 'The Globally Integrated Enterprise', *Foreign Affairs*, 85/3: 127–36. A concise account of the new model of global firm from the CEO of IBM.

United Nations Conference on Trade and Development (2015), *Reforming International Investment Governance* (New York and Geneva: United Nations). The annual UNCTAD report on investment flows.

WEBLINKS

The primary source of data on global investment flows is the United Nations Conference on Trade and Development (UNCTAD). Its publications are available at **www.unctad.org**

For academic research on global value chains in a variety of industries and countries, see **http://www.ids.ac.uk/idsresearch/innovation-and-value-chains** and **www.globalvaluechains.org** Work on social upgrading in global value chains can be found at **http://www.capturingthegains.org/** For an excellent example of one company's global manufacturing footprint, see Nike's interactive map at **http://manufacturingmap.nikeinc.com/**

ONLINE RESOURCE CENTRE

Visit the Online Resource Centre that accompanies this book for more information:
www.oxfordtextbooks.co.uk/orc/ravenhill5e

PART III

Global Finance

8

The Evolution of the International Monetary and Financial System

Eric Helleiner

Chapter contents

Reader's guide

The international monetary and financial system plays a central role in the global political economy. Since the late nineteenth century, the nature of this system has undergone several transformations in response to changing political and economic conditions at both domestic and international levels. The first was the collapse of the integrated pre-1914 international monetary and financial regime during the interwar years. The second transformation took place after the Second World War, when the Bretton Woods order was put in place. Since the early 1970s, various features of the Bretton Woods order have unravelled with the globalization of finance, the collapse of the gold exchange standard, and the move to a floating exchange rate regime among the major economic powers. These various changes have important political consequences for the key issue of who gets what, when, and how in the global political economy.

Introduction

It is often said that money makes the world go round. In this age of globalization, this saying appears more relevant than ever. International flows of money today dwarf the cross-border trade of goods. And the influence of these flows seems only enhanced by their unique speed and global reach.

If money is so influential, it is fitting that it should have a prominent place in the study of global political economy. While perspectives vary enormously, scholars working on the political economy of international monetary and financial issues share the belief that the study of money and finance must embrace a wider lens than that adopted by most economists.

Economists are trained to view money and finance primarily as economic phenomena. From their standpoint, money serves as a medium of exchange, a unit of account, and a store of value, while financial activity allocates credit within the economy. These functions are critical to large-scale economic life, since they facilitate commerce, savings, and investment.

Such descriptions of the economic role of money and finance are certainly accurate, but they are also limiting. Money and finance, after all, serve many political purposes as well (not to mention social and cultural ones). In all modern societies, control over the issuing and management of money and credit has been a key source of power and its distributional consequences have been immense. Consequently, the organization and functioning of monetary and financial systems have rarely been determined just by a narrow economic logics but also by various political rationales relating to the pursuit of power, ideas, and interests (Kirshner 2003; Drezner and McNamara 2013).

The interrelationship between politics and systems of money and finance is particularly apparent at the international level, where no single political authority exists. What money should be used to facilitate international economic transactions and how should it be managed? What should the nature of the relationship between national currencies be? How should credit be created and allocated at the international level? The answers to these questions have profoundly important implications for politics, not just within countries but also between them. It should not surprise us, then, that they provoke domestic and international political struggles, often of an intense kind.

This chapter highlights this point by providing an overview of the evolution of the international monetary and financial system since the late nineteenth century. The first section examines how changing political circumstances, both internationally and domestically, during the interwar years undermined the stability of the globally integrated financial and monetary order of the pre-1914 era. The next section describes how a new international monetary and financial system—the Bretton Woods order—was created in 1944 for the post-war period, with a number of distinct features. The following three sections analyse the causes and consequences of challenges to that order which have emerged since the early 1970s with the globalization of finance, the collapse of the gold exchange standard, and the move to a floating exchange rate regime among the major economic powers. In the next chapter, Louis W. Pauly addresses another feature of the contemporary international financial order: its vulnerability to crises.

The fate of a previous globally integrated financial and monetary order

Debates about contemporary economic globalization often note that this trend had an important precedent in the late nineteenth and early twentieth centuries. This is certainly true in the monetary and financial sector (see McGrew, Chapter 10, and Hay, Chapter 11 in this volume). Cross-border flows of money increased dramatically in this earlier period and, according to some criteria, even surpassed those in the current era in significance for national economies. Some of these flows involved short-term capital movements that responded primarily to interest rate differentials between financial centres around the world. Others involved long-term capital exports from the leading powers. The United Kingdom, in particular, exported enormous amounts of long-term capital after 1870, sums that were much larger as a percentage of its national income than any creditor country is exporting today (James 2001: 12).

These capital flows were facilitated by the emergence of an international monetary regime that was also highly integrated, indeed, much more so than in the current period (Gallarotti 1995; Blytheway and Metzler, 2016). By 1914, the currencies of most independent countries and colonized regions around

---

BOX 8.1

The Theory of the Adjustment Process under the International Gold Standard

In theory, the international gold standard was a self-regulating international monetary order. External imbalances would be corrected automatically by domestic wage and price adjustments, according to a process famously described by David Hume: the 'price–specie flow mechanism'. If a country experienced a balance-of-payments deficit, Hume noted, gold exports should depress domestic wages and prices in such a way that the country's international competitive position—and thus its trade position—would be improved. Hume's model assumed that most domestic money was gold coins, but the domestic monetary system of most countries on the gold standard during the late nineteenth and early twentieth centuries was dominated by fiduciary money in the form of bank notes and bank deposits.

In this context, the monetary authority that issued notes and regulated the banking system had to simulate the automatic adjustments of the gold standard by following proper 'rules of the game'. In the event of a trade deficit, it was expected to tighten monetary conditions by curtailing the issue of notes and raising interest rates. The latter was designed not just to induce deflationary pressures (by increasing the cost of borrowing), but also to attract short-term capital flows to help finance the payments imbalance while the underlying macroeconomic adjustment process was taking place. In practice, however, historians of the pre-1914 gold standard note that governments did not always follow these 'rules of the game', and the financing of, and adjustment to, payments imbalances did not always take place in the automatic manner that the theory of the gold standard anticipated (e.g. De Cecco 1974; Eichengreen 1985; Bryan 2010).

---

the world were linked to the same **gold standard** (see Box 8.1). The result was a fixed exchange rate regime with an almost global reach. Indeed, some European countries went even further, to create regional 'monetary unions' in which the currencies of the member countries could circulate in each other's territory. A high-level international conference was even held in 1867 to consider the possibility of a worldwide 'monetary union' of this kind. As the scramble for colonies intensified after 1870, many imperial powers also often encouraged the circulation of their currencies in the newly acquired colonies during this period (Helleiner 2003: chs 6, 8). These currency unions and imperial currency blocs made economic transactions within each union or bloc easier to conduct.

The end of globalization

What can we learn from this era in our efforts to understand the political foundations of international money and finance? Perhaps the most interesting lesson is the fact that this globally integrated financial and monetary order did not last. In the contemporary period, globalization is sometimes said to be irreversible. Studying the fate of this earlier globalization trend reminds us to be more cautious. In particular, it highlights the importance of the *political* basis of international money and finance.

The first signs of disintegration came during the First World War, when cross-border financial flows diminished in Europe and many countries abandoned the gold standard allowing their currencies to fluctuate in value vis-à-vis each other. After the war ended, there was a concerted effort—led by the United Kingdom and the United States—to restore the pre-1914 international monetary and financial order, and this initiative was initially quite successful. Many countries rejoined the gold standard during the 1920s, and international capital flows—both short-term and long-term—resumed on a very large scale by the late 1920s (Pauly 1997: ch. 3).

But this success was short-lived. In the early 1930s, a major international financial crisis triggered the collapse of both the international gold standard and international lending, contributing to what Harold James (2001) has called 'the end of globalization' in that era. The international monetary and financial system broke up into a series of relatively closed currency blocs. Within each bloc, international movements of capital continued and currencies were usually fixed in value vis-à-vis each other. But between the blocs, large-scale international lending diminished and flows of capital were often regulated tightly by new government controls ('capital controls'). The value of currencies between the blocs also fluctuated considerably for much of the decade and some governments introduced fully fledged exchange controls which restricted private actors from converting the national currency into other currencies freely.

Hegemonic stability theory

What explains this dramatic change in the nature of the international monetary and financial regime? A prominent explanation within international political economy (IPE) scholarship attributes the transformation to a change in the distribution of power among states within the international monetary and financial arena (see e.g. Kindleberger 1973). According to this **hegemonic stability** theory, the pre-1914 international financial and monetary regime remained stable as long as British hegemonic leadership sustained it. Before the First World War, the United Kingdom's currency, sterling, was seen to be 'as good as gold' and it was used around the globe as a world currency. Britain was also the largest creditor to the world and London's financial markets held a pre-eminent place in global finance. The United Kingdom's capital exports helped to finance global payments imbalances and they were usefully counter-cyclical; that is, foreign lending expanded when the UK entered a recession, thus compensating foreign countries for the decline in sales to the UK. During international financial crises, the Bank of England is also said to have played a leadership role in stabilizing markets through lender-of-last-resort activities (see Pauly, Chapter 9 in this volume).

After the First World War, however, the United Kingdom lost its ability to perform its leadership role in stabilizing the global monetary and financial order. The United States replaced it as the lead creditor to the world economy, and the US dollar soon emerged as the strongest and most trustworthy world currency. New York also began to rival London's position as the key international financial centre. In these new circumstances, the United States might have taken on the kind of leadership role that the United Kingdom had played before the war. But it proved unwilling to do so because of isolationist sentiments and domestic political conflicts between internationally orientated and more domestically focused economic interests (Frieden 1988). The resulting leadership vacuum is blamed for the instability and eventual breakdown of the gold standard and integrated financial order during the interwar period.

Hegemonic stability theorists criticize several aspects of US behaviour during the 1920s and early 1930s. Its capital exports during the 1920s were pro-cyclical; they expanded rapidly when the US economy was booming, but then came to a sudden stop in the late 1920s, just as the growth of the US economy was slowing down. The collapse of US lending generated **balance-of-payments** crises for many foreign countries that had relied on US loans to cover their external payments deficits. The United States then exacerbated these countries' difficulties by raising tariffs against imports with the passage of the 1930 Smoot–Hawley Act. As confidence in international financial markets collapsed in the early 1930s, the US also refused to take on the role of international lender-of-last-resort, or even to cancel the war debts that were compounding the crisis.

Changing domestic political conditions

This interpretation of the evolution of the international monetary and financial system from the pre-1914 period into the interwar period is not universally accepted (see e.g. Calleo 1976; Eichengreen 1992; Simmons 1994). A particularly important critique has been that the transformation of the international financial and monetary system was generated more by a change in the distribution of power *within* many states than between them. According to this perspective, the stability of the pre-1914 international monetary and financial order was dependent on a very specific domestic political context: governments were strongly committed to the classical liberal idea that domestic **monetary policy** should be geared to the external goal of maintaining the convertibility of the national currency into gold at a fixed rate.

This commitment stemmed not just from liberal ideology, but also from the fact that governments before 1914 were less responsive to domestic popular pressures. Deflationary policies required to maintain the fixed currency peg in the face of a trade deficit or capital outflows could be very painful for domestic groups, particularly the poor whose wages were forced downwards (or who experienced unemployment if wages did not fall). These policies were politically viable only because many low-income citizens had little voice in the national political arena. In most countries, the electoral franchise remained narrow before 1914. In many countries, central banks were not even public bodies in this period, and in colonial or peripheral regions, foreign interests often controlled monetary authorities.

After the First World War, the domestic political order was transformed in many independent states. The electoral franchise widened, the power of labour grew, and there was increasing support for more interventionist economic policies. These changes generated political pressures for monetary policy to be geared more towards domestic goals, such as addressing domestic unemployment, rather than the goal of maintaining external convertibility of the currency into gold. As governments ceased to play by the 'rules of the game', the 'self-regulating' character of the gold standard began to break down (see Box 8.1). Short-term international financial flows also became more volatile and speculative, as investors no longer had confidence in governments' commitment to maintain fixed rates. Faced with these new domestic pressures, central banks also found it more difficult to cooperate in ways that promoted international monetary and financial stability.

In the context of the international financial crisis and Great Depression of the early 1930s, many governments then chose simply to abandon the international gold standard altogether in order to escape its discipline. In countries facing external payments deficits, the depreciation of the national currency provided a quicker, less painful, method for lowering the country's wages and prices vis-à-vis those in foreign countries in order to boost exports and curtail imports. Abandoning the international gold standard also allowed many governments to insulate their country from deflationary pressures emanating from the US at this time. In addition, a floating exchange rate provided governments with greater national policy autonomy to pursue expansionary monetary policies that could address pressing domestic economic needs. This policy autonomy was reinforced by capital controls that insulated countries from the influence of speculative cross-border financial movements. For this reason, it was not surprising to find such controls supported by John Maynard Keynes, the leading advocate of domestically oriented, activist macroeconomic management, who famously urged governments in the early 1930s to 'let finance be primarily national' (Keynes 1933: 758).

KEY POINTS

- In the late nineteenth and early twentieth centuries, a highly integrated global financial and monetary order existed. By the early 1930s, it had collapsed, and was replaced by a fragmented order organized around closed economic blocs and floating exchange rates.

- Some believe the reason for the breakdown of the pre-1914 order was the absence of a state acting as a hegemonic leader to perform such roles as the provision of stable international lending, the maintenance of an open market for foreign goods, and the stabilization of financial markets during crises.

- Others argue that the pre-1914 order was brought down more by a domestic political transformation across much of the world, associated with expansion of the electoral franchise, the growing power of labour, and the new prominence of supporters of interventionist economic policies.

The Bretton Woods order

If an integrated international monetary and financial order was to be rebuilt, it would need to be compatible with the new priority placed on domestic policy autonomy. The opportunity to create such an order finally arose in the early 1940s, when US policymakers began to plan the organization of the post-war international monetary and financial system.

Embedded liberalism

At the time, it was clear that the United States would emerge from the war as the dominant economic power, and US officials were determined to play a leadership role in building and sustaining a more liberal and multilateral international economic order than the one that had existed during the 1930s. The closed economic blocs and economic instability of the previous decade were thought to have contributed to the Great Depression and the Second World War. Because of the leading international economic position of many US firms, US officials also recognized that their country would benefit economically from a more open international economic order. But US policymakers also did not want to see a return to the classical liberal international economic order of the pre-1930s period. Instead, they hoped to find a way to reconcile their commitment to an open multilateral world economy with new kinds of government intervention in domestic economic life that had become influential in the wake of the Great Depression in the US and many other countries.

This objective to create what Ruggie (1982) has called an **embedded liberal** international economic order was shared by policymakers in many other countries, including Keynes who had emerged as the key policymaker directing UK planning for the post-war world economy during the early 1940s. Keynes and his American counterpart, Harry Dexter White, took the lead in producing detailed blueprints for the post-war international monetary and financial order whose content was discussed and modified in negotiation with officials from many other countries (and even colonies such as India) between 1942 and 1944. At a conference in Bretton Woods, New Hampshire, in July 1944, 44 governments then endorsed a final set of agreements (Conway 2015; Rauchway 2015).

Signatories to the Bretton Woods agreements committed to peg their currency in relation to the gold content of the US dollar, which was convertible into gold at a rate of $35 per ounce. This commitment to interfixed exchange rates reflected the widespread concern that floating exchange rates had been associated with beggar-thy-neighbour competitive devaluations, speculative financial flows, and currency instability that undermined international trade and investment. By pegging national currencies in this way, the Bretton Woods architects were also re-establishing an international gold standard—or, to be more precise, a 'gold exchange' standard or 'gold-dollar' standard. But several other features of the Bretton Woods agreements made clear that this commitment did not signal a return to the same kind of gold standard that had existed during the 1920s or the pre-1914 period.

A different kind of gold standard

To begin with, although each country agreed to make their currencies freely convertible into other currencies for current account transactions (i.e. trade payments), they were given the right to control all capital movements. While the Bretton Woods architects welcomed productive international investment flows, this provision was designed to enable governments to control speculative and 'disequilibrating' private financial flows that could disrupt stable exchange rates and national economic policy autonomy. The new support

for capital controls signalled a dramatic change of views towards private cross-border financial movements from the 1920s. As John Maynard Keynes put it, 'What used to be a heresy is now endorsed as orthodox' (quoted in Helleiner 1994: 25).

The Bretton Woods conference also established for the first time two public multilateral financial institutions to assume some aspects of international lending that had previously been left to private markets: the International Monetary Fund (IMF) and the **International Bank for Reconstruction and Development (IBRD)** (known as the World Bank). The IMF was to provide short-term loans to help countries finance their temporary balance-of-payments deficits, thus providing deficit countries with greater breathing space than they had had under the pre-1930s international gold standard (see Box 8.2). The IBRD was designed to provide and encourage long-term loans for reconstruction and development after the war, a task that the private markets were not trusted to perform well on their own. Support for the new 'development' function of the IBRD was particularly strong among those delegates from non-industrialized regions who made up well over half of the jurisdictions represented at the conference (Helleiner 2014a).

Finally, rather than trust the automatic self-regulating adjustments of the gold standard, the Bretton Woods architects assigned public authorities a more conscious and active role in the management of international economic imbalances. Particularly important was the fact that national governments were given the option of changing the peg value of their national currencies whenever their country was in 'fundamental disequilibrium' (a term whose precise meaning was left ambiguous). In other words, this was to be a kind of **adjustable peg** system, in which countries could substitute exchange rate devaluations for harsh domestic deflations when they experienced sustained payments deficits.

More generally, the IMF was to promote global monetary cooperation and encourage countries to, in the words of its charter, 'shorten the duration and lessen the degree of disequilibrium in the international balances of payments of members' (Article 1-vi). To discourage international economic imbalances, the IMF's lending capacity gave it some potential influence over deficit countries. Another provision in its charter—the scarce currency clause—provided a means for official pressure to come to bear on surplus countries; if the Fund's ability to supply a surplus

BOX 8.2

Quotas and Decision-Making in the IMF

While the World Bank can borrow from the private markets to fund its activities, the IMF's capacity to lend comes primarily from the contributions of member governments. On joining the IMF, all member governments pay a 'quota' to the institution that largely reflects their relative size within the world economy. The amount of money they can borrow from the Fund is determined by their quota size. Quotas also play a very significant role in determining voting shares within the Fund. All countries are allocated 250 'basic votes', but the bulk of their voting share is determined by their quota size. At the time of the founding of the IMF, 'basic votes' made up 11 per cent of total votes, but they have since fallen to a far lower share because of the entrance of new members and quota increases.

Quotas are reviewed at least every five years, and the relative share of various countries has changed over time in response to these reviews. The US quota share, for example, has fallen from more than 30 per cent of the total votes in 1944 to roughly 17 per cent today, while the shares of countries such as Japan, Germany, and Saudi Arabia have increased considerably. One of the key issues on the international policy agenda today is the need to adjust IMF quotas to reflect the growing economic significance of China and other rapidly industrializing countries.

The IMF is governed by its Board of Governors, which meets annually. Day-to-day decision-making, however, is delegated to the Executive Board, which meets several times a week. The Executive Board started with only 12 executive directors, with the five largest country contributors being assigned a single seat and other members being represented by 'constituency' groups. The number of executive directors has subsequently risen to 24 and, in addition to the five largest contributors (presently, the US, Japan, Germany, France, and the UK), single-country constituencies have been created for Saudi Arabia, China, and Russia.

country's currency was threatened (because of excessive demand for it from other members), the IMF could declare that currency 'scarce' and member governments would then be permitted to impose temporary restrictions on trade with that country.

Despite the success of the 1944 conference, it quickly became clear that some of its ambitions would not easily be realized. The Bretton Woods architects had hoped that the agreements they negotiated were building an international monetary and financial order of worldwide scope. But the Soviet Union—which had participated in the Bretton Woods negotiations—refused to join the system and Soviet allies then withdrew once the Cold War began. After the 1949 Chinese revolution, the People's Republic of China (PRC) was also outside the system because China—which had also participated in the Bretton Woods negotiations—was represented in the IMF and IBRD by the government in Taiwan. (The PRC would not join the IMF and World Bank until 1980, while Russia became a member of both institutions in 1992 after the collapse of the Soviet Union).

Even among the countries that remained members of the Bretton Woods system, the IMF and IBRD played only very limited roles for the first decade-and-a-half after the Second World War. Many countries also did not make their currencies convertible in this period, including most West European countries which did not restore current account convertibility

until 1958 (the Bretton Woods agreements had allowed for a 'transition' period during which countries could keep currencies inconvertible). These developments have led some historians to argue that the Bretton Woods system was placed in 'virtual cold storage' in this time (Skidelsky 2003: 125). It is worth noting, however, that during this period most governments outside the Soviet orbit were still committed to the other principles outlined at Bretton Woods: namely, support for capital controls, the gold exchange standard, and the maintenance of an adjustable peg exchange rate regime. Moreover, although the Bretton Woods institutions were sidelined, other bodies—particularly the US government, but also regional institutions such as the European Payments Union—acted in the ways that the Bretton Woods architects had hoped the IMF and IBRD would. Public international lending was provided for temporary balance-of-payments support, as well as for reconstruction and development. United States policymakers also encouraged international monetary cooperation and promoted 'embedded liberal' ideals when they were engaged in monetary and financing advisory roles in a number of places around the world (Helleiner 1994: ch. 3; 2003: ch. 9, 2014a).

During the heyday of the Bretton Woods order, from the late 1950s until 1971, the IMF and World Bank became more active lenders, although they had a less central role in the system than the Bretton Woods architects had hoped for. Governments also remain committed to the other key features of the order. What, then, became of the Bretton Woods order? In some respects, it seems to be still alive. The IMF and World Bank still exist (although some of their purposes have been altered, as described later) and their membership has widened to include almost all countries in the world (including the People's Republic of China and Russia which joined the institutions in 1980 and 1992, respectively); most countries' currencies are convertible for current account transactions; the dollar is still the key international currency; and the broader formal commitment to **multilateralism** has endured. In the following sections, however, I explore the key causes and consequences of challenges that have emerged to various features of the Bretton Woods regime with: the globalization of finance, the collapse of the gold exchange standard, and the move to a floating exchange rate regime among the major economic powers.

KEY POINTS

- The Bretton Woods Conference in 1944 created a new international monetary and financial order that was inspired by an 'embedded liberal' ideology and backed by US leadership.

- Governments joining this order committed themselves to: currency convertibility for current account payments, a gold exchange standard, an adjustable peg exchange rate regime, an acceptance of capital controls, and support for the IMF and World Bank.

- Some of the features of the Bretton Woods order were in place between 1945 and 1958, but this order reached its heyday between 1958 and 1971.

The globalization of financial markets

The globalization of private financial markets has been one of the more dramatic developments of the last few decades. Recall that the Bretton Woods architects endorsed an international financial order in which governments could control cross-border private financial flows, and public international institutions played a new role in international lending. Although the Bretton Woods architects had certainly hoped to revive productive private international investment

flows, few at the time expected the world we now live in which enormous sums of private capital flow around the world quite freely on a 24-hour basis.

Explaining financial globalization

How did we get from there to here? Technological developments have played a role as the growth of global telecommunications networks has enabled money to be moved around the world much more easily and cheaply than in the past. Market pressures have also been important. Private actors were encouraged to diversify their assets internationally by the increasingly volatile currency environment after the breakdown of the Bretton Woods exchange rate system in the early 1970s (see later). The dramatic expansion of international trade and multinational corporate activity in recent decades has also generated growing demand for private international financial services. Financial globalization was also fostered by growing competitive pressures within leading financial systems as well as various market innovations, such as the creation of derivatives products including futures, options, and swaps.

The globalization of finance was a product not just of these technological and market developments but also of political choices by governments to support the emergence of a more liberal environment for cross-border financial flows (Helleiner 1994; Abdelal 2007). The first step in this direction took place when the British government encouraged the growth of the 'euro-market' in London during the 1960s where international financial activity in foreign currencies— primarily US dollars in the early years—could be conducted on a largely unregulated basis. After the early 1970s, many governments then fully dismantled capital controls they had employed at various times during the post-war years. The United States and United Kingdom led the way, abolishing their national capital controls in 1974 and 1979, respectively. They were soon followed by other Organisation for Economic Co-operation and Development (OECD) countries. Indeed, by the 1990s, an almost fully liberal pattern of financial relations had emerged among wealthy 'Northern' countries, giving market actors a degree of freedom in cross-border financial activity unparalleled since the 1920s. Many poorer 'Southern' countries have also abolished capital controls, including many small jurisdictions—such as the Grand Caymans— that offered their territories as locations for 'offshore' international financial activity via loose regulatory environments (Palan, Murphy, and Chavagneux 2009).

What explains states' growing support for financial globalization? The increasing influence of more free market or 'neo-liberal' ideology among financial policymakers in this period played a part in some countries. Neo-liberals argued that removal of capital controls would increase individual choice and enable markets to allocate capital internationally in a more efficient manner. Many neo-liberals were also less sympathetic to Bretton Woods' 'embedded liberal' goal of protecting the policy autonomy of governments. From their standpoint, international financial markets could play a useful role imposing an external discipline on governments pursuing inflationary or fiscally unsustainable policies.

The liberalization of capital controls has also been seen by some policymakers as a kind of competitive strategy to attract mobile financial business and capital to their national territory (Cerny 1994). The British government's support for the euromarkets and its decision to abolish capital controls in 1979 were both designed to help rebuild London's status as a leading international financial centre in this way. The US support for financial liberalization (both at home and abroad) was also designed to bolster New York's international financial position, as well as to attract foreign capital to the uniquely deep and liquid US financial markets in ways that could help finance US trade and budget deficits. The smaller, offshore financial centres also saw the hosting of an international financial centre as a development strategy that could provide employment and some limited government revenue (from licences and fees). Once governments such as these had begun to liberalize and deregulate their financial systems, many other governments felt competitive pressure to emulate their decisions in order to prevent mobile domestic capital and financial business from migrating abroad. As their country's firms became increasingly transnational and had access to foreign financial markets, policymakers also worried that national capital controls were becoming increasingly difficult to enforce in an effective manner that was not costly to the national economy (Goodman and Pauly 1993).

Alongside governments' unilateral decisions to abolish capital controls, there have been efforts to codify a more liberal set of international rules to govern cross-border financial flows (Abdelal 2007; Moschella 2012). Some of these efforts have been successful, such as a 1988 European Union directive to liberalize capital controls among its members and a 1989 amendment to an OECD code which committed OECD countries to liberalize all financial flows. In the mid 1990s, a more ambitious initiative was launched by IMF management to overturn the restrictive Bretton Woods rules by assigning their institution the purpose of promoting financial liberalization and giving it jurisdiction over capital movements. But this effort was abandoned at the height of the 1997–8 East Asian financial crisis, which highlighted to many policymakers, including key figures in US Congress as well as many Southern countries, the potential risks associated with financial globalization. The way in which the crisis generated new scepticism towards the financial liberalization trend was also evident from the high profile decision of the Malaysian government in 1998 to reintroduce capital controls (Beeson 2000).

Although Malaysia's decision provoked very strong opposition from many Western policymakers and financial market actors, these responses to the East Asian crisis signalled that the enthusiasm for financial liberalization had passed its highpoint. The experience of the Global Financial Crisis of 2008 further undercut support, particularly among many Southern policymakers. It was widely noted that countries that had maintained capital controls—such as China and India—were often more insulated from the severe financial turmoil in US and European markets. When US and European authorities dramatically lowered interest rates during and after the crisis, countries such as Brazil and South Korea also reimposed various capital account restrictions to prevent large-scale financial inflows from driving up their exchange rates and/or generating domestic financial bubbles.

These moves elicited much less reaction in the leading financial powers than Malaysia's initiatives had a decade earlier, reflecting the growing scepticism of 'free market finance' after the crisis. Increasingly powerful 'emerging market' countries have also used their new influence in settings such as the G20 (see later) to press the IMF to be more supportive of the use of capital controls. After a formal review, the IMF declared in late 2012 its new institutional view that 'in certain circumstances, capital flow management measures can be useful' (IMF 2012c: 2). The statement was hardly a ringing endorsement of capital controls of the kind expressed at Bretton Woods, but it signalled a less doctrinaire position than existed on the issue a decade earlier (Gallagher 2014). At the same time, no major

Northern country has reimposed capital controls and global financial markets remain an enduring, central feature of the global political economy in the wake of the crisis (although the financial upheaval did encourage some retreat by market actors to the greater safety of domestic markets).

Implications for national policy autonomy

What have been the implications of the post-war globalization of finance? One set of implications is addressed in Chapter 9: the vulnerability of global financial markets to financial crises. A second set of implications relates to the concerns of the Bretton Woods architects. As noted earlier, they worried that a liberal international financial order would undermine their efforts to create a stable exchange rate system and to protect national policy autonomy. We will see later how financial globalization did complicate the task of maintaining fixed exchange rates. But what about its implications for the autonomy of national governments to pursue their preferred economic policies?

This question has generated much debate in the field of IPE. Some have argued that financial globalization has severely undermined national policy autonomy, since it gives investors a powerful 'exit' option to exercise against governments that stray too far from their preferences. Proponents of this view argue that this discipline is felt particularly strongly by governments that pursue policies disliked by wealthy asset holders, such as large budget deficits, high taxation, expansionary macroeconomic policies that risk inflation, or, more generally, policies that reflect left-of-centre political values (Gill and Law 1989; McKenzie and Lee 1991; Kurzer 1993; Cerny 1994; Sinclair 1994; Harmes 1998). These new constraints—what Thomas Friedman (2000) calls the 'Golden Straightjacket'—are said to help explain why many governments across the world have shifted away from these kinds of policies since the 1970s.

Southern governments are seen to be especially vulnerable to the discipline of global financial markets. This is partly because their financial systems are often so small relative to the enormous size of global financial flows. It is also because investors tend to be more skittish about the security of their assets in contexts where economic and political instability may be higher and where there may be a greater possibility of sovereign defaults. In this context, a sudden loss of confidence in a country's prospects among private actors in international financial markets can provoke a serious financial crisis in that country.

The international debt crisis of the early 1980s showed how a sudden stop in international private lending could generate severe sovereign debt crises across many Southern countries. At that time, the external discipline of the markets was reinforced by the IMF which stepped in to prevent defaults by offering emergency loans in return for tough austerity and structural adjustment programmes that promoted liberalization (programmes that were also backed by the World Bank). The IMF's tough conditionality and promotion of neo-liberal policy advice at the time was encouraged by Western governments that controlled the institution with their dominant voting share. It placed the Fund in a very different role from that envisioned by the Bretton Woods architects who had hoped this international institution would protect, rather than undermine, the policy autonomy of borrowing countries. The IMF's new role remained evident in further sovereign debt crises in the 1990s, but analysts have noted that its approach to policy conditionality has begun to change more recently, particularly after the 2008 Global Financial Crisis (Grabel 2011).

In addition to experiencing sudden stops in private international lending, Southern countries have also suffered from the fact that their wealthy citizens have taken advantage of the new global markets to park their assets in Northern financial markets. During debt crises, the size of this 'flight capital' from many debtor countries has often equalled or surpassed that of the country's external debts. In other words, these countries were often creditors to the world economy at the very moment that their governments were managing a severe sovereign debt crisis; if this flight capital could have been repatriated (or prevented from leaving in the first place), these countries would not have experienced the same kind of debt crisis and its associated loss of policy autonomy (Lissakers 1991; Helleiner 2001).

Other scholars suggest that these arguments about the declining policy autonomy of national governments are overstated. They point to open macroeconomic theory which explains that governments face trade-offs among an 'impossible trinity' of monetary policy autonomy, cross-border capital mobility, and stable exchange rates. Governments can achieve two of these goals, but never all three simultaneously (see Box 8.3). As they liberalized cross-border capital

BOX 8.3

The 'Impossible Trinity' of Open Macroeconomics

Economists have pointed out that national governments face an inevitable trade-off between the three policy goals of exchange rate stability, national monetary policy autonomy, and capital mobility. It is only ever possible for governments to realize two of these goals at the same time. If, for example, a national government wants to preserve capital mobility and a fixed exchange rate, it must abandon an independent monetary policy. An independent expansionary monetary policy in an environment of capital mobility will trigger capital outflows—and downward pressure on the national currency—as domestic interest rates fall. In this context, it will be possible to maintain the fixed exchange rate only by pushing interest rates back up and thereby abandoning the initial monetary policy goal. If, however, the government chooses to maintain the expansionary policy, it will

need either to introduce capital controls or to embrace currency depreciation (the latter may also reinforce domestic expansionary pressures by boosting exports and discouraging imports), thereby sacrificing one of the other goals within the 'impossible trinity'.

Historically, during the era of the gold standard, governments embraced fixed exchange rates and capital mobility, while abandoning national monetary policy autonomy. During the early post-1945 years, national policy autonomy and fixed (although adjustable) exchange rates were prioritized, while capital mobility was deemed to be less important. Since the early 1970s, the leading powers have sacrificed a global regime of fixed exchange rates in order to prioritize capital mobility and preserve a degree of monetary policy autonomy. Many governments within this system, however, have embraced fixed rates at the regional or bilateral level by using capital controls or by abandoning national policy autonomy.

movements, governments could still maintain monetary policy autonomy if they were willing to allow their national currency's exchange rate to fluctuate in value (Andrews 1994).

Governments could, for example, continue to pursue autonomous expansionary monetary policies as long as they were willing to accept a depreciation of the national currency. The importance of exchange rate policy in providing a degree of macroeconomic autonomy has also been highlighted in the case of capital flight from Southern countries. Crystal (1994) has shown how Latin American countries maintaining overvalued exchange rates have suffered much more serious capital flight than those that have not, and how government decisions to maintain overvalued exchange rates reflected domestic political constraints rather than the influence of global financial markets.

Other authors suggest that the disciplining effect of global finance on governments with high levels of government spending, high taxation, or a more general left-of-centre political orientation has also been exaggerated (see the discussion in Hay, Chapter 11 in this volume). Garrett (1995) has highlighted how many OECD governments have been able to use borrowing in international capital markets to finance increased government spending (see also Swank 2002). In a detailed study, Mosley (2003) found that international financial market actors were concerned primarily with national inflation rates and aggregate levels of fiscal

deficits; they did not worry about governments' overall level of spending, taxation, or political orientation when considering investment decisions (although this result was less true when they considered investments in Southern countries; see also Johnson and Barnes 2015). Other scholars have shown how states can continue to pursue 'developmental' goals by intervening in various ways within their domestic financial markets (Thurbon 2016). Still others have noted that the policy autonomy of the US, in particular, has been boosted by the globalization of finance for the reasons noted above: private investors around the world have been attracted to its uniquely deep and liquid financial markets in ways that have helped fund US current account and fiscal deficits (e.g. Strange 1986; Helleiner 1994; Schwartz 2009). In recent years, the US and other OECD governments have also launched efforts to try to reduce international tax evasion in various ways, including by applying pressure on offshore tax havens to cooperate with their initiatives (Palan and Wiggan 2014; Emmenegger 2015).

Some scholars have also argued that the discipline imposed by international bankers on Southern countries facing international financial crises should not be overstated. Argentina's experience in 2001–5, showed how debtor governments can exploit creditor divisions and place the burden of adjustment partially back onto international investors (Cooper and Momani 2005). The decisions of Malaysia in 1998 and of other Southern countries more recently to reintroduce capital controls have also demonstrated the enduring capacity of states to assert their authority over international flows of capital (Beeson 2000; Gallagher 2014). Many poor countries have also found their policy autonomy boosted by an aspect of the financial globalization trend that has received less attention from IPE scholars: flows of remittances from rich to poor countries. These flows have been growing rapidly in recent years, and they are sometimes counter-cyclical; that is, they increase when the recipient country is undergoing difficult economic times (see e.g. Kapur and McHale 2003).

Finally, the increasing significance of 'sovereign wealth funds' (SWFs) in global financial markets has also challenged the thesis that these markets are undermining government's policy autonomy. In this context, the analytical distinction between 'global markets' and 'states' has become blurred; the governments that control the largest such funds (especially Abu Dhabi, China, Kuwait, Norway, and Singapore) are significant market actors. Their policy priorities, rather than being constrained by global markets, now play a role in shaping the behaviour of those markets. For example, Norway's SWF is mandated to invest in ways that uphold various international social and environmental conventions that Norwegian politicians have prioritized. The overseas investments of SWFs may also be used to gain economic or political leverage abroad, or to bolster the power of the state that owns them in other ways (see the discussion in Helleiner and Kirshner 2009b; Lenihan 2014).

Distributive and environmental implications of financial globalization

Scholars of IPE have also been interested in some other implications of financial globalization that attracted less attention at Bretton Woods, one of these being its distributive impact within countries. Neo-Marxist scholars have argued that financial globalization has bolstered the power of an emerging, internationally mobile capitalist class, while eroding that of labour. The emerging transnational capital class has gained 'structural power' through its new ability to exit—or simply to threaten to exit—domestic political settings. This power has been used to reinforce neo-liberal ideology and a kind of 'internationalization of the state' that serves the interests of this new class (Gill and Law 1989).

Frieden (1991) has also highlighted new political divisions that have emerged within the business sector. While **transnational corporations** (TNCs) and owners of financial assets and services have gained from financial globalization, businesses that are more nationally based often have not. In a world of heightened capital mobility, he argues, these two groups are, in fact, increasingly at loggerheads over policy choices within the 'impossible trinity'. The former generally prefer exchange rate stability because of their involvement in international trade and finance, even if this involves a cost of abandoning monetary policy autonomy. Those in the non-tradable sector are inclined to defend monetary policy autonomy, even if this involves accepting a floating exchange rate.

Some scholars have also analysed the gendered implications of financial globalization (Singh and Zammit 2000; van Staveren 2002). To the extent that global financial integration has been associated with the retrenchment of the welfare state, the costs have often been borne more by women than men. Cutbacks to government spending in areas such as health, education, public transportation, and other social services frequently have the effect of increasing the role played in these areas by the unpaid sector of the economy, a sector traditionally dominated by women. When countries experience sovereign debt crises, other aspects of the burden of adjustment can also be strongly gendered. For example, during the 1997–8 Asian financial crisis, incomes in the informal sectors—where women were heavily represented—fell particularly sharply, and job cuts in the formal private sector often fell more heavily on women. Aslanbeigui and Summerfield (2000: 87, 91) also note how 'across the region, migrant workers, the majority of whom were women, were expelled from host countries' and they quote the World Bank's observation that 'child labour, prostitution and domestic violence' increased during the crisis. Other analysts have also highlighted the gendered nature of the global financial markets themselves which are constructed and legitimated by gendered narratives and discourses, and made up overwhelmingly of male traders operating with a culture that is hyper-masculinized (McDowell 1997; De Goede 2000; Prügl 2012; Griffin 2013; Brassett and Rethel 2015).

Another important issue concerns the environmental implications of global financial markets. Some analysts have argued that speculative and volatile international financial flows reward instant economic results and short-term thinking in ways that greatly complicate the kind of long-term planning that is required for the promotion of environmental values. During the East Asian financial crisis, for example, governments scrapped environmental programmes and there was an intensification of deforestation, mining, and other economic activities that put pressure on natural ecosystems (Durbin and Welch 2002). Two analysts working with the World Business Council on Sustainable Development have also argued that 'the globalization of investment flows is speeding the destruction of natural forests' as investors push firms to harvest forests for short-term windfall profits (Schmidheiny and Zorraquin 1996: 10). On the other hand, one powerful actor in global finance—the global insurance sector—does have a longer-term perspective that has led it to lobby for action on climate change in order to reduce the risk of future claims in this area (Haufler 1997; Paterson 2001; Thistlewaite 2012). A number of voluntary codes have also been developed in recent years by investor groups and banks to encourage firms to disclose environmentally related material risks. and these initiatives have received some official support, including from the World Bank in the case of the 'Equator Principles' and United Nations Environment Program through its Finance Initiative (Pattberg 2005; Wright and Rwabizambuga 2006; MacLeod and Park 2011). Some IPE scholars remain sceptical, however, of the effectiveness of these standards for addressing issues such as climate change (Harmes 2011).

KEY POINTS

- The globalization of financial markets has been driven, not just by technological and market pressures, but also by the decisions of states to liberalize capital controls that had been popular in the early post-war years.

- A hotly contested subject among IPE scholars concerns the question of whether, and to what extent, global financial markets have eroded the policy autonomy of national governments.

- Financial globalization has also had important distributive consequences along class, sectoral, and gender lines as well as environmental implications.

The collapse of the gold exchange standard and the future of the dollar

While the globalization of financial markets took place in a gradual fashion, the Bretton Woods' gold exchange standard broke down in a more sudden way when the United States President Richard Nixon unilaterally suspended the convertibility of the US dollar into gold in August 1971. Since other currencies had been tied to gold only via the US dollar, this 'Nixon shock' signalled the end of gold's role as a standard for other currencies as well.

This collapse of the gold exchange standard had in fact been predicted as far back as 1960, when Robert Triffin (1960) had highlighted its inherent instability. In a system where the dollar was the central reserve currency, he argued that international **liquidity** could be expanded only when the United States provided the world with more dollars by running larger current account deficits. But the more it did so, the more it risked undermining confidence in the dollar's convertibility into gold.

One potential solution to the **Triffin Dilemma** was to create a new international currency whose supply would not be tied to the balance-of-payments condition of any one country. Keynes had, in fact, proposed such a currency—which he called 'bancor'—during the negotiations leading up to the Bretton Woods conference. In 1965, the United States began to support the idea that the IMF could issue such a currency as a means of supplementing the dollar's role as a reserve currency, and **Special Drawing Rights** (SDRs) were finally created for this purpose in 1969. The SDR was not a currency that individuals handled; it was used only by national monetary authorities as a reserve asset for settling inter-country payments imbalances (and subject to certain conditions). Subsequently, however, IMF members refused to approve the issuance of significant quantities of SDR to enable it to play much of a role in the global monetary system.

During the 1960s, and in particular after the mid 1960s, US currency abroad grew considerably larger than the amount of gold the US government held to back it up. In one sense, the situation was beneficial to the United States: the country was able to finance growing external deficits associated with the Vietnam War and its domestic Great Society programme (which produced rising imports) simply by printing dollars. Indeed, the United States was doing much more than providing the world with needed international liquidity by the late 1960s; it was actively exporting inflation by flooding the world with dollars. In another sense, however, the country was becoming increasingly vulnerable to a confidence crisis. If all holders of dollars suddenly decided to convert the US currency into gold, the US would not be able to meet the demand. Another cost to the US was the fact that the dollar's fixed value in gold was undermining the international competitiveness of US-based firms. If major trading partners in Europe and Japan had been willing to revalue their currencies, this problem could have been addressed, but these governments resisted, preferring to keep their exports to the US market competitively priced.

A crisis of confidence in the dollar's convertibility into gold was initially postponed when some key foreign allies—notably Germany and Japan—agreed not to convert their reserves into gold (sometimes as part of an explicit trade-off for US security protection: Zimmermann 2002). But other countries that were critical of US foreign policy in this period—France in particular—refused to adopt this practice, seeing it as a reinforcement of American hegemony and the 'exorbitant privilege' that the US was seen to gain from issuing the world's leading currency (Kirshner 1995: 192–203). Private speculators also increasingly targeted the US dollar, especially after sterling was devalued in 1967. When speculative pressures against the dollar reached a peak in 1971, the United States chose simply to 'close the gold window' in order to free itself from the constraint on its policies that gold convertibility imposed (Gowa 1983).

The dollar's enduring global role

In the eyes of some observers, the breakdown of the gold exchange standard reflected declining US power, thus providing further evidence to support the hegemonic stability theory. Others, however, suggested US hegemonic power in the international monetary system remained and all that had changed was the country's willingness to lead (for example, Calleo 1976; Strange 1986). Defenders of the latter position pointed to the fact that the US dollar remained the unchallenged dominant world currency after 1971.

When US policymakers ended the dollar's convertibility into gold, some predicted that the US currency's role as the dominant world currency would be challenged quickly, since the dollar was no longer 'as good

as gold'. In fact, however, the dollar's central global role has endured up to the present day (Cohen and Benney 2014). It has continued to be the currency of choice for settling international economic transactions and for denominating international trade and investments across much of the world. Among countries that peg their currencies, the dollar is also the most popular anchor currency. In addition, the greenback has remained the most common currency in which most governments hold their foreign exchange reserves.

The US dollar's enduring central global position is a partly a product of inertia and the enormous size and significance of the US economy in the world. There are many 'network externalities' that reinforce the continued use of existing currencies, particularly when the issuing country is such a major player in the global economy; the more a currency is used, the greater the incentive for others to use it for convenience reasons. Some foreign governments have also continued to hold their reserves in US dollars and denominated their international trade in dollars because of economic and political ties with the US. Particularly important in explaining the dollar's enduring global role has been the fact that US financial markets have remained the most liquid in the world because of their depth, breadth, resilience, and openness to foreigners. This has made the holding and use of US dollars very attractive to private actors and foreign governments. Although some predicted that the yen and Deutschmark might challenge the dollar after 1971, neither Japan nor West Germany were willing and/or able to cultivate the kinds of domestic financial markets in which yen-denominated or Deutschmark-denominated assets could be held to rival their dollar-based counterparts (Helleiner and Kirshner 2009a; Chey 2012).

Emerging challenges to the dollar's dominant position?

Will the dollar's global role continue? Before the 2008 Global Financial Crisis, some scholars argued that the dollar's global status had become increasingly precarious. The country's large current account and fiscal deficits, combined with its growing external debt, raised concerns that foreigners might lose soon confidence in the currency. The fact that these deficits were increasingly financed by foreign governments such as Japan, Russia, and especially China (largely through their dollar reserve holdings) only reinforced concerns, suggesting that the dollar had increasingly become a 'negotiated' currency whose international status rested partly on political bargains that the US could make with its foreign official creditors. With the creation of the euro in 1999, the dollar was also seen to face its most serious post-war challenger, a currency managed by a conservative central bank dedicated to price stability and backed by a powerful and large economic zone with deep financial markets (see various chapters in Helleiner and Kirshner 2009a). As the crisis unfolded in US financial markets in 2007–8, prominent analysts predicted an imminent dollar crisis, triggered by foreign dumping of dollar assets, particularly after US policymakers responded to the crisis with dramatic interest rate cuts and larger fiscal deficits (Soros 2008).

In fact, however, support for the dollar from global investors and foreign governments endured throughout the crisis and even strengthened as the crisis intensified throughout 2008. Despite the US financial difficulties, the US Treasury bill remained the investment of choice for financial institutions, investors and governments scrambling for liquidity and safety (Reinhart and Rogoff 2009: 222). Foreign governments whose economies were heavily dependent on exports to the US—such as China's—also had good reason to continue to hold their large dollar reserves during the crisis to protect the competitiveness of their exchange rate, the health of external market for their products, and the value of their existing reserve assets. Other governments which had accumulated large dollar reserves to defend themselves against external financial pressures also had many reasons to maintain this war chest of 'self-insurance' given the global financial instability of the time (Helleiner 2014b).

The dollar also benefited from the failure of the euro to inspire more confidence at this time. The fragmented nature of European financial markets and the absence of a common fiscal authority in Europe ensured that no equivalent existed in the eurozone to the uniquely liquid and deep US Treasury bill market. Before the crisis, IPE scholars such as Cohen (2003) had argued that foreign confidence in the euro was also held back by uncertainties regarding the governance structure, and thus the broader political credibility of the whole initiative. The crisis that began in 2008 revealed these weak political foundations of the euro very starkly. Because the architects of the euro had failed to specify clear procedures for the prevention and resolution of eurozone financial crises, European

financial institutions facing distress were forced to turn to national governments for support, leading to questions about whether European financial integration and eurozone unity would unravel. These fears were only reinforced with the outbreak of the debt crises in the periphery of the eurozone which demonstrated further weaknesses in the political design of the euro (see below). Until major reforms have been undertaken to strengthen the eurozone's governance, the threat to the international role of the dollar posed by the euro will remain low.

What other challenges might the dollar face in the coming years? Analysts have increasingly focused on China as its economic size and significance in the world economy continues to grow. Speculation about whether its currency, the renminbi (RMB), might begin to challenge the dollar's international dominance has been encouraged by the sudden interest shown by the Chinese government in internationalizing the RMB in response to the 2008 Global Financial Crisis (Helleiner and Kirshner 2014). The crisis highlighted to the Chinese leadership the vulnerabilities associated with its dependence on the dollar, particularly those stemming from the fact that the vast bulk of its foreign assets are held in US dollar-denominated assets. Most powerful creditor countries in the past have lent abroad in their own currency in order to avoid exposure to the kinds of exchange rate risks which China now faces. While this vulnerability has left Chinese officials with strong incentives in the short term to defend the dollar in order to protect the value of its existing assets, it has also encouraged them to explore ways of reducing their dependence on the dollar over the medium term (Kirshner 2014). Promoting the RMB's international use will also reduce exchange rate risks and transaction costs for Chinese firms involved in international commerce. Since the crisis, Chinese authorities have engaged in a flurry of initiatives to promote the internationalization of the RMB, ranging from the removal of many of the controls that were previously imposed on its international use to the signing of bilateral currency swap agreements with many foreign monetary authorities that can help to encourage the growth of RMB use abroad (Liao and McDowell 2015).

How quickly could the RMB become a leading international currency? Because of the growing size of China's economy, some predict that the RMB is destined to take over from the dollar as the leading reserve currency as soon as the early 2020s (Subramanian 2011). But even those ambitious predictions are conditional on the Chinese government launching far-reaching financial reforms. As Eichengreen (2011: 7) puts it, if the euro is challenged by being a 'currency without a state', the RMB faces the opposite situation of being a 'currency with too much state'. The RMB is not yet even fully convertible. And even if it was, the attractiveness of China's currency to foreigners would be inhibited by the absence of well-developed, liquid, and open RMB financial markets that are backed by a stable legal infrastructure and property rights. Like the United States in the late nineteenth century, China's ability to emerge as an international monetary leader still lags very far behind its newfound industrial power (De Cecco 2009). It will depend on the politics of financial reform in China. While some groups within China favour the kinds of reforms that are necessary for RMB internationalization, those reforms also threaten to undermine the regulated financial system that has been core to the Chinese export-oriented state-led development model. They thus have powerful opponents in the Chinese political economy (Helleiner and Kirshner 2014).

Expanded role for the SDR?

Chinese officials have also begun to support the strengthening of the SDR's role in the international monetary system. In March 2009, Chinese central bank governor Zhou Xiaochuan (2009) released a prominent paper that, citing Keynes and Triffin, argued that the SDR should assume a larger role in the international monetary system to pave the way for the longer-term goal of creating a system centred on a 'super-sovereign reserve currency'. To promote the SDR's use, Zhou outlined various ideas to promote the SDR's use (e.g. the issuing of SDR-denominated bonds, the creation of a fund at the IMF where governments could swap their existing reserve currencies for SDRs) and he urged that the SDR's value be determined by a wider basket of currencies than the existing four: the US dollar (which was weighted at the time at 44 per cent of the currency basket), the euro (34 per cent), the yen (11 per cent), and sterling (11 per cent).

Zhou's ideas found considerable support among national policymakers from some other countries, including other large dollar reserve holding countries such as Brazil and Russia. The United Nations' Stiglitz Commission, tasked with investigating the Global Financial Crisis, also put forward some similar ideas in its 2009 report and it added that SDRs should be allocated on the basis of GDP or some measure of need instead of the existing method of using countries' IMF quotas (which ensures that new SDR allocations benefit most the wealthy industrialized countries who need SDRs least) (UN 2009a).

Other policymakers, including US officials, were more sceptical of Zhou's ambitious ideas, but they recognized the usefulness of the SDR for addressing an immediate short-term problem during the financial crisis at the time: the need to bolster the IMF's resources to help buffer countries from balance-of-payments shocks. With this goal in mind, the IMF membership as a whole backed in 2009 the first new SDR allocation since the early 1980s and also the largest at approximately SDR150 billion (US$250 billion). But its role remains a relatively minor one in the international monetary system: the new allocation raised the share of SDRs in the world's non-gold official reserves from less than 0.5 per cent to still only about 5 per cent (Williamson 2009). In the absence of more serious reforms, the SDR's role is likely to remain that of simply supplementing existing international reserve currencies for some time to come (Ly 2012; Helleiner 2014b). In November 2015, however, the IMF did approve the inclusion of the RMB in the basket of currencies that makes up the SDR's value, and it was given a weighting of 11 per cent, above that of the yen (8 per cent) and sterling (8 per cent) but below the euro (31 per cent) and the US dollar (42 per cent).

Consequences of the dollar's declining role?

It thus remains unclear thus whether and how the dollar's international role may be challenged in the coming years. If it were challenged in the future, however, what would be the consequences? To begin with, the United States would lose some benefits it has derived from the currency's status (Eichengreen 2011; Kirshner 2013, 2014). In addition to the international prestige that comes from issuing a dominant world currency, the US dollar's use abroad has produced extra **seigniorage** revenue for the US government (see Box 8.4). When foreigners hold dollar bills, they provide the equivalent of an interest-free loan to the US. According to some estimates, this seigniorage profit has totalled between $16 billion and $22 billion per year recently (Cohen 2008a: 258). To the extent that the dollar's international role generates higher foreign

BOX 8.4

What Is 'Seigniorage'?

Seigniorage is usually defined as the difference between the nominal value of money and its cost of production. This difference is a kind of 'profit' for the issuer of money. In medieval Europe, this source of revenue was often very important for ruling authorities. They could earn it either openly by adding a 'seigniorage' charge (above the normal mint charge that offset the cost of minting) when producing metallic coins, or more secretly by debasing their coin through a reduction of its weight or its 'fineness' (by increasing the proportion of non-precious

alloy). If the surreptitious strategy were to be detected by the public, its effectiveness would be undermined, as people would either not accept the coins or accept them only at a discount. In more modern times, metallic coins no longer dominate the monetary system, and governments now earn seigniorage also through the issuing of paper currency as well as indirectly through their regulation of the creation of bank deposit money. National monetary authorities earn seigniorage not just from the use of the money they issue by citizens within their borders; the international use of their currency will augment the seigniorage revenue they earn even further.

demand for its services (e.g. trade finance, foreign exchange business, the buying and selling of securities), the US financial sector also earns some 'denomination rents'.

The dollar's global role has also bolstered the US capacity to finance current account deficits as well as to deflect the costs of adjustments onto foreigners by depreciating its currency. During international political and economic crises, the US may also have benefited from a 'flight to quality' by investors in ways that boosted its macroeconomic room to manoeuvre (Kirshner 2009: 213). In addition, US authorities have been able to use the dependence of market actors on dollar-clearing networks to encourage worldwide cooperation with US regulatory initiatives (for example, with respect to tax or anti-money laundering regulations) as well as to enforce sanctions against foreign states (e.g. Emmenegger 2015). As the sole producer of the world's key currency, the US also plays a decisive role during international financial crises because of its unique ability to make advances of dollars to foreign governments or private institutions in distress (see Pauly, Chapter 9 in this volume). Foreign dependence on an international currency may also benefit the issuer by encouraging foreigners to identify their interests more closely with those of the issuing country (Kirshner 1995; Andrews 2006).

While these various benefits for the US may be eroded, the issuing of an international currency also comes with some costs that the US would no longer experience. US policymakers might regain some macroeconomic control that had been lost from the dollar's international role. They might also feel less of a burden of responsibility to maintain the stability of the international monetary system as a whole. The US

would also be less vulnerable to the selling of external dollar holdings as well as the overvaluation of its currency that can result from foreign demand for the dollar. In the wake of the 2008 crisis, some prominent US analysts also urged US policymakers to downsize the dollar's global role because it had enabled their country to live recklessly beyond its means and had encouraged a pattern of US growth characterized by large current account deficits, foreign capital inflows, and accumulating foreign debt (Bergsten 2009). Because the issuing of an international currency carries many such costs, some analysts have described it as more of an 'exorbitant burden' than a privilege (Pettis 2011). That judgement is not shared, however, by those groups in American society that experience the benefits of the dollar's international status directly, including those earning 'denomination rents'.

The erosion of the dollar's central global position would also have consequences for the world as a whole. Drawing on the interwar experience, supporters of the hegemonic stability theory might predict that the shift to a more multipolar currency order will generate a more unstable global monetary system. But the opposite may also be true. David Calleo (1987: ch. 8) has long argued that a world monetary order based on more 'pluralistic' or 'balance of power' principles may be more likely to produce stability over time than one based on hegemony. A hegemonic power, in his view, is inevitably tempted to exploit its dominant position over time to serve its own interests rather than the interests of the stability of the system. Then European Commission president, Jacques Delors, advanced a similar argument in defending the euro project in 1993; in his words, the creation of the euro would make the EU 'strong enough to force the

United States and Japan to play by rules which would ensure much greater monetary stability around the world' (quoted in Henning 1998: 565). More recently, Chinese officials have also highlighted benefits that they believe would flow from a more multipolar currency order (Chin 2014; Otero-Iglesias 2014). Even if we accept that a more pluralistic international monetary order may be more stable, however, the transition away from a dollar-centred order is likely to contain risks for the world economy and usher in broader geopolitical shifts (Kirshner 2013, 2014).

KEY POINTS

- In 1971, the United States ended the gold convertibility of its currency, and, by extension, that of all other currencies. The US decision reflected its desire to free itself from the growing constraint on its policies that gold convertibility was imposing.

- The US dollar continued to be a dominant global currency after it ceased to be convertible into gold in 1971 for a variety of economic and political reasons.

- The US dollar's global role may face new challenges over time, particularly from the euro and the renminbi, challenges that would have important implications for the US and international monetary system as a whole.

From adjustable pegs to floating exchange rates

Alongside the gold exchange standard, another feature of the Bretton Woods monetary order that broke down in the early 1970s was the adjustable peg system. This development took place in 1973, when governments allowed the world's major currencies to float in value vis-à-vis one other. The new floating exchange rate system was formalized in 1978, when a second amendment of the IMF's Articles of Agreement came into force. This amendment legalized floating exchange rates, and declared that each country could now choose its own exchange rate regime subject to the rule that each country should 'avoid manipulating exchange rates or the international monetary system in order to prevent effective balance of payments adjustment or to gain an unfair competitive advantage over other members' (Article 4.1(iii)).

The end of the adjustable peg system was partly triggered by the growing size of speculative international financial flows that complicated governments' efforts to defend their currency pegs. Equally important, however, was the fact that influential policymakers began to re-evaluate the merits of floating exchange rates. We have already seen how the Bretton Woods architects took a very negative view of the experience of floating exchange rates before the Second World War. Indeed, the drawbacks of floating exchange rates were deemed to be so obvious that there had been very few serious defences of them at the time. By the early 1970s, however, floating exchange rates had attracted a number of prominent advocates, particularly in the United States (Odell 1982).

These advocates argued that floating exchange rates could play a very useful role in facilitating smooth adjustments to external imbalances in a world where governments were unwilling to accept the discipline of the gold standard. The idea of using exchange rate changes for this purpose had, of course, been endorsed at Bretton Woods; governments could adjust their currency's peg when the country was in 'fundamental disequilibrium'. But, in practice, governments had been reluctant to make these changes because exchange rate adjustments often generated political controversy, both at home and abroad. Governments usually made these adjustments only when large-scale speculative financial movements left them no option. The result had been a rather rigid and crisis-prone exchange rate system, in which countries often resorted to international economic controls to address imbalances instead. A floating exchange rate system, it was hoped, would allow external imbalances to be addressed more smoothly and continuously, and without so much resort to controls.

It was also argued that floating exchange rates had unfairly acquired a bad reputation during the 1930s. From this perspective, there was no necessary reason why floating exchange rates should be associated with either competitive devaluations or a retreat from international economic integration, as they had been in the 1930s. Their role in encouraging destabilizing speculative financial flows during the 1930s was also questioned. Financial movements in that decade, it was argued, had been volatile, not because of floating exchange rates, but because they were responding properly to the highly unstable underlying economic conditions of the time (for example, Friedman 1953).

Has the floating exchange rate system performed in the ways that its advocates had hoped? The proponents of floating exchange rates were certainly correct that this exchange rate regime has not inhibited the growth of international trade and investment, both of which have expanded rapidly since the early 1970s. Floating exchange rates have undoubtedly often also played a useful role in facilitating adjustments to international economic imbalances. But critics have argued that this latter role should not be overstated.

From Plaza to Louvre

Some have echoed the argument made in the 1930s, that floating exchange rates have encouraged destabilizing speculative currency trading which has distorted currency values. It is certainly true that currency trading has grown very dramatically since the early 1970s; the size of daily foreign exchange trading increased from $15 billion in 1973 to $4 trillion by 2010 (Gilpin 2001: 261; BIS 2010). As foreign exchange trading has grown dramatically, exchange rates have sometimes been subject to considerable short-term volatility and longer-term misalignments. In these circumstances, floating exchange rates have often been the source of, rather than the means of adjusting to, external economic imbalances.

One of the more dramatic episodes of a longer-term misalignment involved the appreciation of the US dollar in the early-to-mid 1980s. Speculative financial flows, attracted by the US's high interest rates and rapid economic expansion after 1982, exacerbated the US current account deficit at the time, and generated widespread protectionist sentiments within the United States by 1984–5. This episode led the United States and other major industrial countries to consider briefly a move back towards more managed exchange rates. In September 1985, the G5 (the United States, the United Kingdom, the Federal Republic of Germany, France, and Japan) signed the Plaza Agreement which committed these countries to work together to encourage the US dollar to depreciate against the currencies of its major trading partners. After the dollar had fallen almost 50 per cent vis-à-vis the yen and Deutschmark by February 1987, they then announced the Louvre Accord, which established target ranges for the major currencies to be reached through closer macroeconomic policy coordination (Henning 1987; Funabashi 1988; Webb 1995).

This enthusiasm for a more managed exchange rate system between the world's major currencies proved to be short-lived. The three leading economic powers—the United States, West Germany, and

Japan—were not prepared to accept the kinds of serious constraints on their macroeconomic policy autonomy that were required to make such a system effective. Many policymakers in West Germany and Japan also argued that the US interest in macroeconomic policy coordination seemed designed primarily to reduce its own external deficit by encouraging changes in macroeconomic policy abroad rather than at home. This complaint had been heard before during the late 1970s, when the US policymakers last pressed Germany and Japan to coordinate macroeconomic policies. In both instances, US policymakers sought to address their country's external payments deficit by pressing Germany and Japan to revalue their currencies and pursue more expansionary domestic economic policies. These moves would enable the United States to curtail its deficit without a domestic contraction by boosting US exports.

Bretton Woods II

Arguments for macroeconomic coordination among the leading powers have emerged at other moments, most recently in the context of the growth of East Asian trade surpluses since 2000. In this instance, criticism has been directed not at speculative pressures in foreign exchange markets, but rather at many East Asian governments—particularly China—which are alleged to have deliberately undervalued their national currencies for competitive advantage in ways that have exacerbated global economic imbalances (and undermined the IMF rule that prevents exchange rates from being manipulated 'to gain unfair competitive advantage over other members'). They are accused, in other words, of not allowing their exchange rates to float enough. The rapid accumulation of foreign exchange reserves by these governments is cited as evidence that they have been intervening in foreign exchange markets for this 'mercantilist' purpose, purchasing foreign exchange (usually dollars) in order to keep the value of their currency low (for discussions, see Hamilton-Hart 2014; Steinberg 2015). Since China joined the WTO in 2001, its reserves grew particularly dramatically, expanding within a decade to a massive total of over $4 trillion by mid 2014 (of which a majority were estimated to be held in US dollar-denominated assets). Its reserve holdings became by far the largest in the world.

Some have argued that post-2000 East Asian accumulation of dollar reserves recreated the situation that existed in the 1960s, when Europe and Japan built up dollar holdings as a result of their efforts to keep their exchange rates competitive vis-à-vis the US under the Bretton Woods exchange rate system. Proponents of this viewpoint have argued that the contemporary 'Bretton Woods II' system might be quite durable because it provided the major participating countries with economic benefits (Dooley, Folkerts-Landau, and Garber 2003). East Asian countries have been able to support their export-oriented industrialization strategies, while the US gains cheap imports and low cost foreign funding—in the form of foreign dollar holdings of its large trade and fiscal deficits.

Others have been less sure of the political sustainability of this system. In East Asian countries such as China, the costs of holding such large reserves have become increasingly politicized, as citizens have asked why more of their country's savings are not being invested domestically. Protectionist pressures within the US also call into question that country's willingness to continue to provide an open market to exports from the new industrializing 'periphery'. Protectionist sentiments have also generated growing interest in the US Congress in measures—including trade restrictions—that could penalize countries that are deliberately manipulating their exchange rates to gain an unfair competitive advantage in international trade. Congress has also begun pressing for new international trade agreements to include provisions outlawing currency manipulation. These calls generated their first results in the negotiation of the Trans-Pacific Partnership whose final agreement was accompanied by a 'joint declaration' which promised that each macroeconomic authority in the member countries 'will refrain from competitive devaluation and will not target its country's exchange rate for competitive purposes' (TPP 2015: 1). Although these provisions (and others such as commitments to publicly disclose information about foreign exchange intervention and reserve data) were not legally binding, the US Treasury (2015: 1) trumpeted the fact that 'for the first time in the context of a free trade agreement, countries have adopted a Declaration that addresses unfair currency practices by promoting transparency and accountability'.

The G20 mutual assessment process

In the wake of the 2008 financial crisis, the G20 was another forum in which the issue of macroeconomic coordination arose because of concerns about

'global imbalances' and their role in generating the crisis. At the time of the 2008 crisis, it was clear to all that the G5 or G7 could no longer be effective bodies within which this issue was addressed since many of the key surplus countries were not members. The task fell instead to the new G20 leaders' forum which was created at the height of the financial crisis in November 2008 and included leaders from all the world's major economies (the G20 had already met regularly at the level of finance ministers and central bankers since 1999). During their first two summits, the G20 leaders focused primarily on international regulatory issues designed to minimize future crises (see Pauly, Chapter 9 in this volume). But at their third summit in September 2009, they widened the agenda, announcing that the G20 was now 'the premier forum for our international economic cooperation' and committing to a 'Framework for Strong, Sustainable and Balanced Growth'. This Framework includes a new 'consultative mutual assessment process' to evaluate whether national economic policies are consistent with shared goals outlined by the G20 as a whole.

The IMF (along with the World Bank) was assigned a role of supporting this process through analyses that build on its existing bilateral and multilateral surveillance activities. Those activities emerged after the Bretton Woods exchange rate regime broke down in the early 1970s. In an effort to maintain some semblance of multilateral order over the new floating exchange rate system, IMF members assigned the institution a new mandate to 'exercise firm surveillance over the exchange rate policies of members' under the second amendment to its charter that came into effect in 1978 (quoted in Pauly 1997: 105). The IMF's 'surveillance' activities quickly became an important part of its overall operations, focusing initially primarily on bilateral consultations with individual member countries but with more focus on multilateral surveillance in recent years.

Some hope that the new G20 mutual assessment process will reinvigorate the kind of multilateral exchange rate management and macroeconomic coordination that characterized the Plaza to Louvre period. But the fundamental political challenge identified at Bretton Woods of reconciling countries' desire for national policy autonomy with their commitment to open multilateral world economy remains. And it is now being met in a context which is less 'hegemonic' than the early post-war years, raising new political challenges.

The creation of the euro

Although international efforts to coordinate the relationship between the values of the world's major currencies have been limited since the early 1970s, some governments have moved to create stable monetary relations in smaller bilateral and regional contexts. The most politically charged and elaborate initiative has taken place in Europe. At the time of the breakdown of the Bretton Woods exchange rate system, a number of the countries of the European Community (EC) attempted to stabilize exchange rates among themselves. These initial efforts were followed by the creation of the European Monetary System (EMS) in 1979, which established a kind of 'mini-Bretton Woods' adjustable peg regime in which capital controls were still widely used and financial support was provided to protect each country's currency peg vis-à-vis other European currencies (Mourlon-Druol 2012). Then, with the Maastricht Treaty in 1991, most members of European Union went one step further to commit to a full monetary union in 1999.

The long-standing resistance of many European governments to intra-European floating exchange rates stemmed partly from worries that exchange rate volatility and misalignments would disrupt their efforts to build a closer economic community. Exchange rate instability was deemed to be disruptive, not only to private commerce, but also to the complicated system of regional public payments within Europe's important Common Agricultural Policy. But why go so far as to abandon national currencies altogether in 1999?

One answer is that the adjustable peg system of the EMS became unsustainable after European governments committed themselves to abolish capital controls in 1988. The latter decision left European currency pegs vulnerable to increasingly powerful speculative financial flows, a fact demonstrated vividly in the 1992–3 European currency crisis. By committing to a monetary union, they eliminated the possibility of future intra-regional exchange rate crises altogether.

Some policymakers outside of Germany also saw the currency union as a way to import the German central bank's anti-inflationary monetary policy. Like the German Bundesbank, the new European central bank was given a strict mandate to pursue price stability as its primary goal. For neo-liberal policymakers, whose influence had been growing across Europe, this mandate promised an end to activist national monetary policies which were often associated with inflation (McNamara 1998). Some neo-liberals also hoped that the euro, by eliminating the possibility of national devaluations, might encourage greater price and wage flexibility within national economies as workers and firms were forced to confront the impact of external economic 'shocks' in a more direct fashion.

Interestingly, for a related reason, some European social democrats and unions saw the euro as an opportunity to reinvigorate national corporatist social pacts in which cooperative wage bargaining, employment friendly taxation schemes, and other social protection measures could assume a key role in the process of adjusting to external economic shocks. Because the euro could protect a country from speculative currency attacks, some of these interests also saw monetary union as creating a more stable macroeconomic environment in which progressive supply-side reforms could be undertaken to promote equity, growth, and employment. In some countries, adopting the euro was also seen as a way to lower domestic interest rates by reducing risk premiums that the markets were imposing, a result that improved governments' budgetary positions and prevented cuts to the welfare state. Some on the left also hoped that the euro project might eventually help to dilute the monetary influence of the neo-liberal Bundesbank across Europe, and encourage coordinated EU-wide expansionary fiscal policies (Josselin 2001; Notermans 2001).

The monetary union project also had a broader political meaning. In addition to challenging the US dollar's international role, the creation of the euro has been seen as an important symbol of the process of fostering ever-closer European cooperation. Many analysts also argue that the decision to create the euro was linked to a broader political deal between Germany and other European countries at the time of the Maastricht Treaty. Many European countries—especially France—had become increasingly frustrated by the domination of the European monetary system by the German Bundesbank, and they pressed for European and Monetary Union (EMU) as a way to dilute its influence. Germany is said to have accepted EMU when it came to be seen as a trade-off for European (and especially French) support for German reunification in 1989 (see, for example, Kaltenthaler 1998).

Crisis of the euro

The Global Financial Crisis of 2008 acted as a catalyst to expose weaknesses in the euro's design. We have already noted the absence of clear rules for resolving financial crises in the eurozone. But it was also clear from the start that the eurozone was not what economists call an 'optimum currency area' and that its architecture did not make adequate provisions for adjustments to intra-zone payments imbalances (see Box 8.5). During the first decade of the euro's existence, Germany accumulated large surpluses while payments deficits emerged in a number of poorer eurozone countries in response to differing rates of productivity growth, asymmetric shocks, and other diverging economic trends. Within large national currency zones such as the United States or Canada, imbalances of this kind between regions of the country are paved over by mechanisms such as labour migration and large fiscal transfers from the national government. In the eurozone, however, large labour migration was unlikely and no Europe-wide authority exists with a mandate to mobilize large-scale fiscal transfers of this kind (Cohen 2012).

A monetary union could still function effectively if countries adjusted to imbalances through wage and price flexibility, as under the gold standard. As noted above, many designers of the euro had in fact hoped it would encourage such flexibility with deficit countries being forced to adjust through lower wages and prices. But those kinds of adjustments are slow, painful, and politically difficult in an era of mass democracy, particularly in the absence of strong national corporatist arrangements (Johnston 2016). Many deficit countries found it easier simply to finance payments deficits through private and public borrowing from investors outside their country. Indeed, the euro's creation was accompanied by large capital flows from surplus to deficit countries that often financed domestic consumption booms, property bubbles and/or government deficit spending that only contributed to the country's payments problems as well as to high levels of private and/or public debt.

The 2008 Global Financial Crisis brought this external borrowing to a halt, exposing the underlying payments imbalances as well as unsustainable levels of private and/or public debts in a number of countries. The severe economic downturn only contributed further to the difficulties of servicing debts, particularly for governments who saw tax revenues collapse and spending increase (including for bank bailouts). Greece was the first eurozone country to experience a severe debt crisis, but others (e.g. Ireland, Portugal, Spain, Italy) soon experienced troubles too, as private investors reacted to the new context as well as to the slow and bumbling European management of the crisis.

In this context, the eurozone has faced a set of major challenges. One has been to solve the immediate sovereign debt crises of a number of its poorer members and the associated problems among European banks.

BOX 8.5

Monetary Unions and the Theory of Optimum Currency Areas

The theory of optimum currency areas was first developed by the Nobel Prize-winning economist, Robert Mundell (1961), to evaluate the pros and cons of forming a monetary union among a selected group of countries. While assuming the union will produce microeconomic benefits in the form of lower transaction costs for cross-border commerce, the theory focuses its analytical attention on the potential macroeconomic costs associated with abandoning the exchange rate as a tool of macroeconomic adjustment. If these costs are low, the region is said to approximate more closely an 'optimum currency area' that should be encouraged to create a monetary union.

To evaluate how significant these costs are in each regional context, the theory examines a number of criteria. If selected countries experience similar external shocks, for example, the theory notes that they are more likely to be good candidates for monetary union, since they will each have less of a need for an independent exchange rate. Even if they experience asymmetric shocks, the macroeconomic costs of abandoning national exchange rates may still be low if wages and prices are very flexible within each country, if labour is highly mobile between countries, or if there are mechanisms for transferring fiscal payments among the countries. Each of these conditions would enable adjustments to be made to external shocks in the absence of an exchange rate.

The strategy chosen has relied heavily on austerity programmes and liberalizing structural reforms, an approach reminiscent of the era of the gold standard and one with major distributional consequences both within and between eurozone countries (Blyth 2013; Blyth and Matthijs 2015; Matthijs and McNamara 2015). At the same time, if the euro is to flourish, its member countries must also address the flaws in its governance that have been so bluntly revealed, including the need for region-wide financial regulation and supervision, clearer provisions for the extension of emergency liquidity, and closer fiscal cooperation (including not just larger fiscal transfers but also the issuing of common eurozone debt). In the words of McNamara (2015), what is needed is a more 'embedded currency area'. These reforms have many supporters in Europe and some initiatives have already emerged from the crisis experience that point in these directions, but they require more pooling of sovereignty, which also generates political resistance of various kinds across the continent (Cohen 2012).

The outcomes of these political battles will shape not just the future of Europe. They will also influence the evolution of the international monetary system as a whole. A more politically consolidated and stronger eurozone would accelerate the move towards a more multipolar currency order.

Currency unions elsewhere?

The trajectory of the eurozone may also influence discussions about regional monetary cooperation elsewhere. The euro's creation in 1999 triggered considerable policy and scholarly debate about the prospects of closer monetary cooperation in other regions. Some monetary unions already exist in other regions such as the CFA (Communauté Financière Africaine) franc zone involving many former French colonies in West and Central Africa. Its members chose at independence to maintain a colonial monetary union created by France and its evolution has continued to be shaped by the power and political interests of France in the post-colonial context (Stasavage 2003).

At the time of the euro's creation, there was a brief debate about constructing a monetary union either in North America or the Americas as a whole based on the US dollar. Two countries that were already extensively dollarized—Ecuador and El Salvador—introduced the US dollar as their national currency, in 2000 and 2001, respectively, but the idea of formal **dollarization** attracted little serious political support elsewhere. Most governments were very wary of abandoning the exchange rate tool of adjustment in the absence of any alternative adjustment mechanisms such as free labour movement to and from the US, or arrangements for inter-country fiscal transfers. The high costs of relying on wage and price flexibility alone to maintain a currency peg to the US dollar were also demonstrated very vividly by Argentina's deflation of the late 1990s that contributed to its spectacular financial crisis of 2001 (Blustein 2005). In addition, US policymakers made it clear that the US Federal Reserve would not offer dollarized countries any role in its decision-making, extend lender-of-last-resort support to their banks, or even share seigniorage revenue with them. While European countries have shared sovereignty in creating the euro, countries in the Americas had only the unattractive option of becoming a monetary dependency (Helleiner 2006).

There has also been some talk of monetary unions in the East Asian region in recent years. This discussion builds on initiatives to foster closer monetary and financial cooperation in the wake of the 1997–8 East Asian financial crisis. The crisis exposed the vulnerability of the region to outside market and political pressures, encouraging policymakers from China, Japan, South Korea, and the ASEAN (Association of South East Asian Nations) countries to explore ways to boost their collective monetary and financial independence. The first major cooperative venture of this 'ASEAN + 3' grouping was the Chiang Mai Initiative, created in 2000 to provide short-term financial assistance to member countries suffering from balance-of-payments crises. The initial bilateral swap network was soon transformed under the Chiang Mai Initiative Multilateralization initiative into $120 billion multilateral fund that opened in 2010 (and whose size was doubled to $240 billion in 2012), accompanied in 2011 by a new region-wide economic surveillance operation. In 2003, they also created the Asian Bond Markets Initiative, which seeks to encourage East Asian savings to be reinvested in the region. In 2006, alongside these initiatives, ASEAN + 3 countries backed the creation of an Asian Currency Unit (ACU) whose value is made up of a weighted average of a basket of the region's currencies. Modelled on the European Currency Unit (ECU) that was a precursor to the euro, supporters hope the ACU could reduce the influence of the dollar and bolster monetary cooperation by acting as a unit of account for public and private actors in the region. While this initiative is important, the prospect of a fully fledged East Asian monetary union any time soon is considered remote by most observers. In addition to the usual concerns about monetary sovereignty, this initiative—like all the others—would be complicated by a difficult relationship between Japan and China, each of which appears to have leadership aspirations in this area (Katada 2011; Grimes 2015).

Even if the creation of new monetary unions in East Asia and elsewhere seems unlikely, the closer financial cooperation in East Asia signals the growing decentralization of the balance-of-payments lending role that the IMF was assigned at Bretton Woods. The CMIM has retained a strong link to the IMF: the majority of the funds can be access only if a country has an IMF programme in place (Grimes 2015). Other multilateral funds with partial links to the IMF have been created elsewhere, such as the $100 billion Contingent Reserve Arrangement created by the BRICs (Brazil, Russia, India, China and South Africa) in 2014. This decentralization trend is being intensified by trends in the field of development lending where the creation of new institutions such as the BRICs' New Development Bank and the Chinese-led Asian Infrastructure Investment Bank in 2014-15 are complementing the World Bank's role. This trend is both responding to and reinforcing the broader decentralization of power in the global economy, as well as discontent with lack of reform of the Bretton Woods institutions among emerging powers and their increasingly ambitious financial statecraft (Armijo and Katada 2014, 2015; Wang 2014).

KEY POINTS

- The adjustable peg exchange rate regime of Bretton Woods was replaced in 1973 by a system of floating exchange rates between the currencies of the leading economic powers. The change was caused by heightened capital mobility and by a reconsideration of the merits of floating exchange rates among leading policymakers, particularly in the United States.

- Floating exchange rates have performed an important role in facilitating balance-of-payments adjustments, but critics argue that they have also been subject to short-term volatility and longer-term misalignments.

- There have been occasional intergovernmental efforts since the 1970s to manage the relationship between

the values of the world's major currencies through macroeconomic coordination. The most recent has been driven by a desire to address global imbalances that arose in the years leading up to the 2008 Global Financial Crisis.

- Since the breakdown of the Bretton Woods exchange rate system, there have also been initiatives to create more stable monetary relations at the regional level, most notably in Europe where cooperation culminated in the creation of a monetary union in 1999. Political prospects for the creation of regional monetary unions soon in other regions such as the Americas or East Asia are remote, but other kinds of more decentralized multilateral financial cooperation are growing.

Conclusion

The international monetary and financial system has undergone three important transformations since the late nineteenth century, in response to changing economic and political conditions. During the interwar years, the global integrated monetary and financial order of the pre-1914 period broke down. At the Bretton Woods Conference of 1944, a new order was built on 'embedded liberal' principles. Since the early 1970s, the third change has been underway, as a number of the features of the Bretton Woods system have unravelled with the globalization of finance, the collapse of the gold exchange standard, and the move to a floating exchange rate regime among the major economic powers.

The emerging international monetary and financial system cannot be characterized in simple terms. The highly globalized nature of financial markets is reminiscent of the pre-1914 era, as are some of the neoliberal ideas that have become more prominent in policymaking circles. The floating exchange rate regime between the major powers, new challenges to the dominant currency's international role, and decentralization trends remind some analysts of aspects of the interwar period. The legacy of the Bretton Woods order also clearly lives on in the dollar's enduring global role, ongoing commitments to current account convertibility, the survival of the IMF and World Bank (even if their roles have changed), and the broader formal support for multilateralism (including the near-universal IMF and World Bank membership of the countries of the United Nations, just as the Bretton Woods architects had initially hoped).

Each of the recent transformations in the nature of the international monetary and financial system has had important consequences for the key question of who gets what, when, and how in the global political economy. Monetary and financial systems—at both the domestic and international levels—do not just serve economic functions. They also serve various political projects relating to the pursuit of power, ideas, and interests. For this reason, the study of money and finance cannot be left only to economists, who have traditionally dominated scholarship in this area. It also needs the attention of students of IPE who have an interest in these wider political issues.

 QUESTIONS

1. Is a hegemonic leader necessary for a stable international monetary and financial system to exist?

2. To what extent has financial globalization undermined the power and policy autonomy of national governments? Is financial globalization irreversible?

3. How important has financial globalization been in influencing class, sectoral, and gender relations within countries? What are its environmental consequences?

4. For how much longer will the US dollar remain the world's key currency? Is the renminbi likely to challenge its international status in the coming years? What are the costs and benefits of issuing an international currency?

5. Will the SDR ever become the dominant reserve currency in the world? What would be the costs and benefits?

6. Should the leading powers attempt to stabilize the relationship between the values of the major currencies? Should countries that manipulate their exchange rates 'to gain unfair competitive advantage' be penalized in some way? Should bodies such as the IMF or G20 play a more active role in fostering international macroeconomic coordination?

7. Has the creation of the euro been a positive move for Europeans? Should other regions emulate the European example, and are they likely to do so?

 FURTHER READING

Abdelal, R. (2007), *Capital Rules: The Construction of Global Finance* (Cambridge: Harvard University Press). A history of the changing norms regarding state control of cross-border capital flows in the post-1945 years.

Armijo, L. and Katada, S. (eds) (2014). *The Financial Statecraft of Emerging Powers: Shield and Sword in Asia and Latin America* (New York: Palgrave Macmillan, 2014). Analyses of the increasingly important role of emerging powers in international monetary and financial diplomacy.

Best, J. (2005), *The Limits of Transparency: Ambiguity and the History of International Finance* (Ithaca, NY: Cornell University Press). A history of the evolution of the international monetary and financial governance since Bretton Woods.

Cohen, B. (2015), *Currency Power: Understanding Monetary Rivalry* (Princeton: Princeton University Press). An analysis of the relationship between power and money by one of the pioneers of the study of the GPE of money and finance.

Frieden, J. (2014). *Currency Politics: The Political Economy of Exchange Rate Policy* (Princeton: Princeton University Press). An analysis of the politics of exchange rates from the gold standard era to the contemporary eurozone.

Johnson, J. 2016. *Priests of Prosperity: How Central Bankers Transformed the Postcommunist World* (Ithaca, NY: Cornell University Press). An analysis of the monetary dimensions of incorporation of ex-Communist countries into the global financial order after the end of the Cold War.

Kirshner, J. (ed.) (2002), *Monetary Orders* (Ithaca, NY: Cornell University Press). A collection that highlights the political foundations of national and international monetary systems.

Strange, S. (1998), *Mad Money: When Markets Outgrow Government* (Ann Arbor, MI: University of Michigan Press). A survey and critique of the international monetary and financial system from one of the pioneers of the study of the GPE of money and finance.

WEBLINKS

www.bis.org The website of the Bank for International Settlements. The Bank is the 'central bankers' bank' and it provides detailed analyses of international monetary and financial developments.

www.ft.com World's leading newspaper addressing global monetary and financial developments.

www.brettonwoodsproject.org The website of the Bretton Woods Project, a leading NGO concerned with the activities of the IMF, World Bank, and other international financial institutions.

www.new-rules.org The website of The New Rules for Global Finance, a leading NGO concerned with issues of international financial reform.

www.imf.org The website of the International Monetary Fund.

ONLINE RESOURCE CENTRE

For additional material and resources, please visit the Online Resource Centre at:
www.oxfordtextbooks.co.uk/ravenhill5e

9

The Political Economy of Global Financial Crises

Louis W. Pauly

Chapter contents

Reader's guide

The world economy today reflects an experiment involving, on the one hand, the opening and integration of financial markets and, on the other hand, the dispersion of political authority. The resulting governance challenges are nowhere clearer than in the circumstances surrounding financial crises spilling ever more readily across national borders. In the late twentieth century, most such crises began in emerging-market countries. In 2008, however, the experiment almost failed catastrophically when policy mistakes in the United States combined with an economic downturn to spawn a global emergency. This chapter explores the changing political economy of systemic risk assessment, crisis prevention, and emergency management as the experiment continues.

Introduction

Promoting **interdependence** among the economies of the world was a key strategic objective of the United States and its main allies after 1945. During the 1970s, the logic of interdependence was extended from real economies, where tangible goods are produced, to markets for capital and financial services, which were then entering a new era of expansion and liberalization (Helleiner, Chapter 8 in this volume). From that point on, reminiscent of the experience of global capitalism before the First World War, crises in national financial markets began to have cross-border consequences.

The collapse of the **Bretton Woods** exchange rate system in the early 1970s occurred in tandem with a broadening movement towards more open financial markets around the world. In fact, financial innovation and policy change had been gradually undermining the kinds of **capital controls** many countries had put in place during the 1930s and especially during the Second World War. Although economists still argue about the effect of capital market liberalization on the efficient functioning of real economies, liberalization policies certainly did make it easier for intermittent financial shocks to spread misery beyond the localities where they originated. Policymakers in the leading states did not want to repeat the worst experiences of the nineteenth century, when banking crises and economic depressions commonly coincided. But they eschewed re-imposing controls as they struggled to balance the objectives of efficiency and stability in more open and interdependent markets. **Financial intermediaries** and their clients found it easier and ever more important to diversify their balance sheets internationally. Economies across the industrial and developing worlds gradually became more reliant on the freer movement of both short and long-term capital. Dealing with financial crises, whether sparked by imprudent risk-taking, excessive public or private-sector indebtedness, or a host of other reasons, came once again to the forefront of statecraft.

As they did during the pre-1914 era of market openness, financial panics recurred with some regularity after the 1970s, and they now spread rapidly across both functional and geographic frontiers. Markets that were more integrated cross-nationally often exhibited the behaviour of a manic depressive. Periods of ecstatic euphoria were routinely followed by moments of black despair, marked by runs on banks and more recently, failures of 'shadow banks'—financial intermediaries of various sorts providing instruments roughly analogous to short-term bank deposits. In such situations, financial claims much in demand one day, that is, 'liquid' or easy to sell, suddenly attract no buyers. And without reliable financing, real economies begin to falter.

In the 1980s, crises in Latin American markets sent shock waves through the entire system. In the late 1990s, a financial panic spread rapidly from stock to bond to banking markets in East Asia, and then to their counterparts in Russia, Latin America, and eventually to Wall Street. Ten years later, a much more virulent emergency originated in American housing markets. Not only the experiment in international financial integration but the post-1945 world order itself seemed under threat as intermediaries and their clients around the world lost confidence in the future. Looming over economic policymakers in the United States and elsewhere under crisis conditions was the spectre of the terrible decade spanning the US stock market crash of 1929 and the start of the Second World War in 1939, when economic depression brought widespread unemployment and political extremism in its wake. Their desire to avoid repeating the experience prompted them to reinforce their core payment systems by extending implicit or explicit governmental guarantees to banks and bailing out intermediaries whose failure might have threatened those systems. In 1984, US government agencies took over the Continental-Illinois Bank, the largest bank collapse in American history to that date. Three and a half decades later, they and their counterparts in other advanced countries came to the rescue of much larger institutions around the world.

The idea that financial markets need to be regulated and supervised, both to stop the unscrupulous few from taking advantage of the naive many and to limit the 'moral hazards' that arise when financial managers think they will be bailed out when they make mistakes, is hardly new. The related idea that regulation and supervision are most effectively delivered at local and national levels has a long pedigree. Of more recent vintage is the libertarian insistence that financial markets, like other markets, work best when they are freed from government interference and when bail-outs are credibly forbidden. The ideological debate becomes vivid at moments of crisis. Doubts about the wisdom of the larger systemic experiment in financial liberalization and integration return to the surface. Changing sides in the debate is rare, so many were surprised in 2008 when Alan Greenspan, a libertarian who had recently retired as the head of the American central bank, conceded his 'state of shocked disbelief' that a system that for 40 years had been 'working exceptionally well' came very close to collapsing (Greenspan 2008). Greenspan's cherished belief, in fact, had many decades ago been subjected to withering criticism in the work of John Maynard Keynes and other sceptics, who considered financial markets, especially cross-border markets, to be inherently fragile. Much recent history supports the Keynesian view (Minsky 1986; Wade 1990; Skidelsky 2009; Rodrik 2011). That same history is also well marked by the human proclivity to forget.

The preceding chapter set out the broad context for understanding the changing monetary dimension of our contemporary global economy. This chapter looks in depth at the political economy of recurring financial crises therein. For students of international relations and international economics, such moments in time are worth considerable attention. They open a unique window on the strengths and weaknesses of the political foundations underneath globalizing markets. Those markets seem to promise prosperity and peaceful interaction among the world's still distinctive societies, but they do not by themselves guarantee such outcomes. The early chapters of the book drew

attention to the importance of international collaboration. Global financial emergencies demonstrate its difficulty and necessity when capital is able to flow freely across national borders.

Local politics, global markets

Financial markets exist to support the development of 'real' economies. The prices of most financial assets and liabilities continuously fluctuate. But rapid and severe fluctuations in the value of financial claims can disrupt the fundamental mechanisms through which goods and services are actually produced. In the countries currently lying at the heart of an integrating global economy, financial market ups and downs are typically quite constructive. Well-functioning financial markets may be viewed as a successful tool of policy, an instrument for achieving long-term political ends. When they promote growth and innovation, they can stabilize social orders, create jobs, and underpin prosperity (see Hiscox, Chapter 4 in this volume). There is little doubt that international capital flows in recent decades have facilitated expanding trade and even permitted large national deficits and surpluses to persist (Figure 9.1).

Economic resources are surely distributed and redistributed as financial prices move, but the process

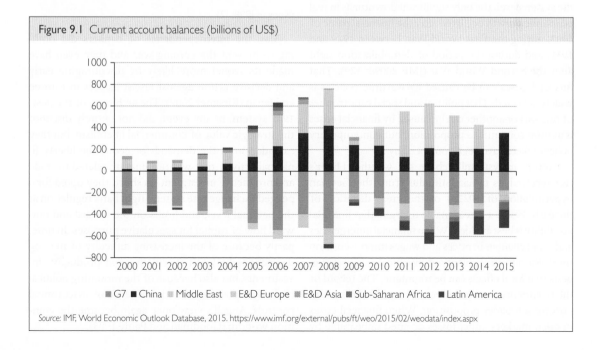

Figure 9.1 Current account balances (billions of US$)

G7   China   Middle East   E&D Europe   E&D Asia   Sub-Saharan Africa   Latin America

Source: IMF, World Economic Outlook Database, 2015. https://www.imf.org/external/pubs/ft/weo/2015/02/weodata/index.aspx

usually occurs in such a way that no particular group or groups with overwhelming political power become aggrieved enough to seek fundamental political and social change. In this regard, it is also worth noting that, with the exception of wartime, highly controlled financial markets tend to be correlated with authoritarian governments and official corruption. Not always, but very often, what economists call the 'repression' of financial markets correlates with deepening poverty. Economic inequality, conversely, is associated with both repressed financial markets and uncontrolled markets.

Some volatility in financial markets is quite normal and expected as buyers and sellers of claims recalibrate risks, respond to changes in tax and other policies, and seek new opportunities. A high degree of volatility may be the consequence of speculative excesses or a symptom of the necessity of deeper economic adjustment. Extreme market instability, however, suggests radical uncertainty about the future and tends to be socially and politically destructive. When markets are open and reliant on the movement of capital inward and outward, that destruction can quickly become systemic.

In modern history, global financial instability has been associated with human-made disasters of the first order. In fact, from the 1870s until today, the world economy has grown rapidly and consistently, except during periods overshadowed by financial crises. At the system level, the only significant downturns in real economic growth occurred after the financial panic of 1907, during the First World War, between 1929 and 1931, and during the period of demobilization right after the Second World War (IMF 2009d: 129). That financial crises can be caused by wartime policies is widely accepted. That political and social catastrophes of one sort or another can be caused by financial crises is a more contentious proposition, but contemporary policymakers have been convinced by it.

Even if analysts still debate, say, whether Hitler's rise received its crucial stimulus from the German hyperinflation of 1922–3 or the great deflation of the early 1930s, it is reasonable to argue that financial instability is best avoided. When financial emergencies and rapid changes in prices and wages impose costs on the politically weak, plenty of historical evidence suggests that local effects can be traumatic. The record of the twentieth century, moreover, provides strong support for a broader proposition. When financial crises in open markets inflict losses deemed unbearable by the politically strong and mobilized, they can set back the prospects for entire societies and shake the foundations of world order.

The global economy gradually and intentionally built up after 1945 rested on the promise of a widening circle of shared prosperity. International economic interdependence formed a core element in the strategy of systemic stabilization and development agreed by the victorious allies (Helleiner 2014a; Rauchway 2015). The central idea of a more secure world based on open-market principles was hardly novel. Mindful of the financial turmoil of the interwar period, however, system architects this time tried to limit the extent to which the strategy depended on unhindered capital flows across national borders.

In the background were the disappointed hopes of liberals like Norman Angell. In the halcyon days before 1914, he had famously opined:

> " Commercial interdependence, which is the special mark of banking as it is the mark of no other profession or trade in quite the same degree … is surely doing a great deal to demonstrate that morality after all is not founded upon self-sacrifice, but enlightened self-interest … And such a clearer understanding is bound to improve, not merely the relationship of one group to another, but the relationship of all men to other men, to create a consciousness which must make for more efficient human cooperation, a better human society. "

(Keegan 1998: 12)

Alas, the interdependence of bankers did nothing to prevent the coming war and may even have made its sequel more likely by discouraging early and decisive action against fascist leaders in Europe and Japan (Kirshner 2007). The architects of the post-1945 system, in any event, did not entirely discount the strategic value of commercial liberalism, but they excluded from the demands of economic liberty financial activity that was not directly related to trade and productive investment. In short, they opted for a pegged exchange rate system, tight bank regulation at the national level, and limits on the inward and outward flow of capital for speculative purposes. In time, partly because of the increasing difficulty of making distinctions between speculative and productive investments, but also because of the mounting political challenges posed by the maintenance of strict capital controls, Angell's view once again became the common wisdom (Goodman and Pauly 1993).

The die was actually cast in favour of the gradual loosening of restrictions over international capital movements when the main creditor in the post-war system, namely the United States, decided to rely on the private sector for the provision of the vast amounts of capital required to help rebuild broken economies and then to promote development in the rest of the world. Public funds, such as those allocated through the **Marshall Plan**, kick-started the process, but they were soon dwarfed by private capital flows in the form of export proceeds, foreign bank borrowing, private remittances, and **foreign direct investment**. That the latter eventually succeeded in building the global corporate structures through which most trade now flowed contributed much to what followed. So too did the rapidly rising offshore demand for and supply of US dollars described by Helleiner in the previous chapter. By the 1970s, changing official and private preferences in advanced industrial countries lay behind a series of explicit and implicit policy choices that cumulatively pushed the system back towards both more flexible exchange rates and freer international capital movements. These came to be mediated mainly by private financial institutions, which were permitted over time to engage in a widening range of commercial and investment activities.

Within 20 years, a similar shift in preferences would be well underway in much of the developing world, despite myriad local crises often characterized by sudden stops in necessary inward capital flows. Such crises provided regular reminders of the need for fairer rules in markets lacking solid legal foundations. **Property rights** had to be established, and adjudicated when conflicts arose. Predictable procedures had to be in place to handle inevitable bankruptcies with cross-border dimensions. Someone had to provide the degree of insurance necessary to limit the chance that specific debt defaults would cascade and engulf otherwise healthy borrowers and lenders. Some agency had to be entrusted with the responsibility and endowed with the capability to act as international lender-of-last resort. In light of the risk that the very existence of such ultimate insurance facilities could tempt potential beneficiaries to act imprudently, a risk that economists call 'moral hazard', this last-resort lending function had to be complemented by the official supervision of cross-border financial intermediaries. Finally, to deal with extreme instability, the lender-of-last resort had to be back-stopped by an investor-of-last resort, an investor capable in extreme circumstances of expropriating troubled cross-border firms or forcing them to merge with stronger

competitors. Even to list such requirements is simply to underline the absence of global government.

After 1945, all advanced industrial states clearly sought to regulate and supervise their national markets. Some gave the bulk of implementing responsibilities to their central banks, while some split them between central banks and official agencies. Most initiated some kind of deposit insurance scheme to ameliorate the risk of domestic bank runs, even as they tried to leave as much scope as local circumstances would allow for prudent self-discipline by market actors themselves. When no one else would provide sufficient funding to intermediaries whose survival was deemed vital to larger national interests, or in the extreme when no one else would hold their stock, some arm of the state was endowed with the mandate to do so. Across the developing world, as discussed more fully below, a challenge repeatedly confronted in recent decades has been to create similar *national-level* capabilities.

National governments in many advanced and emerging-market economies had by the early years of the twenty-first century proved capable of developing the fiscal capacity, emergency liquidity instruments, and regulatory structures needed to govern local financial markets. But as those markets became more integrated internationally, dilemmas of collective political action proliferated. How can the authority to govern integrating markets be transnationalized? More open market—the consequence of increasing systemic reliance on freer international capital movements—promise no escape from the periodic necessity of dealing with crises. Voluntary policy coordination is an obvious response, but inevitable conflict over the final distribution of costs and benefits renders it fragile. What is missing is a global polity willing and able to sustain last-resort lending and investing instruments analogous to those established at the national level. Therein lies the central political challenge posed by the contemporary experiment in international financial openness and integration.

KEY POINTS

- Financial markets are prone to bouts of instability.

- During the twentieth century, leading states built up national fiscal, monetary, and regulatory instruments to limit the dangers of financial crises.

- Cross-national regulatory and supervisory coordination became necessary after international capital movements accelerated in the 1970s, but remained fragile.

The nature and variety of financial crises

Financial crises commence with sharp breaks in the prices of key financial instruments. The expectations of market participants suddenly change. 'Shocks' course through markets, and participants seek to adjust their financial holdings rapidly. Unable to accommodate demands, markets freeze up and very soon the commerce depending on them stops. Historically, the consequences of financial crises have varied in their severity and scope. The moments that particularly interest us here are those characterized most often by runs on bank deposits or their equivalents and by plummeting prices in the value of the assets at the core of national payments systems (referred to as a 'banking crisis') and/or in the value of a national currency relative to other currencies (referred to as a 'currency crisis').

Risk and uncertainty

Capitalist economies rest on foundations of debt. Borrowing and lending fuel economic growth. In principle, the aggregate financial claims created by the interaction of consumers, producers, savers, and investors in an economy are eminently supportable as long as expected future incomes exceed expected future debt repayments. The same logic applies internationally when once-separated economies become more integrated. At base, this involves the integration of markets for information.

Since we cannot know the future, expectations of future balances in national, corporate, or individual accounts are always subject to doubt. When enough borrowers and lenders share the perception that the extent of such doubts can reasonably be estimated, it becomes appropriate to speak of measurable probabilities, or risks (Knight 1921; Arnoldi 2009). Risks can be managed. Indeed, this is precisely what banks do when they accept deposits from savers in the short run, pool them, and make longer-term loans to borrowers. This simple operation lies at the root of modern systems of credit intermediation and maturity transformation. In more advanced economies, the functional equivalent of a bank can take the form of various types of firms involved in buying and selling securities, like stocks, bonds, investment funds, and exotic payment obligations. Through such banking and near-banking activities, money is created and financial claims are generated, priced, and exchanged. The different time horizons of savers and borrowers are 'mediated'. Insurance firms do something similar when they accept premiums, invest the proceeds in diversified portfolios, and estimate future payouts. In the absence of financial intermediaries, the ability of a particular individual, firm, or government to invest would be limited to the amount that individual, firm, or government could save out of its own resources at any given moment in time

Even when financial **intermediation** occurs smoothly, say through efficient and prudent banks, specific financial claims (assets from the point of view of banks, liabilities from the point of view of borrowers) become insupportable all the time. Mistakes are made, misjudgements occur, market conditions change unexpectedly. In the wake of such shocks, the expectations of creditors can shift, assets can be sold, and losses written off. If such shocks become generalized and creditors become entirely *uncertain* about the limits of future losses, panic can ensue. Debtors and creditors, especially creditors late through the exit door, suddenly have no sense of their future prospects. When national financial markets are open to the world, conventional distinctions between risk and uncertainty can break down fairly easily (Nelson and Katzenstein 2014). At any point in time, many variables not easily measurable can interact, many contingencies can arise, and many doubts about the final arbitration of conflicts can come to the fore. Because of those doubts, a radical sense of uncertainty can readily spread like a contagious virus.

The history of global capitalism is replete with such episodes of systemic contagion. As Kindleberger put it in the title of a famous book, manias, panics, and crashes are endemic in a financial market-based system (Kindleberger 1978). Few close observers deny that financial markets can sometimes move from extreme volatility to disastrous instability. Nevertheless, few actual markets participants are prepared to concede the feasibility of alternative non-market or overtly political mechanisms for the authoritative allocation of economic values in complex social systems. The massive human failures associated with planned economies in the twentieth century are not easy to forget.

The theoretical debate over whether the financial crises associated with modern capitalism are self-correcting in the absence of government intervention is a perennial one. Since the 1930s, however, the sceptical argument has proved irresistible to policymakers, except, as we shall see below, at one crucial and brief moment in 2008. The near-disaster that followed reinforced the belief that governments had sometimes to intervene in financial markets to stop them from collapsing. In the face of a confidence-sapping shock, some agency widely perceived to be acting with final authority had to administer a counter-shock capable of bringing market participants psychologically out of the realm of radical uncertainty and back into the realm of risk.

The same logic extends to the international level when national markets begin to open up to one another. Early on in the post-1945 period, the United States was the obvious leader, and all looked to it whenever currency or banking crises threatened to become contagious. As the financial integration project later proceeded and economic power became more dispersed at the global level, more complex and intense collaboration among diverse national and regional authorities seemed required. Questions concerning the reliability of such collaboration, however, rose in tandem with doubts about the distributive justice of a system that ever more tightly linked financial markets across rich and poor countries and appeared to exacerbate local and global social inequalities (Frieden 2006; Sen 2009; Piketty 2014).

Notwithstanding the difficulty of imagining significantly different financial systems conducive to global prosperity, contemporary history highlights three crucial facts. First, financial crises, and especially banking crises, recur; their only reliable predictor seems to be periods of market euphoria suggesting that high debt levels are now tolerable because 'this time is different' (Reinhart and Rogoff 2009). Second, when financial markets cross legal and political borders, the probability of crisis increases as the information embedded in prices becomes less readily accessible for all market participants; in the deep structure of contemporary financial markets, the information asymmetries analysed by economists and the power asymmetries analysed by political scientists overlap. Third, when financial markets are calm, the crisis-borne wisdom of rebuilding national buffers and placing firm limits on the global diversification of financial portfolios becomes politically and practically untenable.

Currency crises and banking crises

Economic historians commonly depict the period 1870 to 1914 as the first to witness the rapid expansion of cross-border financial markets (Flandreau and Zumer

2004; Frieden 2006). Although few countries were involved, by some measures the scale of international financial intermediation far exceeded anything that has developed since then. A golden age only for some, the purchase and sale of financial claims to foreigners boomed. So, too, did defaults, especially around 1875, and then again when the world began marching towards what became known as the Great War. In an era when the values of the main currencies were meant to be firmly pegged to one another (recall the discussion in the previous chapter of the **gold standard**, which itself never worked perfectly), such defaults often translated into bank failures. After 1919, the incidence of banking crises escalated, but so, too, did currency crises when re-pegged exchange rates would not hold. The disastrous decade commencing in 1929 was characterized by the awful coincidence and global explosion of banking and currency crises (Kindleberger 1973).

Currency crises continued to plague the system that eventually emerged from the ashes of the Second World War. Efforts by the United States and its victorious allies to ensure internal financial stability and peg key exchange rates did succeed in reducing the incidence of banking crises in the decades immediately following the war. But even after 1945, recurrent currency crises strained efforts to hold the Bretton Woods exchange rate system together. As Helleiner noted (Chapter 8 in this volume), those efforts finally ended in the early 1970s, when the link between the world's leading currency and the price of gold was broken. After 1973, banking crises once again became a fact of international economic life; so, too, did their coincidence with currency crises, mainly in the developing world (Bordo and Eichengreen, 2002). As we shall see, in 2008 came a powerful reminder that advanced industrial countries remained far from immune to such coincidences.

KEY POINTS

- Financial markets help societies to reduce uncertainty and manage risks, but they are prone to periodic breakdowns.
- The most damaging financial crises occur when banking markets and currency markets simultaneously come under pressure.
- After the end of the Bretton Woods exchange rate system in the early 1970s and before the cross-border crisis of 2007, banking and currency crises occurred with most frequency in emerging market countries.

The changing policy context

In 1974, the failure of a German bank, Bankhaus I. D. Herstatt, to honour its foreign exchange contracts had knock-on effects that ultimately led to the collapse of the Franklin National Bank of New York (Spero 1980). Long memories recalled the failure of the Credit-Anstalt Bank in Austria in 1931 and the contagion it eventually spread through world markets (Schubert 1992). This time, governments intervened to contain the damage, and the international economic system as a whole did not spiral into depression. The lessons of 1931 had apparently been learned, even as critics argued that the moral hazards created by the intervention made integrating markets more, not less, fragile.

Throughout the 1970s, banks based in advanced industrial countries rapidly expanded their international lending operations throughout the 1970s, while **multinational corporations** diversified their investment and trading activities. Individual and corporate investors gradually began buying more bonds and other financial instruments issued by developing-country governments and firms based in Central and South America. Some associated capital flows were trade related, some investment related, and some simply reflected the kind of financial speculation inherent in a market-based system now becoming more global. Not surprisingly, crises with cross-border effects now occasionally occurred (Martinez-Diaz 2009). The consequent question for policymakers became both obvious and difficult to answer. When real economic growth rates were sought in excess of those capable of being generated by domestic savings, how were the benefits and costs of financial openness to be distributed?

Domestic policy reform, international systemic consequences

By the 1980s, it had become clear that states constituting the international economy had collectively moved away from one set of policy trade-offs and towards another. Immediately after the Second World War, they sought to reconcile their newfound desire for exchange rate stability with their interest in maintaining independent **monetary policies**. Both as a matter of logic and of policy, they therefore had to tolerate limits on inward and outward capital flows—the 'unholy trinity' framework discussed in Helleiner's chapter. Four decades later, their priorities had changed.

Capital mobility and monetary autonomy were privileged, and they were willing to tolerate variable exchange rates as well as more openness and more volatility in their expanding financial markets (Obstfeld and Taylor 2004).

In the 1970s, to be sure, some developing countries sought to limit the future role of privately owned international capital, and they demanded a **new international economic order** (Krasner 1985). Over the course of the next decade, though, most of them had abandoned such a quest (Boughton 2001). Few initially joined the leading states in assigning priority to financial openness over exchange rate stability, and the painful earlier experience of leading states in attempting to maintain exchange rate pegs would often be repeated. With the rise of East Asian economies and especially China in ensuing decades, private capital flows would increase rapidly even as control regimes would sometimes only gradually and tentatively be loosened (Figures 9.2 and 9.3).

Over time, exchange rates measure relative price levels across economies that are linked together by trade and investment. They can, however, also gyrate wildly in the face of speculative pressures or unanticipated economic or political shocks. As real economies become more open to trade and foreign investment, such flexibility can be difficult to manage, both economically and politically. In the short run, exporters, importers, and investors may be able to hedge their foreign exposures, but this is costly and gets more problematic as time horizons lengthen. Standard economic theory, if still debatable, suggests that the best way to limit currency fluctuations is to coordinate monetary and fiscal policies cross-nationally. Industrialized economies demonstrated only intermittent interest in that option after the move to floating exchange rates in the early 1970s, despite rhetorical expressions to the contrary at successive high-profile meetings of the G7/G8 and other collaborative bodies (Baker 2006). They have, instead, left it to more open financial markets to attempt to impose on national societies the economic discipline necessary to stabilize the system as a whole. In practice, the stronger the country—that is, the more it was capable of generating and retaining its own domestic savings and/or the more it was capable of attracting foreign capital flows despite its pursuit of unbalanced fiscal and monetary policies—the lower such disciplinary effects turned out to be. In any event, through such macro-policy choices, leading states constructed a system that relied on the possibility of sharp

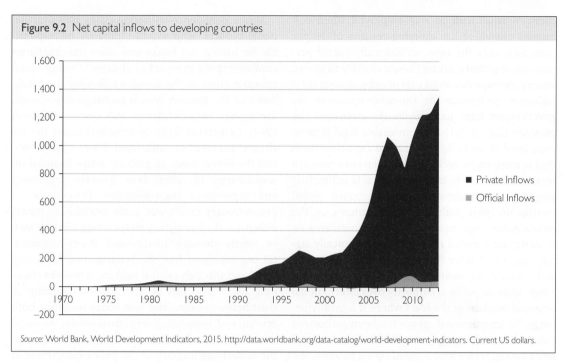

Figure 9.2 Net capital inflows to developing countries

Source: World Bank, World Development Indicators, 2015. http://data.worldbank.org/data-catalog/world-development-indicators. Current US dollars.

reversals in capital flows to force on themselves and others that modicum of coordination required for the interdependence of real economies to deepen. Partly in reaction, European states sought to restore some room for manoeuvre through the establishment of a regional currency union (Abdelal 2007).

Political sovereignty and economic interdependence

When financial markets are booming, participants tend to forget the past—intentionally or not. When a fund manager is earning 5 per cent a year for a

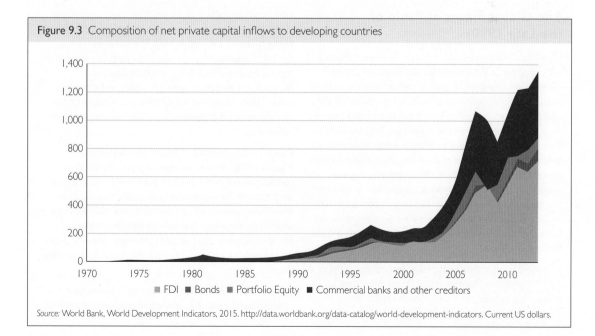

Figure 9.3 Composition of net private capital inflows to developing countries

Source: World Bank, World Development Indicators, 2015. http://data.worldbank.org/data-catalog/world-development-indicators. Current US dollars.

client, it is difficult to stay employed when colleagues elsewhere are claiming returns of 10 per cent. Still, only the most ideologically biased participants in global markets choose entirely to ignore history. Perhaps this helps explain why, despite their collective preference for financial openness, no governments have unambiguously embraced the principle that capital has an inviolable legal right to cross borders, and why the idea that capital controls may sometimes be necessary has even been noted in recent IMF research. In this regard, it is telling that governments continue refusing to match global treaties on trade with robust agreements on the collaborative regulation of capital movements or to designate a global overseer for systemically significant cross-border financial intermediaries. The architects of the post-1973 order will simply not lodge ultimate political authority over international financial markets at the level where it logically belongs. No international agency has been authorized comprehensively to govern international capital movements. States have instead opted to allow the global expansion of the financial intermediaries they themselves continue to license and more or less to monitor.

When confidence-withering crises spill over national borders, who would ultimately be responsible for bailing out banks and other intermediaries confronting the prospect of collapse? During actual financial crises in the decades following the breakdown of the Bretton Woods exchange rate system, the answer became clearer and clearer (Kapstein 1994). Last-resort facilities remained under the exclusive purview of individual states themselves, and the home states of globally active financial intermediaries therefore bore primary regulatory and supervisory responsibilities. Pre-emptive or precautionary credit was made available to others either not at all or by key states acting on their own or jointly through treaty-based intergovernmental organizations like the International Monetary Fund and through central banking networks (Henning 2002). At points of emergency, a modicum of trust between home and host states remained both crucial and tenuous. Every cross-border financial crisis since the 1970s thus refocused attention on the underlying fragility of the policy experiment in financial liberalization in a system fundamentally characterized by dispersed political authority (see Box 9.1). In their aftermath come now-predictable

---

BOX 9.1

The Global Financial Panic of the Late 1990s

In the mid 1990s, interest rates fell and stock markets boomed in North America and Western Europe. Banks and portfolio investors, including rapidly expanding mutual funds and hedge funds that pooled and leveraged the capital of institutional and wealthy investors, increasingly looked abroad for higher returns. With those higher returns came higher risks. They manifested themselves in localized currency crises, as in Mexico in 1994, but they seemed manageable in an expanding array of opening markets. Japanese banks in particular, confronting stagnant demand in a slumping home market, considered it an ideal time to expand aggressively across the East Asian region. Both public sector and private sector borrowers in many emerging-market economies discovered new and ready sources of funds, and they borrowed heavily.

In Thailand, much of this new debt was denominated in the local currency, which the Thai government valued at a pegged, not floating rate. By buying local debt, investors and creditors, in essence, bet that the Thai baht would hold its value. Early in

1997, however, Japanese banks, which then held about half of the country's foreign debt, began to lose confidence. They sought to reduce their exposures in Thailand as well as in a number of neighbouring countries. Their pullback prompted a regional **liquidity** crunch. Soon, generalized fears of a devaluation of the baht became self-fulfilling, and other Asian nations needed to defend the competitive advantages of their own exporting industries by allowing their own currencies to depreciate.

Capital suddenly flew out of South Korea, Indonesia, and Malaysia. Just as a bank hit by a run of depositors is forced hurriedly to raise cash by calling in loans, investment funds had to meet demands for withdrawals by liquidating their assets. As their Thai assets declined in redeemable value, they withdrew what they could as quickly as possible from their Asian portfolios. Liquidity dried up across the region, and very quickly the solvency of local banks recently considered sound came into question.

The government of Malaysia tried to stem the panic by imposing capital controls to forbid the repatriation of what its

BOX 9.1 (continued)

prime minister labelled the immoral gains of speculators. Others took the more conventional route of calling in the IMF to provide emergency funding until the panic subsided. Such borrowing from the Fund and other multilateral agencies came, as usual, with conditions attached. In this case, however, the terms were particularly controversial. Whereas borrowing countries saw themselves struggling against a short-term problem, the Fund began insisting on more fundamental kinds of reform designed to make East Asian markets, including financial markets, more open and more transparent. Talk of neo-imperialism by Western powers, especially the United States, became commonplace as national incomes fell across the region, imports declined, and a cut-throat competition to maintain exports ensued.

In the midst of the East Asian debacle, Russia's post-1991 experiment with frontier capitalism crashed into a wall of unsustainable foreign debt. It certainly seems in retrospect that many foreign investors had unwisely discounted the possibility that Russia's new class of tycoons would take careful measures to spirit their own capital out of the country. By the summer of 1998, even a massive IMF loan could not bolster confidence in the value of the rouble. It also failed to attract back private Russian capital invested in safe Western investments. Not coincidentally, American and European investors pulled out what they could. When the Russian government defaulted in August and simultaneously devalued the rouble, seismic shocks immediately hit the core of the world's financial system. Loans

extended to hedge funds were called in by banks, while stock markets plummeted around the world. Fearing that other emerging-market economies would follow Russia, panicked financiers pulled vast amounts of capital out of Mexico, Brazil, Argentina, and elsewhere.

In September 1998, Long-Term Capital Management (LTCM), a particularly prominent and highly leveraged American hedge fund with little direct exposure in emerging markets, found its heretofore extremely successful investment strategies wrecked as the crisis spread unexpectedly from Asia to Russia (Lowenstein 2001). While the consensus view among American financial market regulators would ordinarily have been to let such an entity bear the cost of its mistakes, and even to fail, panic had by now gripped Wall Street itself. The Federal Reserve encouraged a consortium of LTCM's creditors to take over the firm's dwindling assets, gradually unwind its bad bets, and replace its management. No one doubted that the full faith and credit of the US government would be available if required, but in the end this more limited emergency operation succeeded and calm gradually returned to the markets of industrial countries. For most emerging-market economies toeing the line of policy liberalization in an effort to attract capital investment back again after the panic subsided, the situation soon began to improve (Boughton 2012). Around the world it seemed that the new millennium heralded the dawn of a promising era of financial globalization.

---

collaborative efforts to measure and assess cross-border financial risks more effectively, to improve instruments designed to prevent future crises, and to agree on future procedures for emergency management when such instruments fail. The political energy behind such initiatives, however, tends to dissipate as memories fade and competitive impulses build once again. Despite its fragility, the overarching policy experiment continues.

KEY POINTS

- Crises have not stopped policy moves towards financial openness in advanced or emerging-market economies.

- Sovereignty remains an important legal doctrine in a globalizing economy, but in practical policy terms it is under rising pressure as the need collectively to manage border-spanning risks becomes ever more obvious.

Risk assessment and crisis prevention

No modern financial market exists for long without common standards understood by all participants. At the most basic level, financial information must be expressed in an understandable form so that risks may be recognized and measured. The intermediaries between the buyers of financial claims and the sellers must be deemed trustworthy. Accounting, auditing, and licensing rules form the bedrock. In all but the most limited local markets, or in all but the most libertarian utopias, such rules have not been spontaneously generated. Somebody has to provide the collective goods of standard setting, adjudication, reform, and, ultimately, rule enforcement. Even illegal markets, if they are to persist, require someone to instil confidence in the finality of exchanges. In legal markets, by definition, such collective goods are provided by the authoritative maker and enforcer of binding laws. To be sure, governments can and do delegate the responsibility to define and promote technical standards for risk assessment in many of the world's financial markets. But all contemporary markets that are legal rest on standards, rules, and enforcement procedures associated with governmental authority in one form or another. Even central banks that we now conventionally label 'independent', like the European Central Bank and the central banks of the most advanced countries, derive their authority from constitutional arrangements or interstate treaties widely accepted as legitimate. Risk assessment and crisis prevention policies begin here. They are designed to instil and reinforce confidence in the long-term stability of markets.

Defending public and private interests

International financial crises obviously expose jurisdictional ambiguities. But they have not yet been followed by the establishment of an unambiguous global standard-setter or a global agency capable of final rule enforcement. The frontier of markets integrating across political and legal boundaries therefore remains characterized by intergovernmental bodies and voluntary industry associations expected to negotiate common cross-border understandings (Bryant 2003). Standard-setting bodies with mixed public and private-sector participation are increasingly common. In the United States, the United Kingdom, and elsewhere, governments have often been willing to let market participants attempt to reach agreement among themselves on best operating practices. When such attempts fail and markets are threatened with disruption, however, governments and central banks come out of the shadows.

Contemplating the ever-present possibility that a bank they regulate could fail and thereby compromise the financial system as a whole (systemic risk), governments retain the ultimate capabilities either to dip into national treasuries or to rely on their central banks for the funding required to withstand market turmoil.

Over time, other kinds of financial intermediaries found ways to provide analogous services more cheaply. With the post-1970s emergence and global expansion of a shadow banking system more lightly regulated than its banking counterpart, the logic of international collaboration on standard setting and rule enforcement began to spread beyond the banking

sector. To some extent, most firms in globalizing insurance, securities, and asset-management businesses were supervised in their home markets, but the governmental agencies licensing and overseeing them sometimes tried to minimize their own offshore responsibilities. That is, governments attempted both to limit their own potential liabilities and to reduce the risk that firms would make imprudent judgements in the belief that they would be in all cases bailed out. As in the banking sector though, setting standards, defining enforcement responsibilities, and limiting official liabilities became more complicated as functional and geographic barriers were permitted to erode. Disentangling the links between banks and other kinds of financial firms became more difficult, and drawing a clear dividing line in real time between public interests and private risks was no longer a straightforward task (Pauly 2009).

Recognizing systemic risks

By the 1980s, multilateral collaboration on systemic risk recognition and assessment became focused on central bankers' clubs hosted by the Bank for International Settlements (BIS). Originally established to manage reparations payments after the First World War, the BIS survived attempts to close it down after 1945. Thirty years later, after it had developed a profitable business managing central-bank reserves, it proved a convenient venue for monetary and financial meetings and a source of staff support. The Basel Committee on Banking Supervision (BCBS) was the first of the clubs to benefit.

The focus of the BCBS is at the micro-level, specifically on large banks active across national borders and the core payment systems they operate. In 1999 and having just come through a crisis, G20 governments established the Financial Stability Forum (FSF) to concentrate on the macroeconomic implications of integrating financial markets. 'Macroprudential policies', addressing systemic vulnerabilities that could threaten even healthy and well-managed financial intermediaries, came to the forefront when the FSF became the Financial Stability Board ten years later. Other bodies were also established or expanded to promote regulatory and supervisory collaboration across markets that now bridged diverse financial sectors (Box 9.2). Together, the often-overlapping activities of many of these groups came to be called the 'Basel Process'.

BOX 9.2

Institutions for Financial Policy Collaboration

Bank for International Settlements (BIS)

Established in 1930 to oversee Germany's war reparation payments. After the Second World War, this institution based in Basel, Switzerland, assisted European governments in their monetary and financial interactions. After the 1960s, its role in facilitating a multilateral payments system in Europe made it an obvious venue for intensifying dialogue among central bankers, now including the United States and other non-European countries, on a broad range of regulatory and supervisory issues. Today, the BIS provides a meeting venue and secretariat for several collaborative committees, including the Basel Committee of Banking Supervision (BCBS), the Committee on the Global Financial System, the Committee on Payments and Market Infrastructures (CPMI), the Markets Committee, and the he Central Bank Governance Forum, and the Irving Fisher Committee on Central Bank Statistics.

Basel Committee on Banking Supervision

Established in 1975 to promote collaborative approaches on issues of common concern among its members as a Standing Committee of the Central Bank Governors of the G-10. (Actually numbering 11, the central banks of Belgium, Canada, France, Italy, Japan, the Netherlands, the United Kingdom, the United States, Germany, Sweden, and Switzerland agreed in the early 1960s to provide borrowing arrangements for the IMF. BCBS participants also now include Argentina, Australia, Brazil, China, the European Union, Hong Kong SAR, India, Indonesia, Korea, Luxembourg, Mexico, Russia, Saudi Arabia, Singapore, South Africa, Spain, and Turkey.) The Committee cooperates with other regional groups and as it develops international standards on capital adequacy for banks and core principles for the effective supervision of cross-border banking. Among other activities, it promotes its standards globally through a biennial International Conference of Banking Supervisors. The Committee also works with related central bank committees convening at the BIS as well as with the IOSCO, the IADI, and the IAIS (see below) on issues related to the operations of financial conglomerates, including the division of supervisory responsibilities both functionally and geographically (Goodhart 2011).

Financial Action Task Force

Initiated at the 1989 summit meeting of the G7 to combat money laundering. A small secretariat based in the OECD, but not technically part of that organization, it coordinates national efforts, now also aimed at disrupting the financing of terrorism in a world of more open markets.

Financial Stability Board (FSB)

Following the international financial crises of the late 1990s, the G7 finance ministers and central bank governors brought together national financial regulators from a wide range of countries hosting important international financial centres, together with international organizations involved in financial policy matters. The Financial Stability Forum (FSF) began meeting in April 1999 and maintained a small secretariat at the BIS. In April 2009, the G20 expanded its membership to include Spain and the European Commission and transformed it into a more ambitious effort with the mandate of fostering 'macro-prudential' collaboration among central banks and financial supervisors, that is, on ensuring that the oversight of financial institutions included not only analysis of the effects of institutional failure on the system as a whole but also rigorous assessment of the effects of systemic shocks on the institutions themselves. The FSB, with an expanded but still modest secretariat comprised mainly of officials seconded from central banks, was to be a vehicle for consultation across various standard-setting groups and organizations. It was to link its country-level work to the Financial Sector Assessment Programs of the World Bank and the IMF and to the Fund's surveillance operations. Especially after the crisis of 2008, particular emphasis was placed on complex issues related to the regulation of capital adequacy and liquidity management in cross-border and systemically significant financial institutions.

G7/G20

Dating back to informal meetings of European finance ministers after the collapse of the Bretton Woods exchange rate arrangements, regular annual meetings of financial officials and heads of government now occur under these rubrics. Originally including seven members, the United States, France, the UK, Germany, Japan, Canada, and Italy in recent years also met with Russia and the European Union. The G20, which includes leading emerging market-countries like China, India, Brazil, and South Africa may overshadow smaller groups in the future.
Meetings often involve the confidential sharing of information on financial and economic policies. Personal relationships thereby developed and reinforced can be useful when it comes to coordinating national policies rapidly in the face of international financial crises. There is no secretariat, but the archive of communiques and other group documents is located in the library system of the University of Toronto.

International Accounting Standards Board (IASB) and International Federation of Accountants (IFAC)

Private sector bodies organized by professional accounting associations to encourage international standardization of

BOX 9.2 (continued)

accounting principles and auditing practices. Activities intensified during the 1970s and came to prominence in the 1990s after a series of accounting scandals in the United States and other major markets.

International Association of Deposit Insurers (IADI)

Established in 2002 to enhance the effectiveness of national deposit insurance systems. Its membership includes 80 deposit insurers, and its secretariat is housed at its secretariat has been housed in Basel, Switzerland, where it receives technical assistance from the BIS.

International Association of Insurance Supervisors (IAIS)

Established in 1992 to encourage cooperation among regulators and supervisors of insurance companies. Since 1998, its secretariat has been housed in Basel, Switzerland, where it receives technical assistance from the BIS.

International Bank for Reconstruction and Development (World Bank)

Also originally created at Bretton Woods (see Wade, Chapter 12, and Phillips, Chapter 13 in this volume).

International Monetary Fund (IMF)

Designed at the Bretton Woods Conference, July 1944. (For details on its subsequent evolution, see Helleiner, Chapter 8 in this volume.)

International Organization of Securities Commissions (IOSCO)

With a secretariat based in Montreal, Canada, IOSCO sponsors conferences and other linkages among the regulators of national stock and other securities markets. Designed to facilitate the sharing of information and best practices, it developed during

the 1970s as buyers and sellers of securities increasingly moved their funds across national borders.

Organisation for Economic Co-operation and Development (OECD)

Evolved out of efforts after the Second World War to facilitate the use of Marshall Plan resources. Often now considered a think tank for industrial countries contemplating various forms of economic policy coordination.

Regional Development Banks

With local mandates akin to the global development mandate of the World Bank, these multilateral organizations are now involved in providing technical advice for financial market deepening, regulation, and supervision in Africa, Latin America, East Asia, Eastern Europe, and Central Europe.

United Nations (UN)

Various UN commissions, agencies, and departments, such as the Department of Economic and Social Affairs in the New York-based secretariat, have mandates to review international financial developments and seek to promote understanding among member states on issues of equity and efficiency in the global economy. In recent years, its focus has shifted to ensuring the availability of adequate financing for developing countries and to promoting internationally agreed Millennium Development Goals for poverty reduction and sustainable development (the 'Monterrey Consensus').

World Trade Organization (WTO)

Having grown out of the **General Agreement on Tariffs and Trade (GATT)**, under which national trade policies have been liberalized on a multilateral basis ever since 1948, the WTO has growing responsibilities for trade in goods as well as various services, including a widening range of financial services.

Banking crises initially led the BCBS to propose a concordat to clarify the respective responsibilities of the home and host country supervisors of cross-border banks. It followed this up with efforts to promote minimum standards for bank capital reserves, which were expected to be available to absorb loan losses and reduce the likelihood that national monetary and fiscal resources would be called upon for bailouts (Basel I). It also commenced work with other national and regional bodies to bolster the effectiveness of prudential supervision for banks and a widening range of financial

intermediaries. In 2006, the most extensive and detailed effort to ensure capital adequacy in globally active lenders came in an accord commonly dubbed Basel II. Under its terms, international lenders were encouraged to bring sophisticated and self-disciplined risk-management techniques into calculations of capital adequacy. The politics of policymaking through technocratic clubs here reached a limit, not least because underlying risk-cultures across major states and regions remained distinctive but also because 'self-discipline' in a competitive environment often proved to be an oxymoron.

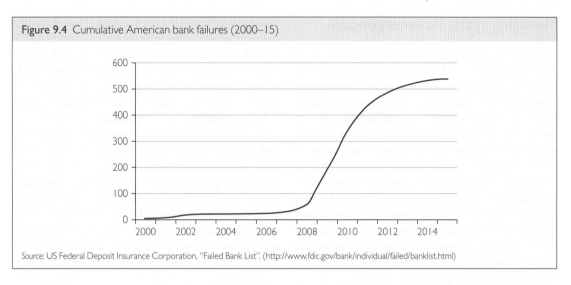

Figure 9.4 Cumulative American bank failures (2000–15)

Source: US Federal Deposit Insurance Corporation, "Failed Bank List". (http://www.fdic.gov/bank/individual/failed/banklist.html)

The fact that the implementation of Basel II left much discretion for national supervisors was only one source of future trouble. The accord enhanced the **competitive advantages** of large money-centre banks. Astute observers pointed out that its impact might also be 'pro-cyclical'. That is, banks around the world would be encouraged excessively to restrict lending during recessions and imprudently to expand lending during booms. They proved to be correct. The Basel Process could promote common risk-assessment standards, but the enforcement of actual operating rules would always depend upon local agencies mainly responsive to diverse and sometimes conflicting domestic policy priorities (Singer 2007).

Policy failures

The main symptom of mounting systemic problems took the form of enduring imbalances in the current accounts of leading countries. By the turn of the twenty-first century, it was clear that the United States was importing too much, saving too little, and depending for its financing needs on vast inflows of capital from China, Japan, Germany, and many middle-income and developing countries. For a time, the situation looked like a happy one for all concerned, not least for the cross-border financial institutions handling the requisite capital flows. Instead of encouraging macroeconomic adjustments, expanding capital markets permitted imbalances to grow.

These imbalances—combined with loose monetary policies, lax regulation, excessively high leverage in key and uninsured financial intermediaries, a dysfunctional

credit-rating system, ill-conceived financial innovations and executive compensation practices, manic speculation, a broadly under-appreciated turn in the business cycle, and, underneath it all in the American economy, an over-reliance on the housing industry—are now all commonly blamed for what happened next. Real-estate related bank failures were not new in American history, but after 2007 staggering numbers occurred (Figure 9.4). In their wake, the capacity of existing multilateral arrangements to pre-empt contagion across the markets to which those banks were now directly or indirectly connected proved inadequate. The politics of tacit intergovernmental understandings, together with reliance on inadequately equipped international organizations and clubs, failed to prevent the worst systemic financial emergency since 1945.

KEY POINTS

- Since the collapse of the Bretton Woods exchange-rate regime, governments have attempted to cooperate more intensively to prevent financial crises.

- Fundamental macroeconomic policy choices condition the flow of capital across national borders, but capital flight can sometimes occur unexpectedly.

- Policy collaboration to reduce the chances that a localized financial crisis will spread has often involved talk about joint moves in fiscal and monetary policymaking, but broad and substantive movement to render global markets more resilient has occurred mainly in regulatory and supervisory arenas. The results have been mixed, and significant challenges remain.

Managing systemic emergencies

As outlined in Box 9.3, governments around the world intervened heavily and directly in global markets in the fall of 2008 and long afterwards. The United States in particular lent and invested monetary and fiscal resources lavishly. The beneficiaries included most of its own large financial institutions and many foreign-headquartered institutions operating within and across its borders. The equivalent of a systemic run had started in securities firms, and it very quickly threatened to bring down the money-centre banks upon which they and everyone else ultimately depended. Central bank funding and eventually fiscal resources managed by the US Treasury flowed to an array of domestic and foreign financial intermediaries. Table 9.1 provides just one insight into the implications. It lists estimated earnings generated by selected banks drawing on US central bank liquidity facilities, the spread between what they paid for their funding and what they likely earned from onward lending. Bank recapitalization, in short, was heavily assisted by publicly funded bailouts.

In circumstances where illiquidity and insolvency were not easy to differentiate, 190 firms benefited from Fed facilities between 2007 through 2010. The total bank earnings resulting from the use of those facilities topped US$13 billion, thus offsetting a large chunk of the US$21.6 billion in losses those same banks recorded during the crisis. Although the specific technique for stabilizing banks at the core of payments systems was hardly novel, the scale and global reach of this particular operation was stunning. Other Federal

---

BOX 9.3

Timeline for the Crisis of 2008

17 May 2007

Following months of rising turbulence in US housing markets, combined with mounting scandals involving government-affiliated agencies that guaranteed $5 trillion in increasingly risky mortgages, Federal Reserve Chairman Ben Bernanke says housing-related defaults will not seriously harm the US economy.

June 2007

Two highly leveraged hedge funds owned by the investment bank, Bear Stearns, report large losses and are forced to begin selling assets at distressed prices. The trouble spreads to major Wall Street firms, which had lent the funds money. Similar problems emerge in the United Kingdom, and it would later emerge that many European and Asian institutions owned vast amounts of subprime mortgage-backed securities.

August 2007

Early in the month, US stock markets fall sharply. 'Credit crunch' spreads around the world as subprime mortgage-backed securities are disclosed in portfolios of banks from BNP Paribas to Bank of China. To provide market liquidity, the Fed cuts interbank interest rates and injects nearly $100 billion into the US banking system. The European Central Bank and the central banks of Japan, England, Canada, and Australia make coordinated moves to provide liquidity in their own markets.

16 August 2007

Stricken by losses in investments related to US subprime mortgages, the German regional bank, SachsenLB, is rapidly sold to Germany's biggest regional bank, Landesbank Baden-Wuerttemberg. The same day, Countrywide Financial Corporation, the biggest US mortgage lender, narrowly avoids bankruptcy by taking out an emergency loan of $11 billion from a group of banks. Shortly thereafter, the UK bank, Northern Rock, requests Bank of England assistance in the face of a run by depositors.

18 September 2007

The Fed starts cutting broader interest rates, and will continue doing so at seven straight monthly meetings and one unscheduled emergency meeting. It also begins providing liquidity to broker-dealers in securities markets and to accept troubled mortgage-backed securities as collateral. Staggering losses soon begin to be announced by international giants like the Union Bank of Switzerland and Merrill Lynch in New York.

2 November 2007

The US Treasury finally implements the Basel II bank capital adequacy accord negotiated by the BCBS.

12 December 2007

The Federal Reserve's Open Market Committee negotiates swap lines with the European Central Bank and the Swiss National Bank for up to $20 billion and $4 billion, respectively.

11 January 2008

Bank of America pays $4 billion for failing Countrywide Financial, the country's biggest and deeply troubled mortgage originator.

BOX 9.3 (continued)

28 January 2008

Four days after the first nationwide decline in housing prices since the 1930s is announced, the Economic Stimulus Act of 2008 is proposed in the US Congress. The next day, the House of Representatives passes a $146 billion aid package to speed up tax rebates to most taxpayers. The Senate increases the package and the legislation is sent to the President on 7 February. Six days later, Northern Rock Bank is nationalized in the UK.

16 March 2008

JPMorgan Chase & Co. acquires what is left of Bear Stearns, in a deal engineered and backstopped by the Fed. The G7 finance ministers launch a review of the global financial regulatory system.

16 June 2008

The New York investment bank, Lehman Brothers, reports a loss of $2.8 billion in the second quarter. Within the firm, funds begin to flow from units overseas back to New York, a development that will cause host countries to raise serious objections. Three days later, ex-Bear Stearns fund managers are arrested by the FBI for allegedly misrepresenting the fiscal health of their funds heavily invested in subprime mortgages.

31 August 2008

German Commerzbank AG takes over Dresdner Kleinwort investment bank. Seven days later, US Treasury Secretary Henry Paulson announces a public 'conservatorship' for cash-starved mortgage-guarantors Fannie Mae and Freddie Mac.

14 September 2008

Lehman Brothers files a Chapter 11 bankruptcy petition after the failure of official attempts to arrange for the 158-year-old firm to be taken over by another private firm. The next day, under pressure from government officials, the Bank of America acquires Merrill Lynch.

16 September 2008

In coordinated operations, central banks around the world pump billions of dollars into money markets. Panic increases, and the US government announces an unprecedented blanket guarantee for money market funds. The same day the Fed lends insurance giant American International Group (AIG), an arm of which had become a key insurer of rapidly depreciating mortgage-backed securities, $85 billion in exchange for nearly 80 per cent of its stock. The price of gold soars by over 8 per cent, equity markets continue a broad global retreat, and governments around the world begin moving to ban the speculative short-selling of financial stocks.

21 September 2008

Goldman Sachs and Morgan Stanley, the two remaining giants in US investment banking markets, change their legal charters to become bank holding companies, thus gaining access to the emergency liquidity facilities of the Fed. Three days later, in the largest bank failure in US history, Washington Mutual collapses and with government support is sold to JPMorgan Chase.

29 September 2008

The US Congress rejects a $700 billion plan to bail out the US financial system. As various banks are nationalized or merged into stronger institutions around the world, the Fed continues supporting markets with massive liquidity operations, while the Securities and Exchange Commission and the Financial Accounting Standards Board announce moves to relax 'mark-to-market' accounting rules that have the effect of exaggerating actual credit losses. The next day, spreads on short-term lending between top-tier banks, normally quite low, spike to 7 per cent, their highest levels ever recorded.

1 October 2008

The US Congress reverses itself and two days later, President Bush signs the $700 billion Emergency Economic Stabilization Act into law. Three days later, EU leaders travel to Paris for an emergency summit. During the next week, stock markets around the world record their worst week since the early 1930s. Iceland's banking system collapses, major British banks are partly nationalized; Germany, France, and other EU countries prepare decisive measures to stabilize failing local banks. Fearing a global economic collapse, central banks around the world simultaneously slash interest rates.

10 October 2008

G7 finance ministers and central bank governors meet in Washington and agree to coordinated monetary and fiscal actions to prevent the credit crisis from throwing the world into depression. Citing provisions of anti-terrorist laws, the UK government freezes Icelandic assets in a bid to force the country to compensate British depositors in failed intermediaries owned by Iceland's main banks.

22 October 2008

The House Oversight and Government Reform Committee grills executives from the country's leading credit-rating companies, which had privately acknowledged for more than a year that conflicts of interest contributed to excessively favourable ratings of mortgage-backed securities.

BOX 9.3 (continued)

10 November 2008

China announces a $586 billion stimulus package, the largest in the country's history. The US Treasury expands a rescue package for troubled insurer, AIG, to $150 billion and allows direct government investment in the company.

28 November 2008

The BCBS provides new guidance on the valuation of assets at fair market prices, while the World Bank launches a Debt Management Facility to help developing countries address future debt problems. Meanwhile, the IMF is busy in central and eastern Europe negotiating large standby arrangements with vulnerable countries.

1 December 2008

The US National Bureau of Economic Research announces that the economy entered a recession in December 2007. A few days later, as global investors seek the relative safety of US government debt, the yield on three-month Treasury bills briefly falls below zero for the first time ever.

17 December 2008

The Fed lowers its base interest rates near 0 per cent and begins planning for highly unusual new measures (quantitative easing) to bolster market liquidity.

9 January 2009

The German government takes a 25 per cent stake in Commerzbank through a €10 billion capital injection in an effort to help Commerzbank acquire Dresdner Bank. Ireland bails out Anglo-Irish Bank. A few days later, Standard & Poor's cuts the credit rating of debt issued by Greece, while Portugal, Spain, and Ireland are put on watch lists.

20 January 2009

Barack Obama is sworn in as the 44th president of the United States. IMF projects world economic growth to fall to just 0.5 per cent this year, its lowest rate since just after the Second World War.

10 February 2009

The US Treasury announces a Financial Stability Plan involving purchases of convertible preferred stock in eligible banks, the creation of a Public-Private Investment Fund to acquire troubled assets from financial institutions, expansion to $1 trillion of the Fed's Term Asset-Backed Securities Loan Facility, and new initiatives to stem residential mortgage foreclosures. One week later, a new $787 billion fiscal stimulus plan, the American Recovery and Reinvestment Act of 2009, is signed into law.

1 March 2009

The Fed and the US Treasury provide $30 billion in capital to AIG and take over two divisions of the company after it announces a $61.7 billion loss, the largest in US corporate history.

2 April 2009

G20 leaders meet in London, where they agree to convert the Financial Stability Forum (FSF), born after the Asian crisis, to the Financial Stability Board (FSB).

9 December 2009

The US Congress begins work that culminates in the sweeping Dodd-Frank Wall Street Reform and Consumer Protection Act on 21 July 2010. Among other things, it establishes the Financial Stability Oversight Council (FSOC) to monitor markets and coordinate policies.

11 January 2010

The Fed records a $46 billion profit for 2009, mainly reflecting interest payments and gains on securities purchased during the crisis. Two days later, the Financial Crisis Inquiry Commission, established by the US Congress to examine the causes of the financial meltdown, holds its first public hearings.

7 June 2010

Euro-area member states establish the European Financial Stability Facility temporarily to provide financing to members in distress. Two years later, it would be succeeded by the permanent European Stability Mechanism and the European Central Bank would become the supervisor of significant cross-border intermediaries in a planned European Banking Union.

January 2011

The Financial Crisis Inquiry Commission (2011) concludes that the crisis was triggered by the sudden collapse of a classic 'bubble' in US housing markets, inflated during many years of low interest rates, loose credit standards, excessive leverage, and new kinds of synthetic and opaque securities—all permitted by inadequate supervision. 'This crisis was avoidable ... Widespread failures in financial regulations and supervision proved devastating ... Dramatic failures of corporate governance and risk management at many systemically important financial institutions were a key cause ... A combination of excessive borrowing, risky investments, and lack of transparency put the financial system on a collision course with crisis... There was a systemic breakdown in accountability and ethics.'

Table 9.1 Estimated earnings attributable to Federal Reserve operations
(1 August 2007–30 April 2010; US$ millions)

Beneficiary	Earnings
Citibank	1,800
Bank of America	1,500
Royal Bank of Scotland	1,200
Wells Fargo	878
Barclays	641
JP Morgan	458
Dexia	350
Credit Suisse	285
Deutsche Bank	253
Unicredit	221
BNP Paribas	175
Société Générale	170
Toronto-Dominion Bank	154
Fortis Bank	106
Sumitomo Mitsui Bank	106
Goldman Sachs	100
Standard Chartered Bank	56
Canadian Imperial Bank of Commerce	20

Source: Federal Reserve data, compiled by *Bloomberg Magazine*, www.bloomberg.com 28 November 2011,
accessed 11 April 2014.

Reserve actions now also suggested longer-term structural changes in the underpinnings of global finance.

Currency swaps between central banks have long been used to keep markets clam and orderly. Typically done at fixed exchange rates for limited terms at modest interest rates, they help central banks meet foreign-currency demand in their local markets. The originating central bank bears no credit risk associated with direct exposure to ultimate beneficiaries and no foreign exchange risk. It does, however, take on the risk that the counterparty central bank may default when it comes time to reverse the swap (sovereign risk). The recipient central bank, in turn, can offer foreign-currency loans to local financial institutions (including the subsidiaries or branches of foreign institutions) under its purview, and by doing so it assumes credit risk. During the crisis of 2008, and especially after the panic caused by the failure of Lehman Brothers, US dollar liquidity in American and foreign markets dried up. Similarly, demand for other reserve currencies, especially the euro and to a lesser extent the Swiss franc and the Japanese yen, spiked. The solution was for the producers of reserve currencies both to open up the tap inside their home markets and to engage in swaps with their primary foreign counterparts. The novelty during this crisis came in the unprecedented scale and speed of such operations, and later in the rendering the most important swap facilities permanent.

In essence, mutually self-interested and informally coordinated actions by key-currency central banks activated and significantly deepened three swap networks centred on the Fed and the dollar, the ECB and euro, and the Swiss National Bank and the Swiss franc. Additionally, regional swap arrangements put in place during and after previous crises in Asia and Latin America were revived. From 2007 onwards, nearly half of all potential foreign-currency demand from local financial institutions around the world was for US dollars, including demand originating from US bank subsidiaries and branches whose parent banks had pulled liquidity home when US markets were dramatically contracting. Swap facilities from the Fed, therefore, played a crucial global role, directly by keeping US dollar markets liquid and indirectly by reassuring market participants that routine funding risks would remain low. In all, 14 swap lines were set up by the Federal Reserve after 2007 (Table 9.2). All but

four eventually drew on them, but whether drawn or not, each country involved benefited from the market-calming influence of their very existence.

The big jump in swap line usage occurred in the fourth quarter of 2008 after the Lehman Brothers' default. It was accompanied by an unprecedented Fed decision to expand without limit the lines available to the central banks of Europe, the United Kingdom, Japan, and Switzerland. These lines expired early in 2010, but new facilities for Canada, Europe, the UK, Japan, and Switzerland were established in the spring in the wake of emergency within the Eurozone. In October 2013, the Fed, the ECB, and the central banks of Canada, the UK, Japan, and Switzerland agreed to make the new swap facilities permanent.

Again, central banks were not alone in their emergency management activities during this period. Between September 2008 and June 2009, advanced-economy governments around the world announced some 34 systemic or institution-specific programs involving bank recapitalization, debt guarantees, asset

Table 9.2 Drawings on US dollar swap facilities provided by the Federal Reserve (US$ millions, end of quarters)

End of	2007Q4	2008Q1	2008Q2	2008Q3	2008Q4	2009Q1	2009Q2	2009Q3
Canada	—	—	—	—	—	—	—	—
ECB	20,000	15,000	50,000	174,742	291,352	165,717	59,899	43,662
Switzerland	4,000	6,000	12,000	28,900	25,175	7,318	369	0
Japan				29,622	122,716	61,025	17,923	1,530
UK				39,999	33,080	14,963	2,503	13
Denmark				5,000	15,000	5,270	3,930	580
Australia				10,000	22,830	9,575	240	0
Sweden					25,000	23,000	11,500	2,700
Norway					8,225	7,050	5,000	1,000
N Zealand	—	—	—	—	—	—	—	—
Korea					10,350	16,000	10,000	4,050
Brazil	—	—	—	—	—	—	—	—
Mexico							3,221	3,221
Singapore	—	—	—	—	—	—	—	—
TOTAL	24,000	21,000	62,000	288,263	553,728	309,918	114,585	56,576

Sources: Federal Reserve Bank of New York data; Allen and Moessner (2010: 45).

purchases and guarantees, and increases in deposit-insurance limits. The politics of emergency management at the national level essentially permitted assertive and informally coordinated fiscal action at the core of the system. Although these ad hoc policy responses appeared quite consistent with earlier technocratic work aimed at crisis prevention, they clearly marked the reassertion of finance ministries and legislatures in the actual face of systemic emergency.

The most visible recent efforts to make the post-crisis system more resilient were coordinated by the FSB as it resumed its project to increase private capital buffers and ensure sound liquidity management in the banking sector, but now also in other sectors like insurance and asset management. By late 2015, leading central banks and supervisors had agreed in principle to impose 'Basel III' rules on systemically important banks. Their 'total loss-absorbing capacity', including capital and subordinated debt, would be expected to rise to 18 per cent of their risk-weighted assets. Proposals were also being developed to reduce the likelihood of future bailouts by ensuring that certain bank creditors, like subordinate bond-holders, would be forced to 'bail in', that is, convert their claims to bank equity, when required. Crisis prevention remained the ultimate objective, but the new standards were once again expected to be implemented at a time of rising cross-national competition and fading memories of crises past. The continuing question was whether they would send an adequate signal to global markets that future government bailouts were actually now a low probability, thus reducing moral hazard and inducing better risk management inside private financial intermediaries. Worth noting in this regard were certain policy reactions to the crisis of 2008 that might complicate life for governments and central banks during the next emergency. The US Congress's Dodd–Frank Act, for example, included clauses specifically aimed at making more difficult a range of Federal Reserve actions in the shadow banking system like those that followed the Lehman Brothers' failure.

The extent to which governments and central banks succeeded in resolving the underlying causes of the crisis of 2008, the allocation of the costs of that success, and the long-term implications of their new policies remain matters of deep analytical and political debate (Gorton 2012; Blinder 2014; Drezner, 2014; Geithner 2014; Helleiner 2014b; Bernanke 2015). The emergency responses to the most damaging financial crisis of the post-1945 period may have avoided even worse outcomes. But vast losses estimated in terms of direct expenditures and systemic economic recession, together with innumerable human tragedies associated with business closures, unemployment, and unpayable debts, dramatically underscored the risks that came with the experiment in systemic financial integration in a world of dispersed political authority.

KEY POINTS

- Managing the systemic crisis of 2008 depended on assertive action by the US government and central bank but also on the collaborative and loosely coordinated complementary policy responses of their counterparts around the world.

- Some emergency management facilities across the leading central banks in the world have been made permanent. But the exercise of some complementary central bank and government crisis-fighting powers may be more difficult in the future.

- One way or another, the fiscal authority of the state provides the foundation for integrating financial markets.

Financial crises in emerging-market economies

Financial emergencies in emerging-market economies are not typically different from that facing the United States and others in 2008. But the fiscal limits of their states tend to be more obvious, and their options for halting runs and redistributing adjustment burdens are fewer. A developing country facing a currency or banking crisis in an open and integrating financial system are in position somewhat analogous to that of a domestic firm unable to meet its obligations, with an important exception. Where the firm, at least inside most capitalist economies, has access to undoubted and binding bankruptcy arrangements, the country does not. When debts are perceived to have become unsustainable, creditors can demand repayment and the resources available to settle accounts can rapidly lose value. Crisis conditions can be generated by government overspending, by excessive imports, or by the building up of private-sector debt that cannot be financed domestically. Any of these situations might motivate the government to increase the rate of production of its monetary printing press. Inflation would normally be the consequence, and if the fundamental problem is one of temporary illiquidity this might just provide the political space for necessary internal adjustments to occur. If much of a country's debt is owed to foreigners and is denominated in foreign currency, however, such a policy may quickly deepen the problem. Inflation in the local currency by definition pushes up the value of foreign currency liabilities. Expecting further declines in the purchasing power of the local currency, domestic as well as foreign creditors and investors rush to preserve their capital or take it out of the country. A deteriorating real exchange rate makes debt repayment more difficult and imports more expensive. The debtor government can default on its loans, or try to allow private firms under its purview to walk away from their obligations to foreign creditors, but then it risks cutting its entire economy off from future capital inflows. The country can be caught in a vicious economic and political trap. The case of Argentina provides a vivid example (Box 9.4).

Missing at the system level is a formal and widely accepted sovereign debt restructuring mechanism. Two successive deputy managing directors of the IMF, in fact, made proposals along this line, one for the Fund to be legally empowered to play the role of lender-of-last resort and the next for the Fund to play the role of ultimate bankruptcy court (Fischer 2000; Goodhart and Illing 2002; Krueger 2002). Even in the aftermath of the Asian and Argentine crises, however, neither proved politically acceptable. What did prove feasible were ideas on the middle ground, including provisions of 'soft law' that would provide incentives for cooperation among bondholders in future debt restructurings (Brummer 2012). Still missing, of course, is a legal system capable of ordering the replacement of government officials and the mandatory adjustment of the national balance sheet. This remains no accident. In the conceptual extreme, the sovereignty of a state

BOX 9.4

The Policy Challenges of Financial Openness: The Case of Argentina

Blessed with abundant natural resources, diversified industries, and a well-educated labour force, Argentina might have become a regional beacon of prosperity during the twentieth century. It was not to be. After decades of troubles, hyperinflation struck in 1989. In April 1991, the government embarked upon a bold policy experiment to reverse the economy's course. The Convertibility Plan rigidly pegged the value of the peso to the US dollar and thereby constrained the ability of the central bank to print money. Simultaneously, the government announced a wide range of structural reforms to make the economy more flexible, competitive, and open. Initially, the plan achieved dramatic results. Inflation fell, international capital flowed in, and the economy grew by an average of 6 per cent through 1997. Late in 1998, however, a surprisingly severe recession began, and its effects were compounded by the unusual turbulence in global financial markets. As capital inflows dried up, some observers say the government did not react quickly enough with domestic policy adjustments. Others point to large loans from the IMF inadequately conditioned on such adjustments, and to a currency devaluation by Brazil that undercut Argentina's export competitiveness. Still others blame the Asia-focused panic then gripping private foreign lenders and investors. In any event, bank runs, the suspension of IMF loans, and severe political and social unrest ensued. In December 2001, the country began defaulting on its international debts; the next month it abandoned its currency peg, and as the peso's value plummeted, the value of its debt, now largely denominated in US dollars, exploded. In 2002,

the economy contracted by 20 per cent and unemployment exceeded 20 per cent of the workforce.

In retrospect, it became clear that either the currency regime should have been abandoned during more halcyon days in 1996 or 1997 or that its continuation should have been supported by tighter **fiscal policies**, a reduction in international borrowing, and lower labour costs. At the time, neither course of action gained any political traction. Even so, according to a key IMF staffer, in 1998 'a crisis might have been avoided with good luck—for example, had the dollar depreciated against the euro, had Brazil not been forced to devalue, or had international capital markets not deteriorated—but Argentina's luck ran out' (Allen 2003: 131; Blustein 2005).

By 2004, a distinct lack of solidarity among Argentina's external creditors provided the policy space necessary to rekindle some domestic production. The government then took several desperate measures to stay afloat, including borrowing from Venezuela at very high interest rates and nationalizing state pension funds. Early in 2010, it engaged in an intense political struggle with its own central bank over the use of the bank's foreign currency reserves and tightened foreign exchange controls. Five years later, still enmeshed in bitter legal battles with recalcitrant foreign creditors who refused to accede to the terms of an IMF-sponsored plan to restructure its debts and restore full access to global capital markets, an election brought a new administration. It struggled to complete the restructuring of its debts, rein in domestic spending, restore balanced trade and investment, and cut a 25 per cent annual inflation rate. The long-term costs of financial instability and default continued to mount.

implies the absolute right both to resort to war and to default on debts. As a classic realist might nevertheless argue, the ability in practice to exercise such a right is in the final analysis dependent on the raw power a state possesses to absorb any negative consequences and the willingness of others states to defer. (In the aftermath of the 2008 crisis, the case of Iceland vividly demonstrated this logic as the country defaulted on debts, imposed draconian capital controls, and embarked on a long and contentious negotiation.)

The architects of the post-1945 system deemed the economic instability threatened by cascading sovereign defaults to be the handmaiden of war. At Bretton Woods, therefore, they took the first steps to design a system that would limit the extent to which sovereign participants in the system would find themselves pushed to renege on their debts. Time and again in succeeding decades, mainly in the midst of crises, the main creditor states redesigned imperfect substitutes for sovereign bankruptcies without establishing a mandatory debt restructuring mechanism. These often took the form of programmes to provide debtor states with the functional equivalent of central bank liquidity facilities and neutral monitors to reschedule foreign-currency denominated debt repayments.

Ad hoc sovereign debt restructurings for developing countries have in fact been commonplace since the 1980s. International banks as well as official agencies providing export credits informally organized themselves into negotiating groups (the so-called London Club and Paris Club, respectively) to manage such arrangements. Frequently, however, the threat of default has drawn attention from creditor governments themselves. In the early decades of the post-1945 period, the initiatives they took to relieve over-extended sovereign debtors were facilitated by the fact that the IMF was on hand to play a coordinating role and that typically only a few large banks were involved. Collective action problems proved challenging but manageable. With the rapid growth of cross-border purchases of bonds, stocks, and other kinds of securities in recent decades, however, the number of potential participants in debt restructurings has increased dramatically, and collective action problems like those faced by Argentina have accordingly become much more difficult to solve.

When it was called upon, the immediate objective of the IMF at such moments was to help break the psychology of fear and mistrust among creditors and debtors. Its ultimate mission, however, was to assist in stabilizing the financial underpinnings necessary for real economies to become more deeply interdependent and more reliably prosperous through expanded trade and investment. That the IMF was not dissolved after 1973, when the exchange rate system it was meant to defend broke down, reflected much more than bureaucratic inertia. Most importantly, the Fund's **balance-of-payments** financing facilities, which had grown over time in both size and flexibility, proved to be extremely convenient to its major member states. In effect, they provided a mechanism for creditors to share the burden of providing emergency financial assistance to debtors and to enforce economic policy adjustments. Through the **conditionality** associated with the use of such facilities, the Fund could exert pressure on borrowers in a manner that would be politically difficult for individual creditor states. Moreover, the Fund's routine surveillance activities offered the promise of holding all members accountable for the external consequences of their economic policy choices (Pauly 1997). Despite many failures and continuing challenges, the Fund evolved into the central crisis manager for emerging markets in a system that moved over time from one based on the interdependence of national exchange rate policies to one based on more open financial markets (Best 2014).

The special needs of emerging-market countries took on a new look in recent decades, as private capital from an array of sources in advanced industrial countries sought higher returns than those available at home. China's turn towards market-based development accelerated the process, the results of which we saw in the first three Figures above. To be sure, this exposed emerging-market economies to the risks associated with excessive speculative inflows, rapid outflows, or sudden stops, albeit not usually as severe as those generated by the US-centred crisis of 2008.

The problem is that this leaves countries dependent on the wisdom of foreign policymakers, something demonstrably in short supply of late (Gallagher 2015). This realization helps in part to account for the massive build-up of official foreign-exchange reserves in many emerging-market and developing countries, especially in East Asia (Figures 9.5 and 9.6). On one hand, those reserves may be viewed as an insurance policy against external shocks. On the other hand, the value of that insurance is limited since it is mainly denominated in the currency of systemic shock-generating countries. Across all emerging markets, 60 per cent of reserves held by emerging-market countries take the form of

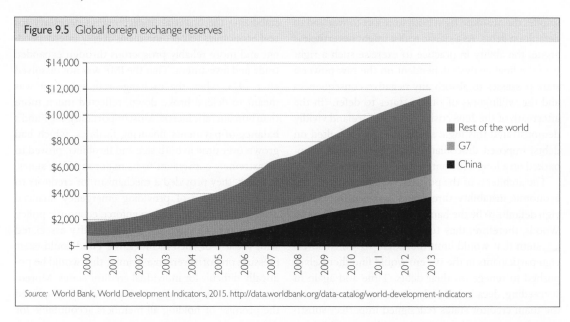

Figure 9.5 Global foreign exchange reserves

Source: World Bank, World Development Indicators, 2015. http://data.worldbank.org/data-catalog/world-development-indicators

short-term dollar investments in American securities, while nearly 30 per cent are invested in euro-denominated assets.

Reserve accumulation above a prudent level required for routine and predictable payments in fact represents the purchase of very expensive insurance policies. The hoarding of reserves and the trade protectionism needed to facilitate it deepened the depression of the 1930s. The idea of multilateralizing such insurance lay at the very centre of the Bretton Woods negotiations, and the IMF eventually became a vehicle

for bringing that idea into policy practice. Reserves reduce the risk that sudden stops in inward capital flows will disrupt domestic economies, making it easier to manage necessary adjustments. The net economic effect of excessive reserves, however, is to suppress balanced economic growth in reserve-accumulating countries. The Fund was meant to counter the self-insurance impulse, and it therefore evolved into the prime crisis manager for developing countries. It was an instrument designed to foster burden-sharing in the process of international economic adjustment. It

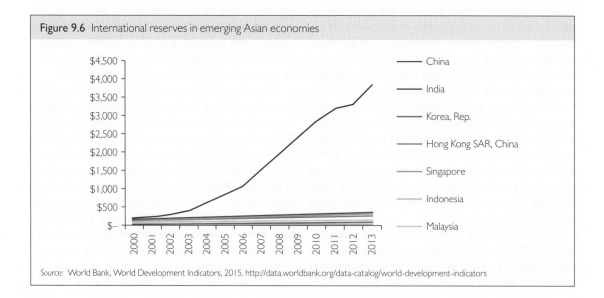

Figure 9.6 International reserves in emerging Asian economies

Source: World Bank, World Development Indicators, 2015. http://data.worldbank.org/data-catalog/world-development-indicators

signified that creditor states and debtor states were embarked together in the construction of global markets.

As in the early years of the Bretton Woods era, the leading states in the system confronted three basic choices every time one country or another could not pay its bills to external customers or service its debts to external creditors:

1. They could do nothing, and risk a crisis spilling over to other countries and perhaps into their own domestic systems as well.

2. They could intervene directly by providing adequate financing from their own resources to the troubled country, and work directly with it to address the fundamental causes of the problem.

3. Or they could do the same indirectly, collectively, and more cheaply through the Fund and other collaborative institutions.

In practice, the third option has often proved to be the least unattractive of the three. For countries whose periodic debt problems were widely perceived to be capable of seriously disrupting the system as a whole, the option of doing nothing, and of thereby letting markets attempt to force necessary adjustments, seldom seemed wise to actual policymakers charged with making such a decision. Moreover, the option of exposing their own taxpayers to the costs of crisis resolution has typically proven itself to be almost as unpalatable as trying unilaterally to impose conditions on recalcitrant debtors. The third option, therefore, nearly always found a sufficient number of advocates, in both creditor and debtor countries alike.

The conventional wisdom before recent financial crises in the United States, Europe, and Asia held that this logic only applied to less powerful economies. Burden-sharing instruments like the post-1970s IMF could therefore be kept limited in scale and scope, combined with technocratic work on toughening common regulatory and supervisory standards, would be adequate to the task of preventing future systemic crises. Despite the near catastrophes of recent years, many apparently retain their faith that more open and integrating markets are all that is required to encourage states, whether powerful or not, to collaborate on matters vital to their own long-run economic interests. The question before policymakers around the word is whether they need to hedge that bet.

KEY POINTS

- International financial crises are more difficult to manage than domestic crises because of jurisdictional ambiguities and intense conflicts of interest.

- Some basic level of cross-national coordination is required in international crisis management and resolution; intergovernmental institutions can play a supportive role, but their main missions have typically focused on reducing the likelihood of the next crisis and helping to manage debt repayment difficulties.

- Foreign exchange reserves provide the policy space required for prudent economic adjustments, but excessively high reserves signal profound domestic and systemic imbalances and complicated political challenges.

Building global governing capacity?

Perhaps there was a moment in time, just after 1945, when one could sense a window opening on a world where states would for the common good delegate coherent pieces of their governing capacities to neutral international agencies with binding, enforceable mandates. By 1973, alas, they had obviously conceded that even necessary monetary and fiscal collaboration in an increasingly interdependent economic system would occur only on a voluntary basis, even as they boldly opened their national financial markets to one another. More integrated, fluid, and much larger markets would develop apace over the next few decades. Those markets would themselves become key instruments for the global distribution and redistribution of political and economic resources. The sovereign authority ultimately required to govern them, however, would continue to be locally bounded.

States at the core of the system then confronted the necessity of coordinating regulatory and supervisory policies aimed at preventing systemic financial crises. When emergencies arose anyway, they improvised. Even inside a European Union formally committed to establishing a single market for financial services, deep political integration remained elusive and compliance with agreed standards imperfect. The prospect of future joint gains from macroeconomic policy coordination proved not to be a very successful motivator for governance innovation. On the other hand, the credible prospect of catastrophic national and systemic losses at moments of emergency has so far concentrated minds and delivered a minimally adequate degree of ad hoc policy collaboration. The costs of repeated financial crises are staggering, and after each one the wisdom of continuing the experiment in incomplete politico-economic integration at both regional and global levels was debated. The expansion of short and long-term capital flows through more open markets nevertheless continued to define the globalizing system of the early twenty-first century.

Global governance, effective and legitimate, seems logically required by the continuing existence and expansion of systemically significant financial institutions (Beck 2009). As memories of emergency fade, however, support can only be mustered for modest voluntary adjustments in policies aimed mainly at measuring systemic risks more precisely and bolstering systemic shock-absorbers. This explains the mission the G20 club has assigned to the Financial Stability Board (FSB) to promote higher and more common capital and liquidity standards for a widening array of intermediaries. It also explains the renewed prominence of central bank networks and the enhancement of currency swap arrangements within them.

The rise of emerging-market economies in the context of increasingly volatile capital movements adds a degree of complexity to the task of building reliable governing capacity beyond the national level. Their leaders and citizens have every right to worry about a process dominated by the great powers that struggles to balance economic efficiency and social justice on a global scale. It remains noteworthy, though, that few have embraced the idea of capital controls on anything other than a temporary or partial basis.

The actual capacity to manage global financial risks is evolving differentially across the spectrum of risk assessment, crisis prevention, and emergency management. Shaping arrangements and future expectations in each of these three policy arenas are different kinds of politics. The politics of risk assessment mainly involves social learning, common knowledge, and technical coordination through international organizations and specialized associations, leavened by competitive market dynamics. The politics of crisis prevention turns on ever more complicated institutional efforts to put the basic principles of insurance systems—risk pooling, portfolio diversification, burden sharing, and joint regulation to reduce moral hazards—into cross-national and cross-sectoral policy practice. Finally, the politics of emergency management continues to incline toward assertive governance

in a hierarchical system periodically spurred into action by the spectre of catastrophic losses.

At a time when systemic power is shifting underneath a globalizing economy, the logic of functional spillovers here meets the hard politics of establishing robust and appropriate governing structures. Global finance is characterized by more complex interdependence *and* more obvious political conflict (Kirshner 2014). Uncertainties abound, but faith in the future remains warranted. Solidarity, after all, has emerged in human communities in the past not from rhetorical appeals but from functional necessity and political struggle. The impulses that gave rise to the governing capacity of the modern state itself suggest the eventual emergence of its successor. The analytically separable logics of risk assessment, crisis prevention, and emergency management—in finance and in other arenas of global policy—open a pathway to imagining its variegated structure. More reliable coordination in risk assessment and crisis prevention may not soon be matched by undoubted global capacity for resolving emergencies. But that does not mean it never can be.

Until some form of fiscal authority moves decisively to the level implied by the scale and scope of global markets, the evolving capacity to govern them will rest on uneasy foundations. Institutional innovations like the Basel Process, the Financial Stability Board, deepening central-bank cooperation, and, within Europe, a nascent banking union and collective supervisory system, may for a time help us cope with rising systemic risks. The actual expansion of cross-national public and private insurance systems, systems that promise to engender a sense of shared fate, might gradually bolster confidence in common governing arrangements. Finally, although straightforward *ex ante* emergency burden-sharing agreements across diverse societies may remain rare for a time, repeated ad hoc burden-sharing practices during systemic emergencies do certainly give rise to reasonable expectations of future cross-national and cross-regional policymaking. In the absence of such confidence, the global experiment in financial integration will ultimately fail. Associated global risks, however, would not then disappear. They would simply be transferred to other policy arenas, including the arena of security policy. The anticipation and resolution of global financial crises therefore call forth at the global level both contentious politics and creative policies. If the experiment proceeds, global governing capacity will develop.

? QUESTIONS

1. What causes financial crises, and why do some quickly spread around the world?

2. What special risks are associated with cross-border finance, and how have regulatory authorities tried to assess them?

3. What measures hold promise for preventing future financial crises?

4. How can international financial crises be more effectively managed?

5. How durable are current political constraints on multilateralizing and formalizing better instruments for managing and resolving financial crises?

6. How should we evaluate issues of distributive justice raised by financial market openness, both for the system as a whole and for specific countries?

≋ FURTHER READING

Abdelal, R. (2007), *Capital Rules: The Construction of Global Finance* (Cambridge, MA: Harvard University Press). An insightful analysis of the normative foundations of contemporary international capital markets.

Drezner, D. (2014), *The System Worked: How the World Stopped Another Great Depression* (Oxford: Oxford University Press). A provocative argument on the management and resolution of the systemic crisis of 2008.

Eichengreen, B. (2003), *Capital Flows and Crises* (Cambridge, MA: MIT Press). A readily accessible account of the causes and consequences of international financial crises.

Financial Crisis Inquiry Commission (2011), *The Financial Crisis Inquiry Report* (New York: Public Affairs). The official report on the crisis of 2008.

Germain, R. (2010), *Global Politics & Financial Governance* (London: Palgrave Macmillan). A concise history of globalizing finance and its regulatory dilemmas.

Helleiner, E. (2014), *The Status Quo Crisis: Global Financial Governance after the 2008 Meltdown* (Oxford: Oxford University Press). A historically rich survey of the policy environment within which the crisis of 2008 played out and ambitious post-crisis reform failed to be achieved.

James, H. (2009), *The Creation and Destruction of Value* (Cambridge, MA: Harvard University Press). A brilliant and historically grounded assessment of the cycles of economic and financial globalization.

Kindleberger, C. P. (1978), *Manias, Panics, and Crashes: A History of Financial Crises* (New York: Basic Books). A path-breaking orientation to the fragile financial underpinnings of modern capitalism.

Kirshner, J. (2014), *American Power after the Financial Crisis* (Ithaca, NY: Cornell University Press). A sceptical view of the durability of an American-led economic order in the aftermath of the 2008 crisis.

Lewis, M. (2010), *The Big Short: Inside the Doomsday Machine* (New York: Norton). Best-selling and accessible account of the unfolding crisis of 2008. A highly successful film version directed by Adam McKay premiered in December 2015.

Martinez-Diaz, L. (2009), *Globalizing in Hard Times: The Politics of Banking-Sector Opening in the Emerging World* (Ithaca, NY: Cornell University Press). A compelling political analysis of financial liberalization in emerging-market countries.

Minsky, H. (1986), *Stabilizing an Unstable Economy* (New Haven, CT: Yale University Press). The original and prescient analysis of the inherent fragility of financial markets.

Obstfeld, M. and Taylor, A. (2004), *Global Capital Markets: Integration, Crisis, and Growth* (Cambridge: Cambridge University Press). A detailed history of international capital mobility since the late nineteenth century by two prominent economists.

Pauly, L. (1997), *Who Elected the Bankers? Surveillance and Control in the World Economy* (Ithaca, NY: Cornell University Press). An examination of the development of the IMF and its principal role in the wake of twentieth-century monetary and financial crises.

Reinhart, C. and Rogoff, K. (2009), *This Time is Different: Eight Centuries of Financial Folly* (Princeton, NJ: Princeton University Press). A comprehensive and controversial empirical examination of the history of financial crises.

Sen, A. (2009), *The Idea of Justice* (Cambridge, MA: Belknap/Harvard University Press). Behind the technical discussions of globally minded financial experts lie significant issues of legitimacy and justice, and this book provides a foundation for beginning to grapple with them.

WEBLINKS

www.imf.org International Monetary Fund.

www.worldbank.org The World Bank Group.

www.financialstabilityboard.org The Financial Stability Board.

www.un.org/esa/desa United Nations, Department of Economic and Social Affairs.

www.bis.org Bank for International Settlements.

www.oecd.org Organisation for Economic Co-operation and Development.

www.g7.utoronto.ca and **www.g20.utoronto.ca** G7/8 and G20 Information Centres.

ONLINE RESOURCE CENTRE

For additional material and resources, please visit the Online Resource Centre at:
www.oxfordtextbooks.co.uk/ravenhill5e

PART IV
Globalization and the State

10

The Logics of Economic Globalization

Anthony McGrew

Reader's guide

In the aftermath of the Global Financial Crisis (GFC) of 2008 the pace of economic globalization has moderated significantly. Some consider the GFC and the responses to it as marking the end of globalization as we have known it. Despite the many obituaries for globalization—understood simply as the widening, deepening, and speeding up of worldwide interconnectedness—this chapter argues that it has proved far more resilient than predicted. Though as recent developments affirm neither is it inevitable nor immutable. Arguably the current 'great moderation' of economic globalization prefigures less its demise than its reformation or to use the World Bank's phrase 'the Next Wave of Globalization' (World Bank 2007b). But this remains a contentious assertion especially given the difficulty of distinguishing cyclical from structural trends in the global political economy. To understand the dynamics of economic globalization invites an examination of its underlying causes which is the principal focus of this chapter.

The chapter is concerned with the underlying causes (or logics) of economic globalization. In comparing and contrasting the principal theoretical accounts of economic globalization, it seeks to establish how these contribute to our understanding of the current phase of globalization and its future prospects. In doing so it leaves to other chapters (see Hay Chapter 11, Wade Chapter 12, and Phillips Chapter 13 in this volume) wider considerations of the implications of globalization for state sovereignty, patterns of inequality, or social democracy. In short, the chapter addresses four related questions:

1. What is economic globalization and what are its principal features?

2. How do theories of international political economy assist us in explaining and understanding economic globalization?

3. What, if anything, is distinctive about economic globalization today?

4. Has the GFC precipitated the demise of globalization or the emergence of a 'new wave'?

Introduction

Obituaries for economic globalization remain, even many years after the GFC, a regularly recurring theme in the media (*Washington Post* 2015; Chancellor 2016; Donnan 2016). Yet, this 'second age of globalization' (the first age being the belle époque of 1870–1914) has proved far more resilient and socially embedded than many (even its most ardent advocates) have acknowledged. Indeed, at the turn of this century, in the aftermath of the events of 9/11, there was a widely shared belief that 'The era of globalisation is over' (Naim 2002; Rosenberg 2005: 2; Saul 2005). Certainly, measured in terms of flows within the circuits of the world economy, economic globalization appeared to stall in the early part of the new century. Yet this slowdown proved temporary as patterns of global economic exchange subsequently intensified, actually peaking prior to the onset of the Global Financial Crisis (GFC) in late 2008 (see Pauly, Chapter 9 in this volume for a discussion of the origins and fallout from the crisis). Some years ago the annual *Foreign Policy* Globalization Index noted: 'The resilience of globalization indicates that it is a phenomenon that runs deeper than the political crises of the day' (Kearney and *Foreign Policy* Globalization Index 2005: 53). Today many years after the GFC, economic globalization appears remarkably resilient despite the fact that for a period global trade, capital flows, and production initially did not just decline (in real terms) but actually went into reverse. While the spectre of deglobalization, as in the Great Depression of the twentieth century, returned it has so far not come to pass (James 2009; Roxburgh *et al.* 2009). One explanation for this resilience, explored later in this chapter, is that economic globalization may be much more 'socially and institutionally embedded' than either its advocates or its critics have presumed (James 2001). This is certainly not to argue that it is either historically inevitable or immutable, but rather to appreciate the ways—structural, institutional, political, and ideational—in which economic globalization continues to constitute the dominant (but not the sole) tendency in the contemporary world economy. Obituaries for this 'second age of globalization' have therefore proved somewhat premature. But this is not to overlook some of the profound changes in recent patterns of economic globalization, which for some heralds a distinctive 'new wave' (World Bank, 2007b; Breznitz and Zysman 2013; DHL 2014; Kelly 2014).

Before examining whether this might be the case it is important to understand the concept of globalization as defined in the global political economy literature. Accordingly, the first section of the chapter will address three interrelated questions, namely:

1. What is globalization?
2. What are the key trends associated with the globalization of economic activity?
3. Is globalization still the dominant trend or tendency in the world economy today?

Following on from this discussion, the second section will reflect upon the primary causes and the dominant theories of globalization. In doing so, it will review an important distinction between what Rosenberg (2000) refers to as 'theories of globalization' and 'globalization theory'. Section three will develop this causal analysis to explore the notion of 'embedded globalization' through a comparison of its first 'golden age' (1870–1914) with the current epoch—the second age of globalization. In the final section, the discussion will consider whether, in the aftermath of the GFC, the world is witnessing a historic retreat or retrenchment of economic globalization or the emergence of a distinctive 'new wave'?

A global economy? 'Embedded globalization' and the rescaling of economic activity

Globalization, at least in the political economy literature, is taken to be synonymous with a process of intensifying worldwide economic integration. Hirst and Thompson assert that: 'We can only begin to assess the issue of globalization if we have some relatively clear and rigorous model of what a global economy would be like' (2003: 99). This economism—i.e. globalization is understood solely, or even principally, as an economic phenomenon—contrasts with a broader understanding of the concept within the social science literatures (see Box 10.1). In this broader literature, globalization (or more accurately globalizations) is conceived as a multidimensional, rather than singular, process—evident across the cultural, political, ecological, military, and social domains—which is both historically open-ended (in so far as it does not prefigure a unified global society) and complex, in that it is associated with patterns of worldwide integration

BOX 10.1

Globalization

Globalization has been variously defined in the literature as:

1. 'The intensification of worldwide social relations which link distant localities in such a way that local happenings are shaped by events occurring many miles away and vice versa' (Giddens 1990: 21).

2. 'The integration of the world economy' (Gilpin 2001: 364).

3. 'the interconnectedness of the world as whole and the corresponding increase in reflexive, global consciousness' (Turner and Holton, 2015: 10)

4. 'the spread of transplanetary—and in recent times also increasingly supraterritorial—connections between people' (Scholte, 2008)

5. '[T]he international integration of markets in goods, services, and capital' (Garrett 2000a: 941).

and fragmentation (Held *et al.* 1999; Keohane and Nye 2003; Axford 2013; Turner and Holton 2015). Underlying these different conceptions are significant methodological disagreements concerning the study of what the famous social historian Charles Tilly referred to as 'Big Structures, Large Processes' or macro-historical change (Tilly 1989; Rosenberg 1995). This suggests the need for some conceptual caution in two significant respects: in automatically privileging the economic in accounting for globalization, but more especially in drawing general conclusions about globalization per se solely from an analysis of economic trends. 'Economizing globalization', in other words, is a methodological oversimplification. That said, no analysis of globalization can, or should, ignore its economic dimension.

Conceptually, globalization is often elided with notions of liberalization, internationalization, universalization, Westernization, or modernization (Scholte 2008). However, as Scholte notes, none of these terms capture its distinctive attributes or qualities. Within the global political economy literature, economic globalization tends to be more precisely specified as 'the emergence and operation of a single, worldwide economy' (Grieco and Ikenberry 2003: 207). It is measured by reference to the growing intensity, extensity, and velocity of worldwide economic interactions and interconnectedness, from trade, through

production and finance, to migration. In this regard, it is conceived as a *process*, rather than a fixed outcome or condition, in so far as it refers to a *historical tendency* towards heightened levels of worldwide economic interconnectedness. Indeed, there is a substantive conceptual difference between the notion of a globalizing world economy and a fully or partially *globalized world economy* that implies a fixed state or condition of economic integration.

This distinction between process and condition (that is 'becoming' and 'being') is emphasized by many scholars seeking to differentiate between globalization—as a historical process—and globalism—the resulting condition at any particular historical moment (Keohane and Nye 2003; Holton 2005; Axford 2013). The implication is that, since globalization is neither an inevitable nor a secular tendency, it is associated, at particular historical moments, with thicker or thinner forms of globalism. Translated into the language of global political economy, globalization is thereby associated historically with deeper or shallower forms of worldwide economic integration.

Understood as a process, economic globalization also implies an evolving *transformation* or qualitative shift in the organization and dynamics of the world economy. Quite simply, cumulative patterns and networks of transborder economic activity over time dissolve the presumed separation of the world into bounded or discrete national economic systems. This process makes the distinction between the domestic and world economy increasingly problematic to sustain—for academics and policymakers alike. In other words, globalization generates emergent tendencies or systemic properties in the world economy such that increasingly it begins to operate as a singular system (Sayer 2000; Goldin and Mariathasan 2015). This structural shift may be evident in, among other things, synchronized worldwide markets, the operation of transnational production networks (see Thun, Chapter 7 in this volume), a worldwide division of labour, together with functioning of institutionalized systems of global regulation ranging from the World Trade Organization (WTO) to the International Accounting Standards Board (IASB).

Underlying these shifts in the scale of economic organization are contemporary informatics technologies and infrastructures of communication and transportation. These have facilitated new forms and possibilities of virtual real-time worldwide economic organization and coordination. In the process, distance and time are substantially reconfigured, such that, for example, economic and other shocks in one region of the world can rapidly diffuse around the globe, often with serious local consequences (see, for example, Pauly, Chapter 9 in this volume). Although geography still matters very much, it is nevertheless the case that globalization is associated with a process of *time–space compression*—literally a shrinking world—in which the sources of even very localized economic developments, from interest rate changes to corporate restructuring, may be traced to economic decisions or markets on other continents.

However, a single worldwide economy is not necessarily coextensive with a universal or planetary economy. More specifically, 'worldwide' is generally taken to refer to *inter-regional or intercontinental* patterns of economic exchange and enmeshment. Accordingly, globalization is best conceived as embodying a *rescaling* of economic space manifested in the intensification of inter- or supraregional and multicontinental networks and flows of economic activity (Brenner 1999). In this respect, it is one (albeit significant) historical tendency operating within the world economy, just as regionalization, nationalization, and localization can be identified as other tendencies—whether as complementary or competing tendencies is a matter of contention. As a principal tendency, globalization denotes a relative *denationalization* of economic relations as significant aspects of economic life become organized increasingly on an inter-regional or multicontinental scale transcending bounded national economic space (Held *et al.* 1999; Scholte 2005;). This rescaling, however, is not experienced uniformly across every region or economy, since globalization is also recognizably an uneven *process*. Differential patterns of enmeshment in, or marginalization from, the worldwide economy define its 'variable geometry' (Castells 2000). Such unevenness generates a distinctive geography of inclusion and exclusion such that the notion of a worldwide or global economy is less (geographically and socially) inclusive than that of a universal or planetary economic order. The implications of this distinction, as will become clear, are highly significant for empirical assessments of economic globalization.

This particular conception of economic globalization invites two related questions:

- What empirical evidence is there to substantiate claims concerning the recent globalization of economic activity?

- Is globalization still a dominant tendency within the contemporary world economy?

There is a huge literature on these basic questions which has been shaped by successive 'waves' of academic controversy and debate (Martell, 2007; Axford 2013; Turner and Holton 2015). Simplifying this literature, two broad schools of analysis can be identified: the globalist and the sceptical. In short, globalists consider that world economic trends disclose significant if not historically unprecedented levels of worldwide economic integration which reflect the operation of a singular world capitalist economy. Globalization, in this account, is the principal or dominant tendency in the world economy. By contrast the sceptics dispute, not only the scale and intensity of globalization, but also conclude that contrary tendencies, from growing regionalism, mercantilism to intensifying geo-economic competition, are much more significant trends in the world economy. At the height of the GFC, for instance, governments responded by nationalizing or bailing out national banks and providing state aid to beleaguered sectors of the national economy. Rather than a more economically integrated world the sceptics emphasize the trend towards a more highly segmented and fragmented world economy. Clearly this is an oversimplification of much more sophisticated analyses but it offers, nevertheless, a useful heuristic device for interpreting the principal trends in the world economy in respect of trade, finance, production, and labour.

Trade

For the globalists the confluence of secular rising trends in patterns of world trade, capital flows, transnational production, and migration affirms the primacy of the globalization tendency. As Samir Amin concludes, while economic globalization is nothing new, it has 'undeniably taken a qualitative step forward during the recent period' (1997: 31). For most of the post-war period, world trade has grown much faster than world output, and significantly so since the beginning of the 1990s (Irwin 2002; WTO 2006c). World exports, measured as a proportion of world output, were three times greater in 1998 than in 1950; the WTO estimates this ratio stood at 29 per cent in 2001 and was about 27 per cent in 2005, in comparison with 17 per cent in 1990 and 12.5 per cent in 1970 and well above 30 per cent in 2015 which is 'at near historic levels' (WTO

2001*a*, 2006*a*; Hoekman 2015 :5; WTO 2015*a*: 17). Despite 9 / 11 and the subsequent downturn in the world economy, world trade measured as a proportion of world output remained at levels well in excess of that of the 1990s until the GFC (Kearney and *Foreign Policy* Globalization Index 2003; WTO 2003*a*, 2006*a*). But even many years after the GFC the ratio of total world trade to world GDP stands at 60 per cent compared to 25 per cent in the 1960s and still 'much higher today than it was twenty years ago' (Hoekman 2015:5; WTO 2015*a*: 17). World merchandise trade peaked in 2008 at almost \$16 trillion compared to \$10 trillion in 2005 (WTO 2009*a*). This is one hundred times the value of world trade in 1963. Services trade stood at \$2,415 billion in 2005, and \$3,778 billion in 2008 (compared to \$365 billion in 1980, an almost 700 per cent increase) (WTO 2006*c*, 2009*a*). However, by the end of 2009, world trade had collapsed at an unprecedented rate, much faster and deeper than in the Great Depression or any subsequent post-war recession (Eichengreen and O'Rourke 2009). In comparison with 2008, the value of world trade in 2009 fell by an unparalleled 33 per cent (goods exports volume fell by 22 per cent and world exports volume by 12 per cent) (WTO 2009*b*: 3; World Bank 2010*a*: 3, 33; WTO 2015*a*: 14;). All major exporters, especially Japan and China, recorded export declines in excess of 20 per cent (Wynne and Kersting 2009). At the height of the GFC, the growth trend of world trade had not just stalled but had reversed with such a 'remarkable degree of synchronization', that in early 2009 all the world's trading economies recorded negative trade growth (Araújo and Martins 2009). The 'Great Trade Collapse' was unprecedented in both the scale and speed of its transmission (Bems and Johnson *et al*. 2012). By 2012, however, there had been a rebound in world trade (value not volume) to \$18.2 trillion (compared with the previous peak in 2008) although the pattern was highly uneven (WTO 2012: 19). Services trade had recovered to \$4.2 trillion while trade volumes were back at 2008 levels but well below trend growth (WTO 2012: 19). But this recovery has not been sustained with trade growth well below historical trend growth accompanied in 2014 / 15 by a further decline in the value of world trade (Evenett 2015: 7; WTO 2015*b*; Donnan, 2016). Underlying this 'sluggishness of trade' as the WTO refers to it is a significant fracturing of the relationship between global economic growth and world trade (in technical terms the income elasticity of trade). More precisely 'the rough two-to-one relationship that prevailed for many years between world

trade volume growth and world GDP growth appears to have broken down' in so far as it currently stands at 1.5 (WTO 2015*b*: 15; Hoekman 2015). This is quite a profound change and if permanent would imply 'a fundamental change in the structure of the global economy' and a potentially significant moderation if not reversal of the historical pattern of trade globalization (UN 2015: 34; Evenett 2015). But the sources of this slowdown in global trade are the subject of significant debate (Hoekman 2015). In particular whether it is the result of slowing global growth (i.e. cyclical factors) or the changing composition of world trade, the growth of global production networks or trade protectionism (i.e. structural factors) matters significantly for the future pattern of trade globalization (Donnan 2016).Whether the great moderation in trade globalization is the new normal remains an open question although the depth and breadth of trade globalization remains much greater today than in the last two decades even if it is below the pre-GFC peak of 2008 (Subrimanian and Kessler 2013).

A significant factor in this synchronized global trade collapse resulted from an expanding number of countries and sectors becoming enmeshed in world trade as a consequence of the rise of global production networks. The changing structure of manufactures production increasingly involving global supply (value) chains now accounts for a very significant proportion of world trade at 49 per cent in 2011 compared to 36 per cent in 1995 (WTO 2015*a*:18). As a consequence, emerging and developing economies now account for a growing share of world export markets and this has intensified further as a result of the Global Financial Crisis (increasing from 19.2 per cent in 1970 to 32.1 per cent in 2005 and an unprecedented 47 per cent in 2011). Trade has become increasingly important to national economic welfare, in particular in emerging economies, as evidenced by the growing share of national **gross domestic product** **(GDP)** accounted for by exports. Over the post-war period, the ratio of exports to GDP for all countries increased from 5.5 per cent in 1950 to 17.2 per cent in 1998, and for many of the major Organisation for Economic Co-operation and Development (OECD) and developing states it more than doubled (Kaplinsky 2005: Table 1.1). Trade now reaches wider and deeper than ever before into more sectors of many more national economies as an expanded array of goods have become tradable.

Of course, world trade for much of the post-war period has been highly concentrated, both geographically—OECD countries accounted for the largest proportion of world merchandise trade (some 65 per cent), and a small number of East Asian countries for the bulk of developing countries' exports—and sectorally. In 2005, manufacturing constituted 58 per cent of total world trade (in value terms), fuels 13.9 per cent, services 20 per cent, and agriculture only 6.7 per cent (Held *et al.* 1999; UNCTAD 2005: 133; WTO 2006*a*). This concentration was hardly surprising, given that OECD countries accounted for the largest share of world economic output and were by far the largest economic units. Yet, since the 1990s, this dominance has become increasingly diluted with developed economies' market share of world merchandise exports declining from 75 per cent in 1970 to 64.8 per cent in 2003 and 54 per cent in 2014 (UNCTAD 2005: 133; WTO 2015*a*: 35). This erosion of trade dominance is associated with the emergence of new trading powers (such as Brazil, Russia, India, and China—the so-called 'BRICs' economies) resulting from structural changes in the world economy associated with a new global division of labour (changes in countries' trade specialization in the world economy) and the intensification of worldwide competition through trade (UNCTAD 2005: 133).

Furthermore, patterns of trade have altered significantly since the 1960s and particularly so in this century accelerating in the wake of the 'great trade collapse'. A new geography of trade exists reflecting the changing location of manufacturing production as East Asia and other **newly industrializing economies** (NIEs) take on the role as the world's factories. At the same time, most OECD economies have expanded markedly their trade in services significantly and these now account for almost a quarter of their exports (WTO 2006*a*). Falling costs of transportation, the communications revolution, liberalization, and the growth of **transnational corporations** have all contributed to a new global division of labour. This restructuring is evident in the shifting pattern of developing country exports from commodities to manufactures and services (fuels account for 18 per cent (by value), commodities 12.7 per cent, and manufactures 68.1 per cent, compared to 38.8 per cent, 26 per cent, and 31.4 per cent, respectively, in 1980 (UNCTAD 2005: 91)).

In just over a quarter of a century, the share of manufactures in developing countries' exports has more than doubled. This shift has also been accompanied in recent years by a significant expansion in trade between developing economies (South–South trade) that has also almost doubled, from 22.9 per cent to 40.9 per cent of their total exports and over 50 per cent by 2010. However, this South–South trade is highly concentrated among East Asian economies, which accounted for some two-thirds of its total in 2003 (UNCTAD 2005). Even so, the NIEs have become increasingly primary engines of global trade, such that the World Bank observes that, 'growth in the global economy will be powered increasingly by developing countries' (World Bank 2007*b*: xiii). In just over three decades, China has evolved from being a negligible force in global trade to the world's largest exporter in 2009, eclipsing Japan, the US, and Germany (WTO 2009*a*: 12). The GFC has accelerated these structural shifts in the geography of trade and the distribution of trade power with the share of world trade accounted for by emerging and developing economies more than doubling in the last three decades (15.9 per cent to 31.5 per cent in 2012 and 39 per cent in 2014) (World Bank 2013*b*; WTO 2015*a*: 24).

These structural shifts constitute a new pattern of specialization (or division of labour) within the world economy, which is also associated with an intensification of global economic competition (Findlay and O'Rourke 2007). In 2003, 40 per cent of manufactured imports into the OECD economies were produced in developing economies, compared with 12 per cent in 1973 (World Bank 2007*b*: xix). In the manufacturing sector, and also increasingly within the services sectors, the expansion of trade increases competitive pressures on domestic businesses, in both the North and the South. It is not just that OECD economies confront cheaper imports from the world's new manufacturing zones, in East Asia or Latin America, or lower-cost services from India and South Africa, but that competition among and between the OECD economies and developing economies has also intensified as production and markets have become globalized.

Lower-cost imports impose greater price competition, while the dominance of **intra-industry trade** (trade in similar products or services) between OECD economies brings domestic business and labour into direct competition with their foreign counterparts. This development has significant distributional consequences for employment and wage levels within countries, although decomposing its effects is a complicated matter such that its implications for labour remain contested (Lawrence 1996*b*). Seeking competitive advantage is articulated either through more efficient domestic production methods or the fragmentation of production—that is, 'slicing up the value chain' or outsourcing production such that firms draw on worldwide networks of suppliers that produce where the greatest **economies of scale** or efficiency gains can be realized (see Thun, Chapter 7 in this volume). Through such mechanisms, productive and competitive forces become globalized while economies in different regions become more tightly integrated. One study suggests that intra-industry and inter-firm trade accounted for at least 30 per cent of the growth of world trade in the period 1970–90 (Hummels 2001). Moreover, as already noted these global production chains account for a major proportion of world merchandise trade. Trade is therefore associated increasingly with the consolidation of a new global division of labour between North and South.

In so far as dense trade flows occur between the major regions of the world economy—namely, the Asia-Pacific, North American Free Trade Agreement (NAFTA), and European Union (EU) cores—there exist global markets in goods and services. The most obvious examples of such markets are those in key primary commodities, such as oil or wheat, which set benchmark world prices. But global markets are far from the textbook notion of the perfectly integrated market. Despite the dramatic trade liberalization since the 1960s, in which formal tariffs have become negligible (average world tariff rates almost halved from 15 per cent to 8 per cent between the 1970s and 1990s), significant **non-tariff barriers** to trade remain, while distance, history, and culture still continue to influence patterns of world trade (Centre for Economic Policy Reform 2002). This makes all the more remarkable both the scale and pre GFC annual rates of trade growth—15 per cent in 2008 and averaging 12 per cent since 2000 (WTO 2006a: 3; 2009b: 3). However, much trade is conducted regionally, leading to the suggestion that the dominant tendency in the world economy is one of regionalization rather than globalization (Chortareas and Pelagidis 2004: 253). This is particularly evident in the significant growth of regionalism (see Ravenhill, Chapter 6 in this volume) over recent decades. Yet, as R. E. Baldwin concludes in an exhaustive study of contemporary regional trading arrangements, there are good theoretical and empirical reasons to believe that 'multilateral and regional liberalisation [have] proceeded in tandem since 1947' (Baldwin 2006: 1487). Moreover, the increasing fragmentation of production creates significant pressures

for competitive liberalization and makes it difficult to sustain any effective trade bloc 'when part of your wall encompasses the enemy camp' (Baldwin 2006: 1495). Despite regionalism, there is also evidence of a tendency for price differentials for traded goods to narrow, as might be expected in a global market place (IMF 2002: 122). Studies suggest that distance is no longer as crucial a determinant of patterns of world trade as in the past or that even if it is of growing relative significance its impact on trade is marginal (Coe *et al.* 2002; Standaert 2015). Nor, too, does regionalism appear to be producing a segmentation of the world economy into separate regional markets. Although patterns of regional trade present a complex picture, *intra-regional* trade as a proportion of world merchandise trade, at an estimated 36 per cent, was lower in 2001 than it was throughout the 1990s (WTO 2001a: 6). As Table 6.3 (Ravenhill, Chapter 6 in this volume) indicates, the evidence does not demonstrate a secular trend towards the regional segmentation of the world economy. In the wake of the GFC there is some evidence of an intensification of intra-regional trade but it remains as yet inconclusive (WTO 2015b; DHL/NYU 2015). Moreover, the trade data conceals the strategic importance to many economies of specific commodities in inter-regional compared to intra-regional trade (for example, oil). While the primacy of transnational production networks, as Baldwin observes, dissolves the distinctions between intra-regional and inter-regional trade activity, which is also obscured in aggregate trade data (Baldwin 2006). For example, the growth of regional trade among East Asian economies is principally a trade in intermediate products that are then assembled (predominantly in China) for export as finished goods to OECD markets in Europe and the US (UNCTAD 2005: 136–8).

Of course, formally, under WTO rules—which have acquired almost universal application—regional arrangements must be compatible with the principles of the multilateral trade regime (see Ravenhill, Chapter 6 in this volume). This institutionalization of global rule-making and adjudication in trade matters marks a seminal development in the political construction of a truly global trade system. Through its very existence and functioning, the WTO defines a global regulatory framework that effectively constitutes the normative and legal foundations of global markets and their operation. In this respect, global markets are not just spontaneous constructions, but partly the product of the regulatory activities of multilateral bodies such as the WTO, not to mention the expanding role of transnational private merchant law (the new *lex mercatoria*) (Gill 1995; Cutler 2003). To this extent, trade globalization is not simply about trends in world trade but also about the critical importance of global and transnational trade authorities in the *constitution* of global markets. In the wake of the GFC the extension of temporary forms of state protectionism (many of which continue in force) has been a factor in the sluggish growth of trade. For some it also represents an increasingly significant institutional restraint on future global trade growth and trade globalization (Evenett 2015).

Finance

Until comparatively recently, international finance was considered to be principally an adjunct to trade, a necessary mechanism enabling the international exchange of goods and services (Eichengreen 1996; Germain 1997). This direct association between finance and trade began to dissolve in the nineteenth century. By the twenty-first century, it became irrelevant, or at best marginal. Daily turnover on foreign exchange markets more than doubled, from $590 billion in 1989 to $1,210 billion in 2001, increasing to $3,500 billion in 2008, peaking at an astonishing $5,344 billion in 2013, and in 2016 averaging $5,088 billion (by comparison daily world exports were approximately $43 billion in 2008) (*BIS Quarterly Review* 2001; Grieco and Ikenberry 2003: 214; BIS 2007: 1, 2010: 7, 2014:1, 2016: 3). Recent growth, generated in part by the instabilities of the financial crisis, has been so spectacular that it has become increasingly a focus of concern amongst global regulators.

As a multiple of world merchandise trade, annual foreign exchange turnover in 1973 was equivalent to twice the value of annual world trade, but by 2008 it was equivalent to more than 60 times the value of annual world trade and significantly exceeds other global financial flows (Held and McGrew 2002: 48). Such activity, facilitated by instantaneous global communications, is conducted around the clock between the world's major financial centres on each continent. This worldwide foreign exchange market influences not just the value of traded currencies but also the level of key financial variables such as national interest rates, since it enables the rapid movement of capital around the globe.

Following the significant liberalization of national financial markets since the 1980s, the level and

geographical scope of global capital flows expanded enormously until the GFC. By comparison with trade, which exhibited a compound growth rate of almost 10 per cent over the period 1964–2001, transborder financial flows grew at a compound rate of almost 19 per cent (Bryant 2003: 141). To put this in context, Bryant calculates for the period 1964–2001 that, if the growth of international bonds—a form of securitized international lending/borrowing measured here in terms of stocks not flows—had been at an equivalent level to the growth rate of all OECD economies, stocks of international bonds would be valued at some $776 billion, only 11 per cent of the actual $7.2 trillion in 2001 (Bryant 2003: 142). Similar patterns are evident for all other types of transborder capital flows, from international issues of shares—which expanded from $8 billion in the 1980s to a peak of $300 billion in 2000, subsequently surpassed in 2005 ($307.5 billion); to cross-border trading in derivatives—which grew (measured in gross value) from $618.3 billion in 1986 to $4,224 billion in 2001 and more than doubled to $10,605 billion in 2005 (equivalent to the annual value of world merchandise trade); and transborder bank lending—which increased more than tenfold from $2,095 billion in 1983 to over $30,000 billion in 2008, but contracted to $25,000 billion in 2009 (Held *et al.* 1999: ch. 4; BIS 2003, 2005, 2006, 2009; Bryant 2003: 140; *BIS Quarterly Review* 2005, 2009). Global capital flows fluctuated between 2 and 6 per cent of world GDP over the period 1980–95, but by 2006 stood at 15 per cent of world GDP and at $17.2 trillion were three times the gross level of 1995 (IMF 2010*a*). In the aftermath of the GFC, global financial flows collapsed dramatically as banks and other financial institutions pursued a 'flight to safety', rapidly reducing international exposure by repatriating capital on a dramatic scale (*BIS Quarterly Review* 2009). Gross cross-border capital flows fell by some 82 per cent from $10.5 trillion (2007) to $1.9 trillion (2008), while global banks not only stopped lending but also drastically reduced their exposure in overseas markets (from $4.9 trillion in 2007 to $1.3 trillion in 2008) (Roxburgh *et al.* 2009: 13). Lending to emerging markets and overall global capital flows declined to levels well below those of the previous decade, such that Roxburgh suggests that, 'Financial globalization has reversed, with capital flows falling by more than 80%' (Roxburgh *et al.* 2009: 7). This trend was reinforced by the eurozone crisis throughout 2010/13 such that in 2012 overall cross-border capital flows (at $4.6 trillion) were some 61 per cent below their 2007 peak ($11.8 trillion) (Lund *et al.* 2013: 15). Repatriation and retrenchment of cross-border banking flows in the eurozone area is responsible for much of this contraction. Relative to world GDP the scale of gross capital flows has contracted dramatically since the GFC: between 2000 and 2007 it reached an average annual peak of 13.3 per cent compared with 6.2 per cent in the period 2008–12 (James 2014). However, this is largely due to the sustained collapse of interbank lending amongst advanced economies and most markedly in Europe (James 2014; BIS 2015). Though, as a recent study notes, this retrenchment conceals the significance of other modes of banking globalization which have expanded since the GFC (Claessens and van Horen 2014). Historically global capital flows remain above much of the period before the peak levels prior to the GFC and as a share of world GDP are comparable with the decade before the turn of the century which at the time was considered a phase of intense financial globalization (James 2014; BIS 2015).

As with trade, the bulk of capital flows (some 66 per cent) until fairly recently, have been concentrated amongst the major OECD economies. Although from the 1980s intercontinental flows have intensified—64 per cent of portfolio investments in stock markets are intercontinental—cross-border financial flows remain highly uneven (IMF 2003). While emerging economies are highly integrated into world financial markets, and increasingly so in the aftermath of the GFC, many of the world's poorest economies remain on the margins of these markets (*BIS Quarterly Review* 2005). Historically capital flows to developing states have fluctuated considerably since the 1970s, peaking in the mid 1990s prior to the East Asian crash and subsequently falling back, although by 2007 they had reached a new high (IMF 2003; World Bank 2007b: 15; World Bank 2010a). These flows are concentrated primarily among the principal emerging economies of Latin America, East Asia, and Eastern Europe which account for the bulk of non-OECD capital flows. Geography and history still exert an influence on capital flows (Thompson 2006). Although even in the wake of the GFC there is little evidence of regionalization of financial markets excepting for Asia where it appears to be an emerging trend (IMF 2015a: 60). But even the Asian economies with strong foreign exchange reserves have been able to insulate themselves fully from the volatility of global financial markets or the consequences of financial contagion in a 24-hour real-time global financial system (Desai 2003). This is particularly evident from

recent studies of the GFC (Wolf 2014; Farlow 2103). Moreover, the GFC has accelerated a profound shift in patterns of cross-border capital flows in that emerging and developing economies now account for almost a third of the global total and South to South flows have attained historic levels of some $1.9 trillion (Lund *et al.* 2013; BIS 2012: 79). In this regard the GFC is associated with a reconfiguration in the geography of global capital flows and while still highly concentrated the dominance of advanced economies has been further diluted. As James concludes: 'While global gross capital flows are now lower than they were in 2007, this reduction has not been broad based across economies and all types of capital flows. Much of the decline reflects a reduction in flows to and from advanced economies … In contrast, capital inflows to some economies have increased since the crisis, in particular those to emerging Asia' (2014: 72). Although cyclical factors, such as historic low interest rates amongst advanced economies in the wake of the GFC, have been significant drivers of huge capital flows to emerging markets, given these economies now account according to the BIS for 50 per cent of world GDP (PPP) this suggests the shifting geographic pattern of global capital flows is much more of a structural phenomenon despite the considerable volatility of such flows (BIS 2015:11; IMF 2015a and b).

Irrespective of the unevenness of transborder capital flows, studies suggest that, since the 1980s, there has been a significant integration of financial markets (Taylor 1996; Lane and Milesi-Ferretti 2003; Obstfeld and Taylor 2004). Financial integration is a matter of degree, or a tendency, expressed in relative measurements of greater or lesser intensity. It is assessed by a variety of measures (including stocks and flows of capital; asset and interest rate price convergence; synchronization of stock markets; foreign liabilities and assets to GDP, and national business cycles), with the consequence that: 'In attacking the problem of measuring [global] market integration, economists have no universally recognized criteria to turn to' (Obstfeld and Taylor 2004: 47). Not to mention the problem that different measures often lead to contradictory conclusions. Not surprisingly, this has produced a considerable debate as to the genuine scale and economic significance of financial globalization assessed in respect of tendencies towards the convergence, deepening, and institutionalization of worldwide financial activity, performance, and regulation (Watson 2001; Obstfeld and Taylor 2004).

Obstfeld and Taylor's (1998, 2003, 2004) econometric studies, among others, identify a narrowing of interest rate differentials between the major OECD economies after 1960 (they returned to their pre-1914 levels), as might be expected under conditions of high capital mobility and openness (Obstfeld and Taylor 1998, 2003, 2004; Fujii and Chinn 2001; Goldberg et al. 2003). Although short of complete convergence, international differentials remain comparable to those within most national economies (for a given financial asset) while they persist for much more limited periods than in the past, an outcome that might be expected in the context of 24-hour global financial trading (Fujii and Chinn 2001; Goldberg et al. 2003; Obstfeld and Taylor 2004). In contrast, Feldstein and Horioka's classic study (1980) concluded that levels of national savings and national investment appeared to be highly correlated (see Hay, Chapter 11 in this volume), signifying much more limited financial integration (Feldstein and Horioka 1980). This finding has also been confirmed by other studies such that in much of the orthodox literature it is regarded as a 'stylized but very robust fact' (Obstfeld and Taylor 2004: 62).

For orthodox economists, these findings present something of a puzzle, in so far as the relative ease of global capital mobility should theoretically imply low (rather than the observed *high*) correlations between domestic savings and domestic investment. Accordingly, the **Feldstein–Horioka puzzle** has attracted much attention as a measure of global financial mobility and integration. Recent studies have 'resolved' the puzzle, in that there appears to be significant empirical evidence that the savings–investment correlation appears to have weakened since the 1990s (indicating significant break points or discontinuities in the data)—a period of significant financial liberalization (Coakley et al. 1998; Abbott and De Vita 2003; Banerjee and Zanghieri 2003; Coakley et al. 2004; Giannone and Lenza 2004; Apergis and Tsoumas 2009; Kumar and Rao 2011). Other studies have questioned the methodological and theoretical robustness of the Feldstein–Horioka puzzle, rather than the empirical findings, as a measure of capital mobility and integration (Baxter and Crucini 1993; Taylor 1996; Hoffmann 1998). These suggest that the observed correlations—probably a product of the theoretical assumptions and econometric modelling—are not inconsistent with high capital mobility, and as such are an imperfect measure of global financial integration.

Other measures, such as the stock of foreign assets as a proportion of world GDP, indicate a much less ambiguous conclusion in so far as this increased from 6 per cent in 1960 to 25 per cent in 1980, and to 92 per cent in 2000 (Obstfeld and Taylor 2004: 55). Similarly, capital flows as a share of world GDP as already noted have grown substantially since the 1960s, although they have not necessarily reached the historic levels of the belle époque nor returned to the pre-GFC peak (Obstfeld and Taylor 2004: 60; James 2014). Lane concludes the IFI ratio (i.e. foreign liabilities/assets to GDP) for major economies has increased significantly since the 1980s and while peaking in 2007 has returned to that level in 2010 indicating that actual financial integration has not lessened despite the global and eurozone financial crises (Lane 2012). Furthermore, there is considerable evidence that **capital controls**—legal restrictions on capital flows—have declined significantly since the 1970s for OECD states, and the 1980s for most developing economies (and were associated with the shift to a floating exchange rate regime) (Obstfeld and Taylor 2004: 165). Though some major emerging economies, such as China, have not liberalized. Bryant accordingly concludes in his study of global finance that, 'the analogy of nearly autonomous national savings [and investment] reservoirs is no longer appropriate' (Bryant 2003: 152). Capital is by no means perfectly mobile in so far as global financial markets are imperfect. Even so, the dominant tendency has been in the direction of greater, rather than lesser, (uneven) financial integration.

Tendencies towards financial integration have also been accompanied by processes of financial deepening (measured in terms of contagion effects, or the synchronization of financial markets and national business cycles) (Obstfeld and Taylor 2004). Finance pervades the operation and management of all modern economies, representing for many—to borrow Hilferding's (1910/1981) vocabulary—a new epoch of 'finance capitalism'. To the extent that national financial systems are increasingly integrated (in real time) with global capital markets, the consequences of financial crisis or volatility abroad is magnified and diffused rapidly at home. Both the unprecedented rapidity with which the GFC spread across the globe and its dramatic consequences for almost all economies, as production and trade collapsed, reflect the significant deepening of global financial integration over the last three decades (Farlow 2013; Wolf 2014; Eichengreen 2015). Moreover, in the aftermath of the GFC the loosening of monetary policy in advanced economies (i.e. historically unprecedented low interest rates combined with quantitative easing) led to huge flows of capital to emerging economies simultaneously deepening global financial integration while generating significant new systemic risks to international financial stability (Wolf 2014; BIS 2015; IMF 2015a, 2015b).

Whether in times of crisis or normalcy, there is also much evidence to suggest that major national stock markets and stock market returns have become increasingly synchronized since the 1970s (Longin and Solnik 1995; Bekaert et al. 2005). This synchrony in financial market movements across the globe is not uniform, since local conditions do make a difference; moreover, it is more evident at times of crisis. Nevertheless, it denotes the heightened significance of global financial conditions for domestic financial stability, and vice versa (Eichengreen 2002). Indeed, M. Bordo and T. Helbling, in a study of business cycles over the last 120 years, points to evidence of a 'secular trend towards increased synchronization' (2003: 42). This process of financial deepening arises out of the interaction between the greater 'financialization' of national economies and its overlapping with global financial activity. Evidence of this is to be found during the 1990s, for example, in increased foreign holdings of national public debt—in the eurozone an increase from 16 to 30 per cent, and in the United States from 19 per cent to in excess of 35 per cent—not to mention increased foreign holdings of shares, private financial assets, and the almost doubling of the ratio of foreign assets to national GDP for most OECD economies (Held et al. 1999; IMF 2002; Mosley 2003). In 2005, foreigners owned some 50 per cent of the total stock of US Treasury Bonds, enabling the US to maintain both lower interest rates than would otherwise be the case, and to fund its historic twin deficits (fiscal and **balance of payments**) (Warnock and Warnock 2006: 1–4). But national responses to the GFC have moderated or reversed this trend amongst some major economies as government debt has been dramatically increased and 'nationalized'. Furthermore, although many studies have pointed to the 'home bias' effect, which refers to investors' preference for domestic assets, such that the international diversification of investment portfolios appears to be relatively low (in the US, foreign equities constitute around 12 per cent of total holdings), recent studies have qualified these findings (Thompson 2006). Cai and Warnock, for example, demonstrate that this finding in part is a product of how home bias is measured, especially a failure to distinguish the

kinds of domestic assets purchased (2006). When such distinctions are made, they 'nearly eliminate the home bias puzzle' (Cai and Warnock 2006: 3).

Associated with this financial deepening is a process of institutionalization as the organization and infrastructures of transborder finance become regularized and systematized through the activities of (public and private) global agencies and networks. This institutionalization is evident in the enormous expansion of multinational banking—for example, HSBC, 'the world's local bank'—as well as the surveillance and global standard-setting activities of the International Monetary Fund (IMF), Bank for International Settlements (BIS), and the multiplicity of official and private transborder networks, from the Financial Action Task Force to the International Accounting Standards Board (IASB) (see Pauly, Chapter 9 in this volume). It is through the operation of these institutions that the essential infrastructure of global financial markets is developed and extended, from the Society for the Worldwide Interbank Transactions (SWIFT) global financial interbank payments system to mechanisms for managing sovereign 'bankruptcy'. In the process, the global or inter-regional integration of financial markets is reinforced.

Production

Although **foreign direct investment** (FDI) is a category of transborder capital flows it is distinctive in so far as it is an indicative measure of the globalization of production (see Thun, Chapter 7 in this volume). Outsourcing production around the world is now widespread in most industrial and many service sectors. Indeed, both investment in overseas production facilities or subsidiaries (FDI) and the creation of global production networks have increased dramatically since the 1970s, dominated by the **transnational corporation** (TNC) (UNCTAD 2002, 2006b, 2009b). By comparison with the 1990s, transnational production rather than trade has become the principal means of servicing global markets. Transnational corporations account for more than 25 per cent of world value added, 80 per cent of world industrial output, approximately 33 per cent of world exports, 25 per cent of world GDP (compared to 7 per cent of world GDP in 1990, $36,365bn in world sales, and employ 75m workers considerably greater than the UK population in 2015 (Gilpin 2001: 289; UNCTAD 2001, 2003, 2006b, 2011, 2015). TNCs are now major determinants of the location and organization of production and services in the world economy, especially within the most advanced and dynamic economic sectors, integrating and reordering business activity between and within the world's three principal economic regions and their associated hinterlands. These developments are characterized by, among other factors: an increased scale and scope; processes of transnational economic restructuring; and the consolidation of a new global division of labour.

Since the 1970s, flows of FDI have not only become more geographically diffuse, but also until the GFC much more intense (Dunning 2000; UNCTAD 2001; for further discussion, see Thun, Chapter 7 in this volume). In 2000, total world (inward) FDI reached a new peak of $1,409.6 billion, almost four times the level of 1995 and over six times that of a decade earlier (UNCTAD 2001: 3; 2006b). After 2001, annual FDI flows initially declined with the slowdown in the world economy, but subsequently increased to a new record of $1,979 billion in 2007 compared to an average of $548 billion in the period 1994–9 (UNCTAD 2003: 2; 2006b: 2; 2009b: 3). In the wake of the GFC, FDI declined by 14 per cent to $1,697 billion (2008) to $1,310 billion in 2012 and $1,230 billion in 2014—the fastest rate of decline in the entire post-war period (UNCTAD 2009b, 2013). This decline has been accompanied by another significant trend as FDI flows to and between emerging and developing economies continue to exceed those to and amongst the developed economies (for the first time in the post-war period). The former remain at 'historically high levels' now accounting for 55 per cent of total FDI compared to 43 per cent in 2008 (UNCTAD 2009b, 2013, 2015:2). The decline in FDI has been accompanied by extensive global divestments as the manufacturing and financial sectors restructured their worldwide activities in the wake of the GFC with the consequence that for some economies, notably the UK and Ireland, net FDI proved negative as divestments exceeded inward investment flows (UNCTAD 2009b: 14). By the end of 2010, FDI to all countries had collapsed by some 37 per cent in comparison with its peak in 2007 (UNCTAD 2011). Even so, FDI flows in 2014 remain considerably in excess of that of two decades earlier (by a factor of 5), and until 2008 had grown at rates in excess of world GDP growth, exports, and overall capital investment while the total stock of FDI in 2014 was $25,875bn more than 10 times the level of 1990 (UNCTAD 2006b: 7; 2015: 18). From 2003 onwards, growth in FDI was

associated with a mergers and acquisition (M&A) boom, as the pressures for global corporate consolidation intensified. This boom exceeded a previous historic high in 2000, with record deals to the value of $3,900 billion in 2006 (Financial Times 2006: 1). With the GFC, funds for M&A rapidly declined by some 35 per cent in 2008 and by over 60 per cent in 2011 compared with the 2007 peak (Roxburgh et al. 2009: 15; UNCTAD 2011: p. xii).

Flows of FDI reflect the 'trend towards integration on ever larger geographical scales ... Supply chains have extended to new areas of the globe and integrated formerly distinct regional production activities' (UNCTAD 2002: 13). Indeed, until the GFC, significant annual flows (more than $10 billion) reached more than 50 countries (including 24 developing economies), compared to 17 (and seven developing economies) in 1985 (UNCTAD 2001: 4). This is a consequence of a variety of factors, including proximity to new markets and technological shifts in the capacity to organize and manage production at a distance (Dicken 2003). However, it is no longer simply manufacturing production that is on the move, but increasingly, with the digitization of information and communications advances, the provision of services, such as call centres, information processing, and legal and banking services (Held et al. 1999: ch. 5; UNCTAD 2001: 6; 2015).

Widely diffused as it is, both flows and stocks of FDI nevertheless remain concentrated among and within the major OECD economies, although as noted above this is increasingly no longer the case (see Thun, Chapter 7 in this volume). Moreover, official FDI flows significantly understate actual levels of foreign investment, since some estimates indicate it constitutes only 25 per cent of the total of such productive investment abroad (Held et al. 1999: 237). In 2000, OECD economies were the destination for some 80 per cent of FDI (inflows), the source of 88 per cent of FDI (outflows), 86 per cent of the world stock of (outward or exported) FDI, and 67 per cent of the world stock of (inward) FDI (UNCTAD 2006b: 7). However, as M. Obstfeld and A. M. Taylor observe, 'this trend may have turned, with FDI to poorer countries increasing in magnitude, and, importantly, reaching a more widely dispersed group of recipient countries' (2004: 83). As noted recent years have witnessed a significant change in the pattern of inward and outward FDI flows—with a dramatic increase in the share accounted for by developing economies (inward from

17.5 per cent in 1990 to 55 per cent in 2014; and outward 6.9 per cent and 35 per cent, respectively)—and in FDI stocks (inward from 20.7 per cent in 1990 to 31.9 per cent in 2014; and outward 8.3 per cent to 18.6 per cent, respectively) (UNCTAD 2006b: 2, 7; 2009b: 4–5; 2015: 5 and A4). This exceeds quite significantly the average shares of FDI invested in or by developing countries throughout the 1990s. Developing economies, particularly in East Asia, are both an increasingly significant destination for, as well as source of, FDI. Such trends have been accelerated by the financial crisis in Western economies and are likely to be magnified in future years if emerging markets continue to grow more rapidly than advanced economies. While there remains a heavy concentration of investment within and between the EU, the United States, and Japan as the largest economies—and between these economies and the NIEs of Asia, Latin America (to a lesser extent), and the East European transition economies—this is being diluted. This concentration has been conceived variously as triadization or regionalization, but this misrepresents the complex matrix of intra-regional and inter-regional flows of FDI and networks of production (Dunning 2000; Dicken 2003). It is the very clustering of FDI around the three major economic regions combined with the intensity of inter-regional flows that reinforces the dynamic of global productive integration.

In linking the dynamics of economies, FDI is also associated with processes of economic restructuring. Although the notion of 'footloose capital' is very much a cliché, the consequences of the mobility of capital are evident in structural changes across many OECD economies and the rise of NIEs in Asia and Latin America (Rowthorn and Wells 1987; Castells 1996; Kapstein 2000; Hoogvelt 2001; Dicken 2003). There is much debate, both about the significance of the deindustrialization of OECD economies in recent decades, and its causes (Piore and Sabel 1984; Krugman 1994; Wood 1994; Lawrence 1996b; Rodrik 1997; Burtless et al. 1998; Schwartz 2001). Although the impact of globalization, as opposed to technological change, on the decline of manufacturing employment in many OECD economies is disputed, there is general agreement that capital mobility and, increasingly, outsourcing nevertheless play a significant role in their continuous economic transformation. Deindustrialization in these economies is linked directly with the industrialization of many developing economies as production is shifted to lower-cost locations,

both through expanded FDI but increasingly through outsourcing arrangements (which require no capital input) (Rowthorn and Wells 1987; Wood 1994; Lawrence 1996b; Rodrik 1997; Munck 2002; UNCTAD 2002, 2006b; Dicken 2003). Furthermore, in the context of the digital economy many services industries have become vulnerable to global outsourcing. This is not to argue that the mobility of productive capital is unconstrained. Proximity to local markets, institutional factors, and productivity differentials limit the potential for industrial capital to relocate abroad, either rapidly or at all. Nevertheless, over time, the cumulative impact of such mobility, along with the expansion of trade, has contributed to major structural changes in the world economy.

Among the most obvious of these structural changes is the evolution and consolidation of a new worldwide division of labour. A significant shift has occurred in the location of manufacturing production, from OECD economies outwards to NIEs in East Asia, Latin America, and other parts of the developing world (Gilpin 2001: 140). Some estimates suggest that between 1977 and 1999 alone, some 3 million US manufacturing jobs were lost as production relocated abroad, but with the contraction in employment almost four times greater than the expansion of employment in developing regions (Harrison and McMillan 2006: 40–1). To a more limited extent, a similar trend is evident in the services sector, most notably in back-office functions, customer services, data and information processing, and so on (WTO 2001a, 2006b). At the same time, the raw material sector has declined, measured as a proportion of world FDI and trade, such that many developing economies have entered, or seek to enter, the manufacturing business. As a result of these shifts, the geography of world economic activity has been transformed in recent years, with important consequences for the distribution of productive power and wealth, and ultimately for the politics of global economic relations (Gilpin 2001; Crafts and Venables 2003). This is patently evident with the rise of China, India, and Brazil as key players in the global political economy.

A second, and related, structural change has been the intensification of transnational and inter-regional competition for market share, technological advantage, and rapid product innovation. Such competition is no longer necessarily best conceived as occurring simply between self-contained national economic units, but, rather, increasingly between firms and businesses in different regions of the globe, in so far as the new geography of world economic activity links distant markets through the operations of giant **multinational corporations** (**MNCs**) and inter-regional production networks (Gilpin 2001: 180–2). Economic and corporate competition becomes globalized, since it transcends regions, biting deeper into national economies and magnifying the consequences of local conditions and differences (Held *et al.* 1999: ch. 5). Domestic competition between supermarket chains for agricultural produce, for example, turns farmers both at home and abroad into direct competitors. Given the existence of instantaneous communications, it is not only the scope but also the rapidity with which global competition evolves that contribute significantly to its intensity (Harvey 1989; Castells 1996).

A third significant change is in the nature of production processes, particularly in manufacturing but also in services, which flows or stocks of FDI do not capture effectively. Outsourcing, or the cross-border fragmentation of production, is increasingly a key means by which production in many sectors is located and relocated abroad to realize efficiency and competitive gains (although it tends to be concentrated in the low-valued-added segments of the production cycle or service provision) (Dicken 2003; Kaplinsky 2005). Since it requires minimal capital investment or ownership, but rather involves collaborative or contractual relationships between producers and a range of suppliers, it is increasingly open to a much wider range of economic agents, from small publishing houses to major TNCs. Outsourcing relies on complex transborder production chains, within and between regions of the world economy, such that, paradoxically, it involves the global integration of productive processes through their increasing geographical fragmentation or dispersion (Gereffi and Korzeniewicz 1994). The significant reliance on production networks presents a challenge to orthodox conceptions of the world economy as a collection of discrete national economic spaces, since it implies a better depiction (although messier but perhaps more accurate) is of a networked global economy—what, in the context of trade, Baldwin (2006) refers to as the spaghetti or noodle-bowl analogy (Castells 2000; Brenner 2004; Sassen 2006). It is also evident that the speed and synchronized collapse of world trade in 2008–9, according to Baldwin, is a result of global integration of production such that, 'Today, Factory Asia is online' (Baldwin 2009). One of the unintended consequences of the GFC has

been to highlight the vulnerabilities of global supply chains provoking some rethinking of the limits to outsourcing. But there is little robust evidence to indicate this is a major reversal of a secular trend. As Amador and Mauro note these global production chains 'have become the paradigm for the production of most goods and services around the world' (Amador and Mauro 2015:14). In 2011 almost half of world trade (49 per cent) was attributable to global production networks compared with 36 per cent in 1995 (WTO 2015*a*:18).

Labour migration

In comparison to capital and goods, labour is relatively immobile. That said, labour flows (especially unskilled) are geographically extensive and, in terms of direction, reflect an almost mirror image of capital flows in so far as they have become primarily South *to* North (Held *et al.* 1999; Castles and Miller 2002; Chiswick and Hatton 2003). As a recent World Migration Report observes the world is experiencing 'an era of unprecedented human mobility' (IOM 2015:17). Outward flows of people are predominantly a developing country phenomenon and, despite significant national restrictions, they are, surprisingly, on a scale of the mass migrations of the early twentieth century (Chiswick and Hatton 2003: 74). Though complex in origin and destination, inter-regional (as opposed to intra-regional) migration has expanded enormously over the period 1950–2014 (Chiswick and Hatton 2003; IOM 2015:37). In 2010, there were some 215 million migrants but by 2014 232m, almost three times the level of 1970 (at 82.5 million), making up over 3 per cent of the global workforce, but over 9 per cent of the workforce in the developed world (Freeman 2006: 2; IOM 2012,2015). Inward migration is highly concentrated, in that 75 per cent of migrants were domiciled in just 23 countries in 1970, 28 countries in 2000 while only 10 high income countries are home to 50 per cent of the world's migrants (IOM 2005: 382; 2015:17). Migration is also an increasingly urban phenomenon, in so far as migrants concentrate in major urban areas (e.g. 25 per cent of Parisians, 37 per cent of Londoners, and 46 per cent of the population of Toronto were born abroad), where there are more employment opportunities (IOM 2015:39). Today, 50 per cent are female, whereas in the past, migrants were overwhelmingly male (Freeman 2006: 4–5). Skilled labour migration from South to North is also on the increase, linked to skills gaps and demographic trends in the North. Significantly, too, the huge expansion of temporary workers moving between world regions, facilitated by low-cost transport infrastructures, is additional to these official figures, and is of growing importance to certain sectors (for example, in construction and agriculture) within many developed economies (for example, in the US, the UK, and even in South Africa, which annually hosts 100,000 guest workers) (Freeman 2006: 8). Furthermore, as with trade and finance the geographical patterns of migration are changing dramatically as South to South, not just South to North, migration has 'gained importance' (IOM 2015: 37).

These developments reflect tendencies towards the integration of distant labour markets (Silver 2003). Such tendencies might be expected to produce some convergence in wage rates (both within the North, and between it and the South) most particularly for the skilled, but overall a growing divergence between rates for skilled and unskilled workers, given the preponderance of the latter among migrants and within the South. There is some evidence to confirm such trends, although the causal role of migration—as opposed to other factors such as trade, technology, or capital mobility—is debated (Galbraith 2002; Firebaugh 2003; Lindert and Williamson 2003). One incontrovertible trend, however, is the growing scale and importance of remittances by migrants, which quadrupled between 1990 and 2004, and which for many labour-exporting countries in the South has become 'an increasingly important source of foreign exchange' (UNCTAD 2006a: 100). According to UNCTAD estimates, the level of migrants' remittances in 1990 was about 50 per cent of total official aid flows, or on a similar scale to FDI flows from North to South. Today, it far exceeds the value of aid flows, and for many countries also exceeds flows of FDI (for example, remittances to India in 2005 totalled $20.5 billion, compared to inward FDI of $11.9 billion) (UNCTAD 2006a: 100). However, the GFC, has considerably impacted migration, as demand for foreign workers has succumbed to rising unemployment and more stringent immigration controls amongst host nations. As a result, 2011 wage remittances by foreign workers declined to $300 billion from a 2008 record of $338 billion (World Bank 2010a: 38). On the other hand, despite falling demand, the GFC has precipitated intensifying international flows of economic migrants such that migration has become a major global political issue.

Globalization: still the dominant tendency?

Although there is fairly widespread agreement among students of global political economy that, in the period since 1945—and in particular since the 1980s—there has been a remarkable intensification of transborder economic activity, nevertheless this is subject to divergent interpretations and explanations (Gordon 1988; O'Brien 1992; Castells 1996; Held *et al.* 1999; Hirst and Thompson 1999; Gilpin 2001; Hoogvelt 2001; Dicken 2003—for further discussion, see Hay, Chapter 11 in this volume). Whatever the scale and significance of economic globalization, as the brief discussion of regionalization and segmentation suggests, it is not the sole tendency within the contemporary world economy. Indeed, those of a more sceptical persuasion give much greater emphasis to these contrary trends. Consequently, they contest the assumption that globalization has been or remains the dominant tendency in the world economy (see Box 10.2). In doing so, they mount a robust challenge to the very idea that globalization best describes the historical trajectory of the world economy. Two related theses inform this sceptical analysis. The first stresses the existing limits to global economic integration; and, the second, the 'exaggerated' scale of contemporary economic

BOX 10.2

Sceptical Argument

1. Globalization is exaggerated and far from historically unprecedented.

2. The world economy was much more integrated and open during the belle époque of 1870–1914, when interest rates, commodity prices, and wages showed significant signs of convergence.

3. Regionalization and triadization, not globalization, are the dominant tendencies in the contemporary world economy.

4. The GFC and responses to it demonstrate both the limits to globalization and the primacy of BRICs (Big and Really Imperial Countries; James uses this term instead of the usual BRICs—Brazil, Russia, India, China) to the effective operation of global markets (2009: 182).

5. Globalization is primarily an ideology or policy discourse that serves to legitimize the interests of dominant political and business interests in expanding their power.

globalization in much of the existing literature, or as Stiglitz refers to it, 'the overselling of globalization' (Stiglitz 2005).

Distance, borders, and market segmentation continue to matter (Feldstein and Horioka 1980; Gordon 1988; Boyer and Drache 1996; Burtless *et al.* 1998; Garrett 1998a; Weiss 1998; Rieger and Leibfried 2003). Gravity models of international trade (a form of regression analysis), which take into account geographic distance, demonstrate an almost exponential decline in trade activity as the distance between trading partners increases (Carrere and Schiff 2004; Thompson 2006). Moreover, border and home bias effects (which measure economic divergence between countries and the tendency of investors or consumers to buy domestic assets / goods, respectively) do not appear to be diminishing. For example, there appears to be very little evidence of a significant trend towards international financial diversification. The implication is that, if globalization is the dominant tendency today, much higher levels of trade and financial flows be expected, as well as much greater economic convergence, than presently exists (Thompson 2006). Globalization in these respects is therefore considerably overstated.

In addition, the sceptics suggest a more critical interrogation of international economic trends since the 1970s would attest to increasing segmentation rather than integration of the world economy (Ruigrok and Tulder 1995; Berger and Dore 1996; Boyer and Drache 1996; Hirst and Thompson 1999; Hay 2000; Ruman 2000). As argued by Hay (Chapter 11 in this volume), the dominant patterns in the world economy over recent years have been the increasing regionalization and triadization of economic activity. This is evident, not just in trade-flow patterns, but has also been reinforced by the recent huge expansion in the numbers of preferential trade agreements (agreements between groups of states, each of which give preferential access to the others' markets) covering an increasing proportion of world trade (Crawford and Florentino 2005; Ravenhill, Chapter 6 in this volume). Regionalization is also to some degree evident in recent international financial trends most especially in Asia where intra-regional capital flows have grown significantly in the aftermath of the GFC (IMF 2015a:60). While Baldwin and Lopez-Gonzalez (2014) have pointed to intensifying 'regional fragmentation' of global production networks (Baldwin and Lopez-Gonzalez 2014). Such segmentation of the world economy along regional

lines, and the continuing dominance of OECD economies, accounts for the absence of the substantive global economic convergence that might be expected under conditions of globalization. It might therefore be concluded that regionalization or segmentation, rather than globalization, is the dominant tendency in the world economy today, or, as Thompson concludes, that the system is 'one poised between "globalization" and supranational "regionalization"' (Hay 2000; Thompson 2006).

Few would dispute that there are limits to economic globalization. National and local economies, to varying degrees, are embedded in global economic networks and systems while, to varying degrees, national and local factors mediate their impact. Distance, borders, and national differences do still matter—but perhaps not quite to the extent that some sceptics assert. Recent studies of the effect of borders on economic interactions suggest they are much less significant than earlier studies have claimed—with only either moderate or negligible impacts on trade flows (Anderson and van Wincoop 2001; Gorodnichenko and Tesar 2005). Moreover, as noted previously, the evidence does not suggest that there exists a significant home bias in financial markets (the Feldstein–Horioka puzzle) or **portfolio investment**. Indeed, the evidence points to the fact that the savings–investment and home bias puzzles, if not solved, are today significantly less puzzling than they were (Baxter and Crucini 1993; Anderson and van Wincoop 2001). Even the most advanced national economies are not as perfectly integrated as orthodox economic theory suggests should be the case, since subregional and sectoral divergences continue to matter. In this respect, indicative limits to globalization are not incompatible with the notion of the world economy as being imperfectly, rather than perfectly, integrated.

Since few economies (apart from Myanmar and North Korea) are significantly isolated, **autarchy**—the pursuit of national self-sufficiency as an economic strategy—appears defunct as national economic fortunes cannot be decoupled entirely from the dynamics of the world economy. This is evident in the manner and speed with which regional crises or slowdowns in world economic activity have a wide and rapid impact across the globe (Bordo and Helbling 2003; Pauly, Chapter 9 in this volume). Furthermore, as the earlier discussion noted, inter-regional flows of trade, capital, and migrants have increased significantly over recent decades. As one leading economic historian has put it, since 1950, 'Interrelations between the different parts of the world economy have greatly intensified' (Maddison 2001: 125). This is not to argue that regionalization and concentration of economic activity are not occurring, but rather to conclude that they are not the dominant trends shaping the world economy. Neither are they necessarily incompatible with economic globalization, since in several respects they reinforce it (Schirm 2002). As Baldwin argues, in a world of fragmented production, the political economy of regionalism can generate an inherent tendency towards trade globalism (Baldwin 2006). Regionalization can magnify the consequences of inter-regional economic integration (and vice versa). The concentration of inter-regional flows within the OECD triad is principally evidence of the unevenness of economic globalization rather than triadization or regionalization per se. That globalization has not measured up to the ideal of neoclassical economic theory, which posits a perfectly integrated world market (of price and income convergence), is readily explicable to theorists of imperfect markets/competition and of institutional economics (Gilpin 2001). Except for the most ardent advocates of neo-liberal economics, few would argue that economic globalization can be assessed solely by measures of economic convergence, because the most pronounced phase of global economic convergence, as economic historians note, was the inter-war period, paradoxically a period of unprecedented deglobalization, when economies rapidly converged, but towards economic collapse (Dowrick and DeLong 2003).

As Garrett remarks, 'No matter how many different numbers are presented … the growth of international economic activity in the past 30 years remains staggering' (2000a: 947). A global economy is in the making, constituted by, and through, the infrastructures and dynamics of economic globalization. This process of economic integration, however, is highly uneven, to the extent that it is associated both with economic convergence and divergence, as different economies/subregions/sectors are integrated differentially into this world economic order. Neither is it inevitable nor is it immutable, as the GFC reminds us. Indeed, as more recent trends disclose, there can be little doubt that, in key respects, in the aftermath of the GFC economic globalization experienced an initial sudden and dramatic reversal. However, for students of global political economy, the critical issue is whether this reversal is cyclical or structural: that is, whether it is simply a temporary hiatus or constitutes a decisive break with the last three decades. In short, does it portend a historic reversal of globalization—i.e. deglobalization?

The eminent economic historian, Harold James, observes that, 'Financial crises are the catalyst for turning the globalization cycle' (2009: 231). The sheer scale of the collapse in global finance, trade and FDI subsequent to the GFC and the unprecedented national responses designed to prevent another Great Depression, James concludes, arguably represent the turning of that cycle: 'In 2009 we can already say that the last great globalization was financial' (2009: 144). As 'state interventionism', with its protectionist impulses, asserted itself in the heartlands of global capitalism, the **Washington Consensus** appeared to have given way to the 'Beijing consensus' (Altman 2009). Combined with national economic adjustments which are necessary to correct the global imbalances (in trade and finance) which many, such as Wolf, argue were at the root of the GFC, the prospects for a rapid return to the historic trend growth of economic globalization—as at the turn of the twenty-first century—appear dramatically muted (2008). Global trade growth has stalled and global financial flows remain well below pre-GFC levels (World Bank 2010a, 2011, 2012c; DHL/NYU 2014; BIS 2015; UN 2015; WTO 2015b). As James concludes, 'the globalization cycle will resume, but not immediately' (2009: 277).

Even so, the GFC and its aftermath provide little support either for the principal arguments of the sceptics or that the world economy is experiencing a period of deglobalization. For both in terms of its severity and the synchronized rapidity with which this global economic shock impacted all economies, the GFC demonstrated, contrary to much sceptical opinion, just how deeply integrated the world economy had become in the last four decades. Furthermore, the aftermath of the GFC has accelerated the structural shift in the global economy towards Asia and the emerging economies, all of which rely significantly on globalization as a both a development and growth strategy. In this respect, the structural adjustments essential to correcting the global economic imbalances which were an important factor in the origins of the GFC appear to be associated with the emergence of a Third Wave of globalization, driven by the emerging economies, rather than any incipient deglobalization (World Bank 2007b; Manyika et al. 2014). As a recent report concludes emerging economies are 'reshaping global connectedness' and 'the 'big shift' of economic activity to emerging economies will have a large influence on the depth of global connectedness' (DHL/NYU 2014: 4, 54). This is evident from the previous discussions of the restructuring of trade, finance, production, and migration patterns in the wake of the GFC. Thus the DHL/NYU globalization index, which measures contemporary global trends, notes that in 2005 the advanced economies accounted for 56 per cent of all international interactions but by 2013 this figure was 48 per cent and declining (DHL/NYU 2014: 61). It is therefore both too simplistic and premature to interpret the current conjuncture as a prelude to incipient deglobalization. Nor is a historical comparison with the 1930s epoch appropriate as Eichengreen amongst others have argued (Temin 2010; Eichengreen 2015). Despite the GFC, the world economy is not experiencing deglobalization so much as the 'great moderation or maturation' of the 'second age of globalization'. Globalization remains the dominant, although not the sole, tendency in the world economy. Explaining the sources and origins of this 'second age of globalization' will be the focus of the next section which will in turn contribute further analytical and historical insights into the principal factors shaping its future trajectory.

KEY POINTS

- Globalization is not a singular process, but its economic dimension is critical.

- Economic globalization defines the principal trend in the contemporary global economy.

- It is associated with growing but uneven worldwide economic integration.

- Regionalization and segmentation are not necessarily incompatible with economic globalization.

- Economic globalization peaked just before the GFC reversed through 2009 but subsequently continues to experience a 'great moderation' compared to the pre-crisis period.

- Recent trends indicate a significant structural shift in the patterns of economic globalization with emerging and developing economies responsible for an increasing share of global economic flows.

The logics of economic globalization

Explaining the causes or drivers of economic globalization is an intellectually challenging and complex task. Challenging because there are multiple dynamics

at work, and complex because the very notion of causation raises some thorny philosophical issues. Casting the latter aside for the moment, it is critical to be clear about what is to be explained: in other words, it is necessary to identify precisely the subject of our explanation i.e. whether the focus is on the *general* determinants of economic globalization, or the particular determinants of its most recent phase namely the 'second age of globalization'. Explaining one is not quite the same as explaining the other (Robertson 2003). Given the story so far, the focus will be primarily, but not exclusively, upon the latter.

To assist this analysis, it is helpful initially to distinguish between thick or thin conceptions of causation. In its thickest sense, causality implies determination in so far as causes are considered both necessary and/or sufficient to produce a particular development or social phenomenon (Mellor 1995: 6). Thus globalization, it is often argued, is principally a product of technological change in so far as technology not only makes it both possible but also propels it forward, i.e. technology is both necessary and sufficient to bring it about such that globalization could not have occurred in its absence. Thinner conceptions of causation refer to dispositions, in the sense of the enabling conditions, tendencies, or factors that make given events or social phenomena more rather than less likely or probable (McCullagh 1998: 173). So, the liberalization of national economies, following the political revolution of neo-liberalism in the 1980s, can be viewed as a cause of economic globalization to the extent that it made it more, rather than less, probable, and thereby not simply a historical accident or arbitrary development. The thinnest conceptions of causation emphasize 'contingent' explanations—that events could readily be otherwise—in so far as globalization results from a coincidence of unique circumstances and the particular actions or interventions of social agencies. However, since many complex social phenomena, such as economic globalization, involve a multiplicity of causes, few theories of globalization develop either a rigidly determinist or a contingent explanatory account. Before examining these theories in some detail, it will be helpful to analyse the principal logics (or social forces) shaping the form and dynamics of economic globalization.

Principal logics

Explanations of economic globalization tend to focus on three interrelated logics or factors, namely:

technics (technological change and social organization); *economics* (markets and capitalism); and *politics* (ideas, interests, agency and institutions). Since they are so closely interrelated, the principal methodological problem for analysts lies in unbundling the causal mechanisms involved (Garrett 2000*a*). Distinguishing them analytically is the first stage.

Technics is central to any account of globalization, since it is a truism that, without modern communications infrastructures in particular, a worldwide economy would not be possible. Transformations in communications and transport technologies have literally and metaphorically 'shrunk the globe'. 'Action at a distance' increasingly transcends national borders, not to mention continents, so that time and space are compressed. In this process, the distinction between domestic economic activity and global economic activity becomes less easy to sustain as global markets evolve. Rather than the liberalization of national economies driving globalization, it can be argued that technological change drives liberalization, especially in the financial sector (Garrett 2000*a*). Modern communication technology not only provides the infrastructure of a real-time global economy but also facilitates new forms of transnational and global economic organization, from production through to regulation.

This informatics revolution has underwritten, not only the infrastructure of an evolving global economy, but, also, according to Dicken and others, a 'global shift' (Dicken 2003). This is expressed in the combined move towards service-based or post-industrial economies within the advanced core of the world economy, and the associated rise of industrial economies in the developing world. To paraphrase Giddens, 'technology is inherently globalizing' in so far as contemporary economic globalization is conceived as a product of the second industrial revolution—the logic of the informatics age (1990).

Crucial as technology is to any account of economic globalization, so, too, is its specifically *economic* logic. This is discussed in two distinct sets of literature: that of orthodox economics, which explains globalization in terms of market dynamics; and that of radical political economy, which explains it in terms of the imperatives of capitalism. In the case of the former, globalization is considered to be a direct consequence of market competition whether, as in the case of trade, in terms of the operation of comparative or strategic advantage, or in relation to transnational production in terms of imperfect competition or the product cycle (Dunning 1993; Gilpin 2001).

The structure and functioning of markets is conceived as being central to understanding the competitive dynamics that lead inevitably to the globalization of economic activity. Drawing on both neoclassical and new economic theories, the principal concern is identifying the specifically economic logic—understood in terms of the pursuit of profit, wealth, and market position—which explains the process of global economic integration and the location or distribution of economic activity (see Box 10.3). By contrast, radical political economy draws on the Marxist tradition that locates economic globalization in the expansionary and universalizing logic of modern capitalism. This expansionary logic is a product of capitalism's structural contradictions—the tendency for overproduction combined with the relative impoverishment of workers—and its insatiable requirement for capital accumulation; that is, profit. Economic globalization is driven by the continual search among the corporate sector for new markets, cheaper labour, and new sources of profitability; a process facilitated and encouraged by governments and the agencies of global economic governance, as they work to reproduce the very system on which their political legitimacy partly depends (Callinicos 2003). In short, the specifically economic logic of globalization arises from both the dynamics of markets and the dynamics of capitalism.

BOX 10.3

Economic Theory and Globalization

1. Neoclassical theory explains globalization in terms of comparative advantage, market forces, and economic convergence.

2. Free trade involves economies trading what they have a comparative advantage or efficiency in producing, thus in theory maximizing both national and global welfare.

3. Market forces and global competition ensure that similar goods and services are produced efficiently and at a minimum cost.

4. Market convergence ensures that prices and interest rates in a globalizing economy become increasingly equalized or differences increasingly narrowed.

5. New trade theory, locational theory, and the theory of imperfect competition explain why perfectly competitive global markets do not exist, and why market segmentation (differences and the lack of complete convergence) occurs even in a globalizing world economy.

Politics—shorthand here for ideas, interests, agency and institutions—constitutes the third logic of economic globalization. Almost all accounts of contemporary globalization make reference to the rise and dominance of neo-liberal ideology throughout the OECD world, along with its associated policies of liberalization, deregulation, and privatization—that is, the infamous 'Washington Consensus'. If technology provides the physical infrastructure of economic globalization, it is the significant movement towards 'market-driven politics' (Leys 2001)—greater emphasis on laissez-faire capitalism—that provides its ideological infrastructure.

Irrespective of the party holding office, the dominant political trend since the 1970s in OECD states has been towards the liberalization of national economies and the easing of restrictions on capital mobility. This has enabled—some might argue, driven—the creation of more integrated global markets and the globalization of production. Governments, or rather states, have been central to the process of economic globalization. They have been instrumental in establishing the necessary national political conditions and policies—not to mention vital regional and global institutions, agreements, and policies—essential to its advancement. Promoted and advocated by a powerful configuration of domestic and transnational coalitions and lobbies, economic globalization is very much a political construction or project; a product of political and economic agents pursuing their separate but also collective interests. This underlying political consensus is critical to economic globalization but in the wake of the GFC everywhere is increasingly under attack from a growing anti-globalization backlash infused with protectionist and nationalist sentiments. The future of economic globalization is thus not simply a result of impersonal technological and market forces. In certain key respects globalization is 'made' by the intersecting decisions and actions of a multiplicity of agents (governments, corporations, social movements, international institutions, etc.) across the world as will be made evident in the subsequent discussion (Holton 2005)

Central to the politics of the current globalization project is the power and role of the United States. To the extent that a liberal world economic order, as Gilpin (2001) and others argue, is a product of US (hegemony) dominance, shifts in the relative power of the US will have significant consequences for economic globalization. To the extent that the relative economic power of the United States has been eroded in recent years, the politics of globalization has become far more complex, with China and other emerging economic powers having a growing impact on the dynamics of economic globalization. In sum, economic globalization has an underlying political logic in so far as it is the product of political ideas and discourses; the political interests of the most powerful states, global institutions, and national and transnational social forces; and the transnational political consensus and public policies which create the conditions which make it possible.

In different measure and combination, these three logics—technics, economics, and politics—inform the principal theories of globalization. How they do so is explored in the following section.

Principal theories

As Rosenberg (2000) observes, there are many theories of globalization—its causes and dynamics—but little substantive globalization theory. This distinction is important in that it suggests that any notional globalization theory must be parasitic upon, if not entirely subservient to, the 'grand theories' of social science. To date, no discrete or singular globalization theory—which seeks to provide a coherent and systematic account of its causes, consequences, and historical trajectory—can be said to exist. Nor is there any singular theory of globalization, only a proliferation of schools and analyses. Accordingly, the emphasis here will be on identifying distinctive theories of globalization, with subsequent elaboration and critical examination of their principal formulations.

Few convincing accounts of economic globalization, given its complexity, locate its origins in a single causal logic. However, existing theories do make judgements either about the relative significance or configuration of different causal logics, in effect privileging some over others in their explanatory narratives. Along the continuum from thicker to thinner forms of causal explanation, accounts vary according to whether they give preference to the structural, the conjunctural, or the contingent sources of economic globalization.

Broadly speaking, structural explanations are thick causal accounts because they tend towards the deterministic: they highlight the imperatives or developmental logic of social and economic systems. Thus, structuralist accounts of economic globalization explain it in terms of the imperatives or drivers of technological advance and/or capital accumulation. Globalization is considered almost an *inevitable* consequence of either modern technologically advanced societies—recall Giddens's dictum that 'modernity is inherently globalizing'—or the expansionary imperatives of capitalism. While structuralist accounts can answer the why and how questions of globalization—why it came about, and how—they are less valuable in explaining its specific historical form (what kind?) or timing (why now?) (see Table 10.1).

In contrast, conjunctural explanations are much better at explaining the specific timing and particular historical characteristics of economic globalization as well as its contemporaneous causes. Conjunctural accounts, which are causally thinner than structural explanations, pay more attention to the confluence of particular historical circumstances, trends, and events, which together combine to produce a given social phenomenon at a specific point in time and in a given form. As McCullagh (1998: 178) summarizes it, 'the cause of an event is a conjunction of things which together have a tendency to produce a certain kind of outcome'. Thus, contemporary economic globalization can be understood as a consequence of a multiplicity of tendencies (technological, economic, and so on), interacting with particular historical conditions and policies (for example, the end of the Cold War), to produce its distinctive (neo-liberal) form. Rather than

stressing the inevitability of globalization, conjunctural explanations stress its **conditionality**.

Finally, accounts that stress the contingency of economic globalization emphasize its causal indeterminacy—the absence of a fully specified causal mechanism. Although such explanations may be less relevant to answering the 'why' question, they are particularly pertinent to addressing 'how, when and what' type questions. As such, these might be considered thin, rather than thick, causal accounts of economic globalization because they stress its almost *incidental* or *consequential* (rather than inevitable or conditional) origins. Attention therefore tends to be focused much more on the role of ideas—economic globalization as an idea or prevailing discourse—rather than seeking to deduce specific causal connections from empirical data concerning global economic interactions (Schirato and Webb 2003: 21; see also Hay, Chapter 11 in this volume). Accordingly, it can be argued that understanding the social or discursive construction of economic globalization is just as—some would say, more—important as identifying underlying causal patterns in the empirical data.

Structural theories of economic globalization can be distinguished in respect of how far they privilege domestic or global structures. Those that emphasize the primacy of domestic structures locate the sources of economic globalization in the nature and dynamics of modern societies. Since the nineteenth-century French philosopher Claude Saint-Simon wrote of the universalizing logic of industrial societies, the primacy of technology as the motor of globalization has figured prominently in the political economy literature. This thesis is to be found, in the more nuanced and less deterministic formulations of Ohmae (1990), Strange (1998*b*), Rosecrance (1999), and Garrett (2000*a*), among others.

Technology is privileged in such explanations, not simply because it has shrunk the globe, but also because it is often conceived as the principal dynamic of social change in advanced societies. Just as the technological revolution of industrialism transformed European agricultural societies, so today the information revolution is transforming the nature of production and social organization. In this 'virtualization' process, to borrow Rosecrance's (1999) label, borders no longer define the boundaries of national economic space, while distance becomes a less significant or costly barrier, although not entirely irrelevant, to the organization of production and economic activity. Moreover,

Table 10.1	Economic globalization: types of theory

	Causal mechanism	Primary concepts
Structural	Imperatives of domestic and international systems	Imperatives Inevitability Determinate
Conjunctural	Emergent properties or confluence of separate logics and circumstances	Conditional Tendencies Dispositions
Constructivist	Ideas and discourses as constitutive	Contingent Incidental Indeterminate

this technological revolution enables firms and national economies, irrespective almost of geographic location, to exploit their comparative economic advantage and specialize further in the production and trading of those goods and services at which they are most efficient. Technological change, in other words, brings in its wake both economic and political change in the form of globalized markets and the liberalization of economies. Since continual technological innovation is a structural (recursive) feature of modern (and modernizing) societies, then economic globalization, notwithstanding its cyclical fluctuations, is an inevitable feature of the contemporary global political economy.

That technology is a necessary requirement of economic globalization is not doubted, but for Marxist theorists (historical materialists) it is by no means a sufficient explanation. It is the capitalist form of the economy that is the crucial explanatory factor, not technology, which is subservient to the dynamics of capitalist accumulation and competition. Wood (2003: 14–15) summarizes this argument well: 'Capitalism … is driven by certain systemic imperatives, the imperatives of competition, profit-maximization and accumulation … globalization is their result rather than their cause.' The sources of globalization are therefore located in the necessary requirement of capitalism constantly to acquire new markets and to produce more efficiently in order to sustain levels of profitability and reproduce itself. Cultivating global markets and producing abroad to maximize profits and corporate efficiency are the consequence of the structural imperatives and contradictions of capitalist economies rather than technological innovation per se.

Moreover, these expansionary tendencies are shaped by intensifying economic competition and the resulting concentration of economic power in huge national and transnational corporations that can readily exploit new technologies and economies of scale to produce more efficiently and compete more effectively, both at home and abroad. Liberalization and the rolling back of the state, reinforced by the disciplines of global institutions such as the WTO and IMF, are conceived ultimately as responses to these developments rather than their author. Such accounts do not deny the importance of political agency or the strategic action of states and other social forces, but, rather, assert that in the very last event these are of only partial relevance in explaining economic globalization (though they are highly relevant to understanding the particular form

it takes; for example, *empire* in the nineteenth century versus *corporate globalization* in the twentieth).

In so far as the main engines of capitalist globalization are located in a small number of OECD economies, there is some disagreement as to whether the contemporary period is best described as a renewed phase of capitalist imperialism, a distinctly new form of globalized capitalism system, or a historically novel, global capitalist empire (Hardt and Negri 2000; Callinicos 2003; Gill 2003; Wood 2003). Irrespective of how it is characterized, the principal logic of contemporary economic globalization is located, in Marxist theory, firmly with the imperatives of capitalist development.

Beyond these domestic-level explanations, other structural theories give priority to international or global system-level structures. Within all the major schools of theory in global political economy—realist, liberal, and Marxist—frequent emphasis is placed on the role of hegemony—or the dominance or pre-eminence of a single power or superpower—in creating and maintaining the conditions for an open world economy, and so economic globalization. In effect, the hierarchical structure of power relations in the global political economy creates the necessary conditions for economic globalization. Despite their otherwise radically different theoretical positions, Gilpin, Ikenberry, and Wallerstein all assert that hegemony is an essential condition for the development and perpetuation of a globalizing world economy (Wallerstein 1983; Gilpin 1987; Ikenberry 2001). Without a hegemonic power capable of establishing a stable and managed world order, through both persuasion and coercion, economic globalization would be little more than an ideal. It is hegemony that makes an open world economy possible. That said, it is also an essential precondition of economic globalization that the hegemonic power is a liberal-capitalist power and thus has a material interest in creating and sustaining a liberal world economic order as opposed to a world empire. In this respect, hegemonic theory is entirely compatible with domestic-level structural accounts, which consider economic globalization as a consequence of the imperatives of capitalist accumulation and market forces. However, to the extent that the hegemonic power becomes predatory or unilateralist, the necessary conditions for economic globalization will be eroded. While in contrast, the relative decline of the hegemon, as Keohane (1984) suggests, may have little impact, to the extent that globalization becomes institutionally embedded.

Whereas structural theories explain economic globalization as a path-dependent outcome of systemic—whether domestic or international—imperatives, by contrast *conjunctural* accounts are rooted in a more context-dependent analysis. This is not to suggest that structural forces or tendencies are ignored—on the contrary, they form the context of any historical analysis—but, rather, they are combined with a greater attention to the unique configuration of political, social, national, and global conditions that precipitated contemporary economic globalization. There is also a greater recognition of the role of strategic action by governments or other key agencies, and the interaction between social forces, political institutions, and ideas in advancing or constraining processes of global economic integration. Rather than an inevitability, economic globalization is understood as being 'rooted in history and shaped by particular political, social and cultural conditions ... a conjunctural correlation of forces that are subject to reversal' (Petras and Veltmeyer 2001: 46). Among the most comprehensive studies in this context is Castells's three-volume study of the rise of 'global informational capitalism' (Castells 1996, 1997, 1998).

Castells sets out to explain the most recent phase of economic globalization, which he dates to the 1980s, rather than to produce a generalizable account of economic globalization per se. Castells identifies the principal sources of this new belle époque in the profound restructuring of the major capitalist economies, itself a response to the economic and political crises of the 1970s (Castells 2000). This period was characterized by historic shifts in the technological, economic, and political spheres that, while insufficient in themselves to forge a new epoch of globalization, in conjunction they provided the vital conditions in which it could flourish. Just as two atoms of hydrogen combine with one atom of oxygen to produce a new substance called water, so, by analogy, the specific configuration and conjunction of developments in these three spheres—technics, economics, and politics—gave rise to the current epoch of globalization. In other words, globalization emerged out of—in more technical language, is an emergent property of—the particular confluence of historical conditions in the technological, economic, and political domains (Sayer 2000: 12). What, then, were these significant developments?

According to Castells, they were, respectively: the information technology revolution; capitalist restructuring; and the political hegemony of the neo-liberal

project (Castells 2000: prologue). Tracing these developments to the dissipation, in the 1970s, of the postwar system of managed capitalism, Castells identifies in the informatics revolution of the 1980s a new production paradigm that facilitated a process of global economic restructuring. Overseas manufacturing production became more technically feasible as well as economically necessary. Production began shifting abroad while the major economies became increasingly service-based (post-industrial) or, in Castells's language, 'informational'.

This deindustrialization in the core economies was accompanied by industrialization in its hinterlands. However, as Castells argues, this:

> Restructuring of business firms, and the new information technologies, while being at the source of globalizing trends, could not have evolved, by themselves, toward a networked global economy without policies of de-regulation, privatization, and the liberalization of trade and investment.

(2000: 147)

Politics—but, more specifically, the advocacy and implementation of neo-liberal (market-enhancing) ideas, policies, and institutional (both national and global) reforms—played a significant role in this process to the extent that he argues that: 'The decisive agents in setting up a new global economy were governments, and, in particular, the governments of the wealthiest countries, the G7, and their ancillary institutions' (Castells 2000: 137). The advance of this political project was also greatly assisted by the collapse of communism and thus any feasible political alternative to the capitalist model of development. For Castells, the emergence of a historically unique 'global informational capitalism' that has 'the institutional, organizational, and technological capacity to work as a unit in real time, or in chosen time, on a planetary scale', can be traced to the specific historical conjuncture of technological, economic, and political circumstances of the 1980s (2000: 104).

Castells's analysis of globalization is among the most comprehensive and sophisticated. However, as with other conjunctural accounts (Scholte 2000; Gill 2003), it is vulnerable to the criticism that in advocating an essentially multi-causal account, it simply avoids specifying a coherent or convincing causal mechanism. In simpler language, since almost every key factor is regarded as a cause of globalization, by definition, nothing in particular can be said to be its specific cause. To critics, conjunctural accounts do not so much explain—that is, identify a causal mechanism or mechanisms—so much as provide a rich description of economic globalization.

This judgement is a little harsh because it presumes a strongly scientific or positivistic model of causation identified with some determinate causal mechanism. By contrast, historical or interpretative models of causation readily acknowledge such causal complexity (McCullagh 1998; Sayer 2000; Benton and Craib 2001). Nevertheless, a more fundamental problem is that conjunctural analyses fail to accept, although they imply, the essential indeterminacy or contingency of complex social phenomena, such as globalization, and thus cannot really claim adequately to explain it (Wendt 1998).

Economic globalization refers, both to a process of growing material interconnectedness, as well as to the 'idea' or consciousness of that process. Obviously, the two are interrelated but in quite complex ways. *Social constructivist* analyses are far more interested in the idea of economic globalization, and why it has become such a pervasive discourse or way of talking and theorizing about the world economy. Although they do not discount the relevance of globalization's material manifestations—in terms of flows of trade and investment—social constructivists are far more interested in its ideational or discursive construction. In this respect, they argue, to paraphrase A. Wendt, that globalization is what states and others make of it, rather than a preordained or objective condition, and as such is a largely contingent phenomenon (Wendt 1992).

Rather than seeking to identify the causal mechanisms that generate globalization, constructivists seek to explore how widely shared ideas or discourses of economic globalization are constitutive of—that is, make real or give intersubjective meaning to—the very process itself; for example, the popular discourse or idea of globalization as an inevitable or irresistible juggernaut of social change (see Box 10.4). In simple terms, there can be no economic globalization without the idea or discourse of economic globalization. This is not to argue that globalization is simply a product of the collective imagination. On the contrary, it is largely to acknowledge that in naming or identifying these material trends in the world economy as a process of 'economic globalization', that very process becomes socially or discursively constructed and is thus

---

BOX 10.4

Causal and Constitutive Theory

1. Causal theories refer to explanations that identify specific or general causal mechanisms which can be said to be both necessary and/or sufficient to produce the social effects or social phenomenon that are the object of analysis.

2. Constitutive theories refer to explanations that demonstrate how ideas, values, and beliefs or discourses about the world construct 'reality' thereby constituting, in part, the very social phenomenon under investigation.

3. An intense debate exists as to whether causal and constitutive theories are different or similar kinds of explanations and, thus, whether in effect reasons (ideas) can be considered, in the strictest sense, to be causes.

---

given intersubjective meaning. Social constructivism, therefore, has an important bearing upon how globalization is interpreted and understood, both within the academy and beyond. Accordingly, to make sense of globalization, it is first necessary to deconstruct or unpack the dominant ideas or discourses that inform how it is generally interpreted or conceived, and the extent to which such ideas or discourses reflect or alternatively misconstrue contemporary world economic trends.

As Petras and Veltmeyer (2001: 11) observe, 'Globalization is both a description and a prescription, and as such, it serves as both an explanation … and an ideology that currently dominates thinking, policymaking and political practice.' Those studies that have drawn on the insights of this kind of social constructivist methodology generally tend to conclude that the genesis and diffusion of the 'idea of economic globalization' is more important to understanding and explaining the contemporary economic condition than is a rigorous assessment of the actual empirical trends (Hay and Watson 1998; Rosamond 2001; Schmidt 2002; Hay, Chapter 11 in this volume). For the constructivists, the evidence is less important than the fact that to the extent that states, social forces, and international agencies perceive and understand the world principally within the discourse of globalization, they reproduce and perpetuate it to a large extent irrespective of what the empirical evidence discloses. There are also very good reasons why they do so, and in this context political interest and motivations—the power of political agency—becomes of critical importance. Irrespective of the objective existence of globalization, it is incontrovertible that the *idea* of economic globalization plays a crucial role in coordinating, communicating, and legitimating a range of diverse political projects, from the politics of anti-globalization movements to the politics of the Neoliberals to the nationalist right (Schmidt 2002). Economic globalization, in such accounts, is therefore distinguished by its essential *contingency* more so than its inevitability. It is as much, if not more of, an ideational, rather than material, phenomenon. As such, it is not so much determined by collective ideas but rather constituted by, and through, them, with significant consequences for the politics of globalization (see Hay, Chapter 11 in this volume).

Making sense of the logics of economic globalization

How are these different accounts of the causes of economic globalization to be reconciled? Do these distinctive types of theory offer competing or complementary explanations? Is a 'grand theory' of economic globalization attainable? Such questions flow naturally from an examination of the theoretical pluralism that is the hallmark of global political economy. If there is no singular theory of globalization this is partly, but not exclusively, a consequence of the fact that there is no universally accepted set of criteria—or **epistemology**—against which the validity of theories of global political economy can be judged. This does not mean that rational judgements cannot be made as to which theories present a more or less convincing account of globalization, but simply that such judgements cannot in any meaningful sense establish their 'truth'—or its true causes. Quite simply, the problem is that, as within the social sciences more generally, an appeal to the evidence or the 'facts' of globalization largely proves inconclusive, since the 'facts' are often compatible with competing theories. That is, theories are underdetermined. Thus, for example, the evidence discussed in the first part of this chapter supports theories that identify both technology and politics as the principal cause of globalization. Accordingly, rather than seeking the unattainable grail of objective truth, a more productive approach may be to explore whether or how these three distinctive types of theory might be conjoined and so contribute to a more comprehensive understanding and explanation of the logics of economic globalization (see Table 10.2).

In a very interesting article, Eric Helleiner (1997) seeks to realize precisely that goal. Drawing on the scholarship of Fernand Braudel, a renowned social historian, Helleiner concludes that to understand and explain economic globalization as a historical and social process, it is necessary to adopt and combine different temporal perspectives. These distinct temporal perspectives reflect the different pace of historical time: from the *longue durée* of centuries over which change can appear to have a glacial momentum, shaped as it is by deeper social structures and recurrent patterns of socioeconomic organization, through the *epochal*, or conjunctural in which the pattern of socioeconomic change over several decades seems to prefigure the emergence of a new era or social formation, to *l'histoire événementielle*, or contemporaneous, in which social agents—from individuals to governments—are daily engaged in reacting to, or in seeking to shape, events and circumstances as they perceive and interpret them. As Helleiner (1997: 95) suggests, these 'three temporal perspectives are useful not just in describing economic globalization, but also in understanding and explaining it'.

A direct correspondence may be observed between these temporal perspectives and the three types of theory elaborated in the preceding section: the *longue durée* is associated with structural accounts; the epochal with the conjunctural; and the contemporaneous with constructivism.

As Gilpin (2001: 364) observes, 'globalization has been taking place for centuries'. Understood as a process of secular historical development, economic globalization might therefore best be explained through the medium of structural theories that locate its causes in the dynamics of enduring systems or recurrent patterns of socioeconomic organization. Thus, economic globalization can be understood as an intrinsic feature of the modern age: of modern societies and the modern international state system or, to use a grand term, modernity. Conceived from a temporal vantage point of the *longue durée*, economic globalization appears as a chronic or persistent—although by no means linear—historical trend that, as Helleiner (1997: 95) comments, 'also makes it seem an almost irreversible one'. To understand and explain economic globalization therefore requires some account of the deeply embedded structures of the global political economy—capitalism, industrialism, hegemony, and so on—which are its underlying drivers. At one level, such accounts are essential, since, while they cannot

Table 10.2 Economic globalization summary: types of theories and forms of explanation

	Principal methodological focus	Causal mechanisms	Focus	Indicative account of globalization
Structural	Focus on organizing principles of domestic and international systems	Tends towards (economic, technological, or political) determinism	Why and How questions	Ohmae (1990)/ Rosecrance (1999)— technics primary causal logic
	Holistic analysis Emphasis on dynamics or 'laws' of the social totality	Emphasis on inevitability, irresistible forces		Woods (2003)— imperatives of capitalism
		Path-dependent outcomes		Gilpin (1987)/ Wallerstein (1983)— political imperatives of hegemony— globalization as Americanization
Conjunctural	Unique configuration of social forces and historical circumstances Political decisions and forces	Emphasis on tendencies and conditional factors Confluence of events and circumstances Emergent properties	How, When and What form	Castells (1996, 1997, 1998, 2000)—global informational capitalism product of conjuncture of technics, economics, and political developments in 1980s
Constructivist	Role of ideas crucial in shaping how agents view and act on the world Discourse of globalization—globe talk— constructs the way the world is understood and acted on by social agents Discourse of economic globalization constitutes it rather than simply mirrors it	Constitutive rather than casual explanation— globalization is made real through discourse Emphasis on motivations, interests, ideas and political agency	When and What form	Schmidt (2002)—how the discourse of globalization came to play the crucial role in coordinating, communicating, and legitimating European government economic strategies in the 1990s

explain its specific historical features or rhythms, they do offer insights into why economic globalization has been a recurring feature of the global political economy for many centuries.

In contrast, particular historical epochs of intensifying global economic integration, like that of today, are better explained by conjunctural theories. Such theories seek principally to account for the cyclical and historical rhythms of economic globalization: how and why it accelerates or contracts at different historical moments, and the specific configuration it

takes—from empire to global markets. In doing so, such accounts emphasize discontinuity, rather than continuity (as in structural accounts) with the past. Thus, the entire debate about whether contemporary globalization is unprecedented by comparison with the belle époque is indicative of an epochal or conjunctural perspective. Understood from such a perspective, the origins of contemporary economic globalization are to be located in a particular conjuncture of factors and forces within a specific historical context. This provides a different frame of reference from the structural, as it suggests that economic globalization is 'also a clearly reversible process' because the conjuncture of forces that hold it together at any given moment may (or will) eventually dissipate (Helleiner 1997: 95). Conjunctural accounts thereby complement structural theories because they provide an explanation of globalization's episodic and discontinuous evolutionary pattern, offering specific insights into what drives it forward (or backwards) at particular moments in history.

Finally, from a contemporaneous perspective, Helleiner notes that economic globalization 'often appears as a political weapon used and promoted by certain groups' as 'a project in which the local is increasingly "globalized" … in an active and deliberate way' (Helleiner 1997: 96). Constructivist explanations that emphasize motivations, strategic actions, and the political struggles over globalization offer significant insights into its contemporaneity. Such accounts complement both structural and conjunctural theories because they can explain how and why economic globalization comes to be constructed through the multiplicity of actions of, and interactions between, individual and collective (political and economic) subjects or agents, from consumers to corporations, and protestors to politicians. From this contemporaneous perspective, economic globalization appears decidedly contingent or fluid. Constructivism privileges the explanation of the motives, interests, ideas, and institutions that are constitutive of such action. In providing this, constructivist theories of economic globalization—which emphasize its essential contingency—function to correct those marked tendencies in structural and conjunctural accounts that play down the significance of social agency—ideas, motivations, and choices. In doing so, the former very much complements the latter.

For much the same reason that economic globalization is considered causally complex, necessitating a multi-causal analysis, so, too, following Helleiner (1997: 102), must it also be conceived as a 'layered' historical process; that is, 'taking place at several different historical speeds'. Accordingly, understanding and explaining the current phase of economic globalization requires a causal analysis that is not only sensitive to its multiple logics—technics, economics, and politics—but also to its multiple speeds—the *longue durée*, epochal, and contemporaneous. No single theory, or account, of economic globalization meets, or is ever likely to meet, such demanding requirements

(Rosenberg 2000). This should not induce academic despondency, because, as has been argued, by drawing on philosophically compatible structural, conjunctural, and constructivist accounts a more systematic and layered analysis of economic globalization is entirely feasible, even if this falls short of the explanatory properties of an ideal globalization theory.

KEY POINTS

- Economic globalization is conceived as having three logics: technics, economics, and politics.

- There are three main types of theory associated with economic globalization: structural, conjunctural, and constructivist.

- These can be distinguished in terms of their distinctive causal terms: imperatives, tendencies, and contingency.

- Understanding globalization as a historical process involves examining it in terms of three speeds of social change: the *longue durée*, the epochal, and the contemporaneous.

- The three theories of globalization correspond with each of these three speeds, explaining economic globalization from a different temporal perspective.

- The three theories of economic globalization are therefore in principle complementary, producing a layered explanation from its structured to its contingent origins.

The second age of globalization: another extraordinary episode?

Remarking on a previous epoch of global economic transformation, John Maynard Keynes wrote of 'an extraordinary episode in the economic progress of man', in which 'the internationalization of…economic and social life…was nearly complete' (quoted in Grieco and Ikenberry 2003: 206). Many of his liberal contemporaries, such as Norman Angell, associated (what later became known as) this belle époque (1870–1914) with the emergence of a new world order in which war was becoming increasingly unthinkable (McGrew 2002). The guns of August 1914 brutally suppressed such liberal idealism. This first age of liberal, or more accurately, imperial, global economic integration has acquired totemic status in the current debates about globalization. For those of a sceptical persuasion, it is the **gold standard** against which the many empirical claims concerning contemporary economic integration can be debunked (Hirst and Thompson 1999). By contrast, for those persuaded that until the GFC the world was in the grip of the second age of globalization, it has become the benchmark against which to validate its historically unprecedented features. This has given rise to a voluminous literature of comparative economic history, dissecting and contrasting the two great ages of globalization in the search for conclusive—or rather, elusive—evidence as to which can lay claim to being the more 'globalized' (see Table 10.3). The real significance of this enterprise, however, is more political than historical. Because the critical issue is not the comparative scale of globalization so much as what the comparison discloses about the limits to, or scope for, national politics under conditions of global economic integration. Or, as Bordo, Eichengreen, and Irwin put it, 'why globalization a century ago did not create the same dilemmas as now' (Bordo *et al.* 1999).

For Gilpin, 'although globalization had become the defining feature of the international economy at the beginning of the twenty-first century', the current world economy, in comparison with the belle époque, remains considerably less globalized and integrated (Gilpin 2001: 3). This is a view shared with other economic historians (for example, O'Rourke and Williamson 1999). The implication is that, far from being unprecedented, economic globalization today is essentially a return to the developmental trajectory of the world economy inaugurated by the birth of the industrial age. In their study of global finance, Obstfeld and Taylor identify a more differentiated picture in which, on some measures (gross capital flows and stocks of foreign capital), globalization is considerably greater today; on others it has converged with pre-1914 levels (interest rate differentials, national savings, and investment correlations); and on yet others still it is below that of the pre-1914 era (flows of capital to the South and net capital flows) (Obstfeld and Taylor 2004). In contrast, for O'Rourke and Williamson (1999) and Gilpin (2002), among others, the world economy still has some way to go in order to achieve the comprehensive levels of global capital, trade, commodity, and labour market integration of the pre-1914 era (O'Rourke and Williamson 1999; Gilpin 2002). As O'Rourke and Williamson (1999: 2, 14) emphasize:

    ❝ By 1914, there was hardly a village or town anywhere on the globe whose prices were not influenced by distant foreign markets, whose infrastructure was not financed by foreign capital, whose engineering, manufacturing, and even business skills were not imported from abroad, or whose labour markets were not influenced by the absence of those who had emigrated or by the presence of strangers who had immigrated. [And] involved the most extensive wage and living standard convergence the Atlantic economy has ever seen. ❞

Indeed, Hoogvelt argues that globalization has involved the implosion of global economic activity as it has become increasingly concentrated in the OECD and a handful of NIEs by comparison with the age of empire (Hoogvelt 2001). The implication is that the significance of the second age of economic globalization is considerably exaggerated and thus its consequences have been significantly overstated, particularly with respect to national politics and the continuing centrality of state power to the proper functioning of the world economy (Hirst and Thompson 1999; see also Hay, Chapter 11 in this volume). This, in some respects, has become the orthodox view.

As many economic historians acknowledge, however, whether this second age of economic globalization is more intensive than the belle époque cannot be determined definitively (Obstfeld and Taylor 2003). A number of economic historians suggest that, on most measures, recent levels of global economic integration are comparable with, if not more so, the period of the belle époque (Geyer and Bright 1995; Bordo *et al.* 1999; Lindert and Williamson 2001; Maddison 2001; Taylor 2002; Findlay and O'Rourke 2007) (see Table 10.3). As Bordo *et al.* conclude, 'the globalization of commodity and financial markets is historically unprecedented' (1999: 56). In particular, while financial integration 'measured in terms of net flows as a percentage of GDP is quite similar in the post-1975 and pre-1914 periods, gross flows are greater today', while the correlation between domestic savings and investment (the Feldstein–Horioka puzzle) is now at 'the levels of the pre-1914 period' (Bordo *et al.* 1998: 17, 3). By comparison, as Findlay and O'Rourke observe, by the end of the twentieth century, 'the ratio of world trade to GDP was higher than ever before in history' (Findlay and O'Rourke 2007: 525). Table 10.3 identifies some of the comparative features of the different historical ages of globalization. It broadly confirms what Dowrick and DeLong, two

Table 10.3 Epochal shifts in globalization since 1820

Epoch	Intercontinental commodity market integration		Migration and world labour markets		Integration of world capital markets
	Change in price gaps between Continents	Why they changed	How migrant shares changed in receiving Countries	Why they changed	What happened to integration (Feldstein–Horioka Slope Coefficient)
1820–1914	Price gaps cut by 81%	72% because of cheaper transport; 28% because of pre-1870 tariff cuts	Migrant shares rise	Passenger transport costs slashed, push and pull (immigration policies remain neutral)	60% progress from complete segmentation towards market integration
1914–50	Gaps double in width, return to 1870 level	New trade barriers only	Migrant shares fall	Restrictive immigration policies	Reversion to complete market segmentation
1950–2000, especially since 1970	Price gaps cut by 76%, now lower than in 1914	74% because of policies freeing trade; 26% because of cheaper transport	Migrant shares rise	Transport costs drop, push and pull again (no net change in immigration policies)	60% progress from complete segmentation towards market integration
Overall 1820–2000	Price gaps cut by 92%	18% because of trade policies; 82% because of cheaper transport	No clear change in US migrant shares, but rises elsewhere	Policy restrictions, offsetting transport improvements	60% progress from complete segmentation towards market integration

Source: Lindert and Williamson (2003).

leading economic historians, conclude that: 'It is hard to argue today that there is any dimension ... save that of mass migration in which we today are less "globalized" than our predecessors at the end of World War I' (2003: 191).

That said, the second age of economic globalization displays some profound *qualitative* differences from that of the pre-1914 era. Most notable are real-time world financial markets; the breadth and depth of trade and financial cross-border activity; the speed of economic exchange; the scale of gross economic flows of goods, and short-term as opposed to long-term capital; the institutionalization of economic relations at an inter-regional level through global and

regional organizations, MNCs, and transnational regulatory bodies; and, finally, the fact that twenty-first-century globalization is experienced much more unevenly than in the belle époque (Obstfeld and Taylor 2004; Held and McGrew 2007). Both the sources and destinations of capital flows today are far more diversified than in the pre-1914 era, while 'gross asset and liability positions were very close to net positions before 1914, in contrast to today where most major industrial countries are both major creditors and debtors' (Wilkins 2003; Bordo 2005: 10). In terms of economic structure, there are profound differences in relation to the global division of labour. The first age of globalization involved deindustrialization on the periphery and industrialization at the core, while the second age has entailed the reverse. This second age of economic globalization undoubtedly displays many unique attributes—from the scale of short-term capital flows to transnational production—and a 'secular trend towards increased synchronization' of national business cycles, as disastrously evident in the GFC. Combined, these trends produce novel political and economic dilemmas for all governments, but most especially democratic states. Garrett's conclusion remains valid today even after the events of the GFC, namely that 'global market integration is qualitatively different and deeper today' (Garrett 2000a). The implications of this for the politics and governance of globalization is the focus of subsequent chapters (especially Hay, Chapter 11 in this volume).

After the crisis: a 'third wave' of economic globalization?

How does this analysis of the distinctive features and underlying causes of economic globalization contribute to an understanding of its future prospects in the aftermath of the GFC? From the preceding discussion, two related observations can be made.

First, as previously highlighted, economic globalization appears to be much more socially and institutionally 'embedded' than is generally acknowledged. Despite the GFC, it has proved far more resilient than even many of its strongest advocates believed would be the case. This is not to argue, as is the tendency with structural theories of economic globalization, that it is either inevitable or immutable. On the contrary, agency and politics matter very much to its future trajectory. As the immediate events of the GFC demonstrated, politics almost everywhere was dominated by the requirement to stabilize the global political economy and to prevent a slide into global depression (Wolf 2014; Eichengreen 2015). This reflects, in part, just how deeply embedded the second age of globalization had become to the functioning of all modern economies most especially the new rising economic powers. But the GFC, as noted, has been associated with a significant slowdown of economic globalization below the peak levels of 2007 although significantly above many earlier periods. This suggests that far from the demise or reversal of economic globalization we appear to be witnessing its 'Great Moderation'. This 'Great Moderation' furthermore is associated with a significant structural shift in patterns of economic globalization as trade, capital, and migration flows have become increasingly shaped by emerging and developing economies, accelerating trends already apparent at the outset of the twenty first century.

Second, as Castells (2000: 147) argues, economic globalization, in a very significant sense, has always been 'politically constituted'. Politics, in other words, provides the ideological, institutional, and motivational resin that binds together the powerful social and economic constituencies that have facilitated, promoted, and benefited from economic globalization. So far, the protectionist and anti-globalization backlash to the GFC has been contained, at least by comparison with the inter-war period (Helleiner 2014a, 2014b; Eichengreen 2015). While elite political support for globalization has not diminished markedly, nevertheless wider public support in the West has eroded dramatically with economic austerity, although significantly the opposite appears to be the case amongst the new rising economic powers. Certainly the vulnerability of globalization has become very much more apparent in the wake of the GFC, from the widespread public opposition to migration not to mention growing fears of 'currency wars' replacing 'trade wars'. As James remarks, 'systemic financial crises like the worldwide catastrophe of the 1930s cause [political] paradigms to shift in ways that threaten to unravel globalization' (2009: 179). With the avoidance to date of such a global catastrophe that unravelling has so far not come to pass. But if catastrophe has been avoided it is also evident that this 'Great Moderation' has been associated with accelerating global economic power shifts. As a consequence, both the politics of, and thereby the future of economic globalization will be increasingly dependent on the economic fortunes and interests of the world's emerging economic powers. This is likely to prove a source of growing friction and instability in the global political economy compounded by the volatility arising from the rebalancing of the world economy as a consequence of the GFC. To interpret the present conjuncture as automatically prefiguring a 'New' or 'Third Wave' of globalization therefore seems decidedly premature (World Bank 2007; Breznitz and Zysman 2013; Kelly 2014).

? QUESTIONS

1. What are the principal causes or logics of globalization?

2. Is economic globalization a product of politics or of capitalism, or both?

3. 'Technics makes globalization.' Discuss.

4. In what sense, if any, do constructivist theories provide a convincing account of the origins of economic globalization?

5. Which is the more convincing: the globalist or the sceptical analysis of economic globalization?

6. Outline the globalist case, and critically evaluate it with reference to the historical evidence.

7. Has the GFC contributed to the demise of economic globalization?

8. How does Braudel's analysis help us to understand the logics of economic globalization?

9. Critically assess the argument that economic globalization is simply a political project.

10. 'Economic globalization is much more limited than many realize' (Gilpin 2001). Critically assess this proposition with reference to contemporary global economic trends.

FURTHER READING

BIS. (2016), *Triennial Central Bank Survey: Foreign Exchange Turnover in April 2016* (Basel: Monetary and Economic Department).

Castells, M. (2000), *The Rise of the Network Society* (Oxford: Blackwell). This is now a contemporary classic account of the political economy of globalization, comprehensive in its analysis of the new global informational capitalism.

Dicken, P. (2014), *Global Shift: Mapping the Changing Contours of the World Economy,* 7th edn (London: Sage). This is an excellent introduction and comprehensive account of the new global division of labour and the globalization of production in the world economy.

Garrett, G. (2000), 'The Causes of Globalization', *Comparative Political Studies,* 33/6: 945–91. A really interesting and thorough exploration of the causal dynamics of globalization written from a rather orthodox political economy position, but, nevertheless, critical of much of the contemporary sceptical analysis.

Giddens, A. (1990), *The Consequences of Modernity* (Cambridge: Polity Press). A classic statement of the rootedness of globalization in the long-term historical processes of modernization or modernity. It is less a political economy than a historical sociological account of globalization which takes it seriously as a transformative force.

Gilpin, R. (2001), *Global Political Economy* (Princeton: Princeton University Press). A more sceptical view of economic globalization which, although taking it seriously, conceives it as an expression of Americanization or American hegemony.

Goldin, I. and Mariathasan, M. (2015), *The Butterfly Defect: How Globalization Creates Systemic Risks and What to Do about It* (Princeton: Princeton University Press).

Held, D. and McGrew, A. (2007), *Globalization/Anti-Globalization* (Cambridge: Polity Press). A comprehensive examination of the academic and political controversies surrounding globalization.

Hirst, P., Thompson, G., and Bromley, S. (2009), *Globalization in Question,* 3rd edn (Cambridge: Polity Press). An excellent and sober critique of the hyperglobalist arguments, it is thoroughly sceptical about the globalization thesis, viewing recent trends as a return to the belle époque and heavily shaped by states.

James, H. (2009), *The Creation and Destruction of Value: The Globalization Cycle* (Cambridge, MA: Harvard University Press). An excellent analysis of the sources and consequences of the Great Crash for contemporary globalization.

Rosenberg, J. (2000), *The Follies of Globalization Theory* (London: Verso). A very erudite and rigorous critique of the globalization literature that, although sceptical about its wilder claims, considers that globalization can only be understood from a historical materialist perspective.

Scholte, J. A. (2005), *Globalization: A Critical Introduction,* 2nd edn (Basingstoke: Palgrave). An excellent introduction to the globalization debate, from its causes to its consequences for the global political economy, from within a critical political economy perspective.

Wood, E. M. (2003), *Empire of Capital* (London: Verso). A novel reworking of the classical Marxist account of imperialism which takes globalization seriously as a new phase of capitalist development accompanied by a unique form of empire.

 ## WEBLINKS

www.isn.ethz.ch Good links to security and global economy nexuses.

www.wto.org Official WTO site, with useful material about its policies and data on world trade.

www.polity.co.uk/global Good site for the globalization debate and related links.

www.voxeu.org An excellent site for current debates about global economic issues and research.

www.indiana.edu/~ipe/ipesection Good site for general material on IPE.

www.nber.org Excellent studies of economic globalization in National Bureau of Economic Research (NBER) Working Paper series.

www.worldbank.org For reports and statistics on economic globalization.

www.imf.org For annual reports on aspects of financial globalization and statistics.

www.unctad.org For annual reports on FDI and statistics on global production.

ONLINE RESOURCE CENTRE

For additional material and resources, please visit the Online Resource Centre at:
www.oxfordtextbooks.co.uk/ravenhill5e/

11

Globalization's Impact on States

Colin Hay

Reader's guide

There is no topic more controversial in the field of global political economy than the impact of globalization on the accountability, autonomy, capacity, and sovereignty of the nation state; and the controversy has only intensified since the onset of the Global Financial Crisis. Arguably, the democratic character of governance in contemporary societies is at stake in such debates. This chapter reviews the extensive controversy that surrounds such questions, focusing attention on the principal mechanisms in and through which globalization is seen to impact upon the nation state and the empirical evidence that might either substantiate or question the existence of such mechanisms. It provides a detailed assessment of the case for and against the globalization thesis, examining the extent to which global economic integration might be seen to restrict the parameters of domestic political autonomy. It concludes by considering the complex and sometimes paradoxical relationship between globalization, democracy and the nation state.

Introduction

It is getting on for 45 years since Charles Kindleberger boldly proclaimed that: 'the nation state is just about through as an economic unit' (1969: 207). Since then, we have witnessed a remarkable profusion of apocalyptic predictions of the demise of the nation state—and a Global Financial Crisis. In such accounts, globalization is invariably cast in the role of prosecutor, judge, jury, and executioner. Yet, despite such doom-laden prognoses, government expenditure continues to account for a significant and, since the Global Financial Crisis, in almost all cases a rising share of **gross domestic product (GDP)**, while the nation state remains the principal focus of political identification and the principal locus of political debate and contestation in an interdependent world. Given this seeming paradox, it is perhaps not surprising that the question of the impact of globalization on the development of the state has become a subject of considerable interest and intense controversy. Opinions range widely.

Though perhaps less influential than it once was, the view that globalization is in the process of, or has already, precipitated a terminal crisis of the nation state is still widespread. Others see such apocalyptic claims as wild and unfounded extrapolations from anecdotal evidence. Proponents of such a view, they suggest, confuse a crisis of the *form* of the nation state for a crisis of the nation state per se. Yet others see globalization as a process driven by states that has, in many cases, served to strengthen and certainly to increase the significance of state intervention for economic performance—a view reinforced by the crucial role played by states in bailing out domestic financial institutions during the crisis (acting in effect as collective public goods providers of last resort). Still others question the role of globalization in such dynamics, suggesting either that globalization—though real—has little to do with the developmental trajectory of the nation state or that the claim that we have witnessed a systematic process of globalization is itself mythical. Finally, there are those who suggest that the very *idea* of globalization as a harsh and non-negotiable economic constraint has itself exerted a powerful influence in confining the political ambitions of elected officials to those consistent with the pervasive neo-liberal orthodoxy. It is this, rather than globalization per se, they suggest, that has given rise to the impression of a waning of the nation state's autonomy, capacity, and sovereignty.

Much more than academic pride is at stake in such debates. For, whether or not we see globalization as restricting the parameters of political choice domestically, and whether or not we see the nation state as having a present or, indeed, a future will have a very significant bearing on the space for political autonomy we perceive there to be. This, in turn, has significant consequences for the extent to which we might legitimately hold elected officials accountable for their conduct in office. Given the significance of the issues we are dealing with, it is important to proceed with a certain degree of caution.

We should perhaps be wary of accepting uncritically, as many have, that globalization leaves states (and the governments which give effect to state power) with no alternative other than to capitulate to the demands and desires of mobile investors. For to do so, is effectively to deny the possibility of the democratic governance of economic processes in contemporary societies, certainly at the national level. In other words, there is a certain danger that in accepting over-hastily an influential conception of the inevitable demise of the nation state's capacity and autonomy, we provide a convenient alibi for politicians keen to justify otherwise unpalatable social and economic reforms by appeal to the harsh economic realities of a global age. Maybe our politicians deserve such an alibi; maybe the constraints of the global economy are so exacting and all-pervasive as to warrant the appeal to such a 'logic of no alternative'; maybe these are valid and defensible conclusions. The crucial point for now is that we cannot allow ourselves to accept at face value such claims without a detailed consideration—both theoretical and empirical—of the arguments for and against such a view.

Though space does not permit a fully comprehensive exploration of the relevant issues, it is my aim in what follows to survey the existing literature in this area and, in so doing, to provide a basis for such an assessment. It is important to emphasize at the outset, however, that there is no agreed or emerging consensus on globalization's impact upon the state—and such debates are only further complicated by the recent Global Financial Crisis. Commentators are divided and they are likely to remain divided. As we shall see, this is—at least in part—due to the rather slippery nature of the term globalization itself, which has come to mean a range of rather different things to a range of different analysts.

The chapter proceeds in four sections. In the first of these, I seek to establish a few necessary preliminaries, distinguishing in particular between the politics of globalization and the globalization of politics. In the second, I identify the principal mechanisms in and through which globalization is seen to impact upon the nation state before turning, in the third, to the empirical evidence which might either substantiate or question the existence of such mechanisms. In the final section, and by way of a conclusion, I consider the complex and sometimes paradoxical relationship between globalization, democracy, and the nation state, looking both at the impact of globalization on states and the state's impact on globalization.

The globalization of politics and the politics of globalization

It is crucial at the outset that we distinguish between the globalization of politics and the politics of globalization. This is particularly important, given the tendency—especially prevalent among international/global political economists—to talk about globalization as if it were a transparent, self-sustaining, and purely economic dynamic (on the dangers of such 'economism', see also Teivainen 2002). It is a key contention of this chapter that globalization is not a tendency that is furthered or, indeed, countered in the *absence of political actors*. As such, it has a politics that must be a central ingredient of any adequate account of its development.

By the *globalization of politics*, I refer to the displacement of political capacities and responsibilities from the national and/or regional levels to the genuinely global level, through the development of institutions of global governance.

By the *politics of globalization*, I refer to the politics of the process of globalization itself, to the political drivers of globalization and to the consequences of such a process for political conflict, practice, and the distribution of political responsibility.

Whether, and to what extent, we observe a globalization of politics is a matter of empirical judgement. It is likely to relate, among other things, to our evaluation of the extent and significance of genuinely global institutions of governance, the relative significance of regional institutions, and the degree to which the emergence of global institutions might be seen to give rise to a politics independent of and irreducible to that between discrete nation states or regions. Yet, whatever specific judgement we reach—and, again,

opinion varies considerably (compare, for instance, Buzan, Held, and McGrew 1998; Krasner 1999; Archibugi 2003)—we must acknowledge that if globalization exists at all, and even if it is confined exclusively to the economic and cultural spheres, it has a politics. While we may well deny the globalization of politics, then, unless we deny globalization itself we cannot deny the *politics* of globalization. It is with the latter that this chapter is principally concerned.

More specifically, I shall focus on three analytically separable, but nonetheless interconnected, dimensions of the politics of globalization:

1. The implications and consequences of globalization (whether economic, political, or cultural) for the capacity and autonomy of the nation state.

2. The interpretation of the opportunities and constraints associated with globalization and the consequent appeal made, in political contexts, to the language of globalization (often, as we shall see, to justify social and economic reforms).

3. The role of political actors, particularly state actors, in the political 'authoring' of globalization and the processes which either sustain or impede its development.

The first of these might be seen as the *structural* dimension, relating as it does to the constraints and opportunities of the external environment for domestic political actors. The second relates to the *ideational* dimension and, more specifically, to the way in which political actors understand the constraints and opportunities that the external environment presents to them. The third relates to the *intentional, strategic,* or *agential* dimension—to the role of political actors in the creation and recreation of the very external environment in which they find themselves. Together, they suggest an approach to the question of the impact of globalization on the state and the state's impact on globalization in which political actors are always present, in which the ideas they hold about their environment shapes their political conduct, and in which they are never unburdened of the constraints (and opportunities) of the environment they have created (for a further elaboration, see Hay 2002*b*: 253–60).

Such a perspective is applied, in the pages that follow, to a series of more substantive issues and controversies. These might together be taken to comprise an

BOX 11.1

The Politics of Globalization: Key Controversies

- The extent to which globalization might be seen to diminish the autonomy and 'perforate' the sovereignty of the nation state (on 'perforated sovereignty', see Duchacek 1990; Jessop 2002).

- The extent to which globalization might be seen to establish powerful tendencies towards global political convergence and homogenization.

- The extent to which it is right to identify a globalization of political problems—the proliferation of issues that require a response in the form of concerted global action.

- The extent to which we can point to a parallel globalization of political solutions and the corresponding emergence of more or less dedicated institutions, mechanisms, and processes of *global governance*.

- The extent to which we can identify the global diffusion of 'best practice' policy solutions (or potential solutions) and/or policy models in the form of the transfer of ideas about 'good' practice between nations (whether by choice or imposition).

- The extent to which globalization might be seen to promote the development of a global polity or *cosmopolis* capable of transcending the state (see e.g. Zolo 1997; Archibugi 2003).

agenda for a consideration of the politics of globalization (see Box 11.1).

Each set of issues, as we shall see, reveals a separate and distinct politics of globalization. By drawing attention to the multifaceted politics of globalization in this way, my aim is to contribute to the attempt to restore political (and one might hope democratic) scrutiny and accountability to processes more conventionally seen as economic and inexorable—and, consequently, as not subject to political deliberation (see, more generally, Hay 2002*a*).

KEY POINTS

- The impact of globalization on the autonomy, capacity, and sovereignty of the nation state is much disputed.

- It is important to distinguish between the politics of globalization (the political drivers of the process of globalization) and the globalization of politics (the displacement of political responsibilities and capacities from the level of the nation state through the emergence of institutions and processes of global governance). Globalization has a politics, whether or not politics has become globalized.

- It is equally important to distinguish between and to acknowledge the structural, ideational, and strategic dimensions of the process of globalization. The first of these relates to the constraints and opportunities presented by globalization; the second to the way in which those structural factors are understood; the third to the role of political actors is 'authoring' the process of globalization itself.

Globalization and the crisis of the nation state

If we are to assess the impact (if any) of globalization on the viability of the nation state, we must first identify the principal mechanisms in and through which globalization is held, in conventional accounts, to limit the capacity, autonomy, and sovereignty of the nation state. Before doing so, however, it is perhaps important to emphasize that most strong variants of the globalization thesis—which present the nation state as a casualty of globalization—tend to do so without pointing directly or explicitly to the mechanism or mechanisms involved (see, for instance, Ohmae 1990, 1995; Reich 1992). At best, it seems, they treat the existence of such mechanisms as self-evident. What we tend to see, instead, is what Andreas Busch (2000: 34) refers to as 'casual empiricism'—the anecdotal appeal to, and extrapolation from, single pieces of evidence that appear to confirm the general tenor of the argument being advanced.

At times, however, casual empiricism gives way to 'casual theoreticism'. Here, tangential reference is made to the increased bargaining power and/or mobility of capital in an era of globalization. In so doing, 'hyperglobalists' appeal, whether they are aware of it or not, to mechanisms derived from neoclassical open economy macroeconomic models (for reviews of the relevant literature, see Obstfeld and Rogoff 1996; Rødseth 2000; Ugur 2001). This is an important point and gives a first clue as to the character of the hyperglobalization thesis. For it serves to indicate that, for such authors, it is *economic* globalization that is the principal factor limiting the capacity and autonomy of the state in the contemporary context. In short, economic globalization gives mobile international investors the upper hand over domestic political authorities.

Without going into any technical detail, it is useful to examine further such open economic macroeconomics models. In particular, it is important that we:

1. Establish the assumptions on which such models are predicated.

2. Assess the plausibility of such assumptions.

3. Consider the sensitivity of the conclusions derived from such assumptions (for the viability or otherwise of the nation state) to modifications in the initial premises from which they are derived.

The hyperglobalization thesis

Arguably, the key factor determining the inevitability of state retrenchment for hyperglobalists is the heightened mobility of capital. The logic to which they appeal is, in fact, very similar to that elaborated by Adam Smith in 1776:

66 The ... proprietor of stock is properly a citizen of the world, and is not necessarily attached to any particular country. He would be apt to abandon the country in which he is exposed to a vexatious inquisition, in order to be assessed a burdensome tax, and would remove his stock to some country where he could either carry on his business or enjoy his fortune at his ease. A tax that tended to drive away stock from a particular country would so far tend to dry up every source of revenue, both to the sovereign and to the society. Not only the profits of stock, but also the rent of land and the wages of labour, would necessarily be more or less diminished by its removal. 99

(1776/1976: 848–9, cited in Swank 2002: 245)

Updated and restated in more familiar terms, the argument goes something like this. In closed national economies, such as those that (supposedly) characterized the early post-war period, capital is essentially immobile and national in character; it has no 'exit' option. In such an environment, governments can impose punitive taxation regimes upon unwilling and relatively impotent national capitals with little cost to the domestic economy (save, except, for the tendency for capitalists to hoard rather than to reinvest their profits). With open economy conditions, such as are conventionally held to characterize the contemporary

era, this is no longer the case. Capital may now exit from national economic environments at minimal cost (indeed, in most neoclassical-inspired models, at zero cost).

Accordingly, by playing off the regulatory regimes of different economies against one another, capital can ensure for itself the highest rate of return on its investment. *Ceteris paribus*, capital will exit high-taxation regimes for low-taxation regimes, comprehensive welfare states for residual states, highly regulated labour markets for flexible labour markets, and economies characterized by strict environmental regulations and high union density for those characterized by lapse environmental standards and low union density. The clear prediction would be that capital will seek out the high-growth regimes of, for instance, **newly industrializing economies (NIEs)** (like Malaysia, for instance) unencumbered by a powerful environmental lobby, burdensome welfare traditions, rigid labour market institutions, and correspondingly higher rates of taxation.

The process pits national economy against national economy, in an increasingly intense competitive struggle. States must effectively clamber over one another in an ever—more frenzied attempt to produce a more favourable investment environment for mobile ('footloose') foreign direct investors than their competitors. Yet, this is not a one-shot game—and an early influx of **foreign direct investment (FDI)** only increases the dependence of the state upon its continued 'locational competitiveness'. If investment is to be retained in such an environment, states must constantly strive to improve the investment opportunities they can offer relative to their competitors. Any failure to do so can only precipitate a haemorrhaging of invested funds, labour shedding and, in turn, economic crisis. A neo-Darwinian survival of the fittest effectively guarantees that states must internalize the preferences of capital, offering ever more attractive investment incentives, ever more flexible labour markets, and ever less restrictive environmental regulations, if they are not to be emptied of investment, economic activity, and employment. Big government, if not perhaps the state itself, is rendered increasingly anachronistic—a guarantor, not of the interests of citizens or even consumers, but a sure means to disinvestment and economic crisis.

Little wonder, then, that the hyperglobalization thesis tends to predict 'social dumping', 'competitive deregulation', and a **race to the bottom** in terms of social and environmental standards, a process lubricated by the 'deregulatory arbitrage' of footloose and fancy-free **transnational corporations**.

The policy implications of such an account are painfully clear. As globalization serves to establish competitive selection mechanisms within the international economy, there is little choice but to cast all regulatory impediments to the efficient operation of the market on the bonfire of welfare institutions, regulatory controls (for instance, of the banking sector), and labour market rigidities.

Plausible, familiar, compelling, and, above all, influential though such a logic may well appear, it serves us well to isolate the assumptions on which it is predicated. For, as we shall see, it is these, rather than any inexorable process of globalization, which ultimately summon the crisis of the nation state. They are principally fivefold, and each can be challenged on both theoretical and empirical grounds (see Box 11.2).

Each of these premises is at best dubious, at worst demonstrably false. Such assumptions, it should perhaps be noted, are not justified in neoclassical economics in terms of their accuracy, but because they are convenient and make possible abstract quasi-mathematical modelling. That defence, whatever one thinks of it, is simply not available to proponents of the hyperglobalization thesis whose borrowings from neoclassical economics rarely extend past the assumptions to the algebra.

Consider each assumption in turn. While it may seem entirely appropriate to attribute to capital the sole motive of seeking the greatest return on its investment, the political and economic history of capital provides little or no support for the notion that capital is blessed either with complete information or even with a relatively clear and consistent conception of what its own best interest is. Moreover, as the political economy of the advanced capitalist democracies demonstrates well, capital has a history of resisting social and economic reforms which it has later come both to rely upon and actively to defend (see, for example, Swenson 2000).

The second assumption is, again, a convenient fiction, used in neoclassical macroeconomics to make possible the modelling of an open economy. Few, if any, economists would defend the claim that markets for goods or services are fully integrated or clear instantly. Indeed, the degree of integration of such markets is an empirical question and, as such, an issue to which we return in the next section.

If the first two assumptions are problematic, then the third is demonstrably false, at least with respect to certain types of capital. For, however mobile portfolio capital may appear in a digital economy, the same is simply not the case for capital invested in infrastructure, machinery, and personnel. Consider inward foreign direct investment. Once attracted to a particular locality, foreign direct investors acquire a range of non-recuperable or **sunk costs**—such as their investment in physical infrastructure, plant, and machinery. Consequently, their exit options become seriously depleted. While it is entirely 'rational' for foreign direct investors to proclaim loudly their mobility, exit is perhaps most effective as a threat.

What this in turn suggests is that predictions of the haemorrhaging of invested capital from generous welfare states are almost certainly misplaced. A combination of exit threats and concerns arising from the hyperglobalization thesis about the *likelihood* of exit may well have had an independent effect on the trajectory of fiscal and labour market reform. But there would seem no a priori reason to hold generous welfare state and high corporate taxation burdens incompatible with the attraction and retention of foreign direct investment. As we shall see in greater

---

BOX 11.2

Core Assumptions of the 'Hyperglobalization' Thesis

- That capital invests where it can secure the greatest net return on that investment and is possessed of perfect information of the means by which to do so.

- That markets for goods and services are fully integrated globally and that, consequently, national economies must prove themselves internationally competitive if economic growth is to be sustained.

- That capital enjoys perfect mobility and the cost of 'exit' (disinvestment) is zero.

- That capital will invariably secure the greatest return on its investment by minimizing its labour costs in flexible labour markets and by relocating its productive activities in economies with the lowest rates of corporate taxation.

- That the welfare state (and the taxation receipts out of which it is funded) represents nothing other than lost capital to mobile asset holders and have no positive externalities for the competitiveness and productivity of the national economy.

detail in the next section, this is precisely what we observe from the empirical record. Not only have the most generous welfare states consistently proved the most attractive locations for inward foreign direct investors (Locke and Kochan 1985; Swank 2002), but volumes of foreign direct investment (expressed as a share of GDP) are, in fact, found to be positively correlated with levels of corporate taxation, union density, labour costs, and the degree of regulation of the labour market (Dunning 1988; Cooke and Noble 1998; Traxler and Woitech 2000; Wilensky 2002: 654–5). As Duane Swank notes:

66 contrary to the claims of the international capital mobility thesis…the general fiscal capacity of democratic governments to fund a variety of levels and mixes of social protection and services may be relatively resilient in the face of internationalisation of markets. **99**

(2002: 276)

Here, it is perhaps instructive to note that, despite a marked tendency for direct corporate taxation to fall in recent years in line with the predictions of such neoclassical-inspired models, the overall burden of taxation on firms has, in fact, remained remarkably constant, rising marginally since the mid 1980s (Kiser and Laing 2001; Steinmo 2003); it is set to do so again in the wake of the Global Financial Crisis.

No less problematic, are assumptions four and five—that capital can only compete in a more intensely competitive environment on the basis of productivity gains secured through tax reductions and cost-shedding (through rationalization, downsizing, and the flexibilization of labour), and that the welfare state is, for business, merely a drain on profits. Such assumptions reflect a narrowly Anglo-US conception of competitiveness which may arguably prove to be one of the conceptual casualties of the crisis—and, as we shall see presently, are difficult to reconcile with the empirical evidence (Hay 2013). Though ever more influential, the hyperglobalization thesis extrapolates wildly and inappropriately from labour-intensive sectors of the international economy in which competitiveness is conventionally enhanced in this way, to the global economy more generally. It fails to appreciate that foreign direct investors in capital-intensive sectors of the international economy are attracted to locations like the Northern European economies, neither for the flexibility of their labour markets nor for the cheapness of the wage and non-wage labour costs

that they impose, but for the access they provide to a highly skilled, reliable, and innovative labour force. High wages and high non-wage labour costs (in the form of payroll taxes) would seem to be a price many **multinational corporations** regard as worth paying for a dynamic and highly skilled workforce.

At this point it might be objected that the above paragraphs relate principally to the investment behaviour of foreign direct investors and not to financial market actors. This is a valid point. Indeed, although the hyperglobalization thesis has rather more to say about the former, it has much to say about the latter, too.

Its assumptions about finance capital and financial markets are similar to those about productive / invested capital and markets in goods and services. Yet, the small differences are significant. Referring again to Box 11.2, the first assumption applies equally to invested and investment capital and is equally problematic. Yet, whether it is accurate or not, arguably matters rather less in the case of portfolio capital. For such investors do not need to act rationally or with perfect information in order to inflict considerable damage on the currencies against which they may be tempted to speculate and the stocks and shares they may be tempted to dump—as the influential literature on 'irrational exuberance' and 'herding instincts' in financial markets makes very clear and as the experience of the Global Financial Crisis perhaps confirms (see e.g. Shiller 2001, 2008; Akerlof and Shiller 2010). Assumption two also applies equally to financial markets and to those in goods and services (see Pauly, Chapter 9 in this volume). All are assumed global and perfectly integrated. This may seem like a more plausible assumption to make of financial markets but, as we shall see in the next section, as an empirical claim it is not easily reconciled with the available evidence. Assumption three, though problematic for productive / invested capital as already discussed, again seems more plausible for portfolio investors. Stocks and shares can certainly be traded, and assets swapped from one denomination to another, in the flickering of a cursor. Yet, whether this *potential* is reflected in the actual behaviour of financial markets is, again, an empirical question and the subject of some debate. This, too, is discussed further in the next section. Assumptions four and five are not directly relevant to finance capital, but they can be adapted to financial actors. Hyperglobalists tend to assume that portfolio investors have a clear interest in, and preference for, strong and stable currencies backed both by implacable independent central banks with hawkish anti-inflationary credentials and governments wedded in theory and in practice to fiscal moderation and prudence. Any departure from this new financial orthodoxy, it is assumed, will precipitate a flurry of speculation against the currency and a haemorrhaging of investment from assets denominated in that currency—or, indeed, a rise in the bond 'yield' charged by financial institutions on national debt. Governments provoke the wrath of the financial markets at their peril. This, again, is an intuitively plausible proposition that would seem to be borne out by a series of high-profile speculative flurries against 'rogue' governments and highly indebted states since the onset of the Global Financial Crisis. It is, however, an empirical claim and, as we shall see later, one that a growing body of scholarship reveals to be considerably at odds with the empirical evidence certainly when considered over any sustained period of time and when one starts to separate out the effect of the crisis itself.

As the above paragraphs perhaps serve to indicate, the theoretical case against the hyperglobalization thesis is strongest with respect to the assumptions made about productive/invested capital. Its assumptions about investment/portfolio capital, if perhaps overly simplistic, are, on the face of it, more plausible. Yet, they give rise to a series of substantive claims and predictions which have prompted an important empirical challenge to the thesis. This provides the principal focus for the next section. Before turning to such issues, however, it is important that we first consider the implications of the hyperglobalization thesis for the question of convergence prior to examining an alternative and rather more political account of the origins of the contemporary crisis of the nation state.

Convergence, dual convergence, or divergence?

Through attempts to enhance competitiveness like labour market flexibility, welfare retrenchment, and the intensification of tax competition between states, the hyperglobalization thesis predicts a simple convergence among previously distinct 'models' or 'varieties' of capitalism—on an Anglo-US or liberal ideal type. This can be represented schematically (see Figure 11.1).

Globalization is the driving force, unleashing an intense competitive struggle between contending models of capitalism. It exposes all economies (A–E in Figure 11.1) to common pressures, which, in turn,

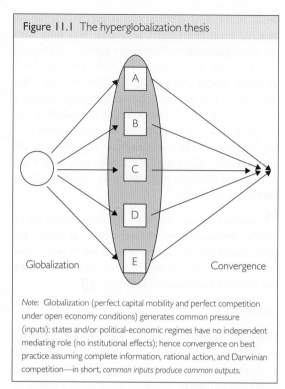

Figure 11.1 The hyperglobalization thesis

Globalization   Convergence

Note: Globalization (perfect capital mobility and perfect competition under open economy conditions) generates common pressure (inputs); states and/or political-economic regimes have no independent mediating role (no institutional effects); hence convergence on best practice assuming complete information, rational action, and Darwinian competition—in short, *common inputs produce common outputs*.

produce common outcomes. Since liberal models of capitalism best approximate the preferences of mobile capital for open markets, low taxation regimes, and light regulation, they rapidly establish themselves as the model to be emulated. Convergence on this Anglo-US ideal type is held to be rapid, lubricated by capital's exit from more highly regulated regimes.

Influential though this simple convergence thesis is, it is not as unquestioned as it once was. An alternative and increasingly influential account points to a rather more complex process of 'dual' or 'co-convergence' (see Figure 11.2), again driven by globalization (see earlier).

In this contending account, more attention is paid to the role of institutional factors in mediating the state's response to globalization. Models of capitalism are differentiated by virtue of the rather different institutions they embody. In the now conventional classification, *liberal market economies* (such as the US and the UK) and *coordinated market economies* (such as Germany, Sweden, and the Netherlands) are contrasted (Hall and Soskice 2001).

The competitive pressures unleashed by globalization may make similar demands of these institutions (such as balanced budgets, flexible labour markets,

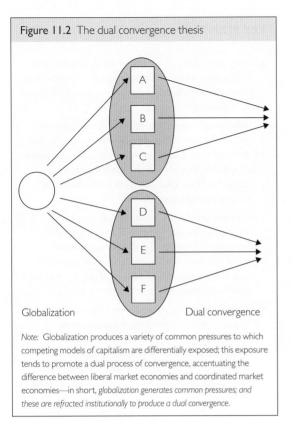

Figure 11.2 The dual convergence thesis

A
B
C

D
E
F

Globalization   Dual convergence

Note: Globalization produces a variety of common pressures to which competing models of capitalism are differentially exposed; this exposure tends to promote a dual process of convergence, accentuating the difference between liberal market economies and coordinated market economies—in short, *globalization generates common pressures; and these are refracted institutionally to produce a dual convergence.*

and the control of inflation), but these can be delivered in different ways in different institutional domains. Consequently, the 'varieties of capitalism' approach, as it has come to be known, predicts not a simple or singular process of convergence on the liberal (or Anglo-US) model, but a complex or dual convergence in which capitalist polities cluster ever more closely around the liberal and coordinated ideal types (Hall and Soskice 2001; see also Kitschelt *et al.* 1999; Garrett 1998*b*, 2000*b*; Iversen, Pontusson, and Soskice 2000; Hay and Wincott 2012).

In its sensitivity to institutional variations among different models of capitalism and in its recognition that common external pressures need not translate into common outcomes, the 'varieties of capitalism' approach represents a considerable advance on the hyperglobalization thesis. Yet, in a number of significant respects it, too, is problematic (see also Blyth 2003; Goodin 2003; Watson 2003; Hay 2004).

1. It may, unwittingly, borrow too much from the hyperglobalization thesis in presenting globalization as the principal agent of convergence (paying insufficient attention to the often regional character of processes of economic integration and/or to the differential exposure of economies to globalization, for instance).

2. In drawing a rigid and rather static distinction between liberal and coordinated market economies, it is not perhaps as sensitive to institutional diversity as it might be (see also Crouch and Streeck 1997).

3. It makes a series of empirical predictions/claims about dual convergence, which are, at best, contestable—as we shall see in the following section.

Finally, in the wake of the recent Global Financial Crisis, it might well be asked whether the liberal market economies (whose propensity to generate asset-price bubbles has been so cruelly exposed and which now look like the key source of systemic risk within the global financial system) can be seen as models of adaptation to globalization (Hay 2009, 2013).

Global problems, national solutions?

Thus far, we have tended to focus exclusively upon mechanisms identifying *economic* globalization as the key determinant of the contemporary crisis of the nation state. Yet, arguably altogether more plausible, is a rather more political mechanism. Strictly speaking, this does not so much point to the diminished capacity and sovereignty of the state in an era of globalization, as to the globalization of the problems with which the nation state is confronted—and its inability to deal with such problems. Indeed, it points to the more general lack of the political capacity to deal with genuinely global problems and risks that results from the continued ascendancy of the nation state as a political unit.

The classic example here, is the problem of high-consequence global environmental risks (Giddens 1990; Beck 1992). This is well expressed in the so-called **tragedy of the commons**, first identified by Garrett Hardin (1968). Hardin provides an intuitively plausible and all too compelling model of the seemingly intractable problem of environmental degradation in contemporary societies. The systematic exploitation and pollution of the environment, it is argued, is set to continue since individual corporations and states, despite a clear collective interest, choose not to impose upon themselves the costs of unilateral environmental action. Their logic is entirely rational, though potentially catastrophic in its cumulative consequences. Such actors know that environmental regulation is costly and, particularly in an open international economy, a burden on competitiveness. Accordingly, in the absence of an international agency capable of enforcing the compliance of all states and all corporations, the anticipation of **free riding** is sufficient to ensure that corporations and states do not burden themselves with additional costs and taxes. The long-term effects for the environment are all too obvious, preventing as it does, a global solution to a genuinely global problem.

The extent to which the narrowly perceived self-interest of states and governments can subvert the development of effective mechanisms and institutions of global governance is well-evidenced by the Bush administration's withdrawal from the 1997 Kyoto Protocol (committing signatories to staged reductions in greenhouse gas emissions); the reliance on the agreement reached in the UN's COP21 negotiation in Paris on the US not using its veto power a second time in a similar way; and, for the critics of both, by the fact that such agreements, even if fully implemented, would only serve to reduce slightly the pace of an ongoing process of environmental degradation.

These are most important examples, and a number of broader implications might be drawn from them (see Box 11.3).

KEY POINTS

- Many of the strongest versions of the globalization thesis fail to specify the mechanism by which globalization might be seen to limit the capacity, autonomy, and sovereignty of the nation state.

- Nonetheless, a variety of such mechanisms have been posited. These are principally economic in character and often rely upon stylized assumptions about the behaviour of capital drawn from open economy neoclassical economics. These assumptions can be questioned theoretically and empirically.

- The hyperglobalization thesis predicts a simple convergence between 'models of capitalism' under conditions of (economic) globalization; the more recent 'varieties of capitalism' perspective predicts a more complex process of dual convergence. There are theoretical problems with both sets of predictions.

- The nation state has always suffered from a limited capacity to deal with genuinely global problems; such problems are proliferating. The 'tragedy of the commons' provides a compelling model of the consequences of this lack of capacity, pointing to the need for effective and democratic institutions of global governance.

BOX 11.3

The Implications of the 'Tragedy of the Commons'

The 'tragedy of the commons' is, effectively, a modern-day morality tale. It is indicative of a more general disparity between the need for and supply of effective institutions and mechanisms of global governance. For, while it is easy to point to genuinely global problems requiring for their resolution coordinated global responses, it is far more difficult to find examples of the latter.

As this perhaps suggests, the 'tragedy of the commons' is not really a story of the crisis of the nation state at all. For, it is the continued capacity of many (if perhaps not all) states to behave unilaterally and to veto international agreements that precludes the appropriate globally coordinated collective response. In other words, political globalization (effective and authoritative institutions of global governance) is impeded by the retention of the nation state's sovereignty. This is less a crisis of the nation

state, then, than a crisis produced by the resilience of the nation state.

While the proliferation of genuinely global political problems does point to the incapacity of a system of sovereign states to deal with the challenges it now faces, it does not indicate any particular incapacity of states to deal with the problems and issues they have always dealt with. This is, then, less of a story of a loss of capacity than of the proliferation of issues which the nation state has never had the capacity to deal with.

Finally, and rather perversely, the disparity between the need for and supply of global solutions to global problems is merely exacerbated by economic globalization. For this has served to drive states, at pain of economic crisis, to elevate considerations of competitiveness over all other concerns, including environmental protection. There is a clear and obvious danger that the narrow pursuit of short-term economic advantage will come at the long-term price of a looming environmental, economic, and political catastrophe.

Globalization and state retrenchment: the evidence assessed

As suggested in the previous section, the hyperglobalization thesis tends to present a theoretical, indeed, largely hypothetical, argument for the contemporary crisis of the nation state. If its assumptions are accepted, then the predicted crisis of the nation state is little more than a logical inference. Yet, as we have seen, there may be good theoretical grounds for challenging some of these assumptions and with them the claimed inevitability of the state's loss of capacity, autonomy, sovereignty, and legitimacy. In the end, however, these are empirical questions—and it is to the empirical evidence itself that we must turn if we are to assess the validity of the hyperglobalization thesis and to assess the impact, if any, of globalization on states. It is to this task that we now turn. We begin first by considering the dependent variable.

The dependent variable: state retrenchment

It is perhaps appropriate to begin with the simplest data that most directly addresses the contemporary condition of the state. If the state were to experience a potentially terminal crisis, we might expect to see clear evidence of systematic state retrenchment. Moreover, we would expect this to be most pronounced in highly open economies whose public spending had traditionally accounted for a high proportion of gross domestic product. Table 11.1 presents data on government expenditure expressed as a proportion of gross domestic product for a number of developed countries from the 1960s, conventionally the point of departure for political economies of globalization.

The evidence itself is fairly unequivocal. These, for the most part extremely open and developed economies, show little sign of systematic retrenchment in the so-called era of globalization. Indeed, in response to the Global Financial Crisis, their levels of public spending have risen steeply. That said, in a number of cases (notably, many of the Anglo-liberal economies such as New Zealand, the UK, and the US), this sharp rise in the period immediately following the crisis has been replaced by a steep and unprecedented decline in state spending as a share of GDP in the period since 2010. It is, of course, too early to judge the significance of this. But it would appear that both the crisis itself

and the subsequent turn to austerity have been more stark in the Anglo-liberal cases (Hay 2014). Yet it is difficult to see this as any simple globalization effect. Moreover, the scale of any such austerity-engendered retrenchment effect would appear to be in inverse proportion to the initial size of the state itself (gauged in GDP terms). What is more clear is that in the two decades or so prior to the crisis there is certainly some evidence of a decline in the proportion of GDP devoted to public spending. Though invariably greatest where unemployment has fallen most, this is consistent with the predictions of the hyperglobalization thesis to some extent. But what is perhaps more important is that in each and every case, the size of the state (as expressed as a share of GDP) has increased considerably over the period, peaking in most cases in the early-to-mid 1990s and, in the Anglo-liberal economies, during the crisis itself.

Of course, state expenditure is not the only means of gauging quantitatively the role of the state. Figure 11.3 presents time-series data on the proportion of the total workforce employed directly by the state since the 1960s.

Again, the evidence is unequivocal. This period, the much-vaunted era of globalization, has witnessed the development of the largest states the world has ever seen and there is little evidence in this data series of this trend being reversed. That said, the Global Financial Crisis has had the effect of driving up levels of public debt—and it is likely that the next decade will see some scaling back of the public sector (and, hence, public employment) in the advanced liberal democracies, as the most recent data in the series seem to begin to attest.

It would certainly seem that globalization is compatible with a far higher level of state expenditure (and employment) than the hyperglobalization thesis would seem to imply—an observation which seems set to endure the crisis and the subsequent turn to austerity, if the evidence of Table 11.1 and Figure 11.3 is anything to go by. This presents something of a paradox: a widely accepted conception of state crisis and retrenchment which seems to stand in some tension to the available empirical evidence. There are at least four potential solutions to this conundrum, each with rather different implications:

1. That the conventional wisdom on the subject is, indeed, correct, that 'big government' represents an ultimately unsustainable drain on

Table 11.1 Government expenditure as a share of GDP

	AUL	AUS	BEL	CAN	DEN	FIN	FRA	GER	IRE
1960	22.1	32.1	34.6	28.9	24.6	26.6	34.6	32.0	28.0
1965	25.6	37.9	36.5	29.1	29.6	30.8	38.4	36.3	33.1
1970	25.5	39.2	42.1	35.7	40.2	30.5	38.9	37.6	39.6
1975	32.4	46.2	51.3	40.7	47.5	38.4	43.5	47.1	46.5
1980	34.1	48.5	58.7	41.5	56.2	39.4	46.2	46.9	50.8
1985	38.5	51.7	62.3	47.1	59.3	45.0	52.2	47.5	54.8
1990	37.7	49.4	55.3	47.8	58.6	46.8	49.9	45.7	41.4
1996	37.2	56.1	52.6	46.6	58.7	59.8	54.5	49.3	39.1
2000	35.2	52.2	49.2	41.1	53.3	48.3	51.6	45.1	31.3
2005	34.8	50.1	52.2	39.9	52.5	50.3	53.4	46.2	33.7
2010	36.7	52.9	52.3	43.3	57.1	54.8	56.5	47.3	66.2
2015	36.1	52.2	53.4	39.5	57.5	59.3	56.9	43.7	36.9
Net growth[a] (%)	63	63	54	37	134	123	64	37	32
Growth to peak (%)	74	75	80	65	158	125	64	54	136
Decline from peak (%)	6.6	7.5	16.7	21.0	3.1	0.8	–	12.8	79.4
	ITA	JAP	NTL	NOR	NZL	SWE	SWZ	UK	USA
1960	30.1	18.3	33.7	32.0	26.9	31.1	17.2	32.6	27.2
1965	34.3	18.6	38.7	34.2	—	36.0	19.7	36.4	27.2
1970	34.2	19.3	45.5	41.0	—	43.7	21.3	39.3	31.6
1975	43.2	27.3	55.9	46.6	—	49	28.7	46.9	34.6
1980	45.6	32.7	62.5	49.4	38.1	65.7	29.7	44.6	33.6
1985	50.8	32.7	59.7	45.6	—	64.3	31.0	46.2	36.4
1990	53.6	32.3	57.5	54.9	41.3	60.8	30.9	42.3	36.6
1996	52.5	36.7	49.4	48.5	41.1	62.9	35.3	42.2	36.6
2000	46.1	39	44.2	42.3	39.2	57.0	35.1	36.6	33.9
2005	48.1	38.4	44.8	42.3	39.1	54.0	35.3	44.1	36.2
2010	49.9	40.7	48.3	45.0	47.8	52.1	32.9	48.3	42.8
2015	50.6	41.6	45.7	47.6	39.4	52.2	33.7	43.1	37.7
Net growth[a] (%)	68	127	36	49	46	68	96	32.2	39
Growth to peak (%)	78	127	85	72	78	111	105	48	57
Decline from peak (%)	5.9	—	37.0	15.3	21.3	25.9	4.7	12.1	13.5

Notes: AUL = Australia; AUS = Austria; BEL = Belgium; CAN = Canada; DEN = Denmark; FIN = Finland; GER = Germany; IRE = Ireland; ITA = Italy; JAP = Japan; NTL = Netherlands; NOR = Norway; NZL = New Zealand; SWE = Sweden; SWZ = Switzerland; UK = United Kingdom; USA = United States
[a] Net growth here refers to the percentage increase in the share of GDP devoted to government expenditure.
Source: Calculated from OECD, *Economic Outlook* (various years).

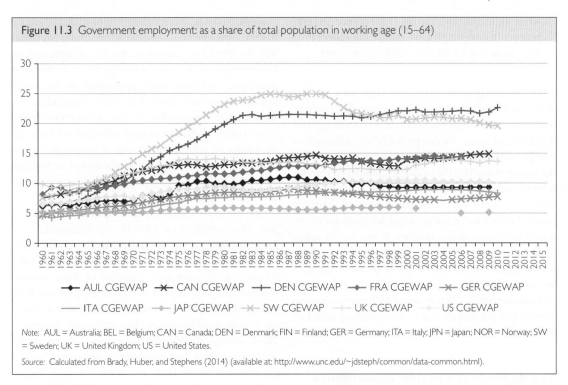

Figure 11.3 Government employment: as a share of total population in working age (15–64)

◆ AUL CGEWAP   ✕ CAN CGEWAP   + DEN CGEWAP   ◆ FRA CGEWAP   ✕ GER CGEWAP

— ITA CGEWAP   ◆ JAP CGEWAP   ✕ SW CGEWAP   + UK CGEWAP   + US CGEWAP

Note: AUL = Australia; BEL = Belgium; CAN = Canada; DEN = Denmark; FIN = Finland; GER = Germany; ITA = Italy; JPN = Japan; NOR = Norway; SW = Sweden; UK = United Kingdom; US = United States.

Source: Calculated from Brady, Huber, and Stephens (2014) (available at: http://www.unc.edu/~jdsteph/common/data-common.html).

competitiveness in an era of globalization, but that the institutional form of the state has become so entrenched and embedded as to make its reform and retrenchment an incremental process down which we are now only slowly embarking on. (Though perhaps the most plausible defence of the 'crisis of the nation state' thesis, this argument is rarely made in the existing literature. It might, however, draw inspiration from the work of historical institutionalists who have consistently pointed to the inertial nature of complex institutions like the state; see, especially, Pierson 1994, 1996.)

2. That the conventional wisdom, though somewhat overstated, is basically correct, since the aggregate empirical evidence, in fact, masks the actual degree of retrenchment. Once we control for demographic and other 'welfare inflationary' pressures (such as higher levels of unemployment and the near exponential growth in health care costs since the 1960s), observed state expenditure is, in fact, substantially below that we would anticipate were consistent levels of generosity and coverage to have been maintained (Barr 1998; Esping-Andersen 1996a, 1996b; Rhodes

1996, 1997; Hay and Wincott 2012). We have not witnessed, nor should we expect to witness, a terminal crisis of the nation state, but we have already experienced a significant process of state retrenchment driven by, or at least simultaneous with, globalization.

3. That while the aggregate evidence may, indeed, mask the real degree of retrenchment that has occurred, the conventional wisdom is still wrong since there is no a priori reason to hold globalization responsible for such retrenchment and/or no consistent evidence of a historically unprecedented process of globalization in recent years (Hirst and Thompson 1999; Wilensky 2002).

4. That, in expecting globalization to precipitate a terminal crisis of the state, the conventional wisdom is simply inaccurate. Far from representing a drain on competitiveness, the state is the very condition of competitiveness in an ever more competitive international/global market (Weiss 1998). Globalization, as has been shown by the crisis, does not discriminate principally between states on their size but on their effectiveness in promoting and sustaining international competitiveness. Consequently,

while we might expect to see convergence on best practice between states, we should not expect to see a withering of the state itself (Cerny 1995, 1997).

As this already serves to indicate, there are a number of ways of rehabilitating an albeit somewhat 'respecified' variant of the globalization thesis in the light of the above evidence. We can probably reject the notion that globalization has precipitated a terminal crisis of the nation state. Yet, the evidence considered thus far is by no means incompatible with the claim that globalization circumscribes the parameters of domestic political choice and is the principal determinant of the state's developmental trajectory. If we are to assess that claim, then we need to turn our attentions from the dependent variable (the extent of state retrenchment) to the independent variable (the process of globalization itself). Before doing so, however, it is important that we first consider one remaining aspect of the dependent variable—the question of convergence.

The dependent variable: convergence or dual convergence

Having originally placed their emphasis upon the crisis and transcendence of the nation state as a political unit responsible for regulating an economic jurisdiction (Ohmae 1990, 1995), proponents of the hyperglobalization thesis now more frequently cast institutional and policy convergence as the dependent variable (Teeple 1995; Gray 1998; Parker 1998). Globalization remains the independent variable and is depicted as a stable equilibrium and as an entirely non-negotiable external economic imperative which exposes all economies within the global system to near identical pressures and challenges. In a highly competitive environment in which only the fittest survive, successful adaptation will rapidly be emulated, resulting in a powerful tendency to convergence.

As we have seen, the institutional sensitivity of the 'varieties of capitalism' approach appeals to a similar logic (and an identical independent variable), in predicting a rather different outcome—a more complex process of dual convergence around liberal and coordinated market economic models.

To what extent are these contending predictions borne out by the empirical evidence? Since we might consider convergence with respect to any number of potential dependent variables, this is a somewhat

contentious issue that we cannot hope to do full justice to here. Space prevents an exhaustive survey. Nonetheless, we would once again expect the convergence or co-convergence theses to be most relevant to the most developed and most open economies in the world system. Moreover, given that welfare expenditure is most frequently described in the globalization literature as the kind of unnecessary indulgence which can no longer be afforded in an era of heightened competition among nations, we might expect to find the strongest evidence of convergence or co-convergence among European welfare states.

Yet, the evidence simply does not bear out that expectation (see also Hay 2003; Hay and Wincott 2012). Limits of space allow us only to consider social transfer payments (expressed as a percentage of GDP). These are, in essence, a measure of basic welfare expenditure. For ease of comparison, they are here standardized at 100 for 1960. Precisely because these are standardized measures, they are bound to show an initial divergence. Yet, the convergence thesis would lead us to expect that initial divergence to be checked considerably by the 1980s and 1990s. It would predict, in short, an oval shaped distribution. And the co-convergence thesis would predict the emergence of two clusters—one grouped around Germany, the other grouped around the UK.

Neither prediction is borne out by the evidence, at least in the period before the crisis—which, of course and as noted earlier, gave rise to a steep increase in state spending at least as a share of GDP (see Figure 11.4). Instead, consistent paths are mapped out from the 1960s, which social models continue to follow for the most part to the present day. The wide initial variance in growth rates is sustained over time. This is not a story of systematic welfare retrenchment, nor is it a story of the diminishing distinctiveness of regime types—which seem, if anything, to be reinforced over time. Indeed, it is the Nordic welfare states that have grown the most. Under globalization, it would seem, the most generous welfare states have thrived.

Second, we might consider the raw unstandardized data itself—i.e. social transfers expressed as a share of GDP. To aid the analysis, European welfare regimes are here grouped in terms of the conventional three-fold classification. The *Nordic* regime type refers to Sweden, Denmark, Finland, and Norway; the *conservative* regime type refers to Germany, the Netherlands, Italy, and France; and the *liberal* regime type to the UK and Ireland.

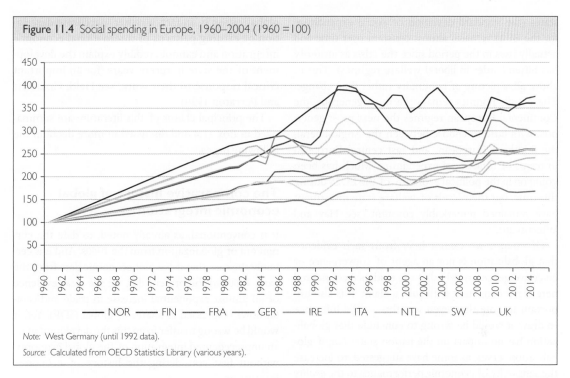

Figure 11.4 Social spending in Europe, 1960–2004 (1960 =100)

Note: West Germany (until 1992 data).

Source: Calculated from OECD Statistics Library (various years).

Again, it seems, the evidence is in some tension with the predictions of the existing literature (see Figure 11.5). For, far from being associated with welfare retrenchment, the period of (supposedly) most intensive globalization has been associated with the consolidation—not the retrenchment—of the most generous welfare states the world has ever known. In recent years, social expenditure has been stable, with little or no evidence of convergence either between geographical clusters or between individual welfare

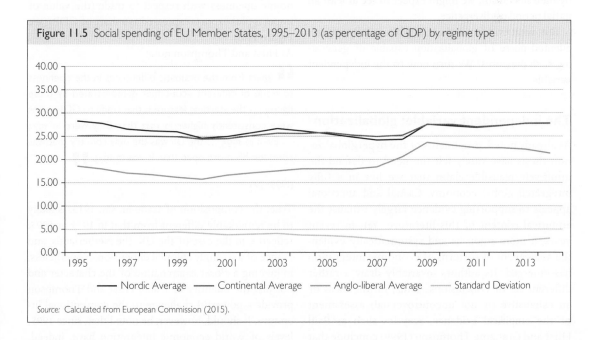

Figure 11.5 Social spending of EU Member States, 1995–2013 (as percentage of GDP) by regime type

Source: Calculated from European Commission (2015).

states (the standard deviation of social expenditure for the EU25 remains almost constant over time and actually rises in the period since the crisis as austerity has bitten harder in liberal welfare regimes). This is, above all, a picture of continuity rather than change. The Nordic regimes remain the most generous, the Continental European regimes the next most generous, with little to choose between the Anglo-liberal, the Southern European, and east central European in terms of total social expenditure. Much has been going on in the political economy of the EU25 during this time, but their levels of welfare state investment have remained remarkably constant (see Hay and Wincott 2012).

Of course, we cannot infer from such evidence that globalization is not an agent of convergence or co-convergence, merely that the evidence considered here is not consistent with such a claim. It is also important to note that, even was this a valid inference to draw, it would be wrong to conclude that globalization has no impact on the nation state. For, if globalization serves, as some have suggested, to increase the sensitivity of economic performance to the *quality* of public policy (see, for instance, Weiss 1998), then there is no particular reason to expect either a crisis of the state or convergence. Moreover, if, as is widely assumed, globalization generates common pressures for neo-liberalization and this has been more enthusiastically embraced in regimes already characterized by their liberalism, we might expect to see at least an initial period of divergence.

But, what evidence is there of a historically unprecedented phase of globalization capable of generating such pressures? We turn now to the independent variable.

The independent variable: globalization

As already noted, proponents of the hyperglobalization thesis have rarely felt the need to defend the intuitively plausible claim that we live in a fully integrated global economy. Casual and anecdotal appeals to supporting evidence largely exhaust the empirical content of this literature. Yet, in recent years, a more rigorous and systematically evidential assessment of patterns of economic integration has emerged. Its authors invariably draw a rather different set of conclusions. Thus, on the basis of an exhaustive (if not uncontroversial) assessment of the empirical evidence, sceptics such as Paul Hirst and Grahame Thompson (1999) conclude that

globalization is, in fact, a rather inaccurate description of existing patterns of international economic integration and cannot credibly explain the development of the state in recent years (for an important critical response to their work, see Held, Goldblatt and Perraton 1999).

The principal claims of this literature are summarized in Box 11.4 and discussed in more detail in the following pages.

The comparative history of global economic integration

It is conventional, as already noted, to date the current era of globalization from the 1960s. And it is certainly the case that if we plot economic data from the early 1960s to the present day, we see clear evidence of an almost exponential increase in trade and capital flows (expressed as shares of global GDP). Yet, it would be wrong to infer from this the development of an unprecedented integration of the global economy, without first considering the history of economic integration.

If we do that, then what becomes very clear is the sensitivity of the conclusions drawn by proponents of the globalization thesis to their preferred start date. If we extend the time frame, choosing as a starting point the late nineteenth or early twentieth century, a rather different picture emerges. Consider, first, economic openness with respect to trade (the value of imports plus exports expressed as a share of GDP) (see Figure 11.6).

As Hirst and Thompson note:

> apart from the dramatic differences in the openness to trade of different economies demonstrated by these figures ... the startling feature is that trade to GDP ratios were consistently higher in 1913 than they were in 1973 ... Even in 1995 ... the US was the only country that was considerably more open than it was in 1913.

(1999: 27)

True, the composition of trade in, say, 1913 is likely to be remarkably different from that in 1973 or 1995, reflective in the case of the UK, the Netherlands, and France of a strongly colonial dimension. Nonetheless, in inviting a closer examination of the character and not just the quantity of trade, Hirst and Thompson provide a powerful challenge to the conventional literature. It should, however, be noted that, since 1995, levels of world economic integration have, indeed,

BOX 11.4

The Empirical Case against the Globalization Thesis

1. Although the period since the 1960s has seen the growing openness of national economies (such that imports plus exports are equivalent to a growing proportion of gross domestic product), there is still some considerable way to go before figures of prior to the First World War are likely to be exceeded (Bairoch 1996; Hirst and Thompson 1999).

2. There continues to be a positive and, indeed, strengthening relationship between public spending (as a share of gross domestic product) and economic openness (Cameron 1978; Katzenstein 1985; Rodrik 1996, 1997; Garrett 1998b).

3. There is no inverse relationship, as might be expected, between the volume of inward foreign direct investment and levels of corporate taxation, environmental and labour market regulations, generosity of welfare benefits or state expenditure as a share of gross domestic product (Dunning 1988; Cooke and Noble 1998; Traxler and Woitech 2000; Wilensky 2002).

4. Trade and international flows of capital (such as foreign direct investment) tend to be extremely concentrated within the core 'triad' (of Europe, North America, and Pacific Asia), providing evidence of regionalization and 'triadization', but hardly of globalization (Petrella 1996; Frankel 1997; Hirst and Thompson 1999).

5. The pace of economic integration is higher *within* regions (such as Europe, North America or Pacific Asia) than it is *between* regions, suggesting that regionalization rather than globalization is the overriding dynamic in the process of international economic integration (Frankel 1997; Kleinknecht and ter Wengel 1998; Hay 2004; Ravenhill, Chapter 6 in this volume).

6. Financial integration has failed to produce the anticipated convergence in interest rates which one would expect from a fully integrated global capital market (Zevin 1992; Hirst and Thompson 1999).

7. Financial integration has failed to produce the anticipated divergence between rates of domestic savings and rates of domestic investment which one would expect in a fully integrated global capital market—the so-called Feldstein–Horioka puzzle (Feldstein and Horioka 1980; see also Epstein 1996: 212–15; Watson 2001).

8. Though the liberalization of financial markets has certainly increased the speed, severity, and significance of investors' reactions to government policy, capital market participants appear far less discriminating or well-informed in their political risk assessment than is conventionally assumed (Swank 2002; Mosley 2003). Consequently, policymakers may retain rather more autonomy than is widely accepted.

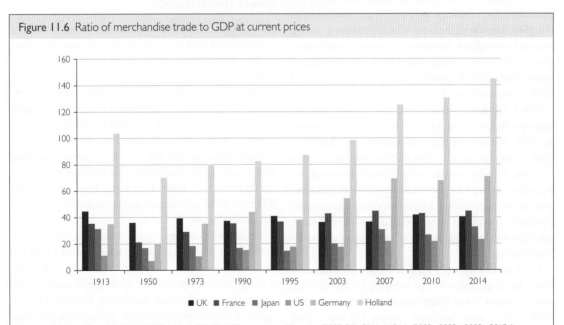

Figure 11.6 Ratio of merchandise trade to GDP at current prices

Legend: UK, France, Japan, US, Germany, Holland

Sources: Calculated from Maddison (1987: table A-23); Hirst, Thompson, and Bromley (2009: 34); ©World Bank (2002c, 2005a, 2009c, 2015e); World Development Indicators Database (available at http://data.worldbank.org/data-catalog); World Bank (2015e) World Development Indicator, "Merchandise Trade (% of GDP)", available at: http://data.worldbank.org/indicator/TG.VAL.TOTL.GD.ZS

surpassed those experienced during the latter half of the nineteenth century.

The data with respect to capital flows reveal a similar pattern. Between 1870 and 1914, international capital flows between the G7 economies averaged some 4 per cent of GDP, peaking at around 6 per cent in 1914. Between 1914 and 1970, they declined to 1.5 per cent of GDP. Since 1970, they have charted a consistent upward trajectory, rising to 3 per cent of GDP by the early 1990s. Yet, they still have a long way to go to reach the figures of the period prior to the First World War (Lewis 1981; Turner 1981; Bairoch 1996: 184; Hirst and Thompson 1999: 28, figure 2.4). In quantitative, if not perhaps in qualitative terms, the current period is not unprecedented or, indeed, unsurpassed.

In sum, then, while from the mid 1970s there has been an increasing trend towards financial and trade integration (albeit one sent into at least a temporary period of reverse with the advent of the Global Financial Crisis), economic openness was greater in the years before the First World War than in the 1990s.

'Stateness' and openness

Arguably more significant, and certainly less contested, are recent attempts to reproduce and update David Cameron's (1978) groundbreaking study of the covariance of economic openness and public expenditure. Such findings are particularly damaging to the globalization orthodoxy which predicts a strong inverse correlation between 'stateness' and openness—high levels of state expenditure (expressed as a proportion of GDP) *should* suppress the globalization of the domestic economy.

What Cameron demonstrated in a now famous paper published in the *American Political Science Review* in 1978, was a strong positive correlation between trade openness and social protection, funded through taxation. In other words, international economic integration seemed to go hand in hand with comprehensive social provision. Moreover, openness was also positively correlated with social democratic tenure, union power, and the degree of regulation of the labour market.

More damaging still to the orthodox globalization thesis has been more recent research in this vein by, among others, Peter Katzenstein (1985), Dani Rodrik (1996, 1997), and Geoffrey Garrett (1998b). What these authors demonstrate is that the strength of the correlation between openness and government

expenditure in OECD countries has only grown in subsequent decades. For proponents of the hyperglobalization thesis, this takes some explaining. Yet, for Rodrik, it is easily explained:

> What should we make of this? I will argue that the puzzle is solved by considering the importance of social insurance and the role of government in providing cover against external risk. Societies that expose themselves to greater amounts of external risk demand (and receive) a larger government role as shelter from the vicissitudes of global markets. In the context of the advanced industrial economies specifically, this translates into more generous social programmes. Hence the conclusion that the social welfare state is the flip side of the open economy!

(1997: 53)

Rodrik's is, of course, not the only possible explanation. Equally plausible, is that high levels of state expenditure are a result of success in international markets—a consequence rather than a condition of the globalization of the domestic economy. Yet, whichever way round it is, economic openness would seem far more compatible with state expenditure than is conventionally assumed.

The determinants of inward foreign direct investment

As we saw in an earlier section, orthodox accounts of globalization tend to make a series of clear and more or less plausible assumptions about the preferences and interests of mobile investors. Such assumptions, as was shown, are directly responsible for the influential thesis that states enhance their locational competitiveness to foreign direct investors by offering targeted investment incentives, eliminating labour market rigidities, reducing the burden of corporate taxation, and ensuring that environmental regulations are not overly restrictive. Alter the assumptions, and a rather different set of inferences (and consequent policy implications) follow.

Recent scholarship, which examines the *revealed* preferences of foreign direct investors as exhibited in actual investment decisions (rather than making a priori assumptions about such preferences), challenges the globalization orthodoxy in important respects. Particularly notable here, is the work of Cooke and Noble on the geographical distribution of foreign direct investment from the US (1998). This work contains a number of significant findings, each troubling to proponents of the hyperglobalization thesis.

1. It is direct market access and/or proximity to market that is the single greatest determinant of investment location. Inward direct investors value, above all else, geographical proximity to a substantial and affluent market. Consequently, the greatest single predictor of the volume of inward investment is total income within a 1,000-kilometre radius of the investment site.

2. Once access and proximity to market are controlled for, educational attainment/skill level is the most critical factor in determining the attractiveness of an industrial relations regime. Yet, the effect is complex and not as anticipated. As Cooke and Noble note, 'with respect to investments in low-skill-low-wage countries, the evidence indicates that US multinational corporations have sought to match lower workforce education with the limited labour skill requirements of operations that get located in low-skill-low-wage countries …[A]cross low-wage-low-skill countries US multinationals invest more in locations with the lowest levels of education' (1998: 596). This much is consistent with the hyperglobalization thesis. Yet, 'in contrast, it appears that, in matching the high labour skills requirements of operations located in high-skill-high-wage countries, US multinationals invest more in countries with both higher average education levels and higher hourly compensation costs' (1998: 596). This reveals a globally segmented market for inward investment, in which it is only developing countries that are compelled to compete in terms of labour costs. Investors, it would seem, are perfectly prepared to pay the price of the highly trained and appropriately skilled workforce that (some) developed economies are capable of providing.

3. Moreover, and in seeming confirmation of this, it is not just the quantity (duration or level of attainment) of education that is important. Though it is difficult to gauge empirically, the evidence strongly supports the thesis that it is the *quality* and not the *cost* of skilled labour that is the key determinant of investment behaviour. Again, it would seem, cost (direct or indirect) is no impediment to investment if the perceived return provides adequate compensation for that cost.

Thus, skill and productivity differences between economies make a significant and additional difference in attracting inward investment. Comparing the UK and Germany, Cooke and Noble explain, 'both have comparable average years of education … but substantially different average hourly compensation costs …Germany's unmeasured skill base has garnered about $2.3 billion more in US FDI per industry than has the UK's unmeasured skill base … high-skill-high-wage countries that further enhance skill levels can attract significant additional US foreign direct investment' (1998: 602).

4. The conclusion is clear, 'countries need not encourage … wage restraint, since high hourly compensation costs do not reduce … foreign direct investment, provided these costs are matched by higher skills and productivity' (1998: 602).

This, and other evidence like it (see e.g. Dunning 1988; Traxler and Woitech 2000; Swank 2002; Wilensky 2002), seriously challenge both the assumptions on which the hyperglobalization thesis is predicated and the predictions it makes about exit from highly regulated labour market regimes with generous welfare states funded out of taxation receipts.

Globalization or 'triadization'

In the highly contentious political economy of globalization, perhaps no issue is more controversial than the geographical character of the process of international economic integration that we have witnessed since the 1960s. It is, in particular, the challenge posed to the conventional wisdom by the recent work of arch globalization sceptics, Paul Hirst and Grahame Thompson (1996, 1999), that has provided the central focus of attention and controversy (see also Petrella 1996: 77–81; Allen and Thompson 1997; and, for a flavour of the critical responses, Held and McGrew 2002: 38–57; Perraton *et al.* 1997).

Hirst and Thompson, along with a growing crescendo of 'sceptics', have questioned the extent to which the term globalization accurately characterizes both the pattern of economic integration within the international political economy today or the trajectory of relations of economic integration and interdependence since the 1960s. Rather than a process of globalization, they suggest, a process of 'triadization' is and has been underway (1996: 2, 63–7). By triadization, they refer to the selective and uneven process of deepening economic integration between the 'triad' economies; and by the 'triad' economies they refer to North America, South East Asia, and Europe. In short, some economies are more globalized than others and this must ultimately lead us to challenge the appropriateness of the appellation 'globalization'. For a significant and rising proportion of international economic activity is conducted within and between the triad economies. This is true of trade, foreign direct investment, and finance. For Hirst and Thompson, then, the developmental path of the international economy is far more accurately characterized by pointing to the effects of two separate processes:

1. A more general process of intra-regional economic integration or 'regionalisation' (discussed in more detail presently).

2. A more specific process of inter-regional economic integration drawing the triad economies into an ever denser web of complex interdependencies.

The appeal, and, indeed, much of the novelty, of Hirst and Thompson's work when first published was its reliance on a substantial body of empirical evidence. Until their contribution, the innumerable empirical assertions made in the literature on globalization were largely unsubstantiated or defended only in a loose and anecdotal sense. Indeed, Hirst and Thompson's iconoclastic claim was that such assertions simply could not be defended evidentially. In so doing, they pointed to the far from global character of flows of trade, investment, and finance. Space does not permit a detailed exploration of this evidence. Suffice it to say that, between 1991 and 1996, over 60 per cent of all flows of foreign direct investment were conducted within and between the triad economies and, in 1995, over 75 per cent of the accumulated stock of foreign direct investment was located within the same triad bloc (Hirst and Thompson 1999: 71; see also Brewer and Young 1998: 58–60). Between 1980 and 1991, the figures were almost identical (Hirst and Thompson 1996: 68). The triadic concentration in the accumulated stock of outward foreign direct investment is even more pronounced (see Figure 11.7). The more recent trends do show a sizeable growth in inbound foreign direct investment destined for the less developed economies. Yet this is largely due to a combination of the opening up of the Chinese economy

and, more recently, the decline in the size of the US and European economies (relative to the world economy) due to their differential exposure to the Global Financial Crisis (and, of course, the eurozone crisis to which it gave rise).

Moreover, in 1996, despite accounting for only 14.5 per cent of the world's population, these economies accounted for some two-thirds of global exports (Hirst and Thompson 1999: 73). This figure is only marginally lower than that for 1992 (70 per cent). Yet, it is significantly greater than that for either 1990 (64 per cent), 1980 (55 per cent), or 1970 (61 per cent) (Hirst and Thompson 1996: 69; Petrella 1996: 79). Finally, as Riccardo Petrella notes, 'during the 1980s, the triad accounted for around four-fifths of all international capital flows … [while] the developing countries' share fell from 25 per cent in the 1970s to 19 per cent' (1996: 77).

How much damage this does to the globalization thesis depends, to a considerable extent, on what one takes that thesis to be. Indeed, arguably the debate is largely semantic (see also Scholte 2000: 14–20). Sceptics such as Hirst and Thompson and Petrella adopt a rather more exacting definition of globalization, it seems, than many of the hyperglobalization theorists. If, to count as evidence of globalization, processes have to be either genuinely global in scope or operative in unleashing such dynamics, then globalization poorly characterizes the condition and trajectory of the international economy. If, on the other hand, globalization means little more than economic openness (as witnessed by greater volumes of trade, investment, and financial flows as a share of global GDP), then globalization is certainly under way but it is unlikely to have the effects so frequently attributed to it. This is the challenge that the sceptics present—one, it would seem, that is largely borne out by the empirical evidence.

Globalization or regionalization?

Hirst and Thompson's (1996) emphasis, particularly in the first edition of *Globalization in Question*, is on the process of 'triadization' and hence on a series of inter-regional processes of economic integration linking North America, East Asia, and Europe. Yet, as indicated above, this rests on the prior identification of a more general tendency towards regionalization (within, and, indeed, beyond, the triad economies). In fact, in the second and subsequent editions of *Globalization in Question*, the significance of triadization is somewhat downplayed as, on

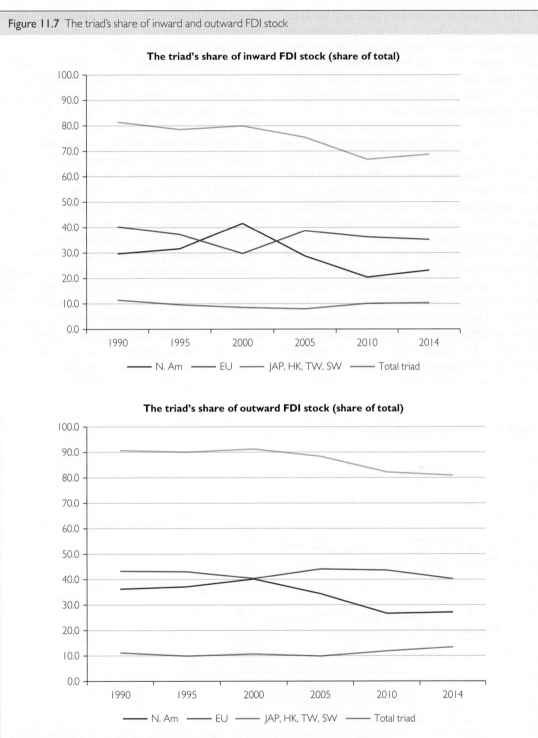

Figure 11.7 The triad's share of inward and outward FDI stock

The triad's share of inward FDI stock (share of total)

— N. Am   — EU   — JAP, HK, TW, SW   — Total triad

The triad's share of outward FDI stock (share of total)

— N. Am   — EU   — JAP, HK, TW, SW   — Total triad

Note: Because of limitations in the data, Pacific Asia here refers only to Japan, Hong Kong, Taiwan, and Singapore.

Sources: Calculated from Brewer and Young (1998: Tables 2.7 and 2.8); UNCTAD (2015b) "FDI inward stock, by region and economy, 1990–2014", World Investment Report 2015; UNCTAD (2015b) "FDI outward stock, by region and economy, 1990–2014", World Investment Report 2015. (both are available at: http://unctad.org/en/Pages/DIAE/World%20Investment%20Report/Annex-Tables.aspx).

the basis of a re-examination and updating of the available evidence, regionalization now emerges as the pervasive tendency within the international economy (Hirst and Thompson 1999: esp. 99–103; Hirst, Thompson, and Bromley 2009). Here, again, Hirst and Thompson's work provides a powerful statement of a developing consensus among sceptical voices.

Yet, it is the work of Jeffrey Frankel that is perhaps the most comprehensive on the question of regionalization (see, especially, Frankel 1997, 1998). On the basis of a detailed examination of the empirical record, he demonstrates that, with respect to trade, any tendency to globalization or even *inter*-regional economic integration has been swamped by the rapid growth in *intra*-regional integration. Due largely to the growth of preferential trading arrangements at the regional level, intra-regional trade accounts for an ever-growing share of global economic activity, suggesting once again that globalization is in fact an increasingly inaccurate characterization of both the process of economic integration and the resulting pattern of economic interdependencies. Figure 11.8 updates Frankel's data, showing the continuing contribution of intra-regional trade to total trade for many of the world's leading economies.

Such findings have been replicated for foreign direct investment flows to and from Europe (Kleinknecht and ter Wengel 1998; Hay 2004).

Finally, so-called gravity models have been used to examine the sensitivity of trade and, indeed, foreign direct investment to distance for a number of European countries (Hay 2003, 2004; see Box 11.5 for further details). A gravity model predicts that trade (and/or foreign direct investment) will decay exponentially with distance. In an era of globalization, in which transportation costs have been diminished and barriers to trade eliminated, we would expect to see the decreasing sensitivity of trade (and investment) to distance. Accordingly, the gravity model should become ever less effective in predicting patterns of trade (and investment).

Yet, unremarkably perhaps given the evidence discussed later, far from showing a consistent pattern of globalization since the 1960s, the gravity model becomes an ever better fit to the data. This demonstrates, once again, a pervasive regionalization tendency in which trade and investment become more not less sensitive to geographical distance. European economies, it would seem, have experienced a consistent and ongoing process of deglobalization since the

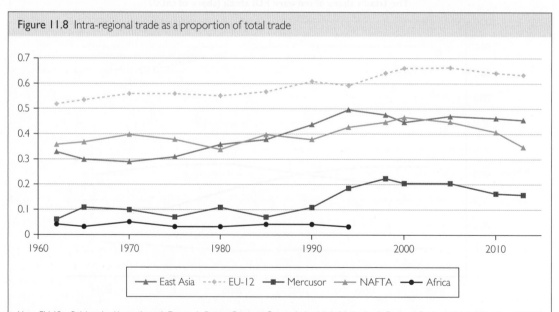

Figure 11.8 Intra-regional trade as a proportion of total trade

Legend: East Asia · · ◆ · · EU-12 ■ Mercusor ▲ NAFTA ● Africa

Note: EU-12 = Belgium (and Luxembourg), Denmark, France, Germany, Greece, Ireland, Italy, Netherlands, Portugal, Spain, and United Kingdom; NAFTA = US, Canada, and Mexico; East Asia = ASEAN-6 (Brunei, Indonesia, Malaysia, Philippines, Singapore, and Thailand), plus China, Hong Kong, Japan, South Korea, and Taiwan; MERCOSUR = Argentina, Brazil, Paraguay, and Uruguay; APEC = East Asia-11, plus NAFTA-3, plus Australia, Chile, New Zealand, and Papua New Guinea; Andean Community = Bolivia, Columbia, Ecuador, Peru, and Venezuela.

Sources: Calculated from Frankel (1997: 22–4); WTO Word Trade Statistics (various years). Such findings have been replicated for foreign direct investment flows to and from Europe (Hay 2004; Kleinknecht and ter Wengel 1998).

BOX 11.5

Gravity Models: The Sensitivity of Trade to Distance

Within a gravity model, trade is assumed to be associated positively with the 'size' of the economies between which it is transacted (usually expressed in terms of their respective shares of global GDP) and to be associated negatively with the distance between them. Geographically proximate countries will trade more with one another than those separated by great distances, just as those economies which account for a substantial share of global GDP will tend to trade more with one another than smaller economies.

The basic model can be written as an equation of the following form:

$$\log T_{ij} = a + b \log(GDP_i/P_i) + c \log(GDP_j/P_j) - d \log(D_{ij}) + \ldots$$

where T_{ij} is the volume of trade between countries i and j; GDP_j/P_j is the GDP per capita of country j; D_{ij} is the distance between country i and j.

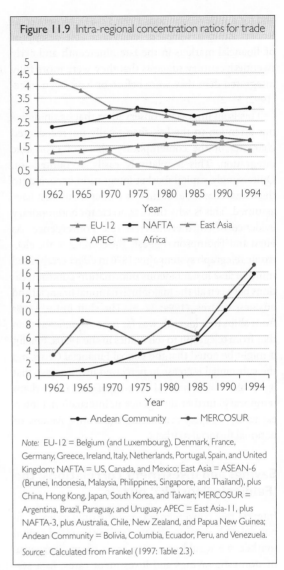

Figure 11.9 Intra-regional concentration ratios for trade

Note: EU-12 = Belgium (and Luxembourg), Denmark, France, Germany, Greece, Ireland, Italy, Netherlands, Portugal, Spain, and United Kingdom; NAFTA = US, Canada, and Mexico; East Asia = ASEAN-6 (Brunei, Indonesia, Malaysia, Philippines, Singapore, and Thailand), plus China, Hong Kong, Japan, South Korea, and Taiwan; MERCOSUR = Argentina, Brazil, Paraguay, and Uruguay; APEC = East Asia-11, plus NAFTA-3, plus Australia, Chile, New Zealand, and Papua New Guinea; Andean Community = Bolivia, Columbia, Ecuador, Peru, and Venezuela.

Source: Calculated from Frankel (1997: Table 2.3).

1960s as the process of European economic integration has accelerated. As Figure 11.9 would suggest, similar tendencies would appear to be underway in many, if perhaps not all, regions within the international economy. As this suggests, globalization is a tendency that has, in the majority of cases, been swamped in recent decades by a regionalizing counter-tendency.

Capital market integration and interest rate convergence

Thus far, we have examined evidence principally relating to trade and foreign direct investment and it is important that we now turn our attention to the degree of integration (or globalization) of financial markets. It is often assumed that, even if the case against the globalization thesis is credible with respect to trade and foreign direct investment (for the reasons discussed above), the thesis is rather more robust with respect to financial markets and, moreover, that the effects of financial market integration on the autonomy of the nation state are most pronounced (see, for instance, Cerny 1995, 1997). Yet, as we shall see, recent evidence casts some doubt on this claim, too.

The first surprising piece of empirical evidence for proponents of the globalization thesis, is the observed failure of interest rates to converge. In a fully

integrated capital market, a common international rate of interest on short-term and long-term loans would emerge almost instantaneously, for fairly obvious reasons. All things being equal, borrowers will seek out the lowest rate of interest available to them, just as investors will seek the highest rate of return (and, hence, interest) on their investments.

Yet, as numerous commentators have noted, and despite some controversy about which precise index to use and what specific inferences to draw from such evidence, interest rate differentials persist and show little sign of being eroded (Kasman and Pigott 1988; Frankel 1991; Osler 1991; Bayoumi and Rose 1993;

and for a review, Simmons 1999: 57–61). Moreover, as Robert Zevin has argued, 'every available descriptor of financial markets in the late nineteenth and early twentieth century suggests that they were more fully integrated than they were before or have been since' (1992: 51–2).

This is an important observation that again draws our attention to the less than totally unprecedented character of the contemporary phase of economic integration. This is relatively easily accounted for. Quite simply, capital market integration occurred (to the extent that it did occur) far earlier than most have assumed. This is why there is no clear contemporary evidence of (further) interest rate convergence. As Hirst and Thompson suggest, 'the coming of the electronic telegraph system after 1870 in effect established more or less instantaneous information communications between all the major international financial and business centres' (1999: 37–8). The shift in the 1870s from ships to telegraph was far more significant than that from telegraph to telematics in the 1970s. Finally, it might be noted that the Global Financial Crisis and the substantial increase in perceived investor risk that it has generated has led to a significant (if perhaps temporary) further divergence in international interest rates, arguably reinforcing the distinctiveness of national financial markets.

Savings and investment correlations: the 'Feldstein–Horioka' puzzle

Interest rate convergence is not the only index of financial globalization. In a perfectly integrated capital market, we would expect to see a clear divergence of domestic savings and investment rates. In a system of closed and bounded national economies, these should correlate absolutely (or very closely). In a genuinely open economy (a perfectly integrated capital market), we would expect the correlation to break down as investors become genuinely global, sourcing their investments from around the world. Indeed, we would expect the correlation to fall to zero (Feldstein and Horioka 1980; see also Bayoumi 1997: 17–19). Consequently, a persistent correlation between domestic savings and investment levels provides strong evidence of a lack of integration of capital markets.

What do we observe? The evidence is again relatively unambiguous. As a large number of commentators have noted, national savings–investment correlations show no consistent pattern of decline in the 1980s and 1990s (Feldstein and Horioka 1980; Feldstein 1983; Bayoumi 1990; Feldstein and Bacchetta 1991; Tesar 1991; Epstein 1996). As Hirst and Thompson suggest, this 'testifies to the continued robust relative autonomy of financial systems' (1999: 38). Indeed, the 'savings retention coefficient' (the proportion of incremental savings invested domestically) remains at 67 per cent for the period 1991–5 (Obstfeld 1993).

This, again, is an important finding and one that continues to trouble international macroeconomists, for whom it remains something of a paradox even after more than two decades. The 'Feldstein–Horioka puzzle', as it has come to be known, has given rise to an extensive literature and considerable controversy (for reviews of which, see Obstfeld and Rogoff 1996: 161–4; Bayoumi 1997: 30–53; Rødseth 2000: 163–4). Unremarkably, a series of challenges have been mounted to the notion that it provides clear evidence of the lack of integration of capital markets. Yet, as we shall see, none of these caveats is ultimately devastating.

1. As a number of commentators have noted, aggregate indices of national investment do not discriminate between public and private investment (see, for instance, Bayoumi 1990). Savings–investment correlations might, then, mask a decrease in the savings–investment correlation for private investors. This is certainly accurate, yet the effect is likely to be relatively small; the essential paradox remains.

2. If, as Hirst and Thompson conjecture, there were 'no significant difference between the return on financial investment' from one economy to the next, 'then we might not expect a large redistribution of capital relative to savings' (1999: 40). Consequently, domestic savings–investment relations might prove persistent. Under such conditions, we would be wrong to infer low levels of capital market integration. Yet, though plausible, the empirical evidence does not bear this out. For, although there was, indeed, some convergence in returns on investment in the 1970s between the developed economies, this has given way to subsequent divergence (Hirst and Thompson 1999: 41). Again, the paradox remains.

3. In growing desperation, perhaps, international macroeconomists have increasingly turned to hypothetical solutions to the paradox. If, they suggest, the global economy had experienced a

productivity shock, we would expect profitability to increase. This would result, in turn, in an increased propensity for both savings and investment. Under such conditions, the anticipated correlation between savings and investment would be spurious, at least in terms of the degree of capital market integration—as it would be generated in the absence of domestic investment being sourced from domestic savings (Ghosh 1995; Rødseth 2000: 164). This hypothetical solution to the paradox is both plausible and ingenious, but it is significantly compromised by the fact that such productivity shocks are both relatively rare and, generally, short-term in nature. The persistent and seemingly long-term character of domestic savings–investment correlations (first observed in 1980) would suggest that a productivity shock is simply not responsible for the Feldstein–Horioka paradox.

4. Rather more plausibly, it has been suggested that economists have tended to draw the wrong (or, at least, an exaggerated) inference from the persistence of domestic savings–investment correlations. For, while in a perfectly integrated textbook capital market we might expect such correlations to tend to zero, in a real-world capital market, even a highly integrated one, we would expect some correlation to persist (Watson 2001). Real markets are not perfectly integrated, nor are they likely to become so. Whether this provides the elusive 'solution' to the 'Feldstein–Horioka puzzle' or merely demonstrates further the dubious nature of the premises which continue to inform influential understandings of globalization (as reflected in unrealistic expectations about the degree of capital mobility we should expect to see) is a moot point.

Finally, although we still lack the time-series data to confirm this, savings-investment correlations are almost bound to have intensified since the advent of the Global Financial Crisis as investors have grown nervous of holdings and stakes denominated in other currencies.

The expressed and exhibited preferences of financial market actors

A persistent theme of this chapter has been the disparity between the a priori theoretical assumptions made in the conventional literature about the preferences of economic actors (principally investors) and the *actual* preferences of such actors (as revealed in their conduct). We have seen how the behaviour of foreign direct investors is rather different in 'reality' from that attributed to them in much of the existing literature. The same is equally true of financial investors, however more intuitively plausible the conventional assumptions may seem for such actors.

Here, the recent work of Layna Mosley (2003) is especially notable. Mosley's work is unique in the existing literature in its attempt to gauge empirically both the *expressed preferences* of market participants through an extensive series of interviews with fund managers, and the *revealed preferences* of market participants through a detailed statistical analysis of their investment decisions. Her conclusions are extremely important and do some considerable damage to the conventional wisdom.

Though the liberalization of financial markets has certainly increased the speed, severity, and significance of investors' reactions to government policy (as the Global Financial Crisis attests well), capital market participants appear far less discriminating or well informed in their political risk assessment than is conventionally assumed. For advanced capitalist democracies, the range of government policies considered by market participants in making investment decisions is, in fact, extremely limited. As Mosley explains:

❝ Governments are pressured strongly to satisfy financial market preferences in terms of overall inflation and government budget deficit levels but retain domestic policymaking latitude in other areas. The means by which governments achieve macropolicy outcomes, and the nature of government policies in other areas, do not concern financial market participants … [G]overnments retain a significant amount of policy autonomy and political accountability. If, for domestic reasons, they prefer to retain traditional social democratic policies, for instance, they are quite able to do so. ❞

(2003: 305)

This is a most important finding, all the more so given the methodological rigour of the study from which it derives. It would seem to support Duane Swank's own important findings. On the basis of a detailed statistic analysis, he demonstrates the existence of a complex interaction effect between welfare state expenditure, on the one hand, and international capital mobility, on the other. When budgets are in balance, capital market liberalization produces a positive effect on welfare effort; when budgets are moderately in deficit there is no effect; and when budget deficits exceed 10 per cent of GDP, the effect becomes negative. As Swank concludes, contrary to the prevailing consensus:

❝ rises in international capital openness, or exposure to international capital markets, do not exert significant downward pressure on the welfare state at moderate levels of budget imbalance [and] when budget deficits don't exist, some expansion of social protection is possible even in the context of international capital mobility. **❞**

(2002: 94)

It would seem that the constraints imposed by financial market integration on domestic political autonomy, certainly in the advanced capitalist economies, have been grossly exaggerated. Yet, the picture is not an undifferentiated one. For developing countries, as Mosley again demonstrates in considerable detail, financial market participants are rather more exacting in the demands they make of government policy and correspondingly more severe in the constraints they impose. Additionally, the Global Financial Crisis will almost certainly result in a certain recalibration of financial market actors' risk assessment and evaluation.

KEY POINTS

- There is little evidence of systematic state retrenchment at the hands of globalization.

- There is little evidence of systematic convergence or dual convergence between models or varieties of capitalism under conditions of globalization.

- The impact of globalization of the nation state suggested in the hyperglobalization thesis has been challenged empirically by a number of authors. They have pointed to the less than unprecedented degree of integration of the global economy today, the positive correlation between openness and public spending, the factors which attract foreign direct investors, the regional and triadic character of international trade and investment, the far from fully integrated character of financial markets, and the investment behaviour of financial market actors.

Conclusions

What are we to make of this? Well, the overall picture that emerges is rather more complex than that we began with. While the economic processes usually labelled 'globalization' have led to a greater degree of economic integration than at any point in the post-war period, current levels of economic interdependence are neither unprecedented historically nor perhaps as genuinely 'global' as is invariably assumed.

The impact of such processes on the capacity, autonomy, and sovereignty of the state is also complex. For, while there is certainly some evidence of state retrenchment in the decades prior to the crisis, especially once one controls for the higher demands placed upon welfare states by demographic change and higher rates of unemployment, there would seem to be no clear evidence that globalization is the driver of this retrenchment—and that retrenchment has since been reversed. Indeed, the evidence reviewed in the previous section would strongly suggest that the constraints imposed upon domestic political autonomy by heightened levels of economic integration (with respect to trade, foreign direct investment, or finance) have been both exaggerated and misunderstood. Yet, this does not mean that globalization has had no impact on the nation state—merely, that we need to be extremely cautious in attributing state retrenchment to globalization.

Rather more plausible, and sadly overlooked in much of the existing literature, is the impact of *ideas* about globalization. If it is conceded that policymakers increasingly view the world they face through a series of assumptions about globalization, then their conduct in office is likely to be shaped significantly by those assumptions. Arguably, then, the idea of globalization may be more influential in shaping the developmental trajectory of the nation state today than the *reality* of globalization (see Box 11.6).

This raises an important point about democratic legitimacy and accountability today. For, it is all very well to argue that state autonomy remains essentially intact in an era of globalization. But, if such autonomy is perceived to have been eroded by all credible candidates for political office, then such autonomy is purely hypothetical. While globalization may not have narrowed the field of democratic choice itself, the idea of globalization may well have done so—as parties across the political spectrum converge on a set of prudent economic and social policies designed to

BOX 11.6

The Role of Ideas about Globalization: Tax Competition between States

Consider tax competition between states. The hyperglobalization thesis suggests that in a globalized context characterized by the heightened mobility of capital, vicious competition between states will serve to drive down the level of corporate taxation. Accordingly, any failure on the part of a state to render its corporate taxation levels competitive in comparative terms, through tax cuts, will result in a punitive depreciation in net revenue as capital exercises its mobility to exit. If governments believe the thesis to be true, or find it to their advantage to present it as true, they will act in a manner consistent with its predictions, thereby contributing to an aggregate depreciation in corporate taxation—whether they are right to do so or not.

To elaborate, were we to envisage a (hypothetical) scenario in which the hyperglobalization thesis were accurate, the free mobility of capital would, indeed, serve to establish tax competition between fiscal authorities seeking to retain existing investment levels while enticing mobile foreign direct investors to relocate (see Figure 11.10). The price of any attempt to buck the trend is immediate capital flight with consequent effects on budget revenue. In such a scenario, any rational administration aware (or assuming itself to be aware) of the mobility of capital will cut corporate taxes with the effect that no exit will be observed (Scenario 1). Any

administration foolish enough to discount or test the mobility of capital by retaining high levels of corporate taxation will be rudely awakened from its state of blissful ignorance or stubborn scepticism by a rapid exodus of capital (Scenario 2). In a world of perfect capital mobility, then, the learning curve is likely to prove very steep, indeed.

Were we to assume instead that we inhabit a world in which the mobility of capital is much exaggerated and in which capital has a clear vested interest in threatening exit, the scenario unfolds rather differently. Here, fiscal authorities lulled into accepting the hyperglobalization thesis by the (ultimately hollow) exit threats of capital will cut rates of corporate tax, (falsely) attributing the lack of capital flight to their competitive taxation regime (Scenario 3). Yet, were they to resist this logic by calling capital's bluff, they might retain substantial taxation receipts without fear of capital flight (Scenario 4). The crucial point, however, is that while politicians believe the hyperglobalization thesis—and act upon it—we cannot differentiate between Scenario 1 (in which the thesis is true) and Scenario 3 (in which it is false). Though in Scenario 1, globalization is a genuine constraint on political autonomy and in Scenario 3 it is merely a social construction, the outcomes are the same. As this suggests, it is ideas about globalization rather than globalization per se that affects political and economic outcomes. This makes the role of international institutions in the dissemination of ideas about globalization especially significant.

Source: Adapted from Hay (2002b: 202–4).

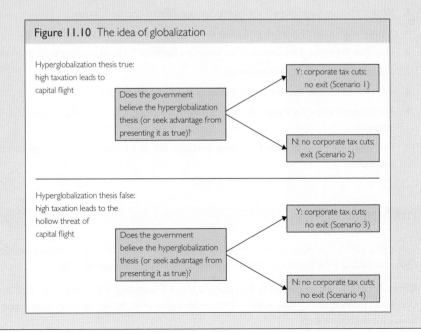

Figure 11.10 The idea of globalization

Hyperglobalization thesis true: high taxation leads to capital flight

Does the government believe the hyperglobalization thesis (or seek advantage from presenting it as true)?

Y: corporate tax cuts; no exit (Scenario 1)

N: no corporate tax cuts; exit (Scenario 2)

Hyperglobalization thesis false: high taxation leads to the hollow threat of capital flight

Does the government believe the hyperglobalization thesis (or seek advantage from presenting it as true)?

Y: corporate tax cuts; no exit (Scenario 3)

N: no corporate tax cuts; no exit (Scenario 4)

appease footloose multinational investors. Arguably, this has much to do with the widespread contemporary disaffection with liberal democratic regimes (see, for instance, Pharr and Putnam 2000; Hay 2007). Democracy is no less a casualty in such a scenario. This makes the public scrutiny of influential assumptions and ideas about globalization a most urgent political priority. It establishes, once again, the phenomenal importance of the ongoing controversy that surrounds the question of globalization's impact on the state.

One final point might also be noted. While there is, in fact, little evidence for the thesis that the nation state's capacity and autonomy has been significantly eroded by virtue of globalization, it is, nonetheless, the case that globalization poses a series of problems for the nation state which it has never had the capacity to deal with. We have seen, and are likely to continue to see, a proliferation of interlinked and genuinely global political, economic, and, above all, environmental problems requiring, for their resolution, effective institutions of global governance. This final point is perhaps the most troubling of all. It is certainly tempting to dismiss globalization as a myth or as a process with minimal impact upon the historical capacities of the state. Yet, the problem of the lack of the political capacity to deal with urgent global problems in an effective and democratic way remains. The challenges we face are essentially twofold:

1. To find ways of designing effective and democratic institutions of global governance capable of commanding political support and legitimacy.

2. To find ways of passing responsibility and, indeed, sovereignty from a system of nation states that still provides the focus of political identification and citizenship to such institutions.

At the point at which we prove ourselves capable of responding to both of these challenges, we might legitimately begin to speak of a transcendence (if not perhaps a crisis) of the nation state. But that point is a very, very long way off.

? QUESTIONS

1. Is there, or has there been, a crisis of the nation state?

2. What is meant by the globalization of politics and has it occurred?

3. What mechanisms can be pointed to suggesting a clear link between globalization and state retrenchment?

4. What are the key assumptions of the hyperglobalization thesis? Are they plausible?

5. Is globalization an agent of convergence, dual convergence, divergence, or continued diversity?

6. How does the model of the 'tragedy of the commons' illuminate the problem of global governance?

7. Assess the evidence for state retrenchment.

8. What impact has globalization had on the development of the nation state?

9. Are the constraints on the autonomy and capacity of the nation state arising from globalization largely real or imagined?

10. How might the Global Financial Crisis serve to change the relationship between the state and the process of globalization?

  FURTHER READING

Cerny, P. G. (1997), 'Paradoxes of the Competition State: The Dynamics of Political Globalization', *Government and Opposition*, 32/2: 251–74. The clearest exposition of the highly influential 'competition state' thesis.

Garrett, G. (2000b), 'Shrinking States? Globalization and National Autonomy', in N. Woods (ed.), *The Political Economy of Globalization* (Basingstoke: Palgrave). A clear and comprehensive survey of the existing literature and supporting evidence by an influential commentator.

Hall, P. A. and Soskice, D. (eds) (2001), *Varieties of Capitalism* (Oxford: Oxford University Press). The definitive statement of the 'varieties of capitalism' perspective linking globalization with a process of dual convergence.

Hay, C. and Wincott, D. (2012), *The Political Economy of European Welfare Capitalism* (Basingstoke: Palgrave). An alternative to Hall and Soskice's influential 'varieties of capitalism' perspective which seeks to chart the complex relationship between globalization, European economic integration, and welfare state trajectories in Europe before and during the crisis.

Hirst, P., Thompson, G., and Bromley, S. (2009), *Globalization in Question,* 3rd edn (Cambridge: Polity Press). The definitive statement of the case against the globalization orthodoxy.

Jessop, B. (2002), *The Future of the Capitalist State* (Cambridge: Polity Press). The product of almost two decades of scholarship, this is perhaps the single most important work on the condition of the state today. Though dense and at times difficult, it rewards close reading.

Mosley, L. (2003), *Global Capital and National Governments* (Cambridge: Cambridge University Press). An exceptionally important recent addition to the existing literature, and a comprehensive reappraisal of the conventional wisdom about the domestic political constraints issuing from financial markets.

Ohmae, K. (1995), *The End of the Nation State: The Rise of Regional Economies* (New York: Free Press). Though widely discredited, still the core exponent and defender of the hyperglobalization thesis.

Weiss, L. (1998), *The Myth of the Powerless State: Governing the Economy in a Global Era* (Cambridge: Polity Press). A clear and accessible defence of the continued centrality and importance of the nation state in an era of globalization.

 WEBLINKS

Useful searchable data sources can be found at:

http://data.worldbank.org/data-catalog

http://www.esds.ac.uk/international/support/user_guides/oecd/mg.asp

http://epp.eurostat.ec.europa.eu/portal/page/portal/eurostat/home

ONLINE RESOURCE CENTRE

For additional material and resources, please visit the Online Resource Centre at:
www.oxfordtextbooks.co.uk/ravenhill5e

PART V
Development, Equality, and the Environment

12

Global Growth, Inequality, and Poverty: The Globalization Argument and the 'Political' Science of Economics

Robert Hunter Wade

Chapter contents

Reader's guide

The head of a Chinese family said to a BBC interviewer, 'You, in the West, all have washing machines, and refrigerators, and TVs. Why shouldn't we Chinese have the same?' Migrants flooding into Europe and North America voice the same aspiration. According to the free market argument, also known as the neo-liberal globalization argument, an international economic order in which nations are as closely integrated to each other as the states of the United States or at least the members of the European Union—so as to make it very easy for goods, services, capital and people to move quickly across borders without having to face government 'intervention'—is the best type of world order to ensure that ordinary people everywhere enjoy substantial improvements in capabilities for human flourishing—including washing machines. The same type of world order also tends to drive political systems towards democracy, as capitalism and democracy fortify each other. The argument concludes that free markets and steady movement towards ever closer integration broadly align the interests of rich countries and poor countries, dominant classes and subordinate classes, thanks to the way that free markets open opportunities and ensure that profit-maximizing firms allocate resources to their most efficient uses (not to cronyism or an easy life). The present income gaps between North and South, core and periphery, and rich and poor people are just lags in the catch-up of the poor world to the prosperity of the rich world, not a result of a global hierarchy inherent in the system of capitalist economies organized into nation states.

In the absence of global government, knowledge of the trends in *global* growth, inequality, and poverty is not of operational interest to any government. But the knowledge is of operational interest to the nearest we have to global economic government, namely the global economic multilateral organizations (GEMs) such as the World Bank, the International Monetary Fund (IMF), the World Trade Organization (WTO), and interstate organizations of more limited scope, such as the Asian Development Bank and the Organisation for Economic Co-operation and Development (OECD). Since the 1980s, these bodies have been mandated by their member states to implement what has come to be known as the Washington Consensus—to deregulate markets, privatize public enterprises, promote 'maximum shareholder value' as the objective of firms, cut taxes and public spending, open national economies to cross-border trade and investment, and harmonize national regulations so as to give economic actors a global 'level playing field', undistorted by state restrictions. The globalization argument provides the intellectual legitimacy for this mandate, and warns that mutual benefits will be at risk if countries start to backslide on market liberalization.

The Washington Consensus is now appropriately called the Washington–Brussels Consensus—as seen in the fact that the 'austerity' agenda imposed by northern Europe and the IMF on southern Europe in the wake of the Eurozone crisis of 2010 is justified by the same broad ideas. Global conditions as of early 2016—with hardening prospects of a new slump in economies still to shake off the crisis of 2008, amplified by tit-for-tat trade wars (notably in steel between the European Union, Japan, and South Korea on one side and China on the other)—raise doubts that it will be possible to return to the pre-2008 growth regime of 'finance-driven globalization'. Developing and developed countries alike must rethink their globalization strategies (UNCTAD 2015a, 2016).

This rethinking is all the more necessary because, as this chapter shows, the evidence for the globalization argument, especially the finance-led variant, is not as robust as the policy mainstream presumes. The chapter begins with an examination of trends in globalization over the past century, and the kind of evidence provided by mainstream economists to support the argument. Then it turns to a description of global-level trends in growth, inequality, and poverty over the past few decades, and shows how our knowledge is dappled with ambiguity, not nearly as favourable to the 'globalization works' argument as the policy mainstream presumes. The penultimate section suggests why the consensus among economists about the virtues of globalization has been so resilient. The conclusion summarizes, and spells out some challenges for economists, especially in the field of professional ethics.

Much of the discussion is framed with the convenient—but too simple—dichotomy between developed and developing countries. Keep in mind the proportions. In 2014 developing countries accounted for 84 per cent of the world's 7.2 billion people, and about 35 per cent of world output. The average resident of developing countries has a share of world output equal to roughly one tenth that of the average resident of developed countries—after decades of 'development'. Why?

❝ The laws of economics are like the laws of engineering. One set of laws works everywhere. [They may be summarized as:] privatization, stabilization and liberalization. ❞

(Lawrence Summers (1991) quoted in Klein 2007: 218)

❝ Today, we have a virtual consensus across the political spectrum in government on at least three points: our public spending must diminish, our economies still have too much inflexibility and we aren't competitive enough. ❞

(Jean-Claude Trichet, former governor of the Banque de France and the European Central Bank, 2016)

❝ Any given decision you make you'll end up with a 30 to 40 per cent chance it's not going to work … You can't be paralyzed by the fact that it might not work out. On top of that, after you have made your decision, you need to feign total certainty about it. People being led do not want to think probabilistically. ❞

(President Obama, quoted in Lewis 2012: 171–2)

Introduction

'Globalization'—a portmanteau word embracing high integration of national economies in terms of trade, investment, and finance, and an ideology, favouring privatization and market liberalization—became a buzz word across the social sciences in the second half of the 1990s. Its ascent was synchronized with the post-Cold War revival of an older Euro-American ideal of the 'mission to civilize'.

The 'international community', as the European and North American states call themselves, sees as its duty to bring capitalism and democracy to less fortunate, poorer nations in the global South; and thereby to expand sources of supply and demand, to mutual benefit. As US Secretary of State Condoleezza Rice explained, it is America's job to remake the world order, in its own image (2008). Where necessary this should be done by 'hard power' military intervention, as in colonial days, or by economic sanctions (Russia, Iran, North Korea); but normally it should be done by 'soft power', by persuading peoples everywhere that capitalist globalization brings large mutual benefits—more than conflicting interests—in terms of higher economic growth, widening opportunities, falling poverty, and falling inequality. International organizations run largely by Euro-American states, such as the World Bank, the IMF, and the OECD are key agencies for propagating belief that a world order based on globalization policy as the best route to higher income and wealth. Liberalizing trade and inward foreign investment, freeing domestic markets from state restrictions, privatizing the provision of infrastructure and public services, cutting taxes, and 'good governance' reforms have become central to their *modus operandi* in developing countries. Bilateral aid programs of Euro-American states and Japan back up their efforts; as does a dense network of neoliberal think tanks devoted to spreading and defending the orthodoxy, many of them spawned and coordinated by the Mont Pelerin Society and the Atlas Economic Research Foundation (since 2011, Atlas Network).

The term 'globalization' only became prominent in the 1990s but the underlying ideas about appropriate public policy—often called 'neo-liberalism'—began to crystallize as 'global policy' around 1980. This happened in the wake of the breakdown of the **Bretton Woods** economic architecture in the early 1970s, followed by rising inflation, the rise of free market political movements starting in the United States and Britain, and the collapse of the West's unifying enemy, the communist bloc, in the late 1980s. Neo-liberalism

has provided the model for global policy ever since. The Crash of 2008 and ensuing great recession have done little to blunt its hold, in contrast to the social democratic response to the Crash of 1929 in North America and parts of western Europe.

What is the meaning of 'neo-liberalism' and 'global policy'? Neo-liberalism is an economic philosophy about the best way for an economy to create wealth and widely distributed material well-being. One of its founding fathers was Friedrich Hayek (1899–1992), who developed it in opposition to the economic philosophies of Nazism, Fascism, Stalinism, and John Maynard Keynes (1883–1946). Hayek emphasized that individuals operating in a market have only fragmented knowledge of particular circumstances close to them, rather than holistic or encompassing knowledge of economy and society. Moreover, no central organization can have reliable knowledge—or knowledge more reliable than the aggregation of undirected market exchanges. So the state should maintain social order, enforce property rights and free entry to sectors, and ensure market competition and a stable financial system. It must not try to stimulate the growth and diversification of production, let alone impart directional thrust, and must not attempt to redistribute income and wealth more than marginally. It should support capitalists in their relations with 'labour', for capitalists are the creators of wealth and employment. Hayek accepted, in passing, that guaranteeing to all 'some minimum of food, shelter and clothing, sufficient to preserve health' would not endanger 'general freedom'; and he approved, in passing, of publicly provided healthcare on grounds that no fair market price could be determined (1944: 120). But beyond these limits, he said, lies 'the road to serfdom', totalitarian regimes. Hayek's melding of neoclassical economics with a political philosophy emphasising maximum freedom of the individual—particularly of the owners and managers of capital—is the basis of modern neo-liberalism.

The philosophy recognizes that markets may sometimes fail, but asserts that—with exceptions related to **public goods**'—the costs of state 'intervention' to fix market failures are generally higher than the benefits (where benefits are calculated with reference to the model of perfect competition as the ideal). In its modern version, it calls for wage growth to be kept below productivity growth (allowing incentivizing profits to grow as a share of national income); for monetary policy to target inflation and let employment take care of itself; for central banks to be 'independent'; and for fiscal policy to sustain no more than low budget deficits in the context of no more than slightly progressive income taxes. It downplays the aggregate demand side of the economy as a subject for public policy; and therefore also downplays how high inequality of income and wealth restrict demand and leave floods of financial capital sloshing around the world in search of higher short-term returns. Western economies applying this doctrine since the 1980s have staved off the resulting tendencies to stagnation mainly by some combination of increased public and private borrowing (notably in the US), booms in financial assets and real estate, and increased exports, this combination generating the impetus to the North Atlantic Crash of 2008, the eurozone crisis of 2010, and perhaps an 'emerging market' debt crisis or US stock market crash to come.

As for 'global policy', the phrase means policy developed by actors who claim to think for the world and who play an advocacy role in multiple states and transnational forums. Examples of global policy actors include the above-mentioned interstate organizations, private bodies like the International Accounting Standards Board, transnational think tanks, and also powerful national agencies like the US Treasury and State Department, and the UK Treasury.

Economists, especially those of the Anglo-American school (the pinnacle of economics worldwide, outside of North Korea, Iran and a few other places), have championed the globalization world order project. They argue that the general movement towards free market policies and mobile production after 1980 caused a general movement towards income convergence rather than divergence, towards less poverty and more equality. According to Martin Wolf, the distinguished columnist for the *Financial Times* and author of *Why Globalization Works* (2004a, 4):

❝ It cannot make sense to fragment the world economy more than it already is but rather to make the world economy work as if it were the United States, or at least the European Union … The failure of our world is not that there is too much globalization, but that there is too little. The potential for greater economic integration is barely tapped. ❞

A senior economist of the premier investment bank Goldman Sachs coined BRICs to bracket Brazil, Russia, India, and China as large and fast growing 'emerging markets', presented as only the top of a wider 'rise of the South', signalling an historic change in the distribution of economic weight and political influence in the world economy—and in where smart investors should put

their money. The president of the World Bank, Robert Zoellick, declared in 2010 that the distinction between developed and developing countries was now obsolete.

❝ If 1989 saw the end of the 'Second World' with Communism's demise, then 2009 saw the end of what was known as the 'Third World'. We are now in a new, fast-evolving multipolar world economy—in which some developing countries are emerging as economic powers; others are moving towards becoming additional poles of growth; and some are struggling to attain their potential within this new system. ❞

(Zoellick 2010)

In effect, Zoellick was saying that we are at the end of the Truman era—which began in the early post-war years when President Truman called on the West to take up the challenge of using 'our' knowledge and resources to deliver development to the rest of the non-communist world.

We can agree that economic development, in production and consumption, has never proceeded so fast and on such a wide front in the world economy as it has since the 1950s. We can also agree that both low- and middle-income countries have grown at some 3 to 5 percentage points faster than the high-income countries from around 2003 to 2012—a historically unprecedented gap in favour of developing countries. The four BRICs shot up the world ranking of gross national income (GNI) between 2000 and 2013 (by the World Bank's Atlas method, in current dollars)—China from seventh to second biggest economy, Brazil from ninth to seventh; Russia from twenty-first to ninth; and India from thirteenth to tenth. China and India's ascent puts them in line to regain their position as the two biggest economies, which—with the two biggest populations—they occupied for about 1,800 of the past 2,000 years.

On the other hand, they remain far down the ranking of average incomes: China in 2013, 85th, up from 123rd in 2000; India in 2013, 145th, up from 148th in 2000. (Take these rankings with a grain of salt, because different ways of comparing income and production produce different rankings.) Never before have the world's ten biggest economies included several far down the ranking of average income. Earlier, the G7 countries, which constituted the top table of global economic governance, were highly ranked in both GDP and GDP per capita, making for a broad homogeneity of interests. Today, the same correlation within the G20, which calls itself the new top table of global economic governance, is much lower, greatly complicating global agreement.

Most analysts present 'the rise of the South' as the pay-off from decades of patient globalization. Implicitly using linear projections, they expect catch-up growth in developing countries to continue indefinitely, with occasional blips. They stress that the world's governments—especially those of developing countries—should keep pushing ahead with market liberalization as the core of their (micro) economic policy agenda; leavened in the past two decades by the magical ingredients of 'good governance' and 'anticorruption'. But while governments should keep expanding the scope for 'exchange', they should not get their hands dirty by directly boosting production capabilities. In particular, they should not undertake 'industrial policy' to accelerate the diversification of production structures (beyond what would result from generic improvements in infrastructure and market institutions), such as the industrial policy practised by the East Asian capitalist governments during their fast-industrialization phase, or the more primitive type of industrial policy practised by the US and continental Europe as these regions caught up with Britain, the first industrializer.

For example, the World Bank has long deployed the Country Policy and Institutional Assessment (CPIA) formula to score countries by the 'goodness-for-development' of their policies and institutions, and then factors the score into its lending decisions and country dialogues. The scoring criteria for the trade regime imply that a completely free trade regime is best for development. The criteria for labour markets give the highest score to countries with minimal worker protection and maximum employer flexibility (Wade 2010). As of 2016 the World Bank and other such organizations no longer preach a hard version of the Washington Consensus; but a fairly hard version remains wired into their cultures and their operating procedures.

Legitimized by the Washington Consensus, most developing country governments have sought to accelerate their integration with developed economies by signing bilateral or regional trade and investment agreements—yet these agreements restrict their ability to complement improved market access with the macroeconomic and industrial policies needed to intensify input-output linkages within the domestic economy. Many of these agreements also require 'investor-state dispute settlement', by which foreign corporations can sue host governments for actions which threaten the corporation's expected future profits (even including regulations to curb cigarette smoking or protect rainforests). They sue governments at an ostensibly neutral international arbitration panel, which operates in high secrecy with a pool of lawyers and arbitrators drawn mostly from western countries, who face obvious conflicts of interest (the prosecutor for a corporation today may be an arbitrator tomorrow for a case prosecuted by today's arbitrator). The panel cannot adjudicate governments suing corporations for failure to fulfil their responsibilities. Such panels have awarded damages against governments running into billions of US dollars, and even just a corporation's threat to bring a suit has been enough to chill socially responsible regulation.

The owners and managers of Western capital remain, post-Crash, powerful advocates and lobbyists for neoliberal globalization. They managed to convert the initial policy response of a Great Re-regulation in 2009 into the Great Escape from regulation by 2011. They have used the Crisis to push governments—seeking to reduce public debt—to privatize public services and thereby convert state provision of public goods out of general taxation into private provision of services (health, education, transport, other infrastructure) financed by arrangements (often state-guaranteed) which generate near-monopoly profits for private capitalists; while governments have also enabled banks to blow politically popular house price bubbles, politically popular because they seem to boost individuals' principal source of wealth and protection against failing pensions. In turn Western governments continue to push the international organizations that intermediate between them and developing country governments to advocate neo-liberal globalization norms, with qualifications at the margins.

Blessed by these norms, the post-Crash system of financial regulation still allows banks to remain 'too big to fail' (a dozen banks now dominate the world's financial system, as before 2008, which each own assets of more than $1 trillion whereas economies of scale in banking fall away beyond assets of around $100 billion). Some banks have been fined, but not senior bankers; yet no company can break the law unless people in the company break the law—to fine companies but not people is like fining Route 66 for speeding. Governments have relied largely on 'quantitative easing' of monetary policy to stimulate aggregate demand, which tends to generate asset booms and raise the share of wealth held by the already rich. The post-Crash system of financial regulation is a recipe for more rounds of the doomsday cycle of bubbles and 'trubbles'—leading to further entrenchment of 'oligarchic-impunity capitalism' in the politically powerful sectors.

The Swahili proverb says, 'Until the lions have their own historians the history of hunting will always glorify the hunters'. The praise for globalization, and the hard-wiring of neoliberal globalization norms into international treaties and the operating procedures of international organizations, illustrates history being written and rules being set by the winners. It is in line with what could be called a 'law' of modern-era power hierarchies: elites legitimize their success in terms of universalistic, meritocratic qualities like initiative, hard work, and Christianity, and legitimize others' lower rank in terms of their failure to match these qualities (their dedication to identity politics, corruption, leisure). Hence we have a vast literature on 'poor economics', but no 'rich economics'. 'Poor people' are a problem for social scientists, 'rich people' are not.

This chapter argues that economists, who collectively have more influence over the life-chances of others than all other social scientists, have oversold the virtues of market liberalization, displaying confidence in derived policy prescriptions well beyond the evidence. Their confidence in advocating always more market liberalization (less crowding out by government), more market integration, in both developing and developed countries ('ever closer integration' in the European Union), overlooking the question of how governments can help to shift the structure of the national economy towards higher value-added activities, is part of a more general pattern of downplaying the limits to their expertise and the dangers associated with their prescriptions. Of course, many academic economists delight in finding theoretical or empirical qualifications to the mainstream prescriptions, and some win so-called Nobel Prizes for doing so. But when they—especially their policy colleagues in organizations like the World Bank, IMF, and the OECD—prescribe what others should do they tend to retreat to 'the free market fundamentals'; and to follow a former editor of *The Economist* who advised young reporters, 'simplify, then exaggerate' (*Economist*, 2011). In theory a government may produce national economic gains by managing trade in line with an industrial strategy, they say, but in practice any such project will be hijacked by special interests, so free trade is best in practice, for national economies and the world.

The most spectacular recent demonstration of hubris is the failure of almost the whole of the mainstream economics profession in the few years before 2007–8 to forecast a major recession. As just two examples among many, Jean-Philippe Cotis, chief economist of the OECD, declared in May 2007, 'the current economic situation is in many ways better than we have experienced in years … Our central forecast remains quite benign … [We expect the OECD to show] strong job creation and falling unemployment' (Cotis 2007). Anne Krueger, the American number two at the IMF, announced in May 2006 that 'the world economy has rarely been in better shape' (lecture at Claremont McKenna College; see also Wade 2016). One reason they got it so wrong is that the OECD, IMF, the Bank of England and most other such organizations have long used macroeconomic models—'dynamic stochastic general equilibrium' models—whose few financial variables are made to depend on real economy variables. They can handle an invasion from Mars better than they can handle a tightening of credit. They continue to be used despite their long track record of failing to forecast recessions even one year ahead. Indeed, the IMF, in its annual forecasts from 1999 to 2014, has failed to anticipate any of the 220 cases when a member country had a recession the following year.

After reviewing evidence on the performance of the world economy in terms of economic growth, income inequality, and poverty, we will have a better idea of the 'epistemic uncertainty' around economists' prescriptions for more globalization, and the dangers posed by the combination of economists' high influence over the life-chances of others, their epistemic certainty, and their epistemic superiority vis-à-vis the public they serve.

Economic growth in long-term perspective

Most national economies have experienced increases in average real income in most years since around 1960. We take this as normal, but on a scale of millennia it is completely exceptional. Earlier, growth of production (perhaps due to the introduction of irrigation or other land-productivity-raising technology) was translated into higher birth rates to the point that the original living conditions were restored, a trend known as the Malthusian trap. Moving from where economic growth is exceptional to where it is normal amounts to a revolution in human civilization, up there with the Greeks and the Renaissance in the annals of human achievement.

One indicator of improving performance is the rate of growth of global production: over the eighteenth century, 0.3 per cent per year; the nineteenth century, 1 per cent; 1900–60, 2.4 per cent; 1960–2000, 4 per cent, meaning that in these 40 years it went up five times (Lucas 2004). Meanwhile world population doubled from about 3 billion to 6.1 billion during 1960–2000, at 1.7 per cent per year; so production per head rose at 2.3 per cent per year.

Another indicator is world average life expectancy at birth. It rose from about 25 years in 1800–1900, to 47.7 years in 1950–5, to 66.4 years in 2000–5. The other side of rising life expectancy is falling childbearing. Eighty-three countries, with 46 per cent of the world's population, now have fertility below replacement rate of 2.1 births per woman. Only 9 per cent of the world's population, almost all in Africa, live in countries with pre-industrial fertility rates of five or six children per woman.

However, until the 2000s average incomes grew more slowly in most of the developing world than in the developed world, especially in the last two decades of the twentieth century (when the globalization policy agenda was most strongly asserted). Today the average income gap between the 20 poorest economies and the United States is around 18–20, three times the figure for 1900. The larger part of global income inequality (inequality in the distribution between all the people of the world shoulder to shoulder, irrespective of country) has been, since the Industrial Revolution, horizontal, meaning inequality of average incomes in different places, rather than vertical. Cecil Rhodes, the nineteenth-century philanthropist and champion of British imperialism and South African apartheid, captured horizontal inequality when he declared, 'Remember that you are an Englishman, and have consequently won first prize in the lottery of life.' The little island off the coast of northwest Europe, Great Britain, in 1913 controlled colonies 125 times larger than itself, covering a quarter of the Earth's land area and 24 per cent of world population. Rhodes could also have identified northern Europeans and North Americans as winners of the first prize, because these regions also forged ahead of the rest of the world in material living conditions through the nineteenth century.

'Catch-up growth' in a late-developing country fast enough and sustained enough for it to attain an average income of, say, 80 per cent of the average of the developed countries within half a century, has been rare. One main reason is that developed countries have typically tried to prevent developing

countries from entering or remaining in dynamic sectors or segments of value chains with increasing returns to scale. That is part of what being a developed country is all about. During colonial times, actors in the European colonial project—governments, militaries, companies—created dependent colonial and New World slave economies to which they outsourced land-intensive production. This structure delivered an 'agricultural windfall', which allowed labour at home to be used for industrialization, and provided an export market for manufacturers. Having created this hierarchical structure, European and then North American actors had multiple means to sustain it. By mid-twentieth century they had established a powerful institutional complex for scientific discovery, where companies, public agencies and universities combine to transform discoveries into technological innovations, generating innovation-led, high value-added growth. A prime example of a developmental state is the US, whose industrial policy has been at least as vigorous and effective as anything in East Asia; but it is a developmental state in disguise, and one could even say that the most effective US industrial policy is to make the rest of the world believe that the US does not do industrial policy (Lazonick 2008; Block and Keller 2011; Mazzucato 2013; Wade 2014, in press).

Just how difficult it is to achieve 'catch-up', let alone 'leapfrog' growth is suggested by the small number of non-Western countries that have become developed in the *past two centuries*, even stretching the categories of 'non-Western', 'developed', and 'country'. The list includes Japan, Russia, Taiwan, South Korea, Hong Kong, Singapore, Israel, maybe a few more. The shockingly small number testifies to the difficulties of sustained economic development. Notice that most of the countries had in common during their fast-industrialization phase both small populations and one or more powerful external enemy states plausibly threatening to end the state's existence. Without this unifying threat, state incumbents might have been tempted to use their power to strangle opponents and redistribute resources to themselves rather than promote a national development project able to create a polity, economy, and society unified enough to dissuade an external enemy.

More evidence comes from a World Bank study (2013). It identifies 101 countries in 1960 as 'middle income'. Only 13 reached 'high income' by 2008, of which four are peripheral western Europe and five are

East Asian. Of the 13, 70 per cent have populations of fewer than 20 million; only one is more than 50 million (Japan). In this study the income thresholds are defined in absolute terms.

A study by IMF researchers (Cherif and Hasanov 2015) defines income thresholds in terms of percentage of US GDP per capita ($PPP 2005, Penn World Tables 8.0). In a set of 167 low- and middle-income countries in 1970, only 9 reached high income by 2010 (the 75th percentile of the income distribution, at 46 per cent of US GDP per capita). Of these, 7 were small European countries, which had already reached upper-middle-income by 1970 (Cyprus, Czech Republic, Greece, Ireland, Malta, Portugal, Slovenia). Only two were non-European: Taiwan and South Korea. The latter shot from around 20 per cent of US income in 1970 to more than 65 per cent in 2010. In contrast, Malaysia was about 20 per cent in 1970 and 26 per cent in 2010. Thailand and Chile had roughly similar performance as Malaysia (Chile doing better over the 2000s thanks to the rise in copper prices).

Other researchers, also at the IMF, find that middle-income countries tend to experience more volatile growth than either low- or high-income countries, with periods of super-fast growth (GDP growth at 6 per cent a year or more) followed by protracted slow-downs (Aiyer et al. 2013).

Putting this and still more evidence together, we can conclude that a country going from lower middle to high income in fewer than four or five decades constitutes something of a 'miracle'. Some researchers conclude that the world economy contains a 'middle-income trap' (or 'non-convergence trap' or 'middle-capabilities trap'). Taken literally the idea of a 'trap' implies no possibility of reaching high-income, which is absurd (Felipe et al., 2014). But taken as a metaphor (like 'glass ceiling'), it highlights that the great majority of middle-income countries have remained in the middle-income range for several decades longer than the East Asian success stories, growing more slowly and with more ups and downs. Also, the phrase, 'middle-capabilities trap' usefully highlights the distinction between countries which achieve high income on a narrow range of exports (oil, diamonds, copper) and those with a diversified production structure (Paus 2014; Ergin 2015). Glass ceiling becomes a 'glass floor' for high income countries, because very few have fallen into the middle income range since 1960.

The fact that only a small number of countries since the 1950s have achieved the diversified production structures of countries now considered to be 'developed', and that virtually all are on the European periphery or in East Asia, sits awkwardly with neo-liberal economics, which encourages the belief that resources of all kinds move fairly easily in a market economy from lower value-added to higher, as easily as toothpaste from a tube. As stated by Adam Smith (1723–90), one of the first theorists of capitalism and a proto-globalist, 'Little else is required to carry a state to the highest degree of opulence from the lowest barbarism, but peace, easy taxes, and a tolerable administration of justice, all the rest being brought about by the natural course of things' (1755). Here Smith was surfing on the ideological revolution of the Reformation, which had reimagined the earlier medieval view of selfishness as a human frailty into self-interest as the basis of the good society; which led on to the conclusion that the wealthy should have not just power but also moral authority over the poor, because the wealthy, having succeeded through their talents and hard work, provide a model for the poor. Smith himself later qualified this argument in The Wealth of Nations and still more in The Theory of Moral Sentiments. But its continuing potency today is suggested by the statement of Harvard economics professor Gregory Mankiw, author of a leading economics textbook and former Chairman of the President's Council of Economic Advisors, that 'Adam Smith was right when he said [the above]' (2006).

The argument implies that the world economy is an open system, with no hierarchical structure of core, and periphery, in which the prosperity of some classes and regions depends on the poverty of others. Development is like a marathon race in which the rank of each runner (country) is a function of its internal strengths, and all runners could conceptually cross the finishing line (prosperity) at the same time. Anyone who believes this should take another look at the short list of non-Western countries that have become developed in the past two centuries; and at the key role of colonial and slave economies in propelling the initial forging ahead of western Europe and northeast United States.

Globalization

Globalization can be traced in quantities as well as in ideas, interests, and institutions (three 'i's' of global political economy). In all these domains the process has increased hugely over the past several decades. For example, the ratio of flows of goods, services, and finance to global GDP rose from around 22 per cent in 1992 to 53 per cent by 2007—and then down to 39 per cent by 2014 (Donnan 2016).

The globalization literature tends to slight the point that this increasing market integration has occurred in the context of a hierarchically structured world economy, with some countries and regions having more activity in dynamic, high profit and high wage activities, and able to set the rules for others. We can think of the structure as a core–periphery model, developed countries at the core and developing countries at the periphery (some more peripheral than others). The two parts are bound together, first, by the tendency for supply to exceed demand in the core (a point emphasized by the classical economists and later by John Maynard Keynes), making the core dependent on the periphery as a source of demand for its (mostly industrial and service) exports; and second, by the core's dependence on imports of natural resources from the periphery. The high-income elasticity of demand for industrial and service imports in the periphery and low income elasticity of demand for natural resources in the core mean that the periphery tends to run trade and current account deficits, financed by credit from the core (and by aid, foreign investment, and military bases). The periphery's foreign debt—which must be repaid in foreign currency, generally US dollars— easily rises above its capacity to repay, resulting in debt traps, followed by emergency loans from core-controlled international organizations and core banks freighted with tough privatizing and market-opening conditionalities. In this way the core–periphery structure tends to reproduce itself, as seen in the 'middle-income trap'. Of course, this is a highly simplified model, which omits major real-world complexities (including hegemonic rivalries within the core, the position of the US as large-scale international debtor, and China escaping periphery traps).

Within the core–periphery hierarchical structure, the period from the 1870s to the First World War saw the first wave of globalization, on the back of technological breakthroughs in coal, steam, iron, and steel, transnational railways, and transcontinental shipbuilding, when the US and Germany emerged to challenge Great Britain. The post-Second World War decades up to around 1980 saw the second wave, led by the US. It was anchored in a new economic structure in the core countries, spanning the 'mass production revolution' and the 'consumer society', based on universal

electricity, cheap oil, cheap suburban housing, plastics and the automobile, and supported by state institutions which recycled taxes back to businesses and various parts of the household income distribution via the welfare state, public employment, and public (including military) procurement, and supported by labour unions which obtained wage increases in line with productivity and expanded non-work time for consumption. Capitalists too supported the compromise and its tax implications ('positive sum game') because the national market was their guaranteed demand space, so they saw wages as a source of demand as well as a cost. Each capitalist still had an incentive to screw down on wages, but capitalists had a collective interest in paying high enough wages to create sufficient demand for their products. On the other hand, the new economic structure depended on access to low cost energy, materials, and manufactured goods in developing countries—depended on core-periphery inequalities (Carlota Perez, personal communication).

Both first and second waves constituted 'shallow integration' between national economies, as compared with the 'deep integration' to come. They were 'trade globalization' with relatively immobile production. Manufacturing companies stayed in one country and produced mostly finished goods for international markets. The second differed from the first in that a growing share of international trade was 'intra-industry' (German cars to France and French cars to Germany) (see Chapter 7).

Financial globalization began in the second wave. One milestone was the abandonment, at the start of the 1970s, of the fixed exchange-rate regime in place since the Bretton Woods agreements in the mid 1940s. Floating currencies transferred currency risk to the private sector and stimulated the development of currency and derivative markets. A second milestone was the oil price hike by the Organization of Petroleum Exporting Countries (OPEC) in 1973. This resulted in large trade deficits in oil-importing countries, including the US, which gave another boost to the international market for US dollars (in which oil transactions were denominated) and for cross-border lending, especially to Latin America, whose sovereign debt first skyrocketed and then tripped the continent into two 'lost decades'.

The third globalization wave, 'production globalization', started around 1980 and lasted till around 2000, again led by the US, on the back of breakthroughs in information technologies (notably the microprocessor launched by Intel in 1971). These innovations enabled Western multinationals to outsource manufacturing and services, so as to use cheap labour or to be nearer final markets (as joint ventures, 'original equipment manufacturers', or arm's-length suppliers). The third wave was intensified by the end of the Cold War and the collapse of the socialist economic system, which merged two separate labour forces and investment pools into one; and at the same time, India became more open to the capitalist world economy than before. Within a short space of time, the world labour supply (workers producing for international markets) roughly doubled. Multinationals became much less dependent on demand from the population of their home countries. The post-war class compromise eroded as western capitalists saw wages only as a cost, demand coming from elsewhere, and as they embraced the norms of 'maximum tax avoidance' and 'winner-take-all' remuneration. The labour share of returns from production fell, the capital share went up, inequality rose in most countries. Production globalization, and 'deep integration', were enthusiastically promoted by the western-dominated international development organizations, including the World Bank and the IMF, under the banner of the Washington Consensus policy agenda for developing countries.

Since around 2000 we have been in the fourth wave, really an intensification and narrowing of the third: 'China-centric production globalization', when Western companies looked to China as the favoured production site for a wide range of manufactured goods. China's ascent marginalized manufacturing in other developing countries like Mexico and Brazil, and generated regional production chains linking subcontracting firms in other parts of East Asia and producers of high value-added components in Japan, North America and Europe, with assembly firms in China making final products for Western markets. By the 2000s Apple, Dell, and many other US tech companies had roughly one employee in America for ten people producing their products in China. Production globalization went with further trade liberalization; average world tariff rates fell to about 6 per cent in 2010 from as high as 40 per cent in the early 1990s. We may recently have entered a fifth wave. With world trade growing at its slowest since the doldrums of the 1970s, individuals and companies are sending some 20 times more data across borders in 2016 than in 2008, including data for 3D printing at the use site of components which would earlier have been shipped in.

Meanwhile financial globalization has been proceeding, intertwined like a double helix with waves of production globalization. It shows itself in both surging volume of cross-border financial transactions and institutional and legal liberalization of national financial systems and cross-border capital movements. The world of producers and consumers becomes the world of creditors and debtors. Giant banks grow at the intersection of credit-creation, saving, and investment, able to extract fast rising returns from the productive economy at every turn. The realm of finance dominates the realm of the 'real economy'—the ratio of global financial transactions to global GDP jumped from 14 in 1997 to almost 70 by 2012. And more than just size, finance now saps industrial capitalism with the prospect of easier profits from financial operations and real estate than from production. The US, with the world's main international currency, biggest capital markets, and population fluent in English (the language of international finance), dominates the financial realm even more than it dominates the GDP realm, which will probably help to sustain its pre-eminent rank among states for decades to come.

As both cause and effect, developed and many developing country governments began to rely less on politically unpopular taxation and more on politically more innocuous borrowing to finance their activities, transitioning from 'taxation states' to 'debt states' (Streeck 2013). They competed to cut taxes and privatize public assets so as to attract foreign capital. Their rising dependence on borrowing, plus high cross-border mobility of finance (hence low cost of 'exit' from any jurisdiction), boosted the *structural* power of finance. The international balance of power shifted in favour of international finance and creditor states (though not away from the biggest debtor state of all, the US). National distributions of power in developed and many developing countries shifted from representatives of domestically oriented groups towards representatives of groups whose interests and ideology aligned with international finance. Wealthy households and giant pension and insurance funds demanded new types of financial instruments in which to store and multiply their rising share of national wealth. Western financial firms looked to developing countries for investment opportunities, and rebranded some of them 'emerging market economies' (EMEs), which sounds more promising than 'developing countries'.

Globalization policy norms acquired a halo of 'success'. 'Reform' came to mean exclusively changes in a free market direction. Reform of a trade regime meant less protection, not making protection work better. Reform of corporate governance meant increasing transparency so that investors can better evaluate the buying and selling of shares, not giving voice to employees. Reform of public enterprises meant privatizing. Reform of macro policies meant making them more friendly to ratings agencies and holders of government debt. Reform of public services meant outsourcing of government responsibilities and making labour contracts 'flexible', tipping power more firmly to employers. On the ground, policy barriers to trade and foreign investment fell away as part of a wider move away from manipulating relative prices. For example, the world average ratio of tariff revenue to GDP fell from about 27 per cent in 1980 to 10 per cent in 2000.

On the other hand, government expenditure as a share of GDP has remained fairly constant, both in developed and developing countries, a disappointment in neo-liberal eyes. One reason is that globalization and its associated technologies have driven a sharp rise in the relative size of the 'precariat' in Western economies and Japan—people engaged in part-time work who want full-time work, people employed for 'tasks' rather than careers, people without employer-provided benefits beyond wages, people employed on 'zero-hour' contracts who are obliged to be at their employer's disposal 24/7 but are guaranteed only, normally, 15 paid hours a week. They are the 'throwaway citizens' (though a small minority flourish as contractors and entrepreneurs on their own). Even as the precariat grows, most Western governments are trying to cut back on social protection and cede more of it to the charity or for-profit sectors, but are somewhat constrained by democratic politics and the need to offset the tendency to depressed private demand. All this underlines the point made by Joseph Schumpeter (1883–1950) that capitalism generally, technological revolutions more specifically, make for 'creative destruction' (sometimes more creative, sometimes more destructive), not just in firms and industries but also in organizational templates and world views, from which comes the ascendancy of those embracing the new 'common sense' and marginalization of those attached to the old common sense (think Detroit to Silicon Valley).

Globalization as key to improved national performance?

The proposition that trade liberalization promotes higher welfare at home and abroad appears to be supported by many cross-country studies which find that more liberal trade and investment policies generate economic dynamism. But these studies often turn out to be less than convincing. Identifying causality is problematic. Finding that faster growth of trade quantities is associated with improved economic performance does not support the conclusion that *trade policy liberalization* is key to faster trade growth. Trade volumes are outcomes of many factors, including an economy's overall growth. They are not something that government controls directly. Studies of the relationship between trade policy (indicated by tariffs and non-tariff barriers) and subsequent economic growth find no strong relationship (Wade 2010, 2013). The only robust relationship is that governments lower trade barriers as their economies become richer. To infer that they became richer because of lowered trade barriers is like inferring that, since rich people tend to live in nice houses, you can become rich by living in a nice house.

With few exceptions, today's rich countries had high tariffs during their rapid growth phase (including the US) and then lowered trade barriers as their domestic industries became competitive. Japan through the 1950s to the 1970s and Korea and Taiwan through the 1960s to the 1980s, had fast growth of trade together with very managed trade regimes. They managed trade so as to intensify the cycle of investment-profits-reinvestment in the domestic economy, which generated fast growth, which generated fast growth of demand for raw materials and capital goods, which prompted strategic trade liberalization (Wade 2004; Chang and Grabel 2014). More recently, China and India began to open their own markets *after* building up entrepreneurship, industrial capacity, internal integration, and fast growth behind high barriers. In 1990, China had the fifth-highest average tariffs in the world, behind Bangladesh, India, Pakistan, and Kenya, at the same time as its exports were surging. India continues to have high trade restrictions.

In Latin America, Chile adopted free market policies under Pinochet in the 1970s and enjoyed substantial economic success. Economists urged other Latin American countries to follow Chile's lead, and many did. Yet they have had poor economic performance. Something is amiss when the good pupils score the low marks (Mexico and many others in Latin America) and the bad pupils score the high marks (Japan, Taiwan, South Korea during their catch-up phase, and China).

The short answer to why East Asia has shown much better economic performance is that gross capital

Table 12.1 Gross capital formation/GDP, selected entities

	1970	1990	2012	1980–2014
China	33	36	47	40
East Asia & Pacific minus China	23	32	30	28
LICs & MICs minus East Asia	22	22	25	23

Notes: LICs = low-income countries, MICs = middle-income countries.
Source: World Development Indicators (22/12/2015).

formation has run at a much higher share of GDP than elsewhere (see Table 12.1).

We can be fairly sure that strong causality runs from investment rates to economic growth (and some causality in the other direction). But the larger point of this section is that our knowledge of the causes of growth in developing and developed countries is not robust. Tatu Westling (2011) estimates an augmented Solow model utilizing the Mankiw–Romer–Weil 121-country dataset and finds that human penis size is statistically highly significant in explaining GDP per capita levels in 1985 and even GDP per capita growth from 1960 to 1985. More seriously, Enrique Moral-Benito (2012: 21) finds that, taking account of endogeneity and model uncertainty, 'There is no variable unambiguously related to economic growth. Hence, economic growth does not appear to be robustly related to the determinants proposed in the literature so far.'

An independent panel of economists tasked with evaluating World Bank research on development policies said of the big cross-country studies, which allegedly show that free market policies constitute the ideal development model:

❝ We see a serious failure in the checks and balances within the system that has led the Bank to repeatedly trumpet these early empirical results without recognizing their fragile and tentative nature … once the evidence is chosen selectively without supporting argument, and empirical skepticism selectively suspended, the credibility and utility of the Bank's research is threatened. **❞**

(Banerjee *et al.* 2006: 53–6)

KEY POINTS

- Sustained increase in average income (economic growth) has been the global norm since the 1950s, but on a scale of millennia it is exceptional. Earlier populations were caught in the Malthusian trap.

- The dominant global economic policy paradigm since the 1980s—neo-liberal globalization—presumes that development is easy, provided governments do not grossly distort market signals, do not undermine incentives to work hard by providing tax-financed benefits, and do provide certain public goods, including enforcement of laws on competition and property rights. This 'exchange-focused' (not 'production-focused') proposition has underpinned the policy prescriptions of Western-dominated international organizations like the World Bank, IMF, and OECD.

- Neo-liberal globalization champions claim solid empirical support for their development theory and for the policy mandates of Western-based international organizations. When examined more closely the evidence looks ambiguous.

- One piece of counter evidence is the small number of non-Western countries that have become developed in the two centuries since the Industrial Revolution. The small number is consistent with the argument that the Washington Consensus policy agenda helps to perpetuate the core-periphery structure of the world economy, by making it difficult for developing countries to keep raising the proportion of economic activities in dynamic, increasing returns sectors.

- Globalization seen as the rising trend of cross-border exchange has gone through several phases. We are now in (and may be nearing the end of) the phase of 'China-centric production globalization', combined with a high level of financial globalization (as seen in the ratio of global financial transactions to global GDP of around 70).

World income and population distribution

In the end our interest is in the outcomes of the world economy for human well-being (and for the whole biosphere), which the globalization trends in quantities, prices, institutions, and rules help to determine. We can measure these outcomes in terms of income, consumption, health, education, accommodation, water, and sanitation, decent working conditions, social inclusion or exclusion, happiness, and more. Here we simplify and stick to income or consumption.

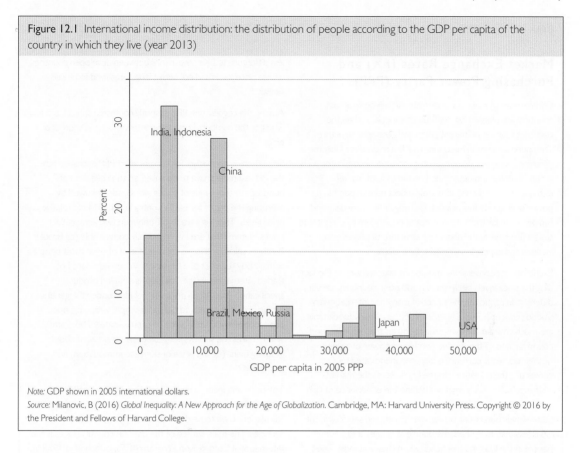

Figure 12.1 International income distribution: the distribution of people according to the GDP per capita of the country in which they live (year 2013)

Note: GDP shown in 2005 international dollars.

Source: Milanovic, B (2016) *Global Inequality: A New Approach for the Age of Globalization.* Cambridge, MA: Harvard University Press. Copyright © 2016 by the President and Fellows of Harvard College.

Today's world income distribution can be shown as the share of the world's population living in countries across the range of average incomes. See Figure 12.1, which measures income at **purchasing power parity** (**PPP**) exchange rates rather than market exchange rates (see Box 12.1). Notice the 'twin peaks' and the 'missing middle'. One peak contains 70 per cent of the world's population living in countries whose GDP per capita is below about PPP$13,000. (The present tense here refers to 2013.) The other peak is the 15 per cent who live in countries with GDP per capita above PPP$30,000—the rich world. Only a small percentage live in countries with average incomes between PPP$20,000 and PPP$30,000. Talk of the 'middle-income' countries can misleadingly suggest that they are 'midway' between the low- and the high-income countries. In fact, the middle-income countries fall towards the low end. And the distribution of world population by the income of individuals is much more skewed towards the tail than the distribution by countries' average income.

Using PPP incomes makes the world distribution look a lot less unequal than FX (market exchange rate) incomes. Economists tend to insist that the question, 'What is happening to world income distribution?' should be answered only with PPP incomes. Sociologists who work on these issues tend to use FX incomes. National governments, too, tend to be more interested in FX incomes than PPP incomes.

Economists are right to emphasize that FX-based income comparisons suffer from all the ways in which official exchange rates do not reflect the 'real' economy (see Box 12.1). In principle, PPP adjustments are better for comparing conditions of living, or material well-being, between countries.

But these are *not* the only questions for which we may be interested in income and its distribution. We may *also* be interested in income distribution as a proxy for the relative purchasing power of residents of different countries over goods and services produced in *other* countries. If we are interested in any of the questions about the impacts of one state, economy, or

BOX 12.1

Market Exchange Rates (FX) and Purchasing Power Parity (PPP)

Comparisons of real income or material well-being across countries are plagued with difficulties, especially when the countries have very different prices and economic structures. They need a common measuring rod. But measures of income in different countries—expressed in a common denominator such as the US dollar and determined on the basis of market exchange rates—do not accurately reflect relative purchasing power over goods and services. Exchange rates vary daily, and can be driven far from any concept of equilibrium by carry-trade capital flows, while the underlying structure of production, income, and expenditure remains fairly stable.

Exchange rate conversions also do not take account of the fact that the price levels between rich and poor countries are very different. In particular, the prices of many not internationally traded services (for example, haircuts), also many food staples, are much cheaper in developing countries than in developed countries, and so the relative purchasing power of a unit of their domestic currency is bigger than indicated by converting the currency into the US dollar at the market exchange rate. This is what lies behind the experience of rich people in India who feel poorer when they visit the United States (their purchasing power over goods and services in the US is less than over the same bundle at home), and poor people in the US who feel richer when they visit India. The market exchange rate is around 50 rupees for 1 dollar. The latest estimate is that around 20 rupees buys about the same amount of a 'typical consumption bundle' in India as $1 in the US. 'Purchasing power parity' (PPP) refers to an adjustment of the market exchange rate so as to give the amount of local currency needed to buy as much as one unit of the currency of the numeraire country, usually the US, in a benchmark year. In the India–US example, today's PPP exchange rate is 20:1, not 50:1, which translates into the statement that India's 'price level' is about 40 per cent of the US price level (20/50). In principle, the PPP adjustment allows real income comparisons, not only between the US and India today, but also—with heroic assumptions—between the US and India before the Industrial Revolution.

Because the price of many services and non-traded goods is lower in poor countries, the main effect of PPP adjustments to national income is to raise the income and consumption of poor countries relative to richer ones. For example, Turkey's average income at market exchange rates (FX dollars) was 10 per cent of the EU-15's in the early 2000s and 24 per cent in PPP dollars. Sub-Saharan Africa's was 2 per cent in FX dollars and 7 per cent in PPP dollars. The development problem looks less daunting when expressed in PPP dollars. The PPP adjustment makes much

less difference to FX comparisons between developed countries, whose price levels and economic structures tend to be fairly similar.

Among the cognoscenti PPP is a hotly contested subject, but few who use the numbers know the controversies and sources of error.

Since there is no market for currencies at PPP exchange rates, the PPP estimates have to be based on the collection of hundreds of thousands of prices worldwide, followed by averaging the prices for each country in order to get relative price levels. There is a trade-off between two aims: collect prices of items that are internationally comparable (eg Brooks Brothers shirt), and items representative of what most people actually buy (eg shirt of a labourer). When items are not traded internationally the 'solution' is detailed product specification (the Africa price list includes, under the generic category of 'fish', 'smoked bonga, in simple wrapping, open product presentation, a piece of approximately 200 grams'); which makes the surveys very expensive. And what about 'housing units' (eg the price of slum accommodation) and 'education'?

The price and income or consumption data are collected locally in line with a common set of procedures, but the core calculations have to be done centrally, not by national statistical agencies. The main source of the data on country prices is the International Comparison Program (ICP), launched in 1968 at the initiative of the UN Statistics Division and the Department of Economics at the University of Pennsylvania, financed by the World Bank and the Ford Foundation; hence the name of the series, the Penn World Tables (PWT). In 1975, Eurostat began to produce PPPs for EU countries as a way to determine more fairly financial contributions to the organization and to settle country disbursements. In 1980, the OECD expanded the work to cover all OECD countries, plus countries of Eastern and Central Europe. Around 1980, the UN Statistics Division took over the task of compiling global estimates and the work of coordinating the collection of international price data. But in the UN the price collection effort soon languished. The World Bank, which had provided technical and financial support to the UN during this time, took over responsibility for coordinating the global exercise in the early 1990s. In the mid 1990s, the World Bank (and the OECD) started to issue their own PPP numbers, using another method of aggregation (EKS) from the one used by PWT (Geary–Khamis). There are now two main series of global PPP data—PWT and the World Bank's. The series show some differences between countries' PPP-adjusted GDPs; and often more substantial differences in estimates of GDP components, such as private consumption, government

BOX 12.1 (continued)

consumption, and the like. The PWT numbers are more frequently used by academics than the World Bank's, in part because the PWT data provide more details on more countries for longer periods.

Dowrick and Akmal (2005) show that the PWT contains a systematic bias towards underestimating world income inequality, due to its use of a 'rich country' price structure to revalue GDP in poor countries (arising from the use of the Geary–Khamis formula that gives greater weight to those prices involved in the larger value of transactions). They urge that the term 'purchasing power parity' be used only in a generic way, with additional specification of whether the numbers come from the PWT or sources based on a different method of making the PPP adjustment.

In addition to the inherently difficult problems of item selection and index numbers, there are other daunting data problems. The price data are spotty in geographic and temporal coverage. The government of China did not allow a price survey in line with the ICP's criteria until 2005 (and then only in 11 cities); the government of India declined to carry one out between 1978 and 2005. For these and other important countries, the PPP numbers were obtained mostly by imputation from other countries or from updating old data. Even for sampled countries, the numbers are collected intermittently, not continuously, making statements of trends in PPP incomes across time problematic. Most of the results of the 1993–5 round of price surveys had still not been made available by the mid 2000s.

The spotty and out-of-date quality of the data reflects the institutional weakness of the ICP, which for much of its existence has hovered on the brink of collapse. While housed in the UN Statistics Division it received little support from senior officials and UN member states, on the grounds that it entailed a big additional burden on participating statistical bureaus and provided data of interest mainly to academics, not policymakers. Since the early 1990s, when the World Bank took it in, it has been carried forward by a few World Bank officials and consultants, who are plagued by shortages of funding and none too keen to let even senior Bank managers see their data computations (Korzeniewicz et al. 2004). They were not able to supervise seriously countries' data collection for the 1993–5 round, and the resulting non-comparability is part of the reason why they delayed releasing data for many years.

The 2005 ICP price survey was more comprehensive than the earlier ones (146 countries participated), and used more strictly specified goods and services so as to ensure international comparability. The results, published in 2008, were a bombshell: they entailed huge revisions of developing countries' GDPs (mostly downwards) and poverty headcounts (mostly upwards, raising the global headcount of those in extreme poverty by half a billion). For example, the World Bank estimated China's PPP GDP per capita in 2005 as $6,760, using the pre-2005 PPP exchange rate; it estimated the figure for the same year as $4,090, 40 per cent down, using the PPP exchange rate derived from the 2005 price survey. India's figure fell from $3,450 to $2,220. (At market exchange rates, the figures for China and India in 2005 are $1,720 and $800.) As Angus Deaton and Alan Heston remark, 'it is hard not to speculate about which previously established econometric results survive the incorporation of these revisions' (Deaton and Heston 2009). They also stress the wide margins of uncertainty around PPP estimates: in the case of the US–China PPP exchange rate, a margin of around 25 per cent on either side.

In 2014 came the results of the 2011 IPC calculations of PPP exchange rates. Another bombshell, but mostly in the opposite direction: most developing countries got large boosts to their PPP GDPs for 2010 compared to the extrapolations for 2010 from the IPC 2005 PPP exchange rates (so China greatly reduced its GDP gap with the US and India got a bigger GDP than Japan). Global inequality between countries now looks to be a lot lower than extrapolation from the 2005 PPP exchange rates would suggest. And one estimate suggests that the 2011 PPPs cut the global poverty rate in 2011 almost by half, compared to the rate extrapolated for 2011 using the 2005 PPPs.

After a detailed technical examination of why the 2011 results are so different from what was expected, Deaton and Bettina Aten conclude, 'our findings suggest that the ICP 2011 estimates are the most accurate we have, and provide no grounds for doubting them ... The revisions that need to be undertaken are to long-standing previous estimates, a process that is likely to be less than straightforward' (2015). On the other hand, Martin Ravallion, who has inside knowledge from being in charge of the World Bank's poverty statistics for many years, finds plenty of grounds for doubting that the 2011 results are superior to the 2005 ones (and extrapolations from 2005 results). He considers that 'the 2011 ICP remains something of a mystery', and concludes more generally that 'the results of this study point to the limitations of PPPs for international comparisons' (2014: 18–19).

The bottom line is that confidence in trends in PPP incomes, inequality, and poverty should be limited by the certainty of wide margins of error in comparisons between rich and poorer countries, however uncomfortable that may be for those who feed them into the econometrics compactor. Good sources for understanding PPPs are Deaton (2010, 2013) and Deaton and Aten (2015).

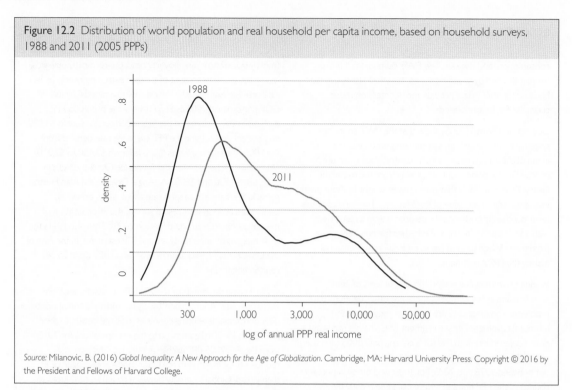

Figure 12.2 Distribution of world population and real household per capita income, based on household surveys, 1988 and 2011 (2005 PPPs)

Source: Milanovic, B. (2016) *Global Inequality: A New Approach for the Age of Globalization*. Cambridge, MA: Harvard University Press. Copyright © 2016 by the President and Fellows of Harvard College.

region on others—including the capacity of developing countries to import, repay their debts, participate in international organizations, and the incentive for people in one country to migrate to another country—we should use incomes compared at market exchange rates lagged over a period of a year or more. FX incomes are a better proxy for relative power and influence, a subject of more interest to sociologists and political scientists than economists.

For example, one reason why many poor small countries are hardly represented in multilateral negotiations that concern them directly is that they cannot afford the cost of hotels, offices, salaries, and consultants in places like Washington, DC, New York, and Geneva, which they must pay for not in PPP dollars but in hard currency bought with their own currency at market exchange rates. Similarly, this is why they cannot afford to pay the foreign exchange costs of living up to many of their international commitments—hiring foreign experts to help them exercise control over their banking sectors so that they can implement their part of the anti-money-laundering regime, for example. International organizations like the World Bank and the IMF allocate voting shares in large part on the basis of relative GDPs, calculated by a formula which gives

more weight to GDPs at market exchange rates than at PPP exchange rates—because by market exchange rates the developed countries are relatively much richer (and get higher voting shares) than they are by PPP exchange rates (Vestergaard and Wade 2013).

Figure 12.2 shows the changes in the distribution of world population by average household income between 1988 and 2011, based on household surveys and 2005 PPPs. The whole distribution shifts to the right, reflecting global economic growth. The shift is pronounced at the poorer end, reflecting a steep fall in the share of world population living on less than, say, $400 a year. The other pronounced shift is the large increase in the share of world population between $1,000 and $10,000 per year, mostly living in China and India. This is often referred to as the growth of the global 'middle class', though no sociologist would describe an income category with fairly arbitrary thresholds as a 'class'. Notice too that the distribution moves from bimodal to unimodal.

We can now look at some of the biggest countries—biggest by population or by share of world GDP (at market exchange rates). See Table 12.2. The disproportion between population shares and GDP shares is striking, and raises again the Adam Smith

Table 12.2 Major economies, share of world population and GDP (%)

	Population 2010	GDP 1980 (FX)	GDP 1980 (PPP)	GDP 2010 (FX)	GDP 2010 (PPP)
USA	4.5	25.7	25.0	22.8	18.2
China	19.3	1.7	6.3	9.2	15.3
Japan	1.8	9.7	8.7	8.4	5.4
Germany	1.2	8.5	6.0	5.2	3.9
France	0.9	6.3	4.9	4.0	2.8
UK	0.9	5.1	4.2	3.7	2.8
Brazil	2.9	2.1	2.6	3.4	2.6
India	17.8	1.7	3.2	2.6	6.1
Russia	2.1	—	—	2.3	3.4
South Africa	0.7	0.7	1.1	0.6	0.7

Source: WDI, Penn World Tables, 8.1. PPP 2005 US$.

question of how the relatively small population of the developed countries got to have such a big slice of world GDP. Other striking points include China's gain in GDP share to make it by 2010 the second biggest economy; India's small share relative to its population and its small gain in GDP share over the past 30 years; and the US's smallish fall in GDP share over the same period, leaving it still the biggest economy by far at market exchange rates.

Growth and geographical distribution

The globalization argument implies that the period since 1980 should have experienced an increase in global economic growth, thanks to the global policy shift towards market-friendly policies and the rise in economic and financial integration between countries. With more integration, ideas, institutions, and goods and services speed faster from societies at the top to those lower down.

In fact, the growth rate of world GDP per capita fell by a third between 1955–80 and 1980–2007, from an average of about 2.2 per cent to 1.7 per cent. Indeed, a majority of the world's countries (56 per cent) experienced negative growth of GDP per person in

1980–2000; though not, of course, a majority of the world's population.

The rich world (24 countries of the 'old' OECD) has slowed almost every decade since the 1960s: from 4 per cent in 1960s, 2.5 per cent in 1970s, 2.2 per cent in the 1980s and 1990s, and less than 1 per cent in the 2000s to 2010. The fall since 1990 is especially telling, because, by this time, the 1980s policies of squeezing inflation, deregulating, privatizing, liberalizing trade and capital movements had worked themselves through into macroeconomic stabilization and free markets; yet the promised upturn in economic growth did not appear. The slowdown since the 1990s partly reflects demographic change, as the post-war baby boomers—the largest and wealthiest generation in history—moved beyond raising children and joined the low-spending 'new old' generation.

World output in 2003 to 2007 grew much faster than during the previous quarter century, at close to 4 per cent a year. Commentators celebrated the 'rise of the South', 'global rebalancing', and the West's 'Great Moderation', the latter meaning modest growth rates with low inflation and high employment. The Crash of 2008 caused a contraction of global output in 2009 of minus 2 per cent, recovering to plus 2.4 per cent in 2012–14. Even the most Pollyannaish pundits before 2008 now recognize that the fast growth and high corporate profits in the earlier part of the decade were based on unsustainable debt on the balance sheets of households and/or governments, especially in the US, Britain, and southern Europe. The Roman playwright, Plautus, got the mechanism 2,300 years ago, when he had one of his characters declare, 'I am a rich man, as long as I do not repay my creditors'. The high global growth rates of 2003 to 2007 are unlikely to be regained any time soon, unless again based on debt—or a baby boom.

The world growth trend hides large variations between regions and classes. Sub-Saharan Africa, with almost 1 billion people, had an average income in the mid 2000s barely above the level of 1980, despite most states having implemented Washington–Brussels Consensus **structural adjustment programmes** for many years. Latin America, with 550 million people, experienced much the same stagnation at a higher income level. The countries of the former Soviet Union, after more than 20 years of transition to capitalism, remain at about the same average income as when the transition started. On the other hand, the North (western Europe and North America) grew faster than these other regions until the early 2000s. China from the 1980s and India from the 1990s grew fast from a very low base, slowing after 2012. India's fast growth reduced the ratio of the average income of the US over South Asia's (constant 2005 $) from 87 in 1980 to 41 in 2014—the fall is large but the gap remains huge. The US to Latin America ratio went from 6 to 7.6 in the same period.

The fact is that, after decades of self-conscious development and market liberalization, the average income for the South is still only around 15 per cent of that of the North (constant 2005 US$). And growth in the South is more erratic than in a typical developed country, with periods of relatively fast growth followed by deeper and longer recessions (Reddy and Minoiu 2009; Pritchett and Summers, 2014). This volatility helps to explain why few developing countries have sustained growth at 6 per cent a year or more for more than 15 years. China holds the world record for number of years of continuous growth at 6 per cent or more: around 40 years (by 2015), followed by Taiwan (32 years) and South Korea (29 years). Brazil languished in the 'lower middle income' range for the last 53 years between 1950 and 2010.

Taking all countries, the spread of average incomes did not fall between 1960 and 2010; in fact, the ratio of the average income of the richest 10 countries over that of the poorest 10 increased from around 33 in 1960 to almost 120 in 2010 (1990 international dollars), contrary

to what a simple version of neo-liberalism might lead one to expect. On the other hand, weighting countries by population, we can say that a large proportion of the world's developing country population experienced fast growth in the two decades up to 2010, thanks to the 38 per cent of the world's population in China and India.

Of the increase in world income or consumption over the 1990s and 2000s, a majority accrued to those already in the top 10 per cent of world income distribution. The absolute income gains of those at the top end in Figure 12.2—four-fifths of whom live in the high-income countries—are much larger than the absolute gains of the so-called 'middle class', most of whom live in China and India.

Evidence of this kind questions the idea of 'the (income) rise of the South'. 'The rise of the South' is mainly 'rise of the East', or, better, 'rise of Asia', and the latter is mainly 'rise of China', with India coming along some way behind. However, China and India, now have big enough GDPs to shift the 'centre of gravity of the world economy' from mid North Atlantic in 1980, around the longitude of Iceland and the latitude of Austin, Texas, Tel Aviv, and Shanghai, eastwards and north to western Turkey (Quah 2011). The smallest circle of territory now containing a majority of the world's population is 3,300 km in radius centred in Myanmar on China's western border (Quah 2015). If global organizations were governed by a 'one person one vote' rule, global power would move towards this circle.

Income inequality between countries

In the past decade trends in world income distribution have become a hot topic of debate in international economics and in sociology (hotter than world poverty). Disagreement about the trends should be no surprise, given the collage of economic performance by region. Different measures emphasize different parts of the collage.

Much of the debate is mathematical, far removed from people's experience of inequality, and focuses less on the 'facts' than on the measures. It turns out that the only valid short answer to the question, 'What is the trend of world income distribution?' is, 'It depends on which of several plausible measures and samples we choose'. Whereas we could get better data on the poor to the extent that the poverty headcount would command general agreement, there is no best measure of world income inequality. Different measures are useful for answering different questions.

The results vary according to which of three core measures of inequality we use: Concept 1: inter- or between-country, using average incomes (this could be called the UN General Assembly measure, one country one vote); Concept 2: inter-country, like Concept 1, but countries weighted by population; and Concept 3: global interpersonal, covering all the world's people as though the world was one country (Milanovic 2006).

Several other choices also affect the results. Incomes may be converted into a common numeraire using market exchange rates or PPP conversion factors. PPP numbers may be drawn from the PWT, or from the World Bank's World Development Indicators, or from Angus Maddison, or still other sources (see Box 12.1). Country sample and time period also matter.

The results also depend on the choice of statistic for calculating dispersion—an integral measure over the whole distribution (such as the **Gini coefficient** or the Theil Inequality Coefficient—see Box 12.2), or a ratio of top decile to bottom four deciles, or average income of a region relative to that of the North or the USA.

BOX 12.2

The Gini Coefficient

How do we know whether one society is more unequal than another? We should measure the distribution of property (including financial assets), which is far more unequally distributed than income. But wealth distribution data are even worse than income distribution data (a sizable fraction of world financial wealth is hidden, at least 13 per cent), so the degree of inequality is normally measured with income or consumption. We should remember that to focus on income rather than property gravely underestimates the extent of inequality.

The workhorse measure of income inequality is the Gini coefficient, a number between zero and one that measures the degree of inequality in the distribution of income in a given society (named after an Italian statistician, Corrado Gini). The coefficient is zero for a society in which each member receives exactly the same income; it reaches its maximum value (bounded from above by 1.0) for a society in which one member receives all the income and the rest nothing.

As normally defined the Gini says that inequality remains constant—growth remains as 'inclusive' as before—if all individuals (or countries by average income) experience the same *rate* of growth, and rises when upper incomes grow faster than lower incomes. So inequality remains constant if a two-person (or two-country) distribution x = (10, 40) becomes y = (20, 80). Yet the income gap has doubled from 30 to 60.

It is at least as plausible to say that inequality remains constant when all individuals (countries) experience the same *absolute* addition to their income; say from x = (10, 40) to y* = (20, 50). If upper income individuals (countries) experience bigger absolute additions, inequality *increases*, growth is less inclusive, which has political implications.

The normal Gini could be called the Relative Gini. The Gini based on absolute changes could be called the Absolute Gini— defined as the Relative Gini multiplied by the mean income. In the above illustration, the Relative Gini for both distributions is the same, at 0.3. But as mean income doubles from 25 to 50 in the transition from x to y, the Absolute Gini doubles, from 7.5 to 15.0. Growth is not 'inclusive'.

The Absolute Gini typically rises much more frequently and by much more than the Relative Gini, and its use could make 'income inequality' into a more salient political issue. The Relative Gini could be called a 'rightist' measure, and the Absolute Gini a 'leftist' measure (Kolm 1976a, 1976b).

Economists' long-standing nonchalance about income inequality is reflected in the rarity of the use of the Absolute Gini. Its unpopularity also reflects the fact that cross-country comparisons of the Absolute Gini are more complicated than for the Relative Gini, because the former depends on the mean of each distribution. This requires that we convert incomes into the same currency (e.g. to compare absolute inequality in India with that in the US we have to convert the two means and income distributions into either rupees or dollars). And to perform comparisons across time we also need to correct for inflation. The choice of appropriate exchange rates and price deflators becomes crucial for making reliable comparisons of absolute inequality. These inconveniences have often been held up as justification for sticking with relative measures of inequality. But as Kolm explains, 'these problems are exactly the same ones which are traditionally encountered in the comparisons of national or per capita incomes ... and they can be given the same traditional solutions. Anyway, convenience could not be an alibi for endorsing injustice' (1976a: 419–20). The bottom line is—all these technical complexities aside—that students of inequality should not ignore trends in absolute income gaps when making inequality comparisons, as most of the literature does, including this text. For more information on measuring inequality, see the World Income Inequality Database page (at http://www.wider. unu.edu/research/Database). Thanks to S. Subramanian, Madras Institute of Development Studies, for help on the Absolute Gini.

Concept 1 inequality: distribution between unweighted countries

Concept 1 gives China the same weight as Uganda. It has the advantage that it requires little information about each country: just per capita GDP or GNP. Of course, we should not weight countries equally if interested in relative well-being of people. But we should weight them equally—treat each country as a laboratory test observation—if interested in convergence or divergence of countries rather than people. We might want to test the effects of different government policies on growth—to see whether (unweighted) countries with more open trade regimes grow faster than those with less open ones, for example.

Whatever our motivating question, the trend of Concept 1 inequality is clear (using PPP incomes): the Gini for unweighted inter-country income distribution held fairly steady from 1960 to 1980, increased steeply from 1980 to 2000, and fell from 2000 to 2007, leaving a large net increase in inequality since 1980 (see Figure 12.3). Is the increase in inequality due only to the collapse of Africa? No. With Africa excluded, the Gini fell from the mid 1960s to the early 1980s, and then increased steeply.

Concept 2 inequality: distribution between weighted countries

Inter-country income inequality, using PPP/PWT dollars, population weights, and the Gini coefficient, was fairly stable from 1960 to the early 1990s, and then fell right up to 2007. This is the good news: it suggests that the centuries-old trend to income divergence between countries has finally gone into reverse.

But here the global Gini conceals as much as it reveals. If we take out just one case, China, the population-weighted inter-country Gini *rises* after 1980 up to 2000, when it, too, begins to turn down; so it goes mostly in the *opposite* direction to the trend with China included. So even with the combination of measures most favourable to the neo-liberal case, falling income inequality between countries is a function of China's fast growth since the early 1980s, not a *widespread* trend of the world economy as the happy result of widespread globalization.

The other bad news is that the result also depends on the use of the Penn World Tables method of calculating PPPs. As noted (see Box 12.1), Dowrick and Akmal (2005) show that the PWT method systematically understates the magnitude of inequality and overstates its fall. The bias comes through the use of

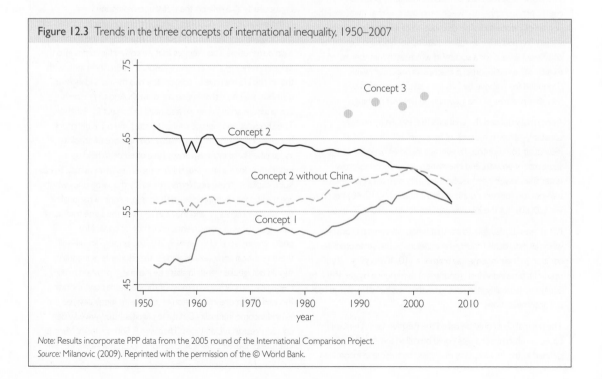

Figure 12.3 Trends in the three concepts of international inequality, 1950–2007

Note: Results incorporate PPP data from the 2005 round of the International Comparison Project.

Source: Milanovic (2009). Reprinted with the permission of the © World Bank.

an average international price structure for revaluing countries' GDPs which results from weighting countries' observed price structures by the relative *global* expenditure at those prices; which means that the average international price structure reflects the price structures of *rich* countries—and so values services (e.g. domestic services, haircuts) much more highly in poor countries, inflating the purchasing power of poor countries' currencies. (This is known as the Geary–Khamis method of aggregation.) When this bias is removed (for example, by switching from Geary–Khamis to the Afriat method), Dowrick and Akmal find that 'true [sic] inequality was stable or increasing slightly … over the 1980s and 90s' (2005: 226). More exactly, three out of their four measures of inequality applied to Afriat-aggregated data show an increase, one shows constancy, *none shows decline*—even when China is included.

That switching from Geary–Khamis to Afriat PPPs reverses the trend towards falling inequality underlines the fragility of the conclusion that world income inequality fell since the 1980s or 1990s. Indeed, a further bias towards rich country prices—hence toward exaggerating poor countries' convergence with rich countries—comes from the self-selection of the countries which participate in the (statistically difficult) ICP. The participating countries tend to be the statistically more advanced, able to handle the complexities; which also tend to be the richer countries. China's and India's non-participation, noted earlier, is part of a wider selection bias.

In any case, this Concept 2 measure—average country incomes weighted by population—is interesting only as an approximation to income distribution among all the world's people or households, regardless of which country they live in. We would not be interested in measuring income inequality in the United States by calculating the average income for each state weighted by its population if we had data for all US households.

Concept 3 inequality: global interpersonal income distribution

Interpersonal or global income inequality could be measured by taking each population-weighted country's average GDP, weighting it by internal income distribution, and calculating the combined between-country and within-country inequalities across the whole sample.

As noted, population-weighted between-country distribution became more equal after the early 1990s with China included and more unequal with China excluded. Within-country distributions have generally become more unequal. A large majority of the world's population lives in countries where income disparities are higher than they were a generation ago.

Trends in industrial wage inequality within countries confirm the broad trend. Wage data has the advantage over income data that pay is a much less ambiguous variable. Also, it has been collected systematically by the United Nations since the early 1960s, and gives many more observation points for each country than any income data set. It is a useful way to get at the impacts of changes in trade policy and trade flows, or of manufacturing innovation, and the like. The disadvantage of pay data is that it treats only a small part of the economy of many developing countries, and provides only a proxy for incomes and expenditure. This is not as limiting as it may seem, because what is happening to pay rates in formal-sector activity reflects larger trends, including income differences between countries and income differences within countries (since the pay of unskilled, entry-port jobs in the formal sector is closely related to the opportunity cost of time in the informal or agricultural sectors).

Pay inequality within a large sample of rich and poor countries was stable from the early 1960s to the early 1970s, then declined till about 1980, then increased from 1980 to the early 2000s, after which it fell to 2008, generally not by much. The countries within continents tend to show closely correlated movements in pay dispersions, suggesting *macro* forces at work (which receive little recognition in studies of causes of inequality trends). James K. Galbraith and associates present analyses of pay dispersions at http://utip.gov.utexas.edu

Countries tend to form high-income and low-income inequality clusters. Most developed countries are in the low-inequality cluster (Gini coefficients for disposable income in the range from 0.20 to 0.35, as of the mid 2000s), and most developing countries are in the high-inequality cluster (0.50 to 0.65). At the low end, Scandinavia's Gini for disposable income was around 0.23–25 in the mid 2000s (down from around 0.42 before taxes and transfers, indicating the redistributive power of the state). The UK's and US's Ginis before taxes and transfers were around 0.45 and 0.49 in the mid 2000s, and 0.33 and 0.38 for disposable income. Japan's Ginis (pre and post) were around 0.44 and 0.32.

China's Gini was around 0.48 in the mid 2000s (the figures for pre- and post-taxes and transfers are not much different). But the China Household Finance Survey, from Southwestern University of Finance and Economics, Chengdu, finds China's real Gini to be about 0.6, the higher figure reflecting determined effort by the surveyors to get information about the richest households. So on the face of it China, ruled by the Chinese Community Party since 1949, has become one of the most unequal countries in the world. But one cannot compare the new figure for China with other countries, because a similarly determined effort in other countries—India and the US, for example—would also yield big increases in their Gini.

Changes in within-country distribution tend to be small relative to the two big Gini clusters, and membership of the clusters shows considerable stability through the second half of the twentieth century. Contrary to what one might expect from the Kuznets inverted U hypothesis (inequality rises in the early stages of development, flattens out, and then falls as rural–urban differentials fall and now better educated citizens demand redistribution), there has been little movement from the high-inequality to the low-inequality cluster as countries become richer. On the other hand, the US—with its history as a hybrid plantation-industrial-financial economy—has been rising out of the low-inequality cluster and by 2000 was well into the zone between the low-inequality and the high-inequality clusters (Korzeniewicz and Moran 2009). Rising income inequality in the US is reflected in the sharp rise in the ultimate inequality—how long you live. Low income middle age men in 1970 had average life expectancy five years less than same age high income men; by 2015 the gap had risen to almost 15 years.

Another way to get at global interpersonal income distribution is to aggregate up from thousands of surveys of household income and expenditure. Branko Milanovic used the resources of the World Bank to do this for five-yearly intervals from 1988. He found a substantial increase in interpersonal income inequality between 1988 and 1993, a smaller fall to 1998, and another increase to 2003, making a large increase in global inequality between 1988 and 2003, followed by a fall to 2008. Of course, this method has its problems. It undercounts free public services such as education, health, and infrastructure that add to welfare but are not counted in household consumption. And there are big problems of comparability between household surveys.

As for the results of the PPP revisions based on the 2005 price data, Milanovic calculates that, compared to estimates based on the earlier price data, they raise the Gini coefficient of global interpersonal income inequality—for the same recent year—from about 0.65 to 0.70 (using only household surveys); a big increase.

The conclusion is that global interpersonal PPP income or consumption distribution (using the Gini coefficient) has probably *not* become significantly more equal since 1980, contrary to neo-liberal assertions. On the other hand, developing countries may have grown sufficiently faster than developed countries during 2003 to 2012 to reduce interpersonal income inequality in this period. The margins of uncertainty are large.

Polarization or relative gap measures

The Gini coefficient is a measure of dispersion across the whole of the distribution. It can mislead by obscuring what is happening to major components and by giving more weight to what is happening in the middle than at the extremes. Simple 'gap' or 'polarization' measures can compensate.

Most such measures show the income caravan to be lengthening. For example, with countries grouped into deciles by their PPP GDP per capita, the ratio between top and bottom deciles almost doubled during the 1960–2000 period, from 19 to 1 to 37 to 1 (Milanovic 2005: 53). Polarization would be even more dramatic if we took the remuneration of the top 1 per cent of the world's population over the median or the average of the bottom 10 per cent's.

Within countries, a simple measure is the share of disposable income accruing to the top 5 per cent. It increased in most OECD countries between the 1980s and 2010. For example, in the US the share of disposable income accruing to the top 5 per cent went from 15 per cent to 19 per cent; in the UK, from 13 per cent to 18 per cent; Australia, 14 per cent to 17 per cent; Germany, 13 per cent to 15 per cent, Sweden, 10 per cent to 13 per cent. The other side is compression of the disposable income share of the population living between 25 per cent and 75 per cent of the national median. For example, in the US, from 32 per cent to 27 per cent; in the UK, from 40 per cent to 33 per cent (Milanovic 2016: ch. IV). This is often described as the squeezing of the middle class, fuelling mass discontent and providing opportunities for populist and/or authoritarian political leaders (see also Palma 2009).

The absolute income gap

Standard measures of inequality refer to relative incomes, not absolute incomes. Box 12.2 set out some reasons why they can be misleading. To extend that discussion, take two countries: A, with a per capita income of $30,000 (e.g. US, Denmark); and, B, with a per capita income of $1,000 (Philippines, pre-war Syria). Their relative income is 30:1 and the absolute gap is $29,000. If A's per capita income increases by 1 per cent to $30,300 and B's also increases by 1 per cent to $1,010, the relative gap remains constant and so 'inequality' as normally defined remains constant; but the absolute gap widens from $29,000 to $29,290. If B jumped to 6 per cent growth while A continued at 1 per cent the absolute gap would widen until year 35 and B would not catch up until year 70. If B grew at 4 per cent and A grew at 2 per cent, the absolute gap would widen for 140 years and catch-up would take the best part of two centuries.

No one questions that world absolute income gaps have been increasing fast—as between, for example, the average income of the top 10 per cent of world income recipients (countries and individuals) and that of the bottom 10 per cent, between the top 10 per cent and the intermediate 60 per cent, and between average incomes in North America and Europe and those in all developing country regions. If, as some evidence suggests, people commonly think about inequality in absolute rather than relative terms—those at the lower end feel more resentful and more inclined to migrate as absolute gaps increase even as relative incomes become more equal—our answer to the question, 'What is happening to income inequality?' should not be blind to absolute gaps.

KEY POINTS

- World life expectancy at birth rose from 47.7 years in 1950–5 to 66.4 years in 2000–5. To what extent the increase was caused by increased income is controversial.

- The average income for the South, with about 85 per cent of world population, is still around 15 per cent of that of the North (constant 2005 US$), after decades of proactive development (http://data.worldbank.org/indicator/NY.GDP.PCAP.KD).

- Incomes should be calculated at PPP-adjusted exchange rates when comparing relative welfare (with acknowledgement of large margins of uncertainty), and at lagged market exchange rates at constant prices when comparing relative ability to participate in cross-border transactions (import, borrow, rent offices in New York and Geneva, hire consultants, and lawyers, etc.)

- The US, with 4.5 per cent of world population (2010), has 22.8 per cent of world FX GDP, by far the biggest share. China, with 19.3 per cent of world population, has 9.2 per cent of world FX GDP (2010), the second biggest share.

- The average income of the richest ten countries relative to that of the poorest ten soared from 33 in 1960 to almost 120 in 2010.

- From around 1980 to the early 2000s, in the post-Bretton Woods economic regime, there was a widespread growth slowdown as globalization intensified from trade globalization to production globalization, as compared with the previous two to three decades. For the OECD countries, output per capita grew more slowly in the period 1990–2010 than in previous decades back to 1960, despite macroeconomic stability and liberal markets.

- Growth rates since 1980 varied substantially between regions. African countries performed poorly; also, from a higher starting point, many Latin American and central and East European countries. In contrast, East Asia's growth rates were the highest in the world.

- A World Bank study found that of the 101 middle-income countries in 1960, only 13 had reached the high-income threshold by 2010. Evidence of this kind underlines the difficulties of economic development, and the reality of a 'middle-income' or 'middle-capabilities' or 'non-convergence' trap or 'glass ceiling'.

- The major determinant of income inequality on a world scale is the choice of measures. The income measure matters most: whether incomes are converted at market exchange rates or PPP exchange rates. The distribution measure is the second most important determinant: whether the Relative Gini, Absolute Gini, or polarization measures.

- Most measures of inequality of average country incomes suggest a significant increase between around 1980 and 2000. Global interpersonal income distribution, as measured by the Relative Gini, increased between 1988 and 2003. Both measures fell over the 2000s, probably for the first time since the Industrial Revolution.

- Most of the absolute increase in world income or consumption between the early 1990s and today accrued to individuals at the upper end of world income distribution, the large majority of whom live in the high-income countries. Only a tiny proportion of the increase accrued to those at the lower end. This is the 'Matthew Effect' on a world scale. Matthew's Gospel says, 'For unto everyone that hath shall be given, and he shall have abundance.'

- The present absolute income gaps in the world economy are so large that they will go on increasing for another half-century at the least, even if developing countries grow significantly faster than developed countries. Many of the negative effects of rising inequality (operating through a sense of stress-deprivation-grievance, for example) probably hold when absolute gaps are widening, even when relative gaps are falling.

- Countries tend to fall into two clusters by internal income inequality: low- and middle-income countries in the high cluster, high-income countries in the low cluster. There is not much evidence of developing countries crossing from the high to the low cluster, contrary to the expectations of the Kuznets inverted U theory of income distribution. The US is transitioning from low to high.

- Trends in income distribution between regions, classes, and individuals or households suggest that the period since 1980 might be called 'the second age of (vertical) inequality', the first one being the period for several decades before 1929.

- The trends in favour of the high-income countries and people may have changed direction in the nearly decade-long period since the early 2000s when low- and middle-income countries grew much faster than high-income countries. But the growth acceleration in the South in 2003–12 was substantially fuelled by unsustainable credit growth in the US and parts of western Europe; and has turned into growth deceleration since 2012.

Poverty

Poverty has attracted more attention from the 'international community' than inequality, as in the World Bank's motto, 'Our dream [now upgraded, under President Jim Kim, to 'plan'] is a world free of poverty', and the United Nations' Millennium Development Goal number one, to halve, by 2015, the proportion of developing countries' population living in 1990 on an income of less than the equivalent of US$1.25 per day. Acting to reduce poverty is sanctioned by all religions and boosts our sense of 'doing good in the world', while acting to reduce inequality inevitably raises questions about the appropriateness of the income of those who voice their concern, and sounds ominously 'political' to international organizations which claim to be 'apolitical'.

The standard way to measure poverty is to use an income or consumption measure, and for the sake of simplicity we stick to this convention here. Counting the number of people living below an income poverty line gives us a measure of the incidence (not severity)

of poverty, and we can measure trends in global poverty by summing the number of people living below a standard international poverty line and tracing the number across time. But we should keep in mind that poverty is about deprivation of basic capabilities, and deprivation is multidimensional, including income, hunger, disease, lack of shelter, lack of water and sanitation, and social exclusion. We should also keep in mind that to observe poverty only through numbers is to miss the tragedy of truncated lives, which would be your and my tragedy if we had the bad luck to be born into the lower deciles of countries where 85 per cent of the world's population lives.

The World Bank is the main source of the poverty numbers. To get the world extreme poverty headcount, the World Bank first defines an international extreme poverty line (IEPL) which (1) reflects the conditions of absolute poverty in the world's poorest economies, and (2) corresponds to the same real level of well-being in all countries. Hence it takes the national poverty lines of a set of very poor countries, uses PPP exchange rates to convert the lines into US dollars, calculates the average, and converts the average back into countries' currencies to get their IEPL in national currency. All countries' IEPLs should have the same notional purchasing power as the dollar line in the United States in the benchmark year; and probably differs from their own national poverty line.

In the Bank's first global poverty estimation (1991), this procedure yielded a conveniently understandable PPP$1 a day for the base year of 1985. Each subsequent round of ICP calculations of PPP exchange rates have required this figure to be updated. The 1993–5 round resulted in the line being raised to $1.08; the 2005 PPPs generated $1.25; and now the 2011 PPPs have generated $1.90. From household surveys, the Bank estimates the number of people in the country living on less than the IEPL in the base year. It sums up the country totals to get the world total of people living in extreme poverty. It then uses national consumer price indices to keep real purchasing power constant across time, and adjusts the IEPL for each country upwards with inflation. As well as the extreme poverty headcount (people living on less than PPP$1 a day, updated) the Bank also estimates the ordinary poverty headcount (people living on less than PPP$2 a day, updated). In 2008, the World Bank presented revised estimates of countries' GDPs and world poverty headcounts, based on the international price survey of 2005. Table 12.3 summarizes the numbers before and

Table 12.3 Key world poverty numbers

	1981		2002		2005	
	No. (bn)	%	No. (bn)	%	No. (bn)	%
Old estimate @ $1.08	1.5	41	1.1	20	0.9	17
New estimate @ $1.25	1.9	52	1.6	31	1.4	25
New estimate @ $2.50	2.7	75	3.3	62	3.1	57
Excluding China						
Old estimate @ $1.08	0.9	32	0.9	23	0.9	22
New estimate @ $1.25	1.1	40	1.2	31	1.2	28
New estimate @ $2.50	1.8	66	2.6	66	2.6	63

Note: Percentage refers to population of the developing world. 'Old' refers to PPP conversion using pre-2005 price data.
Sources: Chen and Ravallion (2008, 2010). See also © World Bank PovcalNet (http://iresearch.worldbank.org/PovcalNet/index.htm?1).

after the revised estimates, with and without China. The size of the revisions suggests the frailty of the poverty numbers.

The numbers living in extreme poverty show a pronounced fall between 1981 and 2005, with both the pre-2005 PPP exchange rates and the ones based on the 2005 price survey. This is good news, indicating substantial progress in cutting the number of people living in extreme poverty. The bad news is that, according to the new estimates, hundreds of millions more people have been living in extreme poverty than earlier estimated, so the extreme poverty problem was and remains much worse than had been thought. As the World Bank's 'poverty czars' summarize, 'While the new data suggest that the developing world is poorer than we thought, it has been no less successful in reducing the incidence of absolute poverty since the early 1980s' (Chen and Ravallion 2008: 33)

More bad news is that the fall in the number under $1.25 a day is due entirely to China. Take out China and the number in extreme poverty increased (though the proportion of the developing world population still fell from 40 per cent to 28 per cent). Still more bad news is the sheer number of people living on less than the scarcely generous PPP$2.50 a day, almost 3 billion by 2010, more than 40 per cent of the world's population. Moreover, the number of people living below this threshold increased substantially between 1981 and 2005, which implies a big bunching between $1.25

and $2.50 a day. People in this income band remain very vulnerable to shocks such as the steep rise in food and fuel prices after 2005, and the economic crisis of 2008.

Still more complications to our understanding of world poverty come from the radical differences between extrapolations forward from the IPC 2005 PPPs and the IPC 2011 PPP results (Box 12.1). The latter give the number of Indians living below the World Bank's extreme poverty line of $1.25 per day as about 300 million *less* than the figure extrapolated from the 2005 PPPs; and the number of extremely poor people in the world as *less than half* the figure estimated by extrapolation from 2005. As noted in Box 12.1, Martin Ravallion, who probably knows more about global poverty statistics than anyone else, considers the 2005 PPPs to be more reliable than the 2011 ones. We are left, again, with the feeling of being on quicksand.

The geographical distribution of extreme poverty has changed. Of the total number of people in 1990 living on less than the PPP$1.25 line (1.8 billion), 48 per cent lived in East Asia and Pacific, 32 per cent in South Asia, and 16 per cent in sub-Saharan Africa. Of the total in 2005 (1.4 billion) the corresponding figures were 23 per cent, 43 per cent and 28 per cent. So world poverty became more 'Southasianized' and 'Africanized'. In terms of the share of total population living in extreme poverty, in 1990, sub-Saharan Africa had 58 per cent, East Asia and Pacific, 55 per cent, South Asia, 52 per cent. By 2005 the corresponding figures were 51 per cent, 17 per cent, and 40 per cent.

These numbers are based on the 2005 PPPs. Recall that the 2011 PPPs give a more upbeat picture for the same years, with a lower level of extreme poverty and a strong downward trend. But whichever source we use, we should not take the Bank's poverty numbers at face value.

Large margin of error

Several reasons suggest that the margin of error is significant. First, the poverty headcount is sensitive to the precise level of the international poverty lines. Figure 12.2 shows that the population–income curve is steep at low levels of income (including at the $1-a-day line), meaning that small shifts in the line make large changes in the number of people below it.

Second, the poverty headcount is sensitive to the reliability of household surveys. Some countries survey income, others, expenditure, others, consumption, and merging the results is not straightforward. The available surveys are of widely varying quality, different countries use different formats and the same country may change the format from one survey to another. For example, surveys may use different reporting periods. A study in India in the late 1990s found that switching from the standard 30-day reporting period (asking people their expenditure over the previous 30 days) to a seven-day period cut the number of poor by half, because the shorter recall period yielded more reported income or expenditure. But a later study found a much smaller effect.

Third, by far the two most important countries for the overall trend, China and India, have PPP-adjusted income figures that contain even more guesswork than for most other big countries. The government of China declined to participate in all the rounds of the ICP until 2005 (see Box 12.1), so the PPP estimations for China have been based on econometric regressions rather than real data; and those for India have been based on extrapolations from the 1978 price survey plus other adjustments. The lack of reliable price surveys for countries accounting for over a third of the world's population—hence the lack of reliable evidence on the purchasing power of even average incomes, let alone incomes of the poor—compromises any statement about levels and trends in world poverty. But China and India did participate in the IPC 2011 price surveys.

Note that other world variables are also subject to large but unquantified margins of error. The absolute income per capita of the poorest countries is implausibly close to the survival minimum, which probably reflects substantial undercounting of agricultural, informal, and black activities. The per capita incomes of the richest countries are undercounted because of deficiencies in measuring inflation and quality improvements, and large-scale concealment of income and wealth at the top.

Downward bias

Other sources of error may bias the poverty numbers downwards, making the number of poor people seem lower than it is; and the bias may increase over time, making the trend look rosier than it is.

First, the Bank's IEPL refers to purchasing power over an 'average consumption' bundle, not to a basket of goods and services that makes sense for measuring poverty (though '$1 a day' does have intuitive appeal to a Western audience being asked to support aid). It probably underestimates the income or expenditure needed for an individual (or household) to avoid periods of food–water–clothing–shelter consumption too low to maintain health; and specifically, needed for manual labour as distinct from sedentary labour. It avoids altogether the problem that basic needs include unpriced public goods like clean water and healthcare. Suppose it costs Rs.30 to buy an equivalent bundle of food in India (defined in terms of calories and micronutrients) as can be bought in the US with $1; and that it costs only Rs.3 to buy an equivalent bundle of services (haircuts, massages) as $1 in the United States (Reddy and Pogge 2003). Current methods of calculating purchasing power parity, based on an *average* consumption bundle of food, services, and other things, may yield a PPP exchange rate of, say, PPP$1 = Rs.10, meaning that Rs.10 in India buys the equivalent average consumption bundle (food, services, etc.) as $1 in the United States. But this is misleading because the poor person, spending most income on food, can buy with Rs.10 only one-third of the food purchasable with $1 in the United States. To take the IEPL for India as Rs.10 therefore biases the number of poor downwards.

We have no way of knowing what proportion of food–water–clothing–shelter needs the Bank's international poverty line captures. But we can be fairly sure that had the Bank used a basic needs poverty line rather than its present one (an average of the national poverty lines of a set of low-income countries) the number of absolute poor would rise, because the national poverty lines equivalent to a global basic needs poverty line would probably rise, perhaps by 25 to 40 per cent.

A 25 to 40 per cent increase in a basic-needs-based international poverty line would, for the reason mentioned earlier, increase the world total of people in extreme poverty by a large fraction, probably at least 25 to 40 per cent. We can be reasonably confident that switching from the Bank's IEPL to one reflecting the purchasing power necessary to achieve elementary human capabilities would substantially raise the number of people in poverty.

The second reason for suspecting that the Bank's poverty numbers make the trend look rosy relates to the effects of changes in average consumption patterns as average incomes rise. Worldwide average consumption patterns are shifting toward services whose prices relative to food and shelter are lower in poor than in rich countries, giving the false impression that the cost of the basic consumption goods required by the poor is falling. As Indians become wealthier and consume more services relative to food, a rupee appears to buy more than it used to; and so the PPP value of Indian incomes goes up. But poor Indians continue to spend most of their income on food, and for them the purchasing power of rupees has not increased. Part of the apparent fall in the number of people below a poverty line defined in PPP-adjusted rupees is therefore a statistical illusion. The widespread removal of price controls on 'necessities' and the lowering of tariffs on luxuries amplify this effect.

All these problems have to be resolved in one way or another in any estimate of world poverty, whoever makes it. The fact that the World Bank is the near-monopoly provider introduces a third possible downward bias. The number of poor people is politically sensitive. The Bank's many critics on Right and Left like to use the poverty numbers as a pointer to the conclusion that it has accomplished 'precious little', in the words of former US Treasury Secretary Paul H. O'Neill. The chairman of a taskforce established by the US Congress to report on the multilateral economic organizations described the fall in the proportion of the world's population in extreme poverty from 28 per cent in 1987 to 24 per cent in 1998 as a 'modest' decline, the better to hammer the Bank (Meltzer 2001). This critique provides a rationale for the US to control

the Bank (appoint the president and maintain a big enough share of votes to exercise a veto, the only country able to do so). For its part, the Bank highlights the fall in the poverty numbers when responding to criticism from powerful member states, to show that it is doing a good job. When trying to enlist support for a bold initiative it may highlight the magnitude of poverty.

The enormous increase in the poverty numbers made in the wake of the 2005 ICP price survey adds to the sense of uncertainty. Angus Deaton argues that the increase is due mostly to the statistical technique for recalibrating the IEPL. The line is calculated as the average national poverty lines in a sample of low-income countries, one of which was India, whose national line was one of the lowest in the sample. When India's average income reached the middle-income threshold its national poverty line was removed from the sample—causing the sample average, hence the IEPL, to rise, causing the global extreme poverty headcount to rise. Having said this, Deaton also says, 'It is all very confused, at least to me' (personal communication, 27 December 2009). However, the Bank now puts its poverty computations online in a way that enables others to recalculate poverty numbers with different assumptions (at PovcalNet).

KEY POINTS

- The good news is that, according to World Bank figures, the number of people living in extreme poverty fell by around 25 per cent between 1981 and 2005; and the proportion of the developing world's population living in extreme poverty fell from half to a quarter. The bad news is that, if China is excluded, the number in extreme poverty increased. The number living on between PPP\$1.25 a day and \$2.50 a day (the new extreme and ordinary poverty lines, based on the post-2005 PPP numbers) increased so much that the world total living on less than \$2.50 a day increased. Almost 3 billion people live on an income of less than PPP\$2.50 a day, more than half of the developing world's population, and more than 40 per cent of the world's population, after decades of development.

- Examination of how the numbers are constructed suggests they contain a large margin of indeterminacy. There are reasons to presume that they may be downwardly biased, and may make the trend look better than it is.

- The international poverty lines have a weak link with the income needed to sustain basic human capabilities.

However, we know enough about trends in other variables—life expectancy, heights, and other non-income measures—to be confident that 'objective' poverty headcounts have, indeed, fallen dramatically over the past 20 to 30 years. Moreover, the magnitude of world population increase is so large that the Bank's poverty numbers would have to be *huge* underestimates for the world poverty rate not to have fallen. This is a historically unprecedented achievement the world can be proud of.

How to explain the globalization consensus

If the evidence is shaky, why the confidence in the global policy community that neo-liberal globalization is the best path of *further* travel for the world? The 'law' of power hierarchies says that elites of a given political economy arrangement tend to believe theories which justify their own position. At the pinnacle of global corporate power is a super-cluster of 147 densely linked firms accounting for a high share of global corporate revenues. It is itself dominated by finance: all of the top 50 except one are financial firms (Coghlan and MacKenzie 2011). Oligopolistic financial firms, at the intersection of the investment, credit, savings processes of the global economy, are able to reap the bulk of the returns from production. This helps to explain the remarkable change noted earlier: the value of financial transactions to global GDP rose from about 14 in 1997 to almost 70 today, so that the realm of finance now swamps the realm of GDP (the 'real economy'). The shift to finance-driven globalization has driven the lift-off of top incomes from the rest, as the 'have-lots' benefit from interest payments and bonuses in the financial system, as well as from dividends. No surprise, then, that the experts invited as media commentators on economic matters come mostly from the financial sector. No surprise that after a short-lived Keynesian response to the crash of 2008, governments gave priority to 'restoring the confidence of financial markets' through fiscal austerity coupled with very cheap credit, much of which flowed into 'emerging markets' and non-productive asset markets, benefiting already rich owners. No surprise that the decades-old idea of taxing financial transactions, originally advanced by James Tobin, which seemed to take root in several European governments after 2008, has been discussed repeatedly only to be left on the shelf.

Giant firms, whether in finance or other sectors, profit from 'first-mover' advantages and other kinds of entry barriers against potential competitors. Facing few competitors, these firms want as open a global playing field for profit maximization as possible; and want to shape state policies to privilege their profit making. Neoliberal ideology helps them. First, it frames the choices as 'market' versus 'state', which obscures how giant corporations constitute a third entity colonizing both markets and states and configuring them to its own advantage. Second, it justifies maximum openness, claiming that maximum openness maximizes GDP growth in the longer run and thereby maximizes the all-important criterion of progress, aggregate consumption. Furthermore, the ideology says that 'there is no alternative': alternative policy directions are infeasible or too costly for consumer welfare. So governments must keep taxes low, avoid trade protection, avoid financial transaction taxes, and so on, all apparently for the sake of consumption, which is equated with consumer welfare, which is equated with well-being.

Neo-liberalism provides a safer justification—because 'apolitical'—than the ones used to justify eighteenth- and nineteenth-century territorial openings, namely nationalism, racism, Christianity, and imperialism. Yet neo-liberal globalization could properly be called the ideology of a 'new imperialism' (Harvey 2005*b*), new because, not being based on colonies, it operates through the combination of open economic policies, an international monetary system based on the US dollar as the primary international currency, and vast numbers of students from across the world attending US and other core countries' universities. The merits of the latter for supporting a modern imperialism were spelled out in 1924 by Robert Lansing, US secretary of state under President Woodrow Wilson: 'We must abandon the idea of installing an American citizen in the Mexican presidency, as that would only lead us, once again, to war … we must open the doors of our universities to young, ambitious Mexicans and make the effort to educate them in the American way of life, in our values, and in respect for the leadership of the United States … these young people will come to occupy important positions and will eventually take possession of the presidency itself. And without the United States having to spend a single cent or fire a single shot, they will do what we want ….' Of course, this modern imperialism also has an iron fist, in the form of a US military budget equal to one third of global military spending and a global network of around 700 bases. The bases are intended to contain Russia and China and to secure governments friendly to the US, especially in energy-rich areas. Beyond marginal figures on the Left and Right, the new imperialism receives remarkably little critical scrutiny, because the clever people who flock into economics and capital management include few like Maynard Keynes, who made a fortune manipulating money on behalf of King's College, Cambridge, while also standing outside such activities and thinking for mankind.

The business community in the West, with its enormous resources, dominates the public debate about world economic order. It commissions studies, endows think tanks and university chairs, and broadcasts appropriate findings ('political' science) with fanfare.

The main political parties depend on the business community for finance, not on members, and present what is good for business as what is good for the nation—centre-left parties almost as much as those of the right. The parties compete to win support of the mass media. To do so they must hesitate to promote projects which run counter to shareholder interests, because media proprietors are beneficiaries of huge market capitalizations and architects of industrial concentration. We saw the power of mass media to contain a continent-wide movement of solidarity with Greece and the Syriza government in 2015, by presenting Greece as a delinquent debtor worsening its responsible creditors' problems, and not as the leader of a European-wide pushback against a failed 'austerity' structural adjustment programme coming from Brussels and the IMF. No wonder that the British Labour Party, while declaring its commitment to reduce poverty, at the same time has long boasted its unconcern about inequality. One of its leading strategists declared, 'We are intensely relaxed about people getting filthy rich.'

These political trends suggest that globalization is working at cross-purposes to democracy, as democratic systems lose their grip to regulate market competition in line with a common good whose characteristics are defined by *political*—therefore compromising—debate. For many globalization champions, stopping democratic processes from interfering with markets and multinational corporations is precisely the point; because the only meaningful common good or national interest is what the marketplace winners think. As stated by a leading neo-liberal economist in the post-war decades, Ludwig von Mises:

❝ Inequality of wealth and incomes is the cause of the masses' well-being, not the cause of anybody's distress … Where there is a lower degree of inequality, there is necessarily a lower standard of living of the masses. ❞

(von Mises 1955)

What held neo-liberalism in check during the long period from the 1930s to the 1970s—when income distribution in Western economies became more equal, dramatically so in the United States—was fear of an external enemy (the Soviet Union) and internal fifth column (trade unions), memory of the calamity brought by free market economics in the 1920s, the need to reward the masses who fought for the nation in two World Wars, and the surging gains in productivity and contentment as the innovations of electricity, telephone, combustion engine and indoor plumbing rolled out across the population. In these circumstances, ruling elites acted like an 'establishment' willing to forge class compromises in order to mobilize consent to their rule, which included redistribution downwards (also to boost domestic demand, given limited export markets, compared to what came later). Social movements—the labour movement, civil rights movement, women's movement, and others—helped to pass legislation which had the effect of raising the share of income at the bottom and middle and lowering the share at the top.

This changed in the 1980s as the generation that experienced the earlier calamities retired and as the angry Right came to public office determined to erode the bargaining power of trade unions and reverse the squeeze on top incomes (in the US the share of income going to the top 1 per cent fell from about 22 per cent in 1929 to about 9 per cent in the late 1970s). Losing fear of the masses, elites in politics, business, and especially finance increasingly began to operate not as an 'establishment' but as an 'oligarchy', using state instruments to redistribute power and income upwards. They justified their coup with the argument that the new structure was necessary to raise the rate of profit, which would raise the rate of growth, which would raise consumer welfare. A top UK civil servant during the Thatcher years, Sir Alan Budd, spelled it out:

❝ The Thatcher government never believed for a moment that [monetarism] was the correct way to bring down inflation. They did however see that this would be a very good way to raise unemployment. And raising unemployment was an extremely desirable way of reducing the strength of the working classes … [This] has allowed the capitalists to make high profits ever since. ❞

(quoted in Cohen 2003)

Deprived of their external and internal adversaries, Western governments, giant corporations, and mass media began to imagine themselves the undisputed victors of the Cold War and the incarnations of global progress, and to lead Western society and the rest of the world in the embrace of further globalization as the direction of human progress. Enabled by technological advances, opening the economies of developing countries in the name of globalization and free market economics became a crucial part of the strategy for building profits at home, redistributing upwards, and undercutting the labour movement.

At home, Euro-American policy elites—the least needy people the world has ever seen—are driving through a neo-liberal agenda in order to gnaw away at wages within their territories, while assuring their voters that there is no alternative. Hence German finance minister Wolfgang Schauble's dictum, 'Austerity is the only cure for the eurozone' (2011: 13).

KEY POINTS

- The shakiness of the evidence that neo-liberal globalization is producing catch-up growth and win-wins all around feeds back only weakly into global policy as advocated by organizations such as the World Bank, the IMF, and the OECD. The story—framed as the application of universal laws (see epigraph 1)—is too good not to be true. It legitimizes the hugely disproportionate gains obtained by the top 10 per cent of world income distribution, by global firms based largely in the West, and by the US state which has adopted a commitment to continuous expansion of private consumption as the basis for domestic peace (also now the Chinese state). The main public-opinion-shaping media outlets are controlled by groups strongly committed to expanding the scope for private profit-seeking. Investors should be able easily to choose between options as diverse as palm oil in the Amazon, oil in the Arctic, and public-private hospital partnerships in Britain.

Conclusions

This chapter began by setting out the neoliberal globalization argument, which has profoundly shaped economic policy in most countries around the world in the last decades of the twentieth century and into the 2000s. It says that national governments can optimize their economy's creation of income and wealth

by adopting free market policies and institutions, thereby extending the geographic and sectoral scope of capitalist exchange and shrinking the scope of non-market social protection. Expanding exchange is the key to a virtuous circle of higher economic growth, stronger rule of law, falling poverty, falling inequality, and stronger democracy. Countries that are poor today can enter this virtuous circle provided the government strengthens capitalist institutions internally, opens the economy to the world, creates institutions of impersonal trust, and stands against corruption; and provided it gets help from the international community. The world economy is an open system; all countries could conceivably enjoy the same high level of prosperity, just as all marathon runners could conceivably cross the line at the same time. There is no *hierarchically structured* relationship between richer parts and poorer parts. The same basic growth strategy is appropriate for all, derived from the immutable laws of economics. The World Bank's newly appointed country economist for Senegal knows what the government should and should not do before she gets off the plane. The champions of this argument—based on the idea of mainstream economics expressing universal truths, free of ideology—tend to ignore contrary evidence or treat it with the annoyance one might direct at a fly.

Globalization in question

We know that evidence underdetermines the acceptance of theories. Nevertheless, it is remarkable how influential the globalization argument became, because the evidence is ambiguous. For example, we have seen that much of the evidence adduced for 'globalization works' and 'the rise of the South' is the story of Asia, and especially China. There is no doubt that most of China's residents have benefited materially, since the 1980s, on a huge scale, by its entrepreneurs, business owners and workers exploiting opportunities in international markets, as the neo-liberal globalization argument expects.

But two big qualifications have to be made. First, the fact that hundreds of millions of people in China (and India) have attained living conditions above extreme poverty in the past 20 years does not support the idea that a general process of globalization is driving a general improvement in global living conditions sufficiently fast to bring most of the caravan of economies and peoples closer together. Much of the evidence for income convergence on a world scale between the

1980s and today disappears when China is removed. Second, China's set of policies and institutions during the past several decades of high growth would earn it a low score on the Washington–Brussels Consensus, unless the scores are reverse-engineered from high subsequent growth rates.

Widespread adoption of neo-liberal prescriptions has not much altered the decades-long coupling of growth in the South to growth in the North, and now also in China; and no developing country has reached the GDP size where its growth has a major impact on global economic conditions, except, again, China. Recall that much of the story about the rise of the South and about globalization being win-win for South and North is based on the fact that over the 2000s low- and middle-income countries experienced much faster economic growth than developed countries, which led many to suggest that the South had 'decoupled' from the North in the sense of being able to generate fast growth endogenously. The bulk of evidence suggests that the unprecedented acceleration of growth in these countries since 2000 was based less on improvements of their 'fundamentals' and more on exceptionally expansionary global economic conditions driven by unsustainable debt-fuelled policies in developed countries and latterly China (Akuz 2013). In 2006 the US's current account deficit was about equal to India's GDP. In the two years of 2011 and 2012 China produced more cement than the US did in the entire twentieth century.

High growth in China has been driven first by fast expansion of exports to the North and more recently by an investment to GDP ratio so high as probably to be unprecedented in world history. Fixed asset investment has risen to nearly 50 per cent of GDP, as compared to 30 per cent to 35 per cent in Japan during its miracle growth decade when it achieved similar growth rates as China over the 2000s. Apartment prices have risen to a dizzying 15 to 20 times the average household income in first tier cities, as compared to 12 to 15 times in late 1980s bubble-era Japan. Two decades later Japan has still not recovered from its burst bubble, and China's crash would have further-reaching consequences for the world than Japan's did.

Evidence adduced in this chapter suggests an analogy between the world economy and the physical universe: a force analogous to 'gravity' hinders upward mobility (and keeps internal inequality high), and a force analogous to 'magnetic levitation' holds up the rich economies (and keeps internal inequality relatively low). Many middle-income countries have languished in a 'middle-capabilities trap', their firms unable to break into innovation-intensive activities or into the market for branded products, where the high profits are to be made, and outcompeted by firms based in China and offshoots in Southeast Asia.

The globalization champions have tended to ignore or downplay not only the poor 'catch up' performance record of the globalization era, but also the tension between more market integration and democracy. There is an 'elective affinity' between more market integration, states relying on borrowing more than taxation, financial crises, stringent fiscal policy to free up resources for debt repayment (mandated by creditors and international organizations), and national executives which strengthen themselves at the expense of legislatures.

In terms of how global thinking about development strategy should change, we should start by setting aside the false dichotomies of open *or* closed economy, globalization as opportunity *or* threat, government limited to umpiring on a level playing field *or* government intervention to influence resource allocation. We can agree that a national incentive structure containing protection of property rights, easy entry into sectors, and encouragement to export gives the foundation for robust economic growth in developing countries. Low scores for these three features constitute significant obstacles. Then the question is how to combine the opportunities offered by international markets and incoming multinational corporations with coordinated strategies for domestic investment, corporate governance and education, so as to stimulate domestic entrepreneurs and create a more nationally integrated economy, with a more diversified production structure and substantial economic sovereignty within the developing country state rather than externalized to foreign firms and foreign governments or international organizations. With this perspective we can consider the possibilities of state-sponsored directional thrust without the discussion being hijacked by a preternatural terror of governments 'picking winners' or a conviction that the private sector can do no wrong, as in the assumption that 'corruption' is only about the public sector (Wade 2004*a*, 2015; Chang and Grabel 2014).

Elsewhere, I have outlined a set of principles that might guide an alternative approach to development strategy with a more active role for the state (Wade

2003*a*, 2003*b*, 2004*a*: ch. 11; 2015). There is not, of course, a single alternative to the Washington–Brussels Consensus. What is appropriate for middle-income, semi-peripheral economies like Malaysia and coastal China may be inappropriate for low-income, peripheral economies like Uganda.

Development strategies have to be geared to the authority structure of states and to leaders' perception of the determinants of their or their group's political survival. Some states are more 'neo-patrimonial' than others, some have a broader class-base than others, and both factors affect the degree to which the state is able to concentrate resources on sensible investment (Kohli 2004). The West is keen to promote democracy and expansion of civil society. But a democratic transition may result in business or religious capture of the state, weakened technocracy, popular disgust of politics, and erosion of a pre-existing growth coalition. In this area of appropriate state structure, we know even less than about alternative principles of development strategy. But the contrast between the development trajectory and present-day living conditions in Seoul/South Korea and Manila/Philippines is sobering for those who believe that democracy, civil society, and a directionless approach to industrial development (the Philippines' story) is the right prescription for development.

In the affluent West, the Crash of 2008 and the long and hesitant recovery suggest a crisis not just *in* the capitalist growth system but *of* the capitalist growth system, resulting from a combination of (a) dominance of the highly concentrated financial sector over politics and the real economy, (b) high income and wealth concentration at the top, and (c) states following a broadly neoliberal agenda. The conundrum is how to curb the plutocracy and its presumption of winner take all, and reverse the growth of the precariat even in the face of rapid automation, while preserving openness to ideas, people, and trade as a core political value.

The solution lies in recognizing that the West and East Asia have already passed a turning point in human history, where female fertility has fallen below replacement levels. The capitalist economy has been dependent on ever more people producing and consuming ever more stuff. An ageing and eventually shrinking population that consumes less takes us into uncharted territory, where further increases in average income are hardly associated with improvements in quality of life.

Climate change and materials shortages likewise take us into uncharted territory. But we can be fairly sure that the direction of economic development for the world has to be: away from mass production and standardized consumption, with 'planned obsolescence' built into production and consumption (the 'American way of life' of the second half of the twentieth century); and towards the reuse of materials (including by hiring and upgrading rather than purchase of new hardware), lower energy consumption, and more renewable energy—but to focus only on switching to renewable energy leaving consumer demand still tethered to energy- and materials-intensive consumption is a recipe for disaster.

These trends have to be complemented by measures to change the opportunity and incentive structure so as to curb income and wealth inequality, especially in developing countries. Not only through redistributive fiscal measures like progressive taxation (and a shift away from income tax towards tax on land and buildings), blocking companies' and wealthy households' ability to hide assets and escape taxation, and public healthcare and early childhood education. Also *predistributive* ones, like measures to greatly expand access to income from capital, via wider share ownership, so that most of the population, not just the wealthy, can earn income while they sleep; and measures to reform corporate governance so as to discourage short-term profit expectations, stock buybacks, and senior executive remuneration three digits more than the average, to encourage R&D and training, and to require financial disclosures of information that 'could' (not just 'would') influence investor decisions, and employee voice in firm management. Governments will have to 'intervene' more than sanctioned by neo-liberal ideology as economies move towards less labour input and more intelligent automation ('no more average'), a trend which, if not buffered through the compromises of the political process, will give more rewards to investors and less to most labour, and will tip the balance even further from 'democratic control *of* capital' towards 'democratic control *by* capital'. All this has to go with efforts to re-energize the (non-material) aesthetic and spiritual dimension of what it means to live well on Earth. Otherwise, the history of hunting (in the Swahili proverb) will foretell the end of human history.

Economics in question

There are two criteria of 'truth' in science. One is consistency, the other, correspondence with evidence.

Mathematics is the home of truth as consistency, observational sciences the home of truth as evidence. Economics claims to combine both. But much of economics, especially macroeconomics, has used another criterion of 'truth' in practice: consistency with faith in free markets, equivalent to faith in religious doctrine or political platform, which unites a group coordinated by deference to a few revered leaders, and encourages disregard of ideas and evidence from people who do not signal their membership of the group (Romer 2016).

This faith holds up the perfectly competitive market as the ideal against which to identify and correct 'imperfections' in the real world. One of the attractions of the perfectly competitive model is that it eliminates 'power'—all actors in the 'democracy of the marketplace' are individually insignificant and cannot shape market outcomes to serve their interests. So 'good' economic policy is policy which sustains competitive markets; 'bad' economic policy is policy which allows individually significant actors to manipulate outcomes in their favour. The faith also presumes that what is derived from a mathematical model has the aura of truth, what is not derived from a model is suspect or irrelevant. As Paul Krugman said about why economists failed to anticipate the Crash of 2008, 'the economics profession went astray because economists … mistook beauty, clad in impressive-looking math, for truth' (Krugman 2009).

The simplicity, elegance, and ease of mathematical formalization of neo-liberal ideas give them persuasive advantages. Presented as 'immutable laws', they endorse politicians', officials' and policy economists' love of brevity and speed. They can readily be deployed to sanction the super-wealthy's opposition to government regulation, taxation, and downwards income redistribution. They obscure the fact that 'the (financial) markets' comprise a small number of organizations powerful enough to hold governments, especially 'debt states', over a barrel. And they connect metaphorically to the wider public's personal experience: 'just as the household has to tighten its belt in hard times, so must the government'; 'a debt problem can't be cured by borrowing'; 'tax cuts generate enough growth to pay for the cuts'; 'wage cuts raise the demand for labour'. They connect not just to personal experience but also to emotional values widely seen as not negotiable, like 'freedom', 'self-reliance', 'level playing field', 'democracy', 'efficiency'.

The political adage says, 'If you are explaining, you are losing'. Keynesian, evolutionary, institutional, and Marxist branches of economics need more explaining than neo-liberal ideas. They are more difficult to formalize mathematically, more difficult to translate into universalistic prescriptions, and more difficult to convince elites of. Also, an economist who is expert in institutional contexts, as distinct from mathematical formalism, is less likely to get published in the 'top' journals and less geographically mobile in the academic job market.

Moreover, both politicians and policy economists face strong incentives to appear certain about policy prescriptions. If they can convince their publics and clients that the alternatives are only two, one of which is obviously inferior (government interventionism or neo-liberal universals), they find it easier to induce action (see epigraph 3).

Economists have tended to harness the neo-liberal apparatus to an implicit 'maxi-max' decision rule: select the policy option which has one of its possible outcomes which is better than any possible outcome of other policy choices, without regard to the probability of that best outcome actually materializing (DeMartino and McCloskey 2016). The combination of the maxi-max decision rule with 'government failure is generally worse than market failure' tends to generate policy prescriptions in line with the interests of the owners and managers of capital. So economists long resisted government regulation of finance on grounds that deregulated financial markets promised bigger benefits than more regulated markets, hardly weighing the possibility that liberalized financial markets—including free cross-border flows—would pose appreciable dangers to the entire society. They have long championed production globalization (transferring factory jobs to cheap labour sites or replacing them at home with machines), which is good for capitalists and the share of profits in national income. They ignore that abandoning today's 'commodity' manufacturing can preclude entry into tomorrow's new industry, because new industries need a whole ecosystem of supplier–customer relations where technological knowledge accumulates and experience builds on experience. (Of course, production globalization has also contributed to a fall in extreme poverty and growth of the middle class in some developing countries, notably China.)

Given the severity of the 2008 Crash and Long Slump, and given what is known about the causal role of the world's leading banks and other financial firms operating in a neo-liberal regulatory framework, the visitor from Mars would be amazed to find that neo-liberalism remains the guiding ideology on the commanding heights of western economies. Politicians and economists have shifted the solution to the crisis from boosting aggregate demand, stronger and simpler regulation of private finance (higher equity requirements, not higher requirements for complex debt securities which can be turned into equity when a bank fails), and investment in infrastructure and new technologies. They focus more on cuts in public spending (especially welfare spending, to stop poor people sponging off the rest of society, unlike the wealthy), and continued reliance on expansionary monetary policy, even after the biggest monetary stimulus in history has failed to regenerate sustained growth.

The clue to the Mars visitor's amazement is the distinction between neo-liberalism as theory and neo-liberalism as source of real-world policy. The former assumes an economy of many competing firms operating in a market to satisfy individual consumers' preferences, and operating in a polity of multiple interests with a strict separation between economic and political power and tight constraints on the political executive. The latter uses the theory of neo-liberalism to disguise the way the state has restructured itself to promote the interests of the owners and managers of oligopolistic corporations. We see this from the way that the latter have emerged from the crisis even wealthier than before, and able to intensify the concentration of economic and political power to the point of allowing only marginal tightening of constraints on their operations (such as the higher capital requirements in the new Basel III banking standards, described by critics as 'a mouse').

One of the big challenges for economists is to reconceptualize the standard 'market' and 'state' polarity, which rests on the neoclassical optimizing theory of the firm, a theory which focuses on the efficiency of allocation of given resources and not on the creation of higher quality and/or lower cost products than were previously available at prevailing factor prices. Development economics must be based on evolutionary ideas, which highlight the potential synergy between innovative, profit-seeking firms and governments acting on economy-wide and international market-wide information of a kind that firms do not have to compile—and acting in line with norms of right conduct arrived at through political debate,

because politicians have to pay at least lip service to collective values, while firms do not. Given that the state is also an arena in which individuals seek their personal advantage, and that states in their dealings with other states seek a delimited national advantage, civil organizations (national and international) and interstate organizations have to help discipline firms and states.

Rethinking the prevailing assumptions about statistics presents another deep challenge. Economists tend to believe that everything that can be measured should be measured, and that statistics are a transparent lens that can be used largely to eliminate ideology and interpretive bias. They tend to be too cavalier about the 'objectivity' of the data they use, forgetting that data is never raw, never disinterested, always structured and measured according to the predispositions and values of someone, even if unaware of it.

Growth in Gross Domestic or National Product has been among the top economic priorities of just about all governments since the 1950s, yet its measurement is egregiously flawed. Nothing increases GDP like a housing boom or a costly healthcare system or a major pollution disaster or a rise in Internet gambling or people eating at restaurants rather than at home. GDP accounting does not discount consumption financed by debt, and does not count the depreciation of natural capital. GDP accounting treats government spending (for example, on education and public health) as *consumption*, not as investment, thus building in a presumption that public spending is wasteful. In low income states, compiling accurate national accounts takes resources generally not made available. Zambia's national accounts in 2010 were compiled by one person. African growth rates commonly have a margin of error of over 3 percentage points; so a country reporting 3 per cent growth might actually be growing at 6 per cent or not at all (Jerven 2013). All the discussion of growth, inequality, and poverty is hobbled by errors in our most basic measure of economic performance.

As a general rule one should always be careful with statistics compiled by organizations whose performance is evaluated against those statistics; and also with statistics used to test propositions vested with high ideological salience (such as, 'countries with higher scores on market liberalization have better subsequent performance'). Who produces the data, what incentives have they to fabricate or bend, what is their relationship to those whose performance is judged? Goodhart's law says that when a policymaker uses a variable as a target (for example, when the central bank targets the money supply) its measurement is liable to be distorted. The Chinese proverb says, 'Officials make the figures, and the figures make the officials'. The English proverb says, 'It is easier to reset the scales than to lose weight'. If the organization producing data on poverty or inequality is judged by its own numbers, its numbers and its presentations may be skewed in a favourable direction to itself and the ideology of its mandate. 'Evidence-based policymaking' becomes 'policy-based evidence-making'.

Plausible estimates of China's GDP growth, by outside analysts using real-economy indicators like railroad freight and diesel equipment sales, suggest it may be two or even three percentage points below the official figure of 6.8 per cent in 2015. India's official figure is over 7 per cent but independent analysts suggest that 5 to 6 per cent is more likely.

The World Bank has been strongly committed to the argument that governance reforms improve subsequent economic growth, and the Bank calculates governance scores for its borrower countries. Marcus Kurtz and Andrew Shrank (2007) examine Bank studies which find that better governance yields higher subsequent growth. Applying careful tests of causality, they find that the governance scores are biased by the 'halo effect' of past growth. Governance scores correlate closely with past growth, not with future growth.

The European Bank for Reconstruction and Development (EBRD) has been strongly committed to advancing neo-liberal capitalism in eastern European countries undergoing the transition from state-socialism to capitalism, one of the most fundamental economic experiments of the second half of the twentieth century. Each year it calculates each country's score on an economic liberalisation index. It finds that countries with higher scores have higher subsequent growth, which confirms the validity of the EBRD's mandate. David Stuckler et al. (2009) compare the EBRD's own country reports with the scores meant to be derived from them. They find systematic bias in translating from reports to scores, to bring the scores (calculated retrospectively) into close correspondence with the growth performance which is known when the scores are calculated.

Again, the Food and Agriculture Organization (FAO) each year publishes a report on 'food insecurity' (hunger), which gives the number of people in the world who are undernourished. The UN's Millennium Development Goals (MDGs) included the goal of halving the number of hungry people in developing countries by 2015 compared to 1990. Over the 2000s FAO several times revised upwards its estimates of the hunger headcount in developing countries *in 1990*, from 789 million in steps up to 995 million. This upwards adjustment of the 1990 estimate allowed FAO to claim in 2014 that the MDG target was within reach, and hence that it and western aid givers had done a good job: 'hunger is being defeated' (Caparros 2014).

'Thumbs on the scales' leads into ethics. Mainstream economists have shifted the discipline from a moral science, where questions like the relationship between freedom and equality could be discussed non-mathematically, to a mathematical allocative science stripped of explicit ethics. Yet the profession should give even more attention to the ethical terrain on which its members operate than do the other social sciences, at least as much as law, civil engineering and medicine (DeMartino and McCloskey 2016). Why? First, economists have more impact on the life-chances of populations around the world than other social scientists. Second, economists deal with those they serve from a position of epistemic superiority compared to other social scientists, based on the unification of the mainstream discipline around mathematical formalism. Third, they tend to operate on an assumption of epistemic certainty or sufficiency, insisting that they know what is the best path for others to achieve their objectives—while leaving their underlying ethical position implicit (the default policy stance for governments should be more market liberalization). In the real world, economists do not know enough to warrant the high confidence they have in their recommended policies. Outside of controlled conditions they necessarily operate with epistemic uncertainty or insufficiency. The ethics of the profession should therefore require them not just to disclose conflicts of interest, but also constantly to emphasize the uncertainties of the data, the limitations of their expertise, the potential dangers of their prescriptions not working out as planned. They should nurture a norm of 'complementary pluralism' in the discipline rather than defend mathematical formalism of neo-classical precepts as the single valid approach. Just how far this is from mainstream faith is colourfully captured by Pontus Rendahl, macroeconomist at

Cambridge, who says that since mainstream economics has 'immutable laws' it would be wrong to teach heterodox theories as though they have equal validity. 'In the same way, I don't think heterodox engineering or alternative medicine should be taught'. The joint head of economics at Manchester University, Ken Clark, recently dismissed non-mainstream economists as pedlars of 'leeches, tobacco-smoke-enemas and homeopathy' (Pilling 2016). It is past time to bring questions of economic ethics up from the ocean of silence. Adam Smith would be first to applaud. Dani Rodrik, one of today's Adam Smiths, can have the last word: 'Too often economists debate a policy question as if one or the other theory has to be universally correct ... In fact, which model works better depends on setting and context ... If we economists understood this, it would make us more humble, less dogmatic, and more syncretic' (quoted in Farrell 2016).

QUESTIONS

1. What is 'the free market'?

2. What arguments and evidence do liberal writers use to make the case that globalization increases growth and reduces poverty and inequality?

3. What are the advantages and disadvantages of using purchasing power parity (PPP) measures for comparing incomes across countries?

4. What are the main difficulties in measuring the number of people living in poverty?

5. What are the advantages and disadvantages of the various ways of examining the extent of inequality within and between countries?

6. How much change has there been in the global distribution of income in the last 40 years?

7. Why might there be problems with the statistics that the World Bank and other international agencies use on poverty and inequality?

8. How can the neo-liberal argument be tested empirically? And how do its assumptions shape its conclusions about the appropriate role of the state?

9. Should one be concerned about rising levels of inequality in the global economy?

10. What are the implications of the trends in growth, poverty, and inequality for the agendas of the multilateral economic organizations?

11. Does it make sense to apply the concept of 'imperialism' to the current world order?

FURTHER READING

Chang, H.-J. and I. Grabel (2014), *Reclaiming Development: An Alternative Economic Policy Manual* (New York: Zed Books). A non-polemical juxtaposition of mainstream development policy prescriptions with counter-arguments.

Chen, S. and Ravallion, M. (2008), 'The Developing World is Poorer than We Thought, But No Less Successful in the Fight Against Poverty', World Bank Policy Research Working Paper, Aug.: 4703 (Washington, DC: World Bank). World Bank update of knowledge about global material well-being.

Deaton, A. (2013), *The Great Escape: Health, Wealth, and the Origins of Inequality* (Princeton: Princeton University Press). Floods of illumination on global trends and public policy.

Donnan, S. (2016), 'Global trade: structural shifts', *Financial Times,* 2 March.

Galbraith, J. K. (2006), 'Global Macroeconomics and Global Inequality', in D. Held and A. Kaya (eds), *Global Inequality: Patterns and Explanations* (Cambridge: Polity Press). A non-technical discussion of inequality trends, including world wage data.

Korzeniewicz, R. P. and Moran, T. P. (2009), *Unveiling Inequality: A World-Historical Perspective* (New York: Russell Sage Foundation). A sociological perspective, accessible to the general reader.

Milanovic, B. (2005), *Worlds Apart: Measuring International and Global Inequality* (Princeton: Princeton University Press). Magnum opus by a heterodox former World Bank economist.

Pilling, D. (2016), 'Crash and Learn', *Financial Times*, 1–2 October.

Rodrik, D. (2007), *One Economics, Many Recipes* (Princeton: Princeton University Press). A powerful argument for development strategy that is not mainly just a liberalization strategy.

Romer, P. (2016), 'The Trouble with Macroeconomics', forthcoming in *The American Economist*.

Sims, A. (2013), *Cancel the Apocalypse: The New Path to Prosperity* (New York: Little, Brown). An optimistic and doable agenda for progressing beyond the race for economic growth as we know it.

UNCTAD. (2016), *Trade and Development Report, 2016: Structural Transformation for Inclusive and Sustained Growth* (New York: UNCTAD). Geneva.

Wade, R. (in press), *Governing the Market: Economic Theory and the Role of Government in East Asian Industrialization* (Princeton: Princeton University Press). A case study of the role of the state in East Asian development, and the rationale of partly non-Washington Consensus policy prescriptions.

Wade, R. (2004), 'The American Paradox: The Ideology of Free Markets and the Practice of Directional Thrust', *Cambridge Journal of Economics*.

Wolf, M. (2004), *Why Globalization Works: The Case for the Global Market Economy* (New Haven: Yale University Press). A sophisticated statement of the neo-liberal globalization argument.

WEBLINKS

http://utip.gov.utexas.edu University of Texas Inequality Project.

www.unido.org United Nations Industrial Development Organization (UNIDO).

www.columbia.edu/~sr793 Monitoring Global Poverty.

www.worldbank.org/poverty World Bank PovertyNet.

www.bris.ac.uk/poverty Townsend Centre for International Poverty Research.

ONLINE RESOURCE CENTRE

For additional material and resources, please visit the Online Resource Centre at:
www.oxfordtextbooks.co.uk/ravenhill5e

13

The Political Economy of Development

Nicola Phillips

Chapter contents

Reader's guide

Despite the many accomplishments since the end of the Second World War, the problems of development in the contemporary global political economy are still of arresting proportions, and the various incarnations of a 'global development agenda' to deal with these problems have had a very mixed record. In fact, there is still little consensus on what development actually is, let alone how it might be achieved, in either academic debates or public discourse. One of the most disputed questions in this context relates to the relationship between globalization and development, and how we should understand the impact of globalization on development across the world. This chapter explores these debates. It starts by reviewing the different (and competing) ways of thinking about development that have emerged since the end of the Second World War, and showing how particular understandings of development have given rise to particular kinds of development strategies, at both the national and global levels. It goes on to consider the impacts and consequences of these strategies for development, and shows on this basis that many of the problems and failures of development have not only persisted but also worsened in the contemporary period. In this context, we move then to consider the key question of how we should understand the relationship between globalization and development, in both empirical and theoretical terms. There is a great deal at stake in this debate, in view of the centrality of globalization to both the panorama of contemporary development strategies and the prospects of achieving genuine improvements in the conditions in which large parts of the world's population live. Having summarized the various positions in the debate, I suggest that the most compelling argument is one which emphasizes and understands how conditions of 'mal-development'—or development failures—both arise from and are reinforced by globalization processes and the ways in which the global economy is governed.

Introduction

It is in some ways remarkable how little we still know, and how little consensus still exists, about the complex processes and conditions summed up in the term 'development'. The second part of the twentieth century and early part of the twenty-first century were marked by a long succession of different approaches to development, each heralded as a magic bullet that would generate growth, eliminate poverty, reduce inequality and attain all the various goals associated with an improvement of the conditions in which huge parts of the world's population live. Yet the record of developmental progress over this period remains very mixed. Many extraordinary advances were made in the period following the end of the Second World War, such as unprecedented increases in life expectancy and improvements in living standards (Corbridge 1998), but the so-called 'Age of Development' has also bequeathed a global economy characterized by a resilience of poverty and a marked increase in inequalities among the world's population. These inequalities have reached levels which can rightly be considered to be 'without historical precedent and without conceivable justification—economic, moral or otherwise' (Pieterse 2002: 1024).

The problems of development in the global economy thus remain of huge proportions, and in many dimensions are growing rather than diminishing. Particularly when we dig beneath the 'global' or 'regional' statistics showing overall reductions in extreme poverty levels, for instance, or increases in annual gross domestic product (GDP), we find a picture of development in which, for very large parts of the world's population, the march of globalization has not led to substantial improvements in their material or social conditions, and in some cases has led to their worsening. The global development agenda, as it evolved over the course of the twentieth century, is considered by many to have failed to provide a framework

for development policy that could deliver the goals of 'global development'. Despite the great fanfare to which the latest 'big idea' was unveiled around the start of the 2000s—namely, the Millennium Development Goals (MDGs), and in 2015 their successor, the Sustainable Development Goals (SDGs)—the global development agenda remains in some disarray, with few unqualified advances on its score card. In many contexts, development processes and strategies have been destabilized by the impact around the world of the economic and financial crisis which engulfed the later part of the decade. To complicate matters further, the extraordinary expansion of the Chinese economy and its emergence as a powerful force on the global political stage, alongside a group of other countries often called the 'rising powers', have challenged the twin notions, dominant from the 1980s onwards, that (a) an unequivocal embrace of neo-liberal 'globalization' is the surest path to growth and development, and (b) that there is or can be an overarching framework for development informing a 'global' development agenda.

Underlying the problems of development and the shortcomings of global development policy is an enduring absence of consensus about what the causes of these trends are, and by extension what is to be done about them. Even more fundamentally, there is little agreement on the very basic question of what development actually is—that is, what we are referring to when we talk about development, what we are aspiring to in trying to advance it, and how we would recognize it when we saw it. The many different theories of development which have emerged in contemporary academic debates and which have informed different kinds of development strategies advance different views on all of these counts. The first task of this chapter is consequently to consider how particular ways of thinking about development have evolved in the period since the end of the Second World War, and to discuss how these theories of development have translated into the evolution of both the global policy agenda and local, national, and regional development strategies. Its second task is then to consider the effects and consequences of these ideas and strategies for development across the world. By reviewing both the empirical picture and competing perspectives on how to explain it, I advance the argument that the most recent phase of globalization, along with the associated policy orthodoxy, is to be judged harshly on the basis of its development outcomes and political consequences. But it is not enough simply to assert this and move swiftly on: instead, we need to think carefully about the relationship between globalization and development, and specifically about what it is about globalization that can be said to cause or contribute directly to the problems of development that we identify as having characterized the contemporary period. The final task of the chapter is then to look forward and, necessarily speculatively, discuss the possibility that we are now moving into a new phase of global development which requires new theoretical perspectives and new policy frameworks.

Ways of thinking about development

Much like the term 'globalization' itself, 'development' is a word that is bandied about in public discourse in frequently glib and unthinking ways (Payne and Phillips 2010). It is a powerful term—one denoting a state of affairs of which everyone, or nearly everyone, can easily and in some cases passionately declare themselves to be in favour. Yet few people would be able to say with much precision what the term actually means. H. W. Arndt captured this well, observing back in 1987 that 'anyone who asked articulate citizens in developed or developing countries what they meant by this desirable objective of "development" would get a great variety of answers':

❝ Higher living standards. A rising per capita income. Increase in productive capacity. Mastery over nature. Freedom through control of man's environment. Economic growth. But not mere growth, growth with equity. Elimination of poverty. Basic needs satisfaction. Catching up with the developed countries in technology, wealth, power, status. Economic independence, self-reliance. Scope for self-fulfillment for all. Liberation, the means to human ascent. ❞

(1987: 1)

He goes on to remark that 'development, in the vast literature on the subject, appears to have come to encompass almost all facets of the good society, everyman's road to utopia' (Arndt 1987: 1). This has perhaps never been more true than in the early years of the twenty-first century, when we have a bewildering array of global institutions, grand policy initiatives, less grand policy initiatives, public campaigns, civil society organizations and individuals, all operating under the banner of 'development', but either advancing no clear conception of what it is they are aspiring to with this label, or else offering widely differing understandings of how to achieve it.

Academic debates around development are also characterized by a lack of agreement—or, put in more constructive terms, a rich diversity of opinion—about how development should be conceived, how development processes should be understood to work, and how development might be achieved. Each of the main theories of development that we will consider here works with different definitions of development and different diagnoses of the causes of either developmental progress or development failures. In what follows we will review briefly the principal ways of thinking about development that have emerged since the end of the Second World War, in order to trace in the next section of the chapter how these have been translated into particular kinds of policies, and with what effects and consequences.

Modernization, structuralist, and underdevelopment theories

Early phases of post-war development theory, like all others, were to a significant degree driven by the changing world order. The onset of the Cold War and the large-scale political, economic, and security shifts that accompanied it yielded a clear recognition in the United States and elsewhere of the centrality of what by then was being called the 'Third World' to the effort to contain communism (Pakenham 1973). The development project was in an immediate sense one of 'winning over' developing countries and societies in order to divert the encroachment of socialist ideas and the influence of the Soviet Union. But, more fundamentally, it was also one of setting the developing world on a path to specifically Western-style development.

The most vigorous expression of this new development agenda was found in modernization theory—a perspective on development which evolved in the

United States in this Cold War context. Its essence was an understanding of development as a 'process of social change whereby less developed societies acquire characteristics common to more developed societies' (Lerner 1972: 386). The emphasis was not only on economic change, but also on a much more sweeping process of social and cultural change that would enable supposedly 'traditional' developing countries and societies both to resemble those of the purportedly advanced, developed West, and to 'catch up' with those societies in terms of levels of wealth, living standards and 'modernity'.

The body of modernization theory grew rapidly, encompassing a range of approaches. Among the most well-known, and harshly criticized, was the version associated notably with W. W. Rostow (1960), in which he developed a notion of the 'stages of economic growth' through which all societies passed in a transition to modernity. These stages were identified as: traditional society; preconditions for take-off; take-off; the road to maturity; and the age of mass consumption, the latter being the indicator of a state of 'development' had been achieved. Modernization theorists in this sense conceived of development as a process with a clear end-point, a state of being 'developed', which was deemed to have been achieved by Western societies (the United States and Western Europe). The rest of the world was thus engaged in catching up to that condition. The other particularly influential version of modernization theory was associated with the notion of 'political development', which took development to refer to the processes by which conditions of liberal democracy were created and institutionalized. Gabriel Almond (1970), in collaboration with others such as James Coleman (1960) and C. B. Powell (1965), was at the forefront of this theoretical effort to extrapolate an understanding of development and prescriptions for development policy from the institutional conditions which had emerged over time in the liberal democracies of the West.

The key characteristics of modernization theory (see Box 13.1)—its ethnocentrism, the equation of modernization (development) with Westernization, and its clear ideological project (Hoogvelt 1978)—generated lasting and trenchant controversy with the other major approach to development of that time. The body of 'underdevelopment theory', which encompassed most notably dependency and world systems theories, emerged as the great rival to modernization theory during the 1960s and 1970s. They

BOX 13.1

Key Dimensions of Modernization Theory

Was developed in the United States in the context of the ideological rivalry of the Cold War.

Conceives of development as both an end-point (a condition of being developed, which had already been achieved by the advanced industrialized countries) and a process of 'catching up' to that condition.

Sees the path to development as being one of 'Westernization'—i.e. a process of catching up by emulating the 'developed' countries—particularly in the nature and sequence of economic change, and in processes of political development to establish liberal democracy.

had a much greater and longer-lasting impact on the ways we think about development than modernization theory, bequeathing to us a 'key vocabulary' of world systems, developmental states, imperialism, neo-colonialism and so on (Harrison 2004: 156).

Unlike modernization theory, which was a distinctively US (and Western) perspective on development, underdevelopment theories had their origins in Latin America, and specifically in a group of economists clustered in the UN Economic Commission for Latin America (ECLA), based in Santiago, Chile. The most famous of them was Raúl Prebisch, who developed a 'structuralist' thesis on the relationship between the global system and the conditions of underdevelopment that he observed in the Latin American region (Prebisch 1950). He advanced the key insight that the global economic system was divided into a powerful 'centre' and weak 'periphery', and identified the ways in which what he called the 'terms of trade'—that is, the ratio of export prices to import prices—worked systematically to favour the centre and disadvantage the periphery. In the periphery, export sectors were unable to generate the levels of national income required for economic development in conditions of rapid population growth, and development problems were perpetuated by the need to increase exports in order to maintain import levels. Competition among countries exporting commodities generated a decline in export prices relative to manufactures imported from industrialized countries. The end result was seen to be the structural entrenchment of a condition of 'underdevelopment' in the periphery, in which the process of industrialization was impeded, leading to a rising gap in incomes between the two parts of the world economy.

Prebisch's insights were picked up and absorbed into more established traditions in the social sciences, specifically into 'neo-Marxist' theories which had long been concerned with notions of imperialism in the world economy. The result was a complex body of thought summed up in the label 'dependency theory', which had at its core a notion that development needed to be understood with reference to the location of economies within the world capitalist system and the interactions of the different parts of this system, and that development and underdevelopment exist in a relationship of structural symbiosis, as 'the two faces of the historical evolution of capitalism' (Sunkel 1972: 520). The obstacles to industrialization that Prebisch had identified were thus seen as rooted in the structure of the global system, which served to perpetuate underdevelopment in the periphery *as a precondition for* development in the centre. Thus, according to a classic definition:

❝ Dependence is a conditioning situation in which the economies of one group of countries are conditioned by the development and expansion of others. A relationship of interdependence … becomes a dependent relationship when some countries can expand only as a reflection of the expansion of the dominant countries, which may have positive or negative effects on their immediate development. **❞**

(Dos Santos 1970: 231)

More and less careful versions of dependency theory emerged, but the impact of the school as a whole on ways of thinking about development during this time was pivotal. Subsequent elaborations by André Gunder Frank and others consolidated its status as an early perspective on inequality between countries and societies, where capitalism was deemed to generate 'economic development for the few and underdevelopment for the many' (Frank 1967: 8). World systems theory subsequently took up the running, most notably elaborated by Immanuel Wallerstein (1974, 1979, 1980), who saw a world market system (what we would now call global economy) as comprising different kinds of states—core, semi-periphery, and periphery—marked by significant asymmetries and jostling for economic advantage. As such, underdevelopment theory was

---

BOX 13.2

Key Dimensions of Underdevelopment and Dependency Theory

Was pioneered in Latin America to explain continued 'underdevelopment' in that region and elsewhere.

Conceives of the world economy as divided into a powerful 'centre' and a weak 'periphery', in which the terms of trade systematically disadvantaged the periphery and perpetuated conditions of underdevelopment.

Identifies development and underdevelopment as 'the two faces of the historical evolution of capitalism' (Sunkel 1972) and explores how conditions of 'dependence'—of the periphery on the centre—serve to reinforce underdevelopment and inequality.

---

clearly a forerunner of many of the debates in which we are interested here about the impact of the changing global political economy on development. Even so, both dependency and world systems theory were subjected to a barrage of criticism, justified and otherwise, to the extent that by the early 1980s they had lost much of their influence and appeal. As we will see in the next section, the failures of the strategies associated with this conception of development, alongside the success of very different development strategies in East Asia, also hastened its decline (see Box 13.2).

Neo-liberalism and neo-statism

A good part of the problem for underdevelopment theories by the 1980s was, quite simply, that they were wrong-footed by events. Aside from the damage caused by the various theoretical critiques, these kinds of theories proved inadequate for understanding and explaining the key trend that was becoming visible in global development—namely, the increasing differentiation and divergence in the development trajectories of countries and economies in different parts of the world. From the 1960s onwards, the big development story was not of underdevelopment, but rather of the spectacular rise of a group of East Asian economies that came to be known as the **newly industrializing economies (NICs)**—Taiwan, Korea, Singapore, and Hong Kong. Their soaring growth rates left economies in Latin America, Africa and other developing regions in the metaphorical dust, and equally left modernization theory and, particularly, underdevelopment theory struggling for anything meaningful to say by way of explanation or theorization. In a nutshell, the rise of East Asia left the notion of a single group of countries and economies, variously termed the 'Third World', 'developing countries', 'periphery' and so on, looking redundant.

Both to take account of these new trends and to conceive of the relationship between development and the processes of globalization that were accelerating at the time, the key debate that emerged from the 1970s onwards was between two schools of thought. The first was the body of theory summed up in the term '**neo-liberalism**', the single most influential paradigm in the contemporary period, which came to define the global development policy agenda and the panorama of development strategies across the world. The second took its cue more concretely from the East Asian experience and can be termed 'neo-statism'. The debate was not about development theories in the sense of those we have just reviewed. It was centrally about the study of political economy in the advanced industrialized world, particularly in the context of the neo-liberal revolutions under the UK Prime Minister Margaret Thatcher and US President Ronald Reagan, and the obsession in the 1980s with the relative performance of Anglo-American economies compared with those organized with greater levels of state intervention in the national economy, such as Germany and Japan. But its expression in the context of development was especially vigorous, oriented to explaining and theorizing the reasons for the divergence in performance between the 'developing regions' of the world.

Neo-liberal theory was, and remains, predicated on a profound cynicism about politics and, more specifically, about states. Its roots in neoclassical economics yield an assumption that individuals are motivated by self-interest, and, therefore, that politics is similarly conditioned. The intervention of states in the workings of national economies, and by extension the global economy, is therefore understood to introduce a wide range of distortions and contradictions which are deemed inimical to the pursuit of growth and development. The core contention of neo-liberalism is consequently, as David Harvey puts it (2005a: 20), that 'human well-being can best be advanced by liberating individual entrepreneurial freedoms and skills within an institutional framework characterized by strong private property rights, free markets, and free trade'. The emphasis fell on 'depoliticizing' economic activity,

and development more broadly, and consolidating market-led mechanisms of organizing economies and allocating resources within them (see Gamble 2001). Crucially, these market-led mechanisms were increasingly 'global' or 'globalizing' in nature.

The era of neo-liberal development thus featured a new and distinctive emphasis on participation in the global economy, conceived both as the accommodation of increasingly unfettered global market activity, and its harnessing in ways that would reap developmental benefits. This was an abrupt break with theories of underdevelopment, despite the common emphasis on the global economy and its role in shaping development. While underdevelopment theories conceived the world economy as imposing structural impediments to development, neo-liberalism understood participation in global economic activity as the prerequisite for development, and development strategy came to be understood as essentially about 'global positioning' (McMichael 2000: 15; Gore 2000). But, at the same time, neo-liberal theories continued to understand development as an inherently national process, and moreover understood the reasons for development failures as lying in internal (endogenous) factors—that is, as rooted in 'incorrect' government policies, institutional underdevelopment, and excessive state intervention in the workings of national economies (see Box 13.3).

BOX 13.3

Key Dimensions of Neo-Liberal Development Theory

Rests on the argument that 'human well-being can best be advanced by liberating individual entrepreneurial freedoms and skills within an institutional framework characterized by strong private property rights, free markets, and free trade' (Harvey 2005a).

Sees the path to development as requiring the consolidation of market-based mechanisms of organizing economies and allocating resources, and therefore the 'depoliticization' of economic activity.

Identifies engagement in the global economy as the key to propelling processes of development, while at the same time attributing development failures to 'internal' factors such as 'incorrect' government policies, institutional underdevelopment, corruption, or excessive state intervention in the economy.

BOX 13.4

Characteristics of the Japanese 'Developmental State'

The first priority of the state is economic development—a priority maintained consistently by the Japanese government in both the pre-war and post-war periods. Economic development is defined in terms of growth, production, and competitiveness, rather than consumption, distribution, and welfare.

A 'small, inexpensive but elite' bureaucracy, recruited on the basis of merit, is responsible for selecting the industries to be developed, identifying the best means of developing these industries, and supervising competition in the selected sectors to guarantee their economic effectiveness.

The legislative and judicial branches of government are restricted to the 'safety valve' functions of ensuring that the bureaucracy responds to the requirements of those groups in society on which the stability of the model rests; put more pithily, 'the politicians reign and the bureaucrats rule' (Johnson 1981: 12).

State intervention in the economy is of a 'market-conforming' nature.

The bureaucracy is led by a 'pilot agency', such as the Japanese Ministry of Trade and Industry (MITI), possessing an array of functions associated with controlling and directing industrial transformation.

Source: adapted from Johnson (1982).

The problem for neo-liberalism was that, as noted, the big development story unfolding at the time was the rise of a group of economies which apparently contradicted this logic, characterized as they were by a very different conception of how development could and should be achieved. The centrepiece of 'neo-statism' was the notion of the 'developmental state' (Johnson 1982; also see White 1988; Woo-Cumings 1999; Kohli 2004), in which the state was recognized to shape, direct, and promote the process of economic development (see Box 13.4). Markets were in this sense 'governed' rather than 'free' (Wade 1990). The forms of 'state developmentalism' observed in East Asia offered in this view a compelling explanation of the divergence in the performance of economies in that region and those in other regions, particularly Latin America, and a way of thinking about development which was ostensibly at odds with the dominant orthodoxy of neo-liberalism. However, things were not quite that simple. Neo-liberal theory also laid claim to the so-called 'East Asian miracle' on the basis of a very different reading of its development trajectory—one based not on the developmental role of states, but on the supposed conformity of the economies in question with the principles of the free market. The debate is of long-standing and has been amply reflected elsewhere (Wade 1990). The point for present purposes is that the battleground for the rivalry between neo-liberal and neo-statist theories of development was precisely the East Asian region, and in theoretical terms the key bone of contention was the relationship between markets and states in development (see Box 13.5).

The rivalry between these schools of thought nevertheless masks a number of similarities between them. We need here to highlight two. First, they both conceive of development as a national process, where what 'develop' are countries or national economies. Second, in both approaches development itself is understood to be about economic growth—only one of the large number of possibilities Arndt mentioned in the list we discussed at the start of this section. While neo-liberalism and neo-statism have dominated thinking about development in the contemporary period,

BOX 13.5

Key Dimensions of Neo-Statist Development Theory

Was developed as a means of explaining the growth trajectory of Japan and other East Asian economies from the 1960s onwards, and the divergence between this region and other parts of the developing world.

Advances a different understanding from neo-liberalism of the relationship between states and markets in East Asian development, emphasizing the role and importance of developmental states in 'governing' markets and shaping development processes.

Along with neo-liberalism and other development theories, sees development as a national process and prioritizes an understanding of development as economic growth.

there have nevertheless been other currents in development theory that have challenged both of these assumptions in interesting ways, some of which have been accepted into these dominant approaches, and some of which have remained on the outside.

'Human development', gender, and environmental theories

The theories grouped together in this section are unified by a commitment to 'human' or 'people-centred' development, and later 'sustainable human development', as a direct challenge to the emphasis on development as aggregate economic growth that has characterized all of the ways of thinking about development that we have looked at thus far. The redefinition of the meaning of development entailed in this commitment was summarized in an early, influential statement by the renowned economist Dudley Seers (1969: 3–4):

 ❝ The questions to ask about a country's development are therefore: What has been happening to poverty? What has been happening to unemployment? What has been happening to inequality? If all three of these have become less severe, then beyond doubt there has been a period of development for the country concerned. If one or two of these central problems have been growing worse, and especially if all three have, it would be strange to call the result 'development', even if per capita income had soared. ❞

In this spirit, 'human development' approaches began to take shape from the 1970s onwards. Their early incarnation was as the so-called 'basic needs' approach, which rested on a recognition that across the world, contrary to the predictions of neoclassical economics and the neo-liberal orthodoxy, economic growth was clearly not always associated with beneficial outcomes for the poor, either in incomes or in employment opportunities. Consequently, it was argued that special redistributive measures were required to target the poor and unemployed (Chenery, Bowen, and Svikhart 1974; ILO 1976). Development in this conception emphasized the meeting of basic material needs (food, shelter, clothing), the need for access to key services (water, sanitation, health care, education), and the need for people to participate in the political and decision-making processes that affected their lives (see Streeten *et al.* 1982).

The approach failed to take root as a result of its unrealistic policy goals, its rejection in poor countries as a result of its 'Western' and 'Northern' flavour in the context of the ideological politics of the Cold War, and the increasing dominance of neo-liberalism. But its essence endured and reappeared in a new generation of human development theory in the 1980s and 1990s, encapsulated most notably in the work of the Nobel prize-winning economist Amartya Sen. Sen advanced an understanding of development as being fundamentally about the enhancement of people's 'capabilities', later reformulated as 'freedoms': stated in seductively simple terms, development was defined as 'a process of expanding the real freedoms that people can enjoy' (Sen 1999: 3). Freedoms were thus understood as both the means and the ends of development. Going further, this approach emphasized the ways in which the agents of development were not governments but ultimately people themselves.

Gender and environmental approaches to development echoed some of the core concerns of human development theories. Ways of thinking about development that privileged gender are varied (see Rai 2002), but are knit together by a core concern with the failures of development to bring about more egalitarian societies, the neglect of the particular needs of women in development processes, and the lack of attention to the ways in which development projects carried particular and distinctive consequences for women. Some of the most influential statements within this broad development project sought to extend the 'basic needs' approach into a 'gender needs' framework (Molyneux 1985; Moser 1989, 1993), which focused on two sets of 'gender interests': 'practical' interests associated with the satisfaction of basic material needs; and 'strategic' interests associated with the rectification of gender inequalities in such areas as political representation, educational opportunity, employment conditions, freedom from domestic violence and exploitation, and so on. These were then extended into a notion of 'empowerment' which, echoing human development approaches, was understood as increasing women's ability to secure 'their own self-reliance and internal strength' (Moser 1989: 107). Other strands of this body of thought which will be of particular relevance to the discussion in the next section of the chapter emphasized the highly gendered impact of globalization processes and particular kinds of development strategies (Elson 1989, 1992, 1995; Marchand 1994, 1996; Pearson 1995; Benería 2003).

Likewise, environmental approaches emerged from the early 1970s onwards as critiques of the view of the relationship between environment and development that had prevailed in post-war growth and modernization theories, as well as neo-liberal approaches. In these latter perspectives, natural resources are not considered to pose obstacles to economic growth and there was a general optimism that technical solutions would be found that allowed human beings to 'harness nature on an ever-larger scale' (Woodhouse 2002: 141). The early critique emerged in a report commissioned by the Club of Rome, entitled *Limits to Growth* (Meadows *et al.* 1972), which advanced the arresting argument that the limits to growth could in fact be reached within the next century if trends in population growth, industrialization, food production, natural resource depletion, and environmental degradation continued. Gradually, the linkages between environment and development thus became a matter of global concern and had moved belatedly, along with poverty and gender, to the centre of global development debates by the end of the 1980s, clothed in the concept of 'sustainable development'. This was defined famously as 'development that meets the needs of the present without compromising the ability of future generations to meet their own needs' (World Commission on Environment and Development 1987). To this end, the ambitious call was issued for a reorientation of economic activity and development strategy to focus on human development and the needs of the poor, noting that unequal distribution of and access to resources, as well as vastly unequal patterns of resource consumption, contributed to both the perpetuation of poverty and the steady destruction of the global environment. These connections between environment and development are discussed in detail by Peter Dauvergne in Chapter 14.

These three approaches, in their quite different ways, advance a critique of the other kinds of development theory that we have looked at in this section. They emphasize the limitations and dangers of the dominant understanding of development as a process of economic growth, and instead highlight a number of the other ways of thinking about development that we noted in the quotation from Arndt at the beginning of the section. Equally, they all take issue with the notion that what develop—the objects of development—are countries or national states and economies, in which national governments are the agents of development. Rather, they conceive of development as being about a process of improvement in the material and social conditions in which people live, and the expansion of opportunities, 'capabilities', and

BOX 13.6

Key Dimensions of 'Human' Development Theories

Take issue with other development theories' definition of development as growth, and instead focus on a range of indicators associated with 'human development' and 'sustainable development'.

Advance a 'people-centred' approach to development, where the objects of development are human beings and groups of people, not simply countries or economies.

Broaden the focus to emphasize inequalities within societies and between groups of people, not simply between countries, and incorporate not only economic inequalities but a range of social inequalities (including those based on gender).

'freedoms' that shape those conditions (see Box 13.6). In this sense, the meaning, process, and goals of development were all redefined to yield a focus on 'sustainable human development'.

KEY POINTS

- Different theories of development reflect differing conceptions of what development is and how it might be achieved, and entail different diagnoses of the causes of either developmental progress or developmental failure.

- The period from the 1940s to the early 1980s was dominated by the controversy between modernization and underdevelopment theories, both of which had been widely discredited by the end of this period.

- The contemporary period (from the early 1980s) was dominated by the controversy between neo-liberalism and neo-statism in seeking to explain the key trend towards divergence in the trajectories of developing economies—a trend which challenged the validity of a notion of the 'Third World' as a single group of countries.

- Both neo-liberalism and neo-statism laid claim to the 'East Asian miracle', the former interpreting it as a triumph of 'export-led growth' and conformity with the free market model, the latter as a triumph of 'investment-led development' and the importance of states in directing and mediating development processes.

- 'Human' or 'people-centred' theories of development challenged the emphasis on economic growth and sought to develop a wider conception of development as being fundamentally about the material and social conditions in which people live.

Development theory in practice

We have seen that a flourishing of development theory has marked the contemporary period, advancing very different ways of thinking about what development means and how to achieve it. Our task now is to trace the translation of these different ways of thinking about development into concrete policies and strategies, and to understand their impact and consequences. The overarching context for this discussion is that the contemporary period of development, from the end of the Second World War to the present time, has taken place in the midst of accelerating processes of globalization. All of these theories provide a different perspective on the relationship between globalization and development—both what that relationship does look like and what it should look like.

The mid 1940s to the early 1980s

Across the regions that constituted what at the time was called the 'Third World', the post-war development context was dramatically different from that which had hitherto prevailed. First, it was marked by the onset of the period of decolonization, in which African and a number of Asian states finally achieved independence from the various European powers, and which initiated the fundamental changes in the international political-economic landscape that defined the development project from that time forwards. Second, the experience of the Great Depression and the two World Wars prompted a reassessment, particularly in Latin America, of the virtues and dangers of the broadly laissez-faire economic policies that had been pursued up to that point, along with the wisdom of dependence on the industrialized states as markets for their exports of primary products and imports of manufactured goods. Third, demographic trends necessitated urgent attention to employment as the key goal of economic policy (Thorp 1998: 128). Finally, the world economy was defined for all developing countries by heightened protectionism in the key European and US markets, the movement towards the formation of the European Economic Community, and the establishment of new institutions under the Bretton Woods system which were dominated by the established powers and in which developing countries, by now vastly increased in number, had no means of effective participation.

This conjunction of circumstances led to two immediate priorities for development strategies. The first was to design policies that would lead to a resumption of growth, achieve the goals of industrialization, and in some cases respond to the demographic urgencies of employment creation. The second was to find ways of mitigating enduring conditions of economic dependence on the 'North' and ensuring effective participation in the new international system which was shaping the possibilities for achieving these goals. The twin imperatives were therefore of 'catching up', on the one hand, and 'breaking out', on the other (Thomas 2008: 418). The emergence of a 'North–South' dynamic was reflected in the key divide in development theory of the time, namely, between modernization theory and underdevelopment theory. The former, as we have seen, viewed the purpose of development strategy as one of catching up with the developed countries by a route of political, institutional, and economic emulation. For this purpose, conditioned by the strategic and ideological imperatives of the Cold War, significant amounts of aid were pumped into the developing world, particularly into regions and countries of key strategic importance. Yet more important in modernization theory than the role of aid was its insistence that export-led growth, and hence trade, were the keys to progress for developing countries.

Underdevelopment theory gained much more traction than modernization theory across most parts of the developing world for both economic and political reasons (although notably it never gained much popularity in East Asia outside the Philippines). The diagnosis of the economic impact of the Great Depression and the two World Wars led to a conviction that a new economic policy direction was required. Governments in Latin America led the way, taking their cue directly from the structuralist theories of Prebisch and others, and advocating a turn not to export-led growth, as advocated by modernization theories and associated policy frameworks, but to 'inward-looking' development strategies. These strategies are known as **import-substituting industrialization (ISI)**. Versions of ISI were implemented widely in Africa and South Asia as well, but its adoption as a region-wide development strategy was most pronounced in Latin America. It had three central goals:

1. Stimulating and consolidating industrialization through a more effective system of state intervention in the economy, restructuring economic activity away from primary products,

and according much greater prominence to foreign capital over trade as the motor of capital accumulation and industrial development;

2. Politically integrating the new and expanding working classes through a programme of social reform and employment generation; and

3. Achieving some degree of autonomy vis-à-vis the international economy.

While ISI strategies were strongly oriented to mitigating economic dependence and achieving greater autonomy from the advanced industrialized nations, the political dimension of development strategy was to achieve more effective participation in the new international system. The nature of this system and the institutions that comprised it have been discussed at length in other chapters. The salient point for our discussion of development is that developing countries were marginalized within this new system. The Bretton Woods institutions were not set up as development institutions—indeed, they did not come to occupy that role until much later—but rather were focused on the needs of the industrialized countries, particularly in the context of post-war reconstruction (see Williams 1994; Woods 2006). It was not until the early 1960s that the World Bank and International Monetary Fund (IMF) began to engage on a substantial scale in lending for developing countries and to acknowledge these countries' demands for special resources. The ability of governments in developing countries to press their demands was also limited by the weighted voting structures that prevailed in these institutions, in which the United States occupied a position of particular privilege and veto power—as indeed it still does today. The GATT system operated similarly to marginalize developing countries. The Kennedy Round of the **General Agreement on Tariffs and Trade (GATT)** negotiations (1964–7) was seen by governments in the developing world as illustrative of the power imbalances in the international system which left them with extremely limited bargaining power and little prospect of achieving cooperation with more industrialized countries.

These concerns entrenched the conviction that developing countries needed to rely on solidarity and cooperation among themselves in order to address the disadvantageous terms on which international, economic, and political interactions were conducted. The **Non-Aligned Movement (NAM)** and the **New International Economic Order (NIEO)** were the two

key political movements that emerged as expressions of this goal. The NAM crystallized in 1955 following the pivotal Asian–African conference held in Indonesia, and provided a platform from which developing countries could organize themselves more effectively to participate and demand representation within international organizations. The establishment of the United Nations Conference on Trade and Development (UNCTAD) and the formation of the Group of 77 (G77), both in 1977, were the first expressions of these greater levels of political organization, the first conceived as an alternative forum to the GATT, and the second designed to afford greater participation and leverage in the UN system. Of greatest influence, however, was the NIEO movement which subsequently took shape in 1974. The call presented to the UN General Assembly for an NIEO in fact constituted a primarily political demand for the sovereignty of developing countries to be taken more seriously, along with a number of economic demands that were oriented particularly to reducing the dependence of developing economies on the international economy, reducing their vulnerability to deteriorating terms of trade for raw materials exports, and increasing their economic 'sovereignty' by enhancing control over **foreign direct investment (FDI)** and natural resources (Thomas 2008: 422). These concerns were articulated in a context of tumultuous change in the international political economy: the delinking of the dollar from a fixed price of gold by the US administration of Richard Nixon in 1971 brought an end to the post-war Bretton Woods era of fixed exchange rates, and international oil prices quadrupled in 1973 as a result of action by the Organization of Petroleum Exporting Countries (OPEC).

These increases in oil prices were especially damaging for oil-importing developing countries in the context of volatile commodity prices at the end of the 1970s, and were a major reason for the vast increase in borrowing among developing countries over the second part of the 1970s and early 1980s. The other reasons were related to the changing form of the ISI experiment, which, contrary to aspirations, remained dependent on inflows of foreign capital and technology. The 'classic' examples of ISI in Latin America—Argentina, Brazil, Chile, Colombia, and Mexico—were thus marked by the heavy participation of **transnational corporations (TNCs)** (Thorp 1998: 133–4). Peter Evans (1979) influentially used the label 'dependent development' to capture the centrality of foreign TNCs and FDI to Latin American development during this time. The foreign capital issue was also sharpened by the explosion in liquidity in international financial markets in the late 1960s and 1970s and its availability to Latin American countries in the form of loans, credit, industrial financing and so on, such that the ISI model in its later stages came to be driven by the massive accretion of foreign debt (see Pauly, Chapter 9 in this volume). The resulting debt crisis, which started in Latin America in 1982, marked the end of experiments with these kinds of inward-looking development based on structuralist underdevelopment theory.

Yet the failures of ISI in Latin America and elsewhere are only a part of the global picture. The crisis of development in Latin America and Africa was unfolding at a time when economies in another supposedly 'developing' region—namely, East Asia—were moving in the opposite direction. From the early 1960s to the early 1980s, the Japanese economy, emerging from the debris of the Second World War, grew at annual rates of around 7 per cent, moving from being the world's twentieth largest exporter to the third largest, and becoming by most indicators the most successful industrialized country in the world (Pempel 1999a). During the same period, the four NICs were also growing at annual rates of over 8 per cent. The articulation of the East Asian model featured a strong concern about the position of Asian economies in the global economy, for the purposes not only of achieving economic prosperity but also of securing a global presence and influence. These goals were formulated in strongly nationalist terms, particularly in the Japanese context, but were not of an inward-looking character. Rather, they were conditioned by a much more unequivocal recognition of the role of the international environment in creating the conditions for East Asian industrialization. In the 1960s, this environment, for Asia, was marked by increasing access to international finance, increasing access to the markets of the industrialized countries, and, perhaps particularly, the increasing relocation of global productive activity to low-cost sites in what was then still thought of as the 'periphery', specifically to Asia (Wade 1990). This process was captured influentially in the notion of the 'new international division of labour' (NIDL) (Frobel, Heinrichs, and Kreye 1980). Moreover, the Japanese and East Asian context differed dramatically from the Latin American 'dependent development' experience, inasmuch as the NICs possessed the strength and autonomy to manage the impact of inflows of foreign capital on the local economies. They were therefore much less conditioned, and certainly less negatively affected, by the dominance of foreign TNCs (Haggard and Cheng 1987).

We can see, therefore, that this period of development—the so-called 'Age of Development'—looked very different for different parts of the developing world. Its record was also very mixed, casting doubt on the utility of the prevalent notions of 'core' and 'periphery', or indeed 'Third World', as homogenous categories of countries. While the East Asian NICs experienced high growth rates, Latin America's aggregate growth performance was more modest. The story in sub-Saharan Africa was the most gloomy, with an average annual increase of only 1 per cent in per capita GDP between 1965 and 1985. An improvement between 1965 and 1974 gave way to a stagnation from the mid 1970s onwards, and by the early 1980s many countries had a lower per capita GDP than before independence some 20 years earlier. Manufactured exports declined between 1970 and 1986 for sub-Saharan African economies, while during the same period they jumped fivefold for Latin America, sixfold for the Middle East and North Africa, and thirteenfold for the East Asian NICs (World Bank 1994: 17–18). Revealingly, in 1965, Indonesia's GDP per capita had been lower than Nigeria's, and Thailand's lower than Ghana's (World Bank 1994: 17). What we saw over this period was thus a complete reordering of the development 'hierarchy' of developing nations, with sub-Saharan Africa sliding backwards as the East Asian NICs surged forwards, and many other developing regions featuring at least moderate improvements in the main indicators of economic development.

The 1980s onwards

From the early 1980s onwards, we see a new phase in the global development project. This was marked by the dominance of the neo-liberal agenda, based, as we outlined earlier, on ways of thinking about development, which sought the freeing of market forces and advanced a political project of 'rolling back' the state. In the advanced industrialized countries, especially the United States and the United Kingdom, neo-liberalism emerged as a specific response to the experiences of Keynesian growth strategies and welfare state policies in Europe, which by the 1970s were seen to have yielded the twin economic problems of stagnant growth rates and accelerating inflation (dubbed 'stagflation'), and the associated political challenges of increased militancy among trade unions. In the developing world, the critique was extended as an attack on ISI and the development problems it was seen to have bequeathed: bloated states, inefficiency, corruption, hyperinflation, the debt crisis, political instability, and a laundry list of other lamentable conditions. Neo-liberal thought in this sense came to consolidate itself as what John Toye (1993) called a 'counter-revolution' in development thinking, which shaped fundamentally the process of globalization and the manner in which countries, economies, and societies participated in it.

The point at which the various currents and elements of neo-liberal thinking were brought together into a blueprint for development came at the end of the 1980s. The US economist John Williamson identified the key elements of the new global policy agenda and attached to it the label **'Washington Consensus'** (**WC**). The resulting framework was quickly assumed not only to reflect the 'consensus' that had emerged in the global network of elite institutions, governments, and market actors associated with the neo-liberal orthodoxy, but also to constitute a list of what governments of countries had to do in order to 'develop'. Its elements are outlined in Box 13.7. Colin Leys put it

well when he observed that, by end of the 1980s, 'the only development policy that was officially approved was not having one—leaving it to the market to allocate resources, not the state' (Leys 1996: 42).

From the start, the WC was presented as common sense which was immune to sensible questioning—Williamson himself famously dismissed dissenters as 'cranks'—and disseminated aggressively across the developing world. The important point is that justification for this new 'orthodoxy' was presented as coming from globalization itself. The 'structural hegemony' of global capital (Gill and Law 1989), which was the cornerstone of globalization processes, was seen to put in place a new structure of rewards and punishments in the global political economy. Capital was understood to respond 'objectively' to particular national macroeconomic and policy conditions, to the extent that putting in place the 'right' policies—namely, those listed in the Washington consensus—was crucial for the achievement of the range of goals associated with development.

The main channels of the dissemination of the new neo-liberal development orthodoxy were the **international financial institutions** (**IFIs**), and specifically the World Bank and the IMF. During the 1980s it was **structural adjustment programmes** (**SAPs**) that ruled the day, reflecting a set of 'one-size-fits-all' policy prescriptions applied widely across Latin America and the Caribbean, sub-Saharan Africa, eastern Europe, and other parts of the developing world. In this model, lending strategies were subject to stringent forms of 'conditionality'—that is, continued lending was dependent on a country's conformity with a range of economic and political policy conditions attached to the loans from the IFIs. By the end of the 1980s, they were seen to have failed, particularly in view of the continued stagnation of most African economies, and resurgent inflation and hyperinflation in many Latin American economies. (The rate of 5,000 per cent in Argentina in 1989 is indicative of a situation of hyperinflation.) Indeed, the 1980s for these two regions were widely seen to be a 'lost decade' of development.

The IFIs changed tack, dropping the term 'structural adjustment' in favour of a new organizing concept—that of 'good governance'—by which the Bank sought to assert a new focus on the centrality of institutions in economic reform and development processes (World Bank 1992a; see Williams and Young 1994; Doornbos 2001). Macroeconomic stabilization (lowering inflation) and adjustment (trade liberalization,

BOX 13.7

The Policy Prescriptions of the Washington Consensus

Maintenance of fiscal discipline (budget deficits should not exceed 2 per cent of GDP).

Reordering of public expenditure priorities (reduction and elimination of subsidies; prioritization of spending in education, health, and infrastructure).

Tax reform (broadening of tax base; maintenance of 'moderate' marginal tax rates).

Maintenance of positive real interest rates (to discourage capital flight and increase savings).

Maintenance of 'competitive' exchange rates.

Trade liberalization.

Elimination of barriers to foreign direct investment.

Privatization of state-owned enterprises.

Deregulation of the economy.

Enforcement of property rights.

Source: Williamson (1990).

financial deregulation, privatization, and so on) remained critical, but were presented as only the 'first generation' of reforms. The 'second generation' comprised an emphasis on sweeping institutional reform for the 'modernization of the state', fiscal reform, tax reform, labour flexibilization, and so on. Whereas the days of the Bretton Woods era and the 1980s had been marked by an insistence on the 'apoliticism' of the IFIs—by which was meant that their agenda would not interfere with domestic political arrangements—the good governance agenda gave the IFIs licence to intervene in highly political ways in developing countries, and the agents of the neo-liberal counter-revolution thus claimed for themselves 'an unprecedented capacity to shape the strategic direction of large parts of the world' (Payne 2005a: 59).

> view of the continued stagnation of African economies, the resurgence of (hyper)inflation in Latin America, and the poor performance of other developing regions, except Asia.
> - The IFIs changed tack and introduced an emphasis on 'good governance' and 'second generation reforms', consolidating the neo-liberal counter-revolution in development thinking and strategy during the 1990s.

The crisis of the Washington Consensus in the 1990s

By the end of the 1990s, the neo-liberal development project was in trouble and the credibility of the WC under great strain. The record of development across Latin America, eastern Europe, and sub-Saharan Africa in particular—the main testing grounds of neo-liberal reform—was disappointing and in some cases disastrous. The Mexican 'peso crisis' of 1995, which saw the collapse of the currency following a speculative attack in the global financial markets, dealt a serious blow to the development orthodoxy. The Asian financial crisis of the late 1990s, explored by Louis Pauly (see Chapter 9, this volume) similarly knocked both neo-liberalism and neo-statism onto the back foot and revealed much about the relationship between globalization and development in that region and more broadly. Let us go into a little more detail about the record of this period before exploring what it can tell us about the developmental implications of globalization.

Growth

We have noted that the East Asian economies continued into the 1980s and 1990s with strong growth rates. The locus of that growth shifted from Japan and the NICs to China and India over this period. In the case of China, average annual GDP growth from the mid 1980s to the early 2000s stood at 9.5 per cent, increasing to 10.7 per cent by 2006 (World Bank 2007a) (see Figures 13.1 and 13.2). For India, the figures were 6 per cent from the late 1980s to the late 2000s, and 8.6 per cent in the 2003–7 period (Panagariya 2008). Both countries' trajectories featured a significant level of integration into global economic processes, at least in production and trade. But, in China especially, engagement

KEY POINTS

- From the end of the Second World War onwards, the twin goals of development were 'catching up' with the more developed economies and 'breaking out' of enduring conditions of economic dependence on the 'North'.

- Underdevelopment theory gained more traction than modernization theory in the developing world, except in Asia, and led to inward-looking development strategies known as import-substituting industrialization (ISI).

- The NAM and NEIO reflected a conviction among developing countries that they needed greater levels of solidarity and cooperation to press their demands more effectively in the international system and key organizations such as the IFIs, the GATT, and the UN.

- The early 1980s were marked by the Latin American debt crisis, reflecting both the contradictions of ISI and the explosion in lending to developing economies.

- At the same time as inward-looking development strategies were failing in Latin America, sub-Saharan Africa and elsewhere, the East Asian economies were achieving impressive rates of growth and moving rapidly up the economic hierarchy.

- From the early 1980s onwards, the landscape of development was defined by the dominance of neo-liberalism and, in particular, the dissemination of policy strategies based on the Washington consensus across the developing world.

- The structural adjustment policies (SAPs) of the 1980s were seen by the end of this decade to have failed, in

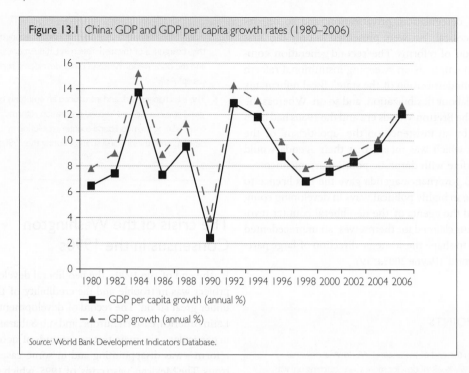

Figure 13.1 China: GDP and GDP per capita growth rates (1980–2006)

GDP per capita growth (annual %)

GDP growth (annual %)

Source: World Bank Development Indicators Database.

with globalization did not extend to financial markets. Equally, both countries engaged in autarkic trade and investment policies until the late 1980s, with liberalization processes initiated only from that time. While growth rates for China and India continued uninterrupted into the 2000s, the Asian crises of the late 1990s brought a setback and new challenges for the East Asian NICs and other economies in South-East Asia.

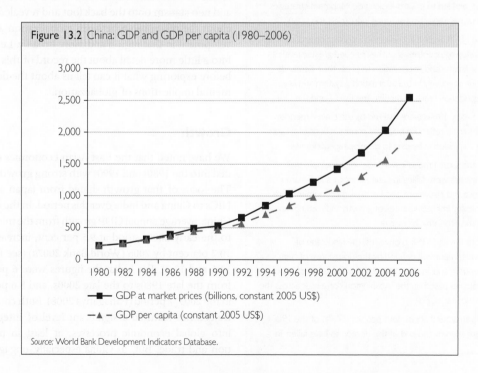

Figure 13.2 China: GDP and GDP per capita (1980–2006)

GDP at market prices (billions, constant 2005 US$)

GDP per capita (constant 2005 US$)

Source: World Bank Development Indicators Database.

The story elsewhere was different. In Latin America, for instance, per capita GDP grew more slowly over the 1990s than during the period between 1950 and 1980, and by 2003 was 1.5 per cent lower than in 1997 (ECLAC 2002). The World Bank's key report on Africa in the 1990s (World Bank 1994) seemed curiously proud of what can only be thought of as a depressing picture: of the 28 countries that had engaged in structural adjustment, exactly half of them had experienced declines in the average annual growth rate of GDP per capita between 1981–6 and 1987–91. Growth figures for the region as a whole picked up pace through the second part of the 1990s, largely driven by export growth. However, for the period 1990–2001, African export growth rates were lower than those recorded for the rest of the world, both in agricultural products and manufactures (Gibbon and Ponte 2005).

Trade

On the trade front, the picture was again one of divergence between developing economies, this time between those which were integrated into international trade patterns as exporters of manufactured goods (mainly the East Asian NICs), and those which remained reliant on the export of primary commodities (mainly some smaller Latin American and sub-Saharan African economies) (Thomas 2008: 426–7). The obstacles to the trade strategies of the exporters of raw materials in Latin America and sub-Saharan Africa were found partly in trends in international commodity prices. In the 1980s, for example, prices collapsed for the key African export crops of cocoa, coffee (each declining by around 70 per cent), and cotton (declining by 28 per cent). But they were also found in the lack of access to the key markets. The problems of protectionism that were identified by the early structuralists and post-war policymakers in developing countries persisted through the 1980s and 1990s, particularly in the key sector of agriculture. Government subsidies to agricultural producers in the countries of the Organisation for Economic Co-operation and Development (OECD) fell slightly between the mid 1980s and the mid 1990s, from levels equivalent to 37 per cent of total farm receipts to around 30 per cent, but this latter figure remained unchanged by the mid 2000s. Levels in the EU have been consistently higher than the average for the OECD, at around 34 per cent of total farm receipts, and in the early 2000s levels were higher still

in Japan and Korea (around 60 per cent), and in Norway, Switzerland, and Iceland (around 70 per cent). In the early 2000s, the US was responsible for some 20 per cent total of global agricultural subsidies, and the European Union (EU) for around 40 per cent (OECD 2003, 2005).

International trade negotiations had expanded continuously to embrace a wide range of areas, including such issues as intellectual property, competition policy or investment policy. Nevertheless, the area of agriculture, for many developing countries fundamental, remained essentially off the negotiating table. In this sense, the expectation was that developing countries would unilaterally liberalize trade in key sectors (that is, with no corresponding liberalization in the developed market economies) and the structure of trade negotiations continued to fail to address the basic trade issues that were critical to their development prospects. The ongoing marginalization of developing countries in trade negotiations themselves compounded the problems, and led to a creeping situation of stalemate in the World Trade Organization (WTO) agenda after the end of the Uruguay Round in the mid 1990s, which persisted throughout the 2000s (Finger and Nogués 2002; Panagariya 2002; Narlikar 2003).

Finance and investment

Much of the commentary about globalization, both enthusiastic and sceptical, notes the huge growth in private investment flows to the developing world, particularly over the course of the 1990s. By the mid 1990s, these had increased sixfold compared with 1990 levels, and were some four times greater than the peak levels reached during the lending boom of 1978–82, which, as we have seen, culminated in the Latin American debt crisis of the early 1980s. Developing economies' share of total global FDI flows stood at 40 per cent, compared with 15 per cent in 1990. Flows to these economies were dominated by FDI, largely associated with large-scale privatization processes, but **portfolio investment** (bonds and equities) rose sharply to account for around a third of the total. By the middle of the 1990s, private flows were also around five times greater than official (aid) flows (World Bank 1997: 9–10). Yet the pattern was much more uneven than these figures suggest at first glance. In the mid 1990s, 95 per cent of these flows were directed to only 26 of the 166 countries classified by the World Bank as 'developing nations' (World Bank 1997: 12). Sub-Saharan Africa, notably, was largely bypassed by this surge in capital flows in comparison with other regions.

Such is the context of the rash of economic and financial crises in the 1990s and early 2000s in the developing world—the Mexican peso crisis of 1995, the Asian financial crisis of 1998, the spread of 'contagion' to Brazil, Russia, Turkey, and elsewhere, and the Argentine collapse of 2001. Financial volatility was both central to the causes of these crises and a result of them. Capital flows to Latin America and the Caribbean, for instance, contracted by more than a third in 2002 alone, the decline being felt most sharply in Mexico and the Caribbean as a result of the additional impact of recession in the US economy (Phillips 2005: 339). While in some cases (Brazil, East Asia), FDI levels picked up quite quickly following the onset of crisis, in others the recovery was much slower and more partial. We will look more closely at debates surrounding the causes of these crises and contending reactions to them in the next section of the chapter.

Debt

The problem of indebtedness among developing countries is of long-standing, but the trajectory of its increase was striking during the 1990s. The total debt stock of the net-debtor developing countries doubled during this decade to US$2.2 billion. Again at an aggregate level, the ratio of debt service payments (that is, either repayments to creditors of money owed, or payments covering some of the interest on the debt) to exports increased from 19.6 per cent in 1991 to 22.3 per cent in 1999. The problem was, and remains, most acute for the heavily indebted countries, where debt levels were equivalent to 103 per cent of total GDP between 1995 and 2000, notwithstanding a small fall since the peak of 120 per cent for 1990–4 (Thomas 2008: 426). But larger and richer developing countries also continued to struggle with high levels of indebtedness. For Argentina in 1998, for example, the ratio of total debt to foreign exchange revenues from exports reached 500 per cent, and its ratio to GDP 41.4 per cent, increasing to 50 per cent by 2000 when the economy was beginning to collapse (Mussa 2002).

The period was marked by a new phase in the global politics of debt, with the announcement in September 1996 of the **Heavily-Indebted Poor Countries**

(**HIPC**) initiative. This policy was not designed to eliminate debt, but rather had the more modest objective of reducing it to 'sustainable' levels, defined as a country's ability to meet its debt service obligations without having to resort to a rescheduling of the debt or accumulating arrears (Payne 2005b: 147). Forty-one countries were initially classified as HIPCs, overwhelmingly from Africa, and some progress was made over time towards reorganizing and alleviating their debt burdens. But, unsurprisingly, the HIPC initiative did not go nearly far enough for the growing concert of non-governmental organizations that began to mobilize around this issue, notably under the umbrella of the Jubilee 2000 movement which demanded the cancellation of the debt of poor countries. In mid-2005 at a summit meeting in Gleneagles, Scotland, the argument was finally accepted by the Group of Seven (G7) countries that the multilateral debt of many poor countries should be cancelled entirely (Helleiner and Cameron 2006), and the Multilateral Debt Relief Initiative (MDRI) came into being. The IMF began to provide the agreed relief from the beginning of 2006, and other institutions and governments have followed suit, on the basis of exacting eligibility criteria.

Poverty and inequality

Trends in poverty and inequality over this period are amply documented in Robert Wade's chapter (Chapter 12, this volume). The important points for our purposes here are twofold. First, the neo-liberal development project did not yield the expected or desired results. While the proportion of the world's population living in conditions of poverty may have diminished at an aggregate level over the course of the 1990s, this improvement was almost entirely accounted for by the performance of East Asia, especially China. The population living below the $1 per day poverty line increased significantly in most other parts of the world, and the recorded increase was even greater using the $2 per day measurement (World Bank 2002a; Kaplinsky 2005). Second, the recurrence of economic crisis in the developing world increased the *vulnerability* of populations to poverty and destitution, along with the range of social phenomena that accompany these conditions. After the Asian financial crisis, for example, the World Bank estimated the incidence of poverty in that region to have increased by around 22 million people (Glyn 2006: 69).

KEY POINTS

- The growth record of the 1990s was highly uneven across regions and countries, with sharp contrasts between the high growth of East Asian economies and the stagnant performance of Latin America and Africa.

- Exporters of manufactured goods did rather better than those economies that remain dependent on primary products, and persistent protectionist barriers in the 'rich' countries, especially in agriculture, have impeded developmentally advantageous participation in the international trading system.

- Finance and investment flows to many developing economies increased significantly over the 1990s, even though sub-Saharan Africa was largely bypassed by this surge. Recurrent crises over the 1990s and 2000s have both reflected and resulted in a marked volatility of financial flows.

- The problem of indebtedness increased over the 1990s, mainly for small and poor economies but also for some large economies.

- Trends in poverty and inequality contradicted the expectations of the neo-liberal orthodoxy.

- the objectives of economic reform did not translate into a single and unique set of policy prescriptions, but rather could be achieved in a number of ways;

- solutions to development problems must be context-specific and the notion of 'models' for emulation was unhelpful;

- rules had been set out in relation to government discretion in ways which introduced undue rigidities into economies and inflexibility into decision-making;

- reform efforts needed to focus on the 'binding constraints' to development, rather than relying on a 'laundry list' of policy reforms that may or may not be appropriate.

The East Asian crisis presented more problems for both neo-liberals and neo-statists, but ultimately the same sorts of arguments emerged. Some explanations sought to emphasize the problems with globalization that impinged on the development experiences of the 1990s, the nature of globalized financial markets, the dynamics of crisis behaviour, and the crisis-management policies of the IMF being among the most notable of these (Sachs 1998; Wade 1998; Higgott and Phillips 2000; Chang 2006; Glyn 2006). Orthodox accounts, by contrast, took aim at levels of corruption and an excessive role for state patronage in the private sector in East Asia—famously labelled 'crony capitalism'—and the deficiencies of banking systems (Henderson 1998; Pempel 1999b; Segal and Goodman 2000; see Kang 2002). Up to this point, neo-liberal claims to the East Asian miracle had sought to play up the role of export-led growth and play down the issues of the role of states and the internal organization of East Asian economies, thus sidestepping the problem of having to account for the growth performance of these economies under conditions held by the neo-liberal orthodoxy to be damaging to development prospects. Now, the emphasis was reversed and the arguments that had previously been avoided were once again used to discredit the East Asian model and explain its 'failure'.

This came after a period in which even the World Bank appeared to have conceded certain ground to the neo-statists in the debate over the role of states. Its *East Asian Miracle* report of 1993, after protracted political wrangling between the Bank and the Japanese government (which was demanding from the Bank a more

Not surprisingly, explanations of the failures of the development project of the 1980s and 1990s ranged widely. The key dividing line was between those who sought explanations in internal factors and those who emphasized the connections with globalization. It was noted earlier that neo-liberal thinking conceived of development failures as being rooted in internal conditions, and as we moved into the 2000s that conviction remained unshaken. John Williamson (2003) set out the clearest statement of the view that the problem lay with the incomplete implementation of neo-liberal reforms. Others saw the Mexican crisis as a 'reality check': it was 'not that the policy recommendations that Williamson outlined are wrong, but that their efficacy—their ability to turn Argentina into Taiwan overnight—was greatly oversold' (Krugman 1995: 30). The World Bank, in a report which addressed itself specifically to the task of 'learning from a decade of reform' (2005c), drew a long list of conclusions summarized well by Dani Rodrik (2006: 976–7):

- insufficient attention had been paid to stimulating the dynamic forces that lie behind the growth process;

explicit acknowledgement of the achievements of the East Asian model), constituted the first acknowledgement of the *fact* of government intervention in East Asian successes and contained a series of mumbled concessions to the benefits of 'selective interventions' in the areas of exports and credit. But it continued staunchly to defend the Bank's line against 'industrial policy' and marshalled an arsenal of (for many, very dubious) evidence to insist on the underlying 'market-conforming' character of the East Asian development model (World Bank 1993; see Wade 1996*b*). The crisis of the late 1990s nevertheless allowed the Bank and other agencies to retreat quickly to much more comfortable terrain, turning these arguments around to argue, in effect, that they had been right all along.

The case for a 'new paradigm for development'— the PWC (Stiglitz 1998, 2001)—was striking for the way it stole a good deal of the thunder from the neo-statists by emphasizing the role of state intervention in economies in order to compensate for market failures and imperfections (Payne and Phillips 2010: 148). But it went a very great deal further, Stiglitz proclaiming that the PWC was, no less, a 'development strategy [which] outlines an approach to the transformation of society'. All aspects of society (including the state, the private sector, the family, community, and individual) needed to be incorporated; it gave precedence to a focus on sustainable and equitable development; it developed the new 'buzzwords' of capacity-building, governance, participation, transparency, civil society, and so on, placing much greater emphasis on democratic governance than its predecessor; and it advocated reform of the IFIs and the 'global governance' of development. It also called for a greater degree of 'ownership' for developing countries of the development policies they pursued, and a correspondingly 'greater degree of humility' on the part of the international financial institutions—an acknowledgement that they 'do not have all the answers' (Stiglitz 1998: 15). The barrage of criticisms was predictable and important—primarily that the PWC represented no significant break from the WC (Standing 2000; Fine 2001; Rodrik 2002). Particularly significant for our purposes is the fact that the treatment of globalization remained largely untouched, with the emphasis still falling on domestic reform rather than on rethinking how the global economy worked.

While the PWC faded quickly from view and parlance, it was particularly interesting for the way in which it coincided with the more explicit incorporation into the global development agenda of the concerns advanced by proponents of a 'human development' approach. This incorporation was not in itself new, inasmuch as by the early 1990s the work of Sen and others at the United Nations Development Program (UNDP) had found a central place in the global development agenda, particularly in the evolving interest in poverty reduction alongside good governance. But the focus on human development became most pronounced in the late 1990s and early 2000s, around the same time as the PWC was being elaborated, and was encapsulated in a focus on poverty reduction as the key global development strategy for the twenty-first century.

Two key frameworks emerged for this purpose: the poverty reduction strategy papers (PRSP) approach, and the MDGs. The PRSP process aimed to emphasize the question of local ownership in global poverty reduction strategies, involving (a) 'promoting opportunity' and pursuing 'pro-poor growth'; (b) 'facilitating empowerment', particularly by promoting 'good governance'; and (c) 'enhancing [human] security', involving such areas as health, education, and sometimes 'social safety nets' or 'social protection measures' (Craig and Porter 2003: 53–4). They have been widely seen, by supporters and detractors, as integral to a PWC-type approach to development. The MDGs, agreed in 2001, were announced with considerably more fanfare as a commitment by the whole international community to achieving an ambitious set of development targets. These are set out in Box 13.8. It is not difficult to see why the MDGs have widely been seen as the practical expression of the human development approach as articulated by the UNDP, expanded to embrace also the World Bank's income poverty monitoring measures (Fukuda-Parr 2004; Saith 2006).

Two aspects of the MDGs are of particular interest to us. First, the MDGs constituted yet another global development initiative which emanated very specifically from the rich-country development community: it was 'a donor-country interpretation of the key issues, for a donor-country audience' (Nelson 2007: 2041). Second, the MDG framework contained no mention of those issues relating to globalization, global politics and unequal power structures. The implicit assumption was, once again, that the development problems of the world could be rectified by a global concert of governments and institutions

BOX 13.8

The Millennium Development Goals

Goal 1: Eradicate Extreme Poverty and Hunger

Goal 2: Achieve Universal Primary Education

Goal 3: Promote Gender Equality and Empower Women

Goal 4: Reduce Child Mortality

Goal 5: Improve Maternal Health

Goal 6: Combat HIV/AIDS, Malaria, and Other Diseases

Goal 7: Ensure Environmental Sustainability

Goal 8: Develop a Global Partnership for Development

pushing sustained market reforms in the relevant national contexts.

The core goal of MDG1, to halve the proportion of the world's population living on less than $1 per day had been achieved by the second part of the 2000s. By late 2015, the end date for the MDGs, the World Bank's forecasts indicated that the number of people living in extreme poverty was likely to have fallen to under 10 per cent of the global population, using its updated poverty line of $1.90 per day (World Bank 2015a). This represented slightly more than a halving of the number of people living in extreme poverty across the world, from 1.9 billion in 1990 to 836 million in 2015 (UNDP 2015).

However, the aggregate figures hide a patchiness in these improvements, the disparities between regions and between countries within regions, and variability between groups of poor people. The World Bank also noted a reversal in the regional composition of poverty. Whereas in 1990, East Asia had accounted for half of the global poor, and around 15 per cent lived in sub-Saharan Africa, forecasts for 2015 indicated that sub-Saharan Africa had come to account for half of the global poor, and some 12 per cent lived in East Asia (World Bank 2015a). China accounts for the bulk of the dramatic news on poverty, with 662 million fewer people living in extreme poverty in 2008 than in 1981; outside China, a decline of the extreme poverty rate from 41 per cent to 25 per cent by the end of the 2000s was not sufficient to reduce the total number of people living in extreme poverty (World Bank 2012a). In Latin America, the data are heavily skewed by trends in the large economies, specifically in Mexico and

Brazil, and most countries of the region were showing either no improvement at all or, in some cases, slight increases in poverty by the end of the 2000s (Phillips 2011a). In sub-Saharan Africa a modest reduction in extreme poverty meant that, for the time since 1981, less than half the population were living in extreme poverty in 2008, but still 47 per cent of the population fell into this category. In addition, while poverty was continuing to decline in all regions, it was noted that it was becoming more entrenched in countries that were either marked by conflict or strongly dependent on commodity exports (World Bank 2015a). Significantly, too, the World Bank has noted a 'marked bunching up' just above the $1.25 extreme poverty line, indicating that while there had been a drop in extreme poverty, there had been much less progress on poverty in general, particularly in getting over the $2 per day hurdle. The number of people living between the $1.25 and $2 per day poverty lines in fact doubled between 1981 and 2008 (World Bank 2012a).

Aside from the poverty figures, the UNDP, in its report assessing the performance of the MDGs, noted such achievements as the following: a tripling of the number of people in the working middle class (living on more than $4 a day); a halving of under-nourishment, the number of primary school age children not in education, and child mortality rates; the achievement of gender parity in schools in a majority of countries; and significant progress in sanitation and disease control or eradication, particularly in relation to conditions such as HIV/AIDS and tuberculosis. Yet the report also highlighted areas in which there remained a long way to go, including on poverty reduction. Even though extreme poverty may have been halved on aggregate, there remained some 836 million people still living in such conditions, and, as we have seen, the progress has been at best patchy. Conflict, environmental degradation and climate change continued to impede development, and gender inequality remained a stubborn problem. Particularly interestingly, given our earlier comments on its neglect in the formulation of the MDGs, the report highlighted the growing problem of inequality, both between households and between rural and urban areas (UNDP 2015).

As David Hulme and James Scott remind us (2010, citing Fischer 2010), it would nevertheless be a mistake to assume that all progress over this period is attributable to the MDGs. In the first place, many of the advances in some parts of the world were made before the MDGs came into being. In the East Asia and the Pacific region, because 1990 was adopted as the baseline for measurements, the targets on poverty reduction were virtually achieved before the MDGs had even been created (Pogge 2004; Hulme and Scott 2010). Second, progress in some key areas has in fact slowed since the introduction of the MDGs, such as in mortality rates of children under 5 years of age, which fell at an annual rate of around 3.5 per cent between 1960 and 2000, while annual progress since 2000 has been around 2.75 per cent (Hulme and Scott 2010). In short, the glass can be either half full or half empty in our assessment of the record of the MDGs (Hulme and Wilkinson 2012: 4).

The debate about what a 'post-2015 strategy' needed to look like yielded a new set of goals to guide the global development agenda between 2015 and 2030, which came to be called the Sustainable Development Goals (SDGs). At the Rio + 20 Summit in 2012, a working group was established to draft an agenda for the SDGs, which operated in tandem with a series of 'global conversations' set up by the United Nations to feed into the drafting of the recommendations. The draft report was completed in 2014, and

agreed following negotiations in the UN in August 2015. The principles guiding the drawing up of the SDGs accommodated the recognition that economic development needed to be rescued from its relative neglect so that any goals are both economic and social in character, that inequality needed to be integrated into a global development agenda, however politically sensitive that may be, and that a much greater voice for representatives of developing countries and associated social groups needed to be realized (Wilkinson and Hulme 2015). Box 13.9 outlines the 17 SDGs that will be adopted from January 2016 onwards.

The focus on poverty reduction and development goals thus came to define the global development agenda in the post-Washington consensus era, as articulated by the development community centred on the United Nations. However, this was not the only alternative that was articulated at this time. Another emanated from observation of the East Asian region. China, in particular, was seen both to be leading a pack of new 'rising powers' and to be articulating a very different route to high growth and development from that advocated in the policy prescriptions of the

---

BOX 13.9

The Sustainable Development Goals

Goal 1: End poverty in all its forms everywhere

Goal 2: End hunger, achieve food security and improved nutrition, and promote sustainable agriculture

Goal 3: Ensure healthy lives and promote wellbeing for all at all ages

Goal 4: Ensure inclusive and equitable quality education and promote lifelong learning opportunities for all

Goal 5: Achieve gender equality and empower all women and girls

Goal 6: Ensure availability and sustainable management of water and sanitation for all

Goal 7: Ensure access to affordable, reliable, sustainable and modern energy for all

Goal 8: Promote sustained, inclusive and sustainable economic growth, full and productive employment, and decent work for all

Goal 9: Build resilient infrastructure, promote inclusive and sustainable industrialization, and foster innovation

Goal 10: Reduce inequality within and among countries

Goal 11: Make cities and human settlements inclusive, safe, resilient and sustainable

Goal 12: Ensure sustainable consumption and production patterns

Goal 13: Take urgent action to combat climate change and its impacts (taking note of agreements made by the UNFCC forum)

Goal 14: Conserve and sustainably use the oceans, seas and marine resources for sustainable development

Goal 15: Protect, restore and promote sustainable use of terrestrial ecosystems, sustainably manage forests, combat desertification and halt and reverse land degradation, and halt biodiversity loss

Goal 16: Promote peaceful and inclusive societies for sustainable development, provide access to justice for all and build effective, accountable and inclusive institutions at all levels

Goal 17: Strengthen the means of implementation and revitalize the global partnership for sustainable development

Western development community. Its perceived success in economic and developmental terms, achieved without conforming with the neo-liberal consensus, led many to ask whether China might not be epitomizing a new development model, capable of being adopted and replicated elsewhere.

The boldest statement of this argument was made by the journalist Joshua Ramo (2004) in his outline of what he called the 'Beijing Consensus'. With this title, he was invoking the globalist and universalizing pretensions of the WC and other Western development frameworks (Payne and Phillips 2010: 154). In its substance, the Beijing Consensus echoed both theories of East Asian development and some of the older theories of 'catch-up' that we reviewed earlier in the chapter. First, it laid emphasis on the 'value of innovation', but rejected 'trailing-edge innovation', which traditional catch-up theories saw as the starting point, in favour of 'bleeding-edge innovation'—a distinction of aspiration illustrated in the juxtaposition of copper wires versus fibre optics. Second, it articulated a notion of 'balanced development', which went beyond indicators such as per capita GDP to emphasize 'sustainability and equality' over luxuries. Third, it proposed a 'theory of self-determination' and 'the use of leverage to move big, hegemonic powers which might be tempted to tread on your toes' (Ramo 2004: 27).

The Beijing Consensus's moment, as it were, was ultimately fleeting. By the late 2000s, it had largely disappeared from debates about development, in large part because of the profound limits to the replicability of the Chinese model in other regions of the world. The economic, political, and social conditions in which the Chinese model was articulated can safely be deemed to be historically unique. More to the point, the Beijing consensus was built on a rejection of the 'one-size-fits-all' Western development thinking that had dominated twentieth century theory and practice—why should we then expect the Chinese model to be any more universally applicable? Yet, leaving the Beijing Consensus itself to one side, it was precisely the challenge represented by China's economic and development performance to one-size-fits-all thinking that was most significant over this period. The 'find your own way' strand of development theory (Schmitz 2007: 55)—based on the idea that paths to development are multiple and contingent—was strongly reinforced by the continued rise of China and East Asia over the 1990s and 2000s, in the latest instalment of the long-running contest between competing development ideas.

KEY POINTS

- Explanations of the crisis of the Washington Consensus—and neo-liberal strategies more generally—were divided between those who emphasized 'internal' factors and those who emphasized factors associated with globalization.
- The East Asian crisis of the late 1990s was taken by neo-liberals to validate the development orthodoxy and used to discredit the East Asian model, even though it had just appeared to concede certain ground to the neo-statists and acknowledge the role of government intervention.
- The post-Washington consensus (PWC) was put forward as a 'new paradigm for development' (Stiglitz), but was seen by critics to depart very little from the original Washington consensus.
- The issue of poverty reduction came by the 2000s to occupy the centre of global development debates, reflected particularly in the Millennium Development Goals (MDGs) and later the Sustainable Development Goals (SDGs).
- Progress towards achieving the MDGs has been significant but uneven, with considerable differences between countries and groups of people.
- While the so-called Beijing Consensus was short-lived as an intervention in development debates in the 2000s, the rise of China challenges the one-size-fits-all development thinking that has dominated mainstream and Western development theory and practice.

Development in times of economic crisis

The contemporary chapter in global development is unfolding in the context of the twin crises of the late 2000s and early 2010s—on the one hand, the crisis of Anglo-American neo-liberalism which erupted primarily in the United States and the United Kingdom, and, on the other, the debt crisis engulfing large parts of southern Europe. At the time of writing, it is probably safe to say that we are now in the period of the aftermath of the former crisis, with global banking and financial volatility largely subdued. At the same time, it is unquestionably the case that we are still living through the fall-out from the crisis, with responses to it still unfolding across the world. For many countries in Southern Europe, the crisis continues, most starkly in the case of Greece. So what can we say of the implications of the economic crisis of the late 2000s for global development?

In one sense, the crisis that began in 2007 was not strictly speaking a 'global' economic crisis. Its origins were concretely in the United States, United Kingdom, and parts of Europe, and these are the parts of the world in which its effects have been felt the most. It had much to do with regulatory failures in globalized financial and banking systems, as did the Asian financial crisis a few years before. But just as we called this an 'Asian' crisis, so, in a sense, was this an 'Anglo-American' crisis. The difference is that, inevitably, an Anglo-American crisis brings with it global repercussions in a way that crises originating in and affecting other parts of the world would not. Indeed, almost all countries and large parts of the world's population were affected by the waves generated by what has come to be called in some quarters the 'Great Recession'. These waves were of varying size and impact, with some economies in the developing world weathering the storm better than others. Large economies such as China, India, and Brazil suffered serious consequences as a result of global recession. China and India maintained appreciable rates of growth through the most intense period of the crisis around 2009, of an order of 7, 8 or 9 per cent (see Figure 13.3). The waves in this context were felt largely as slow-downs in economic growth, rather than recession. The consequences for Brazil were more severe, with

negative growth in 2009 followed by a quick rebound, and an equally quick downturn from 2011 onwards.

The major reasons for these slow-downs are usually depicted as the decline in demand in Europe and the US, and the consequences thereof for exports from economies like China and Brazil. Robert Wade has highlighted the vital point that Chinese growth in turn fuels growth in economies like Germany, Japan and Brazil, as well as in its own East Asian region, which is important in thinking about the mechanisms by which the repercussions of the crisis are transmitted across the global economy. Many East Asian economies are fuelled by exports to China, to the extent that a dollar fall in China's exports is far more significant for East Asian economies than a dollar fall in domestic demand in China (Wade 2009c). Similarly, China functions as a major export destination for a very large number of economies across the world, including in Africa and Latin America, and an increasingly important source of foreign investment and development financing (Dittmer and Yu 2010). However, it bears remembering that the manufacturing economy in China, in particular, is driven heavily by investment and capital from economies like the US and Japan, and the effects of the crisis are channelled through those flows as well as through trade and the dynamics of global demand.

Some of the sharpest challenges to the large emerging economies became apparent in the arenas of inflation,

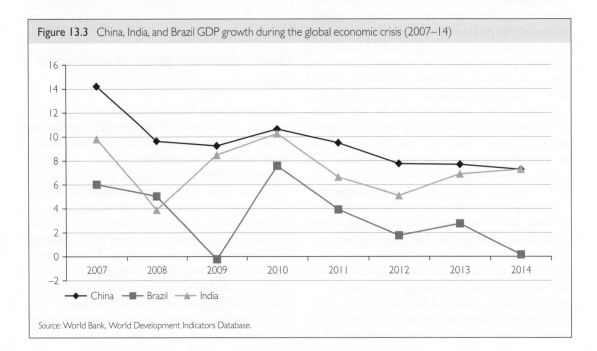

Figure 13.3 China, India, and Brazil GDP growth during the global economic crisis (2007–14)

Source: World Bank, World Development Indicators Database.

currency pressures and pressures on asset prices. The situation in Brazil and China was similar in this respect, except that the Chinese authorities have retained the ability to manipulate the currency in order to avoid the problems of overvaluation that have emerged elsewhere, as in Brazil. However, this strategy on the part of the Chinese government also created problems for other emerging economies, including Brazil, where the combination of currency manipulation in China (an increasingly important trade partner) and strategies of quantitative easing and austerity in the US and elsewhere led to an overvaluation of the Brazilian *real* by the turn of the decade, which became increasingly difficult to manage. In order to meet the twin challenge of reducing inflation and controlling the value of the currency, interest rates were raised, such that by 2012 they were among the highest in the world (over 10 per cent). This measure in turn had the effect of attracting increased inflows of investment and capital, leading the government of President Dilma Roussef to impose capital controls shortly after taking office in 2010. Similarly, the Chinese authorities sought to tackle overheating and inflationary pressures by imposing a range of financial controls, such as on construction and home sales. Indeed, the 'normalization of capital controls' during the crisis—extending to countries ranging from Iceland, Ukraine and Argentina to South Korea, Venezuela, and China, among many others—is perhaps the single most important way in which policy space for development has expanded in the contemporary era (Grabel 2013).

Such an analysis thus focuses on the *repercussions* of the crisis, according to an argument which characterizes it as Anglo-American in character. However, it risks overlooking a different set of insights into what *does* make the crisis 'global' in its character, reflecting an ongoing debate as to its origins and, by extension, the most appropriate solutions. Notwithstanding the need to accept the role of regulatory failure in the causes of the crisis, a different line of argument focuses on the role of 'global imbalances', where China and the other large emerging economies play a pivotal role in creating the conditions for the crisis to occur. The argument runs as follows (Wade 2009*a*). Massive global imbalances were created over the 1990s and 2000s by the interaction of US-type capitalism, dependent on import surpluses, and other types of capitalism espoused by China, Germany, or Japan, dependent on export surpluses. Governments—especially the Chinese authorities—sought to build up large reserves in order to stave off a run

on the currency; households saved a large proportion of their (rising) incomes in case of adversity, in the absence of social services and welfare safety nets provided by the state. The result was a tendency to limit domestic consumption and to increase exports as the basis of the growth model, underpinned generally by an undervalued exchange rate (again most obviously in China). For the global economy, the result was that other economies were forced to run deficits, such that 'world capitalist growth came to depend on insatiable US, UK and other deficit-country demand' (Wade 2009*a*: 10). This demand was financed by capital flows from the surplus countries at low interest rates, connected to increasing indebtedness, and these flows encouraged the proliferation of risky credit instruments. The rest of the story is well known.

This argument thus connects the debate about China and the rising powers to the debate about the causes and consequences of the Global Financial Crisis. Clearly, both perspectives on the crisis can be put to political purposes: the line of argument that this is an Anglo-American crisis with global repercussions is politically useful as further ammunition in the reaction against neo-liberalism as a global development model; the 'global imbalances' line of argument serves valuable political purposes for those, particularly in the US and Europe, who have long sought to force the hand of the Chinese authorities on currency manipulation and other policy positions. But each perspective also generates particular views on the most appropriate directions for the global economy. One focuses on the need for tighter regulation and tempering the excesses of the financial sector; the other focuses on a much broader and deeper set of global reforms and changes to national growth and development strategies, particularly in China and the other rising powers, amounting to a process of 'global rebalancing'. As other chapters in this book have discussed, it is still far from clear which of these—or, better said, which combination of these—will come to prevail.

In the midst of this delicate transition, the position of China as the new global economic powerhouse has been thrown into doubt by ongoing volatility in the Chinese economy. This volatility culminated in the second half of 2015 in a significant market crash following a further devaluation of the yuan in August of that year. More than US$5 trillion was estimated to have been wiped off global stock prices within two weeks of that event, and data indicated a sharp contraction of industrial activity in China. The turbulence had a significant impact on currencies in emerging markets, and the contraction of demand in China augured particular difficulties for national economies dependent on commodity and industrial exports to China, compounded by declining oil and commodity prices. Questions concerning the sustainability of China's high-growth model once more came to the fore, and some saw 'a definitive end to the period of rip-roaring emerging-market growth' in general (*The Economist* 2015). Such an argument was reinforced by grave ongoing difficulties in the Brazilian economy, which by late 2015 was mired in its worst recession since the 1930s, with GDP falling by a record 4.5 per cent in the third quarter, its debt being downgraded to 'junk' status by one credit-rating agency, the budget deficit reaching 9.5 per cent of GDP, and unemployment growing to 7.9 per cent (*Financial Times* 2015). Other large economies, including Russia, were also experiencing economic recession around the same time.

This volatility in emerging markets was not necessarily caused by the Global Financial Crisis of the late 2000s, and we should not confuse the two. Nevertheless, it is clearly highly important for our discussion of the political economy of global development, illustrating that global development prospects are now at least as strongly conditioned—if not more strongly conditioned—by China as by the United States and Europe. While we should not overstate the case, dependence across the developing world on demand in the Chinese economy is becoming increasingly pronounced, and the fall-out from both the global crisis and the emerging-market crisis is significant for our assessment of the changing form that global interconnectedness now takes.

Let us move beyond this focus on national economies to consider the developmental implications of this period of crisis from a different, 'human' perspective. As the financial crisis unfolded from 2007 onwards, it became clear that workers around the world who participate in production linked to global production networks and export markets were the most affected by the crisis, especially as TNCs seek to reduce costs in order to deal with slowing demand in some export markets. Wage employment in non-agricultural activity declined sharply over the first couple of years of the crisis, with the sharpest falls in manufacturing employment. However, even when manufacturing output rebounded during 2009, employment continued to decline, suggesting a sharply increased incidence of self-employment (including home work) in production within global value chains (Ghosh 2010).

The poorest and most vulnerable workers were the ones most affected by these trends, including informal workers who do not enjoy labour protections and work without contracts, migrant workers, and women. The burden also fell largely on the urban poor rather than the rural poor for this reason.

The human developmental implications of the crisis were also transmitted through its connections with global markets for food and fuel. The significant volatility in food and fuel prices through the 2000s are recognized to have been caused largely by the involvement of financial players in those markets, not by 'real' economic forces (Ghosh 2010). The retraction of regulation in global commodity markets permitted an acceleration of speculation, fuelled by an appetite for risk. At the same time, the effects of the global economic crisis constrained the ability of developing countries to import more food or to tailor public spending to distributive ends (Ghosh 2010: 213). Thus, at the height of the crisis, the Inter-American Development Bank was predicting that, in Latin America and the Caribbean, the impact of high food prices was likely to put 26 million people at severe risk of falling into conditions of extreme poverty. Chronic poverty would also be deepened substantially, particularly in food-importing countries like Haiti, Peru, and Nicaragua (IDB 2008).

A third, highly important mechanism by which the human developmental impact of the crisis was transmitted relates to global migration, the sheer scale of which, in all regions of the world, implies a rapid magnification and wide dispersal of the effects of economic crisis. First, the fact that the recession began in industrialized countries and spread outward meant that, as the crisis unfolded, migrants no longer had the ability to move from lagging parts of the world economy to booming parts (Martin 2009). Furthermore, much of the recession was concentrated in sectors that are sensitive to both economic cycles and trade, and traditionally dominated by high numbers of migrant workers. These include construction and manufacturing in economies like those of Spain or the UK and China or Bangladesh. Unemployment in the US construction sector, for example—in which two thirds of workers are foreign born—rose from 7.5 million to 13.2 million between the autumn of 2007 and the spring of 2009 (Martin 2009: 676). As the most economically motivated migrants, unauthorized workers were particularly affected by these patterns. The other sectors in which job losses were concentrated were financial and travel-related services, which tended to affect different groups of migrant workers.

As Philip Martin (2009: 674) observes, 'this means that migrants laid off in boom areas such as Dubai and Singapore include both financial specialists and construction laborers'. Similarly, the contraction of employment opportunities in construction and manufacturing in the principal urban areas of China had serious consequences for the millions of internal migrant workers. Estimates indicate that somewhere between 10 and 20 million Chinese workers returned to rural areas from the coastal industrial centres as a result of the decline in manufacturing activity during the crisis (Skeldon 2010: 10). The employment situation was exacerbated during the crisis by the hardening of political and public attitudes to migration and foreign workers that often occurs in the context of economic hardship, leading to attempts on the parts of governments in countries such as Malaysia, Singapore and a number of European states to seek to restrict migration flows, expel foreign workers, and/or constrain the employment opportunities available to migrant workers (Phillips 2011b).

Remittances—the monies that migrant workers send to families in their home countries—were the other mechanism by which it was expected that the impact of the crisis would be felt, given the rapid growth of global flows of remittances since the 1990s (see Figure 13.4). The employment effects described above would mean that migrants were less able to send remittances, with potentially catastrophic implications for both

households and for economies dependent on remittances (usually in combination with aid). In some of these economies, such as the Philippines or Haiti, remittances in the 2000s were equivalent to some 25 per cent of GDP, and far outstripped overseas development assistance or inflows of FDI. Yet many of the envisaged impacts did not emerge, as remittances to many parts of the world from overseas migrant workers did not decline as much as expected. In fact, remittances remained much more resilient throughout the financial crisis than private capital flows. Notwithstanding some regional variation, a modest decline of around 6 per cent was recorded at the height of the crisis in 2009 (Mohapatra and Ratha 2010), and the 'bottoming-out' process was rapid.

Further slow-downs in the growth of global flows of remittances were caused in 2015, due to weak economic growth in Europe, the deterioration of the Russian economy, and the depreciation of the euro and rouble (World Bank 2015b). Figures for 2015 were expected to show the slowest growth rates since 2008/9 during the Global Financial Crisis, with officially recorded flows to developing countries only predicted to rise by 0.9 per cent over the previous year. Yet they were still expected to reach the arresting total of US$440 billion in 2015. Global remittances, including those to high income countries, were projected to reach US$586 billion. The World Bank's predictions indicated an acceleration by 4.1 per cent in 2016 in

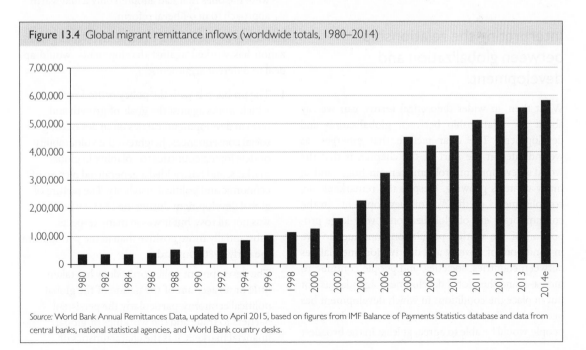

Figure 13.4 Global migrant remittance inflows (worldwide totals, 1980–2014)

Source: World Bank Annual Remittances Data, updated to April 2015, based on figures from IMF Balance of Payments Statistics database and data from central banks, national statistical agencies, and World Bank country desks.

total global remittance flows, to reach an estimated $610 billion, rising to $636 billion in 2017. Remittance flows to developing countries were expected to recover in 2016 to reach $459 billion, rising to $479 billion in 2017 (World Bank 2015b). Notwithstanding the impact of crisis, therefore, remittances remain one of the most important forms of development financing across the world.

Yet, clearly, the economic crisis of this period has highlighted that development, and the problems of development, are not confined to somewhere we would once have called the 'Third World' and now might awkwardly call the 'developing world'. Some of the gravest impacts of the crises and government responses to them were also felt among people in the low-income brackets of societies in countries where the crises have been concentrated, such as the United Kingdom, United States, Greece, or Spain. Significant increases in the numbers living in poverty in these places, hardships for migrant workers, increasing levels of unemployment, and soaring levels of demand on public social services all issue a critical reminder to us that development—and the study of development—is not only about 'poor countries'. Rather, development is a process in which *all* countries and groups of people are engaged, and the relationship between globalization and development needs to be explored and understood in this light (Payne and Phillips 2010).

Interpreting the relationship between globalization and development

What then, in wider theoretical terms, can we say about the relationship between globalization and development? The clear picture that emerges, as we indicated at the start of the chapter, is that the world's development problems remain huge, and in many contexts growing. Despite the remarkable accomplishments of the 'Age of Development', in the contemporary era of globalization a very large proportion of the world's population continues to live in conditions of poverty and deprivation, inequalities between countries, societies, and people continue to increase, and the global development agenda has not put in place the conditions in which development has been able to flourish. On this much it seems that most people would be able to agree, at least in the broadest

terms. Yet participants in the debate about the impact of globalization on development are still able to occupy very distant corners and fight them, as it were, with vigour.

Advocates of what Robert Wade calls the 'globalization works' story have a range of different arguments in their arsenal:

1. It is not globalization, nor the development orthodoxy constructed around it, that have failed. Rather, the issue is the failure of governments to introduce the right kinds of policies, in the right kinds of ways, and to the right extent. Institutions in many developing countries also remain too weak, corruption remains too prevalent, and political conflict too pronounced. What is needed is therefore more reform—more neo-liberalism—not less.

2. The failures of development are due to too little engagement with globalization. Poor people are those who remain 'excluded' from globalization and have not (yet) been able to harness the potential of globalization processes.

3. Financial crisis is not explained by excessive levels of 'openness' or 'vulnerability'—many of the developing economies that were affected by financial crisis over the last 20 years were not the most open. Equally, most of those affected were the ones that had adopted only a lukewarm approach to neo-liberal reform.

Advocates of the contrary perspective—that globalization has worked against development—would appeal to different arguments:

1. The problem is with the policy orthodoxy itself, which works against the goals of growth and human development, carries often devastating social consequences, heightens the vulnerability of developing countries to volatility in global markets, and has yielded a generalized picture of economic and political instability. The picture of global development during the 1945–80 period was not all rosy, but it was in many respects substantially more positive than in the period from the early 1980s onwards.

2. The development policy orthodoxy has taken little or no account of the nature of the global political economy, particularly the persistent barriers to trade and the workings of global financial markets. It is the characteristics of

globalized market activity that impose obstacles to development. More generally, failures of development, persistent forms of poverty and growing levels of inequality are both generated and reinforced by globalization.

3. The recurrent financial crises are crises of globalization and generated by the behaviour of financial markets and the policies of the international financial institutions.

At the heart of the debate is thus a conflict between different interpretations of the dynamics which have produced such an obscene development gap between and within countries, and between different parts of the world's population. It is useful to think about this in the following terms. The orthodox view sees poverty and other signs of what we might call 'mal-development' as 'residual' phenomena—that is, they are residues of a pre-globalization era, bound to be eradicated as the benign forces of globalization spread and reach the world's poor more effectively (Kaplinsky 2005: 50–1). Branko Milanovic (2003: 667) offers a pithy summary of this view:

“ It is only a slight caricaturization ... to state that its proponents regard globalization as a *deus ex machina* for many of the problems, such as poverty, illiteracy or inequality that beset the developing world. The only thing that a country needs to do is to open up its borders, reduce tariff rates, attract foreign capital, and in a few generations if not less, the poor will become rich, the illiterate will learn how to read and write, and inequality will vanish as the poor countries catch up with the rich. **”**

The thrust of the alternative arguments is that the various dimensions of mal-development are instead 'relational' phenomena (Bernstein 1990; Kaplinsky 2005: 51), which arise from and are reinforced by globalization processes. The task is therefore to understand how exactly this relationship works. We have noted many of the relevant issues in this chapter, relating to the workings of global financial markets, fluctuations in the terms of trade and the persistence of trade rules which disadvantage certain kinds of producers and exporters, the politics of the global development agenda, the dynamics of global inequality, and so on.

What this line of reasoning suggests is that the workings of globalization unquestionably present challenges for development. But it is surely too simplistic to state baldly that 'globalization' is intrinsically 'bad' or 'good' for development. It has emerged clearly here that we need to focus on the particular form that globalization takes, and that this is to an important extent politically and ideologically determined. The neoliberal development orthodoxy has shaped heavily the terms on which developing economies and large parts of the world's societies participate in the global economy. The global development agenda has been based on a set of political arrangements which govern how financial markets work, which trade rules prevail, how global value chains are organized, what the lending activities of the IFIs look like, how debt is managed, and so on. The structural dynamics of global capitalism thus combine with particular political and ideological currents, and more specifically particular ways of thinking about development, to shape the evolution of the material and social conditions in which people live. It is thus possible to mount a strong argument for the importance of understanding the 'relational' dynamics of globalization and development.

KEY POINTS

- Opinion is divided on the relationship between globalization and development.

- Some argue that the persistence of poverty, the widening of inequalities, and other manifestations of 'mal-development' are due to too little engagement with globalization and a failure effectively to implement neo-liberal reform. This perspective sees the signs of mal-development as 'residual' phenomena, which will be eradicated as the reach of globalization is extended and its benefits are harnessed.

- Others argue that the problem is globalization itself and the policy orthodoxy that has accompanied it in the contemporary period. They see the problems of mal-development as 'relational' phenomena, which arise from and are reinforced by globalization processes and the workings of the global economy.

Conclusion: a new era of global development?

We conclude this chapter on a note of speculation. First, what will have been the long-term developmental consequences of the global economic crisis of the late 2000s? And second, what does the growth—and latterly instability—of China, east Asia and the rising powers imply for the future of global development? Put together, have these two sets of conditions brought about a waning of the global development agenda that has prevailed to this point? Do they challenge the kinds of development thinking that have underpinned it? Are we moving into a new era of development?

A few years ago, we might have said that the twin economic crises were likely to weaken the neo-liberal orthodoxy—already beleaguered in many regions of the world—to the extent that the credibility of the global development agenda attached to it was fatally undermined. Much has been made of the apparent challenge from China's strategies across the developing world to the foothold of neo-liberalism and the global development agenda in this context, offering other countries and societies an alternative to the institutions and precepts of Western development policy. The gradual emergence of China as a significant actor in the principal institutions of global governance has also prompted discussions about the potential challenge to the global development agenda as articulated over the course of the contemporary period (Gu *et al.* 2008).

Yet, at the time of writing, this assessment seems premature, or at least unsafe. As observers of the fall-out from the crises, we can find ample signs that 'business as usual' has resumed in the centres of Anglo-American capitalism, particularly in political failures to deal decisively with some of the causes of the crises rooted in regulatory failures. Despite its huge social costs, austerity won the day across Europe and elsewhere. By the end of 2015, debate about China and the rising powers featured a core concern not with a spectacular development story but with economic instability and, in some cases, recession verging on economic disaster. Few alternative models seemed robust, leaving ample space for a reassertion of the achievements of the MDGs and the global development agenda. However, unquestionably the world has changed dramatically. We can surely find signs that more space for alternative kinds of development thinking is becoming evident in the post-crisis period, and, despite the downturn in mid 2015, the implications of China's rise for the global economy and global development cannot be understated. Having overtaken the United States for the first time as the world's largest economy in 2014, it is highly significant that the yuan assumes the status of an international reserve currency from 2016 onwards.

Yet, in the midst of a tumultuous period, our challenges in many ways remain unchanged from those which have always faced students and practitioners of development. They are to think carefully and clearly about what we mean by development, to develop theoretical perspectives which will enable us to understand for the contemporary political economy of development, and to work towards local and global strategies which will, at last, put in place the conditions which will produce something very different from the situation that Frank observed back in the 1960s, and still prevails today: 'development for the few and underdevelopment for the many'.

 QUESTIONS

1. What are the key differences between the main development theories that have emerged in the post-Second World War period?

2. Why were both modernization theory and underdevelopment theories largely discredited by the early 1980s?

3. How important were the contributions of 'human development' theories to our understandings of what development means?

4. How did neo-liberal and neo-statist theories of development try to explain the trajectory of divergence between developing regions and countries from the 1960s onwards?

5. What was the Washington Consensus and by what means did it become implanted across the developing world in the 1980s and 1990s?

6. To what extent can the development record of the contemporary period be taken as evidence that the neo-liberal development agenda failed?

7. Explain how both neo-liberals and neo-statists were able to stake a claim to explaining and understanding the 'East Asian miracle'.

8. How has the global economic crisis affected development across the world?

9. Is it more convincing to explain the problems of contemporary development as 'residual' or 'relational' phenomena?

10. Do you think that the economic crises of the late 2000s and the rise of China and the 'East' have changed the way we need to think about the political economy of development?

 ## FURTHER READING

Dittmer, L. and Yu, G. T. (2010), *China, the Developing World, and the New Global Dynamic* (Boulder, CO: Lynne Rienner). A collection of essays exploring the growing engagement of China in the global economy and other developing regions.

Harvey, D. (2005), *A Brief History of Neoliberalism* (New York: Oxford University Press). A discussion of the ideology of neo-liberalism and its global significance.

Hudson, D. (2015), *Global Finance and Development* (London: Routledge). A critical assessment of the complex relationships between finance and development.

Kaplinsky, R. (2005), *Globalization, Poverty and Inequality* (Cambridge: Polity). A detailed exploration of the 'relational' dynamics of globalization, poverty, and inequality.

Kay, C. (1989), *Latin American Theories of Development and Underdevelopment* (London: Routledge). A classic overview of development theories in the context of Latin America—particularly strong on structuralist and underdevelopment theories.

Kohli, A. (2004), *State-Directed Development: Political Power and Industrialization in the Global Periphery* (Cambridge: Cambridge University Press). A detailed comparative exploration of the role of states in development.

Leftwich, A. (2000), *States of Development: On the Primacy of Politics in Development* (Cambridge: Polity). A discussion of the role of states and politics in development.

McMichael, P. (2007), *Development and Social Change: A Global Perspective*, 4th edn (Thousand Oaks, CA: Pine Forge Press). A 'global' perspective on development with detailed historical and comparative discussions.

Payne, A. (2005), *The Global Politics of Unequal Development* (Basingstoke: Palgrave Macmillan). A detailed discussion of the ways in which the global politics of development shape unequal outcomes in key issue areas.

Payne, A. and Phillips, N. (2010), *Development* (Cambridge: Polity Press). An exploration of the key theories of development from the nineteenth century onwards.

Rai, S. (2002), *Gender and the Political Economy of Development* (Cambridge: Polity). An introduction to the key debates around gender and development.

Selwyn, B. (2014), *The Global Development Crisis* (Cambridge: Polity). A Marxist perspective on key development thinkers and ideas, exploring the class relations of poverty and inequality in capitalism.

Wade, R. (1990), *Governing the Market: Economic Theory and the Role of Government in Taiwan's Industrialization* (Princeton: Princeton University Press). An influential statement of the neo-statist position, including critical discussions of the debates surrounding East Asian development.

WEBLINKS

International organizations and multilateral institutions associated with the global development agenda:

www.worldbank.org World Bank

www.imf.org International Monetary Fund

www.ilo.org International Labour Organization

www.unctad.org United Nations Conference on Trade and Development

www.wto.org World Trade Organization

http://www.iom.int/cms/en/sites/iom/home.html International Organization for Migration

www.undp.org United Nations Development Program

www.gdnet.org Global Development Network

www.gfmd.org Global Forum on Migration and Development Regional institutions and regional development banks

www.iadb.org Inter-American Development Bank

www.adb.org Asian Development Bank

www.afdb.org African Development Bank

www.ebrd.org European Bank for Reconstruction and Development

www.eclac.org United Nations Economic Commission for Latin America and the Caribbean

www.uneca.org United Nations Economic Commission for Africa

www.unescap.org United Nations Economic Commission for Asia and the Pacific

 ## ONLINE RESOURCE CENTRE

For additional material and resources, please visit the Online Resource Centre at:
www.oxfordtextbooks.co.uk/ravenhill5e

14

The Political Economy of the Environment

Peter Dauvergne

Reader's guide

The growth of the world economy is transforming the earth's environment. Nothing is particularly controversial about this statement. Yet, sharp disagreements arise over the nature of this transformation. Is the globalization of capitalism a force of progress and environmental solutions? Or is it a *cause* of our current global environmental crisis? This chapter explores these questions by examining the debates around some of the most contentious issues at the core of economic globalization and the environment: economic growth, production, and consumption; trade; and transnational investment. It begins with a glance at the general arguments about how the global political economy affects the global environment. Then, to set the stage for an analysis of more specific arguments about the global political economy of the environment, it sketches the history of global environmentalism—in particular, the emergence of international environmental institutions (including regimes) with the norm of sustainable development. The last section builds on these arguments to assess the effectiveness of North–South environmental financing and international environmental regimes.

Introduction: the political economy of environmental change

The spread of capitalism and the growth of the world economy is altering the global environment. Few scholars of global environmental politics would challenge this statement (see Box 14.1). The nature of the change, however, is hotly debated. Some see the globalization of capitalism as a source of progress and ingenuity and cooperation, of a future world with much better environmental conditions for all. Others argue it is accelerating the process of the exploitation of nature and humanity, spinning the globe faster and faster towards an ecological meltdown.

Towards prosperity and sustainability

The optimists see the globalization of trade, technology, and investment as fostering economic growth and raising per capita incomes, both essential to generate the funds and political will for global environmental management. Optimists see other environmental benefits from globalization as well. It is promoting global integration and cooperation as well as common environmental norms and standards, which are enhancing the capacity of a system of sovereign states to manage problems such as ozone depletion and climate change. It is pushing states to liberalize trade and foreign investment, promote specialization, and eliminate subsidies, which in the past have contributed to **market failures** and suboptimal economic and environmental outcomes. It is enhancing the capacity of developing states to manage environmental change through the transfer of technologies, knowledge, and development assistance. And it is contributing to a host of domestic reforms to policies—such as better environmental laws, stronger institutions, and more secure property rights.

Optimists such as environmental writers Julian Simon, Gregg Easterbrook, and Bjørn Lomborg see a past full of progress and a future full of hope and socioecological triumph. There is every reason to believe that economic growth and technological progress will continue for ever. 'The standard of living', Simon (1996: 12) argues, 'has risen along with the size of the world's population since the beginning of recorded time. There is no convincing economic reason why these trends toward a better life should not continue indefinitely.' Simon's lifetime of work has stirred a hornet's nest of environmental critics. Writers such as Easterbrook, however, see him as profound and brave. 'There was a time', Easterbrook (1995: xxi) argues, 'when to cry alarm regarding environmental affairs was the daring position. Now it's the safe position: People get upset when you say things may turn out fine.' Writers such as Lomborg (2001, 2007) add, too, that little statistical evidence exists of a global environmental crisis—that this common misperception is more a result of media hype and non-governmental organization (NGO) fundraising antics than real problems. 'Mankind's lot', Lomborg (2001: 4) asserts, 'has actually improved in terms of practically every measurable indicator ... We are not running out of energy or natural resources ... Acid rain does not kill the forests, and the air and water around us are becoming

---

BOX 14.1 GLOBALIZATION

This chapter assumes that globalization is an ongoing and accelerating process that is restructuring and increasing connections among economies, institutions, and civil societies. This dynamic and multidimensional process is integrating trade, production, and finance as well as strengthening global norms and global social forces. A constellation of forces drives globalization, including new and faster technologies (such as computers) as well as the increasing dominance of capitalism and Western ideologies. In the simplest terms, it is leading to a 'world as a single place', where changes in distant lands affect people around the globe more quickly, and with greater frequency and intensity (Scholte 1997: 14; also see Scholte 2005; Steger 2013). It is, in the words of Thomas Friedman (2002: 64):

'the integration of everything with everything else ... the integration of markets, finance, and technology in a way that shrinks the world from a size medium to a size small. Globalization enables each of us, wherever we live, to reach around the world farther, faster, deeper, and cheaper than ever before and at the same time allows the world to reach into each of us farther, faster, deeper, and cheaper than ever before.'

This does not assume the process of globalization is even or equal within or across countries. The rich in Europe and North America are unquestionably benefiting far more than the poor of Africa, Asia, and Latin America. The process is also not inevitable. States and societies can resist and reverse globalization.

less and less polluted'. Lomborg (2009) further adds that investing in more real and present global problems, such as curable diseases and malnutrition, will produce far better immediate and long-term results for both people and the global environment.

Simon, Easterbrook, and Lomborg are at the extreme of the optimistic end of the spectrum of opinion. Most supporters of the current trajectory of the global political economy—those in governments such as the United States and the United Kingdom, and in international institutions such as the World Bank and the World Trade Organization (WTO)—emphasize the need for a practical view that looks towards future generations. These supporters argue that some degree of ecological change and loss is inevitable, but the consistent trend as the world economy liberalizes and globalizes is towards a future that looks like Britain, France, and the United States, not one that looks like Burundi, Liberia, and Haiti. History demonstrates the great strides of humanity. Just a hundred years ago, cities such as London and New York were filthy and unhealthy. Today, health conditions in virtually every city in the North are vastly improved. One of the greatest feats has been the increase in food production. In the middle of the twentieth century, close to half of the people in the global South were malnourished or starving. By 1970, it was less than a third; by 2015, it was less than a seventh (Lomborg 2001: 61; FAO 2008, 2009, 2012a, 2015).

Just over two hundred years ago, Thomas Malthus (1798) predicted that exponential population growth would, following the laws of basic maths, inevitably surpass arithmetical food production: and mass starvation would thus ensue. Since then, many scholars, now commonly called Malthusians or neo-Malthusians, have continued to tout the same logic. Yet, optimists stress, Malthus was flat-out wrong, primarily because he discounted the ability of human ingenuity to increase agricultural yields. The Green Revolution of the 1960s saw scientists and farmers work together to produce fast-growing, pest-resistant, high-yield crops able to grow just about anywhere (with the help of irrigation, fertilizers, and pesticides). There is, as a result, plenty of food today. And it is far cheaper—global food prices have fallen by two-thirds in real terms since the 1950s. People starve at present because of inefficient distribution and incompetent governments, not because of insufficient global food supplies. For optimists, perhaps the most revealing statistic of all is global life expectancy at birth: in 1900, it was a mere 30

years; in 1950, 46 years; today, it is over 70 years (Lomborg 2001: 50–1, 61; World Bank 2002c; WHO 2008b: 44; http://data.worldbank.org). Granted, such progress has demanded changes, including some global environmental changes. But, optimists stress, science and human ingenuity have time and again shown the capacity to respond with even more progress.

The view that globalization is a basically positive ecological force dominates global economic and environmental negotiations, and institutional decision-making. The debate here ranges over how best to channel globalization so as to minimize environmental damage and maximize socioeconomic progress (which, in the long run, must occur for effective global environmental management). Some argue for few, if any, restraints. Others see a need to guide economic globalization with national environmental agencies, and strong global norms and institutions. There are, however, many scholars and activists who challenge the core assumptions behind these views—that is, they see the globalization of capitalism as a core cause of the current ecological crisis.

Towards ecological collapse

Environmental critics of the globalization of capitalism worry that it is luring humanity towards a global fate not unlike that of Easter Island of three-hundred years ago, where ecological decay drove a once thriving people to violence and cannibalism in just a few centuries (Rees 2002: 249; Diamond 2005). Particularly worrying for these critics is that so-called progress and scientific reason has created, in the words of Paul Ehrlich's (1968) infamous book title, 'a population bomb', an explosion from fewer than 300 million people at the time of Christ to more than 7.4 billion today (see Figure 14.1). The globalization of capitalism, critics contend, is compounding the ecological impact of more than 200,000 people being added to the planet every day. It reinforces the neoclassical economic assumption that indefinite economic growth is both possible and desirable. Proponents assume, too, that it is possible and logical for the South to follow the development path of the North and continue to industrialize and intensify agricultural production. The globe can barely sustain its current population. How, critics ask, can it sustain another 2.5–3 billion in 2050? How can Africa sustain an additional 1 billion people 50 years from now, more than double its current population?

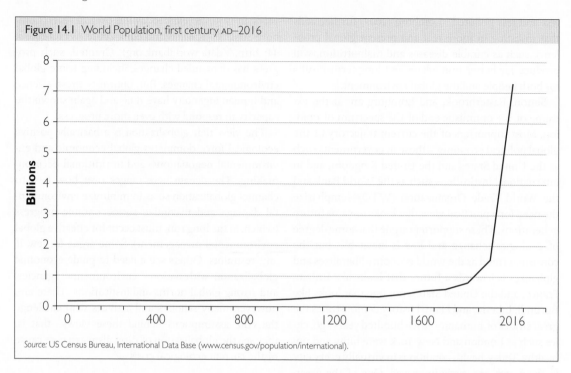

Figure 14.1 World Population, first century AD–2016

Source: US Census Bureau, International Data Base (www.census.gov/population/international).

The net effect of economic globalization, moreover, is to enlarge the **ecological footprint** of *each* person on the planet, by promoting ever more economic growth as well as cultivating an almost religious faith in the value of consumption—in the value of electronic toys, cars, and fast food (Robbins 2013)—all of which requires increasing amounts of natural resources, energy, and infrastructure to produce. The growing integration and disparities among economies are also increasing the reach and intensity of **ecological shadows**, which tend to shift the ecological damage of more powerful economies on to weaker economies and future generations (see Box 14.2).

Critics contend, too, that the globalization of capitalism is encouraging ever more economic growth and production with no real concern about unequal or unsustainable patterns of consumption. It exacerbates the ecological inequality within and between countries, and marginalizes women, indigenous peoples, and the poor. The global political economy is constructing, for critics such as William Rees and Laura Westra (2003), a world of 'eco-apartheid' and 'eco-violence'. Globalization tears, too, at the fabric of local communities, leading to 'food wars' (Bello 2009) and destroying historic patterns of trust, cooperation, and knowledge so essential to ecological and social

balance (Shiva 1997, 2000, 2008; Mander and Goldsmith 2001; Cavanagh and Mander 2004; Barlow 2008, 2014; Broad and Cavanagh 2008; Nixon 2011; Dauvergne and LeBaron 2014). In short, it destroys the living environments of much of the world's people.

There can be, in the view of critics, no environmental justice or biological balance in a globalized world where the super-rich like Bill Gates and J. K. Rowling live alongside (metaphorically, that is, in their mansions) the 1 billion or so who live on less than $1.25 per day, and the 2 billion or so who live on less than $2 per day. Over 650 million people do not have access to clean water (WHO/UNICEF 2015). Around 800 million people suffer from chronic malnutrition (FAO 2015: 3). Unhealthy environments aggravate illnesses, each year contributing to the deaths of millions of children under the age of 5. The future under current patterns within the global political economy, critics argue, is one of still greater horrors: of pandemics such as HIV/AIDS, which killed 1.2 million people in 2014. Around 37 million people are now infected, with 2 million new HIV infections in 2014. Of those living with HIV/AIDS, two-thirds live in sub-Saharan Africa, where average life expectancy in many countries has fallen from above 60 years to below 50 years. What is needed, critics like Colin Hines (2000) argue, is not globalization, but localization.

BOX 14.2 ECOLOGICAL FOOTPRINTS AND SHADOWS

Ecological footprints

Bill Rees and Mathis Wackernagel created the concept of ecological footprint to measure the sustainability of human lifestyles. It translates human consumption of renewable natural resources into hectares of average biologically productive land. A person's footprint is the total area in global hectares (1 hectare of average biological productivity) required to sustain his or her lifestyle: food and water, clothing, shelter, transportation, and consumer goods and services. The concept allows an analyst to compare the average ecological impact of people from Africa to Australia to China to the United Kingdom to the United States. The average global ecological footprint is about 2.7 global hectares per person (as of 2011, the latest data set). There are, however, great differences across the globe. In Africa, the per capita footprint of Eritrea is 0.4, Mali is 1.5, and South Africa is 2.5. In Asia, the per capita footprint of India is 0.9, China is 2.5, and Japan is 3.8. In Latin America, the per capita footprint of Honduras is 1.5, Columbia is 1.7, and Brazil is 2.9. In contrast, the average footprint of someone in the United Kingdom is 4.2, in Canada 6.6, in the United States 6.8, and in Australia 8.3.

This measure also allows an analyst to compare the world ecological footprint with the total biological productive capacity of the earth. The total biocapacity of the earth in 2010 was roughly 12 billion hectares. Between 1961 and 1999, the world ecological footprint grew by 80 per cent, reaching 13.7 billion hectares in 1999. Today, it is over 18 billion hectares and is rising steadily. The state of the globe, according to this measure, is continuing to worsen—and the world's ecological footprint is now equal to about 1.5 planet earths. Humanity, the World Wide Fund for Nature (WWF) laments, is now 'running an ecological deficit with the Earth'.

Sources: Wackernagel and Rees (1996); WWF (2002: 2–4, 22–8); WWF (2006: 28–34); Global Footprint Network (2009) (www.footprintnetwork.org).

Ecological shadows

This concept is designed to capture the extent of the environmental impact of a nation state in jurisdictions beyond its sovereign control. Ecological shadows arise as economies, through both intentional and unintentional patterns of consumption, trade, investment, and financing, transfer the environmental harm of its citizens outside its territory. This concept is particularly useful for analysing the environmental impact of more powerful economies on weaker (dependent) economies. The United States, for example, casts a large ecological shadow over South America. Such shadows can extend down a chain of weaker economies. Japan, for example, casts an ecological shadow over Thailand, which in turn casts a shadow over neighbours such as Cambodia and Laos. Ecological shadows do not arise from straightforward North–South exploitation. Often, elites in weak economies in the South profit personally from these ecological shadows, commonly acting as the agents of the ecological destruction—e.g. as miners, fishers, and loggers.

Sources: MacNeill et al. (1991); Dauvergne (1997, 2008).

The latest biological trends, critics further note, confirm the beginnings of a global Easter Island. Humans are now the dominant predator in every ecosystem (even in the seemingly limitless Pacific and Atlantic oceans), and unless strict restraints are put in place, humans will exhaust the globe's natural resources, fill its sinks, and overstep the earth's capacity to support life. Half the world's forests and wetlands are already gone. Every day another ten to 500 species become extinct. Recent surveys of the world's oceans, say critics, are especially worrying (Hannigan 2015). Coral reefs are degrading and dying, with more than one-fifth now irreparably harmed. Seabirds are faring even worse, with one study calculating a 70 per cent decline since 1950 (Paleczny et al. 2015). Commercial ocean species are in even greater crisis. One analysis of 7,800 species of wild seafood found that catches of 29 per cent of these species are now at least 90 per cent below past averages. At recent harvests rates, predicts the 14-person team of analysts, a 'collapse' of much of the remaining commercial wild seafood will occur before 2050 (Worm et al. 2006). Another ten-year survey by Ransom Myers and Boris Worm (2003) found a 90 per cent decline in the ocean's large predatory fish—such as tuna, swordfish, marlin, cod, and flounder—since the 1950s. The waters of Ernest Hemingway's, The Old Man and the Sea, will soon be empty of the majestic marlin, a startling testimony, critics warn, not to the environmental consequences of the exploits of men such as Hemingway's old man, Santiago, but to the greed of industrial fishing boats plying the oceans to feed global markets.

Supporters and critics of a globalizing world, then, hold starkly different pictures of the current and future state of the global environment. The trends and statistics to support the statement 'globalization is good for the environment' seem convincing. Yet, so do the trends and statistics that say 'globalization is bad for the environment'. The truth seems to lie somewhere in the middle: globalization is producing both constructive and destructive ecological processes. The goal is to harness economic globalization in some way to ensure sustainability. What has the global community done so far to harness the globalization of capitalism and manage global environmental affairs? The next section examines the history of environmentalism with an eye on this question.

KEY POINTS

- Some perceive the net ecological impact of the global political economy as being positive, as a force for progress and better lives. It is fostering economic growth and cooperative institutions—both of these necessary in the long run to manage the global environment.

- Others see the net impact of the globalization of capitalism as negative, as a force sinking the globe into a bog of ecological decay. It is accelerating the destructive process of too many people consuming too many natural resources with no concern for equality or justice.

- Both the pro- and anti-globalization camps present persuasive data and arguments. Globalization involves multiple and complex sets of overlapping processes. Inevitably, there will be manifold and at times cross-cutting effects on the global environment.

History of global environmentalism

Collective human efforts to control nature began in earnest 8,000 to 10,000 years ago, as nomadic hunters-and-gatherers in various locales began to change to settled agriculture. Great civilizations sprang up, inventing such wonders as the plough (animal drawn), the wheel, writing, and numbers. Often, nature was subsumed in the quest for human progress, and many civilizations cut down regional forests, degraded land, and polluted local waters. Environmental decay even toppled a few great civilizations, such as Mesopotamia (a land between the Tigris and Euphrates rivers, part of contemporary Iraq), where a poorly designed irrigation system gradually poisoned the agricultural land with salt. For most of the history of civilization, however, the scale of human activity has been too small to alter the global environment—that is, to induce climate change, deplete

the ozone layer, empty the oceans, or destroy global biodiversity stocks.

This began to change with the dawn of the Industrial Revolution some 250 years ago. Production and energy use (including the burning of coal) began to rise rapidly. The global population of 650 million or so began to multiply. There were 1 billion people by the early 1800s; and 2 billion by the end of the 1920s. The wealthy began to extract more natural resources, more quickly, from increasingly remote parts of the globe (often through colonial administrations). Such activities strained local and regional environments. The evidence was stark. Smog in cities like London and New York killed thousands in the nineteenth and twentieth centuries. Once seemingly boundless species, like the plains bison of North America, were brought to near extinction. Some, like the passenger pigeon, a bird that once migrated through eastern North America in its millions, became extinct (in 1914).

Governments reacted to these environmental disasters with new national and regional policies. At first, these were aimed primarily at either conservation of wildlife or more effective resource management. Canada and the United States, for example, signed the Migratory Birds Treaty in 1918. Colonial powers reacted as well, putting in place policies (such as sustained yield management for logging forests) to try to ensure more efficient and rational resource extraction. After the Second World War, ordinary citizens began to become increasingly worried about the biological impacts of industrialization and agricultural production. Anxiety mounted after Rachel Carson's (1962) best-seller, *Silent Spring*, shocked popular consciousness with images of pesticide-laden food chains and dying ecosystems.

Worries about the health of the 'global environment' also began to emerge around this time. The picture of the earth from space, beautiful and fragile and borderless, became a compelling global ecological image. These concerns fed into the sense of the mutual economic vulnerability of post-war economies (in both the North and the South). Paul Ehrlich's 1968 best-seller, *The Population Bomb*, added a new and perturbing image: the earth left barren by an exploding population. 'In the 1970s', Ehrlich predicted boldly, 'the world will undergo famines—hundreds of millions of people are going to starve to death' (1968: xi).

Concern over the health of the global environment continued to rise in the late 1960s and early 1970s.

Experts met in 1968 at the United Nations Biosphere Conference to discuss global environmental problems. The first Earth Day was held in the United States in April 1970. Twenty million people rallied—one of the largest organized demonstrations in the history of the United States. That same year, the US government founded the Environmental Protection Agency (EPA). Canada created a Department of the Environment the following year. One outcome of this growing societal and political concern was the United Nations Conference on the Human Environment, held in Stockholm, Sweden, in June 1972.

The Stockholm Conference and the 1970s

The Stockholm Conference, organized by Canada's Maurice Strong, was the first global United Nations conference on the environment for state officials. There were 1,200 delegates from over a hundred countries. Swedish Prime Minister Olaf Palme and Indian Prime Minister Indira Gandhi were the only heads of state to attend. Russia and the communist bloc countries boycotted the conference, to protest against the exclusion of East Germany.

The North was interested initially in addressing industrial pollution, nature conservation, and population growth. The South was more worried about development, and did not want the anxieties of rich conservationists to deny poorer countries the benefits of economic growth and industrialization (an ongoing source of conflict). There were tensions, too, over who would pay, and who was responsible for solving global environmental problems. Many Southern delegates saw global capitalism as a core reason for poverty, and there was general anger that global economic institutions were pushing developing countries to export raw materials on declining **terms of trade**. The phrase 'the pollution of poverty' was coined at Stockholm, to express the idea that poverty was the greatest global environmental threat. Many delegates from the South called for global economic reforms to help solve the pollution of poverty.

In the end, conference delegates tried to reconcile the desire (need) for economic development in the South with the need to protect the global environment for all. Most governments came to recognize the mutual **interdependence** and vulnerability of North and South. The official conference documents, however, did not emphasize the Southern calls for global

economic reforms. The conference produced a Declaration on the Human Environment (with 26 principles), an Action Plan for the Human Environment (with 109 recommendations), and a Resolution on Institutional and Financial Arrangements. These were non-binding on signatory states—and most scholars agree that Stockholm produced few practical commitments to address global environmental change.

The Stockholm Conference did, however, signal a growing concern among national governments over the global environment. It also led to a General Assembly decision to create the United Nations Environment Programme (UNEP), launched officially in 1973, with Maurice Strong (2000) as the first executive director. The United Nations Environment Programme was designed as a relatively weak global institution. Its headquarters were in Nairobi, Kenya, rather than New York or Geneva, and it was established as a coordinating programme with a small budget rather than as a specialized agency. This was in the interest of all sides: the North did not want to finance a large institution; and the South did not want a global institution with the power to interfere with development goals. And other United Nations agencies did not want to relinquish significant 'turf' (Elliott 1998: 11–13).

After Stockholm, the Organization of the Petroleum Exporting Countries' (OPEC) success in raising the price of oil dramatically through limiting output in 1973–4 rocked the global economy. Oil prices quadrupled, inflation soared, and economic growth became sluggish worldwide. Many developing economies, particularly those in Latin America and Africa, began to experience debt crises. This economic turbulence deflated some of the potential for more aggressive global environmental initiatives after Stockholm. The South, in particular, became even more worried about the effects on debt levels and prospects for industrial development. Still, the debate over how to handle global environmental change continued, sparked by ground-breaking books such as the Club of Rome's (1972), *Limits to Growth*, and E. F. Schumacher's (1973), *Small Is Beautiful*. The global community also signed noteworthy global environmental treaties just after Stockholm. These include the Convention on the Prevention of Marine Pollution by Dumping of Wastes and other Matter (the London Convention, 1972, which came into force in 1975), and the Convention on International Trade in Endangered Species of Wild Flora and Fauna (CITES 1973, which came into force in 1975).

Environment slid more into the background of global affairs in the second half of the 1970s and first half of the 1980s, as conservative governments came to power in leading industrialized economies, and Southern economies sank further into debt. There was, nevertheless, a great deal of environmental activity. Scientists continued to research global environmental change. Non-governmental organizations continued to campaign and pressure governments and firms. Individual states, including some in the South, continued to establish environmental agencies. States also continued to sign and ratify global environmental agreements, such as the 1980 Convention on the Conservation of Antarctic Marine Living Resources (which came into force in 1982). The global community, too, continued to debate and make some headway on how best to manage the need for development (especially in the South) with the need for a healthy global environment. Problems such as the depletion of the ozone layer, and disasters such as the nuclear accident at Three Mile Island in 1979, the Union Carbide chemical leak in Bhopal in 1984, and the Chernobyl nuclear meltdown in 1986, added a sense of urgency. Slowly, environmental issues began to move once more up the global agenda. The debate by the mid 1980s began to focus increasingly on the concept of *sustainable development*. The publication in 1987 of the World Commission on Environment and Development (WCED) report, *Our Common Future*, synthesized and consolidated the global debates over environment and development, defining sustainable development as 'development that meets the needs of the present without compromising the ability of future generations to meet their own needs' (WCED 1987: 43).

The Brundtland Commission

The World Commission on Environment and Development, commonly known as the Brundtland Commission, was chaired by the former prime minister of Norway, Gro Harlem Brundtland. There were 23 members serving in an expert rather than an official state capacity—and 13 were from the South, including from India, China, and Brazil. Among G7 countries, only France and the United Kingdom did not send representatives. The Commission's report, *Our Common Future*, commonly known as the Brundtland Report, is widely seen as a watershed in the evolution of environmental debates within the global community of state representatives. The content of the Brundtland Report is an ingenious compromise. It did not foresee any necessary limits to growth, and industrialization and natural resource production, under correct management, were viewed as being acceptable, indeed inevitable, for some countries. The report called for a transfer of environmental technologies and economic assistance to support sustainable development in the South. It called, too, for more effective controls on population growth, as well as better education and food security in the South. It portrayed poverty as a core cause of unsustainable development. The source of much of the poverty in the South, it argued, is the position of developing economies within the global structure. The best way forward, then, is to stimulate—not slow down—economic growth: not the unchecked growth of the 1960s and 1970s, however, but growth from sustainable development.

States continued to negotiate and sign global environmental treaties leading up to and after the publication of the Brundtland Report. These include the 1985 Vienna Convention for the Protection of the Ozone Layer, the 1987 Montreal Protocol on Substances that Deplete the Ozone Layer, and the 1989 Basel Convention on the Control of Transboundary Movements of Hazardous Waste and their Disposal. By the late 1980s, global environmental issues had again crept back to the top of the global agenda, culminating in a 1989 United Nations General Assembly resolution to hold the first summit of world leaders on the global environment: what became the 1992 United Nations Conference on Environment and Development (UNCED), held in Rio de Janeiro, Brazil.

The Rio (Earth) Summit

The UNCED is popularly known as the Rio or Earth Summit. It was the largest United Nations conference to date, with most countries and 117 heads of state participating. There were thousands of non-governmental representatives at the official conference as well as at a parallel NGO forum. The recommendations in the Brundtland Report and the notion of sustainable development formed the core of the debate in Rio de Janeiro. Most countries endorsed the Brundtland definition of sustainable development. Many developing countries, however, wanted specific assurances of transfers of environmental technologies and economic assistance from the North to support the additional costs of 'green' growth. Many Northern states, on the other hand, were reluctant to assume further financial commitments (Rogers 1993: 238–9).

The Rio Summit put environment and development on the agendas of global leaders. It reinforced, too, the Brundtland Commission's assumption that more growth was compatible with a better global environment. Two official Rio Summit documents of particular note are the Rio Declaration on Environment and Development, and Agenda 21. The Rio Declaration is a set of 27 principles on the rights and responsibilities of states for environment and development. These principles include far more of the South's concerns about the right to development than the Stockholm Declaration on the Human Environment. Agenda 21 was a 300-page action programme to promote sustainable development (UN 1992).

The Rio Summit also produced the Non-legally Binding Authoritative Statement of Principles for a Global Consensus on the Management, Conservation and Sustainable Development of all Types of Forests. The original intent was to sign a legally binding forest treaty, but after irreconcilable differences arose among negotiators over the terms of an agreement, the conference settled for a non-binding statement of principles (Brack *et al.* 2001: 2). Rio also opened two conventions for signature: the United Nations Framework Convention on Climate Change, and the Convention on Biological Diversity. Negotiations began, too, on a treaty on desertification. Finally, the conference established the United Nations Commission on Sustainable Development to monitor and evaluate the progress on meeting the Rio objectives.

The Rio Summit was a historic global conference, hailed by many states as a great success. Critics from all sides, however, lamented the inadequate amount of 'promised' funds—especially from the North—to implement Agenda 21. More radical environmentalists, too, attacked the Brundtland definition of sustainable development—in particular its support for more economic growth and industrialization. Among activists, there was, in addition, a general concern that the negotiators had ignored the root cause of global environmental change: the inequalities, unsustainable industrial production and growth, and over-consumption that arise from corporate globalization and free trade. In fact, that industry captured the agenda at Rio (Chatterjee and Finger 1994), and the outcomes were little more than an incompetent doctor (the state system) slapping a Band-Aid on to a cancerous tumour

(capitalism). Other critics also felt that the Rio Summit entrenched a top-down set of solutions, without nearly enough focus on the needs of local communities, or the plight of women and indigenous peoples (Shiva 1993; Lohmann 1993).

The decade after Rio saw global environmental issues again slip down the list of state priorities. States turned to the threats of terrorism, chemical and biological warfare, and global financial crises. The global community, nevertheless, kept signing and ratifying environmental treaties. The Convention on Biological Diversity, for example, was opened for signature in 1992 (and came into force in 1993). The United Nations Convention on the Law of the Sea, though first opened for signature in 1982, eventually came into force in 1994. The United Nations Convention to Combat Desertification in Those Countries Experiencing Serious Drought and/or Desertification, Particularly in Africa was opened for signature in 1994 (and came into force in 1996). The Stockholm Convention on Persistent Organic Pollutants (POPs) was opened for signature in 2001 (and came into force in 2004). The Kyoto Protocol to the United Nations Framework Convention on Climate Change was opened for signature in 1998 (and came into force in 2005) (see Table 14.1).

The global community also continued to discuss and review the progress of Agenda 21 and the implementation of sustainable development, including a 1997 special session of the United Nations General Assembly, known as the Earth Summit + 5. The global community also prepared for the World Summit on Sustainable Development, eventually held in Johannesburg, South Africa, in 2002.

Johannesburg and beyond

The World Summit on Sustainable Development is popularly called Rio + 10, or the Johannesburg Summit. The purpose was to evaluate the progress of sustainable development since the Rio Summit in 1992. It was also designed to establish specific targets to improve implementation of the Rio goals as well as to develop a strategy to implement the United Nations' Millennium Development Goals. The Johannesburg Summit—with over 180 nations, over 10,000 delegates, at least 8,000 civil society representatives, and 4,000 members of the press, as well as countless ordinary citizens—was even larger than the Rio Summit. Revealingly, however, only about 100 heads of state attended, fewer than at Rio.

Table 14.1 Examples of international environmental agreements

Name of the agreement	Opened for signature	Entered into force	Website address
International Convention for the Regulation of Whaling	1946	1948	www.iwc.int
Convention on Wetlands of International Importance Especially as Waterflow Habitat (Ramsar)	1971	1975	www.ramsar.org
Convention on the Prevention of Marine Pollution by Dumping Wastes and Other Matter (London Convention)	1972	1975	www.imo.org
Convention on the International Trade in Endangered Species of Wild Flora and Fauna (CITES)	1973	1975	www.cites.org
Convention on the Conservation of Antarctic Marine Living Resources	1980	1982, as part of the Antarctic Treaty System	www.ccamlr.org
Montreal Protocol on Substances that Deplete the Ozone Layer	1987	1989	www.ozone.unep.org
Basel Convention on the Control of Transboundary Movements of Hazardous Wastes and their Disposal	1989	1992	www.basel.int
Convention on Biological Diversity	1992	1993	www.cbd.int
United Nations Convention on the Law of the Sea (LOS)	1982	1994	www.un.org/Depts/los
United Nations Convention to Combat Desertification in Those Countries Experiencing Serious Drought and/or Desertification, Particularly in Africa	1994	1996	www.unccd.int
Convention on the Prior Informed Consent Procedure for Certain Hazardous Chemicals and Pesticides in International Trade (Rotterdam Convention)	1998	2004	www.pic.int
Stockholm Convention on Persistent Organic Pollutants (POPs)	2001	2004	www.pops.int
Kyoto Protocol to the United Nations Framework Convention on Climate Change	1998	2005	www.unfccc.int
Minamata Convention on Mercury	2013	Not in force as of October 2016	www.mercuryconvention.org

The official documents of Johannesburg were similar to Rio and Stockholm in their broad calls for global sustainability. The two most important were the Johannesburg Declaration on Sustainable Development, a list of challenges and general commitments; and the Johannesburg Plan of Implementation, to meet these. Although non-binding, these commitments and implementation plans nevertheless represent significant political compromises. One of the most contentious issues (as was the case too at Rio) was financing. But Johannesburg also added two equally tough topics: the impact of globalization on sustainable development as well as specific timetables/targets to meet goals (Mehta 2003: 122). The Johannesburg Declaration on Sustainable Development (2002) reflects the debates over globalization. Point 12 declares:

❝ The deep fault line that divides human society between the rich and the poor and the ever-increasing gap between the developed and developing worlds pose a major threat to global prosperity, security and stability. ❞

Point 14 states:

❝ Globalization has added a new dimension to [global environmental problems]. The rapid integration of markets, the increasing mobility of capital and significant upsurge in investment flows around the world have opened new challenges and opportunities for the pursuit of sustainable development. But the benefits and costs of globalization are unevenly distributed, with developing countries facing special difficulties in meeting this challenge. ❞

Was the Johannesburg Summit a success? The answer, naturally, depends on your definition of success. No doubt, like Stockholm and Rio, it helped to focus the attention of world leaders on global environmental change. The preparation and outcomes also cemented sustainable development as the core organizing concept for global and national environmental institutions, laying a strong foundation for future international environmental negotiations (for example, on climate change in Copenhagen in 2009, Cancun in 2010, Durban in 2011, Doha in 2012, Warsaw in 2013, Lima in 2014, and Paris in 2015). Some see the outcomes as being constructive and more realistic than the outcomes of Rio. Others, though, see the conference as a symbol of the global failure to tackle sincerely global environmental problems. They see the targets and timetables as weak, and the Johannesburg Declaration as little more than a restatement of the past, doing little to promote global sustainability (Burg 2003: 116–18). These critics also see the official statements on globalization as being little more than bland and evasive whitewash. The Johannesburg Summit added yet another layer to global environmentalism, but as with Stockholm and Rio, in no way did it stem the tide of ecological decay. Paul Wapner (2003: 7), in his assessment of the Johannesburg Summit outcomes, predicted this: 'The strains on the earth's sources, sinks and sites have intensified dramatically since Rio and show no sign of decreasing in the near future'. For critics, the Rio + 20 United Nations Conference on Sustainable Development, held in Rio de Janeiro in June 2012, was one of the most concerning international environmental gatherings to date, doing little more than green-stamping 'business

as usual' and further validating the deep worries of Wapner and many others. In short, critics worry that environmentalism, piloted by the state-led principle of sustainable development, is too weak to manage global environmental change. It does not, in particular, have the depth or content to restrain the ecological impacts of the globalization of production, consumption, trade, and corporations—the focus of the next section of this chapter.

KEY POINTS

- Environmental change began to accelerate some 250 years ago, after the Industrial Revolution intensified production and colonizers reached into distant lands.

- By the late 1960s, governments had begun to recognize the need to cooperate to address global environmental problems. The result was the 1972 United Nations Conference on the Human Environment.

- A global compromise gradually emerged in the 1970s and 1980s around the concept of sustainable development, as defined by the Brundtland Commission in 1987.

- The Rio Summit in 1992 set an ambitious agenda for global sustainable development. Progress, however, was slow and uneven over the following decade. Ten years later, the Johannesburg Summit endeavoured to facilitate the implementation of the Rio goals. Twenty years later negotiators once again met in Rio de Janiero to evaluate and try to energize sustainable development.

- The net result has left thick layers of state-led global environmentalism (treaties, norms, and institutions) with the Brundtland Commission's concept of sustainable development at the core. Supporters see this as evidence of the global community's capacity to handle global environmental change, while critics see it as camouflage for 'business as usual'.

Economic growth, trade, and corporations

What is the ecological impact of economic growth, trade, and corporations under globalization? Some see the net impact as being positive for the health of the planet. It pulls destitute people—who are prone to degrade surrounding environments to survive—out of poverty. And it raises national per capita incomes, which generate the funds, technologies, and political will to implement sustainable development.

In the short run, such growth produces more food and better medical care, which in turn lengthens life expectancy and allows the global population to rise. Undeniably, this creates global ecological pressures. But, contend advocates of economic growth, this is a temporary problem. The global population will stabilize at around 11 billion, probably by the end of the twenty-first century, in part because globalization is raising the standards of living and education levels of women in the South, a development associated historically with smaller family size.

Others see economic growth and corporate globalization as core causes of the global environmental crisis. These forces are distributing environmental effects unequally, where the rich get richer and the poor remain confined in ever-worsening environments. It is also driving up per capita consumption in the South (without improving well-being) and over-consumption in the North. Already, the number of human beings is well beyond the earth's carrying capacity. The global population may well stabilize by the end of the century, but that is still another 3 to 4 billion people to feed, clothe, and shelter. How many earths, these critics wonder, are we planning to live on?

Which side is correct? To begin to address this question, the next section outlines the environmental arguments for more economic growth, more free trade, and more foreign investment.

Trading for growth and a better environment

A world free of poverty, say economists at institutions such as the World Bank, is critical for the long-term health of the planet. The struggle of the poor to survive is a primary cause of problems such as deforestation, desertification, and unsanitary water. The poor forage for wood to cook with and to heat homes. They exhaust nearby natural resources, such as fresh water, seafood, and wildlife. They cultivate unsuitable land to grow food and earn income. And they despoil local waterways with rubbish and sewage. Stating these facts, advocates of economic growth argue, is not an attempt to assign blame. Rather, the point is far simpler: poor people have little choice if they wish to survive.

The poor and uneducated, too, tend to have more children than the rich, which creates a spiral of poverty and ecological collapse as ever more people forage for food, water, and shelter on increasingly fragile lands. This spiral occurs for many reasons besides weak economic growth. Other factors include insecure property rights, the failure of family planning, inadequate government services and regulations, trade distortions, and insufficient investment and development assistance. The downward spiral accelerates during times of slow growth—that is, during an economic recession or depression—since firms are less willing to invest in cleaner technologies, and states are less willing and less able to enforce environmental laws. A quick glance at environmental management in Asia during the 1997–9 financial crisis confirms this (Dauvergne 1999).

Admittedly, advocates note, economic growth can worsen environmental conditions in the short run. Air and water quality, for example, can deteriorate in the early stages of industrial production. Yet, in the long run, once a society harnesses sufficient per capita wealth, environmental standards will invariably rise. Advocates of economic growth commonly illustrate this with the **Environmental Kuznets Curve** (see Figure 14.2). This curve demonstrates that pollution (such as smog and lead) will rise along with economic growth during the early stages of industrial development. This occurs because governments focus on increasing industrial growth and national income rather than on pollution controls. Yet, this is a temporary phenomenon. Once per capita income reaches high enough levels (in the past, often between $5,000 and $8,000), pollution begins to fall (Grossman and Krueger 1995; for an overview, see Dinda 2004). This occurs partly because citizens demand better living environments, and partly because firms and governments now have the financial and institutional capacity to respond effectively. It arises partly, too, because strong economies naturally tend to move away from heavy industry, and towards service and information industries. The Environmental Kuznets Curve usually draws on data for industrial pollution rather than depletion of natural resources. At least one study, however, has found a correlation between lower deforestation and higher national income in Asia, Latin America, and Africa (Bhattarai and Hammig 2001).

Japan's environmental history fits the Environmental Kuznets Curve well. After the Second World War, industrial production and economic growth in Japan soared, and by the 1960s Japan was suffering from acute pollution, 'not unlike many of the heavily polluted areas of India, China, and Southeast Asia today' (Schreurs 2002: 36). Citizen protests over the health

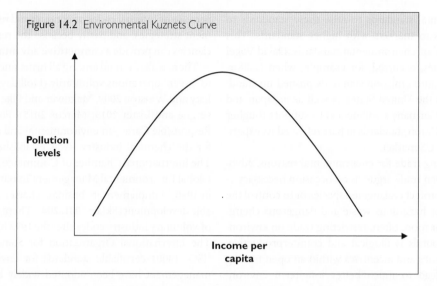

Figure 14.2 Environmental Kuznets Curve

consequences of pollution escalated in the 1960s and 1970s. In response, the Japanese government brought in strict environmental regulations, and Japanese business developed new environmental technologies (McKean 1981; Broadbent 1998; Imura and Schreurs 2005). The result was a dramatic improvement in the domestic environment.

Environmental advocates of economic growth do not generally propose that states with low per capita incomes should blindly pursue economic growth. For most, the Environmental Kuznets Curve suggests two critical lessons: first, that, in the long run, economic growth will improve environmental institutions and governance; and second, that, following the logic of the Environmental Kuznets Curve, it is feasible to use measures such as ecological markets, technological advances, sound policies, and global institutions to help countries with low per capita incomes to 'tunnel' through the middle of the curve, attaining high per capita incomes with less environmental damage.

The globalization of free trade—following the principles of absolute and **comparative advantage**—will also help these weak economies to tunnel through the Environmental Kuznets Curve. Free trade fosters efficient worldwide production as well as the transfer of environmental technologies and higher environmental standards from the North to the South (WTO 1999; Neumayer 2001; Lomborg 2009). It also creates incentives and price signals to ensure more efficient consumption of natural resources, supplying substitutes and more effective production technologies as

scarcity rises (thus, enhancing overall resource availability). This means that humanity is able to produce more goods with fewer resources, which stimulates global economic growth and raises national per capita incomes. The extra income from efficient production is necessary, too, for sustainable development. More income means that more can be spent to preserve the environment as well as to enforce environmental regulations. Former World Trade Organization director-general, Mike Moore, succinctly explains the logic: 'Every WTO Member Government supports open trade because it leads to higher living standards for working families which in turn leads to a cleaner environment' (WTO 1999).

Trade liberalization, too, produces significant environmental rewards. Trade barriers distort price signals for natural resources. Prices therefore do not reflect real scarcities, availability, or pollution costs, which in turn creates waste and overconsumption. Liberalization also fosters cleaner production processes, as firms that produce goods behind trade barriers face less competition and have fewer incentives to upgrade facilities or use resources efficiently. States with more liberal trade policies are also, advocates argue, more likely to meet global environmental standards. 'Liberalized trade', the World Bank (1992b: 67) explains, 'fosters greater efficiency and higher productivity and may actually reduce pollution by encouraging the growth of less-polluting industries and the adoption and diffusion of cleaner technologies'. Trade liberalization can further pressure producers with low environmental standards to raise these standards to gain access to markets with higher standards. This 'trading up' of environmental standards, David Vogel (1995) argues, occurred, for example, when California's strict auto emission standards pushed up standards across the United States as well as in Japan and Germany. Germany's willingness to support tougher European Union standards in part reflected its experience in the US market.

Restricting trade for environmental reasons, advocates of open trade argue, is on occasion necessary—such as to protect endangered species or to control the dumping of hazardous waste and dangerous chemicals. Yet, far more often, restricting trade on environmental grounds is illogical and counterproductive. Sound policies and incentives within an open trading structure lead to much better long-term environmental management. Green markets—where prices throughout a trade chain internalize environmental and social costs, and where consumers voluntarily pay higher prices for these products—are another effective means of promoting sustainable development.

The globalization of corporations, argue supporters, will further promote sustainable development. **Transnational corporations** (TNCs) transfer critical technologies, expertise, and funds into the South. Without this investment, economies stagnate, slip backwards, and sustain environmental degradation—a quick glance at North Korea or conflict areas of sub-Saharan Africa confirms this. Transnational corporations that invest in the South also tend to employ higher environmental standards than local laws require—what Ronie Garcia-Johnson (2000) calls **exporting environmentalism**. This occurs for a host of reasons: partly because of more sophisticated technologies and management techniques; partly because of pressure from states, NGOs, shareholders, and consumers; partly because of internal codes of conduct and risk-management strategies; and partly because the resulting efficiencies can provide a **competitive advantage**.

There is also a trend among all firms since the 1980s to 'green' operations voluntarily (Holliday *et al.* 2002; Esty and Winston 2009; Makower and Pike 2009; Dauvergne and Lister 2013; Marcus 2015). For example, Responsible Care—an environmental and safety code for the chemical industry—was established in 1985. The International Chamber of Commerce created the Global Environmental Management Initiative (GEMI) in 1990 to implement its business charter for sustainable development (Sklair 2001: 204). There was a flood of voluntary industry codes after the 1992 Rio Summit. The International Organization for Standardization (ISO) 14001 certifiable standards for environmental management have been adopted widely by business since the mid 1990s (see Box 14.3). Industry founded the World Business Council of Sustainable Development in 1995 to address 'the challenges and opportunities of sustainable development based on three fundamental and inseparable pillars: the generation of economic wealth, environmental improvement and social responsibility' (Holme and Watts 2000: 5). The 2002 Johannesburg Summit and the Rio + 20 Earth Summit in 2012 saw the business community stress the need for voluntary corporate leadership to promote sustainable development. Corporations are now embracing the principle of corporate social responsibility. Former chairman and chief executive officer of AT&T, C. Michael Armstrong, explains the logic of the greening of the company: 'AT&T understands the need for a global alliance of business, society and the environment. In the 21st century, the world won't tolerate businesses that don't take that partnership seriously, but it will eventually reward companies that do' (quoted in Holme and Watts 2000: 1).

BOX 14.3 ISO 14000 AND ISO 14001

The International Organization for Standardization (ISO), headquartered in Geneva, advances voluntary international standards for particular products, and for environmental management. The ISO develops these standards relying on consensus and voluntary participation among ISO member countries. ISO 14000 is a series of voluntary environmental standards, including for environmental auditing, performance, labelling, and most importantly, the ISO 14001 Environmental Management System (EMS) Standard (launched in 1996 and revised most recently in 2015). The ISO 14001 standard allows for certification from an external authority. By 2016, the ISO had issued some 300,000 ISO 14001 certifications in 171 countries. Certification requires a community or organization to implement practices and procedures that together comprise a system of environmental management. It also requires a policy to prevent pollution and continually improve environmental performance.

Source: ISO 2008 (www.iso.org).

Most states and global institutions accept the need for more economic growth, more open trade, and more foreign investment. There are critics, however, many of whom see the relentless pursuit of growth, trade, and investment under globalization as a primary cause of the global environmental crisis.

Trading away the earth for unequal consumption

Critics contend that the Environmental Kuznets Curve is misleading. They see the link between growth and lower long-term pollution as being simplistic. It is possible, critics argue, for economies to get stuck along the curve, never reaching a point where pollution declines (Arrow et al. 1998; Tisdell 2001: 187). The Curve does not account for the integrity of the ecosystem as a whole, and it ignores irreplaceable losses (such as biodiversity and species loss). It discounts, too, the potential for cumulative ecological change to erupt into a sudden and uncontainable crisis. It does not address the possibility that, as the amount of one toxic substance declines, the amount of another may rise. The Curve, moreover, only works for a limited range of pollutants and resources. It fails, for example, for CO_2 emissions (the leading cause of global warming), which have been rising steadily alongside growth. Finally, a decline of a particular pollutant in one country may occur because industrial production shifts offshore. Japan's domestic environment was able to improve, for example, partly because dirty industries shifted into South-East and North-East Asia (Hall 2002, 2009).

Environmental critics of economic growth argue further that production patterns and unequal consumption—rather than poverty—are the driving forces of global environmental decay. The earth is already beyond its carrying capacity. The push for constant economic growth inherent in today's global political economy, critics contend, means that industrialization, intensive agriculture, and unsustainable natural resource extraction will continue to rise. **Gross domestic product (GDP)** nearly tripled worldwide from 1970 to 2000 (in constant dollar terms). From 2001 to 2006, it then grew more than in any five-year period since the Second World War (World Bank 2007b). The global financial downturn of 2007–9 did slow economic growth. For critics, however, the unprecedented stimulus packages and bailouts of big banks and corporations merely confirm

the unswerving faith of policymakers in the need to keep the global economy growing. For them, the financial crisis is merely a symptom of an unsustainable and unjust global order. And government efforts to stimulate consumption and spending during and since this crisis have simply added to the destructive power of economic globalization.

Globalization also 'distances' production from consumption, so end users do not 'see' the ecological effects of individual purchases or disposal (Princen 1997, 2005, 2010; Clapp 2002; Dauvergne 2008). Products like computers often become obsolete in a few years, partly because of their design. This, along with advertising, is contributing to ever higher levels of consumption in both the North and the South. Private consumption expenditures, for example, increased more than fourfold from 1960 to 2000, even though the world population only doubled during this period. Since 1950, meat consumption has increased more than fivefold, reaching over 295 million metric tons by 2011: an amount some analysts predict will exceed 420 million metric tons by 2050 (FAO 2012b: 8; Nierenberg 2009). These rises, moreover, have not solved the gross inequalities between consumption in the South and the North. In some African countries per capita consumption has declined since the 1980s. The wealthiest one-fifth of the global population accounts for over three-quarters of total private consumption expenditures. This not only translates into far more luxury goods, but also necessities such as food. At the start of the twenty-first century the richest 20 per cent of the world population, for example, was consuming 45 per cent of all meat and fish (UNEP 2002: 35, 37). Inequality in consumption has only grown worse since then, with 1 per cent of the world population now holding 50 per cent of global wealth (Shorrocks, Davies, and Lluberas, 2015). Much of today's consumption, critics argue, is wasteful and excessive—creating a world where obesity is the latest crisis of the middle classes and malnutrition the everlasting crisis of marginalized peoples of the South.

Global free trade, critics contend, merely adds to the earth's unsustainable ecological burden (Daly 1993, 1996, 2002; Rees 2002, 2006; Kissinger and Rees 2010; De Young and Princen 2012). The prices of traded goods generally do not reflect the full environmental and social costs of production—the value, for example, of an old-growth tree as a source of biodiversity—leaving consumer prices far too low and consumption far too high for global sustainability. Environmental critics further argue that trade and trade agreements put downward pressure on environmental standards. This occurs because governments, in a bid to become more competitive in global markets, sometimes lower, or fail to strengthen, environmental management. Some see this as creating a **race to the bottom**; while others see it as leaving countries 'stuck at the bottom' (Esty 1994; Porter 1999). For many, the only solution to the ecological drawbacks of trade is to impose strict controls over trade.

Production under free trade may well become more 'efficient', critics add, but the steady increase in the production of goods overrides any environmental gains—creating, for example, a world heading towards a billion fuel-efficient cars rather than millions of fuel-inefficient cars. Global free trade, moreover, is in fact far from 'free'. Nor is it equal or fair, as highly mobile capital exploits the so-called comparative advantages of weak economies. The ideology of free trade in reality translates into patterns of exchange that exploit the labour and environments of the South and protect the interests of the North (such as farmers). The South ends up exporting unsustainable quantities of natural resources and absorbing ecological damage so that the North can prosper. Production-for-export from the South tends to rely either on unsustainable quantities of natural resources, or on dirty and unsafe factories (and, of course, cheap labour). Logging, mining, and industrial waste sites, and textile and electronic factories in Latin America, Africa, and the Asia-Pacific highlight the ecological damage of such production (Ross 2001; Jackson and Banks 2003; Ali 2004; Tienhaara 2006; Gallagher and Zarsky 2007; Pellow 2007; Smillie 2014; Straumann 2014). Global trade, critics conclude, in effect allows the North to live beyond its carrying capacity, doing so by using up the carrying capacity of the South.

Critics see the rising power of transnational corporations as a fundamental cause of the escalating global ecological crisis. These corporations are viewed as engines of environmental exploitation, plundering the globe's limited resources for quick profits. In particular, critics see *pollution havens* and *double standards* as real or potential threats to sustainability. A pollution haven refers to governments using low environmental standards to induce firms to invest, thus creating a haven for polluters. It does not, as David Wheeler (2002: 1) points out, 'necessarily refer to a region that is seriously polluted'. What really matters is 'the willingness of the host government to "play

the environment card" to promote growth'. A double standard refers to cases where a firm applies one set of standards at home and another set overseas (generally lower standards in countries with weaker laws). Double standards are common and, most economists would agree, a normal outcome of the process of development. The case of the American TNC, Union Carbide, in Bhopal, India, the site of the worst industrial accident in history, is perhaps the best-known case of double standards (the US headquarters was responsible for the plant's design) (MacKenzie 2002; Jasanoff 2007). But there are countless others, too (Ofreneo 1993; Karliner 1997; Korten 2001; Frey 1998, 2003). Over the years the American firms, General Electric, Ford, General Motors, and Westinghouse, for example, have all operated plants in Northern Mexico, in part to avoid California's much tougher regulations on toxic emissions. Critics blame these TNCs for polluting local rivers, soil, and water supplies near these plants.

There is, then, little controversy as to whether double standards exist. The existence of pollution havens, however, is hotly debated. Critics of TNCs commonly assert that corporate globalization is producing pollution havens around the globe. The process of globalization spreads these, because corporations are increasingly willing to relocate for the smallest differences in costs. Governments, meanwhile, are more likely to use lax regulations to entice investors. Most economists, however, argue that the reason for double standards is *not* a result of host governments intentionally and explicitly playing the environment card. There are, they claim, in fact few, if any, permanent pollution havens anywhere in the world (Wheeler 2002). There are many reasons for this. For some industries, it is impractical or too risky to relocate for market or infrastructural reasons. The main reason, however, is that, for most industrial sectors, other costs, such as those for labour and technology, are far higher than environmental costs (Ferrantino 1997: 52). It therefore does not make financial sense for a firm to relocate on environmental grounds alone.

A second and much larger strand of the environmental literature, which is critical of corporations, focuses less on the differential environmental practices of firms across countries and more on practices 'on the ground'. These critics have filled libraries documenting the destructive and illegal practices of loggers, miners, oil companies, chemical companies, and agricultural companies (Clapp 2001; Dauvergne 2001;

Gedicks 2001; Tacconi 2007; Clapp and Fuchs 2009; Nest 2011; Hall 2013; Smillie 2014; Richardson 2015; Clapp 2016). This research not only documents the activities of well-known transnational corporations, but also local and regional firms, such as Malaysian and Indonesian loggers in South-East Asia and the South Pacific. Besides academics, research institutes such as the World Resources Institute and countless numbers of NGOs also research and publish such findings. This research leads popular writers such as Joshua Karliner (1997) to call the world a 'Corporate Planet', and David Korten (2001) to conclude that 'Corporations Rule the World'.

KEY POINTS

Advocates argue that the wealth from the globalization of trade and TNCs creates:

- Poverty alleviation, better education, population controls, and a stronger capacity of states and global institutions to implement sustainable development.

- Technological innovation and less harmful forms of production (e.g. a shift from industry and agriculture to service and knowledge).

- Corporate investment that 'exports environmentalism' by transferring funds, new technologies, and higher standards to the South.

- Opportunities to use creative policies and incentives to tunnel through the Environmental Kuznets Curve.

Critics see unequal and destructive economic growth, trade, and investment that:

- Burden the South with unequal environmental costs and low environmental standards.

- Allow corporations to plunder the globe's fragile ecosystems.

- Generate consumer prices that ignore environmental and social costs of production.

- Drive overconsumption in the North and unbalanced consumption in the South, putting total global consumption well beyond the earth's carrying capacity.

A sustainable future? Financing and regimes

There is, then, a great divide between environmentalists who support and those who oppose economic globalization. Most agree, however, that moving towards a sustainable global economy will no doubt require new consumption patterns, innovative markets, technological advances, corporate ethics, and innovative forms of global governance. Reforms are, indeed, going on in all of these areas. Yet, the global community has put much of its energy into funding sustainable development, and into forming and strengthening global environmental agreements. Is sustainable development an effective core principle? Is funding sufficient? Can international agreements and sustainable development ensure globalization is a positive environmental force? Many in the global community—states and state negotiators in particular—believe in sustainable development and environmental agreements. Others, however, see them as, at best, harmless, and at worst, themselves causes of global environmental harm as the effort to reach a compromise lowers expectations, creates long delays, and ultimately contributes to ineffective policies. The next section addresses these issues, with particular attention to global environmental financing and the political economy of three international regimes: ozone depletion, climate change, and forestry.

Financing sustainable development: the Global Environment Facility (GEF)

Few deny that the South requires assistance to implement sustainable development. How else can the South find the funds and personnel to address issues such as climate change or global biodiversity? Yet, critics lament the failures of existing environmental assistance. Some see total development assistance as being far too low—far below the repeated global promise of total overseas development assistance of 0.7 per cent of gross national income. The total OECD average was just 0.29 per cent in 2014, while the United States is among the lowest of the major donors, supplying 0.19 per cent in 2014 and only 0.16 per cent in 2007 (OECD 2009; www.oecd.org). Although the 2015 Paris Agreement under the UN Framework Convention on Climate Change promises developing countries a minimum of $100 billion a year from 2020 to help mitigate and adapt to climate change, over the past few decades support for sustainable development has been a small portion of total development assistance. At the Rio Summit, for example, the North was only willing to commit to $125 billion of the $625 billion estimated as being needed to implement Agenda 21 (UNEP 2002: 17).

Other critics see development assistance as a cause of global ecological stress. They see the conditions attached to this 'aid' as a tool of donors and corporate allies to exploit labour and natural resources in the South. Multilateral donors such as the World Bank (see Phillips 2009; Park 2010) and bilateral donors such as Japan (the world's largest bilateral aid donor during the 1990s), for example, use loans to require governments to eliminate trade barriers and support foreign investors. Heavy foreign debts, these critics contend, further aggravate ecological pressures as states export natural resources to earn the foreign exchange to service and repay the debt (Rich 1994, 2000, 2009; Babb 2009).

The **Global Environment Facility (GEF)** is one of the few financial sources to fund specific global environmental initiatives in the South. The GEF was first set up as a pilot facility in 1991, just before the Rio Summit, becoming a permanent body formally in 1994. The GEF has three main implementing agencies—the World Bank; the United Nations Development Programme (UNDP); and the UNEP—although seven other agencies that have joined since the GEF was established also participate. The Global Environment Facility is housed formally in the World Bank; although it is functionally independent, many consider this a telling sign of the World Bank's influence over the GEF. The UNDP handles technical assistance and the UNEP coordinates between the GEF and global environmental agreements. Fourteen donor states and 18 recipient states sit on the GEF Council, which has an 'open door policy' towards NGOs. The GEF finances global environmental policies and programmes in developing countries, including ozone depletion, biodiversity, climate change, and persistent organic pollutants (Streck 2001). The GEF has co-financed more than 4,000 projects in more than 180 countries. The total amount of GEF grants allocated by 2015 was over $14.5 billion. The GEF has also managed to leverage over $75 billion in co-financing from other sources (GEF 2009; www.thegef.org).

The GEF disburses grants and technical funds to cover the additional costs for developing countries of a project targeting a global environmental objective (such as to mitigate climate change or protect biodiversity). Some see the GEF as a critical step forward to help the South absorb the financial costs of global sustainability. Others, such as Bruce Rich of the NGO Environmental Defense Fund, have lashed out at the GEF, especially during the pilot phase: 'The

formulation of the Global Environment Facility', he argues (1994: 176–7), 'was a model of the Bank's preferred way of doing business: Top-down, secretive, with a basic contempt for public participation, access to information, involvement of democratically elected legislatures, and informed discussion of alternatives'. These critics see the GEF as little more than a financial Band-Aid that emphasizes top-down technological fixes rather than long-term solutions (Young 2003). These critics worry, too, that the World Bank is tying GEF grants to other World Bank loans financing projects that damage the environment. Korinna Horta of Environmental Defense states: 'The World Bank mocks the principles and policies of the GEF by hypocritically funding and mitigating environmental destruction. The GEF "greenwashes" business as usual for the Bank' (Halifax Initiative 2002; also see Horta *et al.* 2002).

Without doubt, funding for global sustainability is far from adequate, although as this chapter will discuss later, the 2015 Paris Agreement would seem to be a significant commitment to finance climate mitigation and adaptation in developing countries. The global community has in some ways made more progress in developing and strengthening environmental regimes.

Explaining outcomes: the political economy of environmental regimes

The global community has put great faith in international environmental agreements to guide globalization, promote cooperation, rein in **free riders**, and avoid the natural drift of a system of sovereign states towards a **tragedy of the commons** (see Box 14.4). The number of international and regional environmental negotiations has been increasing steadily since the 1970s, and today there are over 1,200 multilateral environmental agreements (including amendments and protocols) (see Mitchell 2014 for a database of agreements; see Table 14.1 for examples).

An international environmental regime encompasses more than just international legal agreements. Steven Krasner's (1983: 2) definition of an international regime is the classic one: 'sets of implicit or explicit principles, norms, rules and decision-making procedures around which actors' expectations converge in a given area of international relations' (see Aggarwal and Dupont, Chapter 3 in this volume). Yet, most international environmental regimes revolve

BOX 14.4 TRAGEDY OF THE COMMONS

Garrett Hardin (1968), in a now famous article in *Science*, drew a vivid analogy of access and historical collapse of the English commons with access and future collapse of modern-day commons (like the high seas, or the atmosphere, or an unregulated forest). Look, he says, at a grazing pasture 'open to all'. It is in the rational self-interest of a farmer to breed and graze as many animals as possible. The addition of one more animal will enhance the wealth of the owner far more than it will degrade the pasture for the owner's herd. Without controls, however, the logic of personal gain will inevitably overfill and destroy the pasture. The process is the same for all commons with rising populations and unrestricted access. 'Ruin is the destination toward which all men rush', he argues, 'each pursuing his own best interest in a society that believes in the freedom of the commons. Freedom in a commons brings ruin to all.' The only solution, he concludes, is 'mutual coercion, mutually agreed upon by the majority of the people affected'.

around an international agreement. Such regimes tend to evolve in four phases. They begin with the recognition of a problem, including the scientific debates about the causes and severity, and the emergence of an agenda. The science here is often speculative, especially if, as with climate change, it involves looking hundreds of years into the future. Working through the science can create decades of delay during this phase as various 'experts' make claims and counter-claims. Dramatic events, such as an oil spill or chemical leak, or a 'hole' in the ozone layer, can catalyse action towards the next stage—the negotiation of the rules and decision-making procedures. Here, coalitions of states or a powerful state such as the United States can play a critical role either in the emergence or the veto of an agreement. States may also shift gears during this phase—for example, signing an agreement then withdrawing later (by refusing to ratify, say). As with the emergence of an agenda, scientists or experts with collective policy preferences can play a key role in defining the content of an agreement (Haas 1992; Lindemann 2008). So can networks of activists who work across traditional sovereign borders (Keck and Sikkink 1998; Pellow 2007; Hironaka 2014; Dauvergne 2016). Once an agreement comes into force, parties to the agreement need to implement policies that meet their obligations. This phase can further strengthen or weaken a regime, as many states, even those striving legitimately to meet obligations, may be unable (or unwilling) to do so for technical or political reasons. Finally, regimes continue to evolve even after implementation begins, strengthening and weakening as norms shift (or sometimes as negotiators amend the formal rules).

There is a growing literature on evaluating the effectiveness of international environmental regimes (Victor *et al.* 1998; Young 1999, 2002; Vogler 2000, 2003;

Mitchell 2002, 2006; Breitmeier *et al.* 2006; Mitchell *et al.* 2006; Stokke and Hønneland 2007; Stokke 2012; Kanie and Andresen 2015; Susskind and Ali 2015). Many global environmental regimes are weak, with little influence over the behaviour of states and firms or, if there is influence, with little impact on global ecological conditions. An array of factors can undermine regime effectiveness. Ongoing research (and resulting debates) within the scientific community can make it hard to create and maintain a scientific consensus on the causes, consequences, and solutions for particular ecological problems (Vogel 2012). Corporations can exploit the resulting uncertainty common to the scientific method to further delay negotiations or weaken regimes (as well as to fund scientific research to try to prolong uncertainty). The domestic political influence of corporations can also weaken the formal rules and procedures for international agreements, undermine international financial commitments to support compliance, and stall national implementation, even in countries with reasonable local environmental records. The priority of all states on maintaining economic growth—and the insistence of many governments in developing countries on ensuring the opportunity to one day reach the levels of economic prosperity the North currently enjoys—can also mean that international negotiators compromise and avoid strict measures entailing economic costs. These factors all shape the scope and nature of international agreements, as well as the strength of the national policies and implementing agencies designed to meet international obligations.

National agencies are generally responsible for monitoring and enforcing international environmental laws. To encourage compliance, however, parties generally submit implementation data to secretariats as well as attend regular meetings to review implementation. Some agreements also link financing to compliance (especially important in the South). The secretariats, however, often lack the staff and funds to verify data (as well as push laggards to submit). The combined total in 1999 of professional staff of the Framework Convention on Climate Change, the Convention on Biological Diversity, the Montreal Protocol, CITES, and the Convention to Combat Desertification was a mere 100 people. The combined total budget was just $43.5 million (Porter *et al.* 2000: 150). Both figures are tiny in comparison with the **international financial institutions (IFIs)**. Non-governmental organizations also play a key role here, publicizing violations and conducting independent studies of national implementation. The NGO, Environmental Defense, for example, was 'critical' in ensuring US regulations in fact implemented the Montreal Protocol after it went into force in 1989 (Porter *et al.* 2000: 149).

Implementation can pose great technical and political problems for governments in the South. Often, these governments do not have the finances, personnel, or technologies to monitor and enforce environmental legislation. Systemic corruption may further hinder enforcement. The cost of compliance, too, is frequently greater in the South than in the North, as the South has less infrastructure and experience in meeting environmental obligations, although, as mentioned earlier, funds such as the ones from the GEF can help to offset the higher costs of compliance in the South. Countries in the North, however, also struggle with implementing international environmental agreements. The process of confirming scientific explanations may create long bureaucratic delays in implementation. Lobby groups and bureaucracies may work to weaken national legislation designed to meet international obligations. In democratic federations, such as Canada, the Canadian federal government may sign and ratify an agreement, but then face stiff opposition from some of the provinces, as happened after the federal government ratified the Kyoto Protocol in 2002.

For all of these reasons, then, it is a formidable challenge for state negotiators and implementers to develop and uphold an effective international environmental regime. Perhaps the most common example of a 'successful' regime is the one to reduce the production and consumption of chlorofluorocarbons (CFCs), the main cause of the depletion of the ozone layer.

Ozone depletion regime

Production and consumption of CFCs, first invented in 1928, rose quickly from the 1950s to the 1970s. The main use was in aerosols, refrigerators, air conditioners, insulation, and solvents. In 1974, Mario Molina and F. Sherwood Rowland (1974) (who went on to win the 1995 Nobel Prize in Chemistry) published an article hypothesizing that CFCs were drifting into the atmosphere, breaking apart, releasing chlorine, then reacting to deplete the ozone layer. Ozone is a molecule of three oxygen atoms able to absorb harmful ultraviolet light. The ozone layer refers to the region of high concentrations of ozone in the stratosphere. (The stratosphere is 10–50 kilometres above the earth's surface. Below this is the troposphere, where weather occurs.) The ozone layer protects us from the harmful effects of ultraviolet radiation from the sun, which can contribute to skin cancer and cataracts, decrease our immunity to diseases, and make plants less productive.

In the decade after Molina and Rowland's seminal article, global negotiators worked slowly towards a collective consensus on the causes and consequences of ozone depletion. This effort gained momentum in 1985, after British scientists found a 'hole' (in fact, a severe thinning) in the ozone layer over Antarctica. This hole, which persisted for three months, was the size of North America. That same year, the global community signed the Vienna Convention for the Protection of the Ozone Layer, a framework convention with no legally binding targets. The 1987 Montreal Protocol on Substances that Deplete the Ozone Layer was adopted two years later, setting mandatory targets to reduce the production of ozone-depleting CFCs and halons (halons are another significant ozone-depleting substance found, for example, in fire extinguishers).

Significantly, in 1990, the South agreed to phase out consumption of CFCs and halons by 2010. The Parties to the Montreal Protocol created the Multilateral Fund for the Implementation of the Montreal Protocol to assist developing countries with implementation. This is unusual, as most international environmental agreements do not contain a funding mechanism, and instead rely on traditional development assistance and, more recently, the GEF. So far, this Fund has approved more than $3 billion to phase out the consumption of ozone-depleting substances in the South (www.multilateralfund.org). Partly as a result of international funding, many developing countries were already 'on

Figure 14.3 Global CFC production, (1931–2004)

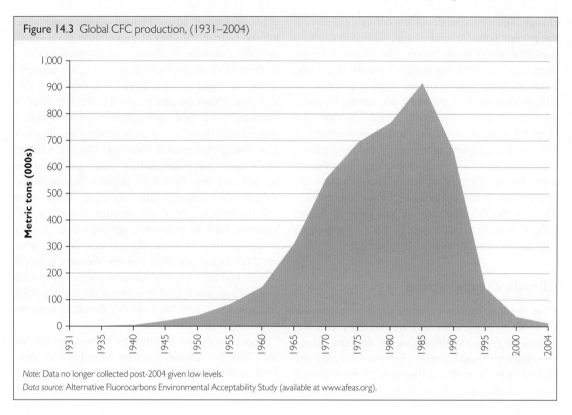

Note: Data no longer collected post-2004 given low levels.

Data source: Alternative Fluorocarbons Environmental Acceptability Study (available at www.afeas.org).

track' by the mid 1990s to phase out CFCs and halons ahead of schedule (Greene 1997: 329), and the South was able to reduce CFC consumption by about 60 per cent from the mid 1990s to 2004 (UNEP 2005).

Conferences of the Parties in London in 1990, Copenhagen in 1992, Montreal in 1997, and Beijing in 1999 amended and strengthened the Montreal Protocol. These conferences also added other ozone-depleting substances and accelerated the phase-out schedules. Over this time, the Vienna Convention and the Montreal Protocol became truly global agreements, and today the Montreal Protocol has 197 Parties. The result has been a dramatic fall in global CFC production (see Figure 14.3), with only very low production levels since 2004.

The damage to the ozone layer, it is important to emphasize, is still a serious problem. The long life of CFCs means that 'old' emissions are still damaging the ozone layer. The ozone hole over Antarctica broke records in September 2006 for depth and average size over a period of time (from 21–30 September). Still, the overall signs are positive, with fewer CFCs allowing the ozone layer to remain fairly stable since the 2000 (Barry and Phillips 2006; also, see NASA Ozone

Watch, http://ozonewatch.gsfc.nasa.gov). (The reasons for changes in ozone are complex—including sunspots, weather, and volcanoes—so some fluctuations are natural.) The World Meteorological Organization (2015) now predicts that the ozone layer will repair itself and return to pre-1980 levels by 2050 (with this occurring a bit later in the Antarctica), thus preventing millions of cases of melanoma cancer and eye cataracts (UNEP 2003: 4). This is, indeed, an exceptional turnaround. 'The ozone layer regime is remarkable', Marvin Soroos (1997: 169) argues, 'not only for the series of agreements limiting and phasing out the production and use of ozone-depleting substances but also for the broad acceptance of them and the apparent high rate of compliance with the controls'. Most other scholars would agree. Edward Parson (2003: vii) calls it a 'striking success', noting: 'With near-universal participation of nations and energetic support from industry, the ozone regime has reduced worldwide use of ozone-depleting chemicals by 95 per cent, and use is still falling'.

Yet, in many ways, this was an exceptional case, one that may well tell us little about our ability to handle future global environmental crises such as climate change. The consequences of less ozone were easy for the general public to understand, with skin cancer a particular worry in the North. The causes and solutions were also relatively straightforward. In the mid 1980s, 21 firms in 16 countries were responsible for CFC production, with the North accounting for about 88 per cent of this. Especially notable, by 1986, the chemical company DuPont, the largest producer of CFCs (accounting for a quarter of global production), had decided to seek substitutes for CFCs (Grundmann 2001; Parson 2003). Two years later, DuPont announced that it would phase out production of CFCs. The shift to CFC substitutes did not harm its profits; indeed, in many ways, it gave DuPont a competitive edge as other producers soon followed suit.

Climate change regime

Most other global environmental problems involve far greater complexities and uncertainties, and will require far greater sacrifices to solve. Climate change is perhaps the most complex of all (see Bulkeley and Newell 2010; Newell and Paterson 2010; Hoffmann 2011; Bulkeley *et al.* 2014; Ciplet *et al.* 2015; Stern 2015; Hickmann 2016). Human activities are altering the relative volumes of greenhouse gases—such as carbon dioxide, methane, and nitrogen oxides—in the earth's atmosphere. Figure 14.4, for example, shows the rapid increase in global emissions of carbon dioxide over the past hundred years. The planet is warming as the 'new' atmosphere traps more heat, a process akin to rolling up a car window on a hot day. The Intergovernmental Panel on Climate Change (IPCC 2001) calculates that the mean global surface temperature rose by 0.3–0.6 degrees Celsius during the twentieth century. This may seem minor, but it was the largest rise of any century in the last millennium. And the problem is getting worse. January 2000 to January 2010 was the warmest decade, January 2011 to January 2016 was the warmest five-year period, and 2015 was the warmest year, since records began. One clear sign of warming is the melting polar ice caps, which have been steadily shrinking since the beginning of the 1980s.

This century will certainly be hotter than the last one. The five hottest years on record are all since 1998, with the US National Aeronautics and Space Administration (NASA) predicting record-high

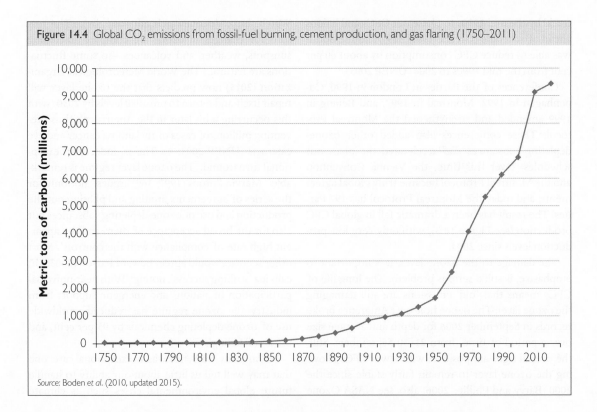

Figure 14.4 Global CO_2 emissions from fossil-fuel burning, cement production, and gas flaring (1750–2011)

Source: Boden *et al.* (2010, updated 2015).

temperatures in future El Niño years (see http://data.giss.nasa.gov). Various IPCC (www.ipcc.ch) scenarios project a possible rise in the earth's average surface temperature of between 1 to 7 degrees Celsius above pre-industrial levels by 2100 (the year 2015 was about 1 degree Celsius above 1880–99 levels). A rise of 3 to 5 degrees Celsius would, according to NASA's Drew Shindell, 'bring us up to the warmest temperatures the world has experienced probably in the last million years' (quoted in Zabarenko 2006). Such a result, the IPCC warns, would cause mass extinctions, prolonged droughts, fierce storms, and seas to rise enough to displace millions of people in low-lying coastal areas in countries such as Bangladesh and low-lying countries such as the Marshall Islands and the Maldives (see also Hansen *et al.* 2015). For this reason, Parties to the UN Framework Convention on Climate Change agreed in 2009 to strive to limit warming to no more than 2 degrees Celsius above pre-industrial levels, later adding an aspirational target of no more than 1.5 degrees Celsius in the Paris Agreement, an outcome of the 21st Conference of the Parties of the UN Framework Convention on Climate Change, held in Paris in 2015.

Climate change alarms environmental critics of economic globalization in particular, as the primary greenhouse gases arise from core economic activities, such as automobiles, power plants, oil refineries, factories, agriculture, and deforestation. At the same time, many of the consequences, such as melting polar ice, rising seas, severe storms, new diseases, and drought, are beyond the lifetimes of politicians and business leaders. No doubt, to lower greenhouse gas emissions will require significant changes to global economic production and consumption patterns. It will require, too, governmental, corporate, and personal sacrifices. Replacing CFCs, these critics note, is simply not a comparable sacrifice (Paterson 1996; Newell 2000; Porter *et al.* 2008).

As highlighted, once again, at the Conferences of the UN Framework Convention on Climate Change leading up to Paris in 2015, the South has commonly portrayed the North as being largely responsible for climate change, because developed countries accounted for three-quarters of cumulative emissions of carbon dioxide between 1950 and 1992. The North, on the other hand, often notes the need for global efforts, as within a few decades carbon dioxide emissions from the South are likely to equal those from the North. Nevertheless, specific views on climate

change do not split cleanly along North–South lines. Over the past two decades the European Union and Japan, for example, have tended to support global efforts to combat climate change, while at various political moments the United States, Canada, and Australia have been sceptical, at times even questioning the science of global warming (although US President Barack Obama made climate protection a top priority during his second term beginning in 2013). Meanwhile, the states in OPEC have generally opposed efforts to reduce the global dependence on oil while, predictably, the 39 countries in the Alliance of Small Island States generally support every possible effort to halt the rise of sea levels. Over the past decade China has also emerged as a global leader in wind and solar power, and has pledged to scale back greenhouse gas emissions, including in 2014 announcing a bilateral climate change commitment with the United States. During the 2015 climate negotiations in Paris, policy positions and alliances crisscrossed North–South lines more than ever before, with, for instance, a 'high-ambition coalition' emerging that brought together more than 100 countries, including the United States, Canada, EU member states, and scores of countries across the Pacific, Africa, and the Caribbean.

Prior to the Paris Agreement, the 1997 Kyoto Protocol to the 1992 Framework Convention on Climate Change was the core agreement in the climate change regime. The Kyoto Protocol required developed countries (including Russia) to reduce emissions of six greenhouse gases, on average, by 5 per cent below 1990 levels between 2008 and 2012 (calculated as an average over these years). (If this had been achieved, emissions levels would have been about 20 per cent lower than they would have been without the Protocol.) Not all governments had the same 'target'. The European Union agreed to reduce emissions by 8 per cent below 1990 levels; the United States by 7 per cent; and Japan and Canada by 6 per cent. The Russian Federation agreed to stabilize emissions at 1990 levels. Australia managed to negotiate an increase of 8 per cent above 1990 levels. Developing countries were exempt from legally binding commitments in the Kyoto Protocol, although some, including India and China, set voluntary reduction targets.

The rules of the Kyoto Protocol required it to come into force 90 days after at least 55 Parties, accounting for at least 55 per cent of the 1990 carbon dioxide emissions of the developed country signatories, had ratified it. This seemed unlikely to occur after the United States, which accounted for 36.1 per cent of 1990 carbon dioxide emissions of developed countries, withdrew support in 2001, and instead vowed to reduce greenhouse gases 'by 18 per cent over the next decade through voluntary, incentive-based, and existing mandatory measures' (Switzer 2004: 293). The Kyoto Protocol did, in the end, come into force in 2005 even without the United States, after Russia, which accounted for 17.4 per cent of 1990 levels, ratified the Protocol and tipped the total over the 55 per cent mark. Many saw the coming into force of the Protocol as a sign of the determination of the global community (minus the United States and Australia) to tackle climate change. Many saw it, too, as a vital foundation for further international dialogue, such as the annual Conference of the Parties of the UN Framework Convention on Climate Change. Still, most analysts agreed that, even with full compliance, the Kyoto Protocol was never going to lower greenhouse gas emissions to levels that would 'solve' climate change. More radical groups, such as Greenpeace, have long argued for a global emission reduction closer to 80 per cent. Almost all analysts came to agree that more effective governance of climate change would require many initiatives at multiple levels, from global to local (e.g. Selin and VanDeveer 2009; Okereke *et al.* 2009): a viewpoint central to the climate negotiations in Paris in 2015.

Representatives from more than 190 countries met in Paris from 30 November to 11 December to negotiate a new international agreement to mitigate and adapt to climate change. The history of the Kyoto Protocol weighed on the minds of many negotiators. The US never did ratify the Protocol; Canada went as far as formally withdrawing. Equally disturbing, many states had failed to meet their reduction targets by the end of the first commitment period in 2012. Parties to the Protocol did agree to a second commitment period from 2013 to 2020 (known as the Doha Amendment), but going into the 2015 Paris meeting not enough states had ratified this amendment to put it in force. The international community, just about everyone agreed, was in desperate need of a new climate change agreement.

Talks in Paris were tense and many compromises were made, but negotiators, nudged along by French diplomats, did manage to reach a general agreement on financing, warming limits, reporting and ratcheting up processes, and national emission-reduction plans. Negotiators also agreed to set aside future liability claims. Initially, many negotiators were seeking legally binding emission-reduction targets as in the Kyoto Protocol; however, with the US Senate declaring it would block ratification of such a treaty, US negotiators pushed for non-binding emission targets and financing pledges to allow President Obama to use his executive powers to commit the US to the Agreement. The Paris Agreement calls for worldwide national plans (with developed economies agreeing to move more quickly) to reduce greenhouse gas emissions with the aim of keeping global warming 'well below 2 degrees Celsius' (United Nations 2015b: 22). Even if fully implemented, the national climate action plans submitted to the Paris conference would not achieve this result; however, the Paris Agreement does require national governments to report on emission reductions every five years, and calls for a ratcheting up of commitments as overall progress is evaluated. As mentioned, the Agreement also includes a new financing pledge to help poorer countries mitigate and adapt to climate change, which by 2020 promises a minimum of $100 billion a year in public and private money (e.g. to fund solar and wind power, support reforestation, and prevent deforestation).

Political leaders around the world hailed the Paris Agreement as a breakthrough in climate governance. President Obama, whose team worked hard to forge a consensus, called it a 'historic agreement' and 'a tribute to American leadership'. British Prime Minister David Cameron said it was 'a huge step forward in helping to secure the future of our planet'. UN Secretary General Ban Ki-moon declared: 'For the first time, we have a truly universal agreement on climate change, one of the most crucial problems on earth'. Indian Prime Minister Narendra Modi tweeted: The 'Paris Agreement has no winners or losers. Climate justice has won and we are all working towards a greener future'. The head of China's negotiating team was equally effusive: The Agreement is 'fair and just, comprehensive and balanced, highly ambitious, enduring and effective' (quoted in Davenport 2015; BBC News 2015). Around the world journalists, policymakers, and climate scientists were also full of praise, seeing the Agreement as an ingenious compromise allowing the US to sidestep the Republican-dominated Senate, bringing on board the emerging economies of Brazil, Russia,

China, and India, and appeasing highly vulnerable countries across the developing world. '[D]ecades of failure were reversed', *Guardian* reporters gushed (Vidal *et al*. 2015). It is 'the world's greatest diplomatic success', pronounced Fiona Harvey (2015) of the *Guardian*. 'The future is bright', declared Lord Nicholas Stern of the London School of Economics: 'If we get this right, it will be more powerful than the industrial revolution. A green race is going on' (quoted in Vidal *et al*. 2015).

Some observers, however, were quick to pan the Agreement for its largely voluntary, loose, and weak nature: ideal for achieving consensus among government negotiators, but a far cry from the mechanisms and measures necessary to decarbonize the global economy and keep fossil fuels in the ground. Emission targets, timetables, and financing, critics railed, fall outside of the legally binding sections of the agreement. Critics also questioned the net value of the new financing pledge, and emphasized that the Agreement excludes future liability claims for compensation as temperatures inevitably rise (likely well over the 'hope' of 2 degrees Celsius). Journalist George Monbiot (2015) captures these sentiments well, arguing the Agreement is replete with 'promises that can slip or unravel' as much of the text 'could mean anything and nothing'. '[W]e will not', he concludes,

'be viewed kindly by succeeding generations'. James Hansen, a world-renowned climate scientist, was similarly dismayed, declaring the Paris talks a 'fraud ... just worthless words. There is no action, just promises' (quoted in Milman 2015).

Forests regime

Most environmental regimes, as with ozone and climate change, contain a core international agreement. But some, such as the international forests regime, have emerged without a core global treaty. The international forests regime includes the norms and principles arising from numerous global meetings since the Rio Summit to discuss the benefits and drawbacks of negotiating a global treaty for forest management. It consists, too, of the forest-related clauses of international conventions such as the ones on biodiversity, desertification, climate change, and wetlands. It also includes the sustainable forest principles of institutions such as the International Tropical Timber Organization (ITTO), and the standards of organizations such as the Forest Stewardship Council (FSC) (see Box 14.5). At the core of the regime is the concept of sustainable forest management. Humphreys (1999: 251) writes, 'The forests regime has coalesced around the core concept of sustainable

---

BOX 14.5 ITTO AND FSC

International Tropical Timber Organization (ITTO)

The 1983 International Tropical Timber Agreement (in force from 1985) created the International Tropical Timber Organization (ITTO), with its headquarters in Yokohama, Japan. Successor agreements were negotiated in 1994 (in force since 1997) and in 2006 (in force since 2011). The ITTO's mandate is to facilitate consultation and cooperation among member countries that produce and consume tropical timber. There are 72 members (as of 2016), representing at least 90 per cent of world trade in tropical timber. The organization is committed to assisting members with meeting the so-called Year 2000 Objective, which calls for members (originally, by the year 2000), to trade only tropical timber products that originate from sustainably managed forests. (This is still being pursued, despite the passing of the target year.)

Source: ITTO website (available at www.itto.int).

Forest Stewardship Council (FSC)

The non-profit Forest Stewardship Council was founded in 1993 to promote more effective forest management. Its members include environmental organizations, forest industries, indigenous, and community groups, and forest certification bodies. The FSC accredits and monitors organizations that certify that forest products come from 'a well-managed forest'—that is, a forest that meets the FSC's Principles and Criteria of Forest Stewardship. The FSC visits certified forests to ensure compliance. It further supports the development of regional, national, and local standards that implement these principles and criteria. The FSC logo on a wood product is ultimately designed to provide a 'credible guarantee' to the consumer 'that the product comes from a well-managed forest'.

Source: FSC website (www.fsc.org).

forest management (SFM) and the norm that forests should be conserved and used in a sustainable manner'. Other global principles include the value of conservation, ecosystem integrity, protected areas, indigenous knowledge and values, and the participation of civil society (Humphreys 1999, 2003, 2006; also, see Cashore *et al.* 2004; Gulbrandsen 2010; Lister 2011; Giessen 2013).

Yet, global norms and principles are only a small part of the basket of rules—both formal and informal—that shape forest management. National and local leaders often ignore the concept of sustainable forest management as well as the non-binding principles of institutions such as the ITTO and FSC. The international forests regime is particularly weak and ineffective in Asia, Africa, and South America, most notably where timber profits prop up corrupt politicians, bureaucrats, and military officers. This explains in part why tropical deforestation has persisted largely unimpeded over the last few decades, despite a global outcry and repeated government promises to do better (Dauvergne 2001; Tacconi 2007; Dauvergne and Lister 2011; Straumann 2014; World Resources Institute 2015).

International regimes, then, can solve global environmental problems. The history of the depletion of the ozone layer confirms this. Yet, the regimes for climate change and deforestation, for different reasons, are still largely ineffective. Supporters of regimes argue this reflects in part the complexity of the causes and consequences of these problems, as well as the need for economic sacrifices to solve them. For them, this suggests a need to work even harder to strengthen these regimes—with outcomes such as the 2015 Paris Agreement demonstrating the prospects for significant progress. For critics of regimes, however, the failure to slow climate change and deforestation suggests the innate limitations of regimes as a mechanism to constrain and guide economic globalization. The energy expended on seemingly endless international negotiations on climate change and deforestation, some critics argue, would be better spent elsewhere, perhaps in labs developing new technologies, or in communities developing new ethics. A few of these critics even see the focus on the development of agreements, such as an international forests convention, as a strategic move by powerful actors to delay real action and ensure that 'business as usual' continues for as long as possible (Dauvergne 2005).

KEY POINTS

- All sides agree that the South needs financial and technical support to pursue global sustainability.
- Some see current efforts—e.g. the GEF—as a critical lifeline for weak economies. Others see such financing as being too small to matter, and still others see global development assistance as a cause of the global environmental crisis, with states exporting natural resources to service and repay foreign debt.
- Environmental regimes are the primary global mechanism for coordinating environmental management across states. It is exceedingly difficult, however, to create and maintain an effective environmental regime.
- Most agree that the ozone regime has been effective, largely because the causes, consequences, and solutions of ozone depletion are straightforward.
- The climate and deforestation regimes are much weaker than the ozone regime. Advocates of regimes see this as temporary, a result of the sheer complexity and difficulty of the science, politics, and economics of climate change and deforestation. These advocates are now hailing the 2015 Paris Agreement as a big step towards financing and ratcheting up commitments to limit global warming to below 2 degrees Celsius. Critics, on the other hand, see weak regimes for problems such as climate change and deforestation as inevitable within the current global political economy; for some, these are not a part of the solution, but, rather, a part of the reasons for failure, as these create illusions of action and progress.
- Most advocates and critics of regimes agree, however, that solutions to climate change and deforestation will require far more than financing and regimes. Solving them will require a level of innovation, cooperation, and sacrifice never seen before in the history of global environmental politics.

Conclusion

What, then, is the nature of global environmental change in an era of globalization? Is the global political economy a force for environmental progress or crisis? Are global environmental regimes and the norm of sustainable development effectively channelling globalization to ensure a sustainable future? The record is mixed. For some problems, such as ozone depletion, global governance has indeed been effective. But for problems such as tropical deforestation, the global community appears to be making no headway at all. Perhaps the greatest environmental problem of all is climate change. Here, it also appears that global efforts are largely failing, although the 2015 Paris Agreement may offer some new pathways forward. Can sustainable development and regimes alone 'solve' deforestation and climate change? The answer seems clear: no. These may, indeed, help. But such great problems will require new national policies, new corporate ethics, more North–South financial transfers, innovative markets, technological advances, and new forms of cooperation. It will be a bumpy path forward: one that will, because of the nature of the global political economy and global environmental change—no doubt, most unjustly—impose the greatest hardships on the world's poorest and least powerful peoples. That much seems certain.

The chapter did not strive to convince the reader to believe in a particular set of arguments. Already far too many globalization and anti-globalization 'environmental ideologues' preach or chant at, rather than talk to, each other. The goal was instead to deepen the understanding of the range of reasonable and logical arguments about the environmental impacts of the ongoing changes to the global political economy. The hope is that, one day, those who choose to act on their beliefs—from joining the World Bank's environment team to protesting at an anti-globalization rally—will do so with the humility of knowing the complexities and uncertainties of the relationship between globalization and the environment.

? QUESTIONS

1. What, in the broadest terms, is the relationship between the global political economy and global environmental change?

2. What is the globalization of environmentalism? Is the overall trend positive or negative?

3. Is the Environmental Kuznets Curve a useful policy tool?

4. Which is more common: 'pollution havens' or 'exporting environmentalism'?

5. What are the effects of inequality and consumption on global environmental conditions?

6. What are the effects of trade and corporations on global environmental conditions?

7. What are the effects of financing and regimes on global environmental conditions?

8. Is there a global environmental crisis? If yes, why? If no, why?

9. Can we solve global environmental problems within the current political and economic structures? If yes, how? If no, why?

10. In what ways is the 2015 Paris Agreement a 'success'? What does this suggest for the potential effectiveness of the international climate change regime?

≋ FURTHER READING

Axelrod, R. S. and VanDeveer, S. D. (eds) (2015), *The Global Environment: Institutions, Law, and Policy*, 4th edn (Washington, DC: CQ Press). Analyses the role of institutions, legal instruments, and policy in shaping global environmental management and change.

Chasek, P. S., Downie, D. L., and Brown, J. W. (2016), *Global Environmental Politics*, 7th edn (Boulder, CO: Westview Press). Introduces the academic study of global environmental politics with a focus on international agreements.

Clapp, J. and Dauvergne, P. (2011), *Paths to a Green World: The Political Economy of the Global Environment*, 2nd edn (Cambridge, MA: MIT Press). Maps out an original typology to classify the dominant world views regarding the impact of the global political economy on the global environment.

Conca, K. and Dabelko, G. D. (eds) (2014), *Green Planet Blues: Critical Perspectives on Global Environmental Politics*, 5th edn (Boulder, CO: Westview Press). Surveys and extracts core concepts and arguments from seminal articles in global environmental politics.

Dauvergne, P. (ed.) (2012), *Handbook of Global Environmental Politics*, 2nd edn (Cheltenham: Edward Elgar). Collection of original and cutting-edge articles by many of the world's premier scholars of global environmental politics.

Dryzek, J. S. (2013), *The Politics of the Earth: Environmental Discourses*, 3rd edn (Oxford: Oxford University Press). Analysis of the history of environmental discourses.

Global Environmental Politics available at www.mitpressjournals.org/loi/glep Scholarly journal that contains the latest innovative and original research on environment and the global political economy (first issue February 2001).

Haas, P. M. (ed.) (2003), *Environment in the New Global Economy* (Cheltenham: Edward Elgar). A collection of 60 seminal articles on environment, globalization, and the global political economy (previously published, dating from 1944 to 2001).

Jinnah, S. and Nicholson, S. (eds) (2016), *New Earth Politics* (Cambridge, MA: MIT Press). Original reflections on the politics and value of environmental scholarship and advocacy.

Nicholson, S. and Wapner, P. (eds) (2014), *Global Environmental Politics: From Person to Planet* (New York: Routledge). Edited and condensed collection of essays surveying the politics of global environmental change, from the consequences of individual behaviour to the value of international institutions.

O'Neill, K. (2009), *The Environment and International Relations* (Cambridge: Cambridge University Press). Draws on theories in international relations to provide a valuable toolkit to analyse global environmental change.

Pojman, L. P., Pojman, P., and McShane, K. (eds) (2015), *Environmental Ethics: Readings in Theory and Application*, 7th edn (Belmont, CA: Wadsworth Publishing). Balanced collection of many of the most influential articles in environmental philosophy and politics, including deep ecology, generational obligations, population, hunger, economics, and sustainability.

Princen, T., Maniates, M. F., and Conca, K. (eds) (2002), *Confronting Consumption* (Cambridge, MA: MIT Press). Breaks new ground in the understanding of consumption as a core problem for the global political economy.

WEBLINKS

www.unep.org United Nations Environment Programme and **www.undp.org** United Nations Development Programme. Provide entries into environment and development data and projects of the United Nations.

www.gefweb.org Global Environment Facility. Outlines projects and programmes to finance protection of the global environment in developing countries.

www.wri.org World Resources Institute. Source of scientific environmental research and non-governmental policy proposals. Includes agriculture, biodiversity, forests, climate change, marine ecosystems, water, and health.

www.iisd.org International Institute for Sustainable Development. Monitors the proceedings of global environmental negotiations and conferences.

www.worldwatch.org WorldWatch Institute. Source of data on the global environmental 'crisis'. Challenges some of the data (and interpretations) of the United Nations, World Bank, and governments.

ONLINE RESOURCE CENTRE

For additional material and resources, please visit the Online Resource Centre at:
www.oxfordtextbooks.co.uk/ravenhill5e

Glossary

Absolute advantage Where a country produces one or more goods or services at lower cost than other countries.

Adjustable peg An exchange rate policy whereby the national currency is largely pegged or fixed to a major currency such as the US dollar or euro, but can be readjusted from time to time within a narrow range.

Agency The capacity to act deliberately.

Alienation A process described by Marx through which an increasingly complex **division of labour** enforces psychological harm onto workers, depriving them of opportunities to realize their full human potential by turning them into purely functional aspects of the broader capitalist system.

Amicus curiae Latin for 'friend of the court'. An individual or group not party to a legal proceeding, but with a strong interest in the case, permitted by the court to submit information intending to influence the outcome of the proceedings.

Anarchy The absence of a centralized authority in the international system capable of enforcing agreements. Literally 'without rule'.

Anthropomorphization Attribution of human form or personality to a non-human entity—typically in GPE either the state or the market. The non-human entity is treated as an actor in its own right and is believed to act in line with its own interests.

Autarchy/Autarky When a country attempts to maximize its self-sufficiency by minimizing contacts with the global economy.

Axioms Assumptions considered to be derived from self-evident principles of social organization and therefore not requiring explanation or justification each time they are used anew.

Balance of payments An account of a country's transactions with foreign countries and international institutions in a specific period. Transactions are divided into **current account**, which consists of the **balance of trade** in goods and services plus profits and interest on overseas assets less those paid to foreign owners of domestic assets, plus net transfers such as worker remittances, and the **capital account**, which

consists of inflows and outflows of money for investment, and for grants and loans (and their repayment). The balance of payments is an accounting identity: the entries in the account should sum to zero with, for example, any imbalances on the current account being offset by net movements of capital.

Balance of trade The difference between a country's total imports and exports in a given period (*see* Balance of payments).

Bank for International Settlements (BIS) Set up in 1930 and located in Basel, Switzerland, the BIS facilitates financial relations and policymaking among many of the world's central banks.

Bounded rationality Rational decision-making in a context of incomplete knowledge.

Bretton Woods The site of the 1944 United Nations Monetary and Financial Conference (the Mount Washington Hotel in the New Hampshire village of Bretton Woods). This conference marked the birth of the International Monetary Fund and the World Bank. 'Bretton Woods' is often used as shorthand for post-war international financial regimes.

British East India Company A stockholding corporation set up by Royal Charter at the beginning of the seventeenth century and funded through the selling of shares. It had the explicit aim of exploiting trading opportunities that arose from bringing back to Europe goods originating from South and East Asia.

Capital account *see* **Balance of payments**

Capital accumulation The process which gives the capitalist economy its essential dynamism: without the accumulation of capital no reinvestment can take place and therefore the economy will not grow over the long term.

Capital controls Restrictions placed by governments on private actors moving funds into or out of the territories they control.

Coase Theorem The argument that economic efficiency will be optimized as long as property rights are fully allocated, and completely free trade in these rights is possible.

Collaboration games A type of game where the **Pareto-optimal** solution the players desire may not be an equilibrium outcome; for example, the pursuit of strategies that are rational for individual players produces a suboptimal outcome, as in the Prisoner's Dilemma.

Common market A **customs union** that also allows free movement of factors (capital, labour) within its boundaries.

Common pool resources Goods that cannot be withheld from those that do not pay for them, and whose consumption comes at the expense of other potential consumers.

Comparative advantage Where a country is relatively more efficient at producing at least one product vis-à-vis others, even though it may lack **absolute advantage** in producing that good or service. Production according to comparative advantage enables specialization in relatively more efficient production, thereby increasing aggregate levels of economic welfare.

Competitive advantage The competitive strength of an economy that derives from the capacity of its firms in various sectors. Whether government intervention can enhance an economy's competitive advantage—remains a matter of considerable controversy.

Conditionality The stipulation by lenders of conditions that borrowers must meet if they are to continue to receive instalments of their loans.

Coordination games A type of game that typically has multiple **Nash Equilibria**, some of which are more preferred by one or more players.

Cross-border production Sometimes referred to as 'the new international division of labour' or 'fragmentation', it occurs when different stages in the making of a single product are geographically dispersed across two or more countries.

Current account *see* **Balance of payments**

Customs unions Agreements between two or more countries to trade freely between themselves, and to adopt a common tariff on imports from countries outside the customs union.

Distributional consequences Who benefits and who loses from particular economic policies or, more broadly, from the institutionalization of a particular type of economic system.

Division of labour The centrepiece of Adam Smith's theoretical system in *The Wealth of Nations*, it refers to a situation in which individual workers specialize in only a small part of the production process rather than trying to undertake every work task involved in the production of a particular good. Efficiency gains—materialize for the economy as a whole when workers specialize in this way and are brought together in large work teams.

Dollarization The adoption by foreign countries of the US dollar as their national currency.

Dumping A situation where a country's exports are sold in foreign markets at a price less than that at which they are sold at home.

Ecological footprint A measure (translated into hectares of average biologically productive land) of the resources required to sustain a person's lifestyle.

Ecological shadow A concept that attempts to capture the environmental impact of a country in jurisdictions beyond its sovereign control.

Economic development The process through which a country, a region, or the world as a whole advances to a new level of economic performance. It is conventionally usually associated explicitly with growth performance, but there are other measures of development such as happiness, security of the means to a good life, and the fulfilment of human potential.

Economic union A **common market** that has also adopted common **monetary** and **fiscal policies**.

Economies of scale Realized when increasing output allows firms to produce each unit at a lower average unit cost.

Embedded liberalism A concept put forward by John Gerard Ruggie, following Karl Polanyi, to capture the compromise in the Bretton Woods economic regimes between liberalization and the pursuit of domestic social and political objectives.

Emerging Market Economy. An economy with low to middle income that is experiencing rapid economic growth.

Enabling clause Formally, the 1979 Decision on Differential and More Favourable Treatment, Reciprocity and Fuller Participation of Developing Countries, it legitimizes **special and differential treatment** in the trade regime for **less developed countries**.

Environmental Kuznets Curve A graph of the relationship between the level of per capita income and pollution, showing that levels of pollution initially increase with economic growth but then decline once per capita income reaches high levels.

Epistemology The study of knowledge and justified belief. It is concerned with questions about the necessary and sufficient conditions of knowledge, the sources of knowledge, and how knowledge is created.

Export-oriented industrialization Strategy for economic development based on domestic production targeted primarily at international markets.

Exporting environmentalism The use by **transnational corporations** in less developed economies of more environmentally friendly technologies than are required by local laws.

Externalities Consequences for societal welfare (costs and benefits) that are not captured in the market price of a good; for example, pollution is a negative externality if the producers do not pay the financial costs it imposes on society. Innovation can be a positive externality if pricing does not capture the full benefits that flow from innovators to the broader society. Externalities are a type of **market failure**.

Factor price equalization The process whereby trade generates a tendency for the prices of factors (capital or labour) to be equalized (a process predicted by the **Stolper–Samuelson Theorem**).

Feldstein–Horioka Puzzle In a world of unfettered capital mobility, savings should flow to those countries offering the highest interest rates, while investment will be financed from the lowest-cost source. Feldstein and Horioka, however, found in a 1980 study that national savings and domestic investment were highly correlated in 16 OECD countries, suggesting the presence of segmented capital markets and low capital mobility.

Financial intermediaries Institutions that match lenders with borrowers, linking those with surplus savings and those who desire to use these funds for investment purposes (*see* **Intermediation**).

Fiscal policies Government policies on taxation and expenditure.

Fixed exchange rate An exchange rate regime under which the value of a currency is tied to that of another currency, a basket of currencies, or another asset such as gold. Post-1945, the exchange rates of most currencies were valued in terms of US dollars.

Foreign direct investment (FDI) An investment made by a company or entity in one country that gives it a controlling interest in a company or entity based in another country.

Formalist Revolution The change in economics which occurred in the 1940s and 1950s, often associated with the mathematicization of the subject field. Here, what made for 'good economics' increasingly privileged sophisticated mathematical models rather than the significance of the economic problems to which they were applied.

Free market economies Those countries generally espousing the ideology that all economic decision-making, if possible, should be left to the commercial self-interest of the private sector, and who try to design their economic institutions according to this doctrine of government non-interference.

Free rider A person or group which benefits from the provision of certain goods or services without paying for them.

Free trade Originally an ideology and latterly an institutionalized system of unrestricted commercial activity, whereby countries are increasingly disqualified from using legal mechanisms to artificially lower the price which domestic consumers pay for home-produced goods relative to the price at which overseas producers can supply them.

Free trade area Agreements between two or more countries to remove tariff and non-tariff barriers on trade between themselves.

General Agreement on Tariffs and Trade (GATT) A 1947 agreement that became the principal component of the international trade regime following the failure of the international community to establish the **International Trade Organization**. Its provisions were incorporated into the World Trade Organization (WTO) when it was established in 1995.

Generalized System of Preferences (GSP) Non-reciprocal programmes of tariff preferences on selected goods for **less developed countries** introduced by industrialized countries after GATT in 1971 permitted a waiver of the MFN requirement to facilitate special and differential treatment for LDCs.

Gini coefficient A measure of income inequality devised by the Italian statistician, Corrado Gini. The Gini coefficient is a number between zero and one, where zero represents perfect equality (everyone has the same income), and one represents perfect inequality (one person has all the income, all others have zero). The Gini coefficient is calculated using the Lorenz curve, a graph showing the relationship between the percentage of households and the share of the country's income they receive.

Global Environment Facility (GEF) A fund established in 1991, jointly managed by the World Bank, the United Nations Development Programme, and the United Nations Environment Programme, which finances environmental projects in less developed economies.

Global value chains (GVCs) The term given to the coordination of different stages of production across various countries.

Gold exchange standard An international monetary system in which it is possible for central banks to convert their foreign exchange holdings into gold (one or more countries must guarantee that they will permit others to convert their currencies into gold, as the US did in 1945–71).

Gold standard A monetary system in which the money supply is linked directly to the country's holdings of gold; citizens are usually entitled to exchange banknotes for gold.

An international gold standard is an international monetary system in which the value of all currencies is set in terms of a unit of gold, and settlement of trade imbalances occurs through the transfer of gold reserves.

Graduation The process by which less developed economies are removed from the list of countries given special trade benefits by industrialized countries once they reach a certain level of development.

Gross domestic product (GDP) The total value of goods and services produced by an economy in a specific time period.

Gross national product (GNP) refers to **Gross domestic product** plus the income earned by domestic residents from investment abroad less the income earned by foreigners in the domestic market.

Heavily Indebted Poor Countries (HIPC) A grouping of the world's poorest countries, identified as those eligible for concessional assistance from the World Bank group's International Development Association and from the IMF's Poverty Reduction and Growth Facility that face an unsustainable debt situation after the full application of traditional debt relief mechanisms. A debt relief initiative for HIPC was initiated by the World Bank and the IMF in 1996 (http://www.worldbank.org/en/topic/debt/brief/hipc).

Heckscher–Ohlin Model A model of international trade in which comparative advantage derives from differences in relative factor endowments across countries and differences in relative factor intensities across industries. Countries will export those commodities that are intensive in the factor (land, labour, capital) in which they are best endowed.

Hegemony Often in international relations treated as a synonym for dominance, whereby a dominant state, institution, or ideology is described as being hegemonic, but in its original form following Gramsci the condition of hegemony also requires the consent of the subordinate to be governed in that way.

Hegemonic stability Argument that liberal (open) international economic regimes are associated with the presence of a dominant state.

Import-substitution industrialization (ISI) Strategy pursued by less developed economies to promote industrialization by domestic production of goods previously imported (usually undertaken behind high levels of tariff protection).

Inclusive club goods Goods that can be withheld from those who do not pay for them, and whose consumption does not reduce their availability to other potential consumers. Examples include cable television and access to copyrighted works.

Infant industry promotion Idea that recently established industries require protection until they are able to produce efficiently and withstand import competition from more advanced economies.

Interdependence A network of relationships among actors that is costly for any of the actors to break.

Intermediation *see* **Financial Intermediation**.

International Bank for Reconstruction and Development (World Bank) The original component of the World Bank group, created at the **Bretton Woods** conference in 1944. Subsequently, two other institutions, the International Finance Corporation (1956) and the International Development Association (1960) were added to the group. Most writers today simply refer to the group of institutions as the 'World Bank'.

International financial institutions (IFIs) The International Monetary Fund (IMF) and the World Bank.

International Monetary Fund (IMF) An institution of 189 members as of early 2016, providing extensive technical assistance and short-term flows of stabilization finance to any of those members experiencing temporarily distressed finances.

International Trade Organization (ITO) Intended to be the third of the major post-war international economic institutions alongside the World Bank and the IMF, the ITO was stillborn when the US Congress failed to ratify the Havana Charter.

Intra-industry trade International trade in products from the same sector.

Invisible hand The phrase most readily associated with the political economy of Adam Smith and today almost always taken to infer the automatically equilibrating tendencies of the market economy, even though it is very difficult to establish this reading from Smith's original work.

Keynesian economics A branch of economic theory associated with the work of John Maynard Keynes and his followers, suggesting that there is no automatic tendency for economies to reach an equilibrium position that sustains full employment, and that governments, through their manipulation of **fiscal policies**, can affect aggregate demand and reduce unemployment.

Laissez-faire An economic doctrine of non-interference into commercial, corporate, and competitive affairs, often associated with the dominance of market ideology. The literal translation from the French comes close to being an argument for allowing events to run their own course.

Least developed countries A UN-designated group of 50 low-income countries, membership of which is defined by per capita GDP under $750, weak human assets (a composite index of health, nutrition, and education indicators), and high economic vulnerability (a composite index based on instability of export earnings, dependence on a limited number of primary product exports, and overall size of the economy). The UN can 'graduate' countries from the category when they meet the thresholds of two of the three criteria (over $900 per capita GDP) for two successive years.

Lender of last resort A financial institution, usually the central bank, that is charged with the responsibility of providing loans to other financial institutions when they need an injection of cash—and no other institution is willing to lend to them.

Less developed countries (LDCs) A self-designated category at the WTO of countries that typically have relatively low per capita incomes, an undeveloped industrial base, and a substantial part of their population living in poverty. Often associated with the Group of 77 (G77), established on 15 June 1964 by 77 developing countries signatories of the 'Joint Declaration of the Seventy-Seven Countries' issued at the end of the first session of the United Nations Conference on Trade and Development in Geneva. At the time of writing, the G77 has 130 members, including such relatively high-income economies as the Bahamas, Singapore, and South Korea.

Liquidity International liquidity comprises the total gold and foreign exchange reserves and **Special Drawing Rights** (that is, all international reserves acceptable to other countries) held by all countries in the international financial system.

Logrolling The practice whereby two or more legislators agree to trade their votes to support legislation in which they have no particular interest in order to gain support for legislation that they regard as more important, for example, financing of projects in their electoral districts.

Magnificent Seven The name that Benjamin Cohen gave collectively to those scholars he considered to be the most important trailblazers in early work in Global Political Economy: Robert Keohane, Robert Gilpin, Charles Kindleberger, Stephen Krasner, Peter Katzenstein, Susan Strange, and Robert Cox.

Marginalist Revolution The establishment of what is now referred to as neo-classical economic theory. Generally dated to the first half of the 1870s when the concept of diminishing marginal utility was introduced by William Stanley Jevons, Carl Menger, and Léon Walras. Whereas classical economic theorists had argued that prices ultimately were determined by relative costs of production (usually labour costs), neo-classical theorists argued that price reflected the marginal utility of a good.

Market failure A situation whereby a market does not achieve the optimal allocation of resources. Causes of market failure include the presence of public goods, externalities, and imperfect information.

Marshall Aid Formally known as the European Recovery Program, this was the loan or gift of US money to help reconstruct war-torn European economies after the Second World War. The only condition on the countries receiving such assistance was that they aligned themselves strategically with the West. *See* **Marshall Plan**.

Marshall Plan A US programme to provide grants and loans to assist in the rebuilding of the economies of Europe and some European colonies after the Second World War.

Mathematical tractability The ability to represent a social model or relationship in purely mathematical terms.

Mercantilism Economic policies based on the premise that national wealth and power are best served by the state acting to increase exports and to run a **balance of trade** surplus (originally with the intention of accumulating precious metals).

Methodology A procedure or set of procedures used to study a subject matter.

Minilateralism Policy coordination among a small number of states.

Monetarism A branch of macroeconomic theory that holds that changes in the money supply affect aggregate demand for goods and services, and thus the rate of inflation. Closely associated with the University of Chicago economist, Milton Friedman.

Monetary policies Government policies on the money supply, the rate of interest, and the exchange rate.

Moral hazard A form of **market failure**: the creation of a situation in which individuals or institutions are encouraged to act irresponsibly because of the guarantees (implicit or explicit) that others provide for them; for example, people with insurance may take greater risks than those without it, because they know they will receive compensation if they suffer adverse consequences from their behaviour.

Most-favoured nation principle (MFN) The principle of non-discrimination, enshrined in Article I of the **GATT/WTO**, that members must give all other members the most favourable trade treatment they offer to any member.

Multifiber Arrangement (MFA) A multilateral agreement (1974–94), a form of **orderly marketing arrangement**, limiting the exports of textiles and clothing by **less developed countries** to industrialized countries. Industrialized countries agreed to phase out the MFA over a ten-year period, as part of the GATT Uruguay Round negotiations.

Multilateral Agreement on Investment (MAI) A proposal made by OECD members in 1995 for a multilateral agreement that would liberalize investment regimes, provide protection for foreign investors, and establish dispute settlement mechanisms. The talks on establishing an MAI collapsed in 1998, following disagreements among industrialized countries and opposition from many **less developed countries** and civil society groups.

Multilateralism Policy coordination by three or more states on the basis of principles that specify appropriate conduct.

Multinational corporation/Multinational enterprise (MNCs/MNEs) (*see* **Transnational corporation**) Companies that have a presence in more than one country and which use the different institutional structures in those countries to organize their activities—from basic decisions about production to how best to limit their tax payments—so as to make the highest possible level of profit.

Nash Equilibrium In game theory, a situation where all participants are pursuing their best possible strategy, given the strategies that other players have chosen; in other words, no player can improve his/her situation by changing their own strategy.

National treatment A **GATT/WTO** principle requiring members to offer foreign goods or services identical treatment in their markets to that given to the same domestic good or service.

Navigation Acts Seventeenth- and eighteenth-century legal statutes through which Britain tried to transpose its naval dominance into commercial dominance, limiting the amount of tradeable cargo that non-British ships could bring through British waters while allowing British ships unrestricted access.

Neo-liberalism A political orientation that came to prominence in the 1980s, celebrating the desirability of market-based economic institutions and a willingness to use the market to discipline the population. It is often closely associated with policies of privatization and the retreat of the state from prominence in economic affairs.

Neo-statism A conception and strategy of development based on the idea that states shape, direct, and promote economic development, and that markets are 'governed' rather than 'free'. It has been associated most strongly with the 'developmental state' model in East Asia, and emerged as the key counterpoint to neo-liberalism as a means of explaining the growth and development trajectory of that region from the 1960s onwards.

New International Economic Order (NIEO) A list of demands by less developed economies in the 1970s that proposed a radical restructuring of international economic regimes.

Newly industrializing economy (NIE) Term originally applied to the 'Gang of Four' economies of East Asia (Hong Kong, Korea, Singapore, Taiwan) that experienced rapid economic growth from the late 1960s. Subsequently sometimes applied to selected rapidly growing South-East Asian and Latin American economies.

Non-aligned Movement A movement formed in 1955 as a platform from which developing countries could organize themselves more effectively to participate and demand representation within international organizations in the context of the Cold War.

Non-tariff barriers (NTBs), also Non-tariff measures (NTMs) A wide variety of official or unofficial devices (other than tariffs) that hinder imports into an economy; for example, quantitative restrictions, health regulations, customs procedures.

ODA Official Development Assistance, popularly referred to as foreign aid.

OEM Original equipment manufacturers. Originally used (primarily in the electronics industry) to describe a company manufacturing a product that was marketed under another company's brand name. Now also used (somewhat confusingly) to refer to companies that sell a final product under their own brand name but it is assembled from components manufactured by others; for example, Toyota, General Motors, and other auto assemblers are often referred to as OEMs.

Oligopoly An industry dominated by a few large suppliers of goods or services.

Ontology Literally, from the Greek, 'the study of being'. Ontology typically focuses on the identification of the core objects of study (for instance, does '*homo economicus*' really exist?), their characteristics and their relationships to other objects.

Opportunism Decisions made on the basis of perceived self-interest without regard for principles or the breaking of relationships with others based on trust.

Orderly marketing arrangement (OMA) An agreement between an importing country and one or more exporting countries whereby the latter pledge to limit their exports of particular products. Outlawed by the **GATT** Uruguay Round Agreements.

Pareto-optimal Outcomes where no actor can be better off without making others worse off. In Pareto-suboptimal (instead of Pareto-deficient) situations, other outcomes could increase some actors' welfare without decreasing that of others.

Plaza Accord Agreement reached by the G5 (West Germany, France, the United States, Japan, and the United Kingdom) at the Plaza Hotel in New York in 1985 for concerted intervention by central banks to produce a currency realignment that resulted in a depreciation of the US dollar against other major currencies.

Portfolio investment The acquisition of interest-bearing foreign securities (either government bonds or company stocks and shares) that do not in themselves give the investor management control over the foreign concern.

Private goods Goods and services that can be withheld from those who do not pay for them, and that cannot be used by others without additional production taking place.

Property rights The legal right of owners of resources to be paid for their usage; for example, fees paid to patent or copyright owners.

Protectionist policies Policies that are designed to enhance the trading position of domestic producers by lowering the price of their goods vis-à-vis those of foreign competitors. Home-produced goods can be made more cheaply if the government is prepared to subsidize production, while overseas-produced goods will be more expensive for final consumers if the government forces their producers to pay an import fee called a tariff.

Public goods Goods that cannot be withheld from consumers who do not pay for them, and whose consumption does not reduce their availability to other consumers. Examples include national security and street lighting.

Purchasing power parity (PPP) A method of computing an appropriate exchange rate between currencies (rather than that determined by the market or fixed by governments), which rests on determining domestic purchasing power by calculating the price of a basket of goods in the two countries in local currencies. To compute the PPP exchange rate between the two currencies, one takes the ratio of the prices for the baskets of goods in local currencies. PPP exchange rates are often used as a means of presenting a more accurate comparison of standards of living across countries than those given by actual exchange rates.

Race to the bottom The idea that, in a globalized economy, some governments will attempt to increase their attractiveness to investors by offering minimal requirements on, for example, environmental and labour standards and taxation.

Rareté Walras's concept which attempts to locate the desirability of a product in its scarcity, so that the higher the underlying level of rareté the greater the intensity of the want satisfaction that it can supply.

Rational choice theory A theory of human behaviour that assumes that social activity reflects the behaviours of individuals who are acting rationally to pursue their interests.

Reciprocity The principle in international trade that countries benefiting from trade liberalization by others should offer equivalent (but not necessarily identical) concessions in return.

Regime A set of international governing arrangements (including rules, norms, and procedures) that are intended to regularize the behaviour of state and non-state actors, and control its effects.

Rents: Any payment to a factor of production in excess of the cost needed to bring that factor into production. Factors of production often enjoy rents when an artificial scarcity is created, e.g. licensing the number of taxis in a given geographical area.

Ricardian Socialists A primarily British group of radical economists in the early nineteenth century who tried to reduce Ricardo's labour theory of value to what they saw as its bare essentials, which in turn allowed them to make the political case for a system of distribution that would have enabled workers to enjoy all of the economic rewards resulting from their labour.

Rules of origin Regulations negotiated as part of free trade agreements that specify the conditions that goods must meet if they are to be considered as originating in a partner country (for example, that a specific share of the good's value must be added locally). Intended to prevent non-partner countries from trans-shipping goods to take advantage of the lower tariffs offered within a free trade agreement.

Safeguards Provisions enabling countries with problems in specific sectors or their economy more generally to seek temporary exemptions from some of their obligations in the trade regime.

Seigniorage The profit that results from the difference between the cost of producing and distributing money and the face value of that money. For instance, a dollar coin may have metal in it that is worth 15 cents.

Singapore issues The 1996 WTO ministerial meeting in Singapore began exploratory work on cooperation on policy harmonization in four areas: investment, competition, transparency in government procurement, and trade facilitation. These subsequently became known as the 'Singapore issues'.

Single undertaking The principle within the **GATT/WTO** that members must accept all parts of an agreement rather than signing on selectively to individual components. The effect is that in WTO negotiations, 'Nothing is agreed until everything is agreed'.

Special and differential treatment Exemptions for **less developed countries** from some of the obligations imposed on other members of the trade regime.

Special Drawing Rights (SDR) An international reserve asset created by the International Monetary Fund in 1969.

Over 200 billion SDRs (equivalent to $285 billion) have been created; these were distributed by the IMF to member countries in proportion to the size of their IMF quota. The SDR is based on a basket of five major currencies (the Chinese renminbi, the euro, the Japanese yen, and the US dollar).

Specific Factors Model Following trade liberalization, the movement of one or more factors of production to different uses may be difficult or impossible. The effects of trade, therefore, contrary to the **Stolper–Samuelson Theorem**, may not benefit/harm different factors across various sectors but rather hurt/benefit *all* factors *within* the same industrial sector. The likely consequence for trade policy formation is that coalitions organized around industrial sectors *rather than* classes will emerge.

Sovereign Wealth Funds Pools of foreign currency reserves managed by governments for profit. According to the Sovereign Wealth Fund Institute, a private agency established to monitor SWFs, the total assets of SWFs in 2016 exceeded $7.25 trillion. Their assets are more than double those of all hedge funds combined.

Statism A predisposition amongst many realist theorists of global political economy to treat the state as the most important actor in the global economy.

Sterilization Efforts by monetary authorities to counter the impact of international monetary flows on domestic economic activity by issuing/selling financial instruments to reduce or increase the domestic money supply.

Stolper–Samuelson Theorem Trade benefits the owners of factors of production that are relatively abundant in an economy while lowering the returns to owners of relatively scarce factors; for example, trade for labour-rich countries such as China should benefit (their relatively abundant) labour while lowering the returns to capital.

Strategic trade policies Efforts by governments to promote domestic companies in international industries characterized by **oligopoly** through policies (for example, investment subsidies) intended to permit them to move strategically (for example, enable them to become early developers of a product) and to earn **rents**.

Structural adjustment programmes (SAPs) These are often designed in association with the international financial institutions, and pursued by countries experiencing debt problems. They usually include privatization of assets, reductions in government expenditure to reduce budgetary deficits, trade liberalization, encouragement of foreign investment, and currency devaluation.

Sunk costs Costs that are difficult for investors to recover; for example, investment in physical infrastructure, plant, and machinery.

Supranational institutions International institutions to which states have ceded some of their sovereignty; for example, the European Union.

Surplus value extraction Usually found in Marxist analysis, refers to how capitalists can pay labour only a fraction of the value that it generates. The difference between the wages paid to labour plus the fixed and variable operating costs on the one hand and the value of labour's output on the other constitutes surplus value.

Swiss formula A method of reducing tariffs that results in higher tariffs being reduced more than lower ones. It was used in the Tokyo Round of **GATT** negotiations.

Temptation to free ride Situation in which actors are tempted to contribute less than their appropriate share to the cost of the goods or services from which they benefit.

Terms of trade The price of a country's exports relative to the price of its imports.

Trade creation Where a preferential trade agreement leads to the replacement of domestic production by lower-cost imports from a party to the trade agreement.

Trade diversion Where a preferential trade agreement leads to the displacement of goods previously imported from a non-preferred trading partner by imports from a party to the preferred agreement (because these preferential imports now enter the local market at a reduced tariff).

Trade-Related Aspects of Intellectual Property (TRIPs) A Uruguay Round WTO agreement that establishes minimum levels of protection that governments must give to the intellectual property of fellow WTO members.

Trade-Related Investment Measures (TRIMs) The title of a Uruguay Round WTO agreement that prohibits governments from applying measures that discriminate against foreign companies or foreign products; for example, requirements that foreign investors must source a certain value of their inputs locally ('local content' requirements) or export a certain value of their output ('trade balancing' requirements).

Tragedy of the commons Garrett Hardin, in a paper published in *Science* in 1968, first put forward the idea that individuals rationally pursuing their self-interest where they have access to a freely available good (a 'commons') will inevitably act in a way that is collectively detrimental; for example, through over-grazing a pasture.

Transaction costs The costs other than the nominal price that are involved in trading goods and services; for example, costs of search and information, bargaining and decision-making, and policing and enforcement. High transaction costs are often viewed as a significant example of **externalities**.

Transnational corporations (TNCs) (also Multinational Corporations or Multinational Enterprises) Companies that engage in **Foreign direct investment**; that is, which own, control, and manage assets in more than one country.

Triffin Dilemma Yale University economist Robert Triffin pointed out in a 1960 book that the Bretton Woods monetary system rested on the confidence of other countries in the **gold exchange standard**—that is, their belief that they could convert their dollar holdings into gold—yet, the capacity of the US to guarantee this conversion was being undermined by dollar outflows that were the principal source of new **liquidity** in the system. If outflows stopped, the system would have insufficient liquidity; if they continued, confidence in the system would be undermined.

Two-level game Term coined by Robert Putnam to refer to negotiations in which governments must negotiate simultaneously at two levels: with domestic constituencies, and with one or more foreign partners.

Utility Literally the condition of being useful, but in economic terms it is much more common to use the word to describe the capacity for the consumption of a particular good to be to an individual's liking: the more use-value the consumption is expected to generate, the higher is its utility.

Utility-maximizing behaviour Self-interested actions that allow the actor (a person, a firm, or a country) to do what is best for themselves without being concerned about whether their actions will have adverse implications for others.

Voluntary export restraint An agreement between an exporting and an importing country under which the exporting country agrees to limit the total (value or volume of) exports of particular products. Outlawed by the GATT Uruguay Round Agreements.

Washington Consensus Phrase coined by John Williamson to refer to the prevailing views held in the late 1980s and early 1990s by the international financial institutions and governments of most industrialized countries regarding the desirable policy agenda for less developed economies; namely, liberalization of their trade regimes, privatization of state-owned enterprises, and reduction of state intervention in the economy.

World Trade Organization (WTO) Established in 1995 with headquarters in Geneva and containing 159 members as of late 2013, it is a permanent institution covering services, intellectual property and investment issues as well as pure merchandise trade.

Other useful sources

Print

Bannock, G., Baxter, R. E., and Davis, E. (2011), *The Penguin Dictionary of Economics*, 8th edn (London: Penguin).

Black, J., Hashimzade, N., and G. Myles (2012), *A Dictionary of Economics*, 4th edn (Oxford: Oxford University Press).

Pearce, D. W. (1992), *The MIT Dictionary of Modern Economics*, 4th edn (Cambridge, MA: MIT Press).

Online

Deardorff's Glossary of International Economics http://www-personal.umich.edu/~alandear/glossary

Economics—Wikipedia, the free encyclopedia http://en.wikipedia.org/wiki/Economics

The Economist's Economics A–Z http://economist.com/research/Economics

References

Abbott, A. J., and De Vita, G. (2003), 'Another Piece in the Feldstein-Horioka Puzzle', *Scottish Journal of Political Economy*, 50/1: 68–89.

Abbott, F. M. (2002), 'The Doha Declaration on the TRIPS Agreement and Public Health: Lighting a Dark Corner at the WTO', *Journal of International Economic Law*, 5/2: 469–505.

Abbott, K. W., and Snidal, D. (2000), 'Hard and Soft Law in International Governance', *International Organization*, 54/3: 421–56.

Abdelal, R. (2001), *National Purpose in the World Economy: Post-Soviet States in Comparative Perspective* (Ithaca, NY: Cornell University Press).

—— (2007), *Capital Rules: The Construction of Global Finance* (Cambridge, MA: Harvard University Press).

—— Blyth, M., and Parsons, C. (eds) (2010), *Constructing the International Economy* (Ithaca, NY: Cornell University Press).

Abernathy, F. H., Dunlop, J. T., Hammond, J. H., and Weil, D. (1999), *A Stitch in Time: Lean Retailing and the Transformation of Manufacturing* (Oxford: Oxford University Press).

Abo, T. (2011), 'The Competition Strategies of Japanese Manufacturing Firms in China, 1990s–2000s: The Positioning Problems in the Competitive Advantages Through Transfer of the Production Systems', in T. Abo (ed.), *Competing Chinese and Foreign Firms in Swelling Chinese Economy: Competition Strategies for Japanese, Western and Asian Firms* (Munster, Germany: Lit Verlag).

Adler, M., Brunel, C., Hufbauer, G. C., and Schott, J. J. (2009), *What's on the Table? The Doha Round as of August 2009*, Working Paper 09-6 (Washington, DC: Peterson Institute for International Economics).

Aggarwal, V. K. (1985), *Liberal Protectionism: The International Politics of Organized Textile Trade* (Berkeley and Los Angeles, CA: University of California Press).

—— (1994), 'Comparing Regional Cooperation Efforts in Asia-Pacific and North America', in A. Mack and J. Ravenhill (eds), *Pacific Cooperation: Building Economic and Security Regimes in the Asia-Pacific Region* (Sydney: Allen & Unwin).

—— (1998) (ed.) *Institutional Designs for a Complex World: Bargaining, Linkages and Nesting* (Ithaca, NY: Cornell University Press).

—— (2001), 'Economics: International Trade', in P. J. Simmons and C. de Jonge Oudraat (eds), *Managing Global Issues: Lessons Learned* (Washington, DC: Carnegie Endowment for International Peace)

—— (2002), '"Goods, Games, and Institutions": A Reply', *International Political Science Review*, 23/4: 402–10.

—— and Ahnid A. (2011), 'Comparing EU and US Linkage Strategies in FTAs', paper presented at the Conference on 'ANU MacArthur Foundation Asia Security Initiative Final Conference', Beijing, China.

—— and Dupont, C. (1999), 'Goods, Games and Institutions', *International Political Science Review*, 20/4: 393–409.

—— and Kristi Govella (eds) (2013), *Linking Trade and Security* (Berlin: Springer).

Aiyer, S., R. Duval *et al.* (2013), 'Growth Slowdowns and the Middle-Income Trap', WP 13/71, International Monetary Fund.

Akerof, G. A. A., and Shiller, R. J. J. (2010), *Animal Spirits: How Human Psychology Drives the Economy and Why It Matters for Global Capitalism* (Princeton, NJ: Princeton University Press).

Akuz, Y. (2013), 'Growth in the South: Resilience, Decoupling, Recoupling', *South Views* (Geneva: South Centre), 54 (11 February).

Ali, S. H. (2004), *Mining, the Environment and Indigenous Development Conflicts* (Tucson, AZ: University of Arizona Press).

Alinsky, S. (1972), *Rules for Radicals: A Practical Primer for Realistic Radicals* (New York: Vintage Books).

Allen, J., and Thompson, G. F. (1997), 'Think Global, and Then Think Again: Economic Globalization in Context', *Area*, 29/3: 213–27.

Allen, M. (2003), 'Some Lessons from the Argentine Crisis: A Fund Staff View', in J. J. Teunissen and A. Akkerman (eds), *The Crisis That Was Not Prevented: Lessons for Argentina, the IMF, and Globalisation* (The Hague: FONDAD).

Allen, W. A., and Moessner, R. (2010), 'Central Bank Co-operation and International Liquidity in the Financial Crisis of 2008–9', *BIS Working Paper*, No. 310, Bank for International Settlements, May: 45.

Almond, G. A. (1970), *Political Development: Essays in Heuristic Theory* (Princeton, NJ: Princeton University Press).

—— and Coleman, J. (eds) (1960), *The Politics of the Developing Areas* (Princeton, NJ: Princeton University Press).

—— and Powell, C. B. (1965), *Comparative Politics: A Developmental Agenda* (Boston: Little, Brown).

Alt, J., and Gilligan, M. (1994), 'The Political Economy of Trading States', *Journal of Political Philosophy*, 2/2: 165–92.

Althusser, L. (1996), *For Marx* tr. B. Brewster (London: Verso).

Altman, R. C. (2009), 'The Great Crash, 2008', *Foreign Affairs*, 88/1: 2–14.

Amador, Joao and Filippo di Mauro (eds) (2015), *The Age of Global Value Chains* (London: CEPR).

Amin, S. (1997), *Capitalism in the Age of Globalization* (London: Zed Books).

Amsden, A. (1989), *Asia's Next Giant: South Korea and Late Industrialization* (New York: Oxford University Press).

Amsden, A. (1990), 'Third World Industrialization: "Global Fordism" or a New Model?', *New Left Review*, 182: 5–31.

Anderson, J. E., and van Wincoop, E. (2001), Gravity with Gravitas: A Solution to the Border Puzzle, NBER Working Paper 8079 (Cambridge, MA: National Bureau of Economic Research).

Andrews, D. M. (1994), 'Capital Mobility and State Autonomy: Toward a Structural Theory of International Monetary Relations', *International Studies Quarterly*, 38/2: 193–218.

—— (ed.) (2006), *International Monetary Power* (Ithaca, NY: Cornell University Press).

Apergis, N., and C. Tsoumas (2009), 'A Survey of the Feldstein-Horioka Puzzle: What Has Been Done and Where Do We Stand?', *Research in Economics*, 63/2: 64–76.

Apple (2015), 'Supplier Responsibility 2015 Progress Report'. retrieved January 7, 2015.

Araújo, S., and Martins, J. O. (2009), 'The Great Synchronisation: What Do High-Frequency Statistics Tell Us about the Trade Collapse?', 8 July, www.voxeu.org/index.php?q=node/3751

Archibugi, D. (ed.) (2003), *Debating Cosmopolitics* (London: Verso).

Arndt, H. W. (1987), *Economic Development: The History of an Idea* (Chicago, IL: University of Chicago Press).

Arndt, S. W., and Kierzkowski, S. (2001), *Fragmentation: New Production Patterns in the World Economy* (Oxford: Oxford University Press).

Arnoldi, J. (2009), *Risk* (Cambridge: Polity).

Arrow, K., Bolin, B., Costanza, R., Dasgupta, P., Folk, C., Holling, C. S., Jansson, B., Levin, S., Mäler, K., Perrings, C., and Pimentel, D. (1998), 'Economic Growth, Carrying Capacity and the Environment', *Science*, 268 (28 April 1995), in J. Dryzek and D. Schlosberg (eds), *Debating the Earth: The Environmental Politics Reader* (Oxford: Oxford University Press).

Arup, C. (2000), *The New World Trade Organization Agreements: Globalizing Law through Services and Intellectual Property* (Cambridge: Cambridge University Press).

Aslanbeigui, N., and Summerfield, G. (2000), 'The Asian Crisis, Gender and the International Financial Architecture', *Feminist Economics*, 6/3: 81–103.

Axelrod, R., and Keohane, R. O. (1986), 'Achieving Cooperation under Anarchy: Strategies and Institutions', *World Politics*, 38/1: 226–54.

Axford, B. (2013), *Theories of Globalization* (Cambridge: Polity Press)

Babb, S. (2009), *Behind the Development Banks: Washington Politics, World Poverty, and the Wealth of Nations* (Chicago, IL: University of Chicago Press).

Bachrach, P., and Baratz, M. S. (1970), *Power and Poverty: Theory and Practice* (New York: Oxford University Press).

Backhouse, R. (2002), *The Penguin History of Economics* (London: Penguin).

Baer, W. (1972), 'Import Substitution and Industrialization in Latin America: Experiences and Interpretations', *Latin American Research Review*, 7/1: 95–122.

Bair, J. (2005), 'Global Capitalism and Commodity Chains: Looking Back and Going Forward', *Competition and Change*, 9/2: 153–80.

Bairoch, P. (1996), 'Globalization Myths and Realities: One Century of External Trade and Foreign Investment', in R. Boyer and D. Drache (eds), *States Against Markets: The Limits of Globalization* (London: Routledge).

Baker, A. (2006), *The Group of Seven: Finance Ministries, Central Banks and Global Financial Governance* (London/New York: Routledge).

Balaam, D., and Veseth, M. (2008), *Introduction to International Political Economy*, 4th edn (London: Pearson).

Baldwin, C. Y., and Clark, K. B. (1997), 'Managing in an Age of Modularity', *Harvard Business Review*, 75/5: 84–93.

—— (2000), *Design Rules*, i. *The Power of Modularity* (Boston: MIT Press).

Baldwin, R. E. (1993), A Domino Theory of Regionalism, Working Paper 4465 (Cambridge, MA: National Bureau of Economic Research).

—— (1997), 'The Causes of Regionalism', *World Economy*, 20/7: 865–88.

—— (2006), 'Multilateralising Regionalism: Spaghetti Bowls as Building Blocs on the Path to Global Free Trade', *World Economy*, 29/11: 1451–1518.

—— (2009), 'The Great Trade Collapse: What Caused It and What Does It Mean?', 27 November, www.voxeu.org/index.php?q=node/4304

—— (2011), *21st Century Regionalism: Filling the Gap between 21st Century Trade and 20th Century Trade Rules* (London: Centre for Economic Policy Research, 56; May): http://www.cepr.org/pubs/policyinsights/PolicyInsight56.pdf

—— (2016), 'The World Trade Organization and the Future of Multilateralism', *Journal of Economic Perspectives*, 30/1: 95–116.

—— and J Lopez-Gonzalez (2014), 'Supply-Chain Trade: A Portrait of Global Patterns and Several Testable Hypotheses', *World Economy*, 38/11: 1682–1721.

Banerjee, A., and Zanghieri, P. (2003), A New Look at the Feldstein-Horioka Puzzle Using an Integrated Panel, CEPII Working Paper 2003-22 (Paris: Centre d'Éudes Prospectives et d'Informations Internationales).

Barber, W. (1991), *A History of Economic Thought*, repr. edn (London: Penguin).

Barlow, M. (2008), *Blue Covenant: The Global Water Crisis and the Coming Battle for the Right to Water* (New York: New Press).

—— (2014), *Blue Future: Protecting Water for People and the Planet Forever* (Toronto: House of Anansi Press).

Baron, H. (1988), *In Search of Florentine Civic Humanism: Essays on the Transition from Medieval to Modern Political Thought*, I (Princeton, NJ: Princeton University Press).

Barr, N. (1998), *The Economics of the Welfare State*, 3rd edn (Oxford: Oxford University Press).

Barrientos, S., Gereffi, G. *et al.* (2011), 'Economic and Social Upgrading in Global Production Networks: A New Paradigm for a Changing World', *International Labour Review*, 150/3: 319–40.

—— Knorringa, P. *et al.* (2016), 'Shifting Regional Dynamics of Global Value Chains: Implications for Economic and Social Upgrading in African horticulture', *Environment and Planning A*.

Barry, P. L., and Phillips, T. (2006), 'Earth's Ozone Layer: Good News and a Puzzle', *Space and Earth Science*, 26 May, www.physorg.com

Bauer, R. A., Pool, I., and Dexter, L. A. (1972), *American Business and Public Policy*, 2nd edn (Chicago, IL: Aldine Atherton).

Baxter, M., and Crucini, M. J. (1993), 'Explaining Saving-Investment Correlations', *American Economic Review*, 83/3: 416–36.

Bayoumi, T. (1990), 'Savings-Investment Correlations', *IMF Staff Papers*, 37: 360–87.

—— (1997), *Financial Integration and Real Activity* (Manchester: Manchester University Press).

—— and Rose, A. D. (1993), 'Domestic Savings and Intra-National Capital Flows', *European Economic Review*, 37/6: 1197–1202.

Beason, R., and Weinstein, D. E. (1993), *Growth, Economies of Scale, and Targeting in Japan*, 1955–90, Harvard Institute for Economic Research Discussion Paper No. 1644 (Cambridge, MA: Harvard University).

Beck, U. (1992), *The Risk Society* (London: Sage).

—— (2009), *World at Risk* (Cambridge: Polity).

Bekaert, G., Hodrick, R. J., and Zhang, X. (2005), *International Stock Return Comovements*, NBER Working Paper 11906 (Cambridge, MA: National Bureau of Economic Research).

Bello, W. (2009), *The Food Wars* (London and New York: Verso).

Bems, R., Johnson, R. C., and Yi, K.-M. (2012), *The Great Trade Collapse*, NBER Working Paper 18632 (Cambridge, MA: National Bureau of Economic Research).

Benería, L. (2003), *Gender, Development, and Globalization: Economics as If All People Mattered* (New York: Routledge).

Benton, T., and Craib, I. (2001), *Philosophy of Social Science* (London: Routledge).

Berg, M. (1980), *The Machinery Question and the Making of Political Economy 1815-1848* (Cambridge: Cambridge University Press).

Berger, S. (2006), *How We Compete: What Companies around the World Are Doing to Make It in Today's Global Economy* (New York: Currency Doubleday).

—— and Dore, R. (eds) (1996), *National Diversity and Global Capitalism* (Ithaca, NY: Cornell University Press).

Bergsten, C. F. (1999), 'America and Europe: Clash of the Titans', *Foreign Affairs*, 78/2: 20–34.

Bernanke, B. (2015), *The Courage to Lead: A Memoir of a Crisis and its Aftermath* (New York: Norton).

Bernard, M., and Ravenhill, J. (1995), 'Beyond Product Cycles and Flying Geese: Regionalization, Hierarchy, and the Industrialization of East Asia', *World Politics*, 47/2: 171–209.

Bernhard, W., and Leblang, D. (1999), 'Democratic Institutions and Exchange Rate Commitments', *International Organization*, 53/1: 71–97.

Bernstein, H. (ed.) (1990), *The Food Question: Profits vs. People* (London: Earthscan).

Besson, M (2000), 'Mahathir and the Markets', *Pacific Affairs*, 73/3: 335–51.

Best, J. (2014), *Governing Failure: Provisional Expertise and the Transformation of Global Development Finance* (Cambridge: Cambridge University Press).

Bhagwati, J. (1988), *Protectionism* (Cambridge, MA: MIT Press).

—— (1991), *The World Trading System at Risk* (New York: Harvester Wheatsheaf).

—— (1995), 'US Trade Policy: The Infatuation with Free Trade Areas', in J. N.Bhagwati and A. O. Krueger (eds), *The Dangerous Drift to Preferential Trade Agreements* (Washington, DC: AEI Press).

—— Brecher, R., Dinopoulos, E., and Srinivasan, T. N. (1987), 'Quid Pro Quo Foreign Investment and Welfare: A Political-Economy-Theoretic Model', *Journal of Development Economics*, 27/1–2: 127–38.

Bhattarai, M., and Hammig, M. (2001), 'Institutions and the Environmental Kuznets Curve for Deforestation: A Crosscountry Analysis for Latin America, Africa and Asia', *World Development*, 29/6: 995–1010.

BIS (Bank for International Settlements) (2003) *Annual Report 2003*. (Basle: BIS).

—— (2005), *Triennial Central Bank Survey: Foreign Exchange and Derivatives Market Activity in 2004* (Basel: BIS).

—— (2006), *OTC Derivatives Market Activity in the First Half of 2006* (Basel: BIS).

—— (2009), *International Banking Statistics* (June) (Basel: BIS).

—— (2010), *Triennial Central Bank Survey of Foreign Exchange and Derivatives Market Activity* (Geneva: BIS).

—— (2012), *Annual Report 2012* (Geneva: BIS).

—— (2014), Triennial Central Bank Survey: Global Forex Market turnover in 2013 (Basle: BIS).

—— (2015), BIS Eighth Annual Report June 2015 (Basle: BIS).

—— (2015b), International Banking Statistics June 2015 (Basle: BIS).

BIS Quarterly Review (2001) (Geneva: Bank for International Settlements).

—— (2005) (Geneva:Bank for International Settlements).

—— (2009) (December) (Geneva: Bank for International Settlements).

Black, R. D. C. (1976), 'Smith's Contribution in Historical Perspective', in T. Wilson and A. Skinner (eds) *The Market and the State: Essays in Honour of Adam Smith* (Oxford: Clarendon Press).

Blackhurst, R. (1998), 'The Capacity of the WTO to Fulfill Its Mandate', in A. O. Krueger (ed.), *The WTO as an International Organization* (Chicago, IL: University of Chicago Press)

Blanden, J., Gregg, P., and Machin, S. (2005), *Intergenerational Mobility in Europe and North America*, Centre for Economic Performance (London: London School of Economics).

Blaug, M. (1996), *Economic Theory in Retrospect*, 5th edn (Cambridge: Cambridge University Press).

—— (1999), 'The Formalist Revolution or What Happened to Orthodox Economics after World War II?', in R. Backhouse and J. Creedy (eds) *From Classical Economics to the Theory of the Firm: Essays in Honour of D. P. O'Brien* (Cheltenham: Edward Elgar).

Blinder, A. (2013), *After the Music Stopped: The Financial Crisis, the Response, and the Work Ahead* (New York: Penguin).

Block, F., and Keller, M. (2011), *State of Innovation* (London: Paradigm Publishers).

Blonigen, B., and Feenstra, R. (1996), *Protectionist Threats and Foreign Direct Investment*, NBER Working Paper 5475 (Cambridge, MA: National Bureau of Economic Research).

Blustein, P. (2005), *And the Money Kept Rolling In (And Out): Wall Street, the IMF, and the Bankrupting of Argentina* (New York: Public Affairs).

Blyth, M. (2003), 'Same as It Never Was: Temporality and Typology in the Varieties of Capitalism', *Comparative European Politics*, 1/2: 215–26.

Blyth, M., and Varghese, R. (1999), 'The State of the Discipline in American Political Science: Be Careful What You Wish for?', *British Journal of Politics and International Relations*, 1/3: 345–65.

Blytheway, S., and Metzler, M. (2016), *Central Banks and Gold: How Tokyo, London and New York Shaped the Modern World* (Ithaca, NY: Cornell University Press).

Boden, T. A., Marland, G., and Andres, R. J. 2010 (updated 10 June 2015), 'Global, Regional, and National Fossil-Fuel CO_2 Emissions', Carbon Dioxide Information Analysis Center, Oak Ridge National Laboratory, US Department of Energy, Oak Ridge, TN, USA, doi 10.3334/CDIAC/00001_V2010.

Bomberg, E. E., and Stubb, A. C. G. (2003), *The European Union: How Does It Work?* (Oxford: Oxford University Press).

Bordo, M. (2005), *Historical Perspectives on Global Imbalances*, NBER Working Paper 11383 (Cambridge, MA: National Bureau of Economic Research).

—— and Eichengreen, B. (2002), *Crises Now and Then: What Lessons from the Last Era of Financial Globalization*, NBER Working Paper W8716 (Cambridge, MA: National Bureau of Economic Research).

—— and Helbling, T. (2003), *Have National Business Cycles Become More Synchronized?*, NBER Working Paper 10130 (Cambridge, MA: National Bureau of Economic Research).

—— Eichengreen, B., and Irwin, D. A. (1999), *Is Globalization Today Really Different than Globalization a Hundred Years Ago?*, NBER Working Paper 7195 (Cambridge, MA: National Bureau of Economic Research).

—— and Kim, J. (1998), *Was There Really an Earlier Period of International Financial Integration Comparable to Today?*, NBER Working Paper 6738 (Cambridge, MA: National Bureau of Economic Research).

Borjas, G. J. (1999), 'The Economic Analysis of Immigration', in O. Ashenfelter and D. Card (eds), *Handbook of Labor Economics* (Amsterdam: North-Holland).

—— Freeman, R., and Katz, L. (1996), 'Searching for the Effect of Immigration on the Labor Market', *American Economic Review*, 86/2: 247–51.

Borrus, M., and Zysman, J. (1997), 'Globalization with Borders: The Rise of Wintelism as the Future of Global Competition', *Industry and Innovation*, 4/2: 141–66.

Boughton, J. (2001), *Silent Revolution: The International Monetary Fund, 1979–1989* (Washington, DC: IMF).

—— (2012), *Tearing Down Walls: The International Monetary Fund, 1990–1999* (Washington, DC: IMF).

Bovard, J. (1991), *The Fair Trade Fraud* (New York: St Martin's Press).

Boyer, R., and Drache, D. (eds) (1996), *States Against Markets* (London: Routledge).

Brack, D., Calder, F., and Dolun, M. (2001), From Rio to Johannesburg: The Earth Summit and Rio + 10, Royal Institute of International Affairs Briefing Paper, ns 19 (London: RIIA).

Brady, D., Huber, E., and Stephens, J. D. (2014), Comparative Welfare States Data Set, Northwestern University and University of North Carolina (available at: http://www.unc.edu/~jdsteph/common/data-common.html).

Brandt, L., and Thun, E. (2010), 'The Fight for the Middle: Upgrading, Competition, and Industrial Development in China', *World Development*, 38/11: 1555–74.

—— (2016), 'Constructing a Ladder for Growth: Policy, Markets, and Industrial Upgrading in China', *World Development*, 80: 78–95.

Brawley, M. (2005), *Power, Money, and Trade: Decisions that Shape Global Economic Relations* (Orchard Park, NY: Broadview Press).

Breitmeier, H., Young, O. R., and Zürn, M. (2006), *Analyzing International Environmental Regimes: From Case Study to Database* (Cambridge, MA: MIT Press).

Brenner, N. (1999), 'Beyond State-Centrism? Space, Territoriality and Geographic Scale in Globalization Studies', *Theory and Society*, 28/1: 39–78.

—— (2004), *New State Spaces: Urban Governance and the Rescaling of Statehood* (Oxford: Oxford University Press).

Brewer, T. L., and Young, S. (1998), *The Multilateral Investment System and Multinational Enterprises* (Oxford: Oxford University Press).

Breznitz, Dan and John, Zysman. (eds) (2013), *The Third Globalization* (New York: Oxford University Press)

Broad, R., and Cavanagh, J. (2008), *Development Redefined: How the Market Met its Match* (Boulder, CO: Paradigm Publishers).

Broadbent, J. (1998), *Environmental Politics in Japan: Networks of Power and Protest* (Cambridge: Cambridge University Press).

Brogger, T. (2008), 'Europe Scrambles as Iceland's Banks Fail', Bloomberg.com, 9 October.

Brown, A.G. (2003), *Reluctant Partners: A History of Multilateral Trade Cooperation, 1850–2000* (Ann Arbor, MI: University of Michigan Press).

Brown, V. (1994), *Adam Smith's Discourse: Canonicity, Commerce and Conscience* (London: Routledge).

Broz, J. L., and Frieden, J. A. (2001), 'The Political Economy of International Monetary Relations', *Annual Review of Political Science*, 4/1: 317–43.

Brummer, C. (2012), *Soft Law and the Global Financial System* (Cambridge: Cambridge University Press).

Brune, N., and Garrett, G. (2005), 'The Globalization Rorschach Test: International Economic Integration, Inequality, and the Role of Government', *Annual Review of Political Science*, 8: 399–423.

Bryan, S. (2010), *The Gold Standard at the Turn of the Twentieth Century* (New York: Columbia University Press).

Bryant, R. C. (2003), *Turbulent Waters: Cross-Border Finance and International Governance* (Washington, DC: Brookings Institution).

Buchanan, A. (1982), *Marx and Justice: The Radical Critique of Liberalism* (London: Methuen).

Bulkeley, H., and Newell, P. (2010), *Governing Climate Change* (London: Routledge).

—— Andonova, L. B., Betsill, M. M., Compagnon, D., Hale, T., Hoffmann, M. J., Newell, P., Paterson, M., Roger, C., and VanDeveer, S. D. (2014), *Transnational Climate Change Governance* (Cambridge: Cambridge University Press).

Burch, K., and Denemark, R. A. (1997), *Constituting International Political Economy* (Boulder, CO: Lynne Rienner).

Burg, J. (2003), 'The World Summit on Sustainable Development: Empty Talk or Call to Action?', *Journal of Environment and Development*, 12/1: 111–20.

Burki, S. J., Perry, G. E., and Dillinger, W. R. (1999), *Beyond the Center: Decentralizing the State* (Washington, DC: World Bank).

Burtless, G., Lawrence, R. Z., Litan, R. E., and Shapiro, R. J. (1998), *Globaphobia: Confronting Fears about Free Trade* (Washington, DC: Brookings Institution).

Busch, A. (2000), 'Unpacking the Globalization Debate: Approaches, Evidence and Data', in C. Hay and D. Marsh (eds), *Demystifying Globalization* (Basingstoke: Palgrave).

Buzan, B., Held, D., and McGrew, A. (1998), 'Realism versus Cosmopolitanism: A Debate', *Review of International Studies*, 24/3: 387–98.

Cai, F., and Warnock, F. E. (2006), *International Diversification at Home and Abroad*, NBER Working Paper 12220 (Cambridge, MA: National Bureau of Economic Research).

Calleo, D. (1976), 'The Historiography of the Interwar Period: Reconsiderations', in B. Rowland (ed.), *Balance of Power or Hegemony: The Interwar Monetary System* (New York: New York University Press).

—— (1987), *Beyond American Hegemony* (New York: Basic Books).

Callinicos, A. (2003), *An Anti-Capitalist Manifesto* (Cambridge: Polity Press).

Calvo, G. A., and Talvi, E. (2005), *Sudden Stop, Financial Factors and Economic Collapse in Latin America: Learning from Argentina and Chile*, NBER Working Paper 11153 (Cambridge, MA: National Bureau of Economic Research).

Cameron, D. R. (1978), 'The Expansion of the Public Economy: A Comparative Analysis', *American Political Science Review*, 72/4: 1243–61.

Caner, A., and Wolff, E. (2004), 'Asset Poverty in the United States, 1984–1999', *Challenge: Magazine of Economic Affairs*, 47/1: 5–52.

Caparros, M. (2014), 'Counting the Hungry', *International New York Times*, 30 September: 7.

Capling, A. (2001), *Australia and the Global Trade System: From Havana to Seattle* (Cambridge: Cambridge University Press).

—— and Low, P. (2010), 'The Domestic Politics of Trade Policy-Making: State and Non-state Actor Interactions and Forum Choice', in Capling, A. and Low, P. (eds), *Governments, Non-State Actors and Trade Policy-Making* (Cambridge: Cambridge University Press): 4–28.

—— and Nossal, K. R. (2009), 'The Contradictions of Regionalism in North America', in R. Fawn (ed.), *Globalising the Regional, Regionalising the Global* (Cambridge: Cambridge University Press).

Carlos, A. M., and Nicholas, S. (1988), 'Giants of an Earlier Capitalism: The Chartered Trading Companies as Modern Multinationals', *Business History Review*, 62/autumn: 398–419.

Carr, E. H. (1939/1946), *The Twenty Years' Crisis 1919–1939: An Introduction to the Study of International Relations*, 2nd edn (London: Macmillan).

Carrere, C., and Schiff, M. (2004), *On the Geography of Trade: Distance Is Alive and Well*, World Bank Policy Research Working Paper 3206 (Washington, DC: World Bank).

Carson, R. (1962), *Silent Spring* (Boston: Houghton Mifflin).

Carver, T., and Thomas, P. (1995), *Rational Choice Marxism* (London: Macmillan).

Cashin, P., McDermott, C. J., and Scott, A. (1999), *Booms and Slumps in World Commodity Prices*, IMF Working Paper 99/155 (Washington, DC: IMF).

Cashore, B., Auld, G., and Newsom, D. (2004), *Governing through Markets: Forest Certification and the Emergence of Non-state Authority* (New Haven: Yale University Press).

Castells, M. (1996), *The Rise of the Network Society* (Oxford: Basil Blackwell).

—— (1997), *The Power of Identity* (Oxford: Basil Blackwell).

—— (1998), *End of the Millennium* (Oxford: Basil Blackwell).

—— (2000), *The Rise of the Network Society* (Oxford: Basil Blackwell).

Castles, S., and Miller, M. (2002), *The Age of Global Migration* (Basingstoke: Palgrave).

Catephores, G. (1989), *An Introduction to Marxist Economics* (London: Macmillan).

Cavalcanti, T. V., Mohaddes, K., and Raissi, M. (2012), *Commodity Price Volatility and the Sources of Growth*, IMF Working Paper 12 (online: International Monetary Fund).

Cavanagh, J., and Mander, J. (eds) (2004), *Alternatives to Economic Globalization: A Better World Is Possible*, 2nd edn (San Francisco, CA: Berrett-Koehler).

Caves, R. E. (1982), *Multinational Enterprise and Economic Analysis* (Cambridge: Cambridge University Press).

Çelikkol, A. (2011), *Romances of Free Trade: British Literature, Laissez Faire, and the Global Nineteenth Century* (Oxford: Oxford University Press).

Centre for Economic Policy Reform (2002), *Making Sense of Globalization*, CEPR Policy Paper 8 (Paris: CEPR).

Cerny, P. G. (1994), 'The Dynamics of Financial Globalization: Technology, Market Structure, and Policy Response', *Policy Sciences*, 27/4: 319–42.

—— (1995), 'Globalization and the Changing Logic of Collective Action', *International Organization*, 49/4: 595–625.

—— (1997), 'Paradoxes of the Competition State: The Dynamics of Political Globalization', *Government and Opposition*, 32/2: 251–74.

Chan, J., Pun, N. *et al.* (2013), 'The politics of global production: Apple, Foxconn and China's new working class', *New Technology, Work and Employment*, 28/8: 100–15.

Chancellor, E. (2016), 'Heed the threats to globalization', blogs.reuters.com 9/2/ 16.

Chandler, A. D. (1977), *The Visible Hand: The Managerial Revolution in American Business* (Cambridge, MA/London: Harvard University Press).

Chang, H.-J. (2002), *Kicking away the Ladder: Development Strategy in Historical Perspective* (London: Anthem).

Chang, H.-J. (2003), *Kicking Away the Ladder: Development Strategy in Historical Perspective* (London: Anthem Press).

—— (2006), *The East Asian Development Experience: The Miracle, the Crisis and the Future* (New York: Zed Books).

Chapman, A. (2015), *Mary Somerville and the World of Science* (London: Springer).

Chase, K. A. (2003), 'Economic Interests and Regional Trading Arrangements: The Case of NAFTA', *International Organization*, 57/1: 137–74.

—— (2005), *Trading Blocs: States, Firms, and Regions in the World Economy* (Ann Arbor, MI: University of Michigan Press).

—— (2006), 'Multilateralism Compromised: The Mysterious Origin of GATT Article XXIV', *Journal of World Trade*, 5/1: 1–30.

Chatterjee, P., and Finger, M. (1994), *The Earth Brokers: Power, Politics and World Development* (London: Routledge).

Chen, S., and Ravallion, M. (2004), 'How Have the World's Poorest Fared since the Early 1980s?', *World Bank Research Observer*, 19/2: 141–69.

—— (2008), *The Developing World Is Poorer than We Thought, But No Less Successful in the Fight Against Poverty*, World Bank Policy Research Working Paper 4703 (Washington, DC: World Bank, August).

—— (2010), 'The Developing World Is Poorer than We Thought, But No Less Successful in the Fight Against Poverty', *Quarterly Journal of Economics*, 125/4: 1577–1625.

Chenery, H., Bowen, I., and Svikhart, B. (1974), *Redistribution with Growth: Policies to Improve Income Distribution in Developing Countries in the Context of Economic Growth* (Oxford: Oxford University Press).

Cherif, R., and Hasanov, F. (2015), 'The Leap of the Tiger: How Malaysia Can Escape the Middle-Income Trap', IMF Working Paper WP/15/131 (Washington, DC: IMF).

Chey, H.-K. (2012), 'Theories of International Currency and the Future of the World Monetary Order', *International Studies Review*, 14/1: 51–77.

Chimni, B. S. (2006), 'The World Trade Organization, Democracy and Development: A View from the South', *Journal of World Trade*, 40/1: 5–36.

Chin, G., and Helleiner, E. (2008), 'China as a Creditor: A Rising Financial Power?', *Journal of International Affairs*, 62/1: 87–102.

China News Digest (2006), 'Survey of China's Second-Tier Cities', 15 June.

Chiswick, B. R., and Hatton, T. J. (2003), 'International Migration and Integration of Labor Markets', in M. D. Bordo, A. M. Taylor, and J. G. Williamson (eds), *Globalization in Historical Perspective* (Chicago, IL: Chicago University Press).

Chortareas, G. E., and Pelagidis, T. (2004), 'Trade Flows: A Facet of Regionalism or Globalisation?', *Cambridge Journal of Economics*, 28/2: 253–71.

Chwieroth, J. M. (2010), *Capital Ideas: The IMF and the Rise of Financial Liberalization* (Princeton, NJ: Princeton University Press).

Ciplet, D., Roberts, J. T., and Khan, M. R. (2015), *Power in a Warming World: The New Global Politics of Climate Change and the Remaking of Environmental Inequality* (Cambridge, MA: MIT Press).

Citrin, J., Green, D., Muste, C., and Wong, C. (1997), 'Public Opinion toward Immigration Reform: The Role of Economic Motivations', *Journal of Politics*, 59/3: 858–81.

Claessens, S. and van Horen, N. (2014), 'The Impact of the GFC on Banking Globalization', IMF Working Paper 14/197 (Washington, DC: IMF).

Clapp, J. (2001), *Toxic Exports: The Transfer of Hazardous Wastes from Rich to Poor Countries* (Ithaca, NY: Cornell University Press).

—— (2002), 'What the Pollution Havens Debate Overlooks', *Global Environmental Politics*, 2/2: 11–19.

—— (2016), *Food*, 2nd edn (Cambridge: Polity).

—— and Dauvergne, P. (2011), *Paths to a Green World: The Political Economy of the Global Environment*, 2nd edn (Cambridge, MA: MIT Press).

—— and Fuchs, D. (eds) (2009), *Corporate Power in Global Agrifood Governance* (Cambridge, MA: MIT Press).

Clark, W. R., and Hallerberg, M. (2000), 'Strategic Interaction between Monetary and Fiscal Actors under Full Capital Mobility', *American Political Science Review*, 94/2: 323–46.

—— and Reichert, U. N. (1998), 'International and Domestic Constraints on Political Business Cycles in OECD Economies', *International Organization*, 52/1: 87–120.

Cline, W. R. (ed.) (1983), *Trade Policy in the 1980s* (Washington, DC: Institute for International Economics).

Club of Rome (D. H. Meadows, D. L. Meadows, W. W. Behrens, and J. Randers) (1972), *The Limits to Growth* (New York: Universe Books).

Coakley, J., Fuertes, A.-M., and Spagnolo, F. (2004), 'Is the Feldstein-Horioka Puzzle History?', *Manchester School*, 72/5: 569–90.

—— Kulasi, F., and Smith, R. (1998), 'The Feldstein-Horioka Puzzle and Capital Mobility: A Review', *International Journal of Finance and Economics*, 3/2: 169–88.

Coase, R. H. (1937), 'The Nature of the Firm', *Economica*, 4/16: 386–405.

—— (1960), 'The Problem of Social Cost', *Journal of Law and Economics*, 3: 1–44.

Coe, D. T., Subramanian, A., Tamirisa, N. T., and Bhavnani, R. (2002), *The Missing Globalization Puzzle*, IMF Working Paper No. 02/171 (Washington, DC: IMF).

Coghlan, A., and MacKenzie, D. (2011), 'Revealed: The Capitalist Network that Runs the World', *New Scientist*, 2835.

Cohen, B. (2003), 'Can the Euro Ever Challenge the Dollar?', *Journal of Common Market Studies*, 41/4: 575–95.

—— (2007), 'The Transatlantic Divide: Why Are American and British IPE So Different?', *Review of International Political Economy*, 14/2: 197–219.

—— (2008a), *Global Monetary Governance* (London: Routledge).

—— (2008b), *International Political Economy: An Intellectual History* (Princeton, NJ: Princeton University Press).

—— (2008c), 'The International Monetary System: Diffusion and Ambiguity', *International Affairs*, 84/3: 455–70.

—— (2009), 'Striking a Nerve', *Review of International Political Economy*, 16/1: 136–43.

Cohen, B. (2012), 'The Future of the Euro: Let's Get Real', *Review of International Political Economy*, 19/4: 689–700.

Cohen, J., and Centeno, M. (2006), 'Neoliberalism and Patterns of Economic Performance, 1980–2000', *Annals of the American Academy of Political and Social Sciences*, 606/1: 32–67.

Cohen, N. (2003), 'Gambling with our Future', *New Statesman*, 13 January.

Colander, D. (2001), *The Lost Art of Economics: Essays on Economics and the Economics Profession* (Cheltenham: Edward Elgar).

Condliffe, J. B. (1950), *The Commerce of Nations* (New York: Norton).

Constantinescu, Cristina *et al.* (2015), The Global Trade Slowdown: Cyclical or Structural? IMF Working Paper 15/6 (Washington, DC: IMF)

Conybeare, J. A. C. (1980), 'International Organization and the Theory of Property Rights', *International Organization*, 34/3: 307–34.

—— (1984), 'Public Goods, Prisoners' Dilemmas and the International Political Economy', *International Studies Quarterly*, 28/1: 5–22.

Cooke, W. N., and Noble, D. S. (1998), 'Industrial Relations Systems and US Foreign Direct Investment Abroad', *British Journal of Industrial Relations*, 36/4: 581–609.

Cooper, A. F. (2010), 'The G20 as an Improvised Crisis Committee and/or a Contested "Steering Committee" for the World', *International Affairs*, 86: 741–57.

—— and Momani, B. (2005), 'Negotiating out of Argentina's Financial Crisis: Segmenting the International Creditors', *New Political Economy*, 10/3: 305–20.

Cooper, B. (1997), 'Family Troubles', in E. Mutari, H. Boushey, and W. Fraher (eds) *Gender and Political Economy: Incorporating Diversity into Theory and Practice* (New York: M.E. Sharpe).

Cooper, R. N. (1968), *The Economics of Interdependence* (New York: McGraw-Hill).

—— (1972), 'Economic Interdependence and Foreign Policy in the Seventies', *World Politics*, 24/2: 159–81.

—— (1975), 'Prolegomena to the Choice of an International Monetary System', *International Organization*, 29/1: 63–97.

Corbridge, Stuart (1998), '"Beneath the Pavement Only Soil"': The Poverty of Post-Development', *Journal of Development Studies*, 34/6: 138–48.

Corea, G., and Kiiski, S. (2001), *Trends in Income Distribution in the Post-World War II Period*, Discussion Paper 89 (Helsinki: WIDER).

Cornes, R., and Sandler, T. (1996), *The Theory of Externalities, Public Goods, and Club Goods*, 2nd edn (New York: Cambridge University Press).

Cotis, J.-P. (2007), 'Editorial: achieving further rebalancing', *OECD Economic Outlook*, 1: 7–10.

Cox, R. W. (1981), 'Social Forces, States and World Orders: Beyond International Relations Theory', *Millennium: Journal of International Studies*, 10/2: 126–55.

—— (1987), *Production, Power, and World Order: Social Forces in the Making of History* (New York: Columbia University Press).

—— (2000), 'Explaining Business Support for Regional Trade Agreements', in J. A. Frieden and D. A. Lake (eds), *International Political Economy: Perspectives on Global Wealth and Power*, 4th edn (New York: St Martin's Press).

—— with Sinclair, T. (1996), *Approaches to World Order* (Cambridge: Cambridge University Press).

Crafts, N., and Venables, A. J. (2003), 'Globalization in History: A Geographical Perspective', in M. D. Bordo, A. M. Taylor, and J. G. Williamson (eds), *Globalization in Historical Perspective* (Chicago, IL: Chicago University Press).

Craig, D., and Porter, D. (2003), 'Poverty Reduction Strategy Papers: A New Convergence', *World Development*, 31/1: 53–69.

Crane, G. (1998), 'Economic Nationalism: Bringing the Nation Back in,' *Millennium: Journal of International Studies*, 27/1: 55–75.

Crawford, J.-A., and Florentino, R.V. (2005), *The Changing Landscape of Regional Trade Agreements*, WTO Discussion Paper 8 (Geneva: World Trade Organization).

Croome, J. (1995), *Reshaping the World Trading System: A History of the Uruguay Round* (Geneva: World Trade Organization).

Crouch, C. (2011), *The Strange Non-death of Neoliberalism* (Cambridge: Polity).

—— and Streeck, W. (1997), 'Introduction: The Future of Capitalist Diversity', in C. Crouch and W. Streeck (eds), *Political Economy of Modern Capitalism* (London: Sage).

Crystal, J. (1994), 'The Politics of Capital Flight: Exit and Exchange Rates in Latin America', *Review of International Studies*, 20/2: 131–47.

—— (2003), *Unwanted Company: Foreign Investment in American Industries* (Ithaca, NY: Cornell University Press).

Cumings, B. (1984), 'The Origins and Development of the Northeast Asian Political Economy: Industrial Sectors, Product Cycles, and Political Consequences', *International Organization*, 38/1: 1–40.

Cutler, A. C. (2003), *Private Power and Global Authority* (Cambridge: Cambridge University Press).

Dahl, R. A. (1963), *Modern Political Analysis* (Englewood Cliffs, NJ: Prentice-Hall).

Daly, H. (1993), 'The Perils of Free Trade', *Scientific American*, November: 50–7.

—— (1996), *Beyond Growth: The Economics of Sustainable Development* (Boston: Beacon Press).

—— (2002), 'Uneconomic Growth and Globalization in a Full World', *Natur und Kultur*, 2/2: 3–22.

Dam, K. W. (1970), *The GATT: Law and International Economic Organization* (Chicago, IL: University of Chicago Press).

Darling, J. and Glendinning, A. (1996), *Gender Matters in Schools: Pupils and Teachers* (London: A&C Black).

Dash, K., Cronin, P. and Goddard, R. (2003), 'Introduction', in R. Goddard, P. Cronin and K. Dash (eds) *International Political Economy: State-Market Relations in a Changing Global Order*, 2nd edn (Basingstoke: Palgrave Macmillan).

Dauvergne, P. (1997), *Shadows in the Forest: Japan and the Politics of Timber in Southeast Asia* (Cambridge, MA: MIT Press).

—— (1999), 'Asia's Environment after the 1997 Financial Meltdown: The Need for a Regional Response', *Asian Perspective: A Journal of Regional and International Affairs*, 23/3: 53–77.

—— (2001), *Loggers and Degradation in the Asia-Pacific: Corporations and Environmental Management* (Cambridge: Cambridge University Press).

Dauvergne, P. (2005), 'The Environmental Challenge to Loggers in the Asia-Pacific: Corporate Practices in Informal Regimes of Governance', in D. L. Levy and P. J. Newell (eds), *The Business of Global Environmental Governance* (Cambridge, MA: MIT Press).

—— (2008), *The Shadows of Consumption: Consequences for the Global Environment* (Cambridge, MA: MIT Press).

—— (2016), *Environmentalism of the Rich* (Cambridge, MA: MIT Press).

—— and LeBaron, G. (2014), *Protest Inc.: The Corporatization of Activism* (Cambridge, Polity).

—— and Lister, J. (2011), *Timber* (Cambridge: Polity).

—— (2013), *Eco-Business: A Big-Brand Takeover of Sustainability* (Cambridge, MA: MIT Press).

Davenport, C. (2015), 'Nations Approve Landmark Climate Accord in Paris', *New York Times*, 12 December, www.nytimes.com

Davey, W. J. (2000), 'The WTO Dispute Settlement System', *Journal of International Economic Law*, 3: 15–18.

De Cecco, M. (1974), *Money and Empire* (Oxford: Blackwell).

—— (2009), 'From Monopoly to Oligopoly: Lessons from the Pre-1914 Experience', in E. Helleiner and J. Kirshner (eds), *The Future of the Dollar* (Ithaca, NY: Cornell University Press).

De Goede, M. (2000), 'Mastering Lady Credit: Discourses of Financial Crisis in Historical Perspective', *International Feminist Journal of Politics*, 2/1: 58–81.

De Gregorio, J. (2001), 'Something for Everyone: Chilean Exchange Rate Policy since 1960', in J. Frieden, P. Ghezzi, and E. Stein (eds), *The Currency Game: Exchange Rate Politics in Latin America* (New York: Inter-American Development Bank).

de la Merced, M. J., and Sorkin, A. R. (2010), 'Report Details How Lehman Hid Its Woes', *New York Times*, 11 March.

De Marchi, N. (1999), 'Adam Smith's Accommodation of "Altogether Endless" Desires', in M. Berg and H. Clifford (eds), *Consumers and Luxury: Consumer Culture in Europe, 1650-1850* (Manchester: Manchester University Press).

de Ville, Ferdi, and Siles-Brugge, G. (2016), *TTIP: The Truth About the Transatlantic Trade and Investment Partnership* (Cambridge: Polity Press).

De Vroey, M. (1975), 'The Transition from Classical to Neoclassical Economics: A Scientific Revolution', *Journal of Economic Issues*, 9/3: 415–439.

Deaton, A. (2010), 'Price Indices, Inequality and the Measurement of World Poverty', Presidential Address, American Economic Association, Atlanta, 17 January.

—— and B. Aten. (2015), 'Trying to understand the PPPs in ICP2011', NBER WP No. 20244, revised 28 April.

—— and Heston, A. (2009), *Understanding PPPs and PPP-Based National Accounts*, NBER Working Paper 14499 (Cambridge, MA: National Bureau of Economic Research).

—— Lustig, N., Rogoff, K., with Hsu, E. (2006), *An Evaluation of World Bank Research, 1998–2005* (Washington, DC: World Bank).

Deibert, R. (1997), *Parchment, Printing and Hypermedia* (Ithaca, NY: Cornell University Press).

Deloitte Consulting. (2014), Business trends 2014: Navigating the next wave of globalization (Deloitte)

DeMartino, G. (2011), *The Economist's Oath: On the Need for and Content of Professional Economic Ethics* (New York: Oxford University Press).

—— (forthcoming), 'Epistemic Aspects of Economic Practice and the Insufficiency of Codes of Conduct in Economics', *Review of Social Economy*.

DeMartino, G. and D. McCloskey. (eds) (2016), *Oxford Handbook of Professional Economics Ethics* (Oxford: Oxford University Press).

Desai, P. (2003), *Financial Crisis, Contagion, and Containment* (Princeton, NJ: Princeton University Press).

Destler, I. M. (1995), *American Trade Politics*, 3rd edn (Washington, DC: Institute for International Economics).

—— and Balint, P. (1999), *The New Politics of American Trade: Trade, Labor, and the Environment* (Washington, DC: Institute for International Economics).

—— and Henning, R. C. (1989), *Dollar Politics: Exchange Rate Policymaking in the US* (Washington, DC: Institute for International Economics).

De Young, R., and Princen, T. (eds) (2012), *The Localization Reader: Adapting to the Downshift* (Cambridge, MA: MIT Press).

DG Trade (2015), 'Client and Supplier Countries of the EU28 in Merchandise Trade', available at http://trade.ec.europa.eu/doclib/docs/2006/september/tradoc_122530.pdf

DHL/NYU (2015), Global Connectedness Index 2014 (New York: DHL/NYU).

Diamond, J. M. (2005), *Collapse: How Societies Choose to Fail or Succeed* (New York: Viking).

DiCaprio, A. and Trommer, S. (2010), 'Bilateral Graduation: The Impact of EPAs on LDC Trade Space', *Journal of Development Studies*, 46/9: 1607–27.

Dicken, P. (2003), *Global Shift: Reshaping the Global Economic Map in the 21st Century*, 4th edn (London: Sage).

—— (2015), *Global Shift: Mapping the Changing Contours of the World Economy*, 7th edn (Thousand Oaks, CA: Sage).

Diebold, W. (1952), *The End of the GATT* (Princeton, NJ: Princeton University Press).

Dikhanov, Y., and Ward, M. (2003), 'Evolution of the Global Distribution of Income in 1970–99', Proceedings of the Global Poverty Workshop, Initiative for Policy Dialogue, Columbia University, New York.

DiMento, J. F. C., and Doughman, P. M. (eds) (2007), *Climate Change: What It Means for Us, Our Children, and our Grandchildren* (Cambridge, MA: MIT Press).

Dinda, S. (2004), 'Environmental Kuznets Curve Hypothesis: A Survey', *Ecological Economics*, 49/4: 431–55.

Dittmer, L., and Yu, G. T. (2010), *China, the Developing World, and the New Global Dynamic* (Boulder, CO: Lynne Rienner).

Donnan, S. (2016), 'Global Trade: Structural shifts', *Financial Times*, 3 March.

Dooley, M. P., Folkerts-Landau, D., and Garber, P. (2003), *An Essay on the Revived Bretton Woods System*, NBER Working Paper 9971 (Cambridge, MA: National Bureau of Economic Research).

Doornbos, M. (2001), '"Good Governance": The Rise and Decline of a Policy Metaphor?', *Journal of Development Studies*, 37/6: 93–108.

dos Santos, T. (1970), 'The Structure of Dependence', *American Economic Review*, 60/2: 231–6.

Downs, G. W., and Rocke, D. M. (1995), *Optimal Imperfection? Domestic Uncertainty and Institutions in International Relations* (Princeton, NJ: Princeton University Press).

Dowrick, S., and DeLong, J. B. (2003), 'Globalization and Convergence', in M. D. Bordo, A. M. Taylor, and J. G. Williamson (eds), *Globalization in Historical Perspective* (Chicago, IL: Chicago University Press).

—— and Akmal, M. (2005), 'Contradictory Trends in Global Income Inequality: A Tale of Two Biases', *Review of Income and Wealth*, 51/2: 201–29.

Dressler, A. E., and Parson, E. A. (2006), *The Science and Politics of Global Climate Change* (Cambridge: Cambridge University Press).

Drezner, D. W. (2007), *All Politics Is Global: Explaining International Regulatory Regimes* (Princeton, NJ: Princeton University Press).

—— (2009), 'Bad Debts: Assessing China's Financial Influence in Great Power Politics', *International Security*, 34/2: 7–45.

—— (2014), *The System Worked: How the World Stopped Another Great Depression* (New York: Oxford University Press).

Dryzek, J. (2006), *Deliberative Global Politics: Discourse and Democracy in a Divided World* (Cambridge: Polity Press).

Duchacek, I. D. (1990), 'Perforated Sovereignties: Towards a Typology of New Actors in International Relations', in H. J. Michelman and P. Soldatos (eds), *Federalism and International Relations* (Oxford: Oxford University Press).

Duffield, J. S. (2007), 'What Are International Institutions?', *International Studies Review*, 9/1: 1–22.

Duhigg, C., and Bradsher, K. (2012), 'How the U.S. Lost Out on iPhone Work', *New York Times*, 21 January.

Dunne, T. (2001), 'Liberalism', in J. Baylis and S. Smith (eds), *The Globalization of World Politics*, 2nd edn (Oxford: Oxford University Press).

Dunning, J. H. (1981), *International Production and the Multinational Enterprise* (London: Allen & Unwin).

—— (1988), 'The Eclectic Paradigm of International Production: An Update and Some Possible Extensions', *Journal of International Business Studies*, 19/1: 1–32.

—— (1993), *Multinational Enterprises and the Global Economy* (Wokingham: Addison-Wesley).

—— (2000), 'The New Geography of Foreign Direct Investment', in N. Woods (ed.), *The Political Economy of Globalization* (Basingstoke: Palgrave).

Dupont, C. (1998), 'European Integration and APEC: The Search for Institutional Blueprints', in V. K. Aggarwal and C. Morrison (eds), *Asia-Pacific Crossroads: Regime Creation and the Future of APEC* (New York: St Martin's Press).

—— and Hefeker, C. (2001), 'Integration Linkages: Between Trade-offs and Spillovers', paper presented at the 4th Pan-European IR conference, Canterbury, 8–10 September.

Durbin, A., and Welch, C. (2002), 'The Environmental Movement and Global Finance', in J. A. Scholte (ed.), *Civil Society and Global Finance* (London: Routledge).

Easterbrook, G. (1995), *A Moment on the Earth: The Coming Age of Environmental Optimism* (New York: Penguin).

Eccles, R. G., Serafeim, G., and Cheng, B. (2012), 'Foxconn Technology Group', Harvard Business School Case no. 9-112-002.

ECLA (Economic Commission for Latin America) (2001), *Panorama Social de America Latina2000-01* (Santiago: ECLA (CEPAL)).

ECLA (Economic Commission for Latin America) (2002), *Globalization and Development* (Santiago: ECLA (CEPAL)).

ECLAC (UN Economic Commission for Latin America and the Caribbean) (1995), *Policies to Improve Linkages with the Global Economy* (Santiago: ECLACC).

—— (2001), *Foreign Investment in Latin America and the Caribbean, 2000 Report* (New York: United Nations).

—— (2002), *Preliminary Overview of the Economies of Latin America and the Caribbean, 2002* (Santiago: United Nations).

—— (2008), *Social Panorama of Latin America: Briefing Paper* (Santiago: ECLACC).

Economist (2003), 'Special Report', 20 September.

—— (2011), 'The Case Against Globaloney', 20 April.

—— (2015), 'The Causes and Consequences of China's Market Crash', 24 August.

Edward, P. (2006a), 'Examining Inequality: Who Really Benefits from Global Growth?', *World Development*, 34/10: 1667–95.

—— (2006b), 'The Ethical Poverty Line: A Moral Quantification of Absolute Poverty', *Third World Quarterly*, 27/2: 377–93.

Edwards, S. (2005), *Capital Controls, Sudden Stops and Current Account Reversals*, NBER Working Paper 11170 (Cambridge, MA: National Bureau of Economic Research).

Ehrlich, P. (1968), *The Population Bomb* (New York: Sierra Club-Ballantine).

Eichengreen, B. J. (ed.) (1985), *The Gold Standard in Theory and History* (New York: Methuen).

—— (1992), *Golden Fetters: The Gold Standard and the Great Depression: 1919–1939* (New York: Oxford University Press).

—— (1996), *Globalizing Capital: A History of the International Monetary System* (Princeton, NJ: Princeton University Press).

—— (2002), *Financial Crises and What to Do About Them* (Oxford: Oxford University Press).

—— (2003), *Capital Flows and Crises* (Cambridge, MA: MIT Press).

—— (2009), *Out of the Box Thoughts about the International Financial Architecture*, IMF Working Paper No. 09/116 (Washington, DC: IMF).

—— (2011), *Exorbitant Privilege* (Oxford: Oxford University Press).

—— (2015), *Hall of Mirrors: The Great Depression, the Great Recession, and the Uses-and Misuses-of History* (Oxford: Oxford University Press).

—— and Bordo, M. D. (2002), *Crises Now and Then: What Lessons from the Last Era of Financial Globalization?* NBER Working Paper 8716 (Cambridge, MA: National Bureau of Economic Research).

—— and O'Rourke, K. H. (2009), 'A Tale of Two Depressions', 1 September, www.voxeu.org/index.php?q=node/3421

—— (2010), 'A Tale of Two Depressions: What Do the New Data Tell us? February 2010 Update', 8 March, http://www.voxeu.org/index.php?q=node/3421 (accessed May 2016).

Elam, M. (1997), 'National Imaginations and Systems of Innovation', in C. Edquist (ed.), *Systems of Innovation: Technologies, Institutions and Organizations* (London: Pinter)

Elliott, James. (2014), 'Cross border capital flows since the GFC', Bulletin of the Reserve Bank of Australia, June: 65–72

Elliott, L. (1998), *The Global Politics of the Environment* (New York: New York University Press).

Elsig, M., and Dupont, C. (2012), 'Persistent Deadlocks in Multilateral Trade Negotiations: The Case of Doha', in A. Narlikar, M. Daunton, and R. M. Stern (eds), *The Oxford Handbook on the World Trade Organization* (Oxford: Oxford University Press).

Elson, D. (1989), 'How Is Structural Adjustment Affecting Women?', *Development*, 1: 67–74.

—— (1992), 'Male Bias in Structural Adjustment', in H. Afshar and C. Dennis (eds), *Women and Adjustment Policies in the Third World* (London: Macmillan).

—— (ed.) (1995), *Male Bias in the Development Process* (Manchester: Manchester University Press).

Encarnation, D. J. (ed.) (1999), *Japanese Multinationals in Asia: Regional Operations in Comparative Perspective* (New York and Oxford: Oxford University Press).

Enright, S., Scott, E. E., and Chang, K. (2005), *Regional Powerhouse: The Greater Pearl River Delta and the Rise of China* (Singapore: Wiley).

Epstein, G. (1996), 'International Capital Mobility and the Scope for National Economic Management', in R. Boyer and D. Drache (eds), *States Against Markets: The Limits of Globalization* (London: Routledge).

Ergin, I. (2015), 'Breaking Out of the Middle-Income Trap: Assessing the Role of Structural Transformation', MSc dissertation, Department of International Development, LSE.

Ernst, D. (2006), 'Searching for a New Role in East Asian Regionalization: Japanese Production Networks in the Electronics Industry', in P. J. Katzenstein and T. Shiraishi (eds), *Beyond Japan: The Dynamics of East Asian Regionalism* (Ithaca, NY and London: Cornell University Press).

—— and Ravenhill, J. (2000), 'Convergence and Diversity: How Globalization Reshapes Asian Production Networks', in M. Borrus, D. Ernst, and S. Haggard (eds), *International Production Networks in Asia: Rivalry or Riches?* (London: Routledge).

Espenshade, T. J., and Calhoun, C. A. (1993), 'An Analysis of Public Opinion toward Undocumented Immigration', *Population Research and Policy Review*, 12: 189–224.

Esping-Andersen, G. (1996a), 'After the Golden Age? Welfare State Dilemmas in a Global Economy?', in G. Esping-Andersen, *Welfare States in Transition: National Adaptations in Global Economies* (London: Sage).

—— (1996b), 'Positive-Sum Solutions in a World of Trade-offs', in G. Esping-Andersen (ed.), *Welfare States in Transition: National Adaptations in Global Economies* (London: Sage).

Esty, D. C. (1994), *Greening the GATT: Trade, Environment and the Future* (Washington, DC: Institute for International Economics).

—— and Winston, A. S. (2009), *Green to Gold: How Smart Companies Use Environmental Strategy to Innovate, Create Value, and Build Competitive Advantage*, rev. and updated edn (Hoboken, NJ: Wiley).

European Commission (1990), 'One Market, One Money', *European Economy*, 44.

—— (2007), *European Economy*, No. 3 (Brussels: DG for Economic and Financial Affairs).

Evans, J. W. (1971), *The Kennedy Round in American Trade Policy: The Twilight of the GATT* (Cambridge, MA: Harvard University Press).

Evans, P. B. (1979), *Dependent Development: The Alliance of Multinational, State, and Local Capital in Brazil* (Princeton, NJ: Princeton University Press).

—— Jacobson, H. K., and Putnam, R. D. (eds) (1993), *Double-Edged Diplomacy: International Bargaining and Domestic Politics* (Berkeley and Los Angeles, CA: University of California Press).

Evenett, S.J. and Johannes Fritz. (2015), *The Tide Turns? Trade, Protectionism, and Slowing Global Growth. 18th Global Trade Alert* (London: CEPR).

FAO (Food and Agriculture Organization) (2008), *The State of Food Insecurity in the World 2008: High Food Prices and Food Security-Threats and Opportunities* (Rome: FAO).

—— (2009), 'More People than Ever Are Victims of Hunger', news release, www.fao.org/fileadmin/user_upload/newsroom/docs/Press%20release%20june-en.pdf

—— (2012a), *FAO Statistical Year 2012: World Food and Agriculture* (Rome: FAO).

—— (2012b), *Food Outlook: Global Market Analysis* (Rome: FAO).

—— International Fund for Agricultural Development, and World Food Programme (2015), *The State of Food Insecurity in the World* (Rome: FAO).

Farlow, Andrew. (2013), *Crash and Beyond: Causes and Consequences of the Global Financial Crisis* (Oxford: Oxford University Press)

Farrell, H. (2016), 'Here's Why Economists Should Be More Humble, Even When They Have Great Ideas', *Washington Post*, 25 March.

Fay, M. (1983), 'The Influence of Adam Smith on Marx's Theory of Alienation', *Science and Society*, 47/2: 129–51.

Feldstein, M. (1983), 'Domestic Savings and International Capital Movements in the Long Run and the Short Run', *European Economic Review*, 21: 139–51.

—— and Bacchetta, P. (1991), 'National Saving and International Investment', in D. B. Bernheim and J. B. Shoven (eds), *National Saving and Economic Performance* (Chicago, IL: Chicago University Press).

—— and Horioka, C. (1980), 'Domestic Savings and International Capital Flows', *Economic Journal*, 90/358: 314–29.

Felipe, J., U. Kumar, and R. Galope (2014), 'Middle-income Transition: Trap or Myth', ADB Economics Working Paper Series No. 421, November, Asian Development Bank.

Feller, D. (2000), 'Introduction', in H. Martineau (1838/2000) *Retrospect of Western Travel* (New York: M.E. Sharpe).

Fernandez, R., and Portes, J. (1998), 'Returns to Regionalism: An Analysis of Nontraditional Gains from Regional Trade Agreements', *World Bank Economic Review*, 12/2: 197–220.

Ferrantino, M. (1997), 'International Trade, Environmental Quality and Public Policy', *World Economy*, 20/1: 43–72.

Fewsmith, J. (2001), *China since Tiananmen* (Cambridge: Cambridge University Press).

Financial Times (2006), 21 December: 1.

Fewsmith, J. (2015), 'Brazil's economy shrinks by record 4.5%', 1 December.

Findlay, R., and O'Rourke, K. H. (2007), *Power and Plenty: Trade, War, and the World Economy in the Second Millennium* (Princeton, NJ: Princeton University Press).

Fine, B. (2001), 'Neither the Washington Nor the Post-Washington Consensus: An Introduction', in B. Fine, C. Lapavitsas, and J. Pincus (eds), *Development Policy in the Twenty-First Century: Beyond the Post-Washington Consensus* (London: Routledge).

Finger, J. M., and Nogués, J. J. (2002), 'The Unbalanced Uruguay Round Outcome: The New Areas in Future WTO Negotiations', *World Economy*, 25/3: 321–40.

Finlayson, J.A. and Zacher, M. (1981), 'The GATT and the Regulation of Trade Barriers: Regime Dynamics and Functions', *International Organization*, 35/4: 561–602.

Firebaugh, G. (2003), *The New Geography of Global Income Inequality* (Cambridge, MA: Harvard University Press).

Fischer, A. M. (2010), 'Towards Genuine Universalism within Contemporary Development Policy', *IDS Bulletin*, 41/1: 36–44.

Fischer, C., and Mattson, G. (2009), 'Is America Fragmenting?', *Annual Review of Sociology*, 35/1: 435–55.

Fischer, S. (2000), *On the Need for an International Lender of Last Resort* (Princeton, NJ: International Economics Section, Department of Economics, Princeton University).

Fitzgibbons, A. (1995), *Adam Smith's System of Liberty, Wealth and Virtue: The Moral and Political Foundations of the Wealth of Nations* (Oxford: Clarendon Press).

Flandreau, M., and Zumer, F. (2004), *The Making of Global Finance, 1880–1913* (Paris: OECD Development Centre).

Fleischacker, S. (2004), *On Adam Smith's Wealth of Nations: A Philosophical Companion* (Princeton, NJ: Princeton University Press).

—— (2005), *On Adam Smith's Wealth of Nations: A Philosophical Companion* (Princeton, NJ: Princeton University Press).

Force, P. (2003), *Self-Interest Before Adam Smith: A Genealogy of Economic Science* (Cambridge: Cambridge University Press).

Foroutan, F. (1998), 'Does Membership in a Regional Preferential Trade Arrangement Make a Country More or Less Protectionist?', *World Economy*, 21/3: 305–36.

Frank, A. G. (1967), *Capitalism and Underdevelopment in Latin America* (New York: Monthly Review Press).

Frankel, J. A. (1991), 'Quantifying International Capital Mobility in the 1980s', in D. Bernheim and J. Shoven (eds), *National Saving and Economic Performance* (Chicago, IL: Chicago University Press).

—— (1997), *Regional Trading Blocs in the World Economic System* (Washington, DC: Institute for International Economics).

—— (ed.) (1998), *The Regionalisation of the World Economy* (Cambridge, MA: National Bureau of Economic Research).

—— (2005), *Contractionary Currency Crashes in the Developing Countries*, CID Working Paper 117 (Cambridge, MA: Center for International Development at Harvard University).

Freedgood, E. (1999), 'Banishing Panic: Harriet Martineau and the Popularization of Political Economy', in M. Woodmansee and M. Osteen (eds) *The New Economic Criticism: Studies at the Intersection of Literature and Economics* (London: Routledge).

Freeman, R. B. (2006), *People Flows in Globalization*, NBER Working Paper 12315 (Cambridge, MA: National Bureau of Economic Research).

Frey, B. S. (1984), 'The Public Choice View of International Political Economy', *International Organization*, 38/1: 199–223.

Frey, D. (2009), *America's Economic Moralists: A History of Rival Ethics and Economics* (Albany, NY: State University of New York Press).

Frey, R. S. (1998), 'The Export of Hazardous Industries to the Peripheral Zones of the World System', *Journal of Developing Societies*, 14/1: 66–81.

—— (2003), 'The Transfer of Core-Based Hazardous Production Processes to the Export Processing Zones of the Periphery: The Maquiladora Centers of Northern Mexico', *Journal of World-Systems Research*, 9/2: 317–54.

Frieden, J. A. (1988), 'Sectoral Conflict and Foreign Economic Policy, 1914–1940', *International Organization*, 42/1: 59–90.

—— (1991), 'Invested Interests: The Politics of National Economic Policies in a World of Global Finance', *International Organization*, 45/4: 425–51.

—— (1994), 'Exchange Rate Politics', *Review of International Political Economy*, 1/1: 81–98.

—— (1997), 'Monetary Populism in Nineteenth-Century America: An Open Economy Interpretation', *Journal of Economic History*, 57/2: 367–95.

—— (2009), *Global Capitalism: Its Rise and Fall in the Twentieth Century* (New York: Norton).

—— Ghezzi, P., and Stein, E. (eds) (2001), *The Currency Game: Exchange Rate Politics in Latin America* (New York: Inter-American Development Bank).

—— and Lake, D. (1995), 'Introduction: International Politics and International Economics', in J. Frieden and D. Lake (eds), *International Political Economy: Perspectives on Global Power and Wealth*, 3rd edn (London: Routledge).

Friedman, M. (1953), 'The Case for Flexible Exchange Rates', in M. Friedman, *Essays in Positive Economics* (Chicago, IL: University of Chicago Press).

Friedman, T. (2000), *The Lexus and the Olive Tree* (New York: Anchor Books).

—— (2002), 'Techno Logic', in 'States of Discord: A Debate between Thomas Friedman and Robert Kaplan', *Foreign Policy*, 129 (March/April): 64–5.

Frobel, F., Heinrichs, J., and Kreye, O. (1980), *The New International Division of Labour: Structural Unemployment in Industrialized Countries and Industrialization in Developing Countries* (Cambridge: Cambridge University Press).

Fromm, E. (2004), *Marx's Concept of Man* (London: Continuum).

Fujii, E., and Chinn, M. (2001), 'Fin de Siècle Real Interest Parity', *Journal of International Financial Markets, Institutions and Money*, 11/3–4: 289–308.

Fukuda-Parr, S. (2004), 'Millennium Development Goals: Why they Matter', *Global Governance*, 10/4: 396–402.

Funabashi, Y. (1988), *Managing the Dollar: From the Plaza to the Louvre* (Washington, DC: Institute for International Economics).

G20 (2009a), 'London Summit: Leaders' Statement 2 April 2009' (G20 Communiqué, 2 April), http://www.g20.org/Documents/g20_communique_020409.pdf

G20 (2009b), 'Leaders' Statement: The Pittsburgh Summit, September 24–25, 2009' (G20 Communiqué, 24–25 September), http://www.g20.org/Documents/pittsburgh_summit_leaders_statement_250909.pdf

Galbraith, J. R. (2002), 'A Perfect Crime: Inequality in an Age of Globalization', *Daedalus*, 131/1: 11–25.

Gallagher, K. (2015), *Ruling Capital: Emerging Markets and the Reregulation of Cross-Border Finance* (Ithaca, NY: Cornell University Press).

Gallagher, K., and Zarsky, L. (2007), *The Enclave Economy: Foreign Investment and Sustainable Development in Mexico's Silicon Valley* (Cambridge, MA: MIT Press).

Gallarotti, G. M. (1995), *The Anatomy of an International Monetary Regime: The Classical Gold Standard, 1880–1914* (New York: Oxford University Press).

Gamble, A. (2001), 'Neo-Liberalism', *Capital and Class*, 75: 127–34.

—— and Payne, A. (eds) (1996), *Regionalism and World Order* (New York: St Martin's Press).

Garcia-Johnson, R. (2000), *Exporting Environmentalism: US Multinational Chemical Corporations in Brazil and Mexico* (Cambridge, MA: MIT Press).

Gardner, R. N. (1969), *Sterling–Dollar Diplomacy: The Origins and the Prospects of our International Economic Order*, 2nd edn (New York: McGraw-Hill).

—— (1980), *Sterling–Dollar Diplomacy in Current Perspective: The Origins and the Prospects of our International Economic Order* (New York: Columbia University Press).

Garrett, G. (1995), 'Capital Mobility, Trade, and the Domestic Politics of Economic Policy', *International Organization*, 49/4: 657–87.

—— (1998a), 'Global Markets and National Politics: Collision Course or Virtuous Circle?', *International Organization*, 52/4: 787–824.

—— (1998b), *Partisan Politics in the Global Economy* (Cambridge: Cambridge University Press).

—— (2000a), 'The Causes of Globalization', *Comparative Political Studies*, 33/6–7: 945–91.

—— (2000b), 'Shrinking States? Globalization and National Autonomy', in N. Woods (ed.), *The Political Economy of Globalization* (Basingstoke: Palgrave).

—— and Lange, P. (1996), 'Internationalization, Institutions and Political Change', in R. O. Keohane and H. V. Milner (eds), *Internationalization and Domestic Politics* (Cambridge: Cambridge University Press).

—— and Weingast, B. R. (1993), 'Ideas, Interests, and Institutions: Constructing the European Community's Internal Market', in J. Goldstein and R. O. Keohane (eds), *Ideas and Foreign Policy: Beliefs, Institutions and Political Change* (Ithaca, NY: Cornell University Press).

Gedicks, A. (2001), *Resource Rebels: Native Challenges to Mining and Oil Corporations* (Boston: South End Press).

Gee, S., and Kuo, W. J. (1997), 'Export Success and Technological Capability: Textiles and Electronics in Taiwan Province of China', in D. Ernst, T. Ganistasos, and L. Mytelka (eds), *Technological Capabilities and Export Success* (London: Routledge).

GEF (Global Environment Facility) (2009), 'What Is the GEF?', www.gefweb.org/interior_right.aspx?id=50

—— (2010), *Investing in the Phase-Out of Ozone-Depleting Substances: The GEF Experience* (Washington, DC: GEF).

Geithner, T. (2014), *Stress Test: Reflections on Financial Crises* (New York: Crown).

Gereffi, G., and Korzeniewicz, M. (eds) (1994), *Commodity Chains and Global Capitalism* (Westport, CT: Praeger).

—— and Pan, M. L. (1994), 'The Globalization of Taiwan's Garment Industry', in E. Bonacich, L. Cheng, N. Chinchilla, N. Hamilton, and P. Ong (eds), *Global Production: The Apparel Industry in the Pacific Rim* (Philadelphia, PA: Temple University Press).

—— Humphrey, J., and Sturgeon, T. (2005), 'The Governance of Global Value Chains', *Review of International Political Economy*, 12/1: 78–104.

Germain, R. (1997), *The International Organization of Credit* (Cambridge: Cambridge University Press).

Gerschenkron, A. (1962), *Economic Backwardness in Historical Perspective* (Cambridge, MA: Harvard University Press).

Geyer, M., and Bright, C. (1995), 'World History in a Global Age', *American Historical Review*, 100/4: 1034–60.

Ghosh, A. R. (1995), 'International Capital Mobility amongst the Major Industrialised Countries: Too Little or Too Much?', *Economic Journal*, 105/1: 173–80.

Ghosh, Jayati (2010), 'Global Crisis and Beyond: Sustainable Growth Trajectories for the Developing World', *International Labour Review*, 149/2: 209–25.

Giannone, D., and Lenza, M. (2004), *The Feldstein-Horioka Fact*, CEPR Discussion Paper 4610 (Paris: Centre for Economic Policy Research).

Giavazzi, F., and Pagano, M. (1988), 'The Advantage of Tying One's Hands: EMS Discipline and Central Bank Credibility', *European Economic Review*, 32/5: 1055–75.

Gibbon, Peter and Stefano Ponte (2005), *Trading Down: Africa, Value Chains and the Global Economy* (Philadelphia, PA: Temple University Press).

Giddens, A. (1984), *The Constitution of Society* (Cambridge: Polity Press).

—— (1990), *The Consequences of Modernity* (Cambridge: Polity Press).

Giessen, L. (2013), 'Reviewing the Main Characteristics of the International Forest Regime Complex and Partial Explanations for Its Fragmentation', *International Forestry Review*, 15/1: 60–70.

Gill, S. (1990), *American Hegemony and the Trilateral Commission* (Cambridge: Cambridge University Press).

—— (1995), 'Globalization, Market Civilization, and Disciplinary Neoliberalism', *Millennium: Journal of International Studies*, 24/3: 399–424.

—— (2003), *Power and Resistance in the New World Order* (Basingstoke: Palgrave).

—— and Law, D. (1988), *The Global Political Economy: Perspectives, Problems and Policies* (London: Harvester-Wheatsheaf).

—— (1989), 'Global Hegemony and the Structural Power of Capital', *International Studies Quarterly*, 33/4: 475–99.

Gilligan, M. (1997), *Empowering Exporters; Reciprocity and Collective Action in Twentieth Century American Trade Policy* (Ann Arbor, MI: University of Michigan Press).

Gilpin, R. (1975), *U.S. Power and the Multinational Corporation* (London: Macmillan).

—— (1981), *War and Change in World Politics* (Cambridge: Cambridge University Press).

—— (1987), *The Political Economy of International Relations* (Princeton, NJ: Princeton University Press).

—— (2001), *Global Political Economy: Understanding the International Economic Order* (Princeton, NJ: Princeton University Press).

—— (2002), *The Challenge of Global Capitalism: The World Economy in the 21st Century* (Princeton, NJ: Princeton University Press).

Glenn, J. (2007), *Globalization: North-South Perspectives* (London: Routledge).

Global Footprint Network (2009), Ecological Footprint Atlas 2009 (Oakland, CA: Global Footprint Network), www.footprintnetwork.org/images/uploads/Ecological_Footprint_Atlas_2009.pdf

Glyn, A. (2006), *Capitalism Unleashed: Finance, Globalization, and Welfare* (Oxford: Oxford University Press).

Goddard, R., Cronin, P., and Dash, K. (eds) (2003), *International Political Economy: State-Market Relations in a Changing Global Order*, 2nd edn (Basingstoke: Palgrave Macmillan).

Goldberg, L. G., Lothian, J. R., and Kunev, J. (2003), 'Has International Financial Integration Increased?', *Open Economies Review*, 14/3: 299–317.

Goldin, C. (1994), 'The Political Economy of Immigration Restriction in the United States, 1890 to 1921', in C. Goldin and G. Libecap (eds), *The Regulated Economy: A Historical Approach to Political Economy* (Chicago, IL: University of Chicago Press).

Goldsmith, M. M. (1990), 'Liberty, Luxury and the Pursuit of Happiness', in A. Pagden (ed.), *The Languages of Political Theory in Early-Modern Europe*, paperback edn (Cambridge: Cambridge University Press).

Goldstein, J. (1993), *Ideas, Interests, and American Trade Policy* (Ithaca, NY: Cornell University Press).

—— and Keohane, R. O. (eds) (1993), *Ideas and Foreign Policy: Beliefs, Institutions and Political Change* (Ithaca, NY: Cornell University Press).

Goodhart, C. (2011), *The Basel Committee on Banking Supervision* (Cambridge: Cambridge University Press).

—— and Illing, G. (eds) (2002), *Financial Crises, Contagion, and the Lender of Last Resort* (Oxford: Oxford University Press).

Goodin, R. E. (2003), 'Choose Your Capitalism?', *Comparative European Politics*, 1/2: 203–14.

Goodlad, L. (2004), *Victorian Literature and the Victorian State: Character and Governance in a Liberal Society* (Baltimore, MA: Johns Hopkins University Press).

Goodman, J., and Pauly, L. (1993), 'The Obsolescence of Capital Controls? Economic Management in an Age of Global Markets', *World Politics*, 46/1: 50–82.

Gordon, D. (1988), 'The Global Economy: New Edifice or Crumbling Foundations?', *New Left Review*, 168: 24–64.

Gore, C. (2000), 'The Rise and Fall of the Washington Consensus as a Paradigm for Developing Countries', *World Development*, 28/5: 789–804.

Gorodnichenko, Y., and Tesar, L. (2005), *A Re-Examination of the Border Effect*, NBER Working Paper 11706 (Cambridge, MA: National Bureau of Economic Research).

Gorton, G. (2012), *Misunderstanding Financial Crises* (Oxford: Oxford University Press).

Gowa, J. (1983), *Closing the Gold Window* (Ithaca, NY: Cornell University Press).

—— (1994), *Allies, Adversaries, and International Trade* (Princeton, NJ: Princeton University Press).

Grabel, Ilene (2013), 'Global Financial Governance and Development Finance in the Wake of the 2008 Financial Crisis', *Feminist Economics*, 19:3, 32–54.

Graham, E., and Krugman, P. R. (1995), *Foreign Direct Investment in the United States* (Washington, DC: Institute for International Economics).

Gray, J. (1998), *False Dawn: The Delusions of Global Capitalism* (London: Granta).

Greene, O. (1997), 'Environmental Issues', in J. Baylis and S. Smith (eds), *The Globalization of World Politics: An Introduction to International Relations* (Oxford: Oxford University Press).

Greenspan, A. (2008), Testimony before the House of Representatives, Committee on Oversight and Government Reform, *Bloomberg News* (online), 23 October.

Grieco, J. M., and Ikenberry, G. J. (2003), *State Power and World Markets: The International Political Economy*, 1st edn (New York: Norton).

Grimes, W. W. (2009), *Currency and Contest in East Asia: The Great Power Politics of Financial Regionalism* (Ithaca, NY: Cornell University Press).

Griswold, C. (1999), *Adam Smith and the Virtues of Enlightenment* (Cambridge: Cambridge University Press).

Grossman, G. M., and Helpman, E. (1994), 'Protection for Sale', *American Economic Review*, 84/4: 833–50.

—— (1995), 'The Politics of Free-Trade Agreements', *American Economic Review*, 85: 667–90.

—— and Krueger, A. (1995), 'Economic Growth and the Environment', *Quarterly Journal of Economics*, 110/May: 353–77.

Grundmann, R. (2001), *Transnational Environmental Policy: Reconstructing Ozone* (London: Routledge).

Gu, J., Humphrey, J., and Messner, D. (2008), 'Global Governance and Developing Countries: The Implications of the Rise of China', *World Development*, 36/2: 274–92.

Gulbrandsen, L. H. (2010), *Transnational Environmental Governance: The Emergence and Effects of the Certification of Forests and Fisheries* (Cheltenham: Edward Elgar Publishing).

Haas, E. B. (1958), *The Uniting of Europe: Political, Social and Economic Forces, 1950–1957* (Stanford, CA: Stanford University Press).

—— (1975), *The Obsolescence of Regional Integration Theory* (Berkeley, CA: Institute of International Studies, University of California).

—— (1980), 'Why Collaborate? Issue-Linkage and International Regimes', *World Politics*, 32/3: 357–405.

Haas, P. M. (1989), 'Do Regimes Matter? Epistemic Communities and Mediterranean Pollution Control', *International Organization*, 43: 377–403.

Haas, P. M. (1992), 'Introduction: Epistemic Communities and International Policy Coordination', *International Organization*, 46/1: 1–35.

Haggard, S. (1988), 'The Institutional Foundations of Hegemony: Explaining the Reciprocal Trade Agreements Act of 1934', *International Organization*, 42/1: 91–119.

—— (1990), *Pathways from the Periphery: The Politics of Growth in the Newly Industrializing Economies* (Ithaca, NY: Cornell University Press).

—— (1997), 'Regionalism in Asia and the Americas', in E. D. Mansfield and H. V. Milner (eds), *The Political Economy of Regionalism* (New York: Columbia University Press).

—— and Cheng, T.-J. (1987), 'State and Foreign Capital in the East Asian NICs', in F. Deyo (ed.), *The Political Economy of New Asian Industrialism* (Ithaca, NY: Cornell University Press).

Hainmueller, J., and Hiscox, M. J. (2007), 'Educated Preferences: Explaining Individual Attitudes toward Immigration in Europe', *International Organization*, 61/2: 399–442.

—— and Yotam Margalit (2015), 'Do Concerns about Labor Market Competition Shape Attitudes towards Immigration', *Journal of International Economics*, 97/1: 193–207.

Halifax Initiative (2002), 'Green Band-Aid Won't Save the Environment', press release, 29 August.

Hall, D. (2002), 'Environmental Change, Protest and Havens of Environmental Degradation: Evidence from Asia', *Global Environmental Politics*, 2/2: 20–8.

—— (2009), 'Pollution Export as State and Corporate Strategy: Japan in the 1970s', *Review of International Political Economy*, 16/2: 260–83.

—— (2013), *Land* (Cambridge: Polity).

Hall, P. A. (ed.) (1989), *The Political Power of Economic Ideas* (Princeton, NJ: Princeton University Press).

—— and Soskice, D. (eds) (2001), *Varieties of Capitalism: The Institutional Foundations of Comparative Advantage* (Oxford: Oxford University Press).

Hankyoreh 21 (2004), no. 513, 9 June.

Hannah, E. N. (2014), 'The Quest for Accountable Governance: Embedded NGOs and Demand Driven Advocacy in the International Trade Regime', *Journal of World Trade*, 48/3: 457–79.

Hannigan, J. (2015), *The Geopolitics of Deep Oceans* (Cambridge: Polity).

Hansen, J. *et al.* (2015), 'Ice Melt, Sea Level Rise and Superstorms: Evidence from Paleoclimate Data, Climate Modeling, and Modern Observations that 2°C Global Warming Is Highly Dangerous', *Atmospheric Chemistry and Physics* 15: 20059–20,179, doi: 10.5194/acpd-15-20059-2015.

Hardin, G. (1968), 'The Tragedy of the Commons', *Science*, 162/3859: 1243–8.

Hardt, M., and Negri, A. (2000), *Empire* (Cambridge, MA: Harvard University Press).

—— (2001), *Empire* (Cambridge, MA: Harvard University Press).

Harlen, C. M. (1999), 'A Reappraisal of Classical Economic Nationalism and Economic Liberalism', *International Studies Quarterly*, 43/4: 733–44.

Harmes, A. (1998), 'Institutional Investors and the Reproduction of Neoliberalism', *Review of International Political Economy*, 5/1: 92–121.

—— (2011), 'The Limits of Carbon Disclosure', *Global Environmental Politics*, 11/2: 98–119.

Harrison, A. E., and McMillan, M. S. (2006), *Outsourcing Jobs? Multinationals and US Employment*, NBER Working Paper 12372 (Cambridge, MA: National Bureau of Economic Research).

Harrison, G. (2004), 'Introduction: Globalisation, Governance and Development', *New Political Economy*, 9/2: 155–62.

Harvey, D. (1989), *The Condition of Postmodernity* (Oxford: Basil Blackwell).

—— (2005a), *A Brief History of Neoliberalism* (New York: Oxford University Press).

—— (2005b), *The New Imperialism* (Oxford: Oxford University Press).

Harvey, F. (2015), 'Paris Climate Change Agreement: The World's Greatest Diplomatic Success', *The Guardian*, 14 December, www.theguardian.com

Haufler, V. (1997), *Dangerous Commerce: Insurance and the Management of International Risk* (Ithaca, NY: Cornell University Press).

Hawkins, A. (2015), *Victorian Political Culture: 'Habits of Heart and Mind'* (Oxford: Oxford University Press).

Hawkins, D. G., Lake, D. A., Nielson, D. L., and Tierney, M. J. (eds) (2006), *Delegation and Agency in International Organizations* (Cambridge: Cambridge University Press).

Hay, C. (2000), 'Contemporary Capitalism, Globalization, Regionalization and the Persistence of National Variation', *Review of International Studies*, 26/4: 509–31.

—— (2002a), 'Globalization as a Problem of Political Analysis: Restoring Agents to a "Process without a Subject" and Politics to a Logic of Economic Compulsion', *Cambridge Review of International Affairs*, 15/3: 379–92.

—— (2002b), *Political Analysis* (Basingstoke: Palgrave).

—— (2003), 'What's Globalisation Got to Do with It?', Inaugural Lecture, University of Birmingham, www.polsis.bham.ac.uk/department/staff/publications/hay_inaugural.htm

—— (2004), 'Common Trajectories, Variable Paces, Divergent Outcomes? Models of European Capitalism Under Conditions of Complex Economic Interdependence', *Review of International Political Economy*, 11/2: 231–62.

—— (2007), *Why We Hate Politics* (Cambridge: Polity Press).

—— (2009), 'Good Inflation, Bad Inflation: The Housing Boom, Economic Growth and the Disaggregation of Inflationary Preferences in the UK and Ireland', *British Journal of Politics and International Studies*, 11/3: 461–78.

—— (2013), *A Very British Crisis* (Basingstoke: PIVOT/Palgrave).

—— (2014), *The Failure of Anglo-Liberal Capitalism* (New York: Palgrave Macmillan).

—— and Rosamond, B. (2002), 'Globalisation, European Integration and the Discursive Construction of Economic Imperatives', *Journal of European Public Policy*, 9/2: 147–67.

—— and Watson, M. (1998), 'Rendering the Contingent Necessary: New Labour's Neo-Liberal Conversion and the Discourse of Globalisation', *Center for European Studies Working Paper* (Boston: Center for European Studies, Harvard University).

—— and Wincott, D. (2012), *The Political Economy of European Welfare Capitalism* (Basingstoke: Palgrave).

Hayek, F. (1944), *The Road to Serfdom* (London: Routledge).

Heilbroner, R. (2000), *The Worldly Philosophers: The Lives, Times and Ideas of the Great Economic Thinkers*, rev. 7th edn (London: Penguin).

Held, D., and McGrew, A. (2002), *Globalization/Anti-Globalization* (Cambridge: Polity Press).

—— Goldblatt, D., and Perraton, J. (1999), *Global Transformations: Politics, Economics and Culture* (Cambridge: Polity Press).

Helleiner, E. (1994), *States and the Reemergence of Global Finance* (Ithaca, NY: Cornell University Press).

—— (1997), 'Braudelian Reflections on Economic Globalization: The Historian as Pioneer', in S. Gill and J. Mittleman (eds), *Innovation and Transformation in International Studies* (Cambridge: Cambridge University Press).

—— (2001), 'Regulating Capital Flight', *Challenge*, 44/1: 19–34.

—— (2003), *The Making of National Money: Territorial Currencies in Historical Perspective* (Ithaca, NY: Cornell University Press).

—— (2005), 'Conclusion: The Meaning and Contemporary Significance of Economic Nationalism', in E. Helleiner and A. Pickel (eds), *Economic Nationalism in a Globalizing World* (Ithaca, NY: Cornell University Press).

—— (2006), *Towards North American Monetary Union? The Politics and History of Canada's Exchange Rate Regime* (Montreal: McGill-Queen's University Press).

—— (2009), 'The Development Mandate of International Institutions: Where Did It Come from?', *Studies in Comparative and International Development*, 44/3: 189–211.

—— (2010), 'What Role for the New Financial Stability Board? The Politics of International Standards after the Crisis', *Global Policy*, 1: 282–90.

—— (2012), 'The Limits of Incrementalism: The G20, the FSB, and the International Regulatory Agenda', *Journal of Globalization and Development*, 2/2: 1–19.

—— (2014a), *The Forgotten Foundations of Bretton Woods: International Development and the Making of the Postwar Order* (Ithaca, NY: Cornell University Press).

—— (2014b), *The Status Quo Crisis: Global Financial Governance After the 2008 Crisis* (Oxford: Oxford University Press).

—— and Cameron, G. (2006), 'Another World Order? The Bush Administration and HIPC Debt Cancellation', *New Political Economy*, 11/1: 125–40.

—— and Kirshner, J. (eds) (2008), 'Special Issue: At Home Abroad? The Dollar's Destiny as a World Currency', *Review of International Political Economy*, 15/3: 335–459.

—— (eds) (2009a), *The Future of the Dollar* (Ithaca, NY: Cornell University Press).

—— (eds) (2009b), 'Special Section: The Geopolitics of Sovereign Wealth Funds', *Geopolitics*, 14/2: 300–75.

—— and Lundblad, T. (2008), 'States, Markets, and Sovereign Wealth Funds', *German Policy Studies*, 4/3: 59–82.

—— Pagliari, S., and Zimmermann, H. (eds) (2009), *Global Finance in Crisis* (London: Routledge).

Helleiner, G. K. (1996), 'Why Small Countries Worry: Neglected Issues in Current Analyses of the Benefits and Costs for Small Countries of Integrating with Large Ones', *World Economy*, 19/6: 759–63.

Henderson, C. (1998), *Asia Falling: Making Sense of the Asian Crisis and its Aftermath* (New York: McGraw-Hill).

Henderson, W. (1995), *Economics as Literature* (London: Routledge).

—— (2006), *Evaluating Adam Smith: Creating the Wealth of Nations* (London: Routledge).

Henning, C. R. (1987), *Macroeconomic Diplomacy in the 1980s* (London: Croom Helm).

—— (1998), 'Systemic Conflict and Regional Monetary Integration: The Case of Europe', *International Organization*, 52/3: 537–73.

—— (2002), *East Asian Financial Cooperation*, Policy Analyses in International Economics, 68 (Washington, DC: Institute for International Economics).

Herrigel, G. (1996), *Industrial Constructions: The Source of German Industrial Power* (Cambridge: Cambridge University Press).

Hickey, S., and du Toit, A. (2007), *Adverse Incorporation, Social Exclusion and Chronic Poverty*, Working Paper No. 81 (Manchester: Chronic Poverty Research Centre).

Hickmann, T. (2016), *Rethinking Authority in Global Climate Governance: How Transnational Climate Initiatives Relate to the International Climate Regime* (New York: Routledge).

Higgott, R. (2004), 'US Foreign Policy and the 'Securitization' of Economic Globalization', *International Politics*, 41/2: 147–75.

—— and Phillips, N. (2000), 'Challenging Triumphalism and Convergence: The Limits of Global Liberalisation in Asia and Latin America', *Review of International Studies*, 26/3: 359–79.

—— and Watson, M. (2008), 'All at Sea in a Barbed Wire Canoe: Professor Cohen's Transatlantic Voyage in IPE', *Review of International Political Economy*, 15/1: 1–17.

Hilferding, R. (1910/1981), *Finance Capital: A Study of the Latest Phase of Capitalist Development*, tr. M. Watrick and G. Gordon (London: Routledge & Kegan Paul).

Hines, C. (2000), *Localization: A Global Manifesto* (London: Earthscan).

Hironaka, A. (2014), *Greening the Globe: World Society and Environmental Change* (Cambridge: Cambridge University Press).

Hirschman, A. O. (1945), *National Power and the Structure of Foreign Trade* (Berkeley and Los Angeles, CA: University of California Press).

Hirst, P., and Thompson, G. (1996), *Globalization in Question*, 1st edn (Cambridge: Polity Press).

—— (1999), *Globalization in Question*, 2nd edn (Cambridge: Polity Press).

—— (2003), 'Globalization: A Necessary Myth?', in D. Held and A. McGrew (eds), *The Global Transformations Reader*, 2nd edn (Cambridge: Polity Press).

—— and Bromley, S. (2009), *Globalization in Question*, 3rd edn (Cambridge: Polity Press).

Hiscox, M. J. (1999), 'The Magic Bullet? The RTAA, Institutional Reform, and Trade Liberalization', *International Organization*, 53/4: 669–98.

—— (2002), *International Trade and Political Conflict* (Princeton, NJ: Princeton University Press).

Hobson, J. A. (1902/1948), *Imperialism* (London: Allen & Unwin).

Hoekman, B. (ed.) (2015), *The Global Trade Slowdown: A New Normal?* (London: CEPR).

—— and Kostecki, M. (1995), *The Political Economy of the World Trading System* (Oxford: Oxford University Press).

—— (2009), *The Political Economy of the World Trading System: The WTO and Beyond*, 3rd edn (Oxford: Oxford University Press).

Hoffmann, M. (1998), *Long Run Capital Flows and the Feldstein-Horoika Puzzle: A New Measure of International Capital Mobility and Some Historical Evidence from Great Britain and the United States*, EUI Working Paper 1998/30 (Florence: European University Institute).

—— (2011), *Climate Governance at a Crossroads: Experimenting with a Global Response after Kyoto* (Oxford: Oxford University Press).

Hoffmann, S. (1966), 'Obstinate or Obsolete? The Fate of the Nation-State in Europe', *Daedalus*, 95/3: 862–915.

Holliday, C. O., Jr., Schmidheiny, S., and Watts, P. (2002), *Walking the Talk: The Business Case for Sustainable Development* (Sheffield: Greenleaf).

Holme, R., and Watts, P. (2000), *Corporate Social Responsibility: Making Good Business Sense* (Conches-Geneva: World Business Council for Sustainable Development).

Holsti, O. R. (1996), *Public Opinion and American Foreign Policy* (Ann Arbor, MI: University of Michigan Press).

Hoogvelt, A. (1978), *The Sociology of Developing Societies* (London: Macmillan).

—— (1997), *Globalisation and the Postcolonial World: The New Political Economy of Development* (Basingstoke: Macmillan).

—— (2001), *Globalization and the Post-Colonial World* (Basingstoke: Palgrave).

Hörnqvist, M. (2000), 'The Two Myths of Civic Humanism', in J. Hankins (ed.), *Renaissance Civic Humanism* (Cambridge: Cambridge University Press)

Horta, K., Round, R., and Young, Z. (2002), *The Global Environment Facility: The First Ten Years—Growing Pains or Inherent Flaws?* (Washington, DC and Ottawa: Environmental Defense and Halifax Initiative).

Huber, E., Ragin, C., Stephens, J. D., Brady, D., and Beckfield, D. (2004), *Comparative Welfare States Data Set* (Northwestern University and University of North Carolina), www.lisproject.org/publications/welfaredata/welfareaccess.htm

Hudec, R. E. (1975), *The GATT Legal System and World Trade Diplomacy* (New York: Praeger).

—— Kennedy, D. and Sgarbossa, M. (1993), 'A Statistical Profile of GATT Dispute Settlement Cases: 1948–1989', *Minnesota Journal of Global Trade*, 2/1: 1–25.

Hufbauer, G. C., and Wong, Y. (2004), 'China Bashing 2004', *International Economics Policy Briefs*, Number PB04-5 (September): 1–53.

Hulme, D., and Scott, J. (2010), 'The Political Economy of the MDGs: Retrospect and Prospect for the World's Biggest Promise', *New Political Economy*, 15/2: 293–306.

—— and Wilkinson, R. (2012), 'Moving from MDGs to GDGs: Development Imperatives Beyond 2015', in R. Wilkinson and D. Hulme (eds), *The Millennium Development Goals and Beyond: Global Development After 2015* (London: Routledge).

Hummels, D. (2001), 'The Nature and Growth of Vertical Specialization in World Trade', *Journal of International Economics*, 54/1: 75–96.

Humphrey, J., and Memedovic, O. (2003), *The Global Automotive Value Chain* (Vienna: United Nations Industrial Development Organization).

—— and Schmitz, H. (2000), *Governance and Upgrading: Linking Industrial Cluster and Global Value Chain Research*, IDS Working Paper 120 (Brighton: Institute of Development Studies, University of Sussex).

—— (2001), 'Governance in Global Value Chains', *IDS Bulletin*, 32/3: 19–29.

Humphreys, D. (1999), 'The Evolving Forests Regime', *Global Environmental Change*, 9/3: 251–54.

—— (2003), 'Life Protective or Carcinogenic Challenge? Global Forests Governance under Advanced Capitalism', *Global Environmental Politics*, 3/2: 40–55.

—— (2006), *Logjam: Deforestation and the Crisis of Global Governance* (London: Earthscan).

Hundert, E. (1994), *The Enlightenment's Fable: Bernard Mandeville and the Discovery of Society* (Cambridge: Cambridge University Press).

Hutchison, T. (1998), 'Ultra-Deductivism from Nassau Senior to Lionel Robbins and Daniel Hausman', *Journal of Economic Methodology*, 5/1: 43–91.

Huzel, J. (2006), *The Popularization of Malthus in Early Nineteenth Century England: Martineau, Cobbett and the Pauper Press* (Aldershot: Ashgate).

Hymer, S. (1976), *The International Operations of National Firms* (Cambridge: MIT Press).

IDB (Inter-American Development Bank) (2008), 'Countries Need to Spend More to Prevent Food Crisis from Deepening Poverty', 12 August, www.iadb.org/features-and-web-stories/2008-08/english/countries-need-to-spend-more-to-prevent-food-crisis-from-deepening-poverty-4718.html

—— (2009), 'Fact Sheet: Poverty Scenarios and the Crisis', http://idbdocs.iadb.org/wsdocs/getdocument.aspx?docnum=1885962

Ikeda, S. (2004), 'Zonal Structure and the Trajectories of Canada, Mexico, Australia, and Norway under Neo-liberal Globalization', in M. G. Cohen and S. Clarkson (eds), *Governing Under Stress: Middle Powers and the Challenge of Globalization* (London: Zed Books).

Ikenberry, G. J. (2001), *After Victory* (Princeton, NJ: Princeton University Press).

—— and Kupchan, C. A. (1990), 'Socialization and Hegemonic Power', *International Organization*, 44/3: 283–315.

ILO (International Labour Organization) (1976), *Employment, Growth and Basic Needs: A One-World Problem* (Geneva: ILO).

IMF (International Monetary Fund) (2002), *World Economic Outlook: Trade and Finance* (Washington, DC: IMF).

—— (2003), *World Economic Outlook: Trade and Finance* (Washington, DC: IMF).

—— (2008), 'Global Financial Stability Report: Constraining Systemic Risks and Restoring Financial Soundness' (Washington, DC: IMF, April) http://www.imf.org/External/Pubs/FT/GFSR/2008/01/pdf/text.pdf

IMF (International Monetary Fund) (2009a), 'Group of Twenty: Meeting of the Deputies January 31–1 February 2009, London UK' (Washington, DC: IMF, Note by the Staff of the International Monetary Fund), http://www.imf.org/external/np/g20/pdf/020509.pdf

—— (2009b), 'Global Financial Stability Report: Navigating the Financial Challenges Ahead' (Washington, DC: IMF, October).

—— (2009c), 'The Multilateral Debt Initiative (MDRI): Factsheet', June, www.imf.org/external/np/exr/facts/mdri.htm

—— (2009d), World Economic Outlook (Washington, DC: IMF, October).

—— (2010a), World Economic Outlook: Trade and Finance (Washington, DC: IMF).

—— (2010b), World Economic Outlook Update: A Policy-Driven, Multi-speed Recovery (Washington, DC: IMF, 26 January), http://www.imf.org/external/pubs/ft/weo/2010/update/01/pdf/0110.pdf

—— (2010c), World Economic Outlook April 2010 (Washington, DC: International Monetary Fund).

—— (2012a), Global Financial Stability Report: Restoring Confidence and Progressing on Reforms, October (Washington, DC: IMF).

—— (2012b), World Economic Outlook, October 2012 Special feature: Commodity Market Review (Washington: International Monetary Fund).

—— (2012c), The Liberalization and Management of Capital Flows: An Institutional View (Washington: International Monetary Fund).

—— (2015a), Global Financial Stability Report April 2015 (Washington, DC: IMF)

—— (2015b), Global Financial Stability Report October 2015 (Washington, DC: IMF)

—— (2015c), World Economic Outlook October 2015 (Washington, DC: International Monetary Fund).

—— (2016), Global Financial Stability Report April 2016: Potent Policies for a Successful Normalization (Washington, DC: IMF).

—— (various years), Financial Statistics Yearbook (Washington, DC: IMF).

Imura, H., and Schreurs, M. A. (eds) (2005), Environmental Policy in Japan (Cheltenham: Edward Elgar in association with the World Bank).

IOM (International Organization for Migration) (2005), World Migration 2005: Costs and Benefits of International Migration (Geneva: International Organization for Migration).

—— (2012), World Migration Report 2012 (Geneva: International Organization for Migration).

—— (2015), World Migration Report 2015: Migrants and Cities (Geneva: International Organization for Migration).

IPCC (Intergovernmental Panel on Climate Change) (2001), Climate Change 2001: The Scientific Basis (Cambridge: Cambridge University Press for IPCC).

Irwin, D. (1996), Against the Tide: An Intellectual History of Free Trade (Princeton, NJ: Princeton University Press).

—— (2002), 'Long-Run Trends in World Income and Trade', World Trade Review, 1/1: 89–100.

—— (2003), 'Explaining America's Surge in Manufacturing Exports, 1880–1913', Review of Economics and Statistics, 85/2: 364–76.

—— (2011), Peddling Protectionism: Smoot-Hawley and the Great Depression (Princeton, NJ: Princeton University Press).

—— and Kroszner, R. S. (1997), Interests, Institutions and Ideology in the Republican Conversion to Trade Liberalization, 1934–45, NBER Working Paper 6112 (Cambridge, MA: National Bureau of Economic Research).

Ismail, F. (2012), 'Towards and Alternative Narrative for the Multilateral Trading System', Presentation of the Ambassador Permanent Representative of South Africa to the WTO to the UNCTAD Trade and Development Board, 18 September, Geneva: UNCTAD.

ISO (International Organization for Standardization) (2008), The ISO Survey: 2007 www.iso.org/iso/survey2007.pdf

Iversen, T., Pontusson, J., and Soskice, D. (eds) (2000), Unions, Employers and Central Banks: Macroeconomic Coordination and Institutional Change in Social Market Economies (Cambridge: Cambridge University Press).

Jackson, J. H. (1969), World Trade and the Law of the GATT (Indianapolis, IN: Bobbs-Merrill).

—— (1998), The World Trade Organization: Constitution and Jurisprudence (London: Pinter).

Jackson, R. H. (1993), 'The Weight of Ideas in Decolonization: Normative Change in International Relations', in J. Goldstein and R. O. Keohane (eds), Ideas and Foreign Policy: Beliefs, Institutions and Political Change (Ithaca, NY: Cornell University Press).

Jackson, R. T., and Banks, G. (2003), In Search of the Serpent's Skin: The Story of the Porgera Gold Project (Brisbane: Boolorong Press).

James, H. (1996), International Monetary Cooperation since Bretton Woods (Washington, DC: IMF).

—— (2001), The End of Globalization: Lessons from the Great Depression (Cambridge, MA: Harvard University Press).

—— (2009), The Creation and Destruction of Value: The Globalization Cycle (Cambridge, MA: Harvard University Press).

Jasanoff, S. (2007), 'Bhopal's Trails of Knowledge and Ignorance', ISIS: An International Review Devoted to the History of Science and Its Cultural Influences, 98/2: 344–50.

Jenkins, R. (1987), Transnational Corporations and Uneven Development (London: Methuen).

Jerven, M. (2013), Poor Numbers: How We Are Misled by African Development Statistics and What to Do About It (Ithaca, NY: Cornell University Press).

Jessop, B. (1998), 'The Rise of Governance and the Risks of Failure: The Case of Economic Development', International Social Science Journal, 50/155: 29–45.

—— (2002), The Future of the Capitalist State (Cambridge: Polity Press).

Jevons, W. S. (1871/1970), The Theory of Political Economy (Harmondsworth: Pelican).

Johannesburg Declaration on Sustainable Development (2002), Official Document of the 2002 World Summit on Sustainable Development, 4 September.

Johnson, C. (1982), MITI and the Japanese Miracle (Stanford, CA: Stanford University Press).

Johnston, A. (2016), From Convergence to Crisis: Labor Markets and the Instability of the Euro (Ithaca, NY: Cornell University Press).

Jones, R. (1971), 'A Three-Factor Model in Theory, Trade, and History', in B. Jagdish, R. Jones, R. A. Mundell, and J. Vanek (eds), *Trade, Balance of Payments, and Growth* (Amsterdam: North-Holland).

Jones, V. C. (2006), 'WTO: Antidumping Issues in the Doha Development Agenda', CRS Report for Congress (Washington, DC: Congressional Research Service, Library of Congress).

Jordan (2003), *New York Times*, 4 October: A15.

Josselin, D. (2001), 'Trade Unions for EMU: Sectorial Preferences and Political Opportunities', *West European Politics*, 24/1: 55–74.

Kahler, M. (1992), 'Multilateralism with Small and Large Numbers', *International Organization*, 46/3: 681–708.

Kaltenthaler, K. (1998), *Germany and the Politics of Europe's Money* (Durham, NC: Duke University Press).

Kang, D. (2002), *Crony Capitalism: Corruption and Development in South Korea and the Philippines* (Cambridge: Cambridge University Press).

Kanie, N., and Andresen, S. (2015), *Improving Global Environmental Governance: Best Practices for Architecture and Agency* (New York: Routledge).

Kaplinsky, R. (2000), 'Governance and Unequalisation: What Can Be Learned from Value Chain Analysis?', *Journal of Development Studies*, 37/2: 117–46.

—— (2005), *Globalization, Poverty and Inequality: Between a Rock and a Hard Place* (Cambridge: Polity Press).

Kapstein, E. B. (1994), *Governing the Global Economy: International Finance and the State* (Cambridge, MA: Harvard University Press).

—— (2000), 'Winners and Losers in the Global Economy', *International Organization*, 54/2: 359–84.

Kapur, D. (2002), 'The Changing Anatomy of Governance of the World Bank', in J. Pincus and J. A. Winters (eds), *Reinventing the World Bank* (Ithaca, NY: Cornell University Press).

—— and McHale, J. (2003), 'Migration's New Payoff', *Foreign Policy*, 139 (November-December): 49–57.

Karliner, J. (1997), *The Corporate Planet, Ecology and Politics in the Age of Globalization* (San Francisco: Sierra Club).

Kasman, B., and Pigott, C. (1988), 'Interest Rate Divergences amongst the Major Industrial Nations', *Federal Reserve Bank of New York Quarterly Review*, 13/3: 28–44.

Katada, S. (2002), 'Japan and Asian Monetary Regionalization: Cultivating a New Regional Leadership After the Asian Financial Crisis', *Geopolitics*, 7/1: 85–112.

Katzenstein, P. J. (ed.) (1978), *Between Power and Plenty: Foreign Economic Policies of Advanced Industriala States* (Madison, WI: University of Wisconsin Press).

—— (1985), *Small States in World Markets: Industrial Policy in Europe* (Ithaca, NY: Cornell University Press).

Kay, C. (1989), *Latin American Theories of Development and Underdevelopment* (London: Routledge).

Kearney, A. T., and Foreign Policy Globalization Index (2003), 'Measuring Globalization: Who's Up, Who's Down?', *Foreign Policy*, 134 (January–February): 60–72.

—— (2005), 'Measuring Globalization', *Foreign Policy*, 148 (May–June): 53–60.

Keck, M. E., and Sikkink, K. (1998), *Activists beyond Borders: Advocacy Networks in International Politics* (Ithaca, NY: Cornell University Press).

Keegan, J. (1998), *The First World War* (London: Random House).

Kelton, M. (2008), 'US Economic Statecraft in East Asia', *International Relations of Asia and the Pacific*, 8/2: 149–74.

Kenealy, Daniel, Peterson, J., and Richard, C. (2015), *The European Union: How Does It Work?* (Oxford: Oxford University Press).

Keohane, R. O. (1984), *After Hegemony: Cooperation and Discord in the World Political Economy* (Princeton, NJ: Princeton University Press).

—— (1997), 'Problematic Lucidity: Stephen Krasner's "State Power and the Structure of International Trade"', *World Politics*, 50/1: 150–70.

—— (2011), 'The Old IPE and the New', in N. Phillips and C. Weaver (eds), *International Political Economy: Debating the Past, Present and Future* (London: Routledge).

—— and Nye, J. S. (eds) (1972), *Transnational Relations and World Politics* (Cambridge, MA: Harvard University Press).

—— (1977), *Power and Interdependence* (Boston: Little, Brown).

—— (2003), 'Globalization: What's New? What's Not? (And So What?)', in D. Held and A. McGrew (eds), *The Global Transformations Reader* (Cambridge: Polity Press).

Keynes, J. M. (1925), *The Economic Consequences of Mr. Churchill* (London: L. and V. Woolf).

—— (1933), 'National Self-Sufficiency', *Yale Review*, 22: 755–69.

—— (1936), *General Theory of Employment, Interest and Money* (New York: Harcourt, Brace).

Keynes, J. N. (1891/1970), *The Scope and Method of Political Economy*, repr. 4th edn (New York: Augustus M. Kelley).

Kindleberger, C. P. (1951), 'Group Behavior and International Trade', *Journal of Political Economy*, 59/1: 30–46.

—— (1969), *American Business Abroad: Six Lectures on Direct Investment* (New Haven: Yale University Press).

—— (1973), *The World in Depression, 1929–1939* (Berkeley and Los Angeles, CA: University of California Press).

—— (1975), 'The Rise of Free Trade in Western Europe', *Journal of Economic History*, 35/1: 20–55.

—— (1978), *Manias, Panics, and Crashes: A History of Financial Crises* (New York: Basic Books).

Kirshner, J. (1995), *Currency and Coercion: The Political Economy of International Monetary Power* (Princeton, NJ: Princeton University Press).

—— (ed.) (2003), *Monetary Orders: Ambiguous Economics, Ubiquitous Politics* (Ithaca, NY: Cornell University Press).

—— (2007), *Appeasing Bankers: Financial Caution on the Road to War* (Princeton, NJ: Princeton University Press).

—— (2011), 'The Second Crisis in IPE Theory', in N. Phillips and C. Weaver (eds), *International Political Economy: Debating the Past, Present and Future* (London: Routledge).

Kiser, E., and Laing, A. M. (2001), 'Have We Overestimated the Effects of Neoliberalism and Globalization? Some Speculations on the Anomalous Stability of Taxes on Business', in J. L. Campbell and O. K. Pedersen (eds), *The Rise of Neoliberalism and Institutional Analysis* (Princeton, NJ: Princeton University Press).

Kissinger, M., and Rees, W. (2010), 'Importing Terrestrial Biocapacity: The U.S. Case and Global Implications', *Land Use Policy*, 27/2: 589–99.

Kitschelt, H., Lange, P., Marks, G. and Stephens, J. (1999), 'Convergence and Divergence in Advanced Capitalist Democracies', in H. Kitschelt, P. Lange, G. Marks and J. Stephens (eds) *Continuity and Change in Contemporary Capitalism* (Cambridge: Cambridge University Press).

—— (eds) (1999), *Continuity and Change in Contemporary Capitalism* (Cambridge: Cambridge University Press).

Klaver, C. (2003), *A/Moral Economics: Classical Political Economy and Cultural Authority in Nineteenth-Century England* (Columbus, OH: Ohio State University Press).

Klein, N. (2002), *No Logo* (New York: Picador).

—— (2007), *The Shock Doctrine: The Rise of Disaster Capitalism* (New York: St Martin's Press).

Kleinknecht, A., and ter Wengel, J. (1998), 'The Myth of Economic Globalization', *Cambridge Journal of Economics*, 22/5: 637–47.

Knight, F. (1921), *Risk, Uncertainty and Profit* (Chicago, IL: University of Chicago Press).

Knight, J. (1992), *Institutions and Social Conflict* (Cambridge: Cambridge University Press).

KOF (2010), 'KOF Index of Globalization 2010', http://globalization.kof.ethz.ch

Kohli, A. (2004), *State-Directed Development: Political Power and Industrialization in the Global Periphery* (Cambridge: Cambridge University Press).

Kolm, S. (1976a), 'Unequal Inequalities I', *Journal of Economic Theory*, 12/3: 416–54.

—— (1976b), 'Unequal Inequalities II', *Journal of Economic Theory*, 13/1: 82–111.

Koopman, R., Wang, Z., and Wei, S.-J. (2008), *How Much of Chinese Exports Is Really Made in China? Assessing Domestic Value-Added when Processing Trade Is Pervasive*, NBER Working Paper 14109 (Cambridge, MA: National Bureau of Economic Research).

Koremenos, B., Lipson, C., and Snidal, D. (2001), 'The Rational Design of International Institutions', *International Organization*, 55/4: 761–99.

Koremenos, B., and Snidal, D. (2003), 'Moving Forward, One Step at a Time', *International Organization*, 57: 431–44.

Korten, D. C. (2001), *When Corporations Rule the World*, 2nd edn (San Francisco: Berrett-Koehler).

Korzeniewicz, R. (2009), *Unveiling Inequality: A World-Historical Perspective* (New York: Russell Sage Foundation).

—— (2012), 'Trends in World Income Inequality and the 'Emerging Middle"', *European Journal of Development Research*, 24/2: 205–22.

—— and Moran, T. (2006), 'World Inequality in the Twenty-First Century: Patterns and Tendencies', in G. Ritzer (ed.), *The Blackwell Companion to Globalization* (Oxford: Blackwell).

—— Stach, A., Patil, V., and Moran, T. (2004), 'Measuring National Income: A Critical Assessment', *Comparative Studies in Society and History*, 46/3: 535–86.

Krasner, S. D. (1976), 'State Power and the Structure of International Trade', *World Politics*, 28/3: 317–47.

—— (ed.) (1983), *International Regimes* (Ithaca, NY: Cornell University Press).

—— (1985), *Structural Conflict: The Third World Against Global Liberalism* (Berkeley and Los Angeles, CA: University of California Press).

—— (1991), 'Global Communications and National Power: Life on the Pareto Frontier', *World Politics*, 43/3: 336–66.

—— (1994), 'International Political Economy: Abiding Discord', *Review of International Political Economy*, 1/1: 13–19.

—— (1999), *Sovereignty: Organized Hypocrisy* (Princeton, NJ: Princeton University Press).

Krikorian, J. D. (2012), *International Trade Law and Domestic Policy* (Vancouver, BC: UBC Press).

Krueger, A. O. (1995), *Trade Policies and Developing Nations* (Washington, DC: Brookings Institution).

—— (1999), 'Are Preferential Trading Arrangements Trade-Liberalizing or Protectionist?', *Journal of Economic Perspectives*, 13/4: 105–24.

—— (2002), *A New Approach to Sovereign Debt Restructuring, Pamphlet Series* (Washington, DC: IMF).

Krugman, P. R. (1990), 'Import Protection as Export Promotion: International Competition in the Presence of Oligopoly and Economies of Scale', in P. R. Krugman (ed.), *Rethinking International Trade* (Cambridge, MA: MIT Press)

—— (1994), 'Does Third World Growth Hurt First World Prosperity?', *Harvard Business Review* (July): 113–21.

—— (1995), 'Dutch Tulips and Emerging Markets', *Foreign Affairs*, 74/4: 28–44.

—— (2009), 'How Did Economists Get It So Wrong?', *New York Times Magazine*, 6 September.

—— and Obstfeld, M. (2000), *International Economics: Theory and Policy*, 5th edn (New York: Addison-Wesley).

Kumar, S., and Rao, B. B. (2011), 'A Time-Series Approach to the Feldstein–Horioka Puzzle with Panel Data from the OECD Countries', *World Economy*, 34/3: 473–85.

Kurtz, M., and A. Shrank. (2007), 'Growth and Governance: Models, Measures and Mechanisms', *Journal of Politics*, 69: 538–54.

Kurzer, P. (1993), *Business and Banking: Political Change and Economic Integration in Western Europe* (Ithaca, NY: Cornell University Press).

Lall, S. (2004), *Reinventing Industrial Strategy: The Role of Government Policy in Building Industrial Competitiveness*, G-24 Discussion Paper Series No. 28 (New York and Geneva: United Nations).

Landreth, H., and Colander, D. (1994), *History of Economic Thought*, 3rd edn (Boston: Houghton Mifflin).

Lane, P. (2012), *Financial Globalization and the Crisis*, BIS Working Paper 397 (Geneva: Bank for International Settlements).

—— and Milesi-Ferretti, G. M. (2003), 'International Financial Integration', *IMF Staff Papers*, 50/Special Issue: 82–100.

Lang, A., and Scott, J. (2009), 'The Hidden World of WTO Governance', *European Journal of International Law*, 20/3: 575–614.

Lasswell, H. D. (1936), *Politics: Who Gets What, When, How* (New York: Whittlesey House, McGraw-Hill).

Lawrence, R. Z. (1996a), *Regionalism, Multilateralism, and Deeper Integration* (Washington, DC: Brookings Institution).

—— (1996b), *Single World, Divided Nations? International Trade and OECD Labor Markets* (Washington, DC: Brookings Institution).

Lazonick, W. (2008), 'Entrepreneurial Ventures and the Developmental State', UNU-WIDER Discussion Paper 2008/01.

Leamer, E., and Levinsohn, J. (1995), 'International Trade Theory: The Evidence', in G. Grossman and K. Rogoff (eds), *Handbook of International Economics*, iii (Amsterdam: North-Holland).

Leftwich, A. (2000), *States of Development: On the Primacy of Politics in Development* (Cambridge: Polity).

Lenin, V. I. (1917/96), *Imperialism, the Highest Stage of Capitalism: A Popular Outline* (London: Pluto Press).

Lerner, D. (1972), 'Modernization: Social Aspects', in D. Sills (ed.), *International Encyclopedia of the Social Sciences*, ix (New York: Collier Macmillan).

Levi-Faur, D. (1997), 'Friedrich List and the Political Economy of the Nation-State', *Review of International Political Economy*, 4/1: 154–78.

Levinson, M. (2006), *How the Shipping Container Made the World Smaller and the World Economy Bigger* (Princeton, NJ: Princeton University Press).

Lewis, A. (1981), 'The Rate of Growth of World Trade, 1830–1973', in S. Grassman and E. Lundberg (eds), *The World Economic Order: Past and Prospects* (London: Macmillan).

Lewis, M. (2012), 'Obama's Way', *Vanity Fair*, October.

Leys, C. (1996), 'The Crisis in "Development Theory"', *New Political Economy*, 1/1: 41–58.

—— (2001), *Market-Driven Politics: Neoliberal Democracy and the Public Interest* (London: Verso).

Lim, C. L., Elms, D. K., and Low, P. (eds) (2012), *The Trans-Pacific Partnership: A Quest for a Twenty-First Century Trade Agreement* (Cambridge: Cambridge University Press).

Lindberg, L. N. (1963), *The Political Dynamics of European Economic Integration* (Stanford, CA: Stanford University Press).

Lindemann, S. (2008), 'Understanding Water Regime Formation: A Research Framework with Lessons from Europe', *Global Environmental Politics*, 8/4: 117–40.

Lindert, P. H., and Williamson, J. G. (2001), *Does Globalization Make the World More Unequal?*, NBER Working Paper W8228 (Cambridge, MA: National Bureau of Economic Research).

—— (2003), 'Does Globalization Make the World More Unequal?' in M. D. Bordo, A. M. Taylor, and J. G. Williamson (eds), *Globalization in Historical Perspective* (Chicago, IL: University of Chicago Press).

Lissakers, K. (1991), *Banks, Borrowers and the Establishment* (New York: Basic Books).

—— (1841/2005a), *National System of Political Economy*, i. *The History* (New York: Cosimo Classics).

—— (1841/2005b), *National System of Political Economy*, ii. *The Theory* (New York: Cosimo Classics).

—— (1841/2005c), *National System of Political Economy*, iii. *The Systems and the Politics* (New York: Cosimo Classics).

—— (1966 [1841–4]), *The National System of Political Economy* (New York: Augustus Kelly).

List, F. (1841/2005a), *National System of Political Economy—Volume 1: The History* (New York: Cosimo Classics).

—— (1841/2005b), *National System of Political Economy—Volume 2: The Theory* (New York: Cosimo Classics).

—— (1841/2005c), *National System of Political Economy—Volume 3: The Systems and the Politics* (New York: Cosimo Classics).

Lister, J. (2011), *Corporate Social Responsibility and the State: International Approaches to Forest Co-Regulation* (Vancouver, BC: UBC Press).

Locke, R. M. (1995), *Remaking the Italian Economy* (Ithaca, NY: Cornell University Press).

—— (2003), 'The Promise and Perils of Globalization: The Case of Nike', in T. A. Kochan and R. Schmalensee (eds), *Management: Inventing and Delivering Its Future* (Boston: MIT Press).

Locke, R., and Kochan, T. (1985), 'The Transformation of Industrial Relations? A Cross-National Review of the Evidence', in R. Locke, T. Kochan, and M. Piore (eds), *Employment Relations in a Changing World* (Cambridge, MA: MIT Press).

Logan, D. A. (2004), 'Introduction', in H. Martineau (1832–4/2004) *Illustrations of Political Economy: Selected Tales* (Orchard Park, NY: Broadview Press).

Lohmann, L. (1993), 'Resisting Green Globalism', in W. Sachs (ed.), *Global Ecology: A New Arena of Political Conflict* (London: Zed Books).

Lohmann, S. (1997), 'Linkage Politics', *Journal of Conflict Resolution*, 41/1: 38–67.

Lomborg, B. (2001), *The Skeptical Environmentalist* (Cambridge: Cambridge University Press).

—— (2007), *Cool It: The Skeptical Environmentalist's Guide to Global Warming* (New York: Alfred A. Knopf).

Lomborg, B. (ed.) (2009), *Global Crises, Global Solutions: Costs and Benefits*, 2nd edn (Cambridge: Cambridge University Press).

Longin, F., and Solnik, B. (1995), 'Is the Correlation in International Equity Returns Constant: 1960–1990?', *Journal of International Money and Finance*, 14/1: 3–26.

Lowenstein, R. (2001), *When Genius Failed: The Rise and Fall of Long-Term Capital Management* (London: Fourth Estate).

Lukes, S. (1974), *Power: A Radical View* (London: Macmillan).

Lund, S., Daruvala, T., Dobbs, R., Härle, P., Kwek, J.-H., and Falcón, R. (2013), *Financial Globalization: Retreat or Reset?*, report (New York: McKinsey Global Institute).

Lynn, B. (2005), *End of the Line: The Rise and Coming Fall of the Global Corporation* (New York: Doubleday).

McCall Smith, J. (2000), 'The Politics of Dispute Settlement Design: Explaining Legalism in Regional Trade Pacts', *International Organization*, 54/1: 137–80.

McCloskey, D. (1990), 'Their Blackboard, Right or Wrong: A Comment on Contested Exchange', *Politics and Society*, 18/2: 223–32.

—— (2006), *The Bourgeois Virtues: Ethics for an Age of Commerce* (Chicago, IL: Chicago University Press).

McCord, N. (1958), *The Anti-Corn Law League 1838-1846* (London: George Allen & Unwin).

McCullagh, C. B. (1998), *The Truth of History* (London: Routledge).

McDonald, L. (2001), 'The Florence Nightingale-Harriet Martineau Collaboration', in M. Hill and S. Hoecker-Drysdale (eds) *Harriet Martineau: Theoretical and Methodological Perspectives* (London: Routledge).

McDowell, L. (1997), *Capital Culture: Gender at Work in the City* (Oxford: Basil Blackwell).

McGillivray, F. (1997), 'Party Discipline as a Determinant of the Endogenous Formation of Tariffs', *American Journal of Political Science*, 41/2: 584–607.

McGinnis, M. D. (1986), 'Issue Linkage and the Evolution of International Cooperation', *Journal of Conflict Resolution*, 30/1: 141–70.

McGrew, A. (2002), 'Liberal Internationalism: Between Realism and Cosmopolitanism', in D. Held and A. McGrew (eds), *Governing Globalization: Power, Authority, and Global Governance* (Cambridge: Polity Press).

McKean, M. A. (1981), *Environmental Protest and Citizen Politics in Japan* (Berkeley and Los Angeles, CA: University of California Press).

MacKenzie, D. (2002), 'Fresh Evidence on Bhopal Disaster', *New Scientist*, 4 December.

McKendrick, D. G., Doner, R. F., and Haggard, S. (2000), *From Silicon Valley to Singapore: Location and Competitive Advantage in the Hard Disk Drive Industry* (Stanford, CA: Stanford University Press).

McKenzie, R., and Lee, D. (1991), *Quicksilver Capital: How the Rapid Movement of Wealth Has Changed the World* (New York: Free Press).

McLaren, L. (2001), 'Immigration and the New Politics of Inclusion and Exclusion in the European Union: The Effect of Elites and the EU on Individual-Level Opinions Regarding European and Non-European Immigrants', *European Journal of Political Research*, 39/1: 81–108.

McLean, I. (2006), *Adam Smith, Radical and Egalitarian: An Interpretation for the 21st Century* (Edinburgh: Edinburgh University Press).

MacLeod, M. R., and Park, J. (2011), 'Financial Activism and Global Climate Change', *Global Environmental Politics*, 11/2: 98–119.

McMichael, P. (2000), *Development and Social Change: A Global Perspective*, 2nd edn (Thousand Oaks, CA: Pine Forge Press).

McNamara, K. (1998), *The Currency of Ideas: Monetary Politics in the European Union* (Ithaca, NY: Cornell University Press).

—— (2009), 'Of Intellectual Monocultures and the Study of IPE', *Review of International Political Economy*, 16/1: 72–84.

MacNeill, J., Winsemius, P., and Yakushiji, T. (1991), *Beyond Interdependence: The Meshing of the World's Economy and the Earth's Ecology* (New York: Oxford University Press).

Maddison, A. (1987), 'Growth and Slowdown in Advanced Capitalist Economies: Techniques of Quantitative Assessment', *Journal of Economic Literature*, 25/2: 649–98.

—— (1989), *The World Economy in the 20th Century* (Paris: Development Centre of the Organisation for Economic Co-operation and Development).

—— (2001), *The World Economy: A Millennial Perspective* (Paris: Development Centre of the Organisation for Economic Co-operation and Development).

Maeil Kyongjae [Maeil Business Newspaper] (2005), 'Global Sourcing: Samsung Electronics', 22 February.

Magee, S. P. (1980), 'Three Simple Tests of the Stopler-Samuelson Theorem', in P. Oppenheimer (ed.), *Issues in International Economics* (London: Oriel Press).

—— Brock, W. A., and Young, L. (1989), *Black Hole Tariffs and Endogenous Policy Theory* (Cambridge: Cambridge University Press).

Maggi, G. (1999), 'The Role of Multilateral Institutions in International Trade Cooperation', *American Economic Review*, 89/1: 190–214.

Makower, J., and Pike, C. (2009), *Strategies for the Green Economy: Opportunities and Challenges in the New World of Business* (New York: McGraw-Hill).

Malthus, T. R. (1798), *Essay on the Principle of Population*, 1st edn, www.econlib.org/library/Malthus/malPop.html

Mander, J., and Goldsmith, E. (eds) (2001), *The Case Against the Global Economy: And for a Turn towards Localization*, rev. edn (London: Earthscan).

Mandeville, B. (1714/1755), *The Fable of the Bees; Or, Private Vices, Public Benefits*, 9th edn (Edinburgh: W. Gray & W. Peter).

—— (1714/1997), 'Selections from The Fable of the Bees, Volume 1', *The Fable of the Bees and Other Writings*, abridged and edited by Edward Hundert (Indianapolis, IN: Hackett).

Manger, M. (2005), 'Competition and Bilateralism in Trade Policy: The Case of Japan's Free Trade Agreements', *Review of International Political Economy*, 12/5: 804–28.

Manheim, J. M. (1991), *All of the People All of the Time: Strategic Communication and American Politics* (Armonk, NY: M.E. Sharpe).

Maniyika, James *et al.* (2014), *Global Flows in a Digital Age* (McKinsey Global Institute)

Mankiw, G. (2009), 'That Freshman Course Won't Be Quite the Same', *New York Times*, 23 May.

Marcet, J. (1833/2009), *John Hopkins's Notions on Political Economy* (London: Dodo Press).

—— (1839/2009), *Conversations on Political Economy*, repr. from 7th edn of 1839, with a new introduction by E. Forget (New Brunswick, NJ: Transaction Publishers).

—— (1851), *Rich and Poor* (London: Longmans).

Marchand, M. (1994), 'Gender and New Regionalism in Latin America: Inclusion/Exclusion', *Third World Quarterly*, 15/1: 63–76.

—— (1996), 'Reconceptualising "Gender and Development" in an Era of "Globalisation"', *Millennium: Journal of International Studies*, 25/3: 577–603.

Marcus, A. A. (2015), *Innovations in Sustainability: Fuel and Food* (Cambridge: Cambridge University Press).

Marshall, A. (1897), 'The Old Generation of Economists and the New', *Quarterly Journal of Economics*, 11/2: 115–35.

—— (1920), *Principles of Economics*, 8th edn (London: Macmillan).

Martell, L. (2007), 'The Third Wave in Globalization Theory', *International Studies Review*, 9: 173–96

Martin, L. L. (1992), 'Interests, Power, and Multilateralism', *International Organization*, 46/4: 765–92.

—— (2000), *Democratic Commitments: Legislatures and International Cooperation* (Princeton, NJ: Princeton University Press).

Martin, L. L. (2002), 'International Political Economy: From Paradigmatic Debates to Productive Disagreements', in M. Brecher and F. P. Harvey (eds), *Conflict, Security, Foreign Policy, and International Political Economy: Past Paths and Future Directions in International Studies* (Ann Arbor, MI: University of Michigan Press).

Martin, Philip (2009), 'Recession and Migration: A New Era for Labor Migration?', *International Migration Review*, 43:3, 671–91.

Martineau, H. (1832–4), *Illustrations of Political Economy* (London: Leonard C. Bowles).

—— (1833), *Cousin Marshall: A Tale* (London: Leonard C. Bowles).

Martinez-Diaz, L. (2009), *Globalizing in Hard Times: The Politics of Banking-Sector Opening in the Emerging World* (Ithaca, NY: Cornell University Press).

Marugami, T., Mimura, T., Saito, K., Suzuki, M., and Kotaka, T. (2005), 'Survey Report on Overseas Business Operations by Japanese Manufacturing Companies', *JBICI Review*, 13 (Tokyo: Japan Bank for International Cooperation, September).

Marx, K. (1867/1996), *Das Kapital: A Critique of Political Economy*, vol. I, translated and abridged by S. Levitsky (Washington, DC: Regnery Publishing).

—— (1890/1930), *Capital: A Critique of Political Economy*, tr. from 4th German edn by E. and C. Paul (London: Dent).

—— (1973), *Grundrisse: Foundations of the Critique of Political Economy* (Rough Draft), tr. from German edn by M. Nicolaus (Harmondsworth: Penguin).

—— and Engels, F. (1848/1948), *The Communist Manifesto* (London: Lawrence & Wishart).

Maskus, K. E. (2000), *Intellectual Property Rights in the Global Economy* (Washington, DC: Institute for International Economics).

Massa, I., Keane, J., and Kenna, J. (2012), *The Euro Zone Crisis and Developing Countries*, Working Paper 345 (London: Overseas Development Institute).

Mazur, J. (2000), 'Labor's New Internationalism', *Foreign Affairs*, 79/1: 79–93.

Mazzucato, M. (2013), *The Entrepreneurial State* (London: Anthem Press).

Meadows, D. H., Meadows, D. L., Randers, J., and Behrens, W. W. (1972), *The Limits to Growth* (New York: Universe Books).

Mearsheimer, J. J. (1990), 'Back to the Future: Instability in Europe after the Cold War', *International Security*, 15/1: 5–56.

Meek, R. (1974), 'Value in the History of Economic Thought', *History of Political Economy*, 6/2: 246–60.

Mehta, S. (2003), 'The Johannesburg Summit from the Depths', *Journal of Environment and Development*, 12/1: 121–8.

Melitz, Marc J. (2003), 'The Impact of Trade on Intra-industry Reallocations and Aggregate Industry Productivity', *Econometrica*, 71/6: 1695–1725.

Mellor, D. H. (1995), *The Facts of Causation* (London: Routledge).

Meltzer, A. (2001), 'The World Bank One Year After the Commission's Report to Congress', *Hearings Before the Joint Economic Committee, US Congress*, 8 March.

Menger, C. (1871/1950), *Principles of Economics*, tr. and ed. J. Dingwall and B. Hoselitz (Glencoe, IL: Free Press).

Mercy, Robert. (2012), 'The crisis of Globalization', *The National Interest*, 18 October.

Mészáros, I. (2005), *Marx's Theory of Alienation*, 5th rev. edn (London: Merlin Press).

METI (Ministry of Economy, Trade and Industry, Japan), 2000 CAU METI (Ministry of Economy, Trade and Industry, Japan) D (2000), C 'The Economic Foundations of Japanese Trade Policy: Promoting a Multi-Layered Trade Policy', Ministry of Economy, Trade and Industry, www.meti.go.jp/english/report/data/g00Wconte.pdf

—— (2004), 'The Report of the Joint Study Group on the Possible Trilateral Investment Arrangements among China, Japan, and Korea' (Tokyo: METI), 29 November.

—— (2006), 'White Paper on International Economy and Trade 2006' (Tokyo: METI), June.

Milanovic, B. (2003), 'The Two Faces of Globalization: Against Globalization as We Know It', *World Development*, 31/4: 667–83.

—— (2005), *Worlds Apart: Measuring International and Global Inequality* (Princeton, NJ: Princeton University Press).

—— (2006), 'Global Income Inequality: A Review', *World Economics*, 7/1.

—— (2009), *Global Inequality Recalculated: The Effect of New 2005 PPP Estimates on Global Inequality*, World Bank Working Paper 5061 (Washington, DC: World Bank, September).

—— (2016), *Global Inequality: A New Approach for the Age of Globalization* (Cambridge, MA: Harvard University Press).

Mill, J. S. (1970), *Principles of Political Economy, with Some of their Applications to Social Philosophy* (Harmondsworth: Penguin).

Miller, J. W. (2010), 'WTO Has Obstacles to Trade in Retreat', WSJ.com, 8 March, http://www.wsj.com/articles/SB100014240527487 04706304575107341978847782 (accessed May 2016).

Milman, O. (2015), 'James Hansen, Father of Climate Change Awareness, Calls Paris Talks "a Fraud"', JT *The Guardian*, 12 December, www.theguardian.com

Milner, H. V. (1997a), *Interests, Institutions, and Information: Domestic Politics and International Relations* (Princeton, NJ: Princeton University Press).

—— (1997b), 'Industries, Governments, and the Creation of Regional Trading Blocs', in E. D. Mansfield and H. V. Milner (eds), *The Political Economy of Regionalism* (New York: Columbia University Press).

Milward, A. S. (1984), *The Reconstruction of Western Europe 1945–51* (London: Routledge).

—— (1992), *The European Rescue of the Nation-State* (London: Routledge).

Minsky, H. (1986), *Stabilizing an Unstable Economy* (New Haven: Yale University Press).

Mitchell, B. R. (1992), *International Historical Statistics: Europe 1750–1988*, 3rd edn (London2n: Macmillan).

—— (1993), *International Historical Statistics: The Americas 1750–1988*, 2nd edn (London: Macmillan).

Mitchell, R. B. (2002), 'A Quantitative Approach to Evaluating International Environmental Regimes', *Global Environmental Politics*, 2/4: 58–83.

Mitchell, R. B. (2006), 'Problem Structure, Institutional Design,and the Relative Effectiveness of International Environmental Agreements', *Global Environmental Politics*, 6/3: 72–89.

—— (2014), 'International Environmental Agreements (IEA) (Version2014.3)', IEA Database Project, 2002–16, http://iea.uoregon.edu

—— Clark, W. C., Cash, D. W., and Dickson, N. M. (eds) (2006), *Global Environmental Assessments: Information and Influence* (Cambridge, MA: MIT Press).

Mohapatra, S., and Ratha, D. (2010), 'Impact of the Global Financial Crisis on Migration and Remittances', *World Bank Economic Premise*, February.

Molina, M. J., and Rowland, F. S. (1974), 'Stratospheric Sink for Chlorofluoromethanes: Chlorine Atom Catalyzed Destruction of Ozone', *Nature*, 249: 810–14.

Molyneux, M. (1985), 'Mobilization without Emancipation? Women's Interests, the State, and Revolution in Nicaragua', *Feminist Studies*, 11/2: 227–54.

Monbiot, G. (2015), 'Grand Promises of Paris Climate Deal Undermined by Squalid Retrenchments', *The Guardian*, 12 December, www.theguardian.com

Moral-Benito, E. (2012), 'Growth Empirics in Panel Data under Model Uncertainty and Weak Exogeneity', Working Papers No. 1243, Banco de Espana, Madrid.

Moran, T. H. (1998), *Foreign Direct Investment and Development* (Washington, DC: Institute for International Economics).

Moravcsik, A. (1998), *The Choice for Europe: Social Purpose and State Power from Messina to Maastricht* (Ithaca, NY: Cornell University Press).

Morgenthau, H. (1948/1960), *Politics among Nations: The Struggle for Power and Peace*, 3rd edn (New York: Knopf).

Morgunbladid and Vidskiptabladid (2007), 17 November.

Morse, E. L. (1976), *Modernization and the Transformation of International Relations* (New York: Free Press).

Moser, C. (1989), 'Gender Planning and Development: Meeting Practical and Strategic Needs', *World Development*, 17/11: 1799–825.

—— (1993), *Gender Planning and Development: Theory, Practice and Training* (London: Routledge).

Mosley, L. (2003), *Global Capital and National Governments* (Cambridge: Cambridge University Press).

Motta, M., and Norman, G. (1996), 'Does Economic Integration Cause Foreign Direct Investment?', *International Economic Review*, 37/4: 757–83.

Mun, T. (1664/1928), *England's Treasure by Forraign Trade*, reset and repr. edn (Oxford: Basil Blackwell).

Munck, R. (2002), *Globalisation and Labour* (London: Zed Books).

Mundell, R. (1961), 'A Theory of Optimum Currency Areas', *American Economic Review*, 51/3: 657–65.

Murphy, C. and Tooze, R. (1991), 'Getting Beyond the "Common Sense" of the IPE Orthodoxy', in C. Murphy and R. Tooze (eds) *The New International Political Economy* (London: Lynne Rienner).

—— and Nelson, D. (2001), 'International Political Economy: A Tale of Two Heterodoxies', *British Journal of Politics and International Relations*, 3/3: 393–412.

Mussa, M. (1974), 'Tariffs and the Distribution of Income: The Importance of Factor Specificity, Substitutability, and Intensity in the Short and Long Run', *Journal of Political Economy*, 82/6: 1191–1203.

—— (2002), *Argentina and the Fund: From Triumph to Tragedy* (Washington, DC: Institute for International Economics).

Muthu, S. (2008), 'Adam Smith's Critique of International Trading Companies: Theorizing "Globalization" in the Age of Enlightenment', *Political Theory*, 36/2: 185–212.

Myers, R., and Worm, B. (2003), 'Rapid Worldwide Depletion of Predatory Fish Communities', *Nature*, 423/6937: 280–3.

Nadvi, K., and Schmitz, H. (1998), 'Industrial Clusters in Less Developed Countries: Review of Experiences and Research Agenda', in P. Cadène and M. Holström (eds), *Decentralized Production in India: Industrial Districts, Flexible Specialization, and Employment* (Thousand Oaks, CA: Sage).

Naím, M. (2002), 'Post-Terror Surprises', *Foreign Policy*, 132 (September–October): 95–6.

Narlikar, A. (2003), *International Trade and Developing Countries: Bargaining Coalitions in the GATT and WTO* (London: Routledge).

Nelson, P. (2007), 'Human Rights, the Millennium Development Goals, and the Future of Development Cooperation', *World Development*, 35/12: 2041–55.

Nelson, S. and P. Katzenstein (2014), 'Uncertainty, Risk, and the Financial Crisis of 2008', *International Organization*, 68/2, 361–92.

Nest, M. (2011), *Coltan* (Cambridge: Polity).

Neumayer, E. (2001), *Greening Trade and Investment: Environmental Protection without Protectionism* (London: Earthscan).

Newell, P. (2000), *Climate for Change: Non-State Actors and the Global Politics of the Greenhouse* (Cambridge: Cambridge University Press).

—— and Paterson, M. (2010), *Climate Capitalism: Global Warming and the Transformation of the Global Economy* (Cambridge: Cambridge University Press).

Nicholson, J. S. (1904/1977), 'Introductory Essay', reprinted in F. List (1841/1977) *The National System of Political Economy* (Fairfield, NJ: Augustus M. Kelley).

Nierenberg, D. (2009), 'Meat Production and Consumption Continues to Grow', in *Vital Signs* (Washington, DC: Worldwatch Institute), http://vitalsigns.worldwatch.org/vs-trend/meat-production-and-consumption-continues-grow

Nixon, R. (2011), *Slow Violence and the Environmentalism of the Poor* (Cambridge, MA: Harvard University Press).

Noble, G., and Ravenhill, J. (eds) (2000), *The Asian Financial Crisis and the Architecture of Global Finance* (Cambridge: Cambridge University Press).

Notermans, T. (2001), Social Democracy and Monetary Union (New York: Berghahn).

Nye, J. S., Jr. (1990), 'Soft Power', *Foreign Policy*, 80: 153–71.

O'Brien, R. (1992), *The End of Geography: Global Financial Integration* (London: Pinter).

—— and Williams, M. (2004), *Global Political Economy: Evolution and Dynamics* (Basingstoke: Palgrave Macmillan).

O'Rourke, K. H., and Williamson, J. G. (1999), *Globalization and History: The Evolution of a Nineteenth-Century Atlantic Economy* (Cambridge, MA: MIT Press).

Oatley, T. (1997), *Monetary Politics: Exchange Rate Cooperation in the European Union* (Ann Arbor, MI: University of Michigan Press).

—— (2006), *International Political Economy: Interests and Institutions in the Global Economy*, 2nd edn (London: Pearson Longman).

Obstfeld, M. (1993), *International Capital Mobility in the 1990s*, NBER Working Paper 4534 (Cambridge, MA: National Bureau of Economic Research).

—— and Rogoff, K. (1996), *Foundations of International Macroeconomics* (Cambridge, MA: MIT Press).

—— and Taylor, A. M. (1998), 'The Great Depression as a Watershed: International Capital Mobility in the Long Run', in M. D. Bordo, C. Goldin, and E. N. White (eds), *The Defining Moment: The Great Depression and the American Economy in the Twentieth Century* (Chicago, IL: Chicago University Press).

—— (2003), 'Globalization and Capital Markets', in M. D. Bordo, A. M. Taylor, and J. G. Williamson (eds), *Globalization in Historical Perspective* (Chicago, IL: University of Chicago Press).

—— (2004), *Global Capital Markets: Integration, Crisis, and Growth* (Cambridge: Cambridge University Press).

Odell, J. S. (1982), *US International Monetary Policy: Markets, Power, and Ideas as Sources of Change* (Princeton, NJ: Princeton University Press).

—— (2002), 'Making and Breaking Impasses in International Regimes: The WTO, Seattle and Doha', paper prepared for the Conference on Gaining Leverage in International Negotiations, Yonsei University, Seoul.

OECD (Organisation for Economic Co-Operation and Development) [various years], *Economic Outlook* (Paris: OECD).

—— (2002), Regional Trade Agreements and the Multilateral Trading System: Consolidated Report, 20 November, www.olis.oecd.org/olis/2002doc.nsf/43bb6130e5e86e5fc12569fa005d004c/db1bbc3ddbadceeec1256c770042bc1b/$FILE/JT00135547.PDF

—— (2003), *Agricultural Policies in OECD Countries: Monitoring and Evaluation* (Paris: OECD).

—— (2005), *Agricultural Policies in OECD Countries: Monitoring and Evaluation 2005: Highlights*, www.oecd.org/dataoecd/33/27/35016763.pdf

—— (2006), *Social Expenditure Database, SOCX* (Paris: OECD), www.oecd.org/els/social/expenditure

—— (2009), 'OECD Data, Table 1: Net Official Development Assistance in 2008', 30 March, www.oecd.org/dataoecd/48/34/42459170.pdf

—— (2013), *Perspectives on Global Development 2013—Industrial policies in a changing world* (Paris: OECD).

—— and WTO (2012), *Trade in Value-Added: Concepts, Methodologies and Challenges* (Paris: OECD).

—— WTO, and UN (2010), *Report on G20 Trade and Investment Measures (September 2009 to February 2010)* (Paris and Geneva: OECD, WTO, UNCTAD, 8 March), http://www.oecd.org/dataoecd/22/16/44739159.pdf

—— (2012), *Reports on G20 Trade and Investment Measures (Mid-May to Mid-October 2012)* (Paris: OECD, 31 October).

Offer, A. (1989), *The First World War: An Agrarian Interpretation* (Oxford: Clarendon Press).

Officer, L. H. (2001), 'Gold Standard', *EH.Net Encyclopedia*, 1 October, http://eh.net/encyclopedia/gold-standard (accessed May 2016).

Ofreneo, R. (1993), 'Japan and the Environmental Degradation of the Philippines', in M. Howard (ed.), *Asia's Environmental Crisis* (Boulder, CO: Westview Press).

Ohmae, K. (1990), *The Borderless World* (London: Collins).

—— (1995), *The End of the Nation State: The Rise of Regional Economies* (New York: Free Press).

Oi, J. C. (1992), 'Fiscal Reform and the Economic Foundations of Local State Corporatism in China', *World Politics*, 45/1: 99–126.

Okereke, C., Bulkeley, H., and Schroeder, H. (2009), 'Conceptualizing Climate Governance beyond the International Regime', *Global Environmental Politics*, 9/1: 58–78.

Okimoto, D. I. (1988), 'Political Inclusivity: The Domestic Structure of Trade', in T. Inoguchi and D. I. Okimoto (eds), *The Political Economy of Japan*, ii. *The Changing International Context* (Stanford, CA: Stanford University Press).

Olson, M. (1965), *The Logic of Collective Action: Public Goods and the Theory of Groups* (Cambridge, MA: Harvard University Press).

Onuf, N. (1997), 'Hegemony's Hegemony in IPE', in K. Burch and R. Denemark (eds), *Constituting International Political Economy* (Boulder, CO: Lynne Rienner).

Osgood, I. (2016), 'Differentiated Products, Divided Industries: Firm Preferences over Trade Liberalization', *Economics and Politics*.

Osherenko, G., and Young, O. R. (1993), 'The Formation of International Regimes: Hypotheses and Cases', in O. R. Young and G. Osherenko (eds), *Polar Politics: Creating International Environmental Regimes* (Ithaca, NY: Cornell University Press).

Osler, C. L. (1991), 'Explaining the Absence of International Factor-Price Convergence', *Journal of Money and Finance*, 10/1: 89–107.

Ostrom, E. (2000), 'Reformulating the Commons', *Swiss Political Science Review*, 6/1: 29–52.

—— (2003), 'How Types of Goods and Property Rights Jointly Affect Collective Action', *Journal of Theoretical Politics*, 15/3: 239–70.

Ostry, S. (1997), *The Post-Cold War Trading System: Who's on First* (Chicago, IL: University of Chicago Press).

Oye, K. A. (1985), 'Explaining Cooperation under Anarchy: Hypotheses and Strategies', *World Politics*, 38/1: 1–24.

—— (1992), *Economic Discrimination and Political Exchange: World Political Economy in the 1930s and 1980s* (Princeton, NJ: Princeton University Press).

Paarlberg, R. L. (1997), 'Agricultural Policy Reform and the Uruguay Round: Synergistic Linkage in a Two-Level Game', *International Organization*, 51/3: 413–44.

Pahre, R. (1999), *Leading Questions: How Hegemony Affects the International Political Economy* (Ann Arbor, MI: University of Michigan Press).

Pakenham, R. (1973), *Liberal America and the Third World* (Princeton, NJ: Princeton University Press).

Palan, R. (2003), *The Offshore World: Sovereign Markets, Virtual Places and Nomad Millionaires* (Ithaca, NY: Cornell University Press).

Palan, R. and Abbott, J. with Deans, P. (1999), *State Strategies in the Global Political Economy* (London: Pinter).

Paleczny, M., Hammill, E., Karpouzi, V., and Pauly, D. (2015), 'Population Trend of the World's Monitored Seabirds, 1950–2010', *PLOS One*, 9 June, doi: 10.1371/journal.pone.0129342

Palma, J. G. (2009), 'The Revenge of the Market on the Rentiers', *Cambridge Journal of Economics*, 33/1: 829–69.

Palmeter, D. N., and Mavroidis, P. C. (1999), *Dispute Settlement in the World Trade Organization: Practice and Procedure* (The Hague: Kluwer).

Palmisano, S. J. (2006), 'The Globally Integrated Enterprise', *Foreign Affairs*, 85/3: 127–36.

Panagariya, A. (2002), 'Developing Countries at Doha: A Political Economy Analysis', *World Economy*, 25/9: 1205–33.

—— (2008), *India: The Emerging Giant* (Oxford: Oxford University Press).

Park, S. (2010), *World Bank Group Interactions with Environmentalists: Changing International Organisation Identities* (London: Manchester University Press).

Parker, B. (1998), *Globalization and Business Practice: Managing across Boundaries* (London: Sage).

Parson, E. A. (2003), *Protecting the Ozone Layer: Science and Strategy* (Oxford: Oxford University Press).

Pastor, R. (1980), *Congress and the Politics of US Foreign Economic Policy, 1929–1976* (Berkeley and Los Angeles, CA: University of California Press).

Paterson, M. (1996), *Global Warming and Global Politics* (London: Routledge).

—— (2001), 'Risky Business: Insurance Companies in Global Warming Politics', *Global Environmental Politics*, 1/4: 18–42.

Pattberg, P. (2005), 'The Institutionalization of Private Governance: How Business and Nonprofit Organizations Agree on Transnational Rules', *Governance*, 18/4: 589–610.

Pauly, L. W. (1997), *Who Elected the Bankers? Surveillance and Control in the World Economy* (Ithaca, NY: Cornell University Press).

—— (2009), 'The Old and the New Politics of International Financial Stability', *Journal of Common Market Studies*, 47/5: 955–75.

Paus, E. (2014), 'Latin America and the Middle Income Trap', CEPAL. Series Financing for Development 250.

Payne, A. (2005a), 'The Study of Governance in a Global Political Economy', in N. Phillips (ed.), *Globalizing International Political Economy* (Basingstoke: Palgrave Macmillan).

—— (2005b), *The Global Politics of Unequal Development* (Basingstoke: Palgrave Macmillan).

—— and Phillips, N. (2010), *Development* (Cambridge: Polity Press).

Pearson, F., and Rochester, M. (1998), *International Relations: The Global Condition in the Twenty-First Century*, 4th edn (New York: McGraw-Hill).

Pearson, R. (1995), 'Male Bias and Women's Work in Mexico's Border Industries', in D. Elson (ed.), *Male Bias in the Development Process* (Manchester: Manchester University Press).

Pellow, D. N. (2007), *Resisting Global Toxics: Transnational Movements for Environmental Justice* (Cambridge, MA: MIT Press).

Pempel, T. J. (1999a), 'The Developmental Regime in a Changing World Economy', in M. Woo-Cumings (ed.), *The Developmental State* (Ithaca, NY: Cornell University Press).

—— (ed.) (1999b), *The Politics of the Asian Financial Crisis* (Ithaca, NY: Cornell University Press).

Perraton, J., Goldblatt, D., Held, D., and McGrew, A. (1997), 'The Globalization of Economic Activity', *New Political Economy*, 2/2: 257–78.

Perroni, C., and Whalley, J. (1994), *The New Regionalism: Trade Liberalization or Insurance?*, NBER Working Paper 4626 (Cambridge, MA: National Bureau of Economic Research).

Petras, J., and Veltmeyer, H. (2001), *Globalization Unmasked: Imperialism in the 21st Century* (London: Zed Books).

Petrella, R. (1996), 'Globalization and Internationalization: The Dynamics of the Emerging World Order', in R. Boyer and D. Drache (eds), *States Against Market: The Limits of Globalization* (London: Routledge).

Pharr, S. J., and Putnam, R. D. (eds) (2000), *Disaffected Democracies: What's Troubling the Trilateral Countries?* (Princeton, NJ: Princeton University Press).

Phillips, D. A. (2009), *Reforming the World Bank: Twenty Years of Trial—And Error* (Cambridge: Cambridge University Press).

Phillips, N. (2004), *The Southern Cone Model: The Political Economy of Regional Capitalist Development in Latin America* (London: Routledge).

—— (2005), 'Latin America in the Global Political Economy', in R. Stubbs and G. Underhill (eds), *Political Economy and the Changing Global Order*, 3rd edn (Oxford: Oxford University Press).

—— (2009), 'The Slow Death of Pluralism', *Review of International Political Economy*, 16/1: 85–94.

—— (2011a), 'Poverty Reduction and the Role of Regional Institutions', in G. Mace, A. F. Cooper, and T. M. Shaw (eds), *Inter-American Cooperation at a Crossroads* (Basingstoke: Palgrave).

—— (2011b), 'Migration and the Global Economic Crisis', in Nicola Phillips (ed.), *Migration in the Global Political Economy* (Boulder, CO: Lynne Rienner): 259–66.

Pickering, P., and Tyrell, A. (2000), *The People's Bread: A History of the Anti-Corn Law League* (London: Continuum).

Pierson, P. (1994), *Dismantling the Welfare State? Reagan, Thatcher and the Politics of Retrenchment* (Cambridge: Cambridge University Press).

—— (1996), 'The New Politics of the Welfare State', *World Politics*, 48/2: 143–79.

Pieterse, J. N. (2002), 'Global Inequality: Bringing Politics Back in', *Third World Quarterly*, 23/6: 1023–46.

Piketty, T. (2014), *Capital in the 21st Century* (Cambridge, MA: Harvard University Press).

Pinto, P. M. (2003), 'Tying Hands vs. Exchanging Hostages: Domestic Coalitions, Political Constraints, and FDI', paper presented at the Annual Meeting of the American Political Science Association, Philadelphia.

Piore, M., and Sabel, C. (1984), *The Second Industrial Divide: Possibilities for Prosperity* (New York: Basic Books).

Pogge, T. (2004), 'The First United Nations Millennium Development Goal: A Cause for Celebration?', *Journal of Human Development and Capabilities*, 5/3: 377–97.

Polanyi, K. (1944), *The Great Transformation* (New York: Rinehart).

Polkinghorn, B. (1993), *Jane Marcet: An Uncommon Woman* (Aldermaston: Forestwood Publications).

Polkinghorn, B. and Thomson, D. L. (1998), *Adam Smith's Daughters: Eight Prominent Women Economists from the Eighteenth Century to the Present* (Cheltenham: Edward Elgar).

Ponte, S. (2008), *Developing a 'Vertical' Dimension to Chronic Poverty Research: Some Lessons from Global Value Chain Analysis*, Working Paper No. 111 (Manchester: Chronic Poverty Research Centre, June).

Poovey, M. (2008), *Genres of the Credit Economy: Mediating Value in Eighteenth- and Nineteenth-Century Britain* (Chicago, IL: University of Chicago Press).

Porter, G. (1999), 'Trade Competition and Pollution Standards: "Race to the Bottom" or "Stuck at the Bottom?"', *Journal of Environment and Development*, 8/2: 133–51.

—— Bird, N., Kaur, N., and Peskett, L. (2008), *New Finance for Climate Change and the Environment* (Washington, DC: WWF and Heinrich Böll Foundation), http://assets.panda.org/downloads/ifa_report.pdf

—— Brown, J. W., and Chasek, P. (2000), *Global Environmental Politics*, 3rd edn (Boulder, CO: Westview Press).

Porter, M. E. (1990), *The Competitive Advantage of Nations* (New York: Free Press).

Prebisch, R. (1950), *The Economic Development of Latin America and its Principal Problems* (New York: United Nations).

—— (1963), *Towards a Dynamic Development Policy for Latin America* (New York: United Nations).

—— (1970), *Change and Development: Latin America's Great Task* (Washington, DC: Inter-American Development Bank).

Preeg, E. H. (1970), *Traders and Diplomats: An Analysis of the Kennedy Round under the General Agreement on Tariffs and Trade* (Washington, DC: Brookings Institution).

—— (1995), *Traders in a Brave New World: The Uruguay Round and the Future of the International Trading System* (Chicago, IL: University of Chicago Press).

Princen, T. (1997), 'The Shading and Distancing of Commerce: When Internalization Is Not Enough', *Ecological Economics*, 20/3: 235–53.

—— (2005), *The Logic of Sufficiency* (Cambridge, MA: MIT Press).

—— (2010), *Trading Softly: Paths to Ecological Order* (Cambridge, MA: MIT Press).

Pritchett, L., and L. Summers. (2014), 'Asiaphoria meets regression to the mean', NBER Working Paper 20573, October.

Putnam, R. D. (1988), 'Diplomacy and Domestic Politics: The Logic of Two-Level Games', *International Organization*, 42/3: 427–60.

—— and Bayne, N. (1987), *Hanging Together: Cooperation and Conflict in the Seven-Power Summits* (Cambridge, MA: Harvard University Press).

Quah, D. (2011), 'The Global Economy's Shifting Centre of Gravity', *Global Policy*, 2/1: 3–9.

—— (2015), 'The World's Tightest Cluster of People', http://www.dannyquah.com/writings/en/2015/09/22/the-worlds-tightest-cluster-of-people

Radelet, S., and Sachs, J. (2000), 'The Onset of the East Asian Financial Crisis', in P. Krugman (ed.), *Currency Crises* (Chicago, IL: University of Chicago Press).

Rai, S. (2002), *Gender and the Political Economy of Development* (Cambridge: Polity).

Ramo, Joshua. (2004), *The Beijing Consensus* (London: Foreign Policy Centre).

Raphael, D. D., and Macfie, A. L. (1982), 'Introduction', in A. Smith (1759/1982), *The Theory of Moral Sentiments*, Glasgow Edition of the Works and Correspondence of Adam Smith, ed. D. D. Raphael and A. L. Macfie (Indianapolis, IN: Liberty Fund).

Rashid, S. (1998), *The Myth of Adam Smith* (Cheltenham: Edward Elgar).

Rauchway, E. (2015), *The Money Makers* (New York: Basic Books).

Ravallion, M. (2014), 'An Exploration of the International Comparison Program's New Global Economic Landscape', NBER working paper 20338, July.

Ravenhill, J. (1995), 'Competing Logics of Regionalism in the Asia-Pacific', *Journal of European Integration*, 18/2–3: 179–99.

—— (2001), *APEC and the Construction of Asia-Pacific Regionalism* (Cambridge: Cambridge University Press).

—— (2003), 'The New Bilateralism in the Asia-Pacific', *Third World Quarterly*, 24/2: 299–317.

—— (2004), 'Back to the Nest? Europe's Relations with the African, Caribbean and Pacific Group of Countries', in V. K. Aggarwal and E. A. Fogarty (eds), *EU Trade Statistics: Between Regionalism and Globalization* (Basingstoke: Palgrave Macmillan).

—— (2006a), 'Is China an Economic Threat to Southeast Asia?', *Asian Survey*, 46/5: 653–74.

—— (2006b), 'The Political Economy of the New Asia-Pacific Bilateralism: Benign, Banal or Simply Bad?', in V. K. Aggarwal and S. Urata (eds), *Bilateral Trade Agreements in the Asia-Pacific: Origins, Evolution, and Implications* (London: Routledge).

—— (2010), 'The "New East Asian Regionalism": A Political Domino Effect', *Review of International Political Economy*, 17/2: 178–208.

Reddy, S. G., and Pogge, T. W. (2003), 'How *Not* to Count the Poor', 26 March, www.columbia.edu/~sr793/count.pdf

—— and Minoiu, C. (2009), 'Real Income Stagnation of Countries, 1960–2001', *Journal of Development Studies*, 45/1: 1–23.

Rees, W. E. (2002), 'Globalization and Sustainability: Conflict or Convergence?', *Bulletin of Science, Technology and Society*, 22/4: 249–68.

—— (2006), 'Globalization, Trade and Migration: Undermining Sustainability', *Ecological Economics*, 59/2: 220–5.

—— and Westra, L. (2003), 'When Consumption Does Violence: Can there Be Sustainability and Environmental Justice in a Resource-Limited World?', in J. Agyeman, R. Bullard, and B. Evans (eds), *Just Sustainabilities: Development in an Unequal World* (London: Earthscan).

Reich, R. (1992), *The Work of Nations* (New York: Vintage Books).

Reinhart, C., and Rogoff, K. (2009), *This Time Is Different: Eight Centuries of Financial Folly* (Princeton, NJ: Princeton University Press).

—— and Christoph Trebesch. (2016), 'The International Monetary Fund: 70 Years of Reinvention', *Journal of Economic Perspectives*, 30/1: 3–28.

Rhodes, M. (1996), 'Globalization and West European Welfare States: A Critical Review of Recent Debates', *Journal of European Social Policy*, 6/4: 305–27.

—— (1997), 'The Welfare State: Internal Challenges, External Constraints', in M. Rhodes, P. Heywood, and V. Wright (eds), *Developments in West European Politics* (London: Macmillan).

Ricardo, D. (1817/2002), *On the Principles of Political Economy and Taxation*, repr. vers. of 3rd edn (London: Empiricus Books).

Rich, B. (1994), *Mortgaging the Earth: The World Bank, Environmental Impoverishment, and the Crisis of Development* (London: Earthscan).

—— (2000), 'Exporting Destruction', *Environmental Forum*, September–October: 32–40.

—— (2009), *Foreclosing the Future: Coal, Climate and Public International Finance* (Washington, DC: Environmental Defense Fund), www.edf.org/documents/9593_coal-plants-report.pdf

Rice, C. (2008), 'Rethinking the National Interest: American Realism for a New World', *Foreign Affairs*, 87/4: 2–28.

Richardson, A. (2002), 'Mary Wollstonecraft on Education', in C. Johnson (ed.), *The Cambridge Companion to Mary Wollstonecraft* (Cambridge: Cambridge University Press).

Richardson, B. (2015), *Sugar* (Cambridge: Polity).

Rieger, E., and Leibfried, S. (2003), *Limits to Globalization: Welfare States and the World Economy* (Cambridge: Polity Press).

Rizvi, S. A. T. (2002), 'Adam Smith's Sympathy: Towards a Normative Economics', in E. Fullbrook (ed.), *Intersubjectivity in Economics: Agents and Structures* (London: Routledge).

Robbins, R. H. (2013), *Global Problems and the Culture of Capitalism*, 6th edn (Boston: Pearson).

Robertson, R. (2003), *The Three Waves of Globalization: A History of Developing Global Consciousness* (London: Zed Books).

Robins, N. (2006), *The Corporation that Changed the World: How the East India Company Shaped the Modern Multinational* (London: Pluto).

Robinson, J. (1964), *Economic Philosophy*, 2nd edn (Harmondsworth: Pelican).

Rodrik, D. (1989), 'Promises, Promises: Credible Policy Reform via Signalling', *Economic Journal*, 99/397: 756–72.

—— (1995), 'Political Economy of Trade Policy', in G. Grossman and K. Rogoff (eds), *Handbook of International Economics*, iii (Amsterdam: Elsevier).

—— (1996), *Why Do More Open Economies Have Bigger Governments?*, NBER Working Paper 5537 (Cambridge, MA: National Bureau of Economic Research).

—— (1997), *Has Globalization Gone Too Far?* (Washington, DC: Institute for International Economics).

—— (1999), *The New Economy and Developing Countries: Making Openness Work* (Baltimore, MD: Johns Hopkins University Press for Overseas Development Council).

—— (2002), 'After Neoliberalism, What?', paper presented to the Conference on Alternatives to Neoliberalism sponsored by the New Rules for Global Finance Coalition, 23–4 May, www.newrules.org/docs/afterneolib/rodrik.pdf

—— (2006a), 'Goodbye Washington Consensus, Hello Washington Confusion: A Review of the World Bank's Economic Growth in the 1990s: Learning from a Decade of Reform', *Journal of Economic Literature*, 44/4: 973–87.

—— (2006b), *The Social Cost of Foreign Exchange Reserves*, NBER Working Paper 11952 (Cambridge, MA: National Bureau of Economic Research).

—— (2011), *The Globalization Paradox* (Oxford: Oxford University Press).

Rødseth, A. (2000), *Open Economy Macroeconomics* (Cambridge: Cambridge University Press).

Roemer, J. E. (1988), *Free to Lose: An Introduction to Marxist Economic Philosophy* (London: Radius).

Rogers, A. (1993), *The Earth Summit: A Planetary Reckoning* (Los Angeles, CA: Global View Press).

Rogowski, R. (1987), 'Trade and the Variety of Democratic Institutions', *International Organization*, 41/2: 203–23.

—— (1989), *Commerce and Coalitions* (Princeton, NJ: Princeton University Press).

Rosamond, B. (2001), 'Discourses of Globalization and European Identities', in T. Christiansen, K. Jorgensen, and A. Wiener (eds), *The Social Construction of Europe* (London: Sage).

Rosecrance, R. (1986), *The Rise of the Trading State: Commerce and Conquest in the Modern World* (New York: Basic Books).

—— (1999), *The Rise of the Virtual State* (New York: Basic Books).

Rosen, D. (2003), 'Low-Tech Bed, High-Tech Dreams', *China Economic Quarterly*, 4: 20–7.

Rosen, M. (1996), *On Voluntary Servitude: False Consciousness and the Theory of Ideology* (Cambridge, MA: Harvard University Press).

Rosenberg, A. (1995), *Philosophy of Social Science* (Boulder, CO: Westview Press).

Rosenberg, J. (2000), *The Follies of Globalization Theory* (London: Verso).

—— (2002), *The Follies of Globalisation Theory* (London: Verso).

—— (2005), 'Globalization Theory: A Post Mortem', *International Politics*, 42/1: 2–74.

Rosow, S. (1997), 'Echoes of Commercial Society: Liberal Political Theory in Mainstream IPE', in K. Burch and R. Denemark (eds) *Constituting International Political Economy* (London: Lynne Rienner).

Ross, M. L. (2001), *Timber Booms and Institutional Breakdown in Southeast Asia* (Cambridge: Cambridge University Press).

Rostow, W. W. (1960), *The Stages of Economic Growth: A Non-Communist Manifesto* (Cambridge: Cambridge University Press).

Roubini, N., and Setser, B. (2004), *Bailouts or Bail-Ins? Responding to Financial Crises in Emerging Markets* (Washington, DC: Peterson Institute for International Economics).

Rousseau, J.-J. (1755/2003), 'A Discourse on a Subject Proposed by the Academy of Dijon: What Is the Origin of Inequality among Men, and Is It Authorized by Natural Law?', in J.-J. Rousseau, *The Social Contract and Discourses*, tr. and introduced by G. D. H. Cole, repr. edn (London: Everyman).

Rowthorn, R., and Wells, J. (1987), *De-Industrialization and Foreign Trade* (Cambridge: Cambridge University Press).

Roxburgh, C., Lund, S., Atkins, C., Belot, S., Hu, W. W., and Pierce, M. S. (2009), 'Global Capital Markets: Entering a New Era' (Paris: McKinsey Global Institute).

Ruggie, J. G. (1982), 'International Regimes, Transactions, and Change: Embedded Liberalism in the Postwar Economic Order', *International Organization*, 36/2: 379–415.

—— (1992), 'Multilateralism: The Anatomy of an Institution', *International Organization*, 46/3: 561–98.

Rugman, A. (2000), *The End of Globalization* (London: Random House; New York: Amacom-McGraw-Hill).

Ruigrok, W., and Tulder, R. V. (1995), *The Logic of International Restructuring* (London: Routledge).

Runyan, A. S. (1997), 'Of Markets and Men: The (Re)Making(s) of IPE', in K. Burch and R. Denemark (eds), *Constituting International Political Economy* (London: Lynne Rienner).

Sachs, J. (1998), 'The IMF and the Asian Flu', *American Prospect*, March-April: 16–21.

Saith, A. (2006), 'From Universal Values to Millennium Development Goals: Lost in Translation', *Development and Change*, 37/6: 1167–99.

Sako, M. (2003), 'Modularity and Outsourcing: The Nature of Co-Evolution of Product Architecture and Organization Architecture in the Global Automotive Industry', in A. Prencipe, A. Davies, and M. Hobday (eds), *The Business of Systems Integration* (Oxford: Oxford University Press).

—— (2006), 'Outsourcing and Offshoring: Implications for Productivity of Business Services', *Oxford Review of Economic Policy*, 22/4: 499–512.

Sandholtz, W. (1993), 'Choosing Union: Monetary Politics and Maastricht', *International Organization*, 47/1: 1–39.

—— and Stone Sweet, A. (eds) (1998), *European Integration and Supranational Governance* (Oxford: Oxford University Press).

—— and Zysman, J. (1989), '1992: Recasting the European Bargain', *World Politics*, 42/1: 95–128.

Sandler, T. (1992), *Collective Action: Theory and Applications* (Ann Arbor, MI: University of Michigan Press).

Sassen, S. (2006), *Territory, Authority, Rights: From Medieval to Global Assemblages* (Princeton, NJ: Princeton University Press).

Saul, J. R. (2005), *The Collapse of Globalism* (London: Atlantic Books).

Sayer, A. (2000), *Realism and Social Science* (London: Sage).

Schauble, W. (2011), 'Austerity Is the Only Cure for the Eurozone', *Financial Times*, 6 September.

Schelling, T. C. (1960), *The Strategy of Conflict* (Cambridge, MA: Harvard University Press).

Schiff, M. W., and Winters, L. A. (2003), *Regional Integration and Development* (New York: Oxford University Press for the World Bank).

Schirato, T., and Webb, J. (2003), *Understanding Globalization* (London: Sage).

Schirm, S. A. (2002), *Globalization and the New Regionalism* (Cambridge: Polity Press).

Schmidheiny, S., and Zorraquin, F. (1996), *Financing Change: The Financial Community, Eco-Efficiency, and Sustainable Development* (Cambridge, MA: MIT Press).

Schmidt, V. (2002), *The Futures of European Capitalism* (Oxford: Oxford University Press).

Schmitter, P., and Lehbruch, G. (eds) (1979), *Trends towards Corporatist Intermediation* (Beverly Hills, CA: Sage).

Schmitz, H. (2007), 'Reducing Complexity in the Industrial Policy Debate', *Development Policy Review*, 25/4: 417–28.

Schnietz, K. (1994), 'To Delegate or Not to Delegate: Congressional Institutional Choice in the Regulation of Foreign Trade, 1916–1934', Ph.D. dissertation (Berkeley, CA, University of California).

Scholte, J. A. (1997), 'The Globalization of World Politics', in J. Baylis and S. Smith (eds), *The Globalization of World Politics: An Introduction to International Relations* (Oxford: Oxford University Press).

—— (2000), *Globalization: A Critical Introduction* (Basingstoke: Palgrave).

—— (2005), *Globalization: A Critical Introduction*, rev. and updated 2nd edn (Basingstoke: Palgrave Macmillan).

—— (2008), 'Defining Globalization', *World Economy*, 31/11: 1471–1502

Schreurs, M. A. (2002), *Environmental Politics in Japan, Germany, and the United States* (Cambridge: Cambridge University Press).

Schubert, A. (1992), *The Credit-Anstalt Crisis of 1931* (Cambridge: Cambridge University Press).

Schumacher, E. F. (1973), *Small Is Beautiful: Economics as if People Mattered* (New York: Harper & Row).

Schumpeter, J. (1954/1994), *History of Economic Analysis* (New York: Oxford University Press).

—— (1954/2006), *History of Economic Analysis* (London: Routledge).

Schwartz, H. (2001), 'Round up the Usual Suspects: Globalization, Domestic Politics, and Welfare State Change', in P. Pierson (ed.), *The New Politics of the Welfare State* (Oxford: Oxford University Press).

Schwartz, H. M. (2009), *Subprime Nation: American Power, Global Capital, and the Housing Bubble* (Ithaca, NY: Cornell University Press).

Scollay, R., and Gilbert, J. (2001), *New Regional Trading Arrangements in the Asia Pacific?* (Washington, DC: Institute for International Economics).

Seers, D. (1969), 'The Meaning of Development', *International Development Review*, 11/4: 2–6.

Segal, G., and Goodman, D. (eds) (2002), *Towards Recovery in Pacific Asia* (London: Routledge).

Selin, H., and VanDeveer, S. D. (eds) (2009), *Changing Climates in North American Politics: Institutions, Policymaking, and Multilevel Governance* (Cambridge, MA: MIT Press).

Sell, S. and A. Prakash (2004), 'Using Ideas Strategically: The Contest between Business and NGO Networks in Intellectual Property Rights', *International Studies Quarterly*, 48/1: 143–75.

Sen, A. (1999), *Development as Freedom* (Oxford: Oxford University Press).

—— (2009), *The Idea of Justice* (Cambridge, MA: Belknap/Harvard University Press).

—— (2012), 'The Uses and Abuses of Adam Smith', *History of Political Economy*, 43/2: 257–71.

Shafaeddin, M. (2005), 'Friedrich List and the Infant Industry Argument', in Jomo K. S. (ed.), *The Pioneers of Development Economics: Great Economists on Development* (London: Zed).

Shah, A., and Thompson, T. (2002), 'Implementing Decentralized Local Governance: A Treacherous Road with Potholes, Detours, and Road Closures', paper presented at 'Can Decentralization Help Rebuild Indonesia?', Andrew Young School of Policy Studies, Georgia State University, Atlanta, GA, 1–3 May.

Shapcott, R. (2001), *Justice, Community, and Dialogue in International Relations* (Cambridge: Cambridge University Press).

Shiller, R. J. (2001), *Irrational Exuberance* (Princeton, NJ: Princeton University Press).

—— (2008), *The Subprime Solution: How Today's Global Financial Crisis Happened, and What to Do about It* (Princeton, NJ: Princeton University Press).

Shiva, V. (1993), 'The Greening of the Global Reach', in W. Sachs (ed.), *Global Ecology: A New Arena of Political Conflict* (London: Zed Books).

—— (1997), *Biopiracy: The Plunder of Nature and Knowledge* (Toronto: Between the Lines).

—— (2000), *Stolen Harvest: The Hijacking of the Global Food Supply* (Cambridge, MA: South End Press).

—— (2008), *Soil Not Oil: Environmental Justice in an Age of Climate Justice* (Cambridge, MA: South End Press).

Shonfield, A. (ed.) (1976), *International Economic Relations of the Western World 1959–1971*, i. *Politics and Trade* (London: Oxford University Press).

Shorrocks, A., Davies, J., and Lluberas, R. (2015), *Global Wealth Report 2015*, October, Credit Suisse Research Institute, www.credit-suisse.com

Sien, I. A. R. (2007), 'Beefing up the Hormones Dispute: Problems in Compliance and Viable Compromise Alternatives', *Georgetown Law Journal*, 95: 565–90.

Silver, B. J. (2003), *Forces of Labor: Workers' Movements and Globalization since 1870* (Cambridge: Cambridge University Press).

Simmons, B. A. (1994), *Who Adjusts? Domestic Sources of Foreign Economic Policy during the Interwar Years* (Princeton, NJ: Princeton University Press).

—— (1999), 'The Internationalisation of Capital', in H. Kitschelt, P. Lange, G. Marks, and J. D. Stephens (eds), *Continuity and Change in Contemporary Capitalism* (Cambridge: Cambridge University Press).

Simon, J. L. (1996), *The Ultimate Resource, 2* (Princeton, NJ: Princeton University Press).

Sinclair, T. (1994), 'Between State and Market', *Policy Sciences*, 27/4: 447–66.

Singer, D. (2007), *Regulating Capital: Setting Standards for the International Financial System* (Ithaca, NY: Cornell University Press).

Singh, A., and Zammit, A. (2000), 'International Capital Flows: Identifying the Gender Dimension', *World Development*, 28/7: 1249–68.

Sirkin, H. L., Zinser, M., and Hohner, D. (2011), 'Made in America, Again: Why Manufacturing Will Return to the US', Boston Consulting Group, August: 9, http://www.bcg.com/documents/file84471.pdf

Skeldon, Ronald (2010), 'The Current Global Economic Crisis and Migration: Policies and Practice in Origin and Destination', Working Paper T-32, Development Research Centre on Migration, Globalisation and Poverty, University of Sussex, May.

Skidelsky, R. (2003), 'Keynes's Road to Bretton Woods: An Essay in Interpretation', in M. Flandreau, C.-L. Holtfrerich, and H. James (eds), *International Financial History in the Twentieth Century* (Cambridge: Cambridge University Press).

—— (2009), *Keynes: The Return of the Master* (New York: Public Affairs).

Sklair, L. (2001), *The Transnational Capitalist Class* (Oxford: Blackwell).

Smillie, I. (2014), *Diamonds* (Cambridge: Polity).

Smith, A. (1759/1982), *The Theory of Moral Sentiments*, Glasgow Edition of the Works and Correspondence of Adam Smith, ed. D. D. Raphael and A. L. Macfie Indianapolis, IN: Liberty Fund).

—— (1776/1976), *An Inquiry into the Nature and Causes of the Wealth of Nations* (Oxford: Oxford University Press), www.econlib.org/library/Smith/smWN.html

—— (1776/1981), *An Inquiry into the Nature and Causes of the Wealth of Nations*, Glasgow Edition of the Works and Correspondence of Adam Smith, ed. R. H. Campbell and A. Skinner (Indianapolis, IN: Liberty Fund).

Snidal, D. (1985a), 'Coordination versus Prisoners' Dilemma: Implications for International Cooperation and Regimes', *American Political Science Review*, 79/4: 923–42.

—— (1985b), 'The Limits of Hegemonic Stability Theory', *International Organization*, 39/4: 579–614.

Snyder, R. (2001), 'Scaling Down: The Subnational Comparative Method', *Studies in Comparative International Development*, 36/1: 93–110.

Solis, M. (2003a), 'On the Myth of *Keiretsu* Network: Japanese Electronics in North America', *Business and Politics*, 5/3: 303–33.

—— (2003b), 'Japan's New Regionalism: The Politics of Free Trade Talks with Mexico', *Journal of East Asian Studies*, 3/3: 377–404.

Sorkin, A. (2009), *Too Big to Fail: The Inside Story of How Wall Street and Washington Fought to Save the Financial System—And Themselves* (New York: Viking).

Soroos, M. S. (1997), *The Endangered Atmosphere* (Columbia, SC: University of South Carolina Press).

—— (2008), *The New Paradigm for Financial Markets* (New York: Public Affairs).

Spatafora, N., and Tytell, I. (2009), *Commodity Terms of Trade: The History of Booms and Busts*, IMF Working Paper 205 (online: International Monetary Fund).

Spectator (2012), 'Glad Tidings', editorial, 15 December.

Spero, J. (1980), *The Failure of the Franklin National Bank* (New York: Columbia University Press).

Standaert, Samuel *et al.* (2016), 'Historical Trade Integration; Globalization and the Distance Puzzle in the Long Twentieth Century', *Cliometrica*, 10/2: doi:10.1007/s11698-015-0130-5.

Standing, G. (2000), 'Brave New Worlds? A Critique of Stiglitz's World Bank Rethink', *Development and Change*, 31/4: 737–63.

Stasavage, D. (2003), 'When Do States Abandon Monetary Discretion? Lessons from the Evolution of the CFA Franc Zone', in J. Kirshner (ed.), *Monetary Orders: Ambiguous Economics, Ubiquitous Politics* (Ithaca, NY: Cornell University Press).

Steans, J., and Pettiford, L. (2001), *International Relations: Perspectives and Themes* (Harlow: Pearson Education).

Steger, M. (2013), *Globalization: A Very Short Introduction*, 3rd edn (Oxford: Oxford University Press).

Stein, A. A. (1982), 'Coordination and Collaboration: Regimes in an Anarchic World', *International Organization*, 36/2: 294–324.

Steinmo, S. (2003), 'The Evolution of Policy Ideas: Tax Policy in the Twentieth Century', *British Journal of Politics and International Relations*, 5/2: 206–36.

Stern, N. (2015), *Why Are We Waiting? The Logic, Urgency, and Promise of Tackling Climate Change* (Cambridge, MA: MIT Press).

Stiglitz, J. E. (1998a), 'Towards a New Paradigm for Development: Strategies, Policies and Processes', Prebisch Lecture at UNCTAD, Geneva, 19 October.

—— (1998b), 'More Instruments and Broader Goals: Moving Toward the Post-Washington Consensus', World Institute for Development Economic Research Annual Lecture, Helsinki, 7 January.

—— (2001), 'An Agenda for Development in the Twenty-First Century', in A. Giddens (ed.), *The Global Third Way Debate* (Cambridge: Polity).

—— (2005), 'The Overselling of Globalization', in M. M. Weinstein (ed.), *Globalization: What's New?* (New York: Columbia University Press).

—— (2006), *Making Globalization Work* (New York: Norton).

Stokke, O. S. (2012), *Disaggregating International Regimes: A New Approach to Evaluation and Comparison* (Cambridge, MA: MIT Press).

—— and Hønneland, G. (eds) (2007), *International Cooperation and Arctic Governance: Regime Effectiveness and Northern Region Building* (New York: Routledge).

Stolper, W., and Samuelson, P. A. (1941), 'Protection and Real Wages', *Review of Economic Studies*, 9: 58–73.

Strange, S. (1986), *Casino Capitalism* (Oxford: Basil Blackwell).

—— (1988), *States and Markets* (London: Pinter).

—— (1994), *States and Markets*, 2nd edn (London: Pinter).

—— (1996), *The Retreat of the State: The Diffusion of Power in the World Economy* (Cambridge: Cambridge University Press).

—— (1998a), 'International Political Economy: Beyond Economics and International Relations', *Économies et Sociétés*, 34/4: 3–24.

—— (1998b), *Mad Money: When Markets Outgrow Government* (Ann Arbor, MI: University of Michigan Press).

Straumann, L. (2014), *Money Logging: On the Trail of the Asian Timber Mafia* (Basel, Switzerland: Bergli Books).

Streck, C. (2001), 'The Global Environment Facility: A Role Model for International Governance?', *Global Environmental Politics*, 1/2: 71–94.

Streeck, W. (2013), *The Politics of Public Debt: Neoliberalism, Capitalist Development, and the Restructuring of the State*. MPIfG Discussion Paper 13/7, Cologne: Max Planck Institute for the Study of Societies.

Streeten, P., with Burki, S. J., Ul Haq, M., Hicks, N., and Stewart, F. (1982), *First Things First: Meeting Basic Human Needs in Developing Countries* (New York: World Bank/Oxford University Press).

Strong, M. (2000), *Where on Earth Are We Going?* (Toronto: Knopf).

Stuckler, D., L. King and G. Patton. (2009), 'The social construction of successful market reforms', working paper, Political Economy Research Institute, University of Massachusetts Amherst, March.

Sturgeon, T. (2002), 'Modular Production Networks: A New American Model of Industrial Organization', *Industrial and Corporate Change*, 11/3: 451–96.

—— and Memedovic, O. (2011), *Mapping Global Value Chains: Intermediate Goods Trade and Structural Change in the World Economy*, Development Policy and Strategic Research Branch Working Paper 05/2011 (Vienna: United National Industrial Development Organization).

Subramanian, A. (2011), *Eclipse* (Washington, DC: Peterson Institute for International Economics).

—— and Martin Kessler (2013), *The Hyperglobalization of Trade and its Future* (Switzerland: Global Citizens Foundation).

Sunkel, O. (1972), 'Big Business and "Dependencia": A Latin American View', *Foreign Affairs*, 50/3: 517–31.

Susskind, L., and Ali, S. H. (2015), *Environmental Diplomacy: Negotiating More Effective Global Agreements*, 2nd edn (Oxford: Oxford University Press).

Svedberg, P. (2002), *Global Capital, Political Institutions and Policy Change in Developed Welfare States* (Cambridge: Cambridge University Press).

—— (2003), *World Income Distribution: Which Way?*, Institute for International Economics Seminar Paper 724 (Stockholm: Stockholm University).

Swenson, P. (2000), *Capitalists Against Markets* (Oxford: Oxford University Press).

Switzer, J. V. (2004), *Environmental Politics: Domestic and Global Dimensions*, 4th edn (Belmont, CA: Thomson/Wadsworth).

Tacconi, L. (ed.) (2007), *Illegal Logging: Law Enforcement, Livelihoods and the Timber Trade* (London: Earthscan).

Tasca, H. J. (1938), *The Reciprocal Trade Policy of the United States* (New York: Russell & Russell).

Taylor, A. M. (1996), *Domestic Saving and International Capital Flows Reconsidered*, NBER Working Paper 4892 (Cambridge, MA: National Bureau of Economic Research).

—— (2002), *Globalization, Trade and Development: Some Lessons from History*, NBER Working Paper 9326 (Cambridge, MA: National Bureau of Economic Research).

Taylor, M. (1987), *The Possibility of Cooperation* (Cambridge: Cambridge University Press).

Teeple, G. (1995), *Globalization and the Decline of Social Reform* (Toronto: Garamond Press).

Teivainen, T. (2002), *Enter Economism, Exit Politics* (London: Zed Books).

Temin, P. (2010), *The Great Recession and the Great Depression*, NBER Working Paper 15645 (Cambridge, MA: National Bureau of Economic Research).

Tesar, L. L. (1991), 'Saving, Investment and International Capital Flows', *Journal of International Economics*, 31/1: 55–78.

Thistlethwaite, J. (2012), 'The Climate Wise Principles: Self-Regulating Climate Change Risks in the Insurance Sector', *Business and Society*, 51/1: 121–47.

Thomas, C. (2008), 'Globalization and Development in the South', in J. Ravenhill (ed.), *Global Political Economy*, 2nd edn (Oxford: Oxford University Press)

Thompson, G. (2006), 'The Supra-national Regionalization of the International Financial System: How Far and with What Prospects?', paper prepared for the GARNET Conference, Amsterdam, 28–30 September.

Thorp, R. (1998), *Progress, Poverty and Exclusion: An Economic History of Latin America in the 20th Century* (Baltimore, MD: Johns Hopkins/Inter-American Development Bank).

Thun, E. (2000), *Growing up and Moving out: Globalization in the Taiwanese Textile/Apparel and Automotive Sectors*, MIT IPC Working Paper 00-007 (Cambridge, MA: Industrial Performance Center, Massachusetts Institute of Technology), June.

—— (2006), *Changing Lanes in China: Foreign Direct Investment, Local Governments, and Auto Sector Development* (New York: Cambridge University Press).

Thurbon, E. (2016), *The Developmental Mindset: The Revival of Financial Activism in South Korea* (Ithaca, NY: Cornell University Press).

Tichenor, D. J. (2002), *Dividing Lines: The Politics of Immigration Control in America* (Princeton, NJ: Princeton University Press).

Tienhaara, K. (2006), 'Mineral Investment and the Regulation of the Environment in Developing Countries: Lessons from Ghana', *International Environmental Agreements: Politics, Law and Economics*, 6/4: 371–94.

Tilly, Charles.. (1989), *Big structures, large processes, huge comparisons* (London: Sage)

Tisdell, C. (2001), 'Globalization and Sustainability: Environmental Kuznets Curve and the WTO', *Ecological Economics*, 39/2: 185–96.

Tooze, R. and Murphy, C. (1996), 'The Epistemology of Poverty and the Poverty of Epistemology in IPE: Mystery, Blindness, and Invisibility', *Millennium*, 25/3: 681–707.

Toye, J. (1993), *Dilemmas of Development*, 2nd edn (Oxford: Blackwell).

Trans-Pacific Partnership (TPP) Countries (2015), Joint Declaration of the Macroeconomic Policy Authorities of Trans-Pacific Partnership Countries, https://www.treasury.gov/initiatives/Documents/TPP_Currency_November%202015.pdf

Traxler, F., and Woitech, B. (2000), 'Transnational Investment and National Labour Market Regimes: A Case of 'Regime Shopping'?', *European Journal of Industrial Relations*, 6/2: 141–59.

Tribe, K. (1995), *Strategies of Economic Order: German Economic Discourse, 1750–1950* (Cambridge: Cambridge University Press).

Trichet, J-C. (2016), *Le Journal du Dimanche*, Paris, 14 February.

Triffin, R. (1960), *Gold and the Dollar Crisis* (New Haven: Yale University Press).

Trommer, S. (2014), *Transformations in Trade Politics: Participatory Trade Politics in West Africa* (London: Routledge).

Truman, E. (2006a), 'A Strategy for International Monetary Fund Reform', *Policy Analyses in International Economics*, 77 (Washington, DC: Institute for International Economics).

Truman, E. (ed.) (2006b), *Reforming the IMF for the 21st Century* (Washington, DC: Peterson Institute for International Economics).

Tullock, G. (1983), *The Economics of Income Distribution* (Boston: Kluwer-Nijhoff).

Turner, B. and R. Holton. (eds) (2015), *The Routledge International Handbook of Globalization Studies* (London: Routledge).

Turner, P. (1981), 'Capital Flows in the 1980s: A Survey of Major Trends', *BIS Economic Papers*, 30 (Geneva: Bank for International Settlements).

Tussie, D. (1987), *The Less Developed Countries and the World Trading System: A Challenge to the GATT* (London: Frances Pinter).

Tyers, R., and Anderson, R. K. (1992), *Disarray in World Food Markets* (Cambridge: Cambridge University Press).

Ugur, M. (ed) (2001), *Open Economy Macroeconomics: A Reader* (London: Routledge).

Underhill, G. (1994), 'Introduction: Conceptualizing the Changing Global Order', in R. Stubbs and G. Underhill (eds) *Political Economy and the Changing Global Order* (Basingstoke: Macmillan).

UN (United Nations) (1992), *Agenda 21: The United Nations Programme of Action from Rio* (New York: United Nations).

—— (2006), *World Economic and Social Survey 2006: Diverging Growth and Development* (New York: United Nations).

—— (2009a), 'Report of the Commission of Experts of the President of the United Nations General Assembly on Reforms of the International Monetary and Financial System', 21 September, www.un.org/ga/econcrisissummit/docs/FinalReport_CoE.pdf

—— (2009b), *The Millennium Development Goals Report 2009* (New York: United Nations).

—— (2015), World Economic Situation and Prospects 2015 (New York: United Nations).

—— (2015b), *Adoption of the Paris Agreement*, Framework Convention on Climate Change, Conference of the Parties Twenty-first session Paris, 30 November to 11 December 2015, FCCC/CP/2015/L.9/Rev.1, 12 December, available at https://unfccc.int

UN Commission on Transnational Corporations (1978), *Transnational Corporations in World Development: A Re-Examination* (New York: UN Publications).

UNCTAD (United Nations Conference on Trade and Development) (1979), *Multilateral Trade Negotiations: Evaluations and Further Recommendation Arising Therefrom*, UNCTAD v (UN Doc. TD/227).

—— (1982), *Assessment of the results of the multilateral trade negotiations* (Geneva: UNCTAD).

—— (1999), *World Investment Report 1999: Foreign Direct Investment and the Challenge of Development* (Geneva: UNCTADC).

—— (2000), *World Investment Report 2000: Cross-Border Mergers and Acquisitions and Development* (Geneva: UNCTADC).

—— (2001), *World Investment Report: Promoting Linkages* (Geneva: UNCTADC).

—— (2002), *World Investment Report 2002: Transnational Corporations and Export Competitiveness* (Geneva: UNCTADC).

—— (2003), *World Investment Report 2003: FDI Policies for Development: National and International Perspectives* (Geneva: UNCTADC).

—— (2004a), *Development and Globalization: Facts and Figures* (Geneva: UNCTADC).

—— (2004b), 'The New Geography of International Economic Relations', TD/B/51/6 Trade and Development Board, 51st Session, Geneva, 4–15 October, GE. 04-52426.

—— (2005), *Trade and Development Report 2005: New Features of Global Interdependence* (Geneva: UNCTADC).

UNCTAD (United Nations Conference on Trade and Development) (2006), *Trade and Development Report 2006: Global Partnership and National Policies for Development* (Geneva: UNCTADC).

—— (2009*a*), 'Global FDI in Decline due to the Financial Crisis, and a Further Drop Expected', *UNCTAD Investment Brief*, 1, www. waipa.org/pdf/InvestmentBriefs/Investmentbrief_01_2009.pdf

—— (2009*b*), *World Investment Report 2009: Transnational Corporations, Agricultural Production and Development* (Geneva: UNCTADC).

—— (2011), *World Investment Report 2011* (Geneva: UNCTADC).

—— (2012*a*), *World Investment Report 2012: Towards a New Generation of Investment Policies* (Geneva: UNCTADC).

—— (2012*b*), *Excessive Commodity Price Volatility: Macroeconomic Effects on Growth* and Policy Options (Geneva: UNCTADC).

—— (2013), *Investment Trends Monitor*, 11 (23 January).

—— (2014), *State of Commodity Dependence* (Geneva and New York: United Nations).

—— (2015*a*), *Rethinking Development Strategies after the Financial Crisis, vol. 1: Making the Case for Policy Space* (Geneva: UNCTAD).

—— (2015*b*), *World Investment Report 2015: Reforming International Investment Governance* (Geneva: UNCTAD).

—— (2016), *Rethinking Development Strategies after the Financial Crisis, vol. 2: Country Studies and International Comparisons* (Geneva: UNCTAD).

UNDP (United Nations Development Programme) (2003), *Making Global Trade Work for People* (London: Earthscan).

—— (2006), *Human Development Report 2005: International Cooperation at a Crossroads: Air, Trade and Security in an Unequal World* (New York: UNDP).

—— (2011), *Towards Human Resilience: Sustaining MDG Progress in an Age of Economic Uncertainty* (New York: UNDP).

—— (2015), *The Millennium Development Goals Report 2015* (New York: United Nations).

UNEP (United Nations Environment Programme) (2002), *Global Environment Outlook 3* (London: Earthscan).

—— (2003), 'Backgrounder: Basic Facts and Data on the Science and Politics of Ozone Protection', www.unep.org/ozone/pdf/Press-Backgrounder.pdf

—— (2005), 'Basic Facts and Data on the Science and Politics of Ozone Protection', Nov. Media Release (Nairobi: UNEP).

UNGA (2013), World Commodity Trends and Prospects. Report of the Secretary General, A/68/204 (New York: United Nations).

UNICEF (United Nations Children's Fund) (2007), 'Child Poverty in Perspective: An Overview of Child Well-Being in Rich Countries', Report Card 7 (Florence: UNICEF Innocenti Research Centre).

US Federal Deposit Insurance Corporation (2012), 'Failed Bank List', updated weekly, www.fdic.gov/bank/individual/failed/banklist.html

US Treasury (2015), Fact Sheet: Joint Declaration of the Macroeconomic Policy Authorities of Trans-Pacific Partnership Countries, 5 November, https://www.treasury.gov/initiatives/Documents/Press%20Release%20-%20Joint%20Declaration%20Fact%20Sheet.pdf

van der Pijl, K. (1998), *Transnational Classes and International Relations* (London: Routledge).

van Dormael, A. (1978), *Bretton Woods: The Birth of a Monetary System* (London: Macmillan).

van Staveren, I. (2002), 'Global Finance and Gender', in J. A. Scholte (ed.), *Civil Society and Global Finance* (London: Routledge).

Vaubel, R. (1986), 'A Public Choice Approach to International Organization', *Public Choice*, 51/1: 39–57.

—— (1991), 'The Political Economy of the International Monetary Fund', in R. Vaubel and T. D. Willett (eds), *The Political Economy of International Organizations: A Public Choice Approach* (Boulder, CO: Westview Press).

Veloso, F. (2000), *The Automotive Supply Chain Organization: Global Trends and Perspectives*, MIT Working Paper (Cambridge, MA: MIT).

Verdier, D. (1994), *Democracy and International Trade: Britain, France, and the United States, 1860–1990* (Princeton, NJ: Princeton University Press).

Vernon, R. (1971), *Sovereignty at Bay* (New York: Basic Books).

—— (1995), 'The World Trade Organization: A New Stage in International Trade and Development', *Harvard International Law Journal*, 36: 329–40.

Veseth, M. (2005), *Globaloney: Unraveling the Myths of Globalization* (Lanham, MD: Rowman & Littlefield).

Vestergaard, J., and Wade, R. (2012), 'The Governance Response to the Great Recession: The "Success" of the G20', *Journal of Economic Issues*, 46: 481–9.

—— (2013), 'Protecting Power: How Western States Retain their Dominant Voice in the World Bank's Governance', *World Development*, 46: 153–64, http://dx.doi.org/10.1016/j.worlddev.2013.01.031

Victor, D., Raustiala, K., and Skolnikoff, E. (1998), *The Implementation and Effectiveness of International Environmental Commitments: Theory and Practice* (Cambridge, MA: MIT Press).

Vidal, J., Goldenberg, S., and Taylor, L. (2015), 'How the Historic Paris Deal Over Climate Change Was Finally Agreed', *The Guardian*, 13 December, www.theguardian.com

Viner, J. (1928/1989), 'Adam Smith and Laissez-Faire', in J. M. Clark *et al.*, *Adam Smith, 1776–1926: Lectures to Commemorate the Sesquicentennial of the Publication of the 'Wealth of Nations'* (New York: Augustus M. Kelley Publishers).

—— (1948), 'Power versus Plenty', *World Politics*, 1/1: 1–29.

—— (1950), *The Customs Union Issue* (New York: Carnegie Endowment for International Peace).

Vogel, D. (1995), *Trading Up: Consumer and Environmental Regulation in a Global Economy* (Cambridge, MA: Harvard University Press).

—— (2012), *The Politics of Precaution: Regulating Health, Safety, and Environmental Risks in Europe and the United States* (Princeton, NJ: Princeton University Press).

Vogler, J. (2000), *The Global Commons: Environmental and Technological Governance*, 2nd edn (Chichester: Wiley).

—— (2003), 'Taking Institutions Seriously: How Regime Analysis Can Be Relevant to Multilevel Environmental Governance', *Global Environmental Politics*, 3/2: 25–39.

von Mises, L. (1955), *Ideas on Liberty* (New York: Irvington).

Wackernagel, M., and Rees, W. (1996), *Our Ecological Footprint: Reducing Human Impact on the Earth* (Gabriola Island, BC: New Society Publishers).

Wade, R. (1990), *Governing the Market: Economic Theory and the Role of Government in Taiwan's Industrialization* (Princeton, NJ: Princeton University Press).

—— (1996a), 'Globalization and Its Limits: Reports of the Death of the National Economy Are Greatly Exaggerated', in S. Berger and R. Dore (eds), *National Diversity and Global Capitalism* (Ithaca, NY: Cornell University Press).

—— (1996b), 'Japan, the World Bank, and the Art of Paradigm Maintenance: The East Asian Miracle in Political Perspective', *New Left Review*, 217: 3–36.

—— (1998), 'The Asian Debt-and-Development Crisis of 1997–?: Causes and Consequences', *World Development*, 26/8: 1535–53.

—— (2003a), 'What Strategies Are Viable for Developing Countries Today? The WTO and the Shrinkage of Development Space', *Review of International Political Economy*, 10/4: 621–44.

—— (2003b), 'The Invisible Hand of the American Empire', *Ethics and International Affairs*, 17/2: 77–88.

—— (2004), *Governing the Market: Economic Theory and the Role of Government in East Asian Industrialization* (Princeton, NJ: Princeton University Press).

—— (2007a), 'The Washington Consensus', in *International Encyclopaedia of the Social Sciences* (New York: Macmillan).

—— (2007b), 'Economic Liberalism and the "Outward Alliance" of State, Finance and Big Companies: A Perspective from the United Kingdom', in P. Bowles, H. Veltmeyer, S. Cornelissen, N. Invernizzi, and K.-L. Tang (eds), *National Perspectives on Globalization: A Critical Reader* (Basingstoke: Palgrave Macmillan).

—— (2009a), 'From Global Imbalances to Global Reorganizations', *Cambridge Journal of Economics*, 33/4: 539–62.

—— (2009b), 'Iceland as Icarus', *Challenge*, 52/3: 5–33.

—— (2009c), 'The Global Slump: Deeper Causes and Harder Lessons', *Challenge*, 52/5: 5–24.

—— (2009d), *Governing the Market* (Princeton, NJ: Princeton University Press).

—— (2010), 'Is the Globalization Consensus Dead?', in N. Castree, P. Chatterton, N. Heynen, W. Larner, and M. Wright (eds), *The Point Is to Change It: Geographies of Hope and Survival in an Age of Crisis* (Oxford: Wiley-Blackwell).

—— (2011), 'Beware What You Wish for: Lessons for International Political Economy from the Transformation of Economics', in N. Phillips and C. Weaver (eds), *International Political Economy: Debating the Past, Present and Future* (London: Routledge).

—— (2012), 'Why Has Income Inequality Remained on the Sidelines of Public Policy for So Long?', *Challenge*, 55/3: 21–50.

—— (2013), 'Trade Liberalization and Economic Growth: Does Trade Liberalization Contribute to Economic Prosperity?', in P. Haas and J. Hird (eds), *Controversies in Globalization: Contending Approaches to International Relations*, 2nd edn (Washington, DC: CQPress).

—— (2014), 'The Paradox of US Industrial Policy: The Developmental State in Disguise', ch. 14 in J. Salazar-Xirinachs *et al.*, *Transforming Economies: Making Industrial Policy Work for Growth, Jobs and Development* (Geneva: UNCTAD and ILO).

—— (2015), 'The role of industrial policy in developing countries', in UNCTAD (2015): 67–79.

—— (2016), 'Economists' ethics in the build-up to the Great Recession', ch. 15 in DeMartino and McCloskey (eds), *The Oxford Handbook of Professional Economic Ethics* (Oxford: Oxford University Press).

Walker, R. B. J. (1993), *Inside/Outside: International Relations as Political Theory* (Cambridge: Cambridge University Press).

Wall Street Journal (2006), 3 January.

Wallace, H. (2000), 'The Policy Process: A Moving Pendulum', in H. Wallace and W. Wallace (eds), *Policy-Making in the European Union*, 4th edn (Oxford: Oxford University Press).

—— Wallace, W., and Pollack, M. A. (eds) (2005), *Policy-Making in the European Union* (Oxford: Oxford University Press).

—— Mark A. Pollack, and Alasdair R. Young (eds) (2015), *Policy-Making in the European Union*, 7th edn (Oxford: Oxford University Press).

Wallbank, A. (2012), *Dialogue, Didacticism and the Genres of Dispute: Literary Dialogues in the Age of Revolution* (London: Pickering & Chatto).

Wallerstein, I. (1974), *The Modern World System*, i (New York: Academic Press).

—— (1979), *The Capitalist World-System: Essays by Immanuel Wallerstein* (Cambridge: Cambridge University Press).

—— (1980), *The Modern World System*, ii (New York: Academic Press).

—— (1983), *Historical Capitalism* (London: Verso).

Walras, L. (1874/1984), *Elements of Pure Economics: Or the Theory of Social Wealth*, tr. W. Jaffé (Philadelphia: Orion Editions).

Waltz, K. N. (1979), *Theory of International Politics* (Reading, MA: Addison Wesley).

Wapner, P. (2003), 'World Summit on Sustainable Development: Toward a Post-Jo'burg Environmentalism', *Global Environmental Politics*, 3/1: 1–10.

Warnock, F. E., and Warnock, V. C. (2006), *International Capital Flows and US Interest Rates*, NBER Working Paper 12560 (Cambridge, MA: National Bureau of Economic Research).

Warwick Commission (2007), *The Multilateral Trade Regime: Which Way Forward?* The Report of the First Warwick Commission, University of Warwick.

Washington Post (2015), 'The End of Globalization', 20 September.

Watson, M. (2001), 'International Capital Mobility in an Era of Globalization: Adding a Political Dimension to the Feldstein-Horioka Puzzle', *Politics*, 21/2: 81–92.

—— (2003), 'Ricardian Political Economy and the Varieties of Capitalism Approach: Specialisation, Trade and Comparative Institutional Advantage', *Comparative European Politics*, 1/2: 227–40.

—— (2005), *Foundations of International Political Economy* (Basingstoke: Palgrave Macmillan).

Watts, J. (2005), 'The Tiger's Teeth', *Guardian*, 25 May.

WCED (World Commission on Environment and Development) (1987), *Our Common Future* (Oxford: Oxford University Press).

Webb, M. (1995), *The Political Economy of Policy Coordination: International Adjustment since 1945* (Ithaca, NY: Cornell University Press).

Weber, M. (1913/1958), 'The Social Psychology of the World Religions', in H. H. Gerth and C. Wright Mills (eds), *Max Weber: Essays in Sociology* (New York: Oxford University Press).

Weingast, B., Shepsle, K., and Johnsen, C. (1981), 'The Political Economy of Benefits and Costs', *Journal of Political Economy*, 89/4: 642–64.

Weiss, L. (1998), *The Myth of the Powerless State: Governing the Economy in a Global Era* (Cambridge: Polity Press).

—— and Hobson, J. M. (1995), *States and Economic Development: A Comparative Historical Analysis* (London: Polity).

Wendt, A. (1992), 'Anarchy Is What States Make of It', *International Organization*, 42/2: 391–422.

—— (1995), 'Constructing International Politics', *International Security*, 20/1: 71–81.

—— (1998), 'On Constitution and Causation in International Relations', *Review of International Studies*, 24/5: 101–17.

Westling, T. (2011), 'Male organ and economic growth: does size matter?', MPRA Paper No. 32706. University Library, Munich.

Whalley, J. (1999), 'Why Do Countries Seek Regional Trade Agreements?', in J. Frankel (ed.), *The Regionalization of the World Economy* (Cambridge, MA: National Bureau of Economic Research).

Wheeler, D. (2002), 'Beyond Pollution Havens', *Global Environmental Politics*, 2/2: 1–10.

White, G. (ed.) (1988), *Developmental States in East Asia* (London: Macmillan).

Whiting, S. H. (2001), *Power and Wealth in Rural China* (Cambridge: Cambridge University Press).

WHO (World Health Organization) (2008), *World Health Statistics: Part 2 Global Health Indicators* (Geneva: WHO).

—— and UNICEF (2015), *Progress on Sanitation and Drinking Water: 2015 Update and MDG Assessment* (Geneva: WHO and UNICEF).

Wilensky, H. L. (2002), *Rich Democracies: Political Economy, Public Policy and Performance* (Berkeley and Los Angeles, CA: University of California Press).

Wilkins, M. (2003), 'Conduits for Long Term Foreign Investment in the Gold Standard Era', in M. Flandreu, C.-L. Holtfrerich, and H. James (eds), *International Financial History in the Twentieth Century: System and Anarchy* (Cambridge: Cambridge University Press).

Wilkinson, R. (2006), *The WTO: Crisis and the Governance of Global Trade* (London: Routledge).

—— and Hulme, D. (eds) (2012), *The Millennium Development Goals and Beyond: Global Development After 2015* (London: Routledge).

—— and Pickett, K. (2009), *The Spirit Level: Why More Equal Societies Almost Always Do Better* (London: Allen Lane).

Williams, D., and Young, T. (1994), 'Governance, the World Bank and Liberal Theory', *Political Studies*, 42/1: 84–100.

Williams, M. (1994), *International Economic Organizations and the Third World* (Hemel Hempstead: Harvester Wheatsheaf).

—— (2004), 'Contesting Global Trade Rules: Social Movements and the World Trade Organization', in L. Benería and S. Bisnath (eds),

Global Tensions: Challenges and Opportunities in the World Economy, London: Routledge: 193–206.

Williamson, J. (1990), 'What Washington Means by Policy Reform', in J. Williamson (ed.), *Latin American Adjustment: How Much Has Happened?* (Washington, DC: Institute of International Economics).

—— (2003), 'Overview: An Agenda for Restarting Growth and Reform', in J. Williamson and P.-P. Kuczynski (eds), *After the Washington Consensus: Restarting Growth and Reform in Latin America* (Washington, DC: Institute for International Economics).

—— (2009), 'Understanding Special Drawing Rights (SDRs)', Policy Brief Number PB09-11 (Washington, DC: Peterson Institute for International Economics, June).

Williamson, O. E. (1975), *Markets and Hierarchies, Analysis and Anti-Trust Implications: A Study in the Economics of Internal Organization* (New York: Free Press).

—— (1981), 'The Modern Corporation: Origins, Evolution, Attributes', *Journal of Economic Literature*, 19/4: 1537–68.

Winch, C. (1998), 'Listian Political Economy: Social Capitalism Conceptualised?', *New Political Economy*, 3/2: 301–16.

Winchester, S. (1991), *Pacific Rising* (New York: Prentice-Hall).

Winham, G. R. (1986), *International Trade and the Tokyo Round Negotiation* (Princeton, NJ: Princeton University Press).

—— (1998a), 'Explanations of Developing Country Behaviour in the GATT Uruguay Round Negotiation', *World Competition*, 21/3: 109–34.

—— (1998b), 'The World Trade Organization: Institution-Building in the Multilateral Trade System', *World Economy*, 21/3: 349–68.

Wintrobe, R. (1998), *The Political Economy of Dictatorship* (Cambridge: Cambridge University Press).

Wionczek, M. (1966), 'Requisites for Viable Economic Integration', in M. Wionczek (ed.), *Latin American Economic Integration: Experiences and Prospects* (New York: Praeger).

Wolf, D., and Zangl, B. (1996), 'The European Economic and Monetary Union: "Two-Level Games" and the Formation of International Institutions', *European Journal of International Relations*, 2/3: 355–93.

Wolf, M. (2000), 'The Big Lie of Global Inequality', *Financial Times*, 8 February.

—— (2004a), *Why Globalization Works* (New Haven: Yale University Press).

—— (2004b), 'States Are Cure and Disease', Special Report: World Economy, *Financial Times*, 1 October.

—— (2006), 'Will Globalization Survive?', *World Economics*, 6/4.

—— (2008), *Fixing Global Finance* (Baltimore, MD: Johns Hopkins University Press).

—— (2009), 'Why President Obama Must Mend a Sick World Economy', *Financial Times*, 21 January.

—— (2014), *The Shifts and the Shocks* (London: Penguin)

Wolff, J. (2002), *Why Read Marx Today?* (Oxford: Oxford University Press).

Womack, J. P., Jones, D. T., and Roos, D. (1990), *The Machine that Changed the World* (New York: Harper Perennial).

Woo-Cumings, M. (ed.) (1999), *The Developmental State* (Ithaca, NY: Cornell University Press).

Wood, A. (1994), *North-South Trade, Employment andInequality* (Oxford: Oxford University Press).

Wood, E. M. (2003), *Empire of Capital* (London: Verso).

Woodhouse, P. (2002), 'Development Policies and Environmental Agendas', in U. Kothari and M. Minogue (eds), *Development Theory and Practice: Critical Perspectives* (Basingstoke: Palgrave).

Woods, N. (2003), 'Order, Justice, the IMF and the World Bank', in R. Foot, J. L. Gaddis, and A. Hurrell (eds), *Order and Justice in International Relations* (Oxford: Oxford University Press).

—— (2006), *The Globalizers: The IMF, the World Bank and Their Borrowers* (Ithaca, NY: Cornell University Press).

World Bank (1992a), *Governance and Development* (Washington, DC: IBRD).

—— (1992b), *World Development Report 1992* (New York: Oxford University Press).

—— (1993), *The East Asian Miracle: Economic Growth and Public Policy* (Oxford: Oxford University Press).

—— (1994), *Adjustment in Africa: Reforms, Results, and the Road Ahead* (Washington, DC: IBRD).

—— (1997), *Private Capital Flows to Developing Countries: The Road to Financial Integration* (Washington, DC: IBRD).

—— (1999a), *Global Development Finance* [electronic resource] (Washington, DC: IBRD/World Bank), computer disks; 3½ in.

—— (1999b), *World Development Report 1999/2000: Entering the 21st Century* (Washington, DC: World Bank).

—— (2000), *Trade Blocs* (New York: Oxford University Press).

—— (2002a), *Global Development Finance: Financing the Poorest Countries* [electronic resource] (Washington, DC: World Bank), 1 CD-ROM; 4¾ in.

—— (2002b), *Globalization, Growth, and Poverty: Building an Inclusive World Economy* (New York: Oxford University Press).

—— (2002c), *World Development Indicators 2002* (Washington, DC: World Bank).

—— (2005a), *World Development Indicators 2005* (Washington, DC: World Bank).

—— (2005b), *World Development Report 2006: Equity and Development* (New York: World Bank and Oxford University Press).

—— (2005c), *Economic Growth in the 1990s: Learning from a Decade of Reform* (Washington, DC: IBRD).

—— (2007a), East Asia and Pacific Update: Ten Years After Asia's Financial Crisis, April, http://siteresources.worldbank.org

—— (2007b), *Global Economic Prospects: Managing the Next Wave of Globalization, 2007* (Washington, DC: World Bank).

—— (2009a), *Global Development Finance* (Washington, DC: World Bank).

—— (2009b), *Global Monitoring Report: A Development Emergency* (Washington, DC: World Bank).

—— (2009c), *World Development Indicators 2009* (Washington, DC: World Bank).

—— (2009d), *World Development Report 2009: Reshaping Economic Geography* (Washington, DC: World Bank).

—— (2010a), *Global Economic Prospects 2010: Crisis, Finance, and Growth* (Washington, DC: World Bank).

—— (2010b), *World Development Indicators* (Washington, DC: World Bank).

—— (2011), *Global Economic Prospects* (Washington, DC: World Bank).

—— (2012a), *An Update to the World Bank's Estimates of Consumption Poverty in the Developing World*, Briefing Note, 29 February, http://siteresources.worldbank.org/INTPOVCALNET/Resources/Global_Poverty_Update201202-29-12.pdf

—— (2012b), *Global Development Finance Database* (Washington, DC: World Bank).

—— (2012c), *Global Economic Prospects—January 2013: Assuring Growth Over the Medium Term* (Washington, DC: World Bank).

—— (2013a), *China 2030: Building a Modern, Harmonious, and Creative Society*.

—— (2013b), *Global Economic Prospects January 2013* (Washington, DC: World Bank).

—— (2015a), World Bank Forecasts Global Poverty to Fall Below 10% for First Time; Major Hurdles Remain in Goal to End Poverty by 2030, press release, 4 October, available at http://www.worldbank.org/en/news/press-release/2015/10/04/world-bank-forecasts-global-poverty-to-fall-below-10-for-first-time-major-hurdles-remain-in-goal-to-end-poverty-by-2030 (accessed May 2016).

—— (2015b), Remittances growth to slow sharply in 2015, as Europe and Russia stay weak; pick up expected next year, press release, 13 April.

—— (2015c), *Global Economic Prospects January 2015* (Washington, DC: World Bank).

—— (2015d), *Global Economic Prospects—The Global Economy in Transition* (Washington, DC: World Bank).

—— (2015e), *World Development Indicator*, 'Merchandise Trade (% of GDP)', available at: http://data.worldbank.org/indicator/TG.VAL.TOTL.GD.ZS

World Commission on Environment and Development (1987), *Our Common Future* (Oxford: Oxford University Press).

World Meteorological Organization Secretariat (2015), 'Highlights from the Most Recent WMO/UNEP Ozone Assessment', *World Meteorological Organization Bulletin*, 64/1: www.wmo.int/bulletin

World Resources Institute (2015), 'New Global Data Finds Tropical Forests Declining in Overlooked Hotspots', WRI press release, 2 September, www.wri.org

WTO (World Trade Organization) (1996), *Guidelines for Arrangements on Relations with Non-Governmental Organizations*, Decision Adopted by the General Council on 18 July 1996, WT/L/162.

—— (1999), *WTO, Trade and Environment*, Special Studies 4 (Geneva: WTO), press release, www.wto.org/english/tratop_e/envir_e/stud99_e.htm

—— (2000a), 'Mapping of Regional Trade Agreements: Note by the Secretariat', Committee on Regional Trade Agreements, WT/REG/W/41 (Geneva: World Trade Organization) 11 October, www.wto.org/english/tratop_e/region_/wtregw41_e.doc (Chart 2: 5).

—— (2000b), 'Overview of the State of Play of WTO Disputes', Informal Paper (Geneva: WTO).

—— (2001a), *World Trade Report* (Geneva: WTO).

—— (2001b), 'WTO Successfully Concludes Negotiations on China's Entry', WTO press release (PRESS/243), 17 September.

—— (2002), *World Trade Report* (Geneva: WTO).

—— (2003a), *Annual Report* (Geneva: WTO).

—— (2003b), 'Decision Removes Final Patent Obstacle to Cheap Drug Imports', WTO press release, PRESS/350/Rev. 1, 4 September.

—— (2003c), *World Trade Report* (Geneva: WTO), www.wto.org/english/res_e/booksp_e/anrep_e/world_trade_report_2003_e.pdf

—— (2005), *World Trade Report 2005: Exploring the Links between Trade, Standards* and *the WTO* (Geneva: WTO).

—— (2006a), *International Trade Statistics 2006* (Geneva: WTO).

—— (2006b), *Report (2006) of the Committee on Regional Trade Agreements to the General Council*, WT/REG/17, http://docsonline.wto.org

—— (2006c), *World Trade Report 2006: Subsidies, Trade and the WTO* (Geneva: WTO).

—— (2008), 'European Communities—Regime for the Importation, Sale and Distribution of Bananas', www.wto.org/english/tratop_e/dispu_e/cases_e/ds27_e.htm

—— (2009a), *World Trade Report 2009: Trade Policy Commitments and Contingency Measures* (Geneva: WTO).

—— (2009b), *International Trade Statistics 2009* (Geneva: WTO).

—— (2009c), 'European Communities—Measures Concerning Meat and Meat Products (Hormones)', www.wto.org/english/tratop_e/dispu_e/cases_e/ds26_e.htm

—— (2011a), 'Cover Note by TNC Chair', TN/C/13, 21 April.

—— (2011b), *World Trade Report 2011: Preferential Trade Agreements and the WTO: From Co-Existence to Coherence* (Geneva: WTO).

—— (2012), *World Trade Report 2012* (Geneva: WTO).

—— (2013), 'Regional Trade Agreements: Facts and Figures', www.wto.org/english/tratop_e/region_e/regfac_e.htm

—— (2015a), *International Trade Statistics* (Geneva: WTO).

—— (2015b), *World Trade Report 2015* (Geneva: WTO).

—— (2015c), 'Overview of the WTO Secretariat', available at https://www.wto.org/english/thewto_e/secre_e/intro_e.htm

Worm, B., Barbier, E. B., Beaumont, N., Emmett Duffy, J., Folke, C., Halpern, B. S., Jackson, J. B. C., Lotze, H. K., Micheli, F., Palumbi, S. R., Sala, E., Selkoe, K. A., Stachowicz, J. J., and Watson, R. (2006), 'Impacts of Biodiversity Loss on Ocean Ecosystem Services', *Science*, 314/5800, 3 November: 787–90.

Wright, C., and Rwabizambuga, A. (2006), 'Institutional Pressures, Corporate Reputation, and Voluntary Codes of Conduct: An Examination of the Equator Principles', *Business and Society Review*, 111/1: 89–117.

WWF (World Wide Fund for Nature) (2002), *Living Planet Report 2002* (Gland, Switzerland: WWF), www.panda.org/downloads/general/LPR_2002.pdf

—— (2006), *Living Planet Report 2006* (Gland, Switzerland: WWF).

Wynne, M. A., and Kersting, E. K. (2009), 'Trade, Globalization and the Financial Crisis', *Economic Letter: Insights from the Federal Reserve Bank of Dallas*, 4/8, www.dallasfed.org/research/eclett/2009/e10908.htm

Xu, Yi-Chong, and Patrick Moray Weller (eds) (2015), *The Politics of International Organizations: Views from Insiders* (London: Routledge).

Yandle, B. (1984), 'Intertwined Interests, Rent Seeking and Regulation', *Social Science Quarterly*, 65/4: 1002–12.

Young, O. R. (ed) (1999), *The Effectiveness of International Environmental Regimes: Causal Connections and Behavioral Mechanisms* (Cambridge, MA: MIT Press).

—— (2002), *The Institutional Dimensions of Environmental Change: Fit, Interplay, and Scale* (Cambridge, MA: MIT Press).

Young, Z. (2003), *A New Green Order: The World Bank and the Politics of the Global Environment Facility* (London: Pluto Press).

Yusuf, S., and Nabeshima, K. (2009), *Tiger Economies under Threat* (Washington, DC: World Bank).

Zabarenko, D. (2006), '2005 Was Warmest Year on Record: NASA', Reuters, 24 January.

Zaller, J. (1992), *The Nature and Origins of Mass Opinion* (New York: Cambridge University Press).

Zevin, R. (1992), 'Are World Financial Markets More Open? If so, Why and with What Effects?', in T. Banuri and J. B. Schor (eds), *Financial Openness and National Autonomy: Opportunities and Constraints* (Oxford: Oxford University Press).

Zhou Xiaochuan (2009), 'Reform the International Monetary System', 24 March, People's Bank of China, Beijing, www.pbc.gov.cn/english/detail.asp?col=6500&id=178

Zimmermann, H. (2002), *Money and Security: Troops, Monetary Policy and West Germany's Relations with the United States and Britain 1950-71* (Cambridge: Cambridge University Press).

Zoellick, R. (2010), 'The End of the Third World?', address to Woodrow Wilson Center for International Scholars, Washington, DC, 14 April.

Zolo, D. (1997), *Cosmopolis: Prospects for World Government* (Cambridge: Polity Press).

Zürn, M. (1992), *Interessen und Institutionen in der internationalen Politik: Grundlegung und Anwendung des situationsstrukturellen Ansatzes* (Opladen: Leske & Budrich).

Zysman, J. (1984), *Governments, Markets and Growth: Financial Systems and the Politics of Industrial Change* (Ithaca, NY: Cornell University Press).

Index